Friuli
Venezia Giulia

The Mountains
p210

Cividale del Friuli & the Valli del Natisone
p173

Pordenone, the Magredi & the Valli Pordenonesi
p187

Udine & Surrounds
p139

Gorizia, the Collio & the Isonzo
p93

Sea & Lagoon
p112

Trieste & the Carso
p50

Luigi Farrauto, Piero Pasini, Cristian Bonetto

PLAN YOUR TRIP

Welcome to
Friuli Venezia Giulia 4

Friuli Venezia Giulia Map. . 6

Friuli Venezia Giulia's
Top 15 8

What's New 16

If You Like 17

Itineraries 20

Month by Month 26

Discovering
Friuli Venezia Giulia 29

Outdoor Activities 42

Family Travel 46

PIAZZA UNITÀ D'ITALIA
(P53), TRIESTE

PIERO PASINI/EDT ©

ON THE ROAD

TRIESTE &
THE CARSO 50
Trieste 52
Costiera Triestina 83
Barcola 84
Grignano 85
Duino-Aurisina 86
The Carso 88
Opicina 88
Sgonico 89
Towards Istria 90
Muggia 90

GORIZIA, THE COLLIO
& THE ISONZO 93
Gorizia 95
The Collio 102
Cormòns 102
Capriva del Friuli 106
San Floriano del Collio . . . 106
Dolegna del Collio 109
The Isonzo 109
Gradisca d'Isonzo 109
Fogliano Redipuglia 110
San Martino del Carso . . . 110
San Michele del Carso 111

SEA & LAGOON 112
Lignano Sabbiadoro 114
The Laguna di Grado &
Marano Lagunare 123
Marano Lagunare 124
Riserva Naturale
delle Foci dello Stella 126
Grado 126
Aquileia &
Surrounds 132
Aquileia 132
Torviscosa 136
Strassoldo 137
Riserva Naturale
della Foce dell'Isonzo
& Valle Cavanata 137
Monfalcone 138

UDINE &
SURROUNDS 139
Udine 141
The Plain
South of Udine 154
Palmanova 154
Clauiano 157
Codroipo 157
The Hills
North of Udine 158
Fagagna 158
San Daniele del Friuli 159
Pinzano al Tagliamento . . . 164
Forgaria nel Friuli 164
Osoppo 164
Ragogna 165
Lago di Cavazzo 166
Gemona del Friuli 166
Venzone 167
Colli Orientali 169
Tarcento 169
Artegna 170
Magnano in Riviera 170
Nimis 171
Attimis 171

PALMANOVA (P154)

MAYKOVA GALINA/SHUTTERSTOCK ©

Contents

Faedis 171
Lusevera 171
Buttrio 172
Manzano 172

CIVIDALE DEL FRIULI & THE VALLI DEL NATISONE 173
Cividale del Friuli 175
Valli del Natisone 181
San Pietro al Natisone . . . 182
Prepotto. 182
San Leonardo 183
Stregna 183
Grimacco. 184
Drenchia 184
Savogna. 184
Pulfero 185

PORDENONE, THE MAGREDI & THE VALLI PORDENONESI 187
Pordenone & the Plain. 189
Pordenone. 189
Sacile 195
Caneva. 197
San Vito al Tagliamento . . 198
Valvasone 199
Spilimbergo. 200
The Magredi 201
Vivaro. 202
The Valli Pordenonesi . . 203
Polcenigo. 204
Maniago. 205
Sequals 206
Travesio 206
Meduno 207
Clauzetto 208

THE MOUNTAINS . . .210
Piancavallo 211
Friulian Dolomites 214
Erto & Casso. 216
Val Zemola. 218
Cimolais. 219
Claut. 220
Val Settimana 220
Barcis. 221
Frisanco & Val Colvera . . .222
Val Tramontina 223
Forni di Sopra & Forni di Sotto 224
CARNIC ALPS 226
Tolmezzo 227
Ampezzo 229
Sauris 230
Prato Carnico 232
Sappada. 234
Zuglio 235
Sutrio 236
Ravascletto 237
Julian Prealps 238
Val Resia 238
Resiutta 239
Julian Alps. 240
Malborghetto Valbruna . . . 241
Tarvisio. 242
Sella Nevea 245

UNDERSTAND

History 248
Arts & Literature 261
Food & Wine 274
Environment 283

SURVIVAL GUIDE

Directory A–Z 288
Transport 291
Index. 297
Map Legend. 303

COVID-19

The economic and social impacts of COVID-19 will continue to be felt long after the outbreak has been contained, and many businesses, services and events referenced in this guide may experience ongoing restrictions. Some businesses may be temporarily closed, have changed their opening hours and services, or require bookings; some unfortunately could have closed permanently. We suggest you check with venues before visiting for the latest information.

Welcome to Friuli Venezia Giulia

Friuli Venezia Giulia is one of Italy's least-known regions. Yet, look behind the three words that make up its name and you'll discover a plethora of worlds. Discover them all, from the Alps to the Adriatic.

A Region with the Lot

It might be a claim made in many parts of the world, but Friuli Venezia Giulia really does have it all. Here, seas lap both sandy, resort-studded beaches and wild, rocky coastline. Mountains can be as wild and extreme as the Dolomites or as genteel and bucolic as the Julian Alps. And while cities like Udine radiate a unique regional charm, capital Trieste is undisputedly worldly and cosmopolitan. Hit the road and soak up ever-changing landscapes as you seek out Roman antiquities, Venetian cities and chic, Habsburg palaces.

Europe's Melting Pot

A borderland and cultural crossroads for millennia, the region has been shaped by many. Venetian influence reveals itself in the art and dialect of Pordenone, while the spirit of the Patria del Friuli – a former territory dating from the Holy Roman Empire – dominates the region's geographic heart, Udine. If Germanic heritage is rooted in the history of Trieste and the culture of the Julian Alps, then Slavic culture is inscribed in the DNA of Gorizia and the Carso. These various elements haven't always coexisted harmoniously, but together they constitute Friuli Venezia Giulia's most unique, valuable asset.

Four Splendid Seasons

Weather is always an important factor when planning a trip. In Friuli Venezia Giulia, every month and every season offers distinct opportunities for a memorable sojourn. Take in the region's beauty with a snowy *settimana bianca* (white week), a spring trek or a cooling August dip. Outdoors or indoors, along trails or on the beach, the options are endless. Come autumn, the Carso turns a reddish hue, Carnia peaks are sprinkled white and the plains are crowned by the bluest of skies. And if it rains, no sweat: cycling in the Collio becomes even more of a thrill.

Slow Travel

When it comes to bike paths and mountain trails, Friuli Venezia Giulia is on the cutting edge. Trails are well maintained and e-bike recharging stations are scattered throughout the region. Consequently, alfresco adventures are as comfortable as they are inspiring. In between hikes and rides, the region reveals its stories, beauty and world-famous flavours. And what a feast it is! Plan a picnic in the mountains or book a tasting, whether in a *malga* (alpine hut) or on the beach.

Why I Love Friuli Venezia Giulia
Luigi Farrauto, Writer

Aside from its excellent food and wine, its seamless transition from mountains to lagoon and sea, its mind-boggling number of hillside villages and not to mention a biocultural diversity with few equals in Italy, Friuli Venezia Giulia takes the breath away with its big heart and impeccable hospitality. I felt it beating everywhere: in ancient cities and modern museums, in castle ruins and old trench lines; in dimly lit taverns and in the trendiest of pubs. It might be a small region, but travelling through it feels like a trip around the world.

For more about our writers, see p304.

Friuli Venezia Giulia

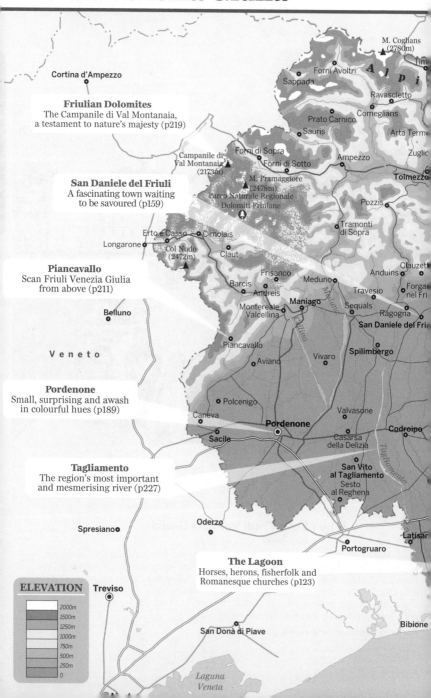

Friulian Dolomites
The Campanile di Val Montanaia,
a testament to nature's majesty (p219)

San Daniele del Friuli
A fascinating town waiting
to be savoured (p159)

Piancavallo
Scan Friuli Venezia Giulia
from above (p211)

Pordenone
Small, surprising and awash
in colourful hues (p189)

Tagliamento
The region's most important
and mesmerising river (p227)

The Lagoon
Horses, herons, fisherfolk and
Romanesque churches (p123)

ELEVATION

2000m
1500m
1250m
1000m
750m
500m
250m
0

0 — 20 km
0 — 10 miles

AUSTRIA

Hermagor

C a r n i c h e

Pontebba

Tarvisio

Laghi di Fasine

Udine
Tiepolo artworks and
lively bars (p141)

Riserva
Naturale
Val Alba

Resiutta

Resia

Jôf di Montasio
(2753m)

Sella Nevea

Cividale del Friuli
Cross the Devil's Bridge and
enjoy the spectacle (p175)

Venzone

Parco Naturale Regionale
delle Prealpi Giulie

Bovec

The Collio
Slow living in magnificent
surrounds (p102)

Gemona del Friuli

SLOVENIA

Tarcento

Nimis

Attimis

Pulfero

Tricesimo

Faedis

Tolmin

Gorizia
A town with many tales
to tell (p95)

Fagagna

San Pietro
al Natisone

Cividale del Friuli

Udine

Aquileia
Echo of an ancient
capital (p132)

Campoformido

Buttrio

Manzano

Cormòns

Nova Gorica

Gorizia

Duino-Aurisina
Where castles seemingly
spring from the sea (p86)

Capriva
del Friuli

Isonzo

Palmanova

Gradisca d'Isonzo

Pocenia

Ronchi dei Legionari

Cervignano
del Friuli

Fogliano
Redipuglia

The Carso
Deep caves and
soul-stirring foliage (p88)

Marano Lagunare

Monfalcone

Aquileia

Duino-Aurisina

Sgonico

Monrupino

Riserva Naturale
Foci dello Stella

Riserva Naturale
della Foce
dell'Isonzo

Miramare

Sežana

Opicina

Lignano
Sabbiadoro

Laguna di Grado e Marano

Grado

*Golfo
di Trieste*

Trieste

Trieste
A cosmopolitan city squeezed in
between the Carso and the sea (p52)

San Dorligo
della Valle

Muggia

MARE ADRIATICO

Koper/Capodistria

Piran/Pirano

Friuli Venezia Giulia's
Top 15

Trieste & Its 'Seas'

1 Trieste is not short of cultural draw-cards, from museums and ancient sites, to industrial archaeology and contemporary architecture. Yet, it's the city's cosmopolitan soul that will win you over, one shaped by Slavic and Germanic influences still palpable in the traditions, food and spirit of its people. Multicultural and interfaith, the city is a melting pot of Mediterranean, Central European and Balkan worlds. Also unique is the locals' bond with the sea: from the terraces of Barcola (p84) to the city's Austro-Hungarian sea baths (p71), you'll be amazed at how easy it is to find a place to take a dip.

Udine & Its Nightlife

2 Udine is the city of Tiepolo (p146) and contemporary art, to which an excellent museum is dedicated. It's also the 'Venice of the Mainland', its historic links to La Serenissima echoed in the elegant loggias, arcades and mullioned windows of Piazza della Libertà. Yet, these historic streets also crackle with the youthful energy of what is a vibrant university town and bastion of Friulian nightlife. Choose a tavern and dive into its lively scene: chances are you'll end up making a friend or two.

MASSANPH/GETTY IMAGES ©

Gorizia

3 A border town with Habsburg traits, Gorizia (p95) warrants more than a brief pitstop, a fact reflected in its nomination for European Capital of Culture 2025 (alongside Nova Gorica). While the atmosphere is Austrian, its vibrant multiculturalism shines through in both its language and architecture. Here, beautiful churches with 'onion-shaped' bell towers share the limelight with a postcard-perfect medieval castle, the latter hovering above Piazza Vittoria. This is a city where history is writ large. And what an intriguing backstory it is.

Castles among the Waves

4 The Trieste coast is more than its magnificent seascapes. From Duino, where Venezia Giulia begins, to Miramare, on the outskirts of Trieste, through to Muggia by the Slovenian border, a string of marvellous castles turned museums add character and culture. On a rocky spur, the Castello di Duino (p86) tells the story of the coast, while Miramare's castle (p85) offers Viennese atmosphere with a Mediterranean twist. Trieste's Castello di San Giusto (pictured; p60) commands the gulf and Muggia's fascinating ruins (p91) reveal an ancient past.

Between Land & Water

5 A succession of lagoons and river mouths, the compact stretch of coastline between Lignano Sabbiadoro (p114) and Monfalcone delivers exceptional natural beauty, much of it protected. It also offers a plethora of unique wildlife encounters, from marine birds to wild horses. From Marano Lagunare (p124) to Grado, on the other hand, the same area recounts the lives of those who settled on this challenging terrain between late antiquity and the Middle Ages, building Romanesque churches and colourful fishermen's houses.

Dolce Vita of the Collio

6 There are many reasons to visit the Collio (p102), but perhaps one is enough: if you fancy escaping the stresses and hassle of modern life, the verdant Collio has your back with vineyards, food artisans and bike-friendly routes to let you savour it all. Starting in Cormòns, set out and explore the *agriturisimi,* wineries and farms that have made this patch of earth world-famous for its wines. Then, as the sun sinks, gaze out over this tranquil landscape and discover a whole new level of sweet, mind-clearing silence.

LUIGI FARRAUTO/EDT ©

The Dolomites & the Campanile di Val Montanaia

7 Protected by a large nature park, the Friulian Dolomites (p214) stand out for their wild, unspoilt beauty, one that is awash with rivers, caves and waterfalls. The park's symbol is the Campanile di Val Montanaia (p219). Reached via a magnificent (albeit demanding) trek, the monumental natural obelisk is dubbed the 'Stone Cry' by mountaineers.

The Carso

8 According to an old adage, the Carso (p88) constitutes the other half of the Triestini's hearts. On this ruggedly beautiful, rocky plateau, locals have managed to coexist harmoniously with nature for many centuries. And while its setting at the meeting point of different languages and cultures has given it a unique charm, it has, at times, also caused great suffering. This is exemplified by the area's distinctive sink holes, linked to the violent settling of scores in the aftermath of WWII.

San Daniele del Friuli

9 San Daniele (p159) is more than the home town of *prosciutto crudo*. Stay a while and discover a medieval town with a sophisticated, literary soul. There's the Biblioteca Guarneriana and its precious manuscripts and miniature books, and the Chiesa di Sant'Antonio Abate and its magnificent interior (pictured; p161). In between exploring San Daniele's lesser-known treasures, there's always time to sample the local delicacies, which include its celebrated trout.

Villas & Castles

10 Fans of battlements, towers, drawbridges and medieval city walls will shriek at the region's wealth of castles and villas. Some are in excellent condition, others have been rattled by time and earthquakes – but all deliver lordly views. While the castles of Miramare (p85), Valvasone (p199) and Artegna (pictured; p170) are unmissable, World Heritage–listed Palmanova (p154) is also worth a visit. The star-shaped fortress-city was built by the Venetians in the 16th century.

Tagliamento River

11 Of the region's wealth of waterways, none stand out quite like the Tagliamento River (p227). Slicing the region in two from north to south (and marking part of the border with Veneto), its imprint on the landscape is both constant and commanding. Expect to spot it from above, from the riverbank and crossing valleys and towns, so much so that it will begin to feel like a faithful friend. Why? Because wherever you go, the Tagliamento will keep you company for part of your journey.

Cividale del Friuli & the Valli del Natisone

12 It's not unusual to find traces of the Lombards in Italian towns and Cividale (p175) is no exception. Perched at one end of the Devil's Bridge, this medieval town is both intriguing and rich in traditions. Not that you'll be the first to cross the threshold: Julius Caesar passed through here too, leaving his mark on the entire region. Outside Cividale, the Valli del Natisone await with their authentic villages and tracts of unspoilt nature. Tempietto Longobardo (p176)

Friuli's Balcony

13 The region's less-trodden south-west is a Slow Travel delight, with beautiful trails best explored by bike or on horseback. Make time also for the Magredi steppes (p201), unique in Italy and with few equals in Europe. From here, a sudden ascent to ski resort Piancavallo (pictured; p211) rewards with a dizzying panorama that takes in Istria, the Magredi, the Grado Lagoon and, on very clear days, the Venetian Lagoon as well.

The Frescoed Palazzi of Pordenone

14 Historically tied to Venice, Pordenone (p189) is an unexpected architectural jewel. Colourful buildings with Gothic windows echo those of the Grand Canal on Corso Vittorio Emanuele II, which leads to Palazzo Comunale and its pair of bell-ringing stone Moors. The Duomo's bell tower is higher still and the cathedral's richly decorated interiors are adorned with frescoes by the great Pordenone. Toast to it all with a *centino*, the city's famous aperitif.

Aquileia & the X Regio

15 Don't be fooled by its modest population: Aquileia (p132) has serious historical clout. Capital of the Roman Empire's X Regio, the town subsequently became the seat of the patriarchs who helmed the Patria del Friuli, among the first governments in the world to adopt a parliament. As you'd expect, its cultural treasures are impressive, among them ancient ruins of a Roman forum, port and burial ground, a well-endowed archaeological museum and a magnificently mosaicked Basilica.

What's New

Aquileia

In Aquileia, 2020 delighted locals and visitors alike with the archaeological discovery of the Mercati Tardo Antichi (p134) and the revamped Domus di Tito Macro (p135). More good news followed in 2021 with the inauguration of new galleries at the Museo Archeologico Nazionale (p134), dedicated to the museum's collection of amber objects, gems, cameos, jewels and coins.

Porto Vecchio, Trieste

Lovers of industrial archaeology will appreciate Trieste's revamped old port. Steeped in the history of the city and its surrounds, the large site has found new purpose as an exhibition space open to the public. (p70)

Sleeping in the Trees at Malga Priu

If one of your childhood dreams was to slumber in a treehouse, you can finally make it come true... big time. Imagine one of the most scenic places in the Julian Alps and waiting there for you is a pair of giant, two-storey 'pine cones' equipped with creature comforts. (p242)

Valli Pordenonesi's Gluttonous Side

Refined palates have two new hotspots to swoon over in Friuli Venezia Giulia. In the Pordenone foothills, among hills and bell towers, await La Stella and Ai Cacciatori. (p207)

Sappada

Friuli Venezia Giulia's chain of mountains grew a little longer in 2018 with the addition of Sappada to the region. Head up for invigorating summer activities, winter skiing or to find the starting point of the famous River Piave. (p234)

Pic&Taste

It's a simple formula: a hamper for two (or more), packed with regional bites, a cutting board, knife, wine bottle, glasses and a blanket, for a perfect picnic in a vineyard or mountain valley. Or you could opt for breakfast in an alpine hut. Offered June to October, you'll find a list of participating businesses at www.turismofvg.it/pic-and-taste.

Galleria de Martiis

In the heart of Cividale, Palazzo de Nordis hosts this gallery of modern and contemporary paintings, with works by greats including Karel Appel, Édouard Pignon and Friuli's own Afro Basaldella. (p177)

Gorizia 2025

Straddling the Italian–Slovenian border, Piazza Transalpina roared with jubilation in December 2020, when Gorizia (p95) and its Slovenian neighbour Nova Gorica were jointly declared European Capital of Culture 2025. It's the first time that a Capital of Culture spans two European countries in what is a highly symbolic achievement. Preparations are in full swing.

If You Like...

Beaches

Lignano The region's most popular seaside stretch consists of three hamlets: Sabbiadoro, Pineta and Riviera. You'll find beach clubs, a slew of activities, and wilder swathes of coastline. (p114)

Grado A holiday destination since Habsburg times, the Grado coast lures with beautiful public beaches, while its lagoon offers a unique setting for a dip. (p129)

Costa Giuliana Northwest of Trieste, the coast is rocky but incredibly varied, ranging from cliffs to coves to the one-of-a-kind Barcola Promenade. (p84)

Trieste A swim in Trieste? The Ausonia and Lanterna bathing establishments have drawn the city's denizens for centuries, even during office hours... That said, it's always more fun when you don't have to rush off after your lunch break. (p71)

Mountains

Tarvisio & Sella Nevea Ski slopes perfect for a week in the snow and no shortage of summer fun too. (p242 and p245)

Parco Naturale delle Dolomiti Friulane Trek up to the Campanile di Val Montanaia, pitch your tent in a valley or follow in the hoofsteps of deer – all adventures waiting in the Friulian Dolomites. (p215)

Tarvisio (p242)

Barcis An anise-coloured lake in a mountain village seemingly frozen in time for centuries. (p221)

Piancavallo Perfect if you have kids in tow and fancy enrolling them in a ski school, or for rookie snowboarders practising their moves. (p211)

Sappada New to Friuli Venezia Giulia, Sappada brings with it stunning landscapes and sporting activities all year round. (p234)

Resia At the end of an idyllic cul-de-sac valley bordering Slovenia, this geographically isolated area claims an unusual dialect, unique cultural traditions and its own variety of Slow Food–recognised garlic. (p238)

Hikes

Napoleonica A 4km trail from Opicina to Prosecco, with the Trieste coast on one side and the Carso on the other. (p88)

Palmanova The old ramparts of this star-shaped city are fully accessible on foot. (p154)

Julian Prealps Hit any one of the trails leading from the alpine huts and soak up the panoramic views. (p238)

Dolomites From strenuous hikes up to the Campanile di Val Montanaia (p219) to easy saunters in search of dinosaur footprints in Claut (p220), the Dolomites has something for everyone.

Cormòns The Sentiero delle Vigne Alte (High Vineyards Trail) crosses the heart of the Collio up to the Castello di Spessa. (p103)

Val Rosandra Hit this nature reserve where you can follow old railway tracks, stopping to photograph waterfalls or old military lookouts. (p90)

Great War Routes The Alps are littered with historic war trails and Friuli Venezia Giulia has its fair share of them, its well-marked routes reaching key sites of WWI. (p111)

Villages

Valvasone A very pleasant village, dominated by a jewel-box castle big on beauty. (p199)

Poffabro Narrow streets, stone houses with wooden balconies and, come spring, a colourful sea of flowers. (p222)

Topolò A typical Valli del Natisone scene of homes huddled snugly on a mountainside. (p184)

Venzone Although partly rebuilt after the earthquake of 1976, Venzone remains a very charming village. (p167)

Malborghetto Valbruna From its troubled past, this town in the heart of the Val Canale inherited beautiful Palazzo Veneziano and tranquil streets. (p241)

Illegio This ancient, atmospheric village feels suspended in time, especially at dusk. (p228)

Muggia A Venetian thorn in the side of the Austro-Hungarian coast, this fishing village south of Trieste is the only Italian coastal settlement on the Istrian peninsula. (p90)

History

Aquileia Once the capital of Imperial Rome's 10th region and seat of the Patriarchate, this town also hosted the world's first parliament. (p132)

Villa Manin Former home of the Doge, with a guest list that has included Napoleon. Today, it hosts a highly regarded concert series. (p157)

Fogliano Redipuglia This military memorial is the final resting place of more than 100,000 soldiers killed in WWI. (p110)

Ossario di Oslavia Also home to the remains of thousands of soldiers, their memory honoured with imposing architecture. (p101)

San Martino del Carso Rediscover battlegrounds described by military volunteer and celebrated poet Giuseppe Ungaretti, starting from the park named in his honour. (p110)

Risiera di San Sabba Located in suburban Trieste, this WWII concentration camp is informative and moving. (p70)

Erto & Casso Despite being devastated by the Vajont dam disaster of 1963, traditions remain strong in this now infamous valley. (p216)

Gorizia Not too long ago, Piazza della Transalpina marked more than the border between Italy and Slovenia. It separated Europe's West from its East. (p95)

Modern & Contemporary Art

Museo Revoltella One of Trieste's cultural treasures, featuring a notable array of contemporary artworks. (p63)

Museo d'Arte Moderna Ugo Carà The fantastical works of sculptor Ugo Carà (1908–2004) are the drawcard at this dedicated museum in his hometown of Muggia. (p91)

Casa Cavazzini – Museo d'Arte Moderna e Contemporanea It's impossible not to be enchanted by this collection in Udine. (p147)

Cycling

Grado The Ciclovia Alpe Adria (p242) takes you all the way to Salzburg, but kickstart your

training by pedalling around the island. (p129)

Carso Isontino If you have a mountain bike, test yourself on the trails scattered throughout the Gorizia region. (p109)

Marano Lagunare Load your bike on a boat and cross the lagoon or the mouth of the Stella River to pedal all the way to Marano. (p125)

Unusual Places

Museo Nazionale dell'Antartide Antarctica in Trieste? That's right. Head here to find out why. (p70)

Pesariis Splendid in its own right, this town is entirely devoted to clocks... of every type imaginable. Tick tock. (p233)

Aiello del Friuli If Pesariis has changed your perception of time, Aiello's sundials await you. (p159)

Cisgne A poignant and fascinating village, literally engulfed by vegetation. (p183)

Laghi di Fusine Want to learn how to drive a dog sled? Head here. (p244)

Gemona del Friuli Climb a rock face flanking the town, then top off the day with a tandem flight. (p166)

Oratorio della Purità You'll walk away with different eyes after viewing the frescoes here. (p146)

Fortezza di Osoppo A mammoth fort bearing the signs of time and the memory of a conflict. (p165)

Torviscosa A tiny town with a curious dream of self reliance. (p136)

Forra del Cellina A gorge that overhangs a fantastic canyon along the old highway. (p221)

Top: Pesariis (p233)
Bottom: Laghi di Fusine (p244)

Plan Your Trip
Itineraries

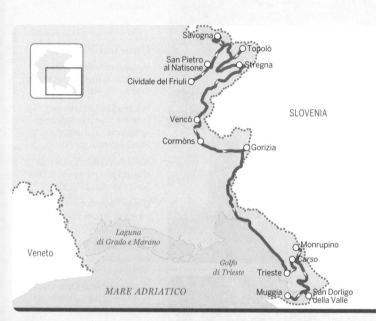

14 DAYS Towards Eastern Europe

This journey explores Friuli Venezia Giulia's Slovenian influences.

Awaiting you in **Cividale del Friuli** are magnificent Lombard relics and the beautiful vistas of the Valli del Natisone. Between **San Pietro al Natisone** and the peak of Matajur, which rises near **Savogna**, you'll find dozens of walking trails, as well as authentic villages rich in tradition, among them **Topolò** and **Stregna**.

From here head south to discover the Collio and let its peaceful atmosphere wash over you: after a bike or Vespa ride and a few glasses of white wine (best in that order), stop in **Vencò**, near Dolegna del Collio, to savour Michelin-starred cuisine at L'Argine, the fruit of centuries of cultural fusion.

Detour to **Cormòns** before heading to **Gorizia**, a border town which spills into Slovenia. Central Europe's influence is especially clear here: note the onion-shaped domes of the Chiesa di Sant'Ignazio, visible from the castle. Saunter through Piazza della Transalpina to put a foot in two countries and lunch on *ljubljanska* (schnitzel stuffed with ham and cheese), which is Slovenia's take on *cotoletta*.

Mandracchio (p91), Muggia's port

In **Trieste**, the Serbian community claims one of the largest Orthodox churches in the West and the Greeks an 18th-century temple by the sea.

Behind the capital, the **Carso** plateau has long been a crossroads, a place where Mediterranean, Central European and Balkan worlds collide. Here, linguistic borders dissolve, the scars of two world wars remain visible, and dishes fuse flavours from the north and east. Explore hidden villages, spectacular sanctuaries such as **Monrupino**, and giant caves.

Venezia Giulia has more surprises in store.

The only remaining Italian municipalities on the Istrian peninsula are **San Dorligo della Valle**, which is a perfect place to get lost on the trails of Val Rosandra, and **Muggia**, a compact fishing village with a Venetian pedigree and an atmosphere that you might find is reminiscent of coastal gems such as Koper (Capodistria) or Novigrad (Cittanova) across the border.

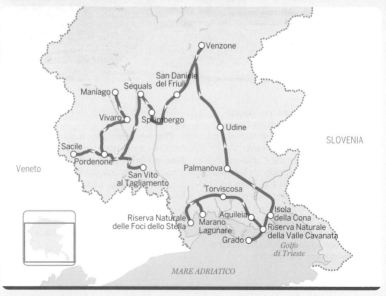

The Heart of the Region

10 DAYS

From the dreamy atmosphere of the lagoon to the relaxed vibe of the Magredi, this is a journey through the region's villages and towns.

PLAN YOUR TRIP ITINERARIES

Unlike in Venezia Giulia, where the coast is rocky, there's no clear demarcation between water and land in Friuli. The coast here is a frayed edge, a mercurial string of lagoons in poignant landscapes.

Start in **Marano Lagunare**, famed for its excellent cockles, and plan a stop at the nearby **Riserva Naturale delle Foci dello Stella**. Continue towards the eastern end of the lagoon, following the state road that passes through **Torviscosa** and **Aquileia** to the spectacular town of **Grado**, once an island and packed with historical sites. The nearby **Riserva Naturale della Valle Cavanata** is ideal for spotting a plethora of bird species, while the nearby **Isola della Cona** is the place to see wild horses.

After a detour to the star-shaped city of **Palmanova**, head to the Venice of the mainland, **Udine**, a city bursting with medieval buildings, museums and atmospheric *osterie*. Next, continue north to Gemona del Friuli and headily scented **Venzone**, towns devastated in the 1976 earthquake but since reborn and thriving.

You'll need at least a couple of days in **San Daniele del Friuli** to properly savour its cultural and culinary riches. Before arriving in Pordenone, stop in **Spilimbergo** for its mosaics and lavishly frescoed castle, or in **Sequals**, birthplace of Giandomenico Facchina, creator of the 'reverse' mosaic.

Easy-going **Pordenone** charms with its frescoed palaces, lively atmosphere and beautiful parks. The town is a convenient base for visiting **Sacile** on the tranquil Livenza River, and the Magredi steppe, where a solitary bell tower soars in **Vivaro**.

Cross over to **Maniago**, the last town before the mountains and birthplace of the utility knife. To the south lies **San Vito al Tagliamento** and its engaging museums.

Top: Grado (p126)
Bottom: Spilimbergo mosaic (p200)

10 DAYS Wild Mountains

Friuli Venezia Giulia's chain of mountains serves up magnificent vistas and alpine villages stretching from the Dolomites to Slovenia.

From the plains of gracious, art-filled **Pordenone**, the SR251 rises rapidly towards the **Forra del Cellina** and **Barcis**. You have two options here: head towards Piancavallo for gobsmacking views of the plain before turning back, or continue along the SR251 to **Cimolais**, an ideal base to walk in the footsteps of dinosaurs in **Claut**, explore the Landre Scur cave and head up to the Rifugio Pordenone in Val Cimoliana, from where you can hike to the **Campanile di Val Montanaia**. Two nights in Cimolais or its surrounds will allow you to do it all.

After Passo Sant'Osvaldo you'll enter the **Valle del Vajont**, where Erto and Casso look out onto the site of the catastrophic Vajont Dam landslide of 1963. You'll pass through the Veneto to reach **Domegge di Cadore** and the Mauria Pass before returning to Friuli Venezia Giulia and the Tagliamento Valley. Here, **Forni di Sopra** offers winter skiing and breathtaking summertime views of the Friulian Dolomites.

Head east along the Tagliamento Valley and after **Ampezzo**, take a sharp turn north to reach the northern valleys of Carnia and **Sauris**, famed for its prosciutto and Carnivale. After another quick detour into the Veneto, you'll find yourself in the northern Pesarina Valley, home to **Pesariis**, the 'capital of time'. Follow the valley eastwards as far as **Comeglians**.

From here, **Sappada** and ski slopes await to the northwest. To the east lies **Monte Zoncolan**, the fearsome Holy Grail of cyclists. Beyond it lie **Sutrio**, the **Terme di Arta** and **Zuglio**, with its Roman history, then **Tolmezzo**, Carnia's 'capital'. While Borgat is no party town, an evening here promises conviviality and good wine.

It's now time to leave Carnia in the direction of the Julian Alps. In **Tarvisio**, walk or ski between Italy and Slovenia or meditate on Mount Lussari. In **Sella Nevea**, opt for any number of winter sports. Whichever you choose, reward yourself with a night in the 'pine cones' of Malga Priu in **Malborghetto Valbruna**.

Top: Sappada (p234)
Bottom: Motorcycling on Monte Zoncolan (p236)

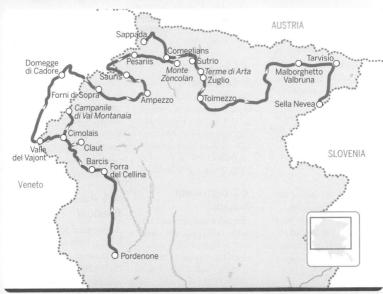

Month by Month

TOP EVENTS

Far East Film Festival, late April

Aria di Festa, late June

Stazione di Topolò, July

Perdòn de Barbana, July

Mittelfest, July/ September

Pordenonelegge, September

La Barcolana, October

January

🎭 Messa dello Spadone

At Cividale's most famous annual mass, a priest raises a large sword as a symbol of religious power, a tradition originating in the 14th century.

☆ Trieste Film Festival

When it's cold, wet or the bora winds are raging, what's better than a good movie? Expect to find all genres at this celluloid shindig. (www.triestefilmfesti val.it)

February/ March

🎭 Carnevale Europeo

Trieste's Piazza dell'Unità fills with confetti and masks to mark this event, though it doesn't take place every year.

🎭 Carnevale di Muggia

Frantic kitchens, packed restaurants and streets jammed with floats and mask-clad revellers mean one thing: Muggia Carnival. A second edition runs in summer. (www.carnevalde muja.com)

🎭 Carnevale di Sappada

The Rollate, a big bear in a wooden mask and cowbells, is the trademark mask of Sappada and the protagonist of the town's carnival parade, which runs for three consecutive Sundays.

🎭 Carnevale Resiano

Five days of festivities: take in the *ballo della Resiana,* the Val Resia's folk dance, as well as live performances using traditional musical instruments.

🎭 Carnevale Saurano

A celebration that is rooted in local crafts, with wooden masks carved using the traditional techniques of Carnian artisans.

April

🎭 Al Veindre Seint

On Good Friday Erto becomes an open-air theatre in which Jesus' final hours are re-enacted around the village. The tradition dates back to the 17th century, with the script handed down from father to son.

☆ Far East Film Festival

Lovers of East Asian cinema know that Udine is the place to be in late April, where this well-established festival serves up films and panel discussions on the region's cinema. (www.far eastfilm.com)

🎭 Pasquetta sui Bastioni

A charming town festival, with activities organised on Palmanova's ramparts: carriage rides, Nordic walking and hot air balloon flights.

May

 Fieste da Viarte

Unmissable if you're in Cormòns on the second last Sunday in May, this event offers access to private houses throughout the Collio, where you can buy homemade products and enjoy sampling endless tastings. (www.fiestedaviarte.org)

Maratona d'Europa

Known locally as *la bavisela,* this historic Trieste marathon draws crowds from all over the region. (www.triesterunningfestival.com)

near/far Premio Terzani

Held in Udine in mid-May, this event includes seminars, panel discussions and photography exhibitions. The winner of the Premio Terzani, a literary prize named after writer and journalist Tiziano Terzani, is also announced at the event. (www.vicinolontano.it)

Bacio delle Croci

In this evocative, ancient ritual, crosses adorned with colourful ribbons, from the different valley communities, are brought to the church of Pieve di San Pietro for a symbolic 'kiss' with the mother cross.

èStoria

A festival dedicated to history in its various forms, held in Gorizia. See the website for program details and locations. (www.estoria.it)

June

Premio Hemingway

Between June and July, Lignano Sabbiadoro remembers the great American writer with this eponymous literary prize. Concerts and other cultural events are held too. (www.premiohemingway.it)

Aria di Festa

Fans of cured meats (and white wines) flock to San Daniele in late June for this big prosciutto fair: producers open their doors to the public and concerts are held nightly. (www.ariadisandaniele.it)

Udine Jazz

At the end of the month, Udine transforms into an epicentre of jazz with this fascinating music festival. Some events are held in Cividale, Palmanova and Aiello del Friuli. (www.euritmica.it)

Magraid

A gruelling three-day, 100km race in the Magredi steppe. (www.magraid.it)

July

Perdòn de Barbana

One of the most heartfelt events in Grado: a procession of boats carries the statue of the Madonna from Grado to Barbana Island. If you're in the area around the first Sunday in July, you might just be invited to assist in the event.

Stazione di Topolò

The Valli del Natisone come alive again and, for a couple of weeks, are inundated by hordes of jugglers, artists, musicians and campers, all of whom converge on Grimacco for this historic event. (www.stazioneditopolo.it)

Maremetraggio

Short-film fans shouldn't miss this week-long fest in Trieste, becoming ever more popular each year. (www.maremetraggio.com)

Mittelfest

Cividale has been celebrating Central European culture with concerts, readings, theatre and dance performances since 1991. The 2020 and 2021 editions were held in September; check the website. (https://mittelfest.org)

Folkest

Rediscover cultures near and far at this folk and pop music festival in Spilimbergo. (www.folkest.com)

August

Palio di San Donato

The villages of Cividale challenge each other with running, archery and crossbow competitions at this historic event, held anually since the 16th century. A three-day party in every street. (www.paliodicividale.it)

Nozze Carsiche

On alternate years, in the last week of August, Monrupino celebrates the 'Karst

Wedding', a folkloric event with roots in local wedding traditions: a public bachelor/bachelorette party with old-world charm.

September

 ### Gusti di Frontiera

On the last weekend of September, Gorizia brings together hundreds of local producers to showcase specialities from Carso Isontino and the province of Gorizia. (http://gustidifrontiera.it)

SUP Race

It's Lignano's answer to the Barcolana, but instead of sailboats, hundreds of athletes race each other on stand-up paddle boards. (www.facebook.com/supracelignano)

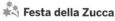 ### Sun & Run

A 10km-track between Sabbiadoro and Pineta for a not-too-demanding run along the coast.

Pordenonelegge

An engaging literary festival featuring prolific Italian and also international cultural figures. Expect book launches, author talks, exhibitions and other special events. (www.pordenonelegge.it)

FriuliDOC

Udine's colourful celebration of Friulian food, wine and crafts. (www.friuli-doc.it)

October

 ### Le Giornate del Cinema Muto

A long-running festival of silent film in Pordenone. Breaking the silence: live tunes. (www.giornatedelcinemamuto.it)

Festa della Zucca

A pumpkin festival complete with masks, fire breathers and jugglers. Held in Venzone at the end of October.

La Barcolana

Spectators crowd into Trieste for this epic regatta on the city's eponymous gulf. If you're heading in, plan ahead. (www.barcolana.it)

Ein Prosit

Tarvisio hosts this wine and food event, as popular with industry professionals as it is with the public. (www.einprosit.org)

December

Sapori di Carnia

A large agri-food fair in Raveo, held on the second Sunday of the month.

Pordenonelegge

Campanile di Val Montanaia (p219)

Discovering Friuli Venezia Giulia

The Best
AT THE TABLE

• •

SALUMI (CURED MEATS)

San Daniele aside, Cormòns and Sauris are also meccas for prosciutto and salami in the region. *Pitina, petuccia* and *peta* are specialities from the slopes of the Dolomites (p223).

CHEESES

Friuli Venezia Giulia's dairy traditions are very old: try the cheeses from Zoff (p106), or those from the alpine huts of the Montasio plateau.

VINEGAR

In the Collio, it's produced at Michelin-starred La Subida (p103) and made strictly from white wine.

GARLIC

It's said that Resia's famous garlic (p239) is kiss-proof; whatever the case, its robust flavour will delight aficionados.

ROSA DI GORIZIA

Reminiscent of a rosebud, this distinctive, delicious radicchio appears on Gorizian dining tables in the winter.

FRICO

It's Friuli's most iconic dish and, according to many, the best version is made in Udine (p151).

COTTO E CREN

An *aperitivo* staple in Trieste, this sandwich is made using cooked ham and a horseradish resembling ginger.

SWEETS

The Austrian influence shines bright on the dessert front. Like dried fruits and lightly boozed sweets? Consider Friuli your culinary Valhalla.

1. San Daniele prosciutto degustation
2. *Fave triestine*, autumnal sweets made with almond flour
3. *Frico di patate*

The Best
DRINKING

The different terms used for beverages (alcoholic or not) offer glimpses into the region's history and unique approach to drinking (and life itself).

OMBRA

That Pordenone refers to a glass of wine as an *ombra* (technically 'shadow') reveals the city's Venetian links: *ombre* were glasses of wine sold in the shadow of San Marco's bell tower in Venice.

TAJ, TAJO OR TAJÙT

The origin of these words – all terms for a glass of wine in Friulian – is uncertain. It may come from 'cut' (as in a 'pause' or 'break'), reflecting the convivial aspect of wine in these parts. It may, however, refer to a 'right amount'; an appropriate pour of *vino*.

BLACK WINE & COFFEE

Would you like white or 'black' wine? This is what the real locals call red.

In Trieste, *nero* is also a coffee served black; *capo* is a macchiato, *cafelate* a cappuccino. It can be served in a cup or 'in B' (a glass). In this city, coffee is a veritable cult, complete with its own terminology.

OSMIZE

Their name derived from *osam* (the Slovenian word for 'eight'), *osmize* originated with an 18th-century Austrian law that gave Carso farmers the right to sell surplus from their barns or cellars for eight days a year. It is mainly vineyards that hold *osmize* today, most running for a few weeks between November and April, and serving farm cheeses and cured meats as well as *vino*.

Finding an *osmiza* is part of the fun: look along Carso roads for the red arrows. Then look up, to signposts, gates or lintels bearing a *frasca* – a leafy branch hung upside down declaring that an *osmiza* is open for business. In many cases, you'll end up quaffing and nibbling in a leafy, private garden, often enclosed by pretty dry-stone walls.

If you don't have the time (or patience) for spotting a *frasca,* cheat by hitting www.osmize.com or its user-friendly app. An insider tip: a *frasca* with fresh-looking leaves hasn't been out long, which means more food and wine at the *osmize.* If it's dry, time and supplies are running out.

WATER & SPIRITS

In the Parco delle Dolomiti Friulane, Val Cimoliana is home to a spring from which mineral water is sourced and sold across Italy. Friuli's mountains are also especially famous for grappa (pomace brandy), produced throughout the region under the Indicazione Geografica Grappa Friulana or Grappa del Friuli appellation.

SLIVOVIZA & PELINKOVAC

The plum brandy *slivoviza* is as popular in Friuli Venezia Giulia as it is in its central and eastern European neighbours. Less common but also loved is *pelinkovac,* a wormwood-based liqueur hailing from Croatia and widespread in the Balkans.

1. *Nero vino* **2.** Collio vineyards (p107)
3. *Osmiza*

In the Footsteps of
ANCIENT HISTORY

Friuli Venezia Giulia has hosted Roman cities, Lombard kingdoms and Byzantine patriarchates, but this ancient land has been inhabited since Paleolithic times.

PALÙ DI LIVENZA

Not far from charming Castello di Caneva (p197) is one of the most important pile-dwelling sites in Italy. While the marshy area surrounding the headwaters of the Livenza River was a stomping ground for the last hunter-gatherers of the late Paleolithic period, it wasn't until the late Neolithic period that an important pile-dwelling settlement developed here, one that has been intensely studied since the late 20th century.

RONCHI DEI LEGIONARI

The town of Ronchi is synonymous with the tumultuous years of Italian history linked to WWI. Yet, there are other reasons to visit this historically important place, among them a Roman villa adorned with mosaicked floors and built between the 1st century BCE and 3rd century CE.

AQUILEIA

It might claim a modest 3000 inhabitants today, but in Roman times 200,000 people lived in Aquileia (p132), fourth city of the Empire and capital of its 10th region, Venetia et Histria. Today, its ancient forum, river port and archaeological museum offer glimpses of this golden age. Both the mosaics of its basilica and the Baptistery that faces it are masterpieces, while excavations offer evidence of a settlement that continued to flourish even after the Huns' incursions.

TERGESTE

Initially a small Illyrian village, Tergeste (Trieste) expanded in Roman times. Despite it remaining a secondary city, a temple with a beautiful propylaeum was erected on the Colle di San Giusto (p57), along with a theatre overlooking the sea. Today, fragments of both survive, alongside other ancient ruins.

IULIUM CARNICUM

Iulium Carnicum (Zuglio; p235) was the northernmost Roman outpost in Italy and the Via Iulia Augusta, which led from Aquileia to Bavaria, passed through it. While most of the finds from the ancient city are now in the museum, the archaeological site itself is stunning in its simplicity.

FORUM IULII

Cividale (p175) occupied a strategic position on the chessboard that is the region's history. Founded by Julius Caesar as the Forum Iulii (ultimately condensed into 'Friuli'), the city's importance grew after the destruction of Aquileia, reaching the height of its splendour in the Lombard era. Explore its many hidden secrets, some of them buried deep underground.

GRADO

In the centre of town, beautiful Piazza Biagio Marin (p127) preserves traces of an ancient early Christian basilica that dates back to the 4th century. Unearthed in 1902, the ruins can be explored along a network of see-through walkways.

1. Castello di San Giusto (p60), Tergeste (Trieste)
2. Mosaic, Aquileia (p132)

Total Relaxation
SEA & WIND

●●●

Friuli Venezia Giulia serves up a plethora of nautical events. Seafaring culture is especially strong in Trieste, where rocky shores and gusty bora winds make its eponymous gulf a thrilling, at times extreme, place to head out in full sail.

A SYMPHONY OF BOATS

Barcola's famous regatta, the **Barcolana** (pictured; p72), is a democratic affair, its starting line heaving with casual sailing enthusiasts, sailors both young and wizened, not to mention world-famous racing greats.

Since its launch by the Società Velica di Barcola e Grignano in 1969, the regatta has grown into one of the most crowded sailing competitions in the world; in 2018, it broke all world records with a whopping 2305 registered boats.

As you would expect, it's a spectacular sight, kicking off with an unforgettable, soul-stirring spectacle of Technicolor sails and foaming white waters.

For the best view, head to the Carso or find an elevated vantage point at Miramare.

Come early September, Lignano Sabbiadoro hosts its own smaller, though much-loved, aquatic battle: the **SUP Race** (p119), where hundreds of rowers paddle for victory on stand-up paddle boards.

Boats also feature in a number of traditional festivals. One of the most evocative is Grado's **Perdòn de Barbana** (p130), celebrated on the first Sunday in July since 1257, the year in which the Virgin Mary miraculously freed Grado from the plague. To give thanks, locals carry a statue of the Madonna from the Basilica di Sant'Eufemia, in the centre of the town, to a sanctuary on the island of Barbana, accompanied by a procession of festively decorated vessels.

On the other side of the lagoon, in Marano, the **Processione di San Vito** (p125) on June 15 is a whirl of religious vestments, banners, saintly statues and prayers. Part of the celebration sees the relics of St Vito and St Modesto taken out to sea, accompanied by their own flotilla.

THE BORA

Boreas was the ancient Greek god of the north wind and from his name comes 'Bora', the region's infamous, katabatic (fast-moving, downward) wind. Originating in Siberia, it picks up fearsome speed on its descent from the Carso into Trieste, with violent gusts capable of overturning buses and forming 'holes' in the sea.

Even when it's not blowing, the bora makes its presence felt, in city place names, in shielded fountains, and even in buildings studded with hand rails and ropes to keep pedestrains steady on blustery winter days.

Get the lowdown on this infamous beast at the Museo della Bora, housed inside the **Magazzino dei Venti** (p66). And if you find yourself in Trieste in June, don't miss **BoraMata**, a festival that celebrates the wind with colourful pinwheels throughout the city.

Total Relaxation
TAGLIAMENTO

It's difficult to ignore the Tagliamento River on your journey through Friuli: its turquoise waters have a way of commanding your attention.

A HYPNOTIC RIVER

The Tagliamento is Friuli Venezia Giulia's longest river, stretching 170km from near the Mauria Pass, some 1200m above sea level, to the Adriatic Sea. It's a torrid, fast-flowing creature, with hypnotic, intertwined channels often the colour of ice. Roaring its way along gravel banks and verdant islands, it revels in surprise, appearing suddenly and spectacularly by the roadside when you least expect it. Gobsmacked, all you seem to be able to do is brake, pull over and grab your camera.

CARNIA

In Carnia, the fledgling Tagliamento is little more than the culmination of a myriad of streams. Between Tolmezzo and Pradis, these waterways mark your journey through valleys and peaks shrouded in time-warped stillness.

PINZANO AL TAGLIAMENTO

Join the motorcyclists who stop near the bridge (p164), which recounts Friuli's turbulent wartime history: the river view here is one-of-a-kind.

RAGOGNA

The walls and towers of the 6th-century castle (p192), a 6th-century structure built on the riverbed of the Tagliamento, offer a beautiful view. The more intrepid can climb Mount Muris, between trenches and observatories, to relax in the greenery and admire the panorama that embraces the Alps. Nearby there is one of the few official beaches on the river.

OSOPPO

Walk up and down the mysterious Fortezza di Osoppo (p165), where the river appears and disappears among hills, woods, tunnels and crumbling walls.

VENZONE

The Tagliamento River flows silently beside the old walls of this town (p167), which welcomes visitors with its unmistakable scent of lavender, rich cultural heritage and wealth of stories.

LIGNANO SABBIADORO

This is where the Tagliamento River ends its journey, its turquoise waters meeting the Adriatic Sea. Chill under a beach umbrella (p114), but also make time for a wander in nature or some water sports.

1. Tagliamento River **2.** Old city walls, Venzone (p167)

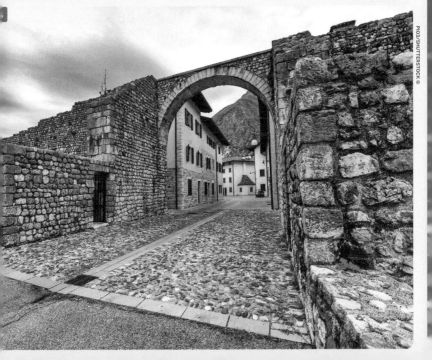

Total Relaxation
ADRIATIC SEA

From Lignano in the west to Miramare in the east, the entire coast of Friuli Venezia Giulia is a unique natural resource.

BETWEEN LAND & WATER

In contrast to the rocky, cliff-strewn coastline in the region's east, Friuli's western coast is low-lying, sandy and punctuated by estuaries and lagoons. Here, land and sea seem to meld into one, creating fascinating landscapes one can explore in a myriad of ways: by car, on foot or horseback, and, above all, by boat.

ALL ABOARD

Don't happen to own a yacht? No problem: sign up for a guided mini-cruise, get from A to B on a charter boat, or rent your own. Rates are relatively low and the thrill factor high.

Hidden coves and majestic castles alternate along the luminous, windswept Gulf of Trieste. Having access to a boat (row or motor) makes all the difference when exploring the deltas of the Tagliamento and Isonzo Rivers.

A plethora of cruise options depart from **Lignano**, **Marano** and **Grado**. The most memorable combine sightseeing with activities or experiences, such as those which stop in Marano and Grado, or those that take you fishing, on the deck or perhaps perched on a *trabocco* (traditional fishing platform) such as **Bilancia di Bepi** (p118).

A SLOW PACE & A SHARP EYE

Much of the coastline is protected by near-pristine nature reserves. The western stretch of the Laguna di Grado and Marano falls within the **Riserva Naturale delle Foci dello Stella** (p126) and the **Riserva Naturale della Valle Canal Novo** (p125), where swarms of

MOTOR BOATS & MORE

Sea&Taste (p118) Beautiful boat experiences.

Motonave Europa (p118) To conquer the Isle of Shells.

Battello Santa Maria (p125) Sail the route of the Patriarchs to Aquileia.

Nico, la Pinta & la Santa Maria (p125) Nico is the captain, *Pinta* and *Santa Maria* his boats. Together they offer boat & bike and dinner cruises.

Nuova Saturno (p125) Fun cruises.

1. Greylag geese, Isola della Cona (p137)
2. Castello di Duino (p86)

waterbirds can be observed from historic *casoni* (hunting shelters). The *casoni* also offer excellent birdwatching at the **Riserva delle Foci dell'Isonzo** and the **Isola della Cona** (p137), where herds of Camargue horses also roam. Consider reaching the reserve via the **Riserva Naturale della Valle Cavanata** (p137), perhaps by bicycle. Take in a fiery sunset, mirrored in the shallow, glassy waters, then continue to the **Falesie di Duino** (p86), precipitous limestone cliffs protected by their own nature reserve.

Here, both landscape and atmosphere take a dramatic turn, the brackish smell of the lagoon replaced by the invigorating scent of the open sea. A walk along the **Rilke trail** is an introspective experience. It's also a perfect prelude to the timeless atmosphere of Miramare, whose own protected waters harbour an abundance of tuna and mussels.

2

European crested

Outdoor Activities

Friuli Venezia Giulia offers a dizzying range of outdoor thrills. The standard of offerings is high in resorts like Lignano on the coast, or Tarvisio and Piancavallo in the mountains. With everything from beaches, lagoons and lakes, to hills, plateaus and mountains, there's no shortage of opportunities to get out into the great outdoors and find your own natural high.

The Best

Nature Watching

Laguna di Grado & Marano (p123) The best way to explore the lagoon is on your own boat. The natural beauty will leave you speechless.

Lago di Cornino (p164) A fairytale lake and reserve, and a great spot to watch the flight of hundreds of griffon vultures. Beyond the walking trails lies the Tagliamento and its tangled channels.

The Magredi (p201) The solitude of the steppe has a haunting quality. This is a place made for aimless wanders in a boundless landscape.

Diving

The best area for diving is between Grignano and Sistiana on the Julian coast: this particular stretch occupies a protected marine reserve.

Hang Gliding & Paragliding

Gemona and Meduno are popular towns for individual and tandem flying. Opportunities also abound around Tarvisio and in the region's ski resorts.

Erto (p216) At the famous 'rock gym with ceiling', an overhanging crag you can scale in any weather.

Lusevera (p171) You can choose the level of difficulty at Ai Ciclamini.

Cycling

Friuli Venezia Giulia has an expansive, well-managed network of cycling paths. Choose from hundreds of trails, in the city or in the mountains, from easy to challenging. Among the most beautiful is the Alpe Adria trail (p242), which leads from Grado to Salzburg. Comprehensive trail information is available at www.alpe-adria-radweg .com/it. Also, check out the Amare in Bici (p102) project, which brings together a network of trails.

Birdwatching

Friuli Venezia Giulia is one of the favourite regions of migratory birds for a stop before flying to Africa. This means that birdwatchers will have a lot of fun at certain times of the year.

Equip yourself with a telescope on Isola della Cona (p137) and throughout the Laguna di Grado & Marano (p123): more than 300 feathered species have been spotted in the area's nature reserves.

Catch a glimpse of the steppe eagle in the Magredi (p201) or spot golden eagles, kites and hawks in the Julian Prealps and Friulian Dolomites (p215).

Lago di Cornino (p164), in Forgaria nel Friuli, is home to a myriad of griffon vultures, part of a protected reserve.

Climbing

You'll be pleasantly surprised to learn that many of the region's towns cater to climbers. The best time to climb is in the coolest, driest months: from spring to summer (even if the rain is always around the corner). The following are especially atmospheric spots to hit the ropes:

Napoleonica (p88) You will find a large crag to climb on the last stretch of this trail (starting from Opicina).

Gemona del Friuli (p166) Climb Monte Glemina, right behind the Duomo.

Hang Gliding & Paragliding

If you're flying for the first time, opt for the area between Gemona and Meduno, or that between Clauzetto and Tarvisio. Not only are the operators especially outstanding, the views are wonderfully diverse, alternating between mountains, hills, plains and the coast. Hang gliding and paragliding are also possible in Piancavallo, near Aviano, though you'll need to keep an eye on the weather; take-offs are only permitted when conditions are deemed completely safe.

Hiking

Hikers will not be disappointed in Friuli Venezia Giulia, with countless trails scattered across the region. All levels are catered for, with everything from short, gentle strolls to steep, calf-toning adventures for pros. Easy or hard, all trails offer an escape into nature.

Walking trails and itineraries are listed throughout this guidebook, so dust off those boots and start planning.

Golf

Friuli Venezia Giulia has seven golf courses, all of them modern and in shipshape. So how to choose? Course technicalities aside, consider the setting.

Would you prefer teeing with a view of the Castello di Spessa or of the Julian Alps? Then again, you could swing through the ball towards the border of three countries at the Golf Club di Tarvisio.

Visit www.turismofvg.it/golf for the lowdown on the courses.

Golf Club Lignano

Golf Castel d'Aviano (📞0434 65 23 05; www.golfclubcasteldaviano.it; Via IV Novembre 13, Aviano)

Golf Club Grado (📞0431 89 68 96; www.tenuta-primero.com; Via Monfalcone 27, Grado)

Golf Club Lignano (📞0431 42 80 25; www.golflignano.it; Via Casa Bianca 6, Lignano)

Golf Club Trieste (📞040 22 61 59; www.golfclubtrieste.it; Loc Padriciano 80, Trieste)

Golf Club Udine (📞0432 80 04 18; www.golfudine.it; Via dei Faggi 1, Fagagna)

Golf Club Without Borders Tarvisio (📞0428 20 47; www.golfsenzaconfini.com; Via Priesnig 5, Tarvisio) Designed by Canadian architect Graham Cooke.

Golf Country Club Castello di Spessa (📞0481 88 10 09; www.golfcastellodispessa.it; Via Spessa 14, Capriva del Friuli)

If you're keen on learning golf but don't feel like tackling an 18-hole course, you'll find a six-hole driving range in Mortegliano: **Tourist Golf** (Via Morsano 79/81, Frazione Chiasellis, Mortegliano). There is also one in Povoletto, **La Faula Golf Club** (members only; www.golfclublafaula.com; Via della Faula, Località Ravosa, Povoletto).

Water Sports

Water is Friuli Venezia Giulia's most significant natural element, shaping and reshaping nature into unique formations. While the coast itself spans a small part of the region, it offers a bumper offering of local experiences, from beach clubs to lagoon expeditions. Indeed, some options may be completely novel to you.

For **diving** and **snorkelling** head to the Trieste coast, between Grignano and Sistiana, around the marine reserve.

Sailing and **windsurfing** can be enjoyed almost everywhere: the beaches are windy and there's a sailing club in every place along the coast. Grado Pineta beach (p129) is one of the best **kitesurfing** spots in Europe.

Cycling on the Strada Napoleonica (p88), Trieste

In Lignano (p115) try **stand-up paddle boarding (SUP)**. Alternatively, don a parachute and be propelled high into the sky by speedboat on a **parasailing** adventure.

Fishing tourism enthusiasts should not miss Marano (p124), from where there are numerous excursions in the lagoon (even at night).

The bad news: the Tagliamento River is not navigable. The good news: **kayaking** and **canoeing** can be enjoyed in many mountain locations, as well as on the lagoon (especially at the mouth of the Stella River).

That said, it's **canyoning** that reigns supreme in this region's valleys. Feel the thrill as you cross rivers on foot, jumping, sliding and climbing your way through deep, wild landscapes. Both Cimolais and Claut (p220) are world-famous canyoning destinations.

The region's many lakes draw athletes in the warmer months, with important sporting events held annually in Barcis, as well as at Lago di Cavazzo (p166).

Mountain Sports

Friuli Venezia Giulia's mountains entertain year round. In winter, the ski resorts come alive, with **downhill skiing**, **snowboarding** and **cross-country skiing** everywhere. If the weather's bad, hit the ice rinks. Snow bunnies with kids in tow should consider Piancavallo, as should skiers and **mountain bikers** who like busting the odd acrobatic move. The Dolomites and Julian Alps offer roughly the same activities: the lifts are good and never too crowded, which makes for hassle-free skiing.

Come summer, you can take to mountain skies in numerous ways: **paragliding**, **hang gliding** and **ultralights** are all extremely popular. Meduno (p207) has no shortage of options. From spring onwards, you can also take advantage of the many **mountain trails** scattered throughout the Alps: contact Alpine Guides (www.guide alpinefvg.it) for more information.

Nevelandia (p23)

Plan Your Trip
Family Travel

In both the cities and smaller towns, little ones are not overlooked in Friuli Venezia Giulia. They can go wild at amusement parks, ski down baby slopes, make a splash at family-friendly bathing establishments, and, at some museums, explore child-friendly exhibitions. Add to this an endless number of family-friendly adventures in nature and you have yourself a near-flawless destination for budding travellers.

Best for Kids

Lignano Sabbiadoro Countless activities, amusement parks, adventures, swimming pools and the sea.

Bathing Establishments of Trieste Tranquil, shallow waters in the heart of the city.

Birdwatching & 'horsewatching' Valleys, estuaries and lagoons have never been so exciting.

Centro Internazionale Vittorio Podrecca Puppets for one and all.

Magazzino dei Venti (Museo della Bora) A warehouse of ideas and creativity guaranteed to bring out your inner child.

Best for Older Kids

Kleine Berlin Chronicling life during the war, Trieste's underground tunnels are as gripping as they are informative.

Risiera di San Sabba Delving into the past can be challenging and painful. This former concentration camp in Trieste tackles its dark history with sensitivity, making it an engaging, educational experience for older kids.

Welcome, Kids!

When it comes to family travel, Friuli Venezia Giulia is well ahead of other Italian regions, with most restaurants, hotels and *agriturismi* well equipped with changing tables, high chairs or cribs for little ones. While the region's traditional flavours are robust, it's not hard to find simpler local food options. Furthermore, restaurant staff are usually more than happy to meet the needs of younger diners. In short, travelling with kids is relatively easy in Friuli Venezia Giulia.

Here Come the Dinosaurs

It was in 1994 that a school group in Claut (p220) in the Dolomites discovered the footprints of a dinosaur that roamed here in the Triassic period. An easy and beautiful guided tour leads you to the prehistoric imprints.

Much younger (by 70 million years) than his Dolomites-roaming compatriot is Antonio the Dinosaur. He has maintained his figure, with an entire skeleton to admire. Find him at Trieste's Civico Museo di Storia Naturale (p69).

Adventures & Acrobatics

Adventure and amusement parks are jewels in Friuli Venezia Giulia's crown. You'll find them throughout the region, from Piancavallo to Tarvisio, Trieste to Lignano.

Lignano (p121) The capital of adventure parks. There's veteran waterpark L'Aquasplash; Strabilia Lunapark with its Ferris wheel and cotton candy; and Parco Junior, complete with fetching miniature train. Little ones love the Gommosi, while Punta Verde Zoo Park delights young and old alike with its lemurs, pink flamingos, pumas and other resident critters.

Rampypark (p211) Scurry up trees and swing between braches at this 'Forest Acrobatic Park', located in Piancavallo.

Trieste Adventure Park (p87) Unleash the Tarzan within your little travel companions at this pulse-racing adventure park in Duino.

Tree Village of Claut (p220) Fancy darting from one tree house to another? Try it here.

Young Nature Fans

The region is rich in pristine yet accessible environments for young nature lovers.

The Magredi (p201) The ideal location for spotting steppe eagles and enjoying experiences in nature, such as going for a gallop at Gelindo's riding school.

Isola della Cona (p137) Observe herds of wild horses in natural surrounds.

Riserva Naturale della foce dell'Isonzo (p137), **dello Stella** (p126) and **della Valle Canal Novo** (p125) Have you ever heard a waterfowl's call in the wild? Hide in a camouflaged lodge and eavesdrop on a call that sounds uncannily like lively, chattery gossip.

Subterranean Secrets

Grotta Gigante (p89) The biggest of the many caves that riddle the Carso (and large enough to hold a cathedral), the Giant Cave is a hidden marvel, which is full of strange natural sculptures and sounds.

Raibl mine (p244) Near Tarvisio, a verified miners' train leads you around tunnels and salt boulders, shafts and hoists, and even to a border: the very one between Italy and Slovenia.

Kleine Berlin (p71) During the war, the people of Trieste took refuge underground. Fortunately, their former shelters are now a fascinating, mysterious route into the city's hidden belly.

Get Adventurous

Landre Scur (p220) The hike up to this cave is within the reach of (almost) everyone, the reward for your efforts worthy of Indiana Jones.

Forra del Cellina (p221) Near Barcis, this canyon is sliced by an emerald green stream, crossed by a Tibetan bridge and accessible via an adorable 'mini train' that runs along an old state road.

Piancavallo (p211) The ideal spot for kids who want to learn to ski.

Hiking Trails

Young hikers have two new trails created just for them: Animalborghetto, starting in Malborghetto (p241), and The Trail of the Sbilfs (elves), which winds around Ravascletto (CAI trail 201, starting from Rifugio De Gasperi).

On & Below the Sea

You'll be spoiled for choice when it comes to a swim along the region's coastline: from Trieste's city-centre bathing establishments to the decked-out beach clubs of Lignano, to the wild ones of Grado.

THE HOLOCAUST IN ITALY

Explaining the horror and tragedy of the Holocaust to children can be challenging. The site of **Risiera di San Sabba** (p70), a concentration camp on Trieste's outskirts, provides thoughtful, sensitive insight into this dark chapter of human history through its didactic museum exhibitions and informative audio guide.

Aquario Marino (p65) A different way to learn about sea creatures in Trieste.

Civico Museo del Mare (p65) For those curious about the relationship between Trieste and the sea.

Magazzino dei Venti (p66) Maritime history is made of sea and... wind, and wind in Trieste means bora. Dedicated to the city's infamous northerly, this engaging museum is a must for inquisitive young minds.

Science for Kids

Immaginario Scientifico are museums tailor-made for kids, where learning, interactive experiences and fun team up to great effect. Find them in Grigano (p85), Pordenone (p193) and Tavagnacco. (The latter, housed inside the Mulino di Adegliacco, is open for special events or by reservation only.)

Magical Marionettes

The puppets at Centro Internazionale Vittorio Podrecca (p178) may stare at you in perfect stillness, but you can't help expecting them to suddenly come alive. Vittorio Podrecca's puppets come in all shapes, hues and outfits. Meet them at this beautiful museum in Cividale del Friuli.

On the Road

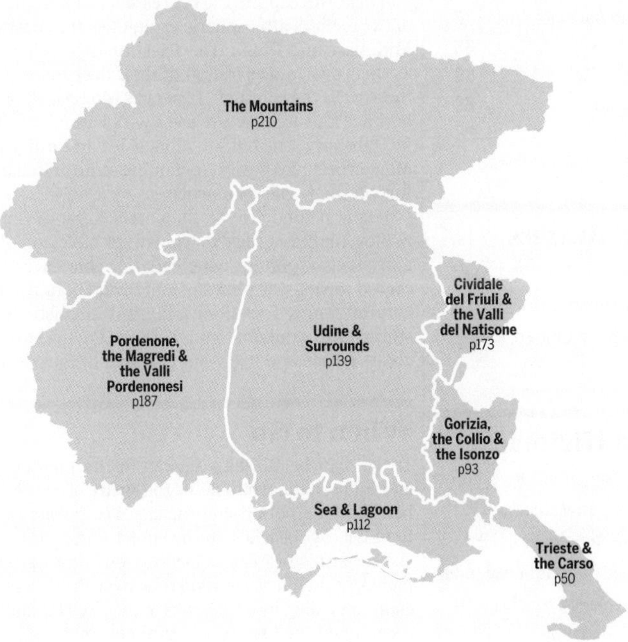

The Mountains
p210

Cividale
del Friuli &
the Valli
del Natisone
p173

Pordenone,
the Magredi &
the Valli
Pordenonesi
p187

Udine &
Surrounds
p139

Gorizia,
the Collio &
the Isonzo
p93

Sea & Lagoon
p112

Trieste &
the Carso
p50

Trieste & the Carso

Includes ➜

Trieste 52
Costiera Triestina 83
Barcola. 84
Grignano 85
Duino-Aurisina 86
The Carso 88
Opicina. 88
Sgonico 89
Muggia. 90

Best Buffets

➜ Da Pepi (p77)
➜ Siora Rosa (p76)
➜ Sandwich Club (p76)
➜ Marascutti (p77)

Best Historic Cafes

➜ Caffè San Marco (p79)
➜ Caffè Tommaseo (p79)
➜ Antico Caffè Torinese (p79)
➜ Caffè degli Specchi (p79)

Why Go?

On a map, Trieste and the Carso look like Italy's index finger, pointing to a region at the crossroads of the Mediterranean, Balkans and Central Europe. This 'collision of worlds' is especially palpable in Trieste, whose melange of cultures, faiths and histories capture the very essence of Europe. Northwest of the region's atmospheric capital lies the coast of Barcola, Miramare and Duino. The Triestini (Trieste locals) claim it as their own, a declaration of their deep, enduring love for the sea. To the south of Trieste lies Muggia, whose Venetian heritage and architecture feel a world away from Trieste and its Habsburg sensibilities. Alongside San Dorligo della Valle, Muggia occupies the last remaining scrap of Italian-governed turf on the Istrian peninsula.

Rising behind Trieste, the Carso (Karst in German, *kras* in Slovenian) is a rugged, windswept tableland of vineyards and *osmize* (pop-up wine cellars), epic caves and stone-carved towns, warming sun and brutal bora winds. With its culturally mixed traditions, blurred linguistic borders and still-painful wounds from WWII, the Carso's story is not just about Trieste and itself, but also that of Europe as a whole.

When to Go

Trieste can be stiflingly muggy in the middle of summer and equally inhospitable in the heart of winter, when the bone-chilling bora lashes the city. Yet, respite can be easily found at city beaches, in the cooler Carso, or in one of Trieste's cosy historic cafes. Each season offers unmissable moments, so there's never a bad time to visit. October is an especially appealing month thanks to the city's famous Barcolana regatta and the Carso's beautiful autumnal hues.

Trieste & the Carso Highlights

1 Piazza Unità d'Italia (p53) You will never tire of admiring it.

2 Colle di San Giusto (p57) Trieste's historic hill.

3 Buffet & osmize (p76 and p86) Sources of pleasures for every self-respecting Triestino.

4 Sea baths (p71) Habsburg traditions live on in the heart of the city, by the sea.

5 Castello di Miramare (p85) One of Italy's most visited museums.

6 Museo Revoltella (p63) Art in a splendid residence.

7 Val Rosandra (p90) Pristine nature a stone's throw from the city centre.

8 Strada Napoleonica (p88) Four kilometres of history between the Carso and the Gulf.

9 Grotta Gigante (p89) You need to see it to believe it.

TRIESTE

POP 199,991 / ELEV 2M

Trieste's greatest talent is its ability to offer big-city sophistication in a compact, welcoming package. After all, this is a place well-versed in contradiction. The same town that serves up austere architecture, ferocious winds and challenging climbs to the Colle di San Giusto, coddles its visitors with its snug, affable buffets (traditional eateries) and seafront cafes alive with bonhomie and chitchat. The city's denizens – the Triestini – reveal themselves in a similar way. Look beyond the reserved exterior and you'll discover a jovial, tolerant bunch with a cosmopolitan world view shaped by centuries of living at the crossroads.

History

The first traces of human activity in the Carso and its caves date back 50,000 years. The development of a distinct Carso civilisation, however, dates from around 2000 BCE, when Illyrians from the Dalmatian coast and hinterland settled where Trieste and Muggia stand today, building fortified villages to defend the coast.

Historical references to Tergeste (from which the name Trieste derives) suggest the existence of a village that developed around the Colle di San Giusto in pre-Roman times. Its role as a strategic junction between the Danube region and the Mediterranean is reflected in its name: 'terg' is the Celtic word for 'market'. In 46 BCE, Julius Caesar incorporated Trieste into the Roman Empire and soon after the first city walls were built. Trieste's most important archaeological relics date from the Roman period.

Under Byzantine rule, the city grew, with a population of around 2000 by the turn of the 13th century. At this time, Trieste was already a cultural melting pot, a place where Latin, Slavic and German worlds met, mingled and traded. Although the trade of wine, oil and salt had made it a prosperous port of the Middle Ages, the city found itself increasingly threatened by its more powerful rival La Serenissima (Venice).

To bolster its own security, Trieste turned to Austria in 1382, seeking its protection. Yet, despite Venice's temporary defeat in 1509, La Serenissima remained a cumbersome presence for Trieste, and the city was eventually left no option but to accept its secondary role in Venice's shadow.

After centuries of decline, Trieste's fortunes reached a decisive turning point in 1700 when the Habsburgs decided that it would make the ideal Mediterranean gateway for their empire. Declared a free port in 1719, Trieste entered a period of great prosperity and growth. The city expanded into the Borgo Teresiano (p65), boosting economic development and providing space to accommodate a growing population.

Towards the end of the 18th century, 200,000 called Trieste home, making the city the empire's third largest. The city's headcount continued to grow after 1797, when Napoleon's invasion of Italy marked the fall of Trieste's long-time maritime rival Venice.

With the 19th century came an expansion of Trieste's port and the arrival of major banks and insurance companies. Belle Époque Trieste was a multicultural city, attracting intellectuals and free thinkers. The freedom of worship granted to the population also drew a large Jewish community, joining one established in the Carso centuries earlier.

At the beginning of the 20th century, Trieste had become a worldly, cosmopolitan hub, whose residents included literary giants Umberto Saba, Italo Svevo and James Joyce. These greats would meet in cafes, cinemas and theatres, places that reverberate with Belle Époque spirit to this day. As a border city during the era of European nation building, Trieste also attracted irredentists and patriots. Italian-spirited locals critical of Austrian rule and in favour of economic reform (among them Trieste's bourgeoisie) looked towards the Italian peninsula.

In contrast, Trieste's Slovenian community was going through its own period of cultural furore, the city's Narodni Dom (Slovene Cultural Centre) fervently organising activities for Slovenian-speaking locals. The assassination of Austria's Archduke Franz Ferdinand in Sarajevo – an event which drew Europe towards WWI – saw Trieste chosen to host his funeral. Shortly afterwards, the Carso became a frontline and critical battleground until Italy's victory in 1918 led to the city's unification with the rest of the Italian peninsula.

Under Fascist rule, Trieste endured a period of forced Italianisation, stifling the city's long-established multicultural identity. Germans, Slovenians and ethnic minorities living in the city endured violence and harassment, aimed at erasing all traces of their present and their past. Arguably, it was this very cosmopolitanism that encouraged the Fascist regime to promulgate its infamous racial laws here in 1938.

Five years later, in 1943, Trieste fell under the direct control of the Third Reich. The old Risiera di San Sabba (p70) was converted into a concentration camp, a place where more than 40,000 Jews, political prisoners and partisans, both Italian and Slavic, would lose their lives.

Trieste would experience one of its most difficult periods with the end of WWII. Despite being heavily bombed and economically depressed, the city had become a nexus in the struggles for a new world order. In 1945, Yugoslav and Allied troops reached it from opposite sides. The Yugoslavs gained initial control, leading to the 'Forty days of Tito', in which Trieste became an autonomous city of the Federal Republic of Yugoslavia, led by a general of the Communist Party. It was a period marked by violence and the settling of scores, culminating in the massacres of the *foibe*. Faced with international pressure, the Yugoslav army withdrew in June 1945 and the city was occupied by Allied troops.

In 1947, the Free Territory of Trieste (FTT) was declared. A region under the guidance of NATO, it was divided into two zones: A included Trieste and the Carso, while B (a buffer state of sorts) included Istria. The FTT lasted seven years. In 1954, zone A was returned to Italy, though its proximity to Yugoslavia and the Iron Curtain saw it surrounded by militarised zones and armoured borders.

It would take the break-up of Yugoslavia and accession of Slovenia to the Schengen Treaty (2007) for Trieste to finally shake off its border-town status and embrace once more its relished role as a cosmopolitan European crossroads.

Orientation

Trieste's *centro storico* (historic centre) is the oldest part of the city, extending down to the waterfront and to Borgo Teresiano. Piazza Unità d'Italia is the area's focal point, as well as the link between the old town and the waterfront area, which includes Le Rive (seafront esplanade) and both the Audace and Bersaglieri piers.

Heading southwest along Le Rive you'll find the Molo Pescheria, Salone degli Incanti and Molo Venezia on one side, and the Borgo Giuseppino (anchored by Piazza Venezia) on the other.

ⓘ FVG CARD

The FVG Card provides free or discounted admission to numerous museums and cultural institutions, as well as discounted public transport. Choose from a 48-hour (adult/concession €25/20) or one week (€39/34) card; both adult cards also cover one accompanying child under 12. See p289.

Heading northwest, Le Rive leads to Piazza Verdi and Piazza della Borsa, where the old town meets Borgo Teresiano. From the old town, the city spreads south, south–east and east. Beyond the Molo Fratelli Bandiera is the city's main port. Viale Gabriele D'Annunzio, Via Cesare Battisti and Viale XX Settembre lead to the city's main residential areas, while to the north of town lie ancient settlements of the Trieste coast (p83).

◉ Sights

◎ The Old Town & Le Rive

Trieste's ancient core – bordered by Piazza Unità d'Italia to the northwest, the Teatro Romano to the northeast, the Colle di San Giusto to the southeast and the remains of the early Christian basilica to the southwest – was the hub of all city life from its origins until the 18th century, with the city rarely expanding beyond its original boundaries.

Excluding Le Rive, this area claims the city's most complicated road network: two of its main thoroughfares are Via del Teatro Romano and Via di Cavana, which cut through much of the area below the *colle* (hill).

★**Piazza Unità d'Italia** PIAZZA
(Map p58) Piazza Unità d'Italia (formerly Piazza Grande) is an ethereal place: at dawn, when it stirs in the half-light; in the afternoon, white and dazzling in the sun; at sunset, cut by shimmering orange blades; and finally at night, when its pavement lights glow blue like the sea.

The grand buildings that flank three sides of the square date from between the late 18th and early 20th centuries. At the far end of the square is eclectic **Palazzo del Municipio**, designed by Triestine architect Giuseppe Bruni, built in 1875 and featuring a distinctive central clock tower. Bruni also designed nearby **Palazzo Modello** (1873), located at the corner of Via Bartoli. The building had been

Trieste

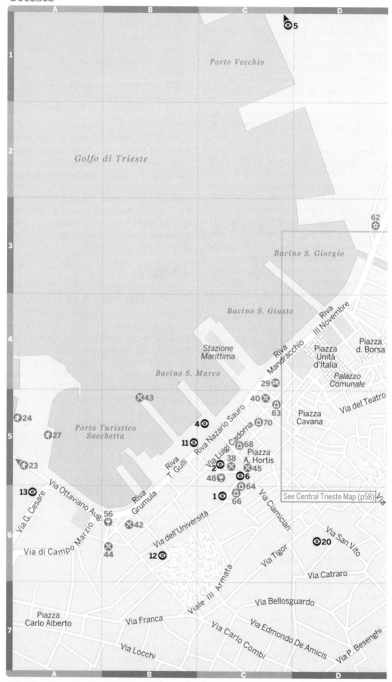

Porto Vecchio

Golfo di Trieste

5

62

Bacino S. Giorgio

Bacino S. Giusto

Riva III Novembre

Riva Mandracchio

Piazza d. Borsa

Piazza Unità d'Italia

Palazzo Comunale

Via del Teatro

Piazza Cavana

29

40

63

70

Stazione Marittima

Bacino S. Marco

43

4

11

Riva Nazario Sauro

Via Luigi Cadorna

68

Piazza A. Hortis

38

2

6

45

Porto Turistico Sacchetta

Riva T. Gulli

48

64

24

27

1

66

See Central Trieste Map (p58)

23

Via Ottaviano Aug.

Riva Grumula

Via Ciamician

13

Via G. Cesare

56

42

Via dell'Università

12

Via Tigor

20

Via San Vito

44

Via di Campo Marzio

Viale III Armata

Via Catraro

Via Bellosguardo

Piazza Carlo Alberto

Via Franca

Via Edmondo De Amicis

Via P. Besenghi

Via Locchi

Via Carlo Combi

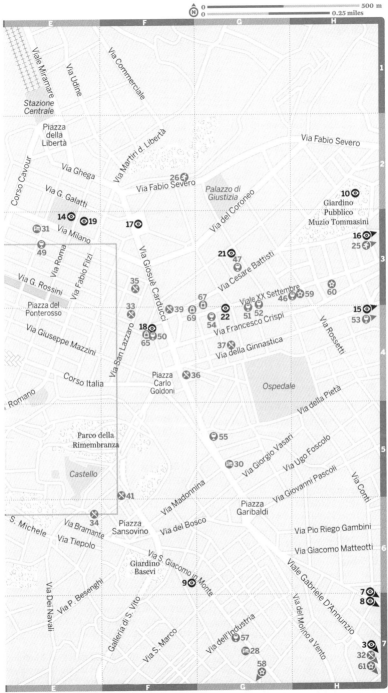

Trieste

◎ **Top Sights**

1 Civico Museo Sartorio C6
2 Museo Revoltella C5
3 Risiera di San Sabba .... off map H7

◎ **Sights**

4 Aquario Marino C5
5 Civico Museo del Mare .... off map C1
6 Civico Museo della Civiltà Istriana,
   Fiumana e Dalmata C5
7 Civico Museo della Guerra per la Pace
   'Diego de Henriquez' .... off map H7
8 Civico Museo
   di Storia Naturale .... off map H7
9 Ex Lavatoio di San Giacomo F6
10 Giardino Pubblico H2
11 Le Rive B5
12 Magazzino dei Venti B6
13 Museo Ferroviario di Trieste –
   Campo Marzio A6
   Museo Nazionale dell'Antartide
   'Felice Ippolito' .... (see 16)
14 Museo Postale e Telegrafico
   della Mitteleuropa E3
15 Orto Botanico .... off map H4
16 Parco di San Giovanni .... off map H3
17 Piazza Oberdan F3
18 Piazza San Giovanni F4
19 Piazza Vittorio Veneto E3
20 Quartiere San Vito D6
21 Synagogue G3
22 Viale XX Settembre G4

◎ **Activities, Courses & Tours**

23 Bagni Ausonia ....off map A5
24 Bagno Marino La Lanterna El Pedocin ... A5
25 City Green .... off map H3
26 Kleine Berlin F2
27 Sub Sea Club A5

◎ **Sleeping**

28 Hotel San Giusto G7
29 Hotel Savoia Excelsior Palace C4
30 Hotel Victoria G5
31 Theresia E3

◎ **Eating**

32 Al Moro .... off map H7

Da Gigi .... (see 3)
33 Da Giovanni F4
34 Da Libero E6
35 Da Roby F3
36 Da Vittorio F4
37 De Scarpon G4
38 Le Botti C5
39 Marascutti F4
40 Marinato C5
41 Osteria di mare Alla Voliga F5
42 Osteria Istriano B6
43 Pier – The Roof B5
44 Sandwich Club B6
45 Siora Rosa C5

◎ **Drinking & Nightlife**

46 Aqvedotto H3
47 Caffè San Marco G3
48 Draw Food C5
49 Giovinoto E3
50 Gran Malabar F4
51 La Preferita 1991 .... G4
52 Lettera Viva G3
53 Oasi del Gelato .... off map H4
54 Il Pane Quotidiano G4
55 Pirona G5
56 Stazione Roger's Outdoor B6
57 Zenzero e Cannella G7

◎ **Entertainment**

58 Casa delle Culture .... off map G7
59 Cinema Federico Fellini H3
60 Politeama Rossetti H3
61 Stadio 'Nereo Rocco' .... off map H7
62 Teatro Miela D3

◎ **Shopping**

63 Blu di Prussia C5
64 Dezen Dezen C5
65 Drogheria Toso F4
66 Laboratorio degli In-perfetti C6
   Lister .... (see 16)
67 Mariabologna G3
68 Record C5
69 Sfreddo F4
70 Vud C5

designed as a prototype for the piazza. The plan was never followed through and (fortuitously perhaps) the older buildings survived.

Next to Palazzo Modello, **Casa Stratti**, built in 1839, houses Caffè degli Specchi (p79). On the same side of the square, the colonnade of **Palazzo del Governo** – built in 1904–5 and the most recent of the buildings on this side – stands out for its decorative detail, a dramatic break from the austere style prevalent in Trieste.

Opposite, the **Palazzo del Lloyd Triestino**, designed by Von Ferstel in neo-Renaissance style around 1880, is named for the shipping company that once had its headquarters here. Today, it's home to the regional government. Note the statues at its base, allegorical representations of both salt and fresh water. Beside it is the Grand Hotel Duchi d'Aosta (p74), itself flanked by the Palazzo Pitteri, dating from 1780.

At its northwestern end, the piazza opens directly onto the sea and its ever-shifting light and colours. Not even the busy road that cuts between the two can detract from the spectacular illusion of the square extending out into the water like a dreamy terrace. Or is it the sea itself that creeps into the city, melding with it?

It's a dynamic that has changed several times over the centuries. In the 14th century, the then-rudimentary square was severed from the waterfront by walls and towers. The snub continued with the Castello Amarina, built by the Venetians. In the 18th century, a tower stood at the centre of the piazza, guarding a small port that separated the city from the open sea. At that time, the square also overlooked a stable, a prison and the Locanda Grande. The most important hotel in the city, it was where art historian Johann Joachim Winckelmann

(p62), one of the fathers of neoclassicism, was stabbed to death in 1768.

One of the largest waterfront squares in Europe, the piazza is speckled with interesting details.

Note the monument to Hapsburg emperor Charles VI (1728), whose declaration of Trieste as a free port ushered in a period of substantial economic growth. Note also the Fontana dei Quattro Continenti (1751) and its allegorical representation of Europe, Asia, Africa and the Americas.

The place from which Mussolini proclaimed his Italian Racial Laws in 1938 is marked on the ground between the fountain and the Palazzo del Municipio. The laws' introduction ushered in one of the darkest chapters in Italy's history and led to the atrocities of the Risiera di San Sabba (p70). At the base of the two flagpoles – erected in 1933 and featuring the halberd (symbol of Trieste) – a group of bronze figures depict the Italian soldiers who, victorious in WWI, achieved the unity from which the piazza derives its name.

Colle di San Giusto   ARCHAEOLOGICAL SITE
(Map p58) As the Roman ruins on its slopes attest, this hill was the very heart of ancient

STROLLING WITH ZENO (& SVEVO)

Trieste plays an integral part in the novels of Italo Svevo, one of Italy's greatest writers. Svevo was born in Trieste as Ettore Schmitz, during the city's time under the Austrian Empire. He would later choose the pseudonym Italo Svevo ('Italian Swabian'), which reflected his German and Italian origins.

Alfonso Nitti, the protagonist of his first novel, *Una vita*, lives in the old city towards San Giusto. The current Via Cesare Battisti and Viale XX Settembre, then known as Corsia Stadion and Via dell'Acquedotto, appear often in Svevo's books, and are where Svevo himself also lived.

Other places to feature are the train station and the city squares – Piazza della Borsa, Piazza Goldoni, Piazza Verdi – as well as the cafes and the Civic Library in Piazza degli Studi, today's Piazza Hortis, in front of which Svevo is remembered by a statue.

Walking between the old town and Borgo Teresiano, it is possible to retrace the movements of Zeno Cosini, the protagonist *of Zeno's conscience*, Svevo's best-known work. The novel tells the crisis of the end of the century through the events of a decadent family of the bourgeoisie and of a city that seems to have lost itself.

As is the case for Trieste's other two literary greats, Umberto Saba and James Joyce, there are several self-guided walking tours dedicated to Svevo, which you can follow via information panels.

One of the houses inhabited by Svevo is now the Musei Svevo e Joyce (Map p58; 040 675 81 82; www.museosveviano.it ; www.museojoycetrieste.it; Via Madonna del Mare 13; 9am-1pm Mon-Sat, also 2-6pm Wed, for reservations call or email museosveviano@comune .trieste.it) FREE. Objects linked to the writers (who were great friends) are kept in two rooms, from manuscripts to private correspondence. The twin museums are study and research centres open to the public.

Central Trieste

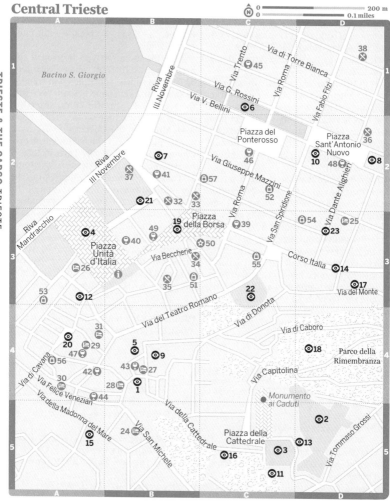

Tergeste, even if medieval-era relics dominate the site today.

Colonised by the Romans in the 2nd century BCE, it was here that the city's construction began, the Roman settlers choosing the site to build important civic buildings like the forum, basilica and theatre.

To reach the hill, cross the porticos of Palazzo del Municipio in Piazza Unità d'Italia and come out in Piazza Piccola. After the short stretch of Via della Muda Vecchia, follow the Scalinata delle Medaglie d'Oro, from where the climb begins.

Basilica di San Silvestro PLACE OF WORSHIP
(Map p58; ☏040 63 27 70; Piazza San Silvestro 1 ⊙9am-6pm Mon-Fri, to 1pm Sat) Heading up the Scalinata delle Medaglie d'Oro (Golden Medals Staircase), you will first come across a small Romanesque basilica consecrated to St Sylvester. While the basilica dates from the 11th century, its beautiful Gothic rose window is a later addition.

Despite its modest size, the building is of considerable importance, being Trieste's oldest place of worship. Its triple-naved interior harbours traces of 14th-century frescoes and a valuable organ.

Central Trieste

◎ Top Sights

1 Arco di Riccardo B4
2 Castello di San Giusto D5
3 Cattedrale di San Giusto Martire C5
4 Piazza Unità d'Italia A3

◎ Sights

5 Basilica di San Silvestro B4
6 Canal Grande C1
7 Chiesa di San Nicolò dei Greci B2
8 Chiesa di Sant'Antonio Taumaturgo D2
9 Chiesa di Santa Maria Maggiore B4
10 Chiesa Serbo-Ortodossa
     di San Spiridione D2
11 Civico Museo d'Antichità
     J.J. Winckelmann & Orto Lapidario .. C5
12 Civico Museo di Arte Orientale A3
13 Colle di San Giusto D5
14 Corso Italia D3
15 Musei Svevo e Joyce A5
16 Museo d'Antichità J.J. Winckelmann..... C5
17 Museo della Comunità Ebraica
     di Trieste 'Carlo e Vera Wagner' D3
18 Parco della Rimembranza D4
19 Piazza della Borsa B3
20 Piazza di Cavana A4
21 Piazza Verdi B2
22 Teatro Romano C3
23 Via Dante Alighieri D3

◎ Sleeping

24 B&B Gens Julia B5
25 Double Tree Hilton D3
26 Grand Hotel Duchi d'Aosta A3
27 Hotel All'Arco B4
28 Hotel Barbacan B4
29 James Joyce Hotel A4

30 L'Albero Nascosto A4
31 Urban Hotel Design A4

◎ Eating

32 Crops B2
33 Da Pepi B2
34 Genuino B3
35 Hostaria Malcanton B3
36 La Bomboniera D2
37 Pep's Fish House B2
38 Rudy - Spaten D1

◎ Drinking & Nightlife

39 Antico Caffè Torinese C3
40 Caffè degli Specchi B3
41 Caffè Tommaseo B2
42 Cemût A4
43 Dream Team B4
44 Hop Store A4
45 Hop&Rock C1
46 James Joyce Cafè C2
47 Maita A4
48 Stella Polare D2
49 Urbanis B3

◎ Entertainment

50 Dhome C3
     Teatro Verdi .... (see 21)

◎ Shopping

51 Achille B3
52 Bischoff C2
53 Katastrofa A3
54 Libreria Antiquaria 'Umberto Saba' D3
55 Oltre la Luna C3
56 Torrefazione La Triestina A4
57 Viezzoli C2

Chiesa di Santa Maria Maggiore
PLACE OF WORSHIP

(Map p58; ☑ 040 63 29 20; Via del Collegio 6; ⊙ 7am-6pm Mon-Fri, 8am-6pm Sat) Located on the same square as the Basilica di San Silvestro lies the Chiesa di Santa Maria Maggiore (also known as dei Gesuiti). Designed by Jesuit Giacomo Briani in 1627 and completed in 1682, its baroque exterior is in sharp contrast to the area's older buildings. Inside, the triple-nave and transept feature 18th-century decoration, while the dome itself was added in the 19th century.

★ Arco di Riccardo
RUINS

(Map p58; Piazza del Barbacan) One of Trieste's most substantial Roman ruins, the Arco di Riccardo rises above a still visible stretch of Roman road (see also p60).

★ Cattedrale di San Giusto Martire
PLACE OF WORSHIP

(Map p58; ☑ 040 260 08 92; Piazza della Cattedrale 2; ⊙ 7am-6.45pm Mon-Sat, until 8pm Sun for mass) The leafy final section of Via della Cattedrale is also the home stretch to the summit. The street spills into a square where, in addition to the cathedral, you'll find the former baptistery, now the **Cappella di San Giovanni**, preceded by a small porch and the **Cappella di San Michele al Carnale**. The latter served as the cemetery chapel. On your way up the hill, you'll have already noticed the cathedral's huge rose window. On closer inspection, you'll also note the Roman-era carvings on the portal, skilfully built using fragments of Roman funerary monuments. This recycling technique dates from the 14th century, the same century in which the cathedral was built by joining together the two older churches of Santa Maria and San Giusto (hence the asymmetrical facade).

The cathedral's squat, 14th-century **bell tower** (⏱9am-5.30pm Apr-Sep, 9am-noon & 2.30-5pm Mar & Oct, call ahead other times ☎393 954 31 31; full/reduced €2/1) incorporates an earlier Romanesque rendition, itself built on a Roman propylaeum. At the top of the once-conical bell tower sat a 'melone', a decorative element destroyed by lightning in 1421; it's now housed in the Castello di San Giusto. Architectural elements from the Roman era are clearly visible in the bell tower. The statue in the *aedicula* (small shrine) depicts St Justus, the patron saint of Trieste, holding a model of the city in one hand and a palm symbolising martyrdom in the other. The bronze busts, added to the Roman-era corbels in 1862, represent important local religious figures: Enea Silvio Piccolomini, bishop of Trieste and later Pius II, and the bishops Rinaldo Scarlicchio and Andrea Rapicio.

Inside, the cathedral is shrouded in a hallowed, mystical air found only in certain very old churches. Its five grand naves and numerous side chapels and spaces reveal a medley of styles and eras. The side apses are decorated with valuable 11th-century Byzantine mosaics, while the mosaic gracing the central apse, by Guido Cadorin, is from 1932. This latter work takes up the theme of the *Coronation of the Virgin*, which was found in the original 15th century apse, itself altered in 1843. The cathedral's **Treasury** includes rare objects, relics and reliquaries, tapestries and paintings. Among these items is St Sergius' halberd, which is the emblem of the city.

★ Castello di San Giusto
CASTLE

(Map p58; ☎040 30 93 62; www.castellodisan giustotrieste.it; Piazza della Cattedrale 3; adult/reduced €5/3; ⏱10am-7pm daily in summer, 10am-5pm Tue-Sun in winter, last entry 30min before closing) One of Trieste's most striking historic landmarks, the Castello di San Giusto is perched on the highest point of the Colle di San Giusto. The castle – unusual for its triangular-shaped walls – was commissioned by Frederick of Habsburg and built as both a fortress and a residence for the imperial

🏃 Walking Tour
Tergeste & Beyond

START VIA DEI CAPITELLI
END TEATRO ROMANO
LENGTH ABOUT 800M; HALF A DAY

The term 'Trieste città romana' (Trieste: Roman City) is more than a claim to noble ancient roots. It's also the theme of this walking tour, whose eclectic mix of sights can be tackled in half a day or, even more evocatively, in the evening, either entirely or in part. Climb and descend the Colle di San Giusto starting from the ❶**archaeological digs** in the vicinity of Via dei Capitelli, more or less in front of Cemût (p78). Look around and you'll notice sections of late-Roman walls, some building foundations and a **tetrapylon**, a square-shaped monument that usually stood at the crossroads of two roads. It's likely that two roads passed through here, of which at least one led from the sea to the city above.

Heading up Via dei Capitelli in a south-easterly direction, you will soon end up in Piazzetta Riccardo, dominated on the left by the ❷**Arco di Riccardo**. One of Trieste's major Roman relics, the arch stands on a stretch of clearly visible Roman road. Part of the arch has since been embedded in medieval-era buildings, as commonly happened in Italian cities. Regardless, it remains an extraordinary sight, perhaps due the incongruity between its monumental scale and claustrophobic setting on a small, bustling square. Over 7m high and 5m wide, the arch dates back to the 1st century CE. Traditionally thought to be part of the ancient city walls, it was more likely one of the access doors to the sanctuary of the Magna Mater. Apparently, its name derives from 'cardo' (one of the Roman city's two main streets) and not from 'Riccardo', a name dating back to Trieste's period of Frankish rule. (Then again, some researchers believe its origin is King Charles VI.)

Passing the arch, take Via della Cattedrale up to Trieste's cathedral and its own unexpected Roman remains. The cathedral was constructed by joining two exisiting previous churches (p59), both of which reputedly sit on the foundations of a classical temple. Salvaged materials used to decorate the cathedral's facade include **sar-**

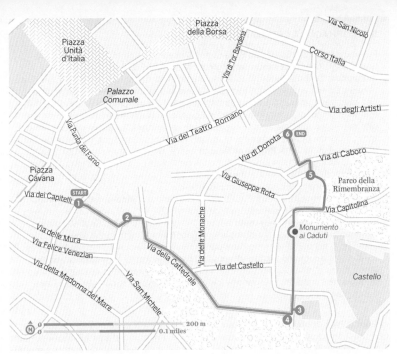

cophagus lids and ancient statues, while lurking inside the bell tower are the architectural remains of the ❸ **Propylaeum of San Giusto** (☑ 338 320 77 90; adult/reduced €2/1; ⊙ 9am-5pm), restored in 2020. Heading up the bell tower, you'll pass the propylaeum's corinthian columns and capitals, as well as a bas-relief depicting Dionysus attending to two thirsty griffins.

To the south of the church (on your left if your back is to the facade) is the entrance to the ❹ **Orto Lapidario** (⊙ 10am-5pm) `FREE`, home to a rich collection of classical finds from the Carso and nearby Aquileia (p132). On the northern side of the church you'll notice columns and other remains brought to light in the 1930s: these belonged to the **basilica civile**, dating from the mid-1st century CE and once overlooking the Roman **square**.

From the square, head down the steps of the Monumento ai Caduti (Monument to the Fallen) and follow Via Capitolina downhill to

the first set of steps leading into the park. Cross the park and turn left into Via di Caboro to reach Via della Chiauchiara and its ❺ **Tor Cucherna**. The tower is the only evidence of the medieval walls that encircled the city until Trieste became a free port in 1719. By this time, the tower had been converted into a dwelling, saving it from demolition. Its strange name probably hails from the German *guken* (peeking), a credible theory given its role as a watchtower. The German word also shaped the Triestine *cucar*, which has the same meaning. Taking Via Battaglia, you'll reach the rear of the ❻ **Teatro Romano** (p62), built between the 1st century BCE and the 2nd century CE and swallowed up by residential buildings in the Middle Ages. Its stalls – visible along the side of the hill – could once accommodate 6000 spectators, who no doubt enjoyed the panoramic view of the gulf. Alas, the view is now blocked by the Questura and other Fascist-era buildings dating from the 1930s.

SARCOPHAGI & A CENOTAPH

Perched atop Colle di San Giusto is the Civico Museo d'Antichità J.J. Winckelmann (Map p58 ☑ 040 31 05 00; www.museoantichitawinckelmann.it; Piazza della Cattedrale ⊙10am-5pm Tue-Sun), founded in 1873 following an expansion of the original collection. The museum collects archaeological finds from Trieste and the Carso, as well Etruscan, Egyptian, Mayan and other antiquities. It's a fascinating trip through time and art, and one that young visitors will especially love. While the Egyptian section is limited, its objects are fascinating, among them sarcophagi, statuettes and canopic jars. The Roman collection is varied, while the Cypriot section claims a large number of vases, used mainly in trade. The museum's real star is the **Rhyton of Taranto**, a silver drinking vessel shaped like a fawn's head and dating from between the 4th and 5th centuries BCE. Discovered in the Puglian city of Taranto and purchased by the museum in 1899, its neck is decorated with a mythological scene depicting Boreas kidnapping Orithyia.

The museum's assets also include the Orto Lapidario and **Winckelmann cenotaph**. Art historian, librarian and archaeologist, Winckelmann (1717–68) achieved a certain notoriety in his life and met an untimely death in Trieste by sheer ill fortune. The German-born classicist was passing through the city on his way back to Rome from Vienna, where he had received honorary medals for his cultural pursuits. In Trieste, he crossed paths with Francesco Arcangeli, a cook and criminal who possibly murdered him for his medals or, perhaps, after a lovers' altercation. Winckelmann's memory is celebrated with a cenotaph among the antiquities of the Orto Lapidario he loved so much, while his remains lie in the Cattedrale di San Giusto.

---

captain, a type of prefect with military duties. Today, the captain's dwellings house the Castle Museum and Lapidarium of Tergeste, with weapons and other 18th-century items. Entering the building, you'll notice, on your right, the famous 'melon with the halberd', which once topped the cathedral bell tower. (The halberd is the emblem of Trieste.) In front of the entrance itself are Micheze and Jacheze, the original automatons that decorated Palazzo del Municipio's clocktower in Piazza Unità d'Italia; the current statues are copies.

Despite being enlarged with additional walls and ramparts over the centuries, the castle has only witnessed two minor battles. Inside the walls, the Cortile delle Milizie now hosts summer festivals and events. Don't leave without wandering around the castle walls, which offer breathtaking views of Trieste and the gulf.

Parco della Rimembranza
MEMORIAL

(Map p58; Via Capitolina) Fascist-era additions to Trieste – some of which radically altered the cityscape – include the Parco della Rimembranza, established in 1926. Crossed by Via Capitolina and Via Ragazzi del 99, the centrally located park occupies the entire northern side of the Colle di San Giusto, which slopes down towards Corso Italia and Teatro Romano (p62). It's pleasant to wander (especially in a downhill direction). Scattered throughout the park is a series of karst stones engraved with the names and units of Trieste's fallen, as well as monuments commemorating various homeland battles.

Teatro Romano
RUINS

(Map p58; ☑ 040 347 83 12; Via del Teatro Romano 3; ⊙ on request) **FREE** The Colle di San Giusto's hillside provides a natural slope for the stalls of this brick-built theatre (see also p61).

Civico Museo di Arte Orientale
MUSEUM

(Map p58; ☑ 040 322 07 36; www.museoarte orientaletrieste.it; Via San Sebastiano 1; ⊙10am-5pm Thu-Sun) **FREE** Great things come in small packages, including Trieste's Museum of Oriental Art. Swoon over exquisite Chinese and Japanese artworks and artefacts, and retrace the Silk Road through the treasures that travelled its route to Europe. The Japanese armour and Hokusai prints alone are worth a visit.

Piazza di Cavana
PIAZZA

(Map p58) Like any self-respecting port area, Piazza di Cavana was, until recently, a disreputable place riddled with brothels and their sailor clientele. Some Triestini remember the place as a childhood no-go zone. Times have changed and now Piazza di Cavana is one of the quietest, most atmospheric corners of the old city. The area's beautiful 18th-century buildings have been restored and the square itself is a mix of old-school raffishness and new-school gentrification; a place where you'll find both greengrocers and quirky bars, many with outdoor tables and a low-key evening buzz.

Expect to pass through here many times on your walks around town. Indeed, you'll be wondering how it was ever possible to get anywhere when the 'hood was off-limits.

Civico Museo della Civiltà Istriana, Fiumana e Dalmata   MUSEUM

(Map p54; ☏040 63 91 88; www.irci.it; Via Torino 8) The museum (temporarily closed on our last visit) consists of 11 themed galleries. The first section sheds light on the ethnology of the Istrian, Rijeka and Dalmatian coasts, all historically linked to Venezia Giulia. The third floor houses the more interesting second section, which deals with the painful (and still somewhat sensitive) topic of the forced expulsion of Italians from areas that passed from Italy to Yugoslavia after WWII.

★ Museo Revoltella   MUSEUM, ART GALLERY

(Map p54; Revoltella Museum - Galleria di Arte Moderna; ☏040 675 43 50; www.museorevoltella.it; Via Diaz 27; adult/reduced € 7/5, free with FVG Card; ☉10am-7pm Mon & Wed-Sun, last entry 6.15pm) The intimate square located at the junction of Via Diaz and Via Torino is where you'll find the entrance to sumptuous Palazzo Revoltella, commissioned by wealthy Triestine merchant Pasquale Revoltella and built in neo-Renaissance style between 1854 and 1858.

Inside, lavish furnishings speak of 19th-century luxury, though the ground floor and the top floors are best known for the interventions of Venetian starchitect Carlo Scarpa (1906–78), who designed the house-museum's current layout.

Indeed, the palace houses a very important collection of late 19th- and 20th-century art, renowned for both its quality and volume. Among the works are paintings by lesser-known Friulano and Central European artists.

➜ Ground Floor

Here you'll find the ticket office, bookshop and, most importantly, Carlo Scarpa's *Fountain with spiral staircase*, which showcases the architect's unique approach to design. Another standout is Canova's *maquette of Napoleon as Mars the Peacemaker*.

➜ First Floor

Featuring their luxurious original furnishings, the seven rooms on this level were the apartment of Baron Revoltella. Among the paintings are evocative landscapes by Ippolito Caffi. Note also the inlaid floor.

➜ Second Floor

Sculptures dominate the second floor, as well as, as in the rest of the building, historic furnishings. Admire the grand staircase, whose panels are decorated with the busts of great historical thinkers and intellectuals (among them Descartes, Newton, Galileo...) and bronze medallions representing poetry, painting, architecture, sculpture, music, physics, and other natural and social sciences.

➜ Third Floor

This floor houses the Galleria di Arte Moderna, which is divided into two sections. One is dedicated to Italian painting of the second half of the 19th century, among them works that depict the Risorgimento (Italy's unification movement). The second focuses on the artists who helped elevate the standing of southern Italian modern painting, among them Giuseppe de Nittis.

➜ Fourth Floor

A staircase designed by Carlo Scarpa leads to the fourth floor, which houses sculptures by Italian and international artists of the late 19th century. Many of the works were featured and subsequently purchased at early Venice Biennales.

➜ Fifth Floor

Together with the floor above it, this section of the museum is dedicated to 20th-century art, with works by great Italian masters such as Carrà, De Chirico, Morandi and Sironi.

➜ Sixth Floor

Home to more 20th-century masters, with paintings and sculptures from the postwar period and A-listers like Guttuso, Fontana, Burri and Vedova. Scarpa's architectural intervention is most evident on the top floor (for instance in the ceiling with its large skylights) and it's from here that you can access a roof terrace that offers a one-of-a-kind view of Trieste.

★ Civico Museo Sartorio   MUSEUM

(Map p54; ☏040 675 93 21; Largo Papa Giovanni XXIII 1; ☉10am-5pm Thu-Sun) FREE A short walk from the Revoltella Museum and with free admission, this unmissable museum isn't short of masterpieces. These include its very

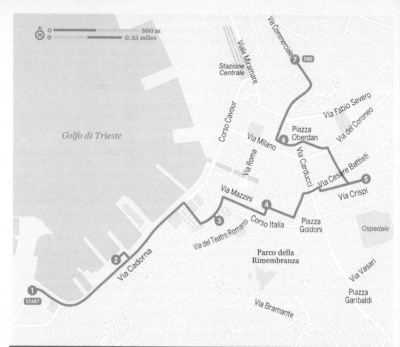

Walking Tour
Liberty Trieste

START STAZIONE CAMPO MARZIO
END VIA COMMERCIALE
LENGTH 4KM; 1HR 30MIN

The Art Nouveau style (known as Stile Liberty in Italy) spread across Europe between the 19th and 20th centuries, its bold, experimental aesthetics reflecting an era of momentous change. This walking tour starts in Art Nouveau's early years, at ❶ **Stazione Campo Marzio**. Built in 1887, it became an important European transport hub in 1906. It now houses the Museo Ferroviario (under restoration). Following the waterfront north (the sea to your left) leads you to another civic veteran: the former fish market. Now the ❷ **Salone degli Incanti (Hall of the Enchanted)**, it was designed in 1913 by architect Giorgio Polli in a style that successfully marries practicality and decorative detail. The section that housed the market now hosts exhibitions, while the main entrance leads to the Aquario Marino. Heading away from the waterfront leads you to two buildings which, while equally sophisticat-

ed in their decorative detail, exemplify different approaches to Art Nouveau: ❸ **Casa Bartoli** in Piazza della Borsa and ❹ **Casa Terni** in nearby Via Dante Alighieri. While the former (1906) charms with elegant floral motifs, the latter focuses its Liberty flourishes in its show-stopping balconies. Lively mouldings also impress at the entrance to ❺ **Palazzo Vivanti-Ghiberti** in Viale XX Settembre. Inaugurated on Christmas Day in 1907, the building was praised for its modernity, elegance and detail, all still evident. Yet, the era was also characterised by rigid, rigorous lines, such as those of ❻ **Hotel Balkan** (also known as 'Nardoni Dom'). Located in Piazza Oberdan, this was the first multifunction civic building constructed in Europe; a commercial, political and social hub for Trieste's Slovenian community. The square itself is flanked by buildings that offer an overview of 20th-century architecture in the city. Your last tour stop is ❼ **Casa Valdoni**, whose style encapsulates the many influences that inspired and informed its designer, architect Giorgio Zaninovich.

setting, an 18th-century villa on the slopes of the Colle di San Giusto, once the home of the Sartorio family. The building preserves its original 19th-century furnishings, a collection of precious ceramics and an extraordinary hoard of artworks. The museum claims the Rusconi-Opuich collection, which includes around 2500 items – everything from paintings, prints and drawings, to jewellery, silverware and textiles – spanning antiquity to the 20th century, as well as important collection of drawings by Tiepolo. Highlights include a 14th-century *Triptych of St Clare*.

Le Rive   SEAFRONT

(Map p54) The seaside streets between the mouth of the Canal Grande (p66) and the Bagno Marino La Lanterna (p71) constitute Le Rive. From north to south, these streets include III Novembre, del Mandracchio, Nazario Sauro, Tommaso Gulli, Grumula and, curving westward, Via Ottaviano Augusto. Fringing Le Rive's waterfront are the *moli* (piers), whose names each give a nod to history. Among them are cruise-ship terminal **Molo dei Bersaglieri** (named for the legendary riflemen of the Italian army) and Molo Fratelli Bandiera (named for 19th-century Italian nationalists Attilio and Emilio Bandiera). The latter wraps itself around the **Sacchetta**, Trieste's tourist marina. Between them lies the **Salone degli Incanti (Hall of Charms)**, a former fish market turned exhibition space.

Civico Museo del Mare   MUSEUM

(Map p54; ☑ 345 715 91 32; museodelmaretrieste.it; Porto Vecchio, Magazzino 26; ⊙10am-7pm Thu-Sun) FREE Could Trieste forego a maritime museum? Absolutely not! After all, this city was the largest port in the Austrian empire, with a long, illustrious nautical heritage reflected in the grand buildings of Piazza Unità d'Italia and Le Rive. This engaging ode to the *mare* (sea) includes nautical charts and instruments, uniforms, models and reproductions (including entire boats), fishing dioramas, not to mention minutely detailed explanations of topics like Austrian navy chevrons. Due to the museum's move to new digs at Magazzino 26 (see p70), only the Lloyd section was open on our last visit.

Aquario Marino   AQUARIUM

(Map p54; Civic Marine Aquarium; ☑ 040 30 62 01; www.aquariomarinotrieste.it; Molo Pescheria 2, Riva Nazario Sauro 1) Undergoing a major revamp at the time of research, Trieste's 'old' aquarium may have already reopened by the time you read these words. Housed in the main building of the *vecchia pescheria* (old fish market), slap bang in middle of Trieste's seaside promenade, the renovated venue will sport larger, more technologically advanced tanks, displays featuring retiles and amphibians, plus new exhibitions designed for young and old.

◉ Borgo Teresiano

Trieste's 'new city', the Borgo Teresiano, was built in the 18th century during a period of economic prosperity and growth. Located directly northwest of the old city, on a site previously occupied by salt pans, the neighbourhood was commissioned by Charles VI. The Habsburg emperor was one of the first monarchs to impose a 'master plan' upon the city. After his death, the project – designed to a rigid grid pattern – was completed by Maria Theresa of Austria, from whom the district takes its name.

Borgo Teresiano's focal point is the Canal Grande, a navigable canal designed on a grand scale. Take a stroll around this area and you'll feel like you're in another Trieste, its elegant buildings and broad, straight streets giving the distinct impression of a Habsburg city, albeit one washed in Mediterranean light.

Piazza della Borsa
& Piazza Verdi   PIAZZAS

(Map p58) Bustling Piazza della Borsa represents the 'checkpoint' between the old and new city, a role it shares with Corso Italia (p66), the street that leads from the waterfront to the heart of the city's residential district. Somewhat triangular in shape, the piazza is dominated by two buildings.

The first is the neoclassical **Palazzo della Borsa Vecchia**, whose dome and statue-graced pronaos deceptively recall a place of worship. In truth, the only god worshipped here is money. Once the city's stock exchange, the *palazzo* – dating from 1806 – now houses the Chamber of Commerce.

To its left is the **Tergesteo**, also known as Palazzo della Borsa Nuova. Built in the first half of the 19th century, it occupies the site of the former Customs House. Another hub of commerce, it also houses a shopping arcade and cafes. The Italian writer Italo Svevo once worked at Unionbank, which had its office on the second floor and in which he set part of his novel *Zeno's Conscience*. The Tergesteo also flanks **Piazza Verdi**, which you can reach by following Via Einaudi between the

THE DIVA & HER MUSEUM

Until a few years ago, whenever the 'diva' rolled into town to shake things up, the city's red-and-white-roped stanchions provided a much-welcomed grip. The diva we're referring to is the **bora**, an infamous wind that stirs in distant Siberia, picks up speed between Slovenia and the Carso, then roars furiously into the Gulf of Trieste as far as Venice. It's a (gusty) beast, capable of flipping over buses, dragging people down the street and tearing ships from their moorings.

Making its presence felt in everything from city shop names to uprooted road signs and the shields that protect fountains from their northeast side, the bora even claims its own quirky museum: the **Magazzino dei Venti** (Map p54; ☑ 040 30 74 78 ; www.museo bora.org; Via Belpoggio 9; ☺ by appointment) **FREE**. A work in progress, the museum is a laboratory, archive and, above all, an engaging, evocative place in which to learn all about Trieste's legendary wind, from ancient legends to scientific facts. You'll even get some travel ideas: for instance, the Val Rosandra (p90) is home to the Sella della Bora, where simply standing up is a feat when the bora blows.

---

two buildings. Elegant and bright, this large, rectangular square acts as a buffer between Piazza Unità d'Italia and Borgo Teresiano.

Overlooking the square is the pink **Teatro Verdi**, inaugurated in 1801. That the theatre's porticoed entrance recalls that of La Fenice in Venice is no coincidence: both were designed by Giannantonio Selva.

Corso Italia   STREET
(Map p58) The northern edge of Piazza della Borsa is bordered by Corso Italia, beyond which lie the gridded *palazzi* of Borgo Teresiano. Heading east along the Corso, you'll pass a number of Fascist-era buildings that loom over the Teatro Romano (p62); some of these are considered fine examples of the Fascist style. Another hundred metres along Corso Italia, on your right, is intimate Piazza Silvio Benco, from which you can easily reach Via del Monte, which runs parallel to Corso Italia.

Head west on Corso Italia (towards the waterfront) and you'll arrive in Piazza Tommaseo. A little to the right is the entrance to the **Chiesa di San Nicolò dei Greci** (Map p58; ☑ 040 36 28 01; Piazza Nicolò Tommaseo; ☺ 9am-12.30pm & 3-7pm Mon-Sat, 11.15am-12.15pm Sun), a hub for the Greek Orthodox community and a testament to Trieste's cosmopolitan heritage. Built in the second half of the 18th century, the church was restored and embellished between 1819 and 1821 with the support of wealthy Greek merchants. The elegant neoclassical facade and domed bell towers date from this time.

The interior features a sanctuary (presbytery) with three apses and two balconies on the back wall; the upper one for the choir, the

second one for the gynaeceum. Three Russian chandeliers illuminate the church and its precious iconostasis.

Museo della Comunità Ebraica di Trieste 'Carlo e Vera Wagner'   MUSEUM
(Map p58; ☑ 040 233 13 18; www.museoebra icotrieste.it; Via del Monte 5-7; adult/reduced €5/3, with synagogue €8/5; ☺ 10am-1pm Mon, Wed & Fri, 4-7pm Tue, 10am-4pm Thu) At the beginning of the 20th century, the building that now houses the Jewish Museum was the headquarters of the Jewish Agency. The organisation played a crucial role in managing the flow of Jewish immigration from northeastern Europe to the area that would become Israel. Given this, there isn't a building more worthy of honouring the history of Trieste's own Jewish community and to display its centuries-old collection of Judaica and other artefacts. Among these are important historical documents and items related to the Holocaust.

In the 'Gal Avanim' lapidary garden lie relics from Trieste's old Jewish cemetery, which sat on the same street, a little further uphill.

Canal Grande   CANAL
(Map p58) From Corso Italia, latticework streets shoot northeast towards the heart of the Borgo Teresiano: the Canal Grande (Grand Canal). Today, only small private boats moor in its still, moss-green waters, but once upon a time, when access to the sea wasn't hindered by bridges and Trieste's main waterfront road, tree-lined canals of flowed right into the heart of the city.

The Canal Grande was conceived between 1754 and 1756 as an axis around which the

Borgo Teresiano would be build. The waterway wasn't dug from scratch but created instead by extending the main collector channel of the salt pans that occupied the area.

Today, the canal is bookended by the Chiesa Sant'Antonio Taumaturgo and the moody, ever-shifting hues of the Adriatic Sea. Historic buildings and cafes flank its banks, which also skirt Piazza Ponte Rosso. The piazza itself is named after the Canal Grande's innermost bridge; the other two crossings are Passaggio Joyce and, closest to the sea, Ponte Verde. Wedged between the canal and Chiesa Sant'Antonio Taumaturgo is Piazza Sant'Antonio, softened by flower beds and often the site of trade fairs.

Chiesa Serbo-Ortodossa di San Spiridione
PLACE OF WORSHIP

(Map p58; ☑ 040 63 13 28; Via San Spiridione 9; ⊙ 8.30am-12.30pm & 4-7pm Tue-Sat, 9am-noon Sun) At the corner of Piazza Sant'Antonio and Via San Spiridione is the church of Trieste's Serbian-Orthodox community,

The declaration of Trieste as a free port in 1719 drew Serbian traders to the neighbourhood, where they conducted business and bought property. Built between 1861 and 1869 on the site of a previous orthodox church dating from 1753, the Chiesa Serbo-Ortodossa di San Spiridionethe was designed by the Lombard architect Carlo Maciachini.

Neo-Byzantine in style, the structure features a Greek cross plan, a lofty central dome and mosaic-embellished facade. The church was built using stone from the Carso and Istria, and marble from Carrara and Verona. Inside, oil paintings that resemble mosaics depict popular Orthodox saints, among them St Spyridon, St Nicholas and St George, as well as Christ and the apostles. Four precious icons decorate the iconostasis, adorned with gold and silver covers made in Russia between 1846 and 1850 and hailing from the former church.

On a visit to Trieste in 1782, the future Tsar Paul I gifted the church the votive lamp that you'll see hanging from the ceiling at the entrance.

Titbit: At the end of the 18th century, Trieste's Serbian community numbered around 200. Today that number is closer to 10,000, with most hailing from Pozarevac (Passarowitz in German), where the Treaty of Požarevac was signed between the Habsburg and Ottoman Empires in 1718.

Chiesa di Sant'Antonio Taumaturgo
PLACE OF WORSHIP

(Map p58; ☑ 040 63 83 76; Via Amilcare Ponchielli 2; ⊙ during services) The church that gives its name to Piazza Sant'Antonio is perfectly aligned with the Canal Grande. Its reflection once rippled in the water, before the last section of the canal was filled in to create the square. The Triestini know it as Sant'Antonio Nuovo (*nuovo* means 'new'), because the current building replaces an older church with the same name.

The current iteration was designed in 1806 by Pietro Nobile, who had originally envisaged a church made entirely of white Istrian stone. Constructed between 1828 and 1849, the building is one of Trieste's finest examples of neoclassical architecture.

The Graeco-Roman influence is strongest in its majestic portico (supported by six Ionic columns), its pediment and Francesco Bosa's six statues depicting the city's patron saints. Meanwhile, its rear facade is dominated by twin bell towers.

Inside, the interior is austere and grand in scale, adorned with Ionic columns, arches and barrel vaults, and a Pantheon-like central dome.

In the chapel to the left of the high altar, known as the Chapel of the Adoration, is Venetian painter Alessandro Longhi's *Visitation of the Virgin* (1769).

Via Dante Alighieri
STREET

(Map p58) Piazza Sant'Antonio is bordered by Via Dante Alighieri, an elegant street awash with beautiful buildings. Strolling along this strip can feel like leafing through an architecture tome, its buildings running the gamut of early modern architectural styles, from Liberty and neo-gothic to Deco. Among its highlights is Liberty show-off

TRIESTE & THE CARSO TRIESTE

PIAZZA SAN GIOVANNI

From behind the Chiesa di Sant'Antonio Taumaturgo, Via delle Torri leads to pretty little **Piazza San Giovanni** (Map p54), flanked by vintage shopfronts and pleasant cafes. The piazza also marks the spot where the axis followed by Borgo Teresiano's streets twists 45° to the north. East of the square, the streets remain gridded, but follow a pattern set by Via Carducci.

Casa Terni (Via Dante Alighieri), worth an admiring look.

Piazza Vittorio Veneto
PIAZZA

(Map p54) On the northern side of the Canal Grande, the gridded streets of Borgo Teresiano extend as far as Piazza della Libertà, home to Trieste's central station. While the buildings at this end of the Borgo enjoy less prestige than those closer to the canal, they are equally elegant.

Although the area is heavily trafficked, it's a pleasant place for an amble, with an industrious, workaday atmosphere and broad streets offering glimpses of the sea.

More or less at its centre is Piazza Vittorio Veneto, rectangular, austere and overlooked by the Palazzo delle Poste, which houses the **Museo Postale e Telegrafico della Mitteleuropa** (Map p54; ☎ 040 676 42 64; Piazza Vittorio Veneto 1; ⊗ 9am-1pm Mon-Sat, also 3-6pm Thu) **FREE**. The museum was temporarily closed on our last visit.

Synagogue
PLACE OF WORSHIP

(Map p54; ☎ 040 37 14 66; www.triestebraica.it/it/culturaturismo/the-synagogue; Via San Francesco d'Assisi 19; adult/reduced €5/3, with Jewish Museum €8/5; ⊗ 5pm Mon & Wed, 10.30am Tue) Trieste has always had a significant Jewish community, a fact reflected in the city's synagogue, which is one of Italy's largest. While its granite exterior appears somewhat bulky, almost oppressive, its vast, breathtaking interior feels light and airy.

The synagogue was built in 1912 to replace the *schole,* places of worship created in the mid-18th-century to meet the needs of an ever-more wealthy, flourishing and growing Jewish community. Guided tours shed light on the synagogue's unique design, which fuses traditional elements with a Christian basilica plan (a marriage based in engineering). Tours also illustrate the history of Trieste's Jews , which is intertwined with that of Jewish people across Europe.

To enter the synagogue, men must wear a headdress or a disposable kippa provided at the entrance.

Viale XX Settembre
PEDESTRIAN STREET

(Map p54) One of the most pleasant places for a stroll in Trieste, this pedestrianised street runs northeast from Largo Francesco Bonifacio, a little square that forms a corner with the Portici di Chiozza. Both the Roman and Teresiano aqueducts once passed along its route, and while the street is named for the Capture of Rome (20 September 1870), some locals still refer to it by its old name Via dell'Acquedotto (Aqueduct St).

A leafy strip scattered with cafe tables and diners, the street claims some notable buildings: at number 16 a plaque indicates the birthplace of Italo Svevo (p57); at number 35/c lies the Eden Palace, Trieste's most important Art Nouveau building; while at number 45 is the Politeama Rossetti (p80), which was inaugurated with Giuseppe Verdi's *A Masked Ball.*

Giardino Pubblico
PARK

(Map p54; btwn Via Giulia & Via Marconi) The Benedictine nuns who lived here sowed this patch of earth between 1854 and 1864, creating a medicinal garden. Today, this little green oasis is much loved by the people of Trieste, who use it to jog, stroll and walk their dogs. The park is also home to what may be the only public toilets in the city; worth keeping in mind when you're out and about.

Piazza Oberdan
PIAZZA

(Map p54) Located on the edge of the Borgo Teresiano, this square is important for two main reasons. The first is its tram stop for the celebrated Opicina Tram (p82), or number 2 tram, expected to be back in service from late 2022.

The second reason is that the square claims the **Museo del Risorgimento e Sacrario Oberdan** (☎ 040 675 40 68/040 675 46 99; www.museodelrisorgimentotrieste.it; Piazza Oberdan ⊗ 10am-5pm Thu-Sun) **FREE**, dedicated to the Triestine patriot Guglielmo Oberdan, an irredentist who became a martyr of the Italian unification movement.

Piazza Oberdan itself is a virtual compendium of Triestine architecture, its sample of buildings leading from the 19th century to the Fascist architecture of the early 20th century.

👁 The Modern City

As Trieste grew, it expanded east of the Borgo Teresiano, namely along Via Battisti and Viale XX Settembre, as well as southeast along Viale D'Annunzio. Here, the first, shy foothills of the Carso meet the city. Behind the Colle di San Giusto and parallel to Viale D'Annunzio, Via dell'Istria crosses the earthy district of San Giacomo.

To the south of the Molo Fratelli Bandiera is the industrial port, which extends into the

TRIESTE: 'GATE OF ZION'

The land now occupied by Trieste's Jewish Museum (p66) was purchased in 1446, but a Jewish presence is documented in the city from the 14th century. Today a Jewish school and the museum remain. Here, on the 50th anniversary of the founding of the State of Israel, a plaque was unveiled to commemorate the deportation of Triestine Jews and 150,000 Jews from Germany and both Central and Eastern Europe between 1920 and 1943: a tragic episode, but also an extraordinary moment of human solidarity. In those years, Jews arrived in Trieste to set sail for Palestine since the city was the only Italian port from which ships sailed to the Levant. Initially, these people were escaping from the Russian and Polish pogroms, but with the onset of Nazi persecutions, displaced people arrived from all of Hitler's occupied territories. And so Trieste became the so-called Gate of Zion: for many, an obligatory passageway towards the 'promised land' and salvation.

The city has always been welcoming to Jews, and it is no coincidence that it is home to the largest synagogue in Italy after the one in Rome. The Jewish presence is also linked to a typical expression in the Triestine lexicon: *far gheto* (to make ghetto). To the Triestini, the saying means 'to cause confusion or great commotion'. While it may sound pejorative, it's anything but. The ghetto, which until 1785 was encircled by walls, encompassed a maze of narrow streets full of antique dealers and secondhand bookshops. These same streets, populated by financiers, Jewish traders and merchants with goods displayed in bulk, swarmed with voices, colours and life. And it's from this that the expression *far gheto* originates, recalling that whirlwind of industrious freneticism that characterised one of the city's commercial hubs.

Trieste's old ghetto was located behind Piazza Unità d'Italia. From the adjacent Piazza della Borsa, historically the city's economic nerve centre, the area is accessed via the Arco della Portizza.

Bay of Muggia, while the outer southern suburbs harbour the Risiera di San Sabba.

Civico Museo di Storia Naturale · MUSEUM

(Map p54; ☎040 675 46 03; www.museostoria naturaletrieste.it; Via dei Tominz 4; adult/reduced €3/2, incl Civico Museo 'Diego de Henriquez' €5/3 ⊙10am-5pm Mon & Wed-Fri) Knowing that Trieste's natural history museum houses the remains of the largest dinosaur found intact in Europe (a 4m-long *Tethyshadros insularis* or hadrosaur) is reason enough to visit. But the recently renovated complex also claims Carlotta, the largest shark in the northern hemisphere (and possibly the world).

Zoology and paleontology aside, the museum also occupies itself with botany and mineralogy.

Although located a little out of the way, you can reach it quickly on bus 22 (alight at bus stop Via Revoltella 83) or on bus 18 (Via Cumano – Museo de Henriquez stop).

Civico Museo della Guerra per la Pace 'Diego de Henriquez' · MUSEUM

(Map p54; ☎ 040 675 46 99, 040 985 24 20; www. museodiegodehenriquez.it; Via Cumano 22; adult/ reduced €3/2; ⊙10am-5pm Mon & Wed-Fri, to 7pm Sat & Sun) Diego de Henriquez was the typical romantic adventurer of the early 20th century. Famously eccentric and contradictory, the Trieste native was also a formidable collector whose hoard is now the focus of his eponymous museum.

While it may be a war museum, it aspires to be a museum for peace; something that becomes clearer as you start exploring the place. Regardless of whether it succeeds or not, the museum does examine 20th-century society at war with its demons and horrors. On the upper floor, the exhibition focuses on the history of Trieste through WWI, Fascist rule and WWII until its reunion with Italy in 1954. Presented chronologically, the exhibition is intertwined with the life of Diego de Henriquez, providing a comprehensive history lesson both general and local.

To reach the museum, catch bus 18 (bus 5 on Sundays and public holidays).

Parco di San Giovanni · PARK

(Map p54; www.parcodisangiovanni.it, lower entrance Via Giovanni Sai, higher entrance Via Edoardo Weiss) Home to Trieste's psychiatric hospital since 1908, in the 1970s Franco Basaglia transformed the hospital into a space where 'the sick are free to leave and the citizens are free to enter'. In addition to the former

THE PORTO VECCHIO (OLD PORT): WHERE ART MEETS INDUSTRIAL ARCHAEOLOGY

West of Piazzale della Stazione lies the entrance to **Porto Vecchio** (Map p54, C1; P. Franco Vecchio), the last and largest historic port in Europe yet untouched by large-scale redevelopment. Not that time has stood entirely still. Plans are already underway to transform the area into a cultural and technological hub (for information on current events: ☑040 675 43 00). The **Centrale Idrodinamica** (Hydrodynamic Power Plant) and its electrical substation are located in an imposing yellow building, home to magnificent machines that powered the port's cranes from 1891 to 1988. The precinct's hub is **Magazzino 26**. A gargantuan hangar built in the 1890s and spanning 30,000 sq metres, it's home to the Lloyd Section of the Civico Museo del Mare (p65), temporary exhibitions, the Sala Luttazzi (used for conventions and special events) and the new Museo delle Masserizie (Museum of Masserizie). The latter houses a somewhat poignant collection of personal objects belonging to refugees who passed through this and other Italian ports.

A walk through Porto Vecchio is also an archaeological adventure of sorts. Explore the 3km of historic waterfront buildings once bustling with port-side activity. Dating from the second half of the 19th century, these industrial relics were among the first to be built using reinforced concrete.

psychiatric hospital, the park now also houses numerous faculties of the University of Trieste, as well as various associations and social cooperatives that make it a pleasant and lively place.

Look for the plasterboard horse symbolising the patients' exit from the hospital; the sculpture was made by the patients themselves.

While here you can also visit the **Museo Nazionale dell'Antartide 'Felice Ippolito'** (☑04056 78 89; www.mna.it; Via Weiss 21; adult/reduced €6/5; ☺ 9.30am-1pm Tue & Wed, 3-6pm Thu, closed Aug), part of a network of research centres dedicated to Antarctica (the others are in Genoa and Siena). The museum showcases videos, old maps and other objects related to the world's southernmost continent and the long-held human desire to 'conquer' it. And while Trieste may seem an incongruous place to find an Antarctic museum, it was from this land of sailors and explorers that one of the first expeditions bound for the South Pole set sail.

The park also harbours a splendid rose garden (a riot of colour in May) and a small restaurant called **Il Posto delle Fragole** (☑ 04057 87 77; www.ilpostodellefragole.eu; Via De Pastrovich 4; meals €5-12; ☺ 6am-6pm Mon-Fri, to 10.30pm summer). Run by a social cooperative, it offers a daily-changing menu.

Orto Botanico BOTANIC GARDEN
(Map p54; ☑040 36 00 68; www.ortobotanico trieste.it; Via Marchesetti 2; ☺9am-1pm Mon & Wed-Sun) FREE Trieste's botanic gardens were established in 1842 on the idea of then Trieste mayor Muzio de' Tommasini, who envisaged a centre for botanical research. Opened to the public in 1873, the gardens are home to over 1000 plant species, including alpine vegetation, medicinal herbs and poisonous plants.

To reach the Orto, catch bus 25 or 26 from Piazza della Borsa.

⭐**Risiera di San Sabba** NATIONAL MONUMENT
(Map p54; ☑040 82 62 02; www.risierasansabba. it; Via Giovanni Palatucci 5; audioguide €2; ☺9am-7pm) FREE Built in 1898 as a large rice husking plant, the Risiera di San Sabba was used by the Nazis as a temporary prison camp for Italian soldiers captured after 8 September 1943.

It was later used as a detention camp, for the sorting of deportees and the storage of looted goods, as well as for the imprisonment and extermination of partisans, political prisoners and Jews.

In Piazza Unità d'Italia (p53) you may have noticed the stone that marks the spot from which, in 1938, Mussolini proclaimed Italy's Racial Laws. To understand just how crucial that moment was in shaping Italy's darkest chapter, a trip to this former concentration camp is a must.

The Risiera di San Sabba is located a few dozen metres from the Stadio Nereo Rocco (p80) and can be reached on bus 8 or 10. While admission is free, the audioguide is an essential tool to fully appreciating the importance of this site, proclaimed a national monument in 1965 and featuring deeply symbolic artistic and architectural interventions by 20th-century architect Romano Boico.

Among them is an iron sculpture. Located near the rice dryer (converted into a crematorium in which thousands were incinerated), it symbolises the oven's chimney. On the ground, a steel walkway traces the footprint of the oven and its pipes. It's an especially powerful gesture given that, shortly before their defeat and escape, the Nazis had tried to destroy evidence of their terrible deeds. Also on view are the tiny cells in which the prisoners awaited death, huddled together amid the dead.

The site is made even more poignant by the addition of an interfaith chapel of remembrance. Don't miss the onsite museum, which movingly explores the complex political situation in which Venezia Giulia was mired, one in which Nazi-fascists, Tito's partisans and Italian anti-fascist partisans clashed.

🏃 Activities & Beaches

Beach Activities & Water Sports

The sea looms large in Trieste: it peeps out among the buildings and dominates the open views, while the urban bathing establishments are so close at hand that locals go swimming during their lunch break from the office.

★ Bagni Ausonia   SEA BATHS

(Map p54; ☑040 30 99 13; Riva Traiana 1; adult/reduced & afternoon ticket €6/5 ⊗8.30am-7.30pm) Located near the historic public baths of La Lanterna, the Bagni Ausonia began life in 1909 as the Nuovo Bagno Militare (New Military Bath). The 1930s saw the addition of the Stabilimento Balneare Ausonia, linked to the original baths (renamed Savoia and opened to the public) by a footbridge.

The original section, still nicknamed 'Savoia' today, is a popular hangout for younger Triestini, who spend most of the summer here in an atmosphere reminiscent of the 1960s.

While the baths are crowded on weekends, they're never too noisy. If you plan on driving here, arrive early or prepare for an exhausting hunt for parking. Alternatively, head in on bus 8 or 9.

The bathing complex includes a bar, showers and a seawater pool with diving boards; the latter hosts Trieste's kooky Olimpiade dele Clanfe (p72).

★ Bagno Marino

La Lanterna El Pedocin   SEA BATHS

(Map p54; ☑04030 59 22; Molo Fratelli Bandiera 3; adult €1; ⊗7.30am-7.30pm Jun-15 Sep, 8am-6.30pm 15-31 May & 16-30 Sep) Aptly located in the shadow of the *lanterna* (the lighthouse on Molo Fratelli Bandiera), these sea baths can also be reached on bus 8 and 9. They're the preferred baths of Triestini of 'a certain age', from the lonely, nostalgic and traditionalist (gender-segregated bathing is still honoured here), to *nonni* out with their *nipotini* (grandchildren). The vibe is earthy, familial and utterly unique. And while the water itself may not be as clean as it is in other parts of the coast, it's the distinctly local, authentic charm of the place that makes them a deeply Triestine experience.

Sub Sea Club   DIVING

(Map p54; www.subseaclubtrieste.it; Fratelli Bandiera Pier 17 ⊗8-10pm Mon Nov-Mar, 8-10pm Mon & Wed Apr-Oct) This association, founded almost 40 years ago with the simple aim of bringing people closer to the sea, organises diving courses, both in the pool and in the Adriatic. If you're in town around Christmas time, you should know that on December 26, a host of local divers (including a priest) gather to celebrate mass inside a diving bell.

E-bike, Segway & E-scooters

Trieste has numerous bike rentals offering e-bikes and other sustainable transport options. The one listed below offers the best value for money.

City Green   E-BIKE

(Map p54; ☑335 838 30 94; www.citygreentrieste. com; Via Giulia 78/c; rental 4hr traditional/electric bike €7/12; ⊗9am-noon & 4-7pm) 🚲 Mountain bikes, fat bikes, city bikes, folding bikes, touring bikes, scooters, hoverboards and two- and three-wheeled scooters, all electric.

🧭 Tour

YesTour   GUIDED TOURS

(☑040 972 00 20; www.yestour.it; Via Antonio Pigafetta 5, south near Risiera di San Sabba) Organises tours with qualified guides in and around Trieste, including museums. Recent additions include the **Hoptour** (adult/reduced €11/6; 75min; ⊗Fri-Sun) a hop-on, hop-off minibus.

Kleine Berlin   AIR-RAID TUNNELS

(Map p54; ☑339 253 97 12; www.cat.ts.it; Via Fabio Severo; adult €3; ⊗ by reservation) During WWII, a huge complex of air-raid tunnels was excavated into the hills of the city. Guides from

TRIESTE & THE CARSO TRIESTE

ANOTHER TRIESTE

To the east of San Giusto lies the district of **Rione San Giacomo**. Back in the day, according to the adage, this was where 'the women have Christ in their heart, the husband at sea and the lover under the bed'. This is a city within a city, a hotbed of humanity in one of the densest, earthiest corners of Trieste. At its heart is Campo di San Giacomo. Take a seat at Zenzero e Cannella (p78), opposite the large church, and let the neighbourhood's atmosphere wash over you, before slipping into its thoroughfares. Via dell'Istria, Via dei Giuliani and Via della Guardia are a jumble of old-school dairy shops, butchers and trattorias, often bursting with the merry chants of Triestina football fans. On these streets, Trieste's raffish, decadent side is on full display, even if many shopkeepers and residents lament the neighbourhood's grimy appearance. If possible, head in for San Giacomo's weekly markets, be it the Coldiretti market on Saturdays or the one in Piazza Puecher on Tuesdays and Fridays. Both showcase San Giacomo's liveliness and multicultural flavour. Another local treasure is the **ex Lavatoio di San Giacomo** (Map p54; ☑ 040 22 55 62; Via San Giacomo in Monte 9; ☻ visitable by reservation only) FREE, Trieste's last standing communal washhouse and a porthole into a lathered chapter of the city's past.

The flip side of the coin is the **Quartierre San Vito** (Map p54). Also on a hill, behind Borgo Giuseppino, it's an elegant residential district of quiet streets flanked by leafy private gardens. Initially used for the defence of Trieste, San Vito's development as a residential area coincided with its popularity among wealthy Britons living in the city. Heading up from Villa Neker, take Viale Terza Armata, Vicolo Calafai, Vicolo De Amicis or Via San Vito in the direction of San Michele and Via Bellosguardo and simply wander aimlessly.

the Club Alpinistico Triestino (which manages the site) lead walking tours through the intricate network, recounting the stories of those who sought shelter here. The tunnels are divided into two sectors, one built by the Italians and intended for civilians, the other by the Germans and used mainly as a storage area. Snooping around the tunnels is a thrill and stepping out of the last one to find yourself in the heart of the city is utterly surreal. Tours (which should be booked in advance) start at the tunnels' entrance (Via Fabio Severo 11). It's a damp, occasionally wet place, so wear waterproof shoes and, if you have one, bring a flashlight.

★✩ Festivals & Events

Trieste Film Festival   JANUARY
(www.triestefilmfestival.it) Italy's pre-eminent festival of Central and Eastern European cinema. Feature films, shorts and documentaries, as well as a program dedicated to directors from Friuli Venezia Giulia. Screenings are held at the Teatro Miela and Sala Tripcovich (p80). Like the Barcolana, the festival attracts hordes of locals. Book accommodation in advance to avoid rate hikes.

Horti Tergestini   APRIL
(www.hortitergestini.it) Nature, gardening and horticulture are the themes of this market show, held on a spring weekend in Parco San Giovanni.

Bioest   JUNE
(www.bioest.org) Eco farmers, small-scale producers and artisans working with toxin-free materials meet at Parco San Giovanni every summer to do their bit to help protect the planet.

Olimpiade dele Clanfe   JULY
(www.spiz.it) The ironic, rollicking spirit of the Triestini comes to the fore at the Olimpiade dele Clanfe, held on the last Saturday in July. In Triestine dialect, *clanfe* refers to creative 'bomb dives' aimed at making the biggest splash, and this offbeat 'Olympics' – conceived by a group of friends – is dedicated to just that. Held at the Bagni Ausonia (p71), the event begins with the 'Hymn of the Clanfe', after which competitors battle it out. Splash size aside, participants are also judged on the creativity of their outfit and their ability to bribe the judges with gifts of alcohol and food. A summer carnival bound to have you in stitches.

★ Barcolana   OCTOBER
(www.barcolana.it) A bit like a maritime New York Marathon, Trieste's world-famous regatta is open to everyone from amateur boaters to professional sailors. Running since 1969, it's the region's most important event, trans-

forming the Gulf of Trieste into a spectacular tapestry of sails with over 2000 vessels of all shapes and sizes. For the best view (and shots), watch the race from the Napoleonica in Opicina, p88). The Barcolana attracts tourists from all over the world, so book your accommodation well in advance.

Barbacan Produce
5 TIMES ANNUALLY

Five times a year, established and emerging artists, artisans and designers peddle their creations in (and around) Piazza Barbacan. Check its Facebook page (www.facebook.com/BarbacanProduce) for dates.

🛏 Sleeping

⭐ Hotel All'Arco
HOTEL €€

(Map p58; ☑040 260 73 89/348 662 60 90; www.hotelallarco.com; Piazzetta San Silvestro 4; s/d €60/80; ✴️🛜) Eleven brand-new, well-equipped rooms in the Old Town. The hotel can be an appealing, great-value option, though fluctuations in price can be quite considerable at times. Reception closes at 9pm: if you're arriving late, let the hotel know in advance. The location, next to the Chiesa di San Silvestro, is wonderful though not accessible by car. Thankfully, the walk isn't too long and hotel guests enjoy a 10% discount at Park San Giusto.

Hotel San Giusto
HOTEL €€

(Map p54; ☑040 76 38 26; www.hotelsangiusto.it; Via Cristoforo Belli 1; s/d €75/95, buffet breakfast €5.50; 🅿️✴️🛜) A nondescript but functional hotel in the middle of Rione San Giacomo, a very local area off the tourist path. Rooms are modern, quiet, and well suited to both business travellers and families on vacation. Buffet breakfast and parking available.

B&B Gens Julia
B&B €€

(Map p58 ☑347 151 06 33/340 605 60 39; www.gensjulia.it; Via San Michele 7; s/d €50/90; 🅿️✴️🛜) Little more than 100m from the cathedral, in the heart of the old town, this B&B combines the charm of a townhouse with the comfort of a hotel. You'll find terracotta floors and large windows, brick arches and wrought-iron beds, all in rooms with private bathrooms and hypoallergenic linen.

James Joyce Hotel
HOTEL €€

(Map p58 ☑040 30 20 65; www.hoteljamesjoyce.com; Via dei Cavazzeni 7; s/d €80/130; ✴️🛜) Although part of the same hotel group as Urban, itself a few steps away, the James Joyce has much simpler, more classically styled rooms, with wooden furniture and few frills. Regardless, standards are high. Check the website for regular great deals.

Hotel Victoria
HOTEL €€

(Map p54; ☑040 36 24 15; www.hotelvictoriatrieste.com; Via Alfredo Oriani 2; d from €108 🅿️✴️🛜🏊) If the thought of sleeping in the same hotel, if not in the same room, as James Joyce isn't impressive enough, you will be satisfied with this hotel's quality and location, ever so slightly removed from Trieste's frenetic centre. The property itself is elegant, stately and well renovated, with 44 rooms, beautiful common areas and excellent transport links. Don't miss the wellness centre, which comes with hammam (€20; free for stays over four nights). Parking €13 for 24 hours.

Theresia
SERVICED APARTMENTS €€

(Map p54; ☑040 372 73 79; www.residencetheresiatrieste.it; Via Trento 12; apt from €60 per person; 🅿️✴️🛜) On the ruler-straight streets of Borgo Teresiano, these serviced apartments (complete with reception) are ideal for self-caterers wanting to take advantage of an equipped kitchen. The apartments are well maintained and decked out with all the essentials. Parking in the area, however, can be a challenge.

⭐ L'Albero Nascosto
HOTELS & APARTMENTS €€ /€€€

(Map p58; ☑040 30 10 88; www.alberonascosto.it; Via Felice Venezian 18; s €75-95, d €95-175; ✴️🛜) The smallest of details are taken care of at this special hotel, tucked away in the heart of the Piazza Cavana area and within walking distance of almost everything. Breakfast here

---

SECRETS OF TRIESTE

Trieste Arcana: i fantasmi di Cittavecchia (Arcane Trieste: The Ghosts of Cittavecchia; ☑040 347 83 12) is one of a number of guided tours offered by Trieste's tourist office. In the dark of night, you'll be introduced to the mysteries and legends that make Trieste a city of the occult on par with London, Prague, Venice and Turin. Evocative night tours that lead to the Colle di San Giusto can also be booked through the tourist office, which sells tickets for Trieste's hop-on, hop-off tourist bus too.

is an unexpected treat. One of the apartments offered by the hotel – on the top floor of a building on Via Armando Diaz – comes with breathtaking views.

Hotel Barbacan
HOTEL €€ /€€€

(Map p58; 📱040247 10 15; www.hotelbarbacan trieste.com; Piazza del Barbacan 3; s/d €65/90, ste €70-180; 🅿️🛜) Despite being a newer addition to the Old Town's accommodation scene, the Barbacan has established itself as a major player. Excellent value for money, with small but well-furnished rooms occupying two buildings. The hotel also manages two large apartments in the centre (only one with air-conditioning). Breakfast is served in a nearby bar and guests enjoy a 10% discount at Park San Giusto.

Double Tree Hilton
HOTEL €€ /€€€

(Map p58; 📱040 971 29 50; www.hiltonhotels.it; Piazza delle Repubblica 1; d from €150; 🅿️🛜🈂️) The latest addition to the Trieste hotel scene needs no introduction. And yet, this Hilton is different from the others because of its location in a marvellous early-20th-century building adapted to the highest modern standards. Parking is €15 for 24 hours.

Grand Hotel Duchi d'Aosta
HOTEL €€ /€€€

(Map p58; 📱040 760 00 11; www.duchi.eu; Piazza Unità d'Italia 2; s/d with breakfast from €120/145; 🅿️🛜) One of Trieste's great classics, this richly historic hotel occupies a landmark period building on Piazza Unità d'Italia (some rooms overlook the square). Opened in 1873, it has epitomised luxury travel in the city ever since. The 19th-century furnishings are opulent, the service is top tier, and parking is available for €25 per day.

★ Hotel Savoia Excelsior Palace
HOTEL €€€

(Map p54; 📱040 779 41; www.starhotels.com; d from €170; 🅿️🛜🈂️) If you're willing to blow the budget, do it here. This is the best hotel in town, for quality, elegance and its spectacular sea-view address (enjoyable in any season) on Le Rive. All details are taken care of and the service is excellent. Parking will set you back €26 per night. Even if you're not staying here, treat yourself to an *aperitivo* in the light-filled, ground-floor hotel bar.

Urban Hotel Design
DESIGN HOTEL €€€

(Map p58; 📱040 30 20 65; www.urbanhotel.it; Androna Chiusa 4; s/d €110/200; 🛜) Among the Roman ruins of the old town, contemporary design dominates the rooms and suites of this carefully furnished hotel. There's a loft for larger groups. Rooms on Via di Cavana can be a bit noisy on weekends. Breakfast is served in the basement, where you can glimpse the ruins of ancient Roman walls. Hotel guests have access to nearby car parks (from €10 per day; nightly €5). Reception is shared with the James Joyce Hotel.

✗ Eating

A crossroads between Mediterranean, Germanic and Slavic worlds – not to mention a former port of the Habsburg Empire – Trieste has absorbed a slew of culinary influences. Its trademark buffets have Austro-Hungarian roots, while its homegrown dishes have been strongly shaped by the coast, the produce of the Carso, as well as Venetian, Istrian and Dalmatian traditions.

Humble in origin, Trieste's local cuisine consists of simple dishes which, in some cases, have become mighty classics. Among these are *buzara,* a stew of tomatoes, chilli and seafood (mainly scampi).

On these streets, time-warped institutions serving faithful recipes rub shoulders with next-gen eateries springing from the city's dynamic dining scene. The quality is generally high and, little by little, vegetarian and vegan options are also making inroads.

La Bomboniera
PASTRIES €

(Map p58; 📱040 63 27 52; Via XXX Ottobre 3; meals €10; ⏱8am-8pm Tue-Sat, to 1pm Sun) Better loosen your trouser belt beforehand because one sweet treat leads to another at this traditional, worldly, creative pastry shop in Borgo Teresiano.

Genuino
GOURMET FAST FOOD €

(Map p58; 📱040 064 04 90; www.genuino.com; Via delle Beccherie 13; sandwiches from €5, hot dishes €5-14, salads €7.50-10.90; ⏱noon-3pm & 6-10pm; 📱) Can fast food be seasonal, wholesome and genuine? Genuino says *si* with its fresh, tasty, additive-free chicken, hamburgers, salads and craft beers, yours to gobble at the bar or at a table. Vegetarian, vegan and gluten-free options available.

Crops
SOUPS & SALADS €

(Map p58; 📱040 982 81 41; www.cropsandco.it; Via Einaudi 2b; salads from €5.90, sandwiches from €3; ⏱9am-4pm & 6.30-9pm Mon-Fri, 9am-4pm Sat) Fresh, seasonal, light and simple: for Irene and Luca, these are the four basic pillars of any dish. The rest is up to you: choose from a list of ingredients, condiments and dressings and customise your salad, soup and more, exactly how you like it.

Pep's Fish House
SEAFOOD

(Map p58; ☑040 36 26 03; Riva III Novembre 3; fish & chips €12; ⊙11.30am-3pm & 6-11pm Mon & Tue, 11.30am-10.30pm Wed-Sun) Literally a stone's throw from the Mediterranean, Pep's is a bit like the fast-food fish joints flanking the North Sea, places where you can chow down a salmon tartare sandwich. This is Southern Europe's answer, an upbeat, smart-casual joint serving grub like *insalatone* (large salad) pimped with shrimps and generous serves of fresh fried fish.

★ Osteria di mare Alla Voliga
SEAFOOD €

(Map p54; ☑040 30 96 06; www.allavoliga.it; Via della Fornace 1; meals €20; ⊙noon-2pm & 7-10pm Wed-Sun) As you sit here, you may notice the pride with which the owner points out how many years this *osteria* – blue, white and smelling of the sea – has been in business: just over 40. And it's only right to mention it because there's a lot of skill and experience behind the simple seafood dishes, served with candour and speed.

The sardine skewer is fabulous, though the sesame sardines and mussel soup are also worth trying. Adding to the homeliness: moka-brewed coffee.

Marinato
PIZZERIA € /€€

(Map p54; ☑040 31 04 12; http://marinato.it; Riva Nazario Sauro 4; meals €15-30; ⊙noon-3.15pm & 7-11pm Mon-Thu, noon-11pm Fri-Sun summer, noon-3pm & 7-11pm daily winter) At Marinato, the all-Neapolitan staff serve one of the best pizzas in town. While it may not quite compare to a pie from Napoli, it's still a satisfying bite.

★ De Scarpon
OSTERIA €€

(Map p54; ☑040 36 76 74; www.osteria-de-scarpon. business.site; Via della Ginnastica 20; meals about €25; ⊙noon-2.15pm & 7-10pm Tue-Sun) In luminous, high-ceilinged rooms hung with old theatre posters, Scarpon's affable staff serve homely, top-quality *cucina giuliana* (Julian cuisine).

Expect everything from stockfish, spaghetti *allo scoglio* (with mixed seafood), bread gnocchi with sea-bass *ragù*, to Barcola sardines and Duino mussels.

Al Moro
TRATTORIA €€

(Map p54; ☑040 246 26 55; www.trattoriaalmoro trieste.com; Via del Destriero 1; meals €25; ⊙6.30-11pm Mon-Thu, noon-3pm & 6.30-11pm Fri-Sun) A lot has changed since hay and cows were traded on Piazza dei Foraggi. One thing that hasn't is this *osteria,* owned by the same family and in the same building for 120 years. Living upstairs is Nevia, whose *nonno* built the place and opened the trattoria.

In this corner of suburbia, the Trieste of old lives on. Settle in under the pergola or bunker down inside for comforting dishes like gnocchi with goulash, Austrian Liptauer (spicy cheese spread) and Slovenian *cevapcici* (grilled meat).

★ Da Libero
SEAFOOD €€

(Map p54; ☑040 30 11 13; www.hostariadalibero .com; Via Risorta 7a; meals €35; ⊙7.30-10pm Mon, 12.30-2pm & 7.30-10pm Tue-Sat) Libero's grandson, Sebastiano, has taken over this revered Trieste institution, a deeply historic *osteria* once frequented by Joyce, who lived nearby. For many locals and out-of-towners, Da Libero means one thing: regional cuisine, with turf-centric *primi* (first courses), homemade pasta and desserts, and warming dishes like pork shoulder and pumpkin flan. Trumping them all is the cult-status *patate in tecia* (pan-fried potatoes).

Da Gigi
ISTRIAN €€

(Map p54; ☑040 81 23 38; Via di Servola 117; meals €20-30; ⊙noon-2.30pm & 7.30-10pm) While Gigi's decor may hurl you back to the 1970s, its food will transport you just across the border. Honest, no-frills Istrian cooking is what you get here, prepared using one rule only: fresh, local seafood. (Gigi's at the counter, cleaning the latest delivery of spider crabs.) Find comfort in fried fish, *brodetto* (fish soup) with polenta, or other time-honoured recipes made using just-caught scallops, razor clams and mantis shrimps.

Located near the Risiera di San Sabba, it's always best to call ahead as it's known to close if the fresh fish runs out.

Osteria Istriano
OSTERIA €€

(Map p54; ☑040 30 66 64; Riva Grumula 6; www. osteriaistriano.com; meals €30-40; ⊙noon-2pm & 7-9pm Tue-Sat) Istriano's manager is an unusual chap. While he may give you the impression he doesn't know which way to turn, he has everything under control. Chances are you'll be too busy swooning over perfectly crumbed fried sardines or one of the more creative dishes, all made using prime ingredients.

The restaurant itself is spacious and welcoming, with outdoor tables looking out at the shimmering Sacchetta.

REBECHIN: ANY TIME IS THE RIGHT TIME

A *rebechin* is a snack eaten at any time of the day, though most locals indulge mid-morning. The most classic *rebechin* is the *rodoleto de coto*, served as a mini sandwich or as a plate of sliced Trieste *prosciutto cotto* (cooked ham) and bread. Pair with a beer, Terrano wine or spritz.

Hostaria Malcanton   RESTAURANT €€

(Map p58; ☎040 241 0719; Via Malcanton 10; meals €30; ⊘noon-3pm & 7-11pm Mon & Wed-Sun) Hostaria Malcanton is the ultimate people pleaser. Yes, it's a seafood restaurant, but not strictly traditional and not just serving seafood. It's in the city centre, but not in the hustle and bustle. And while it's popular with young people, it's just as appealing to mature diners, all of whom appreciate the prime produce and excellent wines. A top choice before a night out on the town.

Pier - The Roof   RESTAURANT €€€

(Map p54; ☎040 322 92 96; www.facebook.com/pier.theroof; Molo Venezia 1; meals €45; ⊘8am-midnight Mon-Thu & Sun, to late Fri & Sat) As the name implies, you're on a pier (Molo Venezia) and a rooftop (or rather a top floor to be precise). Needless to say, it makes for a beautiful setting. To the tinkle of sailboat masts, feast on fish (cooked and raw), prepared in both traditional and contemporary ways. The staff is young and professional, the place practically always open, and the sunset *aperitivo* something to behold.

Buffets

While they may be a legacy of the city's Austro-Hungarian past, buffets have become a quintessentially Triestine experience. These rowdy bar-restaurants are popular with groups and solo punters alike, who drop by for a quick *rebechin* (snack) on their feet (usually a sandwich of Trieste ham, grated horseradish and mustard) or for a sit-down *misto di caldaia* (mixed boiled meats) with steaming sauerkraut.

The *misto di caldaia* is the most typical and popular of the buffet dishes, consisting of a platter of mixed meats cooked in a boiler: *porzina* (pork neck or shoulder), *cotechino* (pork sausage), *carrè* (pork loin), tongue, *zampone* (pig's trotter), pancetta (bacon),

mild 'Vienna' sausage and 'Cragno' sausage, the latter a Carso speciality.

★ Sandwich Club   BUFFET €

(Map p54; ☎335 662 51 30; Via Giovanni e Demetrio Economo 10/b; sandwiches €2-7; ⊘8am-11pm Mon-Fri, 8am-3pm Sat & Sun) While it can't claim the history of its more famous rivals (it's only been in business since 1993), this younger buffet has found a place in the heart of locals (well, some of them at least). It's located near the Molo Fratelli Bandiera, at the southern end of Le Rive, in an area of the city centre rarely trodden by tourists.

Its benches are never short of seafarers, truck drivers and opinionated pensioners, here for the standout sandwiches and snacks, from golden fried morsels to cooked whole hams. An authentic, salty joint at its best at lunch.

Da Giovanni   BUFFET €

(Map p54; ☎040 63 93 96; www.trattoriadagiovanni.com; Via San Lazzaro 14; meals €10-20; ⊘bar 9am-3pm & 4.30-11pm, trattoria noon-3pm & 7-10pm Mon-Sat) The house motto says it all: 'At Giovanni's, two *bicieri* (glasses) if you drink them willingly'. Da Giovanni is an institution, a traditional trattoria with a top-quality, rotating repertoire of Triestine dishes. It's a simple, convivial spot, ideal for a *rebechin* (local snack) among folk of all ages and walks of life, happily clutching prosciutto sandwiches and glasses of Carso white.

Le Botti   BUFFET €

(Map p54; ☎040 260 14 64; www.lebotticavana.it; Via Torino 15; meals €15-20 ⊘8am-midnight; 🖉) Le Botti buffet is located on ever-bustling Via Torino, between Piazza Hortis and Piazza Venezia. With longer opening hours than its competitors, young and helpful staff, ample outdoor seating and a counter never short of fried and boiled bites, it's a lifeline for peckish night owls and vegetarians. Try the *polpette* (meatballs) or *verdure impanate* (crumbed fried vegetables), best washed down with a cold Slovenian beer.

★ Siora Rosa   BUFFET €

(Map p54; ☎04030 14 60; Piazza Hortis 3; meals €20; ⊘8am-3pm & 5-10pm Tue-Sat) When it comes to the title of Trieste's top buffet, it's a strict contest between Pepi and Siora Rosa. Here, traditional meat dishes are offered alongside morsels rooted in the custom of *rebechin* (local snacks), among them crumbed fried vegetables and local-style fish; try the *sardine in saor* (sweet-and-sour sardines cooked with raisins and pine nuts). To guarantee a table (perhaps one on Via Torino), book ahead.

Da Vittorio
BUFFET €

(Map p54; ☎ 040 760 57 09; Via Giosuè Carducci 30; meals €20; ⏰ 9.15am-8pm Mon-Fri, to 2pm Sat) Trieste's buffet may be an Austro-Hungarian tradition, but the dishes served are heavily influenced by local cuisine. At bustling Vittorio's, seafood prevails. And while its mouthwatering counter may recall a fishmonger, everything you see is prepared, cooked and served fresh to peckish crowds who head in for a sit-down family feast, a quick drink at the bar, or to simply read the newspaper while chomping on fried mullet.

Rudy - Spaten
BUFFET €

(Map p58; ☎ 040 63 94 28; Via Valdirivio 32; meals €20 ⏰ 10am-midnight Mon-Fri, from 10.30am Sat) Entering Rudy feels like crossing the threshold of a Bavarian beer hall. It's a classic layout, cosy and dimly lit, with a long counter of fried bites, boiled meats on standby and rivers of Spaten beer fuelling a boisterous, Central European vibe.

Try the Bavarian platter or a hearty *jota.*

Da Roby
BUFFET €

(Map p54; ☎ 040 372 00 02; Via Torrebianca 32; meals €20 ⏰ 9am-9pm Mon-Fri & Sun, 9am-3pm & 6-9pm Sat) Specialising in seafood dishes, enjoyed indoors or alfresco, this buffet on the edge of Borgo Teresiano (just south of Piazza Oberdan) caters mainly to workers, who eagerly dig into its creative, mouthwatering creations.

The risotto is ready at 1.30pm, so whet the appetite with some *antipasti,* a showcase for the kitchen's talents. Prompt, cheerful service to boot.

★ Marascutti
BUFFET € /€€

(Map p54; ☎ 040 63 37 19; www.buffetmarascutti.it; Via Battisti 2/b; sandwiches €3.50, meals €15-30; ⏰ 10am-3pm & 6-10.30pm Mon & Wed-Sun) With Pepi and Siora Rosa by its side, Marascutti completes the triptych of classic Trieste buffets. This is the right place to try *jota,* a soup of sauerkraut and beans (and sometimes potatoes) and other dishes of Austrian origin: from potatoes in *tecia* to pork, you'll be spoilt for choice.

While the wine selection is more limited, the quality is fantastic, with regional drops including Tocai Friulano and Sauvignon.

★ Da Pepi
BUFFET €€

(Map p58; ☎ 040 36 68 58; www.buffetdapepi.it; Via della Cassa di Risparmio 3; boiled pork with side dishes €25; ⏰ 8.30am-10pm Mon-Sat & 10am-4pm Sun) This is undoubtedly the most famous buffet in Trieste. And in this case, fame equals quality. Pepi S'ciavo (*s'ciavo,* in the Julian dialect, means 'from Dalmatia') has been here since 1897, when a certain Pepi Klajsnic opened the doors. Through various vicissitudes (read its story in the leaflet printed for the restaurant's 120th anniversary) it finds itself here today, authentic atmosphere intact. This authenticity extends to its opening hours, which pays no heed to tourist convenience (the place is closed on religious holidays).

Head in to sample the original Austro-Hungarian buffet (Cragno sausage, Vienna sausage, pork, cooked ham and tongue, all sprinkled with freshly grated horseradish) and wash it down with an easy-drinking blonde or Terrano wine from the Carso.

🍷 Drinking & Nightlife

★ Stazione Roger's Outdoor
BAR

(Map p54; ☎ 324 082 85 60; Riva Grumula 14; ⏰ 5.30pm-midnight end of Apr-Barcolana) As good for a sunset toast as it is for an after-dark tipple, this outdoor kiosk occupies a converted 1950s petrol station (note the oil-barrel bar tables). From spritzes to mojitos, drinks are prepared with care and served to a soundtrack of reggae and dance-hall tunes.

Events and private parties are held here in the restored service-station building (www.stazionerogers.eu).

★ Draw Food
LOUNGE BAR

(Map p54; ☎ 040 322 93 70; Via Torino 26 ⏰ 5pm-2am) Via Torino is the hub of Trieste's pre- and post-dinner nightlife, and a standout among its many buzzing bars (especially crowded on Fridays and Saturdays) is Draw. Decked out in tasteful vintage furniture, it's a fine spot for a weekend *aperitivo,* listening to DJ-spun tunes on the sofa, long drink in hand. (Cocktails tend to be on the lighter side, but are tasty nonetheless.)

Maita
TIKI BAR

(Map p58; ☎ 351 684 54 94; Androna dell'Olio 2; ⏰ 5-10pm) Among alleyways and ruins, and with seating on a hidden square, Maita channels the tropics with its colourful, mostly rum-based cocktails (appropriately served in tiki mugs). Located in the city centre.

LOCAL KNOWLEDGE

IT'S NOT JUST A COFFEE

Macchiato, corretto, d'orzo, in tazza grande o piccola, decaffeinato: in Italy, ordering coffee is a highly customised affair. Trieste ups the ante (or confusion) with its very own coffee terminology. Here, an espresso is a *'nero,'* which can be ordered *'normale'* (in a cup) or *'in B'* (in a shot glass). 'Stained' with a dash of milk it becomes a *'capo,'* but spiked with a drop of cream it's a *'gocciato'*. As for a cappuccino, in Trieste it's a *'cafelate'*.

Hop&Rock
CRAFT BREWERY

(Map p58; ☑ 339 599 37 30; Via Machiavelli 10; ◷ noon-midnight Mon-Fri, from 4pm Sat & Sun) A light-filled space in Borgo Teresiano where you can sample and guzzle dozens of craft beers (including some very special brews), devour top-notch sandwiches and listen to rock.

Hop Store
PUB

(Map p58; ☑ 340 787 82 33; Via Felice Venezian 24a; ◷ 7pm-1am Mon-Sat) Wide choice of beers to accompany sandwiches (including club sandwiches). Good value for money, friendly staff, central location.

Oasi del Gelato
BEER

(Map p54; ☑ 380 210 61 04; www.lanuovaoasidel gelato.it; Via dell'Eremo 259; ◷ 6pm-1am Tue-Fri, noon-3pm & 6pm-1am Sat & Sun) Don't let the name fool you: while you will find good *gelato* here (as well as pastries and other treats), it's mainly a beer garden, complete with spacious terrace and surrounded by the greenery. Pastries are prepared on sight and there's a selection of excellent sandwiches to pair with the long list of beers.

Giovinoto
WINE BAR

(Map p54; ☑ 040 965 23 04/333 466 96 54; Via Trento 9; ◷ 10am-2.30pm & 5-9.30pm Mon-Sat) This small, neighbourly wine shop/bar in Borgo Teresiano offers a wide range of traditional and natural wines to buy, as well as many you can quaff onsite.

Lettera Viva
CAFE

(Map p54; ☑ 040 203 83 88; www.letteraviva.it; Viale XX Settembre 31/b; ◷ 9am-10.30pm Mon-Thu, until midnight Fri & Sat, 10am-10pm Sun) Spacious as it may be, it's easy to miss this stylish, bookish cafe-bar in the heart of Viale XX Settembre. It's an ideal spot to sip tea, surrounded by shelves lined with books. Af-

ter something stiffer? There's wine on stand-by too.

Cemût
WINE BAR

(Map p58; ☑ 350 516 82 96; Via dei Capitelli 11 ◷ 11am-midnight) Just like the owners, the wines and bites at this dinky little wine bar are Friulian. Popular with young Triestini (Trieste locals), expect a hip, upbeat vibe.

Gran Malabar
WINE BAR

(Map p54; ☑ 040 63 62 26; Piazza San Giovanni 6; ◷ 7am-9pm Mon-Fri, 8am-9pm Sat, 8am-4pm Sun) A chill, easy-going wine shop/bar popular with affable locals. Buy a bottle to go or savour a drop in house.

A tranquil pit stop on bustling Piazza San Giovanni.

Il Pane Quotidiano
BAKERY

(Map p54; ☑ 040 347 85 42; Viale XX Settembre 11; ◷ 5.30am-midnight Mon-Fri, 24hr Sat & Sun) Slap bang on Viale XX Settembre, 'The Daily Bread' is a trusty standby in this town, being one of few places open (almost) round the clock. Handy on weekend nights, when those post-drinks munchies hit.

Other branches include a magnificent one between Barcola and Grignano (Viale Miramare 72).

La Preferita 1991
PUB

(Map p54; ☑ 388 816 98 89; Viale XX Settembre 29; ◷ 5pm-2am) A classic pub pouring spirits, beers and wines to constant crowds. It's a popular spot for graduation and birthday bashes. If you stumble upon one, don't be shy: jump into the fray and dance.

Aqvedotto
COCKTAIL BAR

(Map p54; Viale XX Settembre 37/c; ◷ 3pm-2am Mon-Sat in summer, also 5pm-1am Sun rest of yr) You'll recognise it by its mascot: a huge black fibreglass horse at the end of the room. Much-loved by locals, it's a fabulous spot for a relaxing *aperitvo*, with on-point tunes, soft lighting and a chill-out vibe.

Zenzero e Cannella
PASTRY SHOP

(Map p54; Campo San Giacomo; ◷ 6.30am-9pm Tue-Thu, to 10.30pm Fri, Sat & Mon) Find a table on the large terrace overlooking Campo San Giacomo and while away the time with an ice-cream or a homemade juice spiked with ginger, cinnamon or other tasty ingredients. Good breakfasts too.

Dream Team
LOUNGE BAR

(Map p58; ☑ 392 333 42 55; Via Riccardo Bazzoni 2; ◷ 6pm-2am Mon-Sat, from 8.30pm Sun)

The Arco di Riccardo neighbourhood is quiet and contemplative in itself, but if you're after something even more discreet, bunker down at this lounge-bar among the many restaurants.

With a boudoir-inspired interior, it's aimed at a generally older crowd seeking good times and well-mixed drinks.

Historic Cafes

Trieste's love affair with coffee is an enduring one, and nowhere is this passion more evident than in the city's historic cafes, beautiful monuments to an esteemed libation.

Of course, you'll find more than *neri* and *capi* at these institutions, with everything from cocktails to full meals on offer.

★ **Caffè San Marco** HISTORIC CAFE
(Map 54; ☑040 203 53 57; Via Battisti 18; ⊙8.30am-11pm Mon-Thu, until 2pm Fri & Sat, 9am-3pm Sun in summer, until 9pm Sun in winter) This splendid Viennese Secession giant opened in 1914 and has been a destination for intellectuals and young activists ever since. At the beginning of WWI it hid a clandestine workshop producing counterfeit passports for patriots. Consequently, it was devastated and closed by Austro-Hungarian soldiers in 1915.

Reopened after WWII, it now houses a **restaurant** (⊙noon-3pm & 7-10pm Mon-Thu, 7am-11pm Fri & Sat, lunch only Sun) and a **bookshop** (⊙same opening times).

★ **Caffè Tommaseo** HISTORIC CAFE
(Map 58; ☑040 36 26 66; www.caffetommaseo .it; Piazza Tommaseo 4/c; ⊙9am-midnight Mon & Wed-Sun) Opened in 1830 between Piazza Unità and Le Rive, this was the first place to offer *gelato* in Trieste. Very quiet and elegant, it also includes a restaurant.

★ **Antico Caffè Torinese** HISTORIC CAFE
(Map 58 ☑040 260 01 53; www.anticocaffetori nese.ts.it; Corso Italia 2 ⊙8.30am-2am) The smallest of Trieste's historic cafes, founded in 1919 and very well preserved.

Drop in for a quick coffee or for a cocktail at the magnificent period counter.

★ **Caffè degli Specchi** HISTORIC CAFE
(Map 58; ☑040 36 80 33; www.caffespecchi.it Piazza Unità d'Italia 7; ⊙8am-midnight) In business since 1839, this veteran's biggest selling point is its splendid setting on Piazza Unità d'Italia. The cafe is adorned with leather sofas, a handsome counter and three of the original mirrors *(specchi)* from which it gets

its name. Back in the day, the mirrors were engraved with important events.

★ **Pirona** HISTORIC PASTRY SHOP
(Map p54; ☑040 233 54 76; www.pirona1900.it; Largo Barriera Vecchia 12; ⊙7.30am-2pm Mon, 7.30am-7.30pm Tue-Sat, 8.30am-12.30pm Sun) Founded in 1900, this pastry shop was loved by Joyce and it's said that he came up with the idea for *Ulysses* right here. Recently reopened, it is once again one of Trieste's enchanting institutions.

Stella Polare HISTORIC CAFE
(Map p58; ☑040 76 54 20; Via Dante 14 ⊙7am-10pm) Opened in 1867, in the shadow of the under-construction Chiesa di San Spiridione, the 'North Star' was a meeting place for Austrian soldiers and officials, the much-loved hangout of Joyce and Saba and, during the Free Territory period, a dance hall for American soldiers.

Urbanis HISTORIC CAFE
(Map p58; ☑040 36 65 80; Piazza della Borsa 15; ⊙7am-1am Mon-Thu, to 2am Fri & Sat, 8am-midnight Sun) Founded in 1832 as a pastry shop, Urbanis is now a bar pulling a young crowd. Note the mosaic on the floor.

James Joyce Cafè CAFE
(Map p58; ☑040 36 42 06; Via Roma 14; ⊙7am-9pm Mon-Sat) Always busy, this place impresses with its 1940s decor and counter. It's hard to choose whether to come here for coffee, a generous salad or an aperitif. Note that the cafe may close at lunch in the summer, when the neighbourhood's office workers are all on vacation.

☆ Entertainment

From *aperitivo* hour onwards, the area between Piazza Unità and Piazza della Borsa becomes one long terrace, packed with punters and thumping, loud tunes. Later in the evening, the scene picks up in Via Torino and Viale XX Settembre.

In summer, keep in mind that the Slovenian coast and its own diversions are a stone's throw away.

Dhome CLUB
(Map p58; ☑333 887 80 15; Via delle Beccherie 18 ⊙10pm-4am Sat) As often closed as it is open (it was temporarily closed when this guidebook was researched; call ahead) this pub, which turns into a club, is a rarity in the heart of the Ghetto. You'll find it right beside Genuino (p74).

SABA'S TRIESTE

Svevo and Joyce aren't the only literary giants linked to Trieste. Another great is the poet and novelist Umberto Saba, for whom the city's everyday life and culture roused both inspiration and a deep personal affection. The writer is honoured with a statue on Via San Nicolò. Sadly, the work is frequently vandalised, occasionally with anti-Semitic intent.

In the same street is the wonderful **Libreria Antiquaria 'Umberto Saba'** (Map p58 ☑ 040 63 17 41; www.libreriasaba.it; Via San Nicolò 30; ☺ 9am-12.30pm & 3.30-7.30pm Tue-Sat), an historic bookstore once run by Saba himself. Its shelves still heave with rare and precious printed works, making it a worthy stop. A vestige of local Jewish heritage, the bookstore is also a stop on the **Jewish Trieste** (www.triestebraica.it) walking tour.

Casa delle Culture
SOCIAL CENTRE

(Map p54; Via Giovanni Orlandini 38) This 'den of antagonists' is one of the few social centers in Trieste and a porthole into the city's alternative scene. Look for news online (www.facebook.com/casa.delle culture) or just head there; you'll always find someone willing to have a chat.

Politeama Rossetti
THEATRE

(Map p54; ☑ 040 359 35 55; www.ilrossetti.it; Viale XX Settembre 45) Trieste's foremost theatre occupies a large, eclectic building, its 1500 seats often filled to capacity on occasion of major theatre productions, musicals, dance performances and concerts.

Teatro Verdi
THEATRE

(Map p58; ☑ 040 672 21 11; www.teatroverdi-trieste.com; Riva III Novembre 1) Trieste's home of opera. Originally called Teatro Nuovo, it was the first theatre in Italy to be named in honour of the famous Italian composer.

Teatro Miela
THEATRE

(Map p54; ☑ 040 36 51 19; www.miela.it; Piazza Duca degli Abruzzi 3) Founded by a cooperative in 1990, this theatre hosts a variety of concerts, independent plays and musicals, as well as film screenings. Check the website for its jam-packed program.

Cinema Federico Fellini
ARTHOUSE CINEMA

(Map p54; ☑ 040 63 64 95; Viale XX Settembre 37) Among the dozens of bars and clubs on Viale XX Settembre is this arthouse cinema and its program of highly sought-after flicks.

Stadio 'Nereo Rocco'
FOOTBALL

(Map p54; piazzale Azzurri d'Italia 2) The city's stadium bears the name of legendary coach Nero Rooco, who led Trieste's beloved football team, Triestina, in the 1940s. If you have the chance, catch a game to see first-hand the passion locals feel towards Trieste.

🔒 Shopping

Lister
FASHION & ACCESSORIES

(Map p54; ☑ 040 399 72 43; www.listersartoriasociale.it; Via Guglielmo de Pastrovich 1, Parco di San Giovanni; ☺ 8.30am-5.30pm Mon-Fri) Beautiful creations, mostly accessories, made exclusively using recycled materials.

Blu di Prussia
ARTS & CRAFTS

(Map p54; ☑ 331 754 9097; Via Cadorna 10; ☺ 5-8pm Tue-Fri, 10am-8pm Sat) Wood is the star material at this enchanting artisan workshop. Keep an eye out for the series of whales, perfect for hanging from the ceiling or for adding intrigue in the lounge room (the creatures are cleverly cut to look like they're diving into your furniture).

Vud
ARTS & CRAFTS

(Map p54; ☑ 040 461 2452; www.vud-design.com; Via Diaz 15a; ☺ 10am-1pm & 3.30-7.30pm Tue-Sat) You could call them handcrafted design pieces or custom-made furniture: tables, cabinets and beautiful cutting boards all put together using little more than joints and glue (no screws) and finished with a signature hole.

Dezen Dezen
ARTS & CRAFTS

(Map p54; ☑ 040 265 14 57; www.dezendezen.com; Via Emanuele Filiberto Duca d'Aosta 6b; ☺ 11am-7pm Tue-Sat) The call of the Balkans is strong at this artisan workshop, where traditional Eastern European patterns find their way onto everything from locally printed sweatshirts, scarves and t-shirts, to bags, handkerchiefs and notebooks.

Laboratorio degli In-perfetti
DESIGN

(Map p54; ☑ 347 460 59 04; www.artelegnoinperfetti.it; Via Emanuele Filiberto Duca d'Aosta 6a; ☺ 9am-5pm Mon, 10am-1pm & 3.30-8pm Tue-Sat, 9am-8pm Sun) The signature item here: decorative timber sculptures shaped like sailing boats. Beyond them is a cachet of stylish, contemporary design pieces, from bookcases and desk lamps, to cutting boards and tables, all made here.

Drogheria Toso   GIFTS

(Map p54; ☑ 04063 62 88; Piazza San Giovanni 6; ⊙ 8am-1pm Mon & Wed, 8am-1pm & 4.30-7pm Tue & Thu-Sat) Time stands still at this vintage *drogheria* (grocery store) from 1906. These days, it's stocked with an assortment of beauty products and items for the home, including a large number of enormous natural sponges.

Sfreddo   FOOD & DRINKS

(Map p54; ☑ 040 76 44 65; www.sfreddo.it; Via Battisti 10; ⊙ 8am-2pm & 4-8pm Mon-Sat) Those wanting to to take home the flavours of the Carso and Friuli Venezia Giulia should drop by this gorgeous deli. Not only does it produce much of what it sells, it's all perfectly packaged and vacuum-packed.

Mariabologna   FOOD & DRINKS

(Map p54; ☑ 040 36 81 66; Via Battisti 7; ⊙ 8am-1.30pm Mon & Wed, 8am-1.30pm & 5-7.30pm Tue & Thu-Sat) Not only has this artisan pasta factory been selling quality fresh pasta since 1919, it's also a deli and rotisserie to boot. Buy the plum gnocchi: whether they're a starter or a dessert is hotly debated.

Viezzoli   FOOD & DRINKS

(Map p58; ☑ 040 36 86 24; Via della Cassa di Risparmio 7; ⊙ 7am-8pm Mon-Sat, 9am-2pm Sun) If you fancy getting your mitts on some *putizza* and *priesnitz* – Trieste's take on Austro-Hungarian rolled sweets – join the queue of locals and tourists at Viezzoli. The desserts are top-notch (and reflected in the price).

Katastrofa   DESIGN

(Map p58; ☑ 335 829 84 32; Via Armando Diaz 4; ⊙ 10am-12.30pm & 4-8pm Tue-Sat) Everything from cult-status design objects to the vintage item you've been looking for to complement your Kartell furniture collection. Fair prices.

Oltre la Luna   TOYS

(Map p58; ☑ 351 843 30 10; www.oltrelaluna.com; Via del Teatro Romano 1; ⊙ 9am-7.30pm Mon-Sat) Modern and vintage toys.

Bischoff   FOOD & DRINKS

(Map p58; ☑ 040 63 14 22; www.bischoff.it; Via Mazzini 21; ⊙ 9.30am-1pm & 4-7.30pm Mon-Sat) Founded in 1777, this vaulted *enoteca* takes its *vino* very seriously: the choice of wines and other spirits is endless, the quality high and the store simply beautiful. Drop in if only to browse.

Record   MUSIC

(Map p54; ☑ 040 30 46 69; Via Diaz 19; ⊙ 8.30am-12.30pm & 3.30-7.30pm Tue-Sat) This small music store survives by selling records that it squeezes into its every nook and cranny. Classical music is the speciality, though you'll also find an interesting selection of folk and military music. Works by Trieste music legend Lelio Luttazzi are noticeably absent, but we're told only because they can't be found.

Torrefazione La Triestina   FOOD & DRINKS

(Map p58; ☑ 040 30 65 86; www.torrefazionela triestina.it; Via di Cavana 2; ⊙ 8am-8pm) This roasting company has been selling kilos of La Triestina coffee to its customers since 1948, not to mention over 300 varieties of tea (including herbal varieties). That it's always packed with locals is a testament to its quality.

Achille   BOOKS

(Map p58; www.libreriaachille.com; Piazza Vecchia 4; ⊙ 9am-12.30pm & 3.30-7pm Tue-Sat) Valhalla for treasure hunters, this large antiquarian bookshop – family run and in business since 1934 – is a trove of pre-loved tomes and beautiful old maps (including nautical ones). Take as much time as you like browsing or let the staff lead you to your next shelf favourite.

ℹ Information

EMERGENCY
Ambulance (☑ 118)
Fire Brigade (☑ 115)
Police (☑ emergencies 113, traffic police 040 419 43 11, emergency response 040 36 61 11)
Roadside Assistance (☑ 803 116 ACI, ☑ 803 803 Europe Assistance)
Sea Rescue (☑ 15 30)

INTERNET ACCESS
Trieste Free Spots (freespots.comune.trieste.it) Provided by the city council and offering free wi-fi for a total of four hours a day.

MEDICAL SERVICES
Ospedale Maggiore (☑ switchboard 040 399 11 11; asugi.sanita.fvg.it, Piazza dell'Ospitale 1)

POST
Piazza Verdi post office (☑ 040 777 23 11; ⊙ 8.20am-7.05pm Mon-Fri, 8.20am-12.35pm Sat) Very central and also open in the afternoon.

TOURIST INFORMATION
Trieste Infopoint (Map p58, B3; ☑ 040 347 83 12; www.turismofvg.it; Piazza Unità d'Italia 4/b

⊙9am-6pm Mon-Sat, to 1pm Sun in winter, 9am-7pm daily in summer; seasonal periods vary annually) Friuli Venezia Giulia's tourist board is located on a corner of Piazza Unità d'Italia. Drop in for free maps and information on sights, activities and transport. It also sells the useful FVG Card (p53), has audio guides and organises guided tours.

❶ Getting There & Away

AIR

Aeroporto Friuli Venezia Giulia (☑0481 77 32 24; www.triesteairport.it; Via Aquileia 46, Ronchi dei Legionari) Located 33km from Trieste, 40km from Udine, 20km from Gorizia and 80km from Pordenone, with daily connections to the main Italian airports, as well direct flights to London, Munich, Paris and Valencia. The airport includes a tourist **Infopoint** (☑0481 47 60 79; www.turismofvg.it ⊙daily, hours vary).

BOAT

From June to September, boat services connect Trieste to Grado and the Istrian coast. Stazione Marittima (Molo Bersaglieri 3) ferry terminal is the main port of call.

WORTH A TRIP

THE OPICINA TRAM
....

The *tram di Opicina* (Opicina tram) holds a special place in the hearts of the Triestini and has taken them from Piazza Oberdan to the Carso town of Opicina for over a century. But this city's beloved old rattler, known locally as the 'number 2 tram', has been idle for over four years. Don't despair: work to replace the sleepers and rails is progressing, albeit slowly, and it's hoped that by the end of 2022 passengers should be back on board the tram. After all, the tram is the only one capable of making it up to the town (elevation 330m) on a route so steep it takes the aid of a funicular to reach the top. If it is running, don't miss the chance to take a ride, perhaps heading back down along the panoramic Napoleonica road (p88). Just keep in mind that it's a tight fit, so leave the stroller at the hotel. When the tram isn't running, bus 2 (every 20 minutes, 7.11am to 8.11pm, €1.25) makes the trip up from Via Galatti, near Piazza Oberdan. Needless to say, it's no substitute for Trieste's charming centenarian.

TPL FVG (☑800 05 20 40, mobile 040 971 23 43; https://tplfvg.it; departing Molo Bersaglieri) sails to Grado (one way/return €7.40/11.25; 8.30am & 5pm Jul & Aug; 2 bicycles allowed per trip; €0.90), to Muggia (10 times daily Mon-Sat, six times daily Sun; one way/return €4.25/7.90; 30min) and to Sistiana (one way/return €6.60/€11.30; four times daily Jun-Sep) via Barcola (one way €2.90) and Grignano (one way €4.60). Purchase tickets on board. Twenty bicycles are allowed on board on the route to Muggia and five bicycles on the route to Barcola, Grignano and Sistiana (€0.90).

BUS

Trieste's main bus station (ticket office ☑040 41 44 82; ⊙6.30am-6.50pm Mon-Sat, 6.30am-2.10pm Sun; www.autostazionetrieste.it; Piazza della Libertà 9) is located beside the train station and houses ticket offices for the main bus companies. Alternatively, buy tickets online on the user-friendly website. International routes reach Slovenia, Croatia, Serbia, Bulgaria, Romania and Hungary.

CAR & MOTORCYLE

From Milan take the A4 and, after Venice, exit at Trieste-Cattinara. Take the SS202 and follow the signs for the centre. **From southern Italy**, follow the A1 to Bologna, continue on the A14 to Padua, then switch to the A4 to Trieste. After the tollbooth you can choose between the panoramic coastal road (SS14) and the so-called 'truck-friendly' route.

Parking

Your best option if arriving by car is to find a parking spot near the centre and then explore the city on foot or using public transport. Parking options include the following:

Foro Ulpiano (informazioni@saba.eu; www.saba.it; Foro Ulpiano 1; €1.70 per hr or part thereof, 3hr €5, daily rate €16; ⊙24hr)

Il Giulia (information@saba.eu; www.saba.it; Via Giulia 75; €1 per hr; ⊙24hr)

Parcheggio Molo IV (€1.50 per hr up to 4hr, 12hr €10, daily rate €15; ⊙24hr).

Parcheggi Rive (paid parking areas ⊙8am-8pm, excluding holidays); red zone €1.40 pr hr (min payment 30min €0.70), yellow zone €1 pr hr (min payment 30min €0.50), green zone €0.80 pr hr (min payment 30min €0.40), Lanterna zone €0.60 pr hr (min payment €0.50).

Park San Giusto (☑040 36 32 65; www.parksanjust.it; Via del Teatro Romano 16; €1.60 per hr, daily rate €15; ⊙24hr)

Saba Campo San Giacomo (information@saba.eu; www.saba.it; Campo San Giacomo 16/1; €1.60 per hr or part thereof, daily rate €14; ⊙24hr)

Saba Ospedale Maggiore (informazioni@saba.eu; www.saba.it; Via Pietà 7 ⊙24hr); €1.80 per hr; 12hr from 7am to 7pm €9; daily rate €15.

Silos (informazioni@saba.eu; www.saba.it; Piazza della Libertà 9; first 3hr €1.50, fourth hr €2, fifth & sixth hr €2.50; one day €10, subsequent days €9 ⊙24hr).

Trieste Terminal Passeggeri (☑ 040 673 25 50; www.triesteterminal.it; Molo Bersaglieri 3) Manages the car parks on Le Rive and at Molo IV. On Sundays, when cruise ships dock, parking is prohibited in the specially signposted area in front of the passenger terminal.

TRAIN
Stazione Centrale (Map p54, E1; Piazza della Libertà 8) Services across the region as well as some international destinations (www.trenitalia.com).

ℹ Getting Around
TO/FROM THE AIRPORT
Polo Intermodale An elevated walkway connects the terminals to the airport car parks, bus station and new airport train station (on the Trieste-Venice line). For more detailed information, see www.triesteairport.it/it/airport/polo-intermodale.

TPL FVG (☑ 800 05 20 40, mobile 040 971 23 43; https://tplfvg.it) Bus G51 connects the airport to the city; departures every 30 minutes. Many hotels offer airport shuttle services for guests.

PUBLIC TRANSPORT
Bus
TPL FVG (☑ 800 05 20 40, mobile 040 971 23 43; https://tplfvg.it) operates city buses, including those formerly run by Trieste Trasporti (www.triestetrasporti.it). Services are efficient and frequent between 5.30am and 9pm on most routes. Unfortunately, services outside this time are scarce; late evening routes are marked with an orange letter, while after-midnight services are marked with an orange number. See the website for routes and timetables, and download the app to purchase tickets from your smartphone. Useful bus routes for visitors include the following: **routes 8 and 10** reach the Risiera di San Sabba (alight at the stop in front of Caffè Tommaseo), **routes 6 and 36** reach Gragnano and the Castello di Miramare, while **route 20** leads to Muggia, from where route 7 reaches the Slovenian border.

A one-hour ticket (valid four hours on Sunday) costs €1.35. A daily ticket costs €4.30. If you have an FVG Card (p53) you can buy a *bollino* (48hr/72hr/1 week €3/4/6) and enjoy unlimited use of public transport.

Ferries
See p84 and p92.

Taxi
Radio Taxi Trieste (☑ 040 30 77 30, active 24hr; www.radiotaxitrieste.it) A trip from the city to the airport costs €60, excluding the motorway toll.

COSTIERA TRIESTINA

Heading northwest from Trieste, the Castello di Miramare appears like a sentinel keeping watch over the gulf. While this Gothic-Revival castle is the undisputed star of the Trieste coast, it's not its only asset.

The neighbourhood of Barcola has 4km of seafront, good for a summertime dip or year-round ocean gazing. The scenery becomes lusher and more evocative as you continue towards Grignano, surrounded by pine trees, marine reserves and crumbling old buildings. Visible from the Castello di Miramare is the less fanciful but equally charming Castello di Duino.

The stretch of coastline between these two castles is riddled with fascinating sights and ravines, the latter hiding the favourite beaches of the Triestini. While tricky to reach, these beaches are wonderfully secluded, wild and worth the effort.

If planning to explore the Costiera Triestina by car, consider that the Strada Costiera (coastal road) is narrow, with tricky parking and easily missed cross roads. A better bet may be a scooter or (if your legs can handle the distances and inclines) a bike.

Beyond the coastal towns closest to Trieste, which in summer become a veritable extension of the city, lies Duino-Aurisina. A sprawling municipality whose hamlets include Marina di Aurisina and Canovella degli Zoppoli, the area is home to the Castello di Duino.

From it, the nature reserve, Sistiana and Marina Aurisina lie to the south, towards Miramare.

To the north, towards Monfalcone, are the Villaggio del Pescatore (Fisherman's Village) and Bocche del Timavo.

ℹ Information
Sistiana Infopoint (☑ 040 29 91 66; www.turismofvg.it; Sistiana 56/b; ⊙9am-1pm & 2-6pm Apr-Oct) Tourist information for the Carso coast.

ⓘ Getting There & Away

BOAT

TPL FVG (☑ 800 05 20 40, mobile 040 971 23 43; https://tplfvg.it/it/il-viaggio/servizi-marittimi) sails from Molo Bersaglieri in Trieste to Barcola, Grignano and Sistiana from early June to early September.

BUS

TPL FVG (☑ 800 05 20 40, mobile 040 971 23 43; https://tplfvg.it) Bus 6 and 36 connect Trieste with Barcola and Grignano; catch them from Piazza Oberdan or Stazione Centrale (every 15 minutes; 5.30am to 11.30pm) and stop at the small piazza near the Pineta di Barcola and at the *bivio* stop. From the latter, Castello di Miramare is a 15-minute walk. The Duino-Aurisina area is served by bus 51 (€3.50, 30 minutes, every 15 minutes), which departs from Piazza della Libertà in Trieste. Bus 44 also reaches the area (€1.35, 60 minutes, every 30 to 40 minutes).

CAR & MOTORCYLE

From Trieste Follow the signs for the SS14 and Miramare to reach Barcola. To reach the Faro della Vittoria, look out for the signs immediately after the Stazione di Trieste (Trieste station): they lead to the old Strada del Friuli, which passes in front of the monument.

From Venice Follow the A4 and exit at Sistiana, then take the scenic coastal road to reach all the destinations covered in this section.

TRAIN

Trenitalia (www.trenitalia.com) runs from Trieste's Stazione Centrale to Miramare (€1.65, nine minutes, roughly every hour from 11am to 7pm, less frequently at other times). The castle is a 20-minute walk from the station. To reach Duino, catch a Monfalcone-Trieste line train to Bivio d'Aurisina station (€3.50, 16 minutes, hourly).

Barcola

POP 2801 / ELEV 2M

It is from this small seafront hamlet that the most important event in the region, the Barcolana, takes its name. And while it may appear as little more than a modest seaside strip between Trieste and Miramare to visitors, Barcolana is a much-loved summer hangout for the Triestini, who turn the place into a veritable offshoot of their city (and a nightmare for anyone looking for a parking spot). The scenario flips in the winter, when the streets are somber and quiet. Come on an especially clear day and the view is soul-stirring, taking in lagoons and Dolomite peaks.

◉ Sights

Barcola lies behind Trieste's Stazione Centrale and Porto Vecchio, its starting point marked by the enormous **Faro della Vittoria** (☑ 04082 12 10; www.farodellavittoria.it; Strada del Friuli 114; ⊘ 3-7pm Fri, 10am-1pm & 3-7pm Sat & Sun Apr-Jun & Sep, 10am-1pm & 4-7pm Wed-Sun Jul & Aug, 3-6pm Fri, 10am-1pm & 3-6pm Sat & Sun Oct, 9.30am-5.30pm during Barcolana, 9.30am-4.30pm Nov 1-4) **FREE**. The lighthouse, almost 70m high and standing on a summit 115m above sea level, was built between 1923 and 1927 to commemorate those who lost their lives at sea in WWI. The base is made of Karst stone and the lantern is enclosed in a bronze and crystal cage, topped by a statue of a woman greeting travellers. Although not obvious, the lighthouse is shaped like an upside-down fasces.

To reach the lighthouse, take bus 42, 44 or 46 from central Trieste.

Heading further north, you'll end up in Barcola's main nightlife hub (which in summer is lively even by day). The hamlet's main thoroughfare is Viale Miramare, which connects Trieste to Duino. The avenue is the heart of Trieste's colourful summertime beach scene, when dozens of families set up sun beds and picnic tables along the Pineta di Barcola, a shady pine grove wedged between Viale Miramare and the Lungomare di Barcola (Barcola Promenade). The latter doubles as Trieste's one-of-a-kind 'beach'. The pine grove itself is divided in two by a large fountain, and at the end of it begin the *topolini*, little terraces with stairs that lead into the water. The terraces themselves are a hit with sunbathers.

From Barcola, it's another 4km to the Castello di Miramare. Halfway there you'll come across Porticciolo del Cedas (also called 'Molo G'). It's said that the small marina has served as a landing place since Roman times. Today it's one of the places where the *muli* go diving.

✕ Eating

Fritolin   SEAFOOD €
(Viale Miramare; meals €10-15; ⊘ 10am-11pm in summer) At this old, whitewashed kiosk, fish is fried 12 hours a day. Devour it at communal tables, a stone's throw away from the *pineta* (pine grove). A simple, unpretentious affair.

Al Pescatore   SEAFOOD €€
(☑ 040 41 11 34; Viale Miramare 211; meals €25-35; ⊘ noon-2.30pm & 7-10pm Mon, Tue & Thu-Sun) For

over 25 years, this restaurant has been serving up the best fish dishes in Barcola. The first courses are unforgettable and the appetisers unmissable.

Prices are higher than average and utterly justified.

Al Faro SEAFOOD €€
(☑ 040 41 00 92; Scala Sforzi 2; meals €30; ☉ 11am-3pm & 6.30-11.30pm Mon & Wed-Sun) A short walk from the Faro della Vittoria, historic Al Faro enjoys a breathtaking location, with a lovely garden shaded by three horse-chestnut trees planted by the owners in the 1930s.

The trattoria retains an authentic air, with a 1500-bottle wine cellar and Trieste-style fresh fish prepared by Dario, a Croatian chef smitten with Italy.

 Drinking & Nightlife

Chioschi nella pineta KIOSKS
(☉ 10am-5pm) The Pineta di Barcola is scattered with *chioschi* (kiosks), all of which overlook the sea. Glass in hand, perched on a stool or chilling on a rug (provided for guests), they're the ideal place to kick back and soak in Barcola's village-meets-beach vibe.

Grignano

POP 474 / ELEV 2M

The Castello di Miramare is so famous that it completely overshadows the name of the hamlet in which it's found: Grignano, located immediately after Barcola.

To the north of the castle, the bay opens up to the area which is overlooked by the marine park. It's an enviable position, with a view of hundreds of boats docked at the port; at sunset prepare your lenses for the perfect photograph.

⊙ **Sights**

★**Castello di Miramare** CASTLE
(☑ 040 22 41 43; www.miramare.beniculturali.it; Viale Miramare; adult/reduced €10/2, free with FVG Card; ☉ 9am-7pm, last entrance 6.30pm) On the Trieste coast, it's impossible not to direct your gaze towards the Castello di Miramare. One of Italy's most visited monuments, its hauntingly elegant profile has a way of searing itself into your mind, becoming an image of the country you will long remember.

The origin of the castle's name becomes clear the moment you step inside this magnificent 19th-century residence: the sea *(mare)* is omnipresent, framed in large windows that capture a magical light. The manor was completed in 1860 at the behest of Archduke Maximilian of Austria, as a private residence where he lived with his wife Charlotte of Belgium. The exterior decorative elements and interior furnishings reflect the tastes of a romantic and idealistic man, the mix of Gothic, Romanesque and Renaissance styles creating one whimsical whole. It's a custom-made fairytale, crafted by the very finest carpenters and artisans of the day.

In the 22-hectare *park* (☉ 8am-4pm Jan, Nov & Dec, to 5pm Feb & Oct, to 6pm Mar, to 7pm Apr-Sep) behind the castle, Maximilian had various botanical species planted, including exotic ones discovered on his globetrotting travels. In summer, when Trieste's heat and humidity can feel unbearable, a stroll through this cool, green wonderland is priceless. The park includes the not-so-modest *gartenhaus* in which the archduke lived with his wife during the castle's construction. On the pier behind the castle is the unexpected sight of a small sphinx, gazing out at the gulf.

Parking (1/2/3hr €1/3/6, €3 every hr thereafter) is available onsite.

Riserva Naturale Marina di Miramare NATURE RESERVE
(☑ 04022 41 47; www.riservamarinamiramare.it; Viale Miramare 349) The first marine nature reserve established in Italy covers an area of 30 hectares around the promontory of Grignano, including some 2km of coastline and up to 200m of ocean off it (note the buoys that mark its boundary).

The reserve's headquarters occupy the Castello di Miramare's *gartenhaus,* where you'll find information about diving and wildlife tours, as well as educational workshops.

Immaginario Scientifico MUSEUM
(☑ 040 22 44 24; www.immaginarioscientifico. it; Riva Massimiliano e Carlotta 15; admission €5, free for children under 6 & FVG Card; ☉ 10am-6pm Tue-Sun) Children can have fun while learning about the world of science at this interactive, multimedia museum in Grignano. Explore the laws of physics through experiments and games that even adults will find intriguing. The Cosmo planetarium is also interesting.

The centre is part of a museum network with six facilities throughout Friuli Venezia Giulia.

OSMIZE HOPPING

One of the unique features of Trieste and the Carso are *osmize*. Not only great for a cheap, authentic bite, these pop-up wine cellars offer an unforgettable portal into the region's culinary traditions and history. They're also a great reason to properly explore the Carso Plateau. Finding the *osmize* is an experience in itself, a curious treasure hunt involving branches and arrows. To learn more, see p32.

🛏 Sleeping

Ostello Tergeste   HOSTEL €
(☑040 22 41 02; http://it.ostellotergeste.com; Viale Miramare 331; dm from €20, d from €60 ☺Mar-Nov;❋☷☎) A hostel by the sea, in a villa from the 1920s, a stone's throw from Castello di Miramare and Barcola's nightlife. Part of the AIG Hostels network, it follows the standard rules: same-sex dorms, afternoon shut-outs for cleaning, and evening curfews. Dorms and private rooms all have private bathroom.

Duino-Aurisina

POP 8238 / ELEV 144M

Beyond Grignano, the cliffs and Castello di Duino take centre stage, signalling that you've arrived in Duino-Aurisina, a sprawling municipality on the road between Trieste and Monfalcone. Home to unspoilt nature and quaint little villages, this stretch of the Julian coast bubbles with energy and surprise, a bit like the natural springs and underground caves that riddle the area where Carso and ocean collide.

👁 Sights & Activities

⭐ Castello di Duino   CASTLE
(☑040 20 81 20; www.castellodiduino.it; Via Castello di Duino 32; adult/reduced €10/5; ☺9.30am-1pm Mon & Wed-Fri, to 5.30pm Sat & Sun) Since 2003, 18 rooms of the private residence of the Thurn und Taxis family have been open to the public, making it possible to snoop around the Castello di Duino. Built in the 14th century and a cultural centre since the 17th century, the castle now exhibits objects, photographs and musical instruments belonging to the family.

The star attraction, however, is the castle tower, which offers a breathtaking view of the coastal cliffs. Looking towards the promontory, seek out the outline of the Dama Bianca (White Dame), an enormous, pale-coloured rock that, according to the legend, recalls a chatelaine (woman of the house) who took her own life for love.

The castle is surrounded by a beautiful park which bursts with colour in the spring. Wandering among the fountains and sculptures you'll stumble upon a bunker from WWII.

On the adjacent promontory are the ruins of the old castle, which dates from the 11th century.

Riserva Naturale delle
Falesie di Duino   PARK
(☑040 201 71 11/040 201 73 72; falesie@comune.duino-aurisina.ts.it; www.falesiediduino.it; Viale Miramare 349) Outlined by the enormous Karst cliffs looming over the Adriatic, this protected area of woods and Mediterranean shrub, where flora and fauna abound, stretches between Duino and Sistiana.

The best way to enjoy it is to hit the Sentiero Rilke, a panoramic, 2km hiking trail that runs along the reserve (allow 30 minutes to complete it).

Bocche del Timavo   NATURE
(SS14, Località San Giovanni di Duino) Mother Nature's love of surprises is clear at these springs, mentioned by the Roman poet Virgil. Their source is the Timavo, a river that sinks underground kilometres from its headwaters in Slovenia only to re-emerge 40km later in San Giovanni. This seemingly 'mystical' reappearance has long bestowed the place with a sacred aura, evidenced in the presence of the Chiesa di San Giovanni in Tuba.

The church itself occupies the site of an early Christian basilica.

Grotta del Mitreo   CAVE
(☑040 452 75 11; ☺10am-noon Sat or on request) **FREE** Hidden in a small cavity at the foot of Monte Hermada is a mithraeum, a Roman temple dedicated to the god Mithras. What makes this temple unique is its setting in a natural grotto; a karstic cavity not unlike many others in the area.

Step inside to see two benches, as well as the block of limestone at which the Eucharist was celebrated.

Adventure Park ADVENTURE PARK

(☑346 632 61 33; www.triesteadventurepark.it; Località Ceroglie; admission up to 5/6/8/10/13yr €5/11/14/17.50/18.50, over 14yr €20.50; ☺10am-7pm Sat & Sun Jun, Thu-Sun Jul-mid Sep, 10am-sunset Sat & Sun mid-Sep-mid-Oct) From trails for little ones not yet ready to climb trees to a zipline 95m above the ground.

Marina di Aurisina

If you love lush landscapes, the Carso's unique take on Mediterranean flora, and secret (often semi-deserted) beaches, Marina di Aurisina will leave you swooning.

Coming from Trieste and Miramare, your first beach option is **Filtri di Aurisina**, which can be reached by taking Via Piccard, immediately after the Grignano tunnel (on the SS14). At the end of the street a steep set of stairs leads to the free, public beach (you can also follow the signs to the Laboratorio di Biologia Marina). If you don't have your own wheels, take bus 44 and alight at the Santa Croce stop. The beach itself is small and pebbly, with a bar and restaurant. If you follow the road from the *porticciolo* (small marina) that skirts the cliff, you'll find another beach, marked by the sign 'FKK – zona naturista': once you cross the threshold, you must be strictly naked.

Canovella of the Zoppoli (*zoppoli* were long boats dug from tree trunks and used by local fishermen) is considered one of the most pleasant beaches on the Trieste coast. From the state road, follow the signs to Canovella, then continue on foot down the small staircase. In summer, it's a hit with young Triestini, who hang around the seafood restaurant. Walk southeast along the beach for 10 minutes and you'll stumble upon another nudist beach, the **Liburnia** (www.liburniats.org).

Lastly, the **Le Ginestre** bathing establishment (www.ginestre.ts.it, adult/reduced €12/5 Sat & Sun, €9/4 Mon-Fri; ☺9am-7.30pm Jun-Sep) charms with its nostalgic 1960s vibe (indeed, it was opened in 1960). You'll find it between Marina di Aurisina and Sistiana: to get here, you need to deviate off the state road, head downhill to the car park and then follow the stairs that lead directly to the sea. The small beach club includes a restaurant for those who wish to beach bum all day long.

Sistiana

The main town in Duino-Aurisina, Sistiana played a strategic role in both World Wars and was an elegant holiday destination between the 19th and 20th centuries. Today it's best known for its **Baia of Sistiana**, an inlet of pleasant, well-equipped beaches and the eastern bookend of the Riserva Naturale delle Falesie di Duino.

To reach the inlet (and its car parks) you'll need to do a very quick switch from the SS14 to the SP3. Follow the signs for Camping Village Mare Pineta (p88) and the **Parco Caravella** (☑348 098 25 93), dotted with bars, nightclubs and small private beaches where you can rent sunbeds, deckchairs and umbrellas, and enjoy the view of the cliffs. You'll also find a children's park with inflatable pools.

Sports enthusiasts can play volleyball, kayak, windsurf or book a diving course (also open to children).

At the southeastern end of the inlet lies the historic Castelreggio bathing establishment, now managed by **Portopiccolo** (www.portopiccolosistiana.it), a large resort whose restaurant, bar and spa services are available to nonguests.

Further southeast along the coast lies the **Costa dei Barbari**, a series of inlets with

LA FOIBA OF BASOVIZZA (SINKHOLE OF BASOVIZZA)

The very name of Basovizza – a Slovenian-speaking village in the northeast of the Carso – is linked to the *foibe* (sinkholes) which mark the Carso plateau. In the final stages of WWII, and in the period that immediately followed, these cavities were mostly used by the Yugoslav troops to dispose the bodies, in some cases still alive, of its Nazi-Fascist enemies. The town's **national monument** and **documentation center** (☑040 36 53 43; www.foibadibasovizza.it; ☺10am-6pm daily Mar-Jun, 10am-2pm Mon, Tue & Thu-Sun Jul-Feb) FREE recount this gruesome chapter in history, in which thousands lost their lives. Curiously, Basovizza itself has no actual *foiba*, just a mineshaft. And while the site itself is of great historical importance, it's not a must-see, so only consider making the trip if you're an especially keen history buff.

small rocky beaches mainly popular with naturists. If you're heading to Sistiana on public transport from Trieste, catch bus 44.

🛏 Sleeping

Camping Village Mare Pineta CAMPING €/€€
(📞 04029 92 64; www.marepineta.com; Sistiana 60/d; pitches €27-70, full-board €51-76; 🅿 ☒ 🛜)
A top-quality campsite whose cabins offer a level of quality and comfort that rivals that of hotels. Open from May to October.

Villaggio del Pescatore

This little village was built around a small harbour in the 1950s to accommodate Giulian and Dalmatian exiles from areas ceded to Yugoslavia. Today, it's known mainly for its fishing tourism, with local catches put to good use at **Al Pescaturismo** (📞 339639 04 73; www.alpescaturismo.it; Villaggio del Pescatore, Zona Cava, Duino-Aurisina; meals €30; ☺ noon-2.30pm & 7-10pm Fri & Sat, noon-4pm Sun Mar-Dec, also 7-10pm Wed in summer), where you can feast on mussels while sipping Friulian wines by the sea.

The area is also paradise for palaeontologists: the former Sertubi quarry zone is one of the largest known dinosaur cemeteries in Italy and the very place where 'Antonio' p69) was discovered.

THE CARSO

The people of Trieste have always divided their affection between the sea before them and the lofty tableland behind them. Stretching from the Julian Alps to Istria, the calcareous Carso (Karst) plateau is geologically unique. Its rock is sensitive to the acid contained in rain, which over millennia has helped erode and shape it, creating a process known as karstification. All water on the ground is absorbed and channelled into underground rivers which pass through caves, re-emerge on the surface, then disappear for miles. Not surprisingly, this land is a speleologist's dream.

At ground level, the Carso is a cheerful place: genteel and coarse in equal measure, alternating between farmland, vineyards, semideserted villages, ancient quarries, windswept sanctuaries and curious *dolinas* (hollows in the ground), the blue of the Adriatic Sea appearing occasionally in the distance.

LOCAL KNOWLEDGE

NAPOLEONICA OR VICENTINA?

The official name of the Napoleonica road is Strada Vicentina. While the route was opened by French soldiers, it was actually designed by engineer Giacomo Vicentini in 1821.

❶ Getting There & Away

BUS

TPL FVG (📞 800 05 20 40, mobile 040 971 23 43; https://tplfvg.it) Bus 42 runs from Piazza Oberdan in Trieste to Sgonico (32 minutes) and its hamlet Borgo Grotta Gigante every 20 minutes, passing through Monrupino and Opicina (38 minutes) en route.

CAR & MOTORCYCLE

From Trieste Head northbound out of the city and take the E70; once passed Opicina, you'll find signs for Sgonico.

TRAM
See p82.

Opicina

POP 7950 / ELEV 330M

There are two worthy reasons for visiting Opicina. The first is the trip itself, on the famous 'number 2 tram' (resuming service in late 2022; see p82) that connects Trieste to the town. The second is the splendid Napoleonica trail. Both can be combined in one pleasant afternoon. You will see the entrance to the **Napoleonica** when you step off the tram at the Obelisco stop in Opicina (near the car park). The road was opened in 1797 by Napoleonic troops engaged in the Italian campaign. Today, around 4km of the route is accessible to pedestrians and cyclists, serving up exceptional views of the landscape.

The route is beautiful in any season. In winter, the trail is protected from the brutal bora wind that lashes Trieste, allowing you to comfortably take in the natural beauty of the Carso and the panoramic views of the gulf, the latter particularly spectacular during the Barcolana regatta.

Starting the route in Opicina (therefore from south to north), you'll end at the San Nazario car park in the hamlet of Prosecco. If you're a fan of free climbing, you'll find some vertical rock walls on the last section of the trail.

🛏 Sleeping

Obelisco CAMPING €

(☑ 040 21 27 44; www.campeggiobelisco.it; Strada Nuova per Opicina 37; adult €5-6, child €2.50-3.50, tent €3.50-4.50, caravan €5-6, camper €6-9) A pleasant, picturesque campsite close to the Opicina Obelisk and a good base for sightseeing, climbing or trekking in the Carso. It's also handy for visiting Trieste, with the Tram di Opicina (Opicina Tram) nearby and, when it's not running, a bus stop an easy five-minute walk away. The campsite has a small **bar-restaurant** (🕑 8am-11pm summer, 8am-11pm Tue-Sun winter).

Le Casite B&B €€

(☑ 339 846 45 40; http://lecasite.com; Località Trebiciano 100; s/d/tr €45/79/85) In addition to being an excellent B&B (four rooms, all with private bathrooms), Le Casite is also a bastion of local history, housed in a traditional and beautifully preserved Carso abode (only the farmers are missing). Best of all, the owners are happy to share information about its history with the curious.

To get here, catch bus 39 (or the Opicina Tramway once services resume), or use one of the useful maps offered by the B&B upon booking.

Sgonico

POP 1991 / ELEV 278M

The area around Sgonico is classic Carso, a place where the plateau flattens and sinkholes hint at the many cavities beneath. Quarried heavily since Roman times, this is a land where wilderness and farmland alternate, a place where the blue of the Adriatic makes unexpected cameos beyond the trees and hills.

◎ Sights

★ Grotta Gigante CAVE

(☑ 040 32 73 12; www.grottagigante.it; Borgo Grotta Gigante 42/a; adult/reduced €13/10, free with FVG Card; 🕑 10am-4pm Tue-Sun) Of the many accessible caves in the Carso, the 'Giant Cave' is hands down the most interesting. True to its name, its main chamber is almost 100m high, 167m long and 76m wide, making it one of the largest caves in the world. Littered with stalactites, stalagmites, ravines, stairways and tunnels, it's an atmospheric, ever-changing wonderland.

The cave houses two enormous pendulums which study the movement of the Earth's crust and monitor seismic activity. Guides are highly knowledgeable, pointing out other peculiar and beautiful features, among them the 12m-high Colonna Ruggero (Ruggero Column).

Make sure to rug up when visiting as the cave is chilly (warm threads are available if you've forgotten your trusty jumper). Upstairs there are fossils and objects that were found in the cave, including the skeleton of a now-extinct karst bear.

🛏 Sleeping

Barbara B&B €€

(☑ 340 558 69 05; www.bbbarbaratrieste.it; Borgo Grotta Gigante 17; d/tr/q €90/120/160; 🅿) 200m from the entrance to the Grotta Gigante, this B&B has two double rooms and a room with mezzanine which can accommodate up to four people; all rooms are thoughtfully furnished.

TRIESTE & THE CARSO SGONICO

OFF THE BEATEN TRACK

A GENEROUS SERVE OF THE CARSO

A 12km drive from Trieste along the SP29B leads to one-of-a-kind **Monrupino**. The village name is linked to a local fortress, home to a *castelliere* (fortified borough) in prehistoric times and, since 1512, the **Santuario della Beata Vergine (Sanctuary of the Blessed Virgin)**. Head up (you can drive to the top) to enjoy a 360-degree view of the Carso and the sea. In the village itself, you can visit the **Museo della Casa Carsica** (☑ 040 327 2 40; www.kraskahisa.com/ita; admission by donation; 🕑 11am-12.30pm & 3-5pm Easter-Oct), a house museum depicting a traditional Carso abode. On the last week of August in odd-numbered years, you can attend Monrupino's Slovenian-flavoured **Nozze Carsiche**. A folk festival based on the Carso's traditional four-day-long wedding celebrations, the shindig involves all the villagers, who dress up in traditional garb and partake in various rituals farewelling celibacy. The event culminates on the Sunday with a procession to the sanctuary, where the bride is 'given away' to the family of the groom.

There's a large, tranquil courtyard for all guests to enjoy. Trieste and the beaches are not far away.

ℹ️ Information

Grotta Gigante (☑ 040 32 73 12; www.grotta gigante.it; Borgo Grotta Gigante 42/a).

TOWARDS ISTRIA

South of Trieste, the final strip of Italian territory also marks the beginning of the Istrian peninsula. In the few kilometres separating Trieste from the small fishing village of Muggia, one passes from a territory historically linked to the Austrian Empire to one tied to the Republic of Venice. This Venetian connection is still palpable in the *calli* (alleys) of Muggia's old town, a place that recalls the villages of the Venetian coast as well as those of the Slovenian coast, for centuries under Venetian domination. It's an interesting, off-the-beaten-track kind of place, and one worth your time.

From Trieste, you can reach Muggia via the coastal road or by boat from the Stazione Marittima.

Muggia

POP 12,899 / ELEV 2M

Muggia became a Venetian entity in 1420 and it was the Venetians who bestowed the town with its Venice-like *calli* (alleys) and waterfront. Yet, Muggia's history is much older.

A fortified village had already appeared on Colle di Santa Barbara in prehistoric times, over which the Romans built Castrum Muglae to defend the area from Istrian invaders. In 931 CE, under the Carolingian Empire, Muggia's territory was gifted to the Patriarchate of Aquileia; the 9th-century Basilica of Muggia Vecchia is the only surviving relic from this period. Around 1000, the inhabitants of the area's hill towns migrated down towards the coast and in the 13th century the Muggia we know today was born. The Duomo and Palazzo Comunale, both on Piazza Marconi, date from this period. Under Venetian rule until 1797, Muggia fell under Napoleonic rule (1805–14) before passing to the Habsburgs. The town's Muglsian dialect, which originated in Ladin, became extinct during the long Venetian period, making way for the current Muggesian dialect of Istrian-Venetian origin.

Muggia was united to Italy alongside Trieste and Istria at the end of WWI. After the 1947 peace treaty, the 1954 London Memorandum (which handed over much of the Istrian territory to Yugoslavia) and the 1975 Treaty of Osimo, the city remained, together with San Dorligo della Valle, the only Istrian city in Italian territory.

🔆 Sights

Piazza Marconi   HISTORIC CENTRE
Punctuated by laidback bars and restaurants, Muggia's historic centre claims the town's most beautiful architecture. Dating from 1263, the gothic **Duomo** features a gracious spire and white-stone facade embellished with a large rose window. Also on Piazza Marconi is the 14th-century **Palazzo Co-**

SAN DORLIGO DELLA VALLE & VAL ROSANDRA

The municipality of San Dorligo della Valle (Dolina in Slovenian) straddles the border between the Carso and Istria, and through it flows the Karst Plateau's only surface-level waterway, the Rosandra. The torrent is the reason for the rich diversity of flora and fauna in the 750-hectare **Riserva Naturale della Val Rosandra** (Visitor Center ☑ 329 128 63 25; www.riservavalrosandra-glinscica.it; Bagnoli della Rosandra-Boljunec 507; ⊙ 9am-5pm Fri-Sun). The abundance of water here led to the construction of 16 water mills in the 18th century. Look for traces of them along the valley or simply lose yourself among the limestone canyons, the latter popular with climbers from around the world. You can drive as far as the suburb of Bagnoli della Rosandra, from where the reserve is accessible on foot. Park trails lead to waterfalls (the highest, at 36m, can be reached by following the Via delle Acque), bat-riddled caves, the remnants of a Roman aqueduct that once connected the valley to Trieste, as well as castle ruins. There's also a beautiful cycling trail, which starts in Cattinara and follows an old railway track. Red-and-white signs marked with a '1' indicate an easy, relatively level hiking trail from Bagnoli della Rosandra to Bottazzo, a popular option that leads to the Chiesa di Santa Maria in Siaris e al Monte Carso.

munale, where the Lion of Venice flanks the coats of arms of the *podestà*.

Mandracchio PORT

Known as the Mandracchio, Muggia's small, picturesque port seems to almost reach the doors of this town. It's a deep, sleepy inlet, speckled with wooden boats and fishing nets drying in the sun.

To reach it, simply follow the waterfront, a very pleasant walk (even if it's a tight fit between sea and traffic).

Castello di Muggia CASTLE

(Calle Lauri) Commissioned by the patriarch of Aquileia and built in 1400, Muggia's hilltop castle is currently a private residence, with public access limited to special events and festivals. Nonetheless, it's worth heading up to admire the coastal views from the panoramic staircase. The castle itself is also impressive, complete with crenellated tower. At the turn of both the 17th and 18th centuries, the building fell into ruin and was stripped of all its splendour. Much of the stone was reused for building houses in the town below.

Muggia Vecchia
(Old Muggia) PARCO ARCHEOLOGICO

(☏ 040 27 11 64; www.parcodimuggiavecchia.it; Salita Muggia Vecchia 53; ⊙ 8am-6pm) Located south of the town centre, this archaeological site preserves what remains (not much) of the medieval village, including columns, fragments of walls and patches of road.

Definitely worth a pit stop is the 11th-century **Basilica di Muggia Vecchia**, home to beautiful Romanesque frescoes.

Museo d'Arte Moderna Ugo Carà MUSEUM

(☏ 040 927 86 32; Via Roma 9; ⊙ 5-7pm Tue-Sat mid-Sept–mid-Jun, 6-8pm Tue-Sat mid-Jun–mid-Sept, also 10am-noon Sat & Sun year-round) `FREE` Modern art has found a home in Muggia thanks to the work of Ugo Carà, a local sculptor (1908–2004) whose creations are inspired by dreams and mythological themes.

Colle di Santa Barbara HISTORIC VILLAGE

(SP16) Leaving Muggia in a south-easterly direction on the SP16 (follow the signs for Slovenia) you can visit Santa Barbara, a village that gives you, with a little imagination, an idea of what the landscape of Muggia was like in ancient times. The small church of Santa Barbara, made of sandstone blocks, dates back at least to the 17th century, while the adjacent cemetery is the result of a late 19th-century renovation. The remains of the prehistoric *castelliere* (fortified borough), the ancient necropolis and the sandstone quarries are also worth a look.

🏃 Activities

Circolo della Vela Muggia SAILING

(☏ 040 27 24 16; www.cdvmuggia.org; Largo Nazario Sauro 5/d) Organises sailing courses. The sailing club itself is lovely.

🎊 Festivals & Events

Carnevale di Muggia FEBRUARY/MARCH

During Carnivale, a Venetian tradition some believe dates back to the 15th century, the streets of Muggia come alive with colourful floats and festive masks. If driving in, expect road closures.

🛏 Sleeping

San Bartolomeo CAMPING €

(☏ 040 27 12 75; www.campeggiosanbartolomeo.it; Road to Lazzaretto 99, San Bartolomeo; adult/child €9/5.50, tent €6, camper €12.50, car & tent €10; ⊙ Jun-Sep) Istria is a land of campers and this tiny Italian patch of it is no exception. The campsite comes with private beach, bar, restaurant and a decent supermarket. If you do stay here, don't forget to take a tour of the small, picturesque port of San Bartolomeo, its beach clubs never short of a crowd in summer.

Dulcinea HOTEL €€

(☏ 040 27 12 66; www.albergodulcinea.com; Via Battisti 1; s/d €65/90; ❄ 🖰) Right on the doorstep of the *centro storico* (historic centre), this charming hotel offers very comfortable single rooms (with spacious single beds) or double rooms at reasonable prices. The property is well-equipped for guests with limited mobility.

🍴 Eating

Trattoria Splendor TRATTORIA €€

(☏ 040 27 52 62; Via Dante 47; meals € 25; ⊙ 8am-2pm & 5.30-10pm Wed-Mon) A trattoria as old and simple as the surf-based cuisine it serves. Chances are you'll have to wait for a table. If so, enjoy the tranquility of the surrounds until it's time for those Dalmatian-style mussels.

Alla Marina RESTAURANT €€/€€€

(☏ 040 27 13 29; Via Manzoni 7; meals €40; ⊙ noon-2.30pm & 7.30-9.30pm Wed-Sun) A terrace overlooking the sea where you can put yourself in chef Guido's hands and enjoy delicious seafood dishes.

Sal de mar
RESTAURANT €€€

(☑ 040 927 89 08; www.saldemar.it; Largo Nazario Sauro 10; meals €40; ⊙ noon-2.30pm & 7-9.30pm, open all day Sun) A top-notch restaurant in the Venetian castle that once protected that precious commodity: salt. Locally sourced ingredients conspire to create dishes like spaghetti with clams, mussels and chanterelles, or surf-and-turf sea bass with San Daniele prosciutto.

ℹ Information

For visitor information, contact the tourist offices in Trieste.

ℹ Getting There & Away

BOAT

TPL FVG (☑ 800 05 20 40, mobile 040 971 23 43; https://tplfvg.it/it/il-viaggio/servizi -marittimi) Sails year-round between Trieste (Molo Bersaglieri) and Muggia (around 10 departures, 30 min).

BUS

TPL FVG (☑ 800 05 20 40, mobile 040 971 23 43; https://tplfvg.it) Bus 20 connects Trieste with Muggia; buses depart from Stazione Centrale and stop at Piazza Oberdan (€1.35, every 15 minutes between 4.55am and 12.40am, 35 minutes).

CAR & MOTORCYCLE

From Trieste Drive south towards Stadio Nereo Rocco (Nereo Rocco Stadium), then take the SS15 to Muggia.

Gorizia, the Collio & the Isonzo

Includes ➔

Gorizia 95
The Collio. 102
Cormòns 102
Capriva del Friuli. 106
San Floriano
del Collio 106
Dolegna del Collio . . . 109
The Isonzo. 109
Gradisca d'Isonzo . . . 109
Fogliano Redipuglia . . 110
San Martino
del Carso 110
San Michele
del Carso 111

Best Farms

➔ D'Osvaldo (p106)

➔ Zoff (p106)

➔ La Subida (p103)

➔ Picech (p103)

➔ Gradis'ciutta (p107)

Best Restaurants

➔ Trattoria at the Subida (p103)

➔ L'Argine a Vencò (p109)

➔ Lokanda Devetak 1870 (p111)

Why Go?

In this corner of the region, which extends from the Isonzo eastward to the national border, you'll be roaming towns with a distinctly Slovenian and Habsburg flavour. You'll also have the opportunity to experience the traditions and rhythms of borderland farms whose gastronomic products are anything but peripheral.

Trilingual Gorizia is all about history and landscapes. While holding onto its frontier-town charm, it has shrugged off its Cold War stiffness, becoming a symbol of renewed camaraderie between Italians and Slovenes. The dramatic events that unfurled on its surrounding rivers and mountains have marked both the territory and its people, and many of these history-making places can be easily explored between Gorizia and the Isonzo, along old trails leading to traces and memories of the Great War.

For those simply wanting to decompress, there's the Collio, an area of gently rolling hills, vineyards, assiduous farmers and silent twilights. The area surrounding Cormòns merits a trip on its own, where it's rather easy to get used to the fabulous food and heartfelt hospitality.

When to Go

It's not folly to plan your trip around the grapevine cycle: during harvest season, the Collio is lively, the climate cool and the landscape lush. Winters are wet and cold. Rain is frequent, forest trails are muddy, but the atmosphere is snug and bewitching. Come springtime, Friuli is enchanting: nature stirs from its slumber, local activities resume, *agriturismi* reopen and cellar doors buzz.

Gorizia, the Collio & the Isonzo Highlights

1 Castello di Gorizia
(p95) The archetypal castle and its magnificent panorama.

2 Piazza della Transalpina
(p98) A leap into the recent past (and into Slovenia).

3 Cormòns (p102)
Explore the town and its family-run farms.

4 Collio on a Vespa
(p102) Fasten your helmet and roam the hills.

5 Sentiero delle Vigne Alte
(p103) Panoramic views and appetite-piquing taverns.

6 Sacrario Militare di Fogliano Redipuglia (p110) Resting place of 100,000 soldiers.

7 Ossario di Oslavia
(p101) Another moving site commemorating the fallen of the Great War.

8 Itinerari della Grande Guerra (p111) A journey along frontlines and trenches, with beautiful trails to wander.

GORIZIA

POP 33,479 / ELEV 84M

It only takes a short walk around Piazza della Vittoria to discern Gorizia's multicultural soul. At its cafes, chatter weaves between Friulian, Italian and Slovenian. It's the same in local offices: in this city, trilingualism reigns supreme. Gorizia's medieval castle rises behind the piazza, whose baroque flourishes hint at the city's former Habsburg splendour.

From Borgo Castello, Gorizia's strategic position is clear: the city sits in a valley between mountains, an ideal spot from which to control the area. It's also located near the Soča River, which marked a very important geographical boundary.

The heart of town lies between the piazza, Via Roma and Corso Verdi, where most of Gorizia's restaurants and bars are concentrated.

One of the oldest streets in the historic centre is Via Rastello, lined with once-busy, time-warped stores now 'reopened' for special events. The name Rastello is said to be the ancient form of *rastrello*, which referred to the gates once lowered across the city's entry points at night. Indeed, a gate was located on this very street in medieval times, separating the city from what was then the surrounding countryside.

History

Although the area around Gorizia was inhabited as early as the 1st century BCE, the city's name was first officially documented in 1001 CE, when Emperor Otto III ceded a villa called Gorizia to the patriarch of Aquileia. In the Middle Ages, Gorizia was a county ruled by various families, who expanded their domains from the Tyrol to Istria. Although the county (which had developed into a walled city) was annexed to the Venetian Republic in 1424, it swiftly fell under Habsburg control in 1500. During this period, the city was one of the transit hubs for merchants heading to Central and Eastern Europe.

In the 19th century it was incorporated, along with Gradisca (and the Collio area), into the Austrian Littoral, an administrative region of the Habsburg Empire with Trieste as its capital. The area between the Soča River and present-day Slovenia remained under Habsburg domination until the 20th century. During this period, Gorizia's relatively mild climate and tranquil disposition saw it become a favourite holiday destination for Central European nobility and imperial officials, earning it the moniker 'The Austrian Nice'.

During WWI, Gorizia was contested between the Italian and Austrian armies in the Battles of the Isonzo (see p255), and the Carso Isontino (Isonzo Karst) became the scene of long, gruelling battles in which 300,000 soldiers lost their lives. Prominent figures who took up arms included the poet Giuseppe Ungaretti. Although Italian troops took control of the city in 1916, they lost it in the Battle of Caporetto the following year. Heavily damaged, Gorizia and its province were finally annexed to the Kingdom of Italy in 1919.

The city's reconstruction began under Fascist rule. New roads were laid out and infrastructure was built, including Duca d'Aosta Airport in 1935. During this period, the region's Slovenian minority was subjected to persecution and violence. Mussolini's intense policy of Italianisation had already forced them to Italianise their names and renounce their mother tongue. At the end of WWII, after heinous clashes between Italians and Slavs and 40 days of Titoist occupation, Gorizia was split. Much of the city and some of its hamlets fell to Yugoslav Slovenia and were renamed Nova Gorica in 1948. And so, one city became two, separated by a border checkpoint and an Iron Curtain.

Today, Gorizia has a very different atmosphere. In 2004, after the collapse of the Eastern Bloc and Slovenia's subsequent entry into the European Union, the fence that divided Piazza della Transalpina in two was dismantled (see p99). Meanwhile, on the Carso Isontino, the Soviet-uniformed soldiers that had for decades kept guard were relayed to the history books. With Slovenia's signing of the Schengen Treaty in 2007, Gorizia's reunification came full circle, the city and its residents no longer restricted by international borders.

⊙ Sights

★ **Castello di Gorizia**   CASTLE
(☑ 0481 53 51 46; Borgo Castello 36; adult/reduced €3/1.50, free with FVG Card; ⊗ 9am-6pm Tue-Sun) It's the archetypal castle found in storybooks: a crenellated mass of stone walls and hulking keeps. Accessed via the mid-17th-century **Porta Leopoldina**, this hilltop *castello* was built around the 12th century to house the Count of Gorizia, combining numerous existing architectural structures and changing shape several times over the years.

Gorizia

What you see today is a meticulous reconstruction, undertaken in 1938 after the castle was almost razed to the ground during WWI. The 16th-century stone lion above the main entrance recalls Gorizia's brief period of Venetian rule. Inside, you can visit the **Museo del Medioevo Goriziano** (⏱ same as castle) and rooms filled with period furnishings and armaments. Highlights include the Sala del Conte, the Salone degli Stati Provinciali (home to a magnificent wooden choir), and the torture chamber.

The castle's pride and joy is the Corte dei Lanzi, a brooding, atmospheric courtyard surrounded by 15th- and 17th-century buildings. Before leaving, make sure to walk around the castle's defensive walls; expect to take impressive photographs on clear days.

Borgo Castello, the little village that developed around the castle, is home to the **Cappella di Santo Spirito** (☎0481 53 01 93; Borgo Castello), a small Romanesque chapel built in 1414 and restored after WWI. Although not open to the public, its window offers a glimpse of 16th-century frescoes attributed to the son of Tintoretto. Note that the castle itself was closed for restoration on our last visit.

Musei Provinciali, Borgo Castello
MUSEUMS

(☎0481 53 39 26; https://musei.regione.fvg.it; Borgo Castello 13; adult/reduced €6/3, combined ticket with Pinacoteca & Palazzo Coronini Cronberg €12/6, free with FVG Card; ⏱9am-7pm Tue-Sun) Below the castle in three adjacent buildings (Casa Domberg, Tasso and Formentini) are three of Gorizia's provincial museums.

The **Museo della Grande Guerra** documents the tragic history of the WWI Italian-Austrian front.

Next door, **Museo della Moda e delle Arti Applicate** displays three centuries of fashion and textiles, including some fine examples of Gorizian lace.

Lastly, the **Collezione Archeologica** houses local archaeological finds. The Pinacoteca at Palazzo Attems Petzenstein (p98) is another of Gorizia's provincial museums.

Gorizia

◎ Top Sights

1 Castello di Gorizia C2
2 Piazza della Transalpina .... off map C1
3 Piazza della Vittoria C2

◎ Sights

4 Chiesa di Sant'Ignazio B2
5 Duomo B3
6 Giardino Viatori .... off map A1
7 Musei Provinciali, Borgo Castello C2
8 Musei Provinciali, Palazzo Attems
   Petzenstein C1
9 Museo del Contrabbando D1
10 Museo Goriški .... off map C1
11 Palazzo Coronini Cronberg B1
12 Palazzo Lantieri C3
13 Palazzo Werdenberg B1
14 Porta Leopoldina C3
15 Synagogue C1

◎ Sleeping

16 1848 - Chef's Rooms C2
17 Al Castello C3
18 Flumen .... off map A1
19 Grand Hotel Entourage C3

◎ Eating

20 Chef You Too B3
21 Osteria ai Tre Amici B2
22 Pasticceria Centrale B3
23 Pasticceria L'Oca Golosa ....off map A3
24 Pizzeria al Lampione C1
25 RebeKin B2
26 Trattoria alla Luna B2
27 Trattoria da Gianni B2

◎ Drinking & Nightlife

28 Atmosfere La Stüa C3
29 Borgo Castello 3 .... C2
30 Caffè Teatro B3
31 Il Giardino dei Vizi C3
32 Mama Angela C2
33 Mister Blu B2

◎ Entertainment

34 Teatro Verdi B3

◎ Shopping

35 Libreria Editrice Goriziana B2
36 Mercato Coperto di Corso Verdi B2

Duomo   PLACE OF WORSHIP
(☑0481 53 01 93; Corte Sant'Ilario; ⊘8.30am-6.30pm) Although Gorizia's cathedral dates from the 13th century, it underwent numerous alterations up to the postwar period. Dedicated to St Hilary and St Taziano, it's the city's main place of worship, if not its most significant architectural asset.

Behind the gabled facade are richly stuccoed interiors that house the tombstone of Leonardo, the last count of Gorizia, and the 15th-century side chapel of Sant'Acazio.

★ **Piazza della Vittoria**   PIAZZA
Flanking Via Roma and in the shadow of the castle, Piazza della Vittoria makes for a wonderful spritz-o-clock pitstop. Criss-crossed by streets only a few years ago, the piazza was once home to a large lawn from which it derived its Slovenian name of Piazza Travnik (Lawn Square).

At its centre is the beautiful **Fountain of Neptune**, designed by Italian-Austrian architect Nicolò Pacassi and built in 1756.

Chiesa di Sant'Ignazio   PLACE OF WORSHIP
(☑0481 53 51 06; Piazza della Vittoria; ⊘8am-6pm Mon-Fri, to 7pm Sat, 9am-6pm Sun) When it comes to Gorizian landmarks, only the cas-

tle trumps this church, whose onion-shaped domes make frequent cameos on the horizon. A baroque-shaped beauty overlooking Piazza della Vittoria, it houses a precious altar from 1716 and a pulpit frescoed by the church's architect Christoph Tausch.

Built in the mid-17th century, the church was commissioned by the Jesuits, who arrived in Gorizia at the behest of the Vatican to counter the rise of Protestantism.

Palazzo Lantieri   HISTORIC BUILDING
(☑0481 53 32 84; www.palazzo-lantieri.com, contact@palazzo-lantieri.com; Piazza Sant'Antonio 6; ⊘guided tours by appointment) Sadly, only part of the cloister of this beautiful building remains, which, in the 15th century, was the epicentre of Gorizia's cultural and artistic life.

Originally a fortress, Palazzo Lantieri became an aristocratic residence whose illustrious guests included Napoleon.

Today, its private collections can be visited upon request.

The Lantieri's gracious hospitality also extends to the palazzo's elegant **hotel** (s/d/ste €100/140/100-170), complete with onsite parking.

Palazzo Werdenberg
HISTORIC BUILDING

(Via Mameli 12) The Jesuits built Palazzo Werdenberg in the 17th century to house a seminary. After the order was suspended in 1773, Maria Theresa of Austria transformed the palace into a public gymnasium. Since the postwar period, it's been home to the **Biblioteca Statale Isontina** (☑ 0481 58 02 11; ⊘ 7.45am-6.45pm Mon-Fri, 7.45am-1.15pm Sat), whose architectural highlights include a baroque staircase and 18th-century stucco.

Palazzo Coronini Cronberg
HISTORIC BUILDING

(☑ 0481 53 34 85; www.coronini.it; Viale XX Settembre 14; adult/reduced €8/6; ⊘ 10am-1pm & 3-6pm Wed-Sun, last admission 1hr before closing) Bearing the name of one of Gorizia's oldest noble families, this 16th-century residence is jammed with magnificent 17th- and 18th-century furnishings, artworks and objects – clocks, ceramics, weaponry and more – from near and afar.

Surrounding it is a tranquil, five-hectare, English-style park planted with Himalayan cedars, ash, limes and bamboo.

Synagogue
PLACE OF WORSHIP

(☑ 0481 53 21 15; Via Ascoli 19; ⊘ 5-7pm Tue & Thu, 10am-1pm first Sun of the month) This is all that remains of Gorizia's old Jewish ghetto, established in 1698 to accommodate the city's large Ashkenazi community. After the Shoah, most of the city's Jewish population was deported to concentration camps and the ghetto on Via Ascoli gradually disappeared. The synagogue, which dates from 1756, now houses the **Gerusalemme sull'Isonzo** museum, which sheds light on Gorizia's Jewish history.

Musei Provinciali, Palazzo Attems Petzenstein
GALLERY

(☑ 0481 38 53 35; admission €6, incl other provincial museums €7; ⊘ 10am-6pm Tue-Sun) Gorizia's main art gallery holds some 100 works, including paintings, canvases and drawings by Veneto artists from the 18th to 20th centuries. Collection highlights include the Klimt-esque works of Josef Maria Auchentaller and canvases by Luigi Spazzapan and a small group of local Futurists.

Housed in a magnificently frescoed, 18th-century *palazzo*, the gallery also regularly hosts temporary exhibitions (included in the admission fee).

★ Piazza della Transalpina
PIAZZA

Don't leave Gorizia without visiting this square, which straddles two countries. Between 1947 and 2004, a fence split the square in two, separating Slovenians and Italians and East from West. Part of the fence has been retained for posterity, while a metal plaque in the middle of the piazza also marks the border point. Overlooking it is the grand old Transalpina Railway Station, which connected Trieste to Jesenice in Slovenia. Today, the station lies on Slovenian turf, though you won't be needing your passport to visit.

Giardino Viatori
PARK

(www.giardinoviatori.it, www.aglv.org; Via Forte del Bosco; 10am-7pm Fri-Sun & holidays Mar-Jun) **FREE** Passionate gardener and botany lover Luciano Viatori had the idea for this botanical garden, located just across the Isonzo (Soča) River. The grounds comprise three terraces, with a water-lily pond and rose garden to boot. While the jewel in its crown is the 'valley of azaleas', the garden also claims impressive magnolias, at their blooming best in spring.

☆☆ Festivals & Events

èStoria
MAY

(www.estoria.it) A festival dedicated to Gorizia's history and more, held annually since 2005. See the website for program details and locations.

Gusti di Frontiera
SEPTEMBER

In late September, hundreds of local producers unite to showcase the area's borderland culinary offerings. Feasting aside, the festival serves up concerts and other special events, with up to 200,000 punters filing into town for its grand finale.

🛏 Sleeping

Al Castello
B&B €/€€

(☑ 340 314 16 72; www.alcastellogorizia.it; Via Gabriele d'Annunzio 36; s/d with breakfast from €40/65; P ✷ 🐲) If you fancy crashing near the atmospheric Borgo Castello (and you should), this B&B is an excellent option. Its beautiful, verdant location is the slope that leads up to the castle. Rooms are clean and spacious, while the terrace means breakfast with a view of the castle village. Free private parking.

Flumen
B&B €/€€

(☑ 0481 39 18 77; www.bbflumen.it; Via Brigata Cuneo 20; s/d with breakfast from €30/65; P ✷ 🐲) Located near the Isonzo, Flumen isn't especially convenient if you're relying on public transport; it's just under 2km from the train station. Of course, this isn't an issue if

THE LAST WALL CRUMBLES IN EUROPE

Only a few hundred metres from the centre of Gorizia lies the last major border to fall in Europe. On 1 May 2004, under pouring rain, crowds filled **Piazza della Transalpina** to celebrate Slovenia's entry into the European Union in an atmosphere reminiscent of Berlin in 1989. The day was marked with the tearing down of the wall that ran across the square, one which, from 1947, had separated two cities, two countries, two worlds. A plaque commemorates the border, where people now take photos with one foot in Italy and the other in Slovenia. For many locals, the historic event marked the end of their separation from loved ones and the bureaucratic tribulations involved with crossing the border (despite the conditions set out in the Osimo Treaty of 1975). Piazza della Transalpina is one of several defunct checkpoints in Gorizia. Another, **Casa Rossa (Red House)**, was the scene of the famous **domenica delle scope (Sunday of the Brooms)** in 1950, when thousands of Yugoslavians defied border restrictions and peacefully marched into Gorizia. The shops opened and people began to buy and exchange food and other items. Among these were sorghum brooms, which – unavailable in Nova Gorica – were snapped up and became the symbol of this meeting between the two communities. In Nova Gorica, the **Museo del Contrabbando** (Muzejska Zbirka Pristava; ☎00386590 238 47; www.facebook.com/rafutpristava; Kostanjeviška cesta 32, Nova Gorica; tickets €2; ⏰1-5pm Mon-Fri, noon-6pm Sat & Sun) sheds light on the tactics used by smugglers to get goods across the border. It's part of the **Museo Goriški** (Goriški Muzej; ☎ 00386533 598 11; www.goriskimuzej.si; Grad Kromberk, Grajska cesta 1, Nova Gorica; adult/reduced €4/2; ⏰ 10am-6pm summer, 9am-5pm winter), whose numerous sites include the Castello di Kromberk. Located 6km from Gorizia, the castle harbours a beautiful collection of artworks from the late Gothic period to the 20th century.

you have your own wheels. The B&B offers three superior-category rooms with garden, as well as a private riverside beach. In addition, the staff organises various sporting, historical and cultural excursions throughout the region.

Grand Hotel Entourage HOTEL €€
(☎0481 55 02 35; www.hotelentourage.it; Piazza San Antonio 2; s/d per person from €65/43) Palazzo Strassoldo houses one of Gorizia's most fascinating hotels, chosen by 19th-century French royalty as their preferred lodgings in town. Biedermeier-style furniture and wooden floors hark back to the Habsburg era, while the hotel's assets include a restaurant and historic winery.

(The property was temporarily closed for maintenance during our last visit; check the website for updates.)

1848 - Chef's Rooms B&B €€
(☎320 675 52 85; www.milleottocentoquarantotto.it; Via Rastello 63; rm from €80; ❄📶) Squint hard and you could be in a 19th-century workshop (albeit one with modern-day perks). A riot of marble, granite and timber, this sumptuous B&B comes with fabulous, thoughtfully equipped rooms. The owner is very gracious and accommodating.

Eating

'Qui si mangia goriziano' (Here we eat Gorizian style): you'll notice this sign proudly displayed at the entrance of many restaurants; a declaration of authenticity and respect for local culinary traditions. In Gorizia, Central Europe's influence is palpable in its dishes: you'll find excellent goulash, strudel and *ljubljanska* (a sort of cordon bleu), which sit comfortably among local specialties like *frittata alle erbe e il musetto* (omelette with herbs and local pork sausage), served with *brovada* (fermented white turnip).

Trattoria da Gianni TRATTORIA €
(☎0481 53 45 68; Via Carlo Morelli 8/b; meals €15-20; ⏰6pm-midnight Wed-Fri, 11am-3pm & 6pm-midnight Sat & Sun) If you're only after a snack, stay away from Gianni: his *ljubljanska* is the size of a pizza. If, on the other hand, you're up for the challenge, leap into this memorable, easy-going trattoria. To avoid a long wait for a table, book ahead.

Pasticceria L'Oca Golosa PASTRY SHOP
(☎0481 215 49; www.pasticceriaocagolosa.it; Corso Italia 201; ⏰7am-1pm Mon & Sun, 7am-1pm & 3-7pm Tue-Sat) Gluttony may be a sin, but it's hard to resist at this sweet-tooth Valhalla. Options include brioche and vegan cakes,

as well as baked goods for those with dietary intolerances.

Pasticceria Centrale
PASTRY SHOP

(☑ 0481 53 01 31; Via Garibaldi 4/a; ☺ 7.30am-7.30pm Mon-Sat) This unmissable patisserie has been baking bread and desserts since 1940. Try the *putizza:* a concoction of puff pastry filled with dried fruit, it's Gorizia's version of the Valli del Natisone's *gubana* (see p183).

Pizzeria al Lampione
PIZZA €

(☑ 0481 327 80; www.pizzerialampione.it; Via Silvio Pellico 7; pizzas €5.70-10.70; ☺ noon-2.30pm & 6-11.30pm Mon & Wed-Sun) Al Lampione's pizza maker won the 2013 World Championships in Rimini with his 'Calabrisella' pizza. The only way to discover all of its ingredients is to order one. You won't be disappointed.

RebeKin
GORIZIAN €/€€

(☑ 0481 090 000; www.facebook.com/RebeKin Gorizia; Via Carlo de Morelli 13/a; meals €15-25; ☺ 10am-9.30pm Mon-Thu, 10am-10.30pm Fri & Sat) Small and welcoming, furnished in Central European style, this tavern takes taste buds on a journey across the local culinary landscape. Try the *gnocchi di pane* (bread dumplings) with goulash or the *jota* soup with sauerkraut.

Osteria ai Tre Amici
GORIZIAN €€

(☑ 340 632 39 92; Via Guglielmo Oberdan 11; meals €30; ☺ 11.30am-3.30pm & 6.30-11.30pm Fri-Tue, 11.30am-3.30pm Thu) Under a red-and-white striped ceiling, locals tuck into top-quality Central European dishes; do not miss the *bigoli* pasta with prosciutto crudo and smoked ricotta. Both the pasta and the gnocchi are homemade, and the bread is baked in a wood-fired oven.

★ Chef You Too
ITALIAN €€

(☑ 800 170 013; www.chefyoutoo.it; meals from €30; ☺ 11am-9pm) Celebrity chef Massimo De Belli is behind this highly popular eatery, whose attention to quality produce is obsessive. Edibles range from soups and pizzas, to Friulian classics. For a tasty introduction to the house style, order the sea bass turban or the scalloped pork.

Trattoria alla Luna
GORIZIAN €€

(☑ 0481 53 03 74; www.trattoriaallaluna.com; Via Oberdan 13; mains €8-16; ☺ 11am-3pm & 6.30-11.30pm Wed-Sun) Couples will appreciate the intimate vibe at this rustic trattoria. Garbed in traditional costume, the waitstaff are run flat off their feet serving hearty local fare such as salami cooked in vinegar and grilled *cevapcici* (minced-meat sausages). Its two small rooms aren't short of a crowd, so it's always smart to book ahead.

🍷 Drinking & Nightlife

Il Giardino dei Vizi
BAR

(☑ 347 821 65 83; Piazza Sant'Antonio 12/13; ☺ 10.30am-1.30pm & 5.30pm-1am Tue-Thu, to 2am Fri & Sat) Locals know it as 'da Lollo' and it's a favourite *aperitivo* option for younger punters, who schmooze over spritzes and *salumi* (cold cuts) platters. Despite being small, the bar's choice of wines is epic and staffers will happily guide the undecided. Tip: focus on the Collio whites.

★ Borgo Castello 3
WINE BAR

(☑ 366 391 54 58; www.bc3gorizia.it; Borgo Castello 3; ☺ 5-9pm Mon, Wed & Thu, 11.30am-2pm & 5-9pm Fri-Sun) The idea of kicking back on a lawn in Borgo Castello, glass of vino in hand, idly looking out over Gorizia, comes to fruition at this charming wine bar. Prices are low, the wines strictly local, and the gracious service free.

Mama Angela
WINE BAR, CAFE

(☑ 0481 09 10 98; www.mamaangela.com; Piazza della Vittoria 53; ☺ 9am-1am) A pleasant cafe-wine bar on Piazza della Vittoria, where you can catch your breath on your way to or from the castle. It generally hosts a younger crowd, drawn by the affable staff, scrumptious toast and solid selection of Collio wines.

Atmosfere La Stüa
WINE BAR

(☑ 0481 336 74; www.atmosferelastua.it; Piazza Sant'Antonio 16; cocktails €5-8.50; ☺ 5.30-11pm Tue, 11.30am-1.30pm & 5.30-11pm Wed, Thu & Sun, to 1am Fri & Sat) In the heart of Piazza Sant'Antonio, this wine bar sports a large, all-weather terrace and cool, hipsterish vibe. Very popular on weekends.

Mister Blu
OSTERIA

(☑ 335 707 59 40; Via Boccaccio 4; meals €15-20; ☺ 7.30am-3pm Mon-Sat) A small, long, narrow tavern, with a friendly chef and both hot and cold lunch bites. Ingredients are strictly local, hailing from Collio producers and those directly across the Slovenian border.

Caffè Teatro
CAFE, BAR

(☑ 0481 28 01 87; http://caffe-teatro.edan.io; Corso Italia 1; ☺ 8am-9pm Mon-Fri, 8am-1pm & 4pm-1am Sat, 9am-1am Sun) A spacious, centrally located spot. Its outdoor area is a treat in sum-

OSLAVIA: HISTORY, MEMORIES & VINEYARDS

North of Gorizia, beyond the Isonzo (Soča) River, lies the hamlet of **Oslavia**. Home to 600 souls, it's known for two reasons: Ribolla gialla wine (which is especially delicious here) and the **Ossario di Oslavia** (☑0481 48 90 24; ⊙9am-noon & 2-5pm Tue-Sat Oct–mid-Mar, 9am-noon & 2-5pm Tue-Fri, 9am-12.30pm & 1.30-6pm Sat & Sun Sep-mid-Mar) **FREE** , built on the slopes of Monte Calvario in the 1930s.The ossuary houses the remains of soldiers who fell in the area during WWI. Its architect, Ghino Venturi, envisaged a triangular, fort-like structure with a stout tower at each corner and a large, taller tower rising from the centre. The complex houses the remains of almost 60,000 soldiers, listed alphabetically, as well as about 36,000 unknown persons. It's a deeply moving place and well worth a visit.

Directly opposite the monument is **Klanjscek** (☑0481 190 66 80; www.klanjscek.it; località Ossario; rm from €105), an outstanding *agriturismo* whose restaurant is just the place to discover local wines. After all, Oslavia is Italy's home of **orange wines**, made by macerating white-wine grapes (usually Ribolla gialla) in a process similar to red-wine production. One of Italy's orange wine pioneers is **Gravner** (☑0481 30 882; www.gravner.it; Località Lenzuolo Bianco 9) owner Josko Gravner, who learned the technique in Georgia and now macerates in underground amphorae (vases). **Radikon** (☑0481 32 804; Località Tre Buchi 4) is another. Known for their somewhat savoury, *umami* flavour, the drops can be savoured at either winery by booking a tasting. If you're exploring by bike, Oslavia's gentle hills make for a memorable pedal. Keep your eyes open for the **percorso delle panchine arancioni** (path of the orange benches; www.ribolladioslavia.it/il-percorso), whose seven benches, located near the cellar doors, allow travellers to catch their breath while drinking in panoramic views.

mer, when young folk from all over head in to mingle, spritz in hand.

☆ Entertainment

Teatro Verdi   THEATRE
(☑0481 38 36 01; www3.comune.gorizia.it/teatro; Via Garibaldi 2/a; ⊙box office 7am-7pm Mon-Sat) Opened in 1740 and rebuilt after a fire in 1782, Teatro Verdi has been closed, re-opened, tweaked and frescoed several times over its career; the current facade dates from 1861. Today the theatre hosts the city's most important cultural events.

Check the website or call the box office for the current program.

🔒 Shopping

Mercato Coperto di Corso Verdi   MARKET
(btwn Corso Verdi & Via Boccaccio) Whether you simply want to admire the beauty of a *rosa di Gorizia* (p279) or stock up on the first fruits of the season, make a beeline for this historic market, just a few minutes' walk from Teatro Verdi.

Libreria Editrice Goriziana   BOOKS
(☑0481 337 76; www.leg.it; Corso Verdi 67; ⊙9am-12.30pm & 3.30-7.30pm Mon-Sat) A lovely bookshop specialising in history titles.

You'll find various books on WWI, many of which recount events played out on the Carso Isontino.

ℹ Information

TOURIST INFORMATION
Gorizia Infopoint (Map p96, B3; ☑0481 53 57 64; www.turismofvg.it; Corso Italia 9; ⊙9am-1pm & 2-6pm Mon-Sat, 9am-1pm Sun) Gorizia's tourist office offers free maps, as well as information on local sights and activities. It also sells the FVG Card (see p53).

ℹ Getting There & Away

BUS
TPL FVG (☑800 05 20 40, mobile 040 971 23 43; https://tplfvg.it) operates buses to/from Gorizia. If heading to Udine (€5.70-7, 2hr) or Trieste (€6.65, 1hr 55min), you'll need to pass through Monfalcone (€4.35, 1 hr 7min) or Aquileia (€5.05, 1 hr 46min).

CAR & MOTORCYLE
If heading in on the A4 from Milan, take the Gorizia exit after Venice. From Trieste, follow the signs for Monfalcone, then take the SS55.

TRAIN
Gorizia's train station (Piazzale Martiri Libertà d'Italia) is served by very frequent services to Udine (€3.40, 30min) and Trieste (€4, 44min).

ℹ Getting Around

BUS

APT di Gorizia (☑ 800 95 59 57; www.aptgorizia .it) manages local transport and is part of the **TPL FVG** (☑ 800 05 20 40, mobile 040 971 23 43; https://tplfvg.it) consortium. Buses depart from the train station. Bus 1 crosses the city, passing by the main attractions (every 20min). A single ticket costs €1.35 and is valid for 60 minutes; a day tickets is €4.60.

A bus service to Nova Gorica (€1, 35min, hourly between 8.35am and 7.20pm) leaves from the train station and is managed by the Gorizia Tourist Board and Slovenian-owned AVRIGO.

TAXI

Taxi ranks are located at the train station square (☑ 0481 220 33, 24 hours) and in Corso Italia (☑ 0481 340 00).

Fait (☑ 348 225 95 97; www.taxigorizia.com)

THE COLLIO

There is one overarching reason to visit the Collio – a rolling patch of green stretching from the Isonzo (Soča) River to the Slovenian border, 12km west of Gorizia, and that is to feel good. Here, time slows down to the rhythm of the locals – folk known for their 'rugged hands and refined minds' – and the area's natural beauty casts a bewitching spell. Lose yourself in the sunsets on the hills around Cormòns, the changing hues of endless vineyards, the scent of cherry trees and the mind-clearing, soul-soothing quiet.

In between tranquil ambles and panoramic Vespa rides (scooter hire and tours are readily available), sample the Collio's DOC whites (and emerging orange wines), drops that have made the area famous across the world. And we haven't even mentioned the area's celebrated *salumi* (cured meats), cheeses and honey. When it comes to grazing, lazing and savouring simple pleasures, few places do it better.

ℹ Getting There & Away

BUS

TPL FVG (☑ 800 05 20 40, mobile 040 971 23 43; https://tplfvg.it) buses reach the Collio. Frequent services connect Cormòns to Gorizia (€3.85, 48min), Udine (€3.50, 40min), Capriva del Friuli (€1.65, 25min), Gradisca d'Isonzo (€4.25, 56min), Cividale del Friuli (€2.95, 30min) and Palmanova (€3.50, 40min). Bus G23 runs between Cormòns and Dolegna del Collio (€2.25, 15min). You'll need to depart from Gorizia to reach San Floriano del

Collio (€1.65, 18min) and Capriva del Friuli (€3.25, 28min).

CAR & MOTORCYLE

Driving from Milan on the A4, exit at Villesse-Gorizia after Venice to join the A34. Exit at Gradisca d'Isonzo, then take the SR305var, followed by the SP16. Once in Cormòns, follow the signs for all the neighbouring villages.

TRAIN

Cormòns (Map p104, B3; Via A. De Gasperi 16) is the most convenient train station. From here, frequent services reach Gorizia (€1.80, 8min) and Udine (€2.80, 22min). Trains also reach Trieste (€5.75, 1hr). See www.trenitalia.com for current timetables.

Cormòns

POP 7100 / ELEV 56M

This mini Habsburg town, which was part of the Austro-Hungarian Empire up until WWI, is the beating heart of the Collio wine region. Its Austrian past is echoed in its onion-shaped domes and 19th-century buildings, some of which conceal magnificent courtyards.

Start your explorations in **Piazza della Libertà**, home to the **Chiesa di Santa Caterina** (☉ 7am-noon & 3-7pm), dating from 1778 and better known as the Santuario di Rosa Mistica. The fountain in the middle of bar-flanked **Piazza XXIV Maggio** features the so-called Statue of the Stone Thrower by sculptor Alfonso Canciani.

The **Duomo di Sant'Adalberto** (☉ 9am-noon Mon, Fri & Sat, 9am-noon & 4-7pm Sun), the main place of worship in Cormòns, made its debut in 1700, built on the site of a 13th-century chapel dedicated to St Adalbert. Its soaring bell tower makes for a handy reference point when wandering around the compact town centre.

Indeed, it only takes a short walk from central Cormòns to find yourself staring out at vine-fringed **Monte Quarin** (274m), a green mantle scattered with the odd bell tower.

🏃 Activities

Bicycles, E-bikes, Scooters

Amare in Bici   CYCLING

Amare in Bici (www.amareinbici.it) is a series of hyper-connected cycling routes in the region, equipped with e-bike charging stations, trail maps, points of interest and affiliated restaurants, wineries and other establishments. From Cormòns, for example, you can cycle to Grado (73km), passing through

Palmanova and Aquileia. See the website for details on all the routes, which range from rookie to pro.

Zorgniotti SCOOTER & E-BIKE HIRE
(📞 0481 605 95; www.zorgniotti.com; Via Vino della Pace 18; ⊙ 8.30am-12.30pm & 1.30-6.30pm Mon-Fri, 9am-noon Sat) Zipping around on a Vespa is the most enjoyable way to take in the views from the hills and hop between cellar doors, and this long-established rental company is a reliable place to rent one.

Hiking

Sentiero delle Vigne Alte WALKING TRAIL
For a bird's eye view of the vineyards, hit the lovely Sentiero delle Vigne Alte for an undulating hike, gallop or bike ride through the hills, from Subida to Castello di Spessa. The trail starts from Subida (behind the riding school).

🎊 Festivals & Events

Fieste da Viarte MAY
(www.fiestedaviarte.it) On the second last Sunday in May, private homes on the route from Via Dante to the top of Monte Quarin in Cormòns open their doors to sell wine, cold cuts, cheese and fruit. In one fell swoop you can combine a picturesque jaunt through the hills with a progressive tasting of local delicacies.

🛌 Sleeping

The Collio hills are littered with dozens of sleeping options. Keep in mind that just like many of the *agriturismi* have excellent restaurants, many of the area's farms offer accommodation in converted barns and other restored rural buildings.

In the high season it can be difficult to find a free bed in the *agriturismi*. If you're not having much luck, ask at establishments along your way: who knows, you may discover a new guesthouse attached to a local farm.

Al Benandant B&B €€
(📞 338 314 78 08; www.albenandant.com; Via Battisti 61; d €80-90; 🅿 ❄ 🛜) Only a few hundred metres from the centre of Cormòns and easily reached on foot, Al Benandant is one of the best options for those wanting to slumber among the vineyards without being too isolated. The B&B's location is enchanting, on the slopes of Monte Quarin and surrounded by greenery. Rooms are neat and clean, and the breakfast generous. To reach the central building, look for the sign at the intersection of Viale Roma and Via Colombar.

Magnàs AGRITURISMO €€
(📞 0481 609 91; www.magnas.it; Via Corona 47; d from €80); 🅿 ❄ 🛜) Another *agriturismo* with its own winery, just south of Cormòns. The vibe here is especially rustic, with furnishings echoing the area's peasant past. Rooms are bright with bucolic views, and the bountiful breakfast focuses on local produce. Bicycles and scooters can be rented on request. (Note that the *agriturismo* was closed indefinitely on our last visit; contact the property for updates.)

La Casa di Alice B&B €€
(📞 335 37 79 94; www.lacasadialicebb.it; Via Ara Pacis 22; rm from €110-125; ⊙ mid-Mar–mid-Dec; 🅿 ❄ 🛜) Each of the four rooms at this fabulous B&B – set in a converted barn close to the centre of Cormòns – features a dominant hue: red, blue, green or yellow. While all four have private bathroom, the red room cranks up the glee with a Jacuzzi. Whichever room you snooze in, you'll have access to the garden swimming pool.

★ Picech AGRITURISMO €€
(📞 0481 603 47; www.picech.com; Location Pradis 11; d €110; turret €130, apt with 2 double bedrooms €130-160; 🅿 ❄ 🛜)An historic Collio winery turned *agriturismo*, whose attention to detail extends to the hedgehog (Picech's mascot) embroidered on the sheets and towels. Choose between three double bedrooms, a small apartment and a lofty tower; the latter offers a gobsmacking view over the hills. Warm and attentive hosts Roberto and Alessia welcome guests with local wines and *prosciutto crudo,* and even provide a yellow Vespa to explore the hills.

The breakfast is equally memorable, with apple strudel, homemade jams, cheeses and local cold cuts.

★ La Subida RESORT €€/€€€
(📞 0481 605 31, 0481 623 88; www.lasubida.it; Via Subida 52; d from €160-180; 🅿 ❄ 🛜) Tricky to define, La Subida consists of a dozen design-literate cabins immersed in the woods, paired with a swimming pool, tennis court, riding stable and vinegar factory (with adjacent sauna, naturally). An onsite store stocks La Subida's house-made products, including Josko Sirk's artisan vinegar. And if that wasn't enough, there's also an *osteria* and the Michelin-starred **Trattoria at the Subida** (Al Cacciatore della Subida set menus €60-75; ⊙ 7-10pm Mon & Thu, noon-2.30pm and 7-10pm Sat & Sun), where game is king.

Cormòns & the Collio

N

0   400 m
0   0.2 miles

CORMÒNS

Via Subida

SR409

Via Faet

Via Dante

Via Battisti

Viale Roma

Via San Giovanni

Via Ascoli

Via Armistizio

Viale Friuli

SR409

Via Gorizia

Via San Daniele

Viale Venezia Giulia

Via De Gasperi

Via Filanda

Via Bancaria

Via Gorizia

SR56

Via Ara Pacis

Via San Quirino

Via Brazzano

Via Novare

Via Savean

SR56

Cormòns & the Collio

⊙ Sights
1 Chiesa di Santa Caterina C3
2 Duomo di Sant'Adalberto C2
3 Piazza della Libertà C3
4 Piazza XXIV Maggio D2

⊙ Activities, Courses & Tours
5 Sentiero delle Vigne Alte G1
6 Zorgniotti .... off map C4

⊙ Sleeping
7 Al Benandant D3
8 La Casa di Alice B4
9 La Subida G1
10 Magnàs .... off map C4
11 Picech...F4

⊗ Eating
12 Al Confine .... off map G1
13 Al Giardinetto.................................... C2
14 Da Marcello .... off map B4
15 Nonno Lince F4
16 Osteria Caramella C3

⊙ Drinking & Nightlife
17 Enoteca di Cormòns D2
18 Jazz&Wine C2

⊙ Shopping
19 A.tipiko C3
20 Alimentari Tomadin............................ C2
21 Chiarosa C3
22 D'Osvaldo D2
23 El Condor B3
24 Zoff .... off map C4

🍴 Eating

Al Confine   AGRITURISMO €€
(☑ 0481 63 04 51; www.russianagricola.it; Località Plessiva 3; meals from €20; ⊙ Fri dinner-Sun dinner) End the week with Al Confine's local specialities, dictated by the season's ingredients: the *blecs (maltagliati)* and gnocchi with *marcundelle ragù* never disappoint. There's no shortage of classic hits either, from *frico* and goulash, to *cotechino* and sausages.

⭐ Osteria Caramella   OSTERIA €€
(☑ 0481 63 93 41; Via Matteotti 1; meals from €20; ⊙ 10am-3pm & 5.30-9.30pm Mon-Sat) A small, family-run tavern with polished, welcoming interiors. Drop in for a decent selection of local wines (which you can also take home) and Friulian bites that include an exceptional *frico*.

If the weather's on your side, kick back in the outdoor area and enjoy the Friulian *dolce vita* with a glass of Sauvignon.

Nonno Lince   AGRITURISMO €€
(☑ 329 066 45 65; Località Pradis 19; www.nonnolince.it; meals from €25-30; ⊙ 5-10pm Fri, from 10am Sat & Sun) Nonno Lince's *agriturismo* is perched on a hilltop in the heart of the Collio and, when you dine here, surrounded by vineyards, woods and hills, time seemingly stands still. Too bad it's only open on weekends.

Al Giardinetto   RESTAURANT & HOTEL €€
(☑ 0481 602 57; Via Matteotti 54; meals from €30-35; ⊙ noon-3.30pm & 7pm-midnight Wed-Sun) Al Giardinetto started life in 1907 as a village tratto-

ria serving Central European dishes. Climbing the culinary ladder in the 1970s, it's now Cormòns' best and most exclusive restaurant. House specialties range from meat to fish, and lunch offers the option of a single dish with five tastings and a glass of wine. The venue also includes a cafe peddling buttery Central European-inspired desserts, as well as three double rooms. Call for details.

Da Marcello   OSTERIA €€ / €€€
(☑ 339 270 25 89; Via Corona 34; meals incl drinks from €35-45; ⊙ 10am-2.30pm & 5-10pm Mon & Thu-Sun) If you're a fan of grilled meat, Da Marcello has an excellent selection, paired with appropriately juicy wines. The quality is very high, reflected in the slightly higher-than-average prices. (The latter are offset by a breathtaking view of the vineyards.)

🍷 Drinking & Nightlife

⭐ Enoteca di Cormòns   WINE BAR
(☑ 0481 63 03 71; https://enotecadicormons.com; Piazza XXIV Maggio 21; ⊙ 11am-10pm Mon & Wed-Sun) In the heart of Cormòns, this wine shop/bar and tourist office in one is as handy for getting the lowdown on Collio activities as it is for savouring local *vino* and edibles from local farms.

Jazz&Wine   PUB
(Via Matteotti 76; ⊙ 5pm-midnight Tue-Thu & Sun, to 2am Fri & Sat) A small, much-loved pub in Cormòns. It's the town's go-to for live tunes in the summer and often hosts jazz evenings. That said, check the posters as it dishes up

music gigs of all kinds. Expect a discerning selection of Friulian wines and a young vibe.

🛍 Shopping

A.tipiko FASHION & ACCESSORIES
(📞338 302 15 57; Via Matteotti 41; ⏱9.30am-12.30pm & 4-7pm Tue-Sat Sep-May, 9.30am-12.30pm & 4-7.30pm Mon-Fri Jun-Aug) Few women fail to stop at A.tipiko's shop window. Fortunately, designer Alessandra Franco's captivating creations are democratically priced. Choose from new collection threads, bags and accessories.

★ Alimentari Tomadin FOOD & WINE
(📞0481 613 05; www.alimentaritomadin.com; Via Cumano 5; ⏱7.30am-1pm & 4.30-7pm Tue & Thu-Sat, 7.30am-1pm Wed) If you're keen on stocking your pantry with Collio's bounty, you'll find practically everything at this providore, including Resia's cult-status garlic.

Chiarosa BAKERY
(📞0481 63 06 64; www.chiarosa.it; Via Gorizia 7; ⏱6.30am-1pm & 4.30-7pm Mon-Sat) This historic Cormòns bakery has been baking bread and sweet treats for over a century. The biscotti claps, *zimui* (shortbread) and *friulini* are all popular choices.

★ D'Osvaldo FOOD & WINE
(📞0481 616 44; www.dosvaldo.it; Via Dante 40; ⏱9am-1pm & 3-7pm Mon-Fri, 9am-1pm Sat) This family-run business has been making its subtly smoky prosciutto, aged for 14 to 24 months, since 1940. Visitors are welcome (it's best to call first) and staff happy to show the various stages of production, which ends with a tasting. If you're in a hurry, the ham is also sold at Alimentari Tomadin.

★ Zoff FOOD & WINE, B&B
(📞0481 672 04; www.borgdaocjs.it; Via Parini 18, Località Borgnano; ⏱4-7pm Mon, 8am-noon Tue, Thu & Sat, 8am-noon & 4-7pm Wed & Fri Jun-Oct, 8am-noon & 3-6pm Mon-Fri, 8am-noon Sat Oct-May) This small shop, linked to a family-run farm, peddles a variety of cheeses, all derived from the prized milk of Italian Red Pezzata cows.

Also onsite is B&B **Borg da Ocjs** (s/d with breakfast from €60/85; 🅿❋🛜), set in a converted stable and rustically furnished.

El Condor SPORTING GOODS
(📞331 303 61 60; www.elcondorsport.it; Viale Friuli 117; ⏱9am-12.30pm & 3.30-7.30pm Tue-Sat) A reliable sporting goods shop stocking everything you need for the outdoors, plus an artisan workshop crafting skis and snowboards.

ℹ Information

Cormòns Infopoint ((map p104, D2; 📞0481 38 62 24; www.turismofvg.it; Piazza XXIV Maggio 15; ⏱9am-1pm & 2-6pm)

Capriva del Friuli
POP 1627 / ELEV 49M

With villages including Budignacco, Russiz di Sopra e di Sotto and Spessa, the municipality of Capriva del Friuli is a fine place to stroll aimlessly among the hills, catching glimpses of vineyards and filling your lungs with fresh air.

History buffs wanting a fix can get it at splendid **Castello di Spessa** (📞0481 80 81 24; www.castellodispessa.it; Via Spessa 1), nestled in a huge park which includes a golf course. Reputedly built on the site of a Roman settlement, it became a castle in around 1200 and was for centuries the home of noble Friulian families and illustrious personalities. The interior is glorious – the barrel-lined cellar is connected to an old military bunker.

Today, the castle is an elegant **hotel** (d€125-230, ste€260-310) with an in-house **Wine Spa** (www.castellodispessa.it/vinum-spa) specialising in wine therapy. The adjacent **wine shop** (📞0481 80 81 24; ⏱9am-7pm) stocks excellent *vino* produced by the castle winery. If you're hungry, **La Tavernetta al Castello** (📞0481 80 82 28; meals €40; ⏱12.30-2.30pm & 7.30-9.30pm Tue-Sat, 12.30-2.30pm Sun) serves excellent lagoon fish and Collio delicacies.

🍴 Eating

Panificio Iordan BAKERY
(📞0481 805 79; www.panificioiordan.it; Piazza Vittoria 16; ⏱7am-2pm Mon & Sat, 7am-2pm & 4-7pm Tue-Fri, bar only service 8am-1pm Sun) Home to one of the last remaining wood-burning ovens in the area, this bakery has been following traditional recipes since 1890. Fill up on pizzas, focaccias, *grissini* (bread sticks) and pastries. Follow your nose to find it.

San Floriano del Collio
POP 746 / ELEV 276M

Northeast of Cormòns, a stone's throw from the Slovenian border, the charming medieval village of San Floriano is famous for both its vineyards and delicious cherries.

One of its most noteworthy buildings is the **Castello Formentini** (📞0481 88 42 74; www.castelloformentini.com; Piazza Libertà 3), once part of the defensive system that included the for-

CIN CIN TO COLLIO DOC

You'll recognise the wines of the **Consorzio Tutela Vini Collio** (www.collio.it; Via Gramsci 2, Cormòns) as they often have a yellow stamp on the bottle. Established in 1964, the consortium is one of the oldest in Italy, created to better promote local DOC-appellation wines. Think of it as a dense network of wineries spread over 1500 hectares of Collio territory. Not only can you book a tasting at many of these wineries, but you can also stay overnight at the wineries' *agriturisimi*. The consortium website lists all the accommodation options, which are plentiful and high quality. In addition to those already mentioned, we recommend the following:

Renzo Sgubin (☑ 0481 63 02 97, 338 207 78 09; Via Faet 15/1, Cormòns; ☺ 9-11.30am & 2-6pm Mon-Fri, 9-11.30am Sat, by reservation) Produces a fantastic Sauvignon.

Livio Felluga (☑ 0481 602 03; www.liviofelluga.it; Via Risorgimento 1, Brazzano di Cormòns; ☺ by reservation) Famous for its indigenous varieties, with an especially notable Picolit.

Ronco dei Tassi (☑ 0481 601 55; www.roncodeitassi.it; Strada della Montona 19, Cormòns; ☺ by reservation) Stock up on their Bianco Fosarin.

Renato Keber (☑ 0481 63 98 44; www.renatokeber.com; Località Zegla, Cormòns; r from €80; ☺ by reservation) On the hills of Zegla, bordering Slovenia, Renato Keber produces, among other things, a much-lauded Pinot Grigio.

Venica & Venica (☑ 0481 612 64; www.venica.it; Località Cerò 8, Dolegna del Collio; ☺ by reservation) An elegantly rustic wine resort where you can enjoy nonstop tastings of the house drops. Try the Friulano and Chardonnay, or the Sauvignon Riserva.

Ronco Blanchis (☑ 0481 805 19; www.roncoblanchis.it; Via Blanchis 70, Mossa; ☺ by reservation) Excellent organic wines and delicious honey too.

Cantina Produttori Cormòns (☑ 0481 624 71; www.cormons.com; Via Vino della Pace 31, Cormòns; ☺ 8.30am-12.30pm & 3-7pm Mon-Sat by reservation) This winery is famous for its Vino della Pace (Wine of Peace), made by blending varieties from every corner of the world. It's a symbolic drop, celebrating human fellowship and delivered to the head of state of each country (including religious leaders). You'll recognise the bottle by its label, designed each vintage by a different artist. (Previous contributors include Enrico Baj, Arnaldo Pomodoro, Yoko Ono and Dario Fo.)

Still not satiated? Then hit the **Strada del Vino e dei Sapori** (Road of Wine & Flavours; www.turismofvg.it/strada-del-vino-e-dei-sapori), a collection of six culinary-themed routes that lead to local winemakers and artisan food producers. While one of the routes traverses the Collio, the others are spread across the region, from the mountains to the coast, crossing rivers, plains and the Carso. See the website for details.

tresses of Gorizia and Gradisca, and the residence of Baron Giuseppe Formentini from the mid-19th century; the castle is open to the public for special events.

🍴 Eating & Drinking

DVOR
OSTERIA, WINE BAR € / €€
(☑ 338 408 81 87; Via Castello 5; tasting menu €30; ☺ noon-10pm Mon & Fri-Sun summer, noon-5pm Mon & Sat, noon-10pm Tue-Fri & Sun winter) While lunching with a view of a vineyard is hardly novel in the Collio, there's something especially personable about DVOR's hospitality. The food is Friulian and its tasting menu a locavore adventure that takes in everything from *salumi* (cold cuts) to gnocchi with aubergines, ravioli and vegetables picked fresh from the garden.

★ **Gradis'ciutta**
WINERY, AGRITURISMO
(☑ 0481 39 02 37; www.gradisciutta.com; Gasbiana 32/a; ☺ 8am-6pm by reservation) A historic family-run winery in San Floriano, known for its elegant white and Sinefinis ('Without Borders') Rebolium. The latter is a sparkling Ribolla gialla, symbolically combining grapes from both Italian and Slovenian vineyards.

During our research, the winery's **agriturismo** (which offers accommodation in a renovated farmhouse) allowed September guests to take part in the grape harvest; see the website for updates.

Cycling or Vespa Tour: Collio Dolce Vita

START: CORMÒNS
END: SAN FLORIANO DEL COLLIO
LENGTH: 22KM; 90 MINUTES

There's nothing better than a cycle along the Collio's tranquil, vine-graced hills to savour the Friulian *dolce vita*. Cellar-door visits booked and large backpack at the ready (who knows how many bottles you may end up buying?), start in ❶ **Cormòns** with a coffee at the Enoteca di Cormòns (p105), perhaps paired with a D'Osvaldo board (p106) to charge the batteries.

Fuelled up, head east out of town, following the signs for ❷ **La Subida** (p103). Once here, browse the farm's artisanal products, take a stroll in the woods and, if you're peckish once more (or simply love game), stop at the restaurant.

Subida is the starting point for the Sentiero delle Vigne Alte (p103), so follow the deer-shaped signs and head towards Capriva del Friuli, home to ❸ **Castello di Spessa** (p106). Clearly, the sublime, rolling panorama was lost on Giacomo Casanova, who holidayed here for over a month and described it as one of the most boring periods of his life. Leave your bike on the lawn, stretch your legs, then toast to the infamous playboy in the castle *osteria* (be sure to order the outstanding house wine).

From Spessa, return to the Regionale 409 and hit the undulating stretch that leads to the Slovenian border. In Giasbana you can visit ❹ **Gradis'ciutta** (p107); if there's space left in your backpack, bag one of its excellent whites (or, as is the case at most wineries, have it shipped it back home).

If you have a wee bit of energy left, continue to the centre of San Floriano del Collio to catch your breathe and sample local delicacies at ❺ **DVOR** (p107).

ℹ️ Information

Consorzio per la Salvaguardia dei Castelli Storici del Friuli Venezia Giulia (Consortium for the Protection of the Historic Castles of Friuli Venezia Giulia; 📞 0432 28 85 88; www.consorzio castelli.it; Piazzetta del Pozzo 21, Udine; ⊙ 9am-1pm Mon-Fri)

Dolegna del Collio

POP 323 / ELEV 90M

Not far from Manzano and **the Valle dello Judrio**, which once marked the border between Italy and Yugoslavia, lies Dolegna del Collio, a village of farmers nestled among the hills and is cloaked, like all the Collio villages, in vineyards. Among its attractions is the two-towered **Castello di Trussio**, originating in the 12th century and rebuilt several times over the centuries.

🍴 Eating

⭐ **L'Argine a Vencò**　　　RESTAURANT €€€
(📞 0481 199 98 82; www.largineavencò.it; Locality Vencò; 5/6/10 course tasting menu €70/80/120; d from €100, gourmet breakfast €25; ⊙ lunch 1-4pm Thu-Sun, dinner 7.45pm-midnight Mon & Wed-Sun) Antonia Klugmann has earned the respect and affection of an entire region in a very short time. Her restaurant secured a Michelin star in record time thanks to her extraordinary culinary creations. Influenced by Slovenia, Klugmann describes her seasonally determined dishes as the result of six centuries of integration.

As for the cherry on the cake: it's the ability to slumber at the onsite B&B and start the next day with the region's tastiest breakfast in blissfully tranquil surrounds.

THE ISONZO

After more than a century, the scars of the Great War are still raw in the **Carso Isontino**, a long, crushing chapter which has helped shape its people and environment.

Indeed, it's impossible to visit the area without acknowledging the events that took place in these valleys, mountains, rivers and cities.

Eleven of the 12 famous Battles of the Isonzo were fought in the Carso between June 1915 and October 1917, forever stamping their mark on the history of the area (for more on this topic, see p101 and p255).

ℹ️ Getting There & Away

BUS

TPL FVG (📞 800 05 20 40, mobile 040 971 23 43; https://tplfvg.it) buses connect Gorizia with Monfalcone, passing through San Michele del Carso (€3.25, 25 minutes) and San Martino del Carso (€3.25, 30 minutes). The trip from Gorizia to Fogliano Redipuglia takes just over half an hour (€3.85), ditto for Gradisca d'Isonzo (€3.25).

CAR & MOTORCYLE

Savogna d'Isonzo is 6km from Gorizia on the SP8. For San Michele del Carso, look for signs for the SP13. For Fogliano, take the Venezia-Trieste motorway and exit at Redipuglia, then follow signs for Fogliano Redipuglia (about 2km).

TRAIN

It's not easy moving around the Isonzo by train: you'll need to get to Sagrado (from Trieste €4.25, 40 minutes; from Udine €5, 34-40 minutes) on the line connecting Udine to Trieste and take a bus from there.

Gradisca d'Isonzo

POP 6346 / ELEV 32M

Included on the list of Italy's most beautiful towns, Gradisca is the kind of place you stumble upon by accident and leave grateful for the serendipity.

A few hours is enough time to explore: start from 19th-century **Piazza Unità d'Italia**, where a column surmounted by the Lion of St Mark gives you a sense of the town's Venetian origins. Due to its proximity to the Isonzo River, Gradisca became one of Venice's bastions against Ottoman raids. The town's **castle** was fortified in 1473, and its walls are marked by six towers and two gates (Porta del Soccorso and Porta Nuova, recognisable by the bust of Leonardo da Vinci).

From the elliptical piazza, Via Ciotti leads to the late 15th-century **Chiesa della Beata Vergine Addolorata**. Close by is the **Duomo**. Dedicated to St Peter and St Paul, it features a baroque facade and interiors dating from the 16th and 17th centuries.

Completed in 1705, **Palazzo Torriani** is one of the most beautiful buildings in Gradisca; today it houses the Town Hall and the Library, as well as the **Galleria d'Arte Contemporanea Luigi Spazzapan** (📞 0481 96 08 16; www.facebook.com/galleria spazzapan/; Via Ciotti 51; adult/reduced €3/2, free with FVG Card; ⊙ 10am-1pm & 3-7pm Wed-Sun). The latter's collection includes works by its namesake local artist and other Friulian artists.

On Via Cesare Battisti, **Casa dei Provveditori Veneti** is one of the few 16th-century buildings left in the town; it dates back to when Gradisca was the seat of Venetian Republic magistrates.

Eating

★**Hostaria Mulin Vecio**   OSTERIA **€€**
(📋0481 997 83; Via Gorizia 2; mains €8-12; ⏰10.30am-2.30pm & 5-11pm Fri-Tue; 🛜) Gradisca's oldest tavern plates up excellent local dishes in an old mill with Habsburg vibes. It's a spacious place with a gorgeous garden, making it a good bet if you don't have a reservation. Don't miss the *jota,* a bean and sauerkraut soup, and if you happen to be in the area on a Saturday, order the *gnocchi al gulash,* one of the house specialties.

ℹ️ Information

Gradisca d'Isonzo Tourist Office (www.prolocogradisca.it; Via Ciotti 49, ⏰9.30am-12.30pm Wed, 9.30am-12.30pm & 3-6pm Thu-Sun)

Fogliano Redipuglia

POP 2946 / ELEV 23M

Fogliano Redipuglia (whose name derives from the Slovenian *sredi polje,* literally 'in the middle of the fields') lies on the left bank of the Isonzo River, near the WWI battleground of **Monte Sei Busi**. The town is home to Italy's largest war memorial, the **Sacrario Militare** (Via Terza Armata 27) FREE . Inaugurated in 1938, its monumental white staircase is the final resting place of over 100,000 soldiers, 60% of whom are unknown. The shrine's solemn sarcophagus, crafted from a 75-ton slab of porphyry, is that of Emanuele Filiberto, Duke of Aosta and commander of Italy's 3rd Army. Recently restored, the site is a moving place: the word *'presente'* (present) is carved above the names. Among them is that of the one woman buried here: Margherita Kaiser Parodi, a volunteer Red Cross nurse who died in 1918, at the age of 21. Below three huge bronze crosses lies a small chapel and a museum displaying items that belonged to the fallen soldiers.

A short walk north of the memorial is the multimedia **Museo della Grande Guerra 'Casa della III Armata'** (📋0481 48 91 39; www.museodellagrandeguerra.com; Via Terza Armata 37; ⏰9.30am-12.30pm & 3.30-6.30pm Mon-Sat, 9.30am-12.30pm Sun) FREE, whose interesting collection of WWI memorabilia includes photographs, gas masks, a reconstructed trench and WWI documentaries. Between the memorial and museum lies **Trattoria al Chiosco**, a spacious eatery and bar (lunch €15 to €22).

ℹ️ Information

IAT Fogliano Redipuglia Office (📋 0481 48 91 39; www.prolocofoglianoredipuglia.it; Via III Armata 37; ⏰9.30am-12.30pm & 3.30-6.30pm Mon-Sat, 9.30am-12.30pm Sun)

San Martino del Carso

POP 258 / ELEV 163M

Founded in the 15th century, this small hamlet in the municipality of Sagrado is sadly known for having been completely razed to the ground during WWI. Like nearby San Michele, it's a good starting point for hitting the Routes of the Great War.

🛏️ Sleeping

B&B San Martino   B&B **€€**
(📋 335 786 69 21; Via Piantella 3, Sagrado; d €60-70; ❄️🛜) If you plan on cycling or hiking the Carso Isontino's trails, this B&B makes for an excellent, low-cost base. Book ahead to secure one of its two double rooms, both with private en suite. If you're traveling by train, the owners are happy to pick you up from Sagrado station.

THE BURIED PORT

Giuseppe Ungaretti, one of the greatest Italian poets of the 20th century, took part in the Great War as a volunteer of the 19th infantry regiment. He wrote some of his most famous poems during the Carso's fiercest battles, later published in *Il porto sepolto* (The Buried Port; 1916). Among these works is *San Martino del Carso,* whose namesake town has since become a symbol of the suffering caused by conflicts. In Castelnuovo, in the municipality of Sagrado, the **Parco Letterario Ungaretti** (📋0481 997 42; Via Castelnuovo 2; temporarily closed, call first) was established in his memory. At the heart of the verdant park is a villa surrounded by vineyards, whose tranquility belies their history as a battlefield. Gracing the park is a series of works in stone, wood and steel inspired by the life and words of the great Friulian poet.

ROUTES OF THE GREAT WAR

An interregional project involving Friuli Venezia Giulia, Trentino Alto Adige, Veneto and Lombardy, **Itinerari della Grande Guerra** (Routes of the Great War) aims to preserve the memory of WWI through the conflict's most significant sites. Friuli Venezia Giulia alone has 24 walking routes, with information on each available at www.turismofvg.it/Grande Guerra, including route map, distance, duration, difficulty and highlights.

Other interesting options include the **Peace Park of Mt. Sabotino Route**, a few kilometres north of Gorizia. The trail crosses the second Austro-Hungarian defensive line on Sabotino (609m), passing through shelters and gun emplacements, hideouts and lookouts. Its starting point is 2km east of the Slovenian village of Gonjače, near the stone pyramid. From San Martino del Carso, however, the Open-Air Museum of Mt San Michele and San Martino del Carso Route starts at the **Museo della Grande Guerra del Monte San Michele** (☑ 0481 920 02; Via Zona Sacra at the top of Monte San Michele, Sagrado; adult/reduced €3/1.50; ☉ 10am-4pm Tue-Sun). Thereafter, the **Museo all'Aperto del Monte San Michele** leads through ancient caves and gun tunnels, skirting the ridge of Monte San Michele alongside the **Path of the Cippi**. The path reaches the trench near the cemetery. Launched in 2021, the 420km-long Walk of Peace project links all of the most significant WWI sites along the Isonzo front, from Slovenia to Trieste. The route is divided into 25 stages, with 12 in Slovenia and 13 in Friuli Venezia Giulia.

San Michele del Carso

POP. 253 / ELEV. 49M

A good reason to visit the Savogna d'Isonzo area (San Michele is one of its hamlets) is to hit the trails that lead to WWI sites around **Monte San Michele** (275m), gripping for both their history and natural beauty.

🏃 Activities

Historical Route of Mt Brestovec
WALKING TOUR

The Historical Route of Mt Brestovec, one of the Routes of the Great War, is a very enjoyable and fairly easy walk. Starting from the car park of the Centro Sportivo di San Michele del Carso, proceed along Via Devetaki to the intersection, where you'll spot the first signs for Brestovec: follow them and around 30 minutes later you'll arrive at the well-preserved, labyrinthine **Italian trench line**. Information panels along the entire route recount the tales of these trenches, while touching traces of the soldiers' lives survive as messages engraved in the stones. The most famous of these declares: '*Voliamo la pace*' (We want peace).

Continuing along the path for a few minutes, passing a **lookout** dating from the Cold War, you'll reach the **Monte Brestovec gun tunnel**, the most interesting feature on the trail. Built around 1917 between the municipalities of Doberdò del Lago and Savogna d'Isonzo, it's part of a system of ancient caves that were fortified in WWI with Austrian trenches and Italian shelters. Among those who passed through here were Italian officer and writer Gabriele D'Annunzio and British journalist Rudyard Kipling. During the Cold War, the tunnel became a bunker.

It remains a highly atmospheric place; from the central cavity you can admire the panorama offered by **Monte Brestovec** (209m). Although you can't see it, Slovenia lies just behind the trees (during the war, the hill wasn't covered in vegetation). Continuing along the Brestovec route, you'll be back at the car park in less than 30 minutes.

🛏 Sleeping & Eating

⭐ **Lokanda Devetak 1870**   INN €€

(☑ 0481 88 24 88; www.devetak.com; Via Brezici 22, Savogna d'Isonzo; meals €35; ☉ noon-3pm & 7-10.30pm Fri-Sun, 7-10.30pm Wed & Thu; ❄ ☎) Tuck into exquisite, seasonal Carso specialties with Slovenian and Habsburg influences, including potato and turnip *spätzle*, dumplings with rabbit *ragù (snidjeno testo)* and *baccalà della nonna Žuta* (salted cod with polenta). Gluten-free options available.

The old stables beside the trattoria now house eight beautiful, clean and spacious **rooms** (s/d/tr starting from €70/120/150), each named after a plant.

Sea & Lagoon

Includes ➡

Lignano
Sabbiadoro 114

The Laguna di Grado
& Marano Lagunare . . 123

Marano Lagunare 124

Riserva Naturale
delle Foci dello Stella . . 126

Grado 126

Aquileia 132

Torviscosa 136

Strassoldo 137

Riserva Naturale
della Foce dell'Isonzo
& Valle Cavanata 137

Monfalcone 138

Best Nature Reserves

➡ Riserva Naturale
della Foce dell'Isonzo
& Valle Cavanata (p137)

➡ Riserva Naturale
delle Foci dello Stella (p126)

➡ Riserva Naturale
della Valle Canal Novo (p125)

Why Go?

Stretching from the Veneto border to Monfalcone, the Friulian coast is one of the region's most unique features. Here, hectares of lagoons, river mouths and wetlands are interspersed with inviting and well-equipped beaches. This part of the Upper Adriatic is an extensive transition zone between land and sea, teeming with bird and marine life, and lit by sunsets that glow and shift like auras. Photographers will be struck by its photogenic beauty, as was Ernest Hemingway, who set part of his work – and his life – here.

Lignano is a quintessential holiday destination, Grado a small culinary rival to Venice, luminous Marano an oasis of tranquility. Further inland, Aquileia is a testament to a millennia-old civilisation that built forts and temples in Roman times and that once rivalled both Rome and Byzantium as a religious powerhouse. Above all, it is water that makes this corner of Friuli Venezia Giulia so special, so do not miss the opportunity to head out onto the lagoon, on a boat tour or in a canoe.

When to Go

The area is humid, making both cold and heat here feel more intense and uncomfortable. Not that a visit in summer or winter (particularly either side of their peaks) should be excluded. The amount of daylight is always worth considering, given that longer days mean more time to enjoy the waterways and their spectacular play of light. Summer and autumn sunsets are almost as magnificent as the mosaics of Aquileia, while the area's clear, brisk winter and spring mornings give the colder months unexpected appeal.

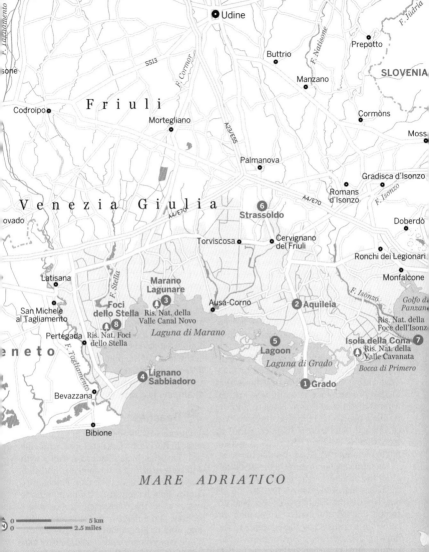

Sea & Lagoon Highlights

1 Grado (p126) Historic churches, a charming port, beaches and seafood restaurants.

2 Aquileia (p132) Important Roman and Byzantine city with noteworthy mosaics. Don't miss the museum.

3 Marano Lagunare (p124) An unspoiled corner of the lagoon and a quiet, welcoming town.

4 Lignano Sabbiadoro (p114) It's time to play sport!

5 Lagoon (p118 and p125) A cruise among seemingly floating churches.

6 Strassoldo (p137) A medieval village with matching castles built between the springs.

7 Isola della Cona (p137) A tranquil oasis inhabited by Camargue horses (don't forget your camera!).

8 Foci dello Stella (p126) Yours to discover by boat, passing by historic Bilancia di Bepi on your way.

LIGNANO SABBIADORO

POP 6765 / ELEV 2M

Lignano's retro vibe will win over fans of '60s Italy. And if you're looking for a beach holiday, you'll be spoiled for choice, with everything from fully decked-out beach clubs to wilder swathes of coast. Fancy some outdoor thrills, perhaps an activity you've never tried? This sports-loving town delivers.

Technically, Lignano covers three coastal localities – from north to south **Sabbiadoro**, **Pineta** and **Riviera** – extending 8km right down to the mouth of the Tagliamento River in Marina Punta Faro. For a sense of what the area would have looked like before its mass development, head to Pineta, where you'll find the last patch of woodland that once carpeted the area. Until the early 20th century, there was only one fishing village here, accessible by sea from Marano Lagunare and surrounded by a giant pine forest rich in wild game. According to one theory, the peninsula's ancient name, Lugnanum ('lupi' is the Latin word for 'wolves') refers to the large population of wolves believed to have roamed here. According to another, however, the peninsula's name is rooted in that of a local landowner from Roman times.

What is certain is that Lignano's first bathing establishment was established in 1903. That said, it wasn't until Fascist times that Lignano's destiny as a seaside resort was set, when a direct road link to Latisana and the Friulian plain was built and the area was christened 'Sabbiadoro' (Golden Sand) in 1935. Indeed, the sand here really is golden, not to mention very clean all along the coast.

Lignano's big boom came in the 1950s and of all the architects who put their mark on the place, Marcello D'Olivo (1921–91) stands out. He was the Friulian architect who designed Pineta's distinctive street plan, its spiral form inspired by the concepts of Renaissance garden city and organic architecture. Further design kudos came in 1972 with architect Aldo Bernardis' iconic Terrazza a Mare, an enduring symbol of the town and the era.

◉ Sights

Terrazza a Mare   TERRACE

(☑0431 713 00; Lungomare Trieste 5; ⊙8.30am-1am summer and 20 Dec-7 Jan; 🐾) Hard to miss from the beach (especially in Sabbiadoro), Lignano's iconic sea terrace sits at the end of a pier lined with shops peddling sports-wear and beachwear. The terrace includes an appealing restaurant and bar, with indoor and outdoor tables along the perimeter, as well as deck chairs. The *antipasti* and seafood *primi* (first courses) are exquisite, not to mention unforgettably served right in the 'middle' of the sea.

Villa Gattolini   HISTORIC BUILDING

This beautiful Art Nouveau villa, decorated with the odd neo-Gothic detail, dates from Lignano's early development. Built in 1910 and originally known as Villa Zuzzi, it was the town hall. Back then, only the building to the right existed, and the surrounding sea. Despite the encroachment of Sabbiadora's more recent buildings, the villa has lost none of its beauty, which you can admire from the seafront promenade.

Chiesa Votiva
di Santa Maria del Mare   PLACE OF WORSHIP

Although Lignano's oldest building dates from the 15th century, it has only been standing here since 1965. Previously, it was located along the banks of the nearby Tagliamento River, in Bevazzana. Threatened by river erosion, the church was dismantled and rebuilt in Sabbiadoro. It's a simple building, set in the heart of the pine forest and home to 15th-century frescoes and sinopias, as well as a stoup by Pordenone-born sculptor Giovanni Antonio Pilacorte.

🏖 Beaches

In Lignano, the beach comes in various formats. In Riviera, it's less developed, with only basic facilities. In Sabbiadoro, it comes with waterside *aperitivi,* afternoon gigs and endless crowds. In tranquil, verdant Pineta, it's a family affair. Bathing establishments sit side by side along this coast, each marked with a number and a flag (there are seven in Riviera, nine in Pineta and 19 in Sabbiadoro). While convenience and crowd density varies between them, all have toilets, showers, baby-changing facilities, as well as access for strollers and those with limited mobility. Wi-fi is widespread.

Admission varies, depending on the season, the establishment's proximity to the sea, and the length of your stay. Expect to pay between €10.30 and €21 per day; discount are available for FVG Card holders. In general, the more you pay, the greater your options, which range from sun loungers (sans umbrella) to 'elite' spots that might come with pagoda-shaped umbrella, additional services and more space. On the other hand, the coast's free beaches will cost you nothing: you'll find a very peaceful one near the eastern tip of the coast, close to the dock.

Spiaggia di Lignano Sabbiadoro BEACH
(www.lignanosabbiadoro.it) You'll find the highest concentration of bathing establishments here. Day and night, the **Beach Village** (☑0431 72 40 33; Bagno 7; ◷9.30am-12.15pm & 4-11pm 1 Jun-5 Sep) is the hub for activities, with entertainment for both adult and kids, as well as fitness facilities. Indulge in sports (including beach volleyball, football and rugby) at **Beach Arena** (Bagno 7) or hit **Lidocity** (Bagno 13; ◷8.30am-11pm) which, aside from its beach umbrellas and bumper activities, claims an excellent restaurant.

If you have four-legged friends in tow, there's **Doggy Beach** (www.doggybeachlignano.com; before Bagno 1; rates vary, daily from €24 in high season), the only section of the beach where dogs are legally permitted.

Spiaggia di Lignano Pineta BEACH
(www.lignanopineta.com) Heading in the direction of La Pagoda (a bar on stilts at the end of a pier), you'll reach **FunVillage** (Bagno 4), which runs free activities between 10am and 6pm. Right next door is Piazza D'Olivo (Bagni 2-3). Cultural events, book launches and wine tastings take place during the summer.

Spiaggia di Lignano Riviera BEACH
(www.lignano-riviera.it) Come here for what you haven't found at the other beaches: space and silence. This stretch of coast, which extends from the mouth of the Tagliamento to Pineta, is clean and less crowded, though not exactly wild. It too has activity zones (including a 'baby club' where you can drop the kids off), as well as areas where you can enjoy activities such as water aerobics and pilates. It's also home to **Sport Beach Village**, which is similar to the one in Pineta.

🏃 Activities

Anchedomani PARASAILING & WATER SPORTS
(☑348 237 37 40; Pagoda Wharf, Via Lungomare Alberto Kechler) Organise exciting flights with an parasail: tied by a rope to a motorboat, you will be pushed into the sky at a height of 100m and gently towed in flight for about 20 minutes. From up there you will see the whole peninsula of Lignano, the lagoon and the mouth of the Tagliamento from top to bottom. If you suffer from vertigo, you will have as an alternative the 'Banana Boat' or the donuts, always dragged by the hull, water skiing and the wakeboard.

SEA & LAGOON LIGNANO SABBIADORO

THE OLD MAN & THE LAGOON: HEMINGWAY IN LIGNANO

Ernest Hemingway would tie his name eternally to Lignano (then known as Latisana) on 14 April 1954, a few months before receiving the Nobel Prize for literature. The writer had been visiting Italy frequently at the time (notably Venice) to recover after a string of road and plane accidents. In 1954 he was invited to Udine by his friend Alberto Kechler, and he went hunting and mingled with the intellectuals of the time. Kechler, a nobleman and major shareholder in Ligneto Pineta's masterplan, had met the American novelist in Cortina. On his return trip to Venice, Hemingway stopped a few hours in Lignano Pineta, where he met Marcello d'Olivo, the architect responsible for the town's distinctive layout. In order to promote the fledgling seaside resort, Kechler gifted Hemingway a plot of land and a residence. In gratitude, Hemingway signed a map of Pineta (marking the very spot of his new digs) and famously declared: 'This is the Florida of Italy'. Sadly, the literary giant never had the chance to enjoy Kechler's generous gift. After leaving Friuli, Hemingway never returned, committing suicide in 1961.

Hemingway was deeply drawn to the lagoons of the Friulian coast: he visited them on several occasions and claimed to be at ease among the reeds and canals that perhaps reminded him of his beloved Florida. Indeed, he writes about this land in *Across the River and Into the Trees,* finding inspiration in the views of the Càorle and Marano lagoons, and in his relationship with Adriana Ivancic, the 19-year-old cousin of Carlo Kechler whom he had met on a hunting trip in 1948. Although Hemingway's sojourn in Lignano was for but a few brief hours, he would leave an indelible mark on the place, inspiring everything from a park to a renowned literary festival and prize.

Lignano Sabbiadoro

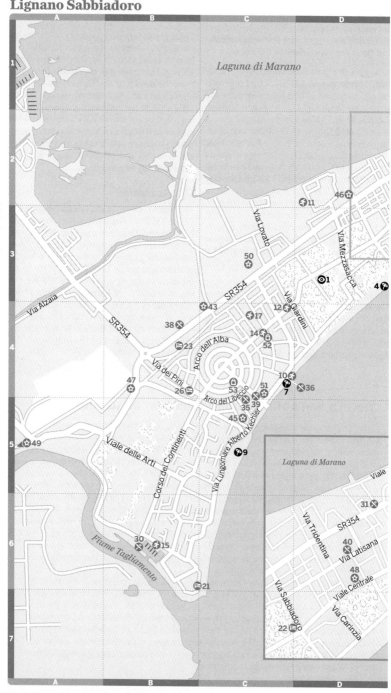

Wind Village
SAILING & WINDSURFING

(sailing ☑ 340 338 84 65, windsurfing ☑ 339 210 40 24; btwn Bagno 6 & 7, Lignano Sabbiadoro) Step forward if you have always dreamed of steering a sailboat or windsurf board. This place rents both, with helpful, professional staff to boot.

Island
WATERSPORTS

(☑ 0431 42 22 48; www.islandsurf.it; Corso degli Alisei 52, Lignano Sabbiadoro) SUP (stand-up paddling), surfing, windsurfing, kitesurfing or wakeboarding?

A.S.D. Nordic Walking Lignano
NORDIC WALKING

(☑ 348 133 24 09; www.nordicwalkinglignano.it If you're intrigued by the idea of Nordic walking on the beach (or right in the water), head to Terrazza a Mare and request the gear: it's free to use.

Walking, Cycling & Horseback Tours

There are 30km of cycling paths in Lignano (marked on Google maps), along with free bike hire at Terrazza a Mare, p114). That said, you may prefer a spot of jogging or Nordic walking. For a quiet pedal, make your way to **Parco Hemingway**, outfitted with play equipment and outdoor performance areas. A section of the park remembers Ernest Hemingway with an installation of images and text. If you fancy exploring the peninsula on horseback, contact the **A.S.D. Circolo Ippico Lignanese** (☑ 0431 738 44; Via Brescia 1; ☺ 9am-6pm).

🎓 Courses

Misterblu
DIVING

(☑ 333 978 91 74; www.misterblu.com; Viale Adriatico 11, Lignano Riviera) If you're interested in exploring the seabed, this outfit will make it happen. Rookie? No problem: courses cover all levels.

Be Free Sport p.a.s.d.
SAILING

(☑ 347 278 19 39, 345 614 69 49; www.befreesport. it; Viale Centrale 29, Lignano Sabbiadoro) This association aimed at promoting sailing sports and nautical culture organises sailing courses for children and teenagers; young people reluctant to try water sports can take tennis courses.

Yacht Club Lignano
SAILING & WINDSURFING

(☑ 0431 731 61; www.yclignano.it; Via Monte Ortigara 3/m, Lignano Sabbiadoro) Runs weekly introductory sailing courses in the summer.

Lignano Sabbiadoro

◎ Sights

1	Chiesa Votiva di Santa Maria del Mare	D3
2	Terrazza a Mare	F6
3	Villa Gattolini	F6

🏖 Beaches

4	Beach Arena	D3
5	Beach Village	F6
6	Doggy Beach	F1
7	FunVillage	C4
8	Lidocity	E7
9	Sport Beach Village (Riviera)	C5

◉ Activities, Courses & Tours

10	Anchedomani	C4
11	A.S.D. Circolo Ippico Lignanese	D2
	A.S.D. Nordic Walking Lignano	(see 2)
12	Be Free Sport p.a.s.d.	C4
13	Circolo Canottieri Lignano	F1
14	Island	C4
15	Misterblu	B6
16	Motonave Europa	F5
17	Parco Hemingway	C4
18	Sea&Taste (boarding)	F1
19	Wind Village	E6
20	Yacht Club Lignano	F1

🛏 Sleeping

21	Camping Pino Mare	C6
22	Camping Sabbiadoro	C7
23	Hotel Alex	B4
24	Hotel Bellavista	F6
25	Hotel Diva	F5
26	Hotel Friuli	B4
27	Hotel Italia Palace	F5
28	Hotel La Goletta	F1
29	Hotel Monaco	F5

⊗ Eating

30	Al Cason	B6
31	Bidin	D6
32	Da Miro	E1
33	Divino	F5
34	Farmacia dei Sani	E5
35	La Buca dei Papi	C5
36	La Pagoda	D4
37	Marechiaro	F1
38	Oasi del Pesce	B4
39	Perbacco	C4
40	Rosa	D6
41	Sacheburache	F5
42	Terrazza di Crema	F1

◎☺ Entertainment

43	Aquasplash	C4
44	Club Italia	F5
45	I Gommosi	C5
46	L.Hub Park	D2
47	Mister Charlie	B4
48	Parco Junior	D6
49	Parco Zoo Punta Verde	off map A5
50	Strabilia Lunapark	C3
51	Tenda	C4

◉ Shopping

52	Island Surf	C4
53	Libreria Pineta	C4

Circolo Canottieri Lignano ROWING
(☏ 347 509 07 36; www.canottaggiolignano.it; Via Lagunare c/o Porto Casoni, Lignano Sabbiadoro) Runs three-week rowing courses for adults and children in the summer.

Tours

Boat Tours

Not all boat excursions in Lignano are created equal. Tour operator **Travel One** (☏ 043 172 04 28; https://travelone.it) runs **Sea&Taste** tours, which include fishing, bird-watching and kayaking experiences. Particularly interesting are its tours to Aquileia, both of which sail on the charming *Santa Maria* boat. Transfers are available to **Bilancia di Bepi** (☏ 340 363 67 33), a traditional fisherman's stilt house that is the starting point for an adventurous canoe tour. Boat tours leave from both Ligna-

no and Marano Lagunare. **Motonave Europa** (☏ 338 606 76 20; www.motonaveeuropa.it) offers tours to the Isola delle Conchiglie (Monday to Saturday; departs 9.30am, returns noon) and the Laguna di Grado (adult €20; departs 2pm, returns 7pm)..

Cycling Tour

If you're interested in joining a bike tour, enquire at Terrazza a Mare (p114): a different tour is offered daily Monday to Friday, running between Lignano, Marano and Latisana.

 Festivals & Events

Premio Hemingway JUNE
(www.premiohemingway.it) Lignano's top cultural event includes book launches, exhibitions and panel discussions with prominent writers.

Incendio del Mare
AUGUST

Every year, on Pineta beach, 'fire magician' Ciro Manfredonia serves up a spectacular fireworks display that will make you think the sea is bursting into flames.

SUP Race
EARLY SEPTEMBER

Lignano's answer to the Barcolana, with hundreds of athletes, young and young-at-heart, up on their boards, paddling for glory.

Sun & Run
SEPTEMBER

Runners should enquire about the date of this race, which follows a 10km route between Sabbiadoro and Pineta.

🛏 Sleeping

Hotels dominate Lignano's skyline, so you won't have much trouble finding a room. Most of the offerings are of similar quality: big buildings with generally clean, well-kept interiors, able to accommodate large numbers. Rates are among the highest in the region, so if you're planning on a long stay, you might want to consider renting an apartment or camping; there are many excellent options in both categories.

The tourist office can provide you with lists of all accommodation offerings. When choosing, consider which of Lignano's hamlets you'd prefer as your base. To help you out, we've divided our recommendations by locality.

🛏 Sabbiadoro

★ Camping Sabbiadoro
CAMPING €

(📞 0431 714 55/0431 717 10; www.campingsabbiadoro.it; Via Sabbiadoro 8; adult €7.20-13.50, child €4.40-7.60, standard pitches €12.50-28; 🅿 🚲 ❄ 🛜) Saving Euros while staying in the centre (and a stone's throw from the sea) is possible at this good-quality, 13-hectare campsite, immersed in a pine forest. Decent facilities include a beautiful private beach.

Hotel La Goletta
HOTEL €€

(📞 0431 712 74; www.hotelgoletta.it; Viale Italia 44; s/d €78/140; 🅿 ❄ 🛜 🍴) If your love of the sea goes deeper than sand and sunscreen, this hotel overlooks Lignano's atmospheric, boat-filled dock. Of course, those golden sands are but a few minutes' walk away.

Hotel Monaco
HOTEL €€ /€€€

(📞 0431 715 23; www.hotelmonaco.net; Via Gorizia 24; d €130-540; 🅿 ❄ 🛜 🍴 🏊) Overlooking Piazza Fontana, the Monaco's location is undisputedly central, right in the heart of Sabbiadora's pedestrian precinct (noise from neighbouring restaurants and bars might be an issue for some). Rooms are pleasant and comfortable, and the vibe refined. Parking is €5 per day.

Hotel Diva
HOTEL €€€

(📞 0431 193 80 86; www.divahotellignano.it; Viale Italia 4/a; d from €160; 🅿 ❄ 🛜 🍴) Filling a niche in an otherwise family-orientated market, svelte Hotel Diva is for adults only. It's a sophisticated, beautifully appointed place, with Italian furnishings and a contemporary look. Especially ideal for single travellers.

Hotel Italia Palace
HOTEL €€€

(📞 0431 711 85; www.hotelitaliapalace.it; Viale Italia 7; d from €190; 🅿 ❄ 🛜 🍴) While Lignano's general image is of a modern town, its seaside fame began in the 20th century. Channel its Belle Époque days at this grand veteran, dating from early last century. Rooms are elegant and luxurious, complimenting onpoint service, a splendid roof-top restaurant and bar, spa and swimming pool.

★ Hotel Bellavista
HOTEL €€€

(📞 0431 713 13; www.bellavistalignano.it; Lungomare Trieste 70; d from €200; 🅿 ❄ 🛜 🍴 🏊) Teak deckchairs by the pool, the sound of the sea and holidaymakers in the distance, and bright, tastefully decorated rooms overlooking the Adriatic.

The onsite restaurant is attentive and accommodating, and the hotel offers special rates for families, making it ideal if you're travelling with kids.

Parking is €10 per day.

🛏 Pineta

Hotel Alex
HOTEL €€

(📞 0431 42 87 73; www.hotelalex.it; Via Tarvisio 82; d €90; 🅿 ❄ 🛜 🏊) A very large hotel, just north of Pineta's iconic spiral street, with TV and balcony in all the rooms. The hotel has a number of bikes available to guests; you'll need them to get to the beach, which is a couple of kilometres away.

★ Hotel Friuli
HOTEL €€

(📞 0431 42 86 83; www.hotelfriuli.it; Via dei Pini 11; per person €40-55, incl breakfast €46-59, half board €62-75; 🅿 ❄ 🛜) Very close to both the sea and Lignano's pine forest, this is one of the best hotels in the area.

While the room decor is retro (which some will actually love), the revamped bathrooms are contemporary. Staff are kind and helpful, and the hotel pool refreshing after a jaunt on one of the hotel bikes.

🛏 Riviera

Camping Pino Mare
CAMPING €

(☑ 0431 42 44 24; www.campingpinomare.it; Lungomare Riccardo Riva 15; adult/child €15/9, pitches €32.60-85.80; P ☒ ✿ 🤶) Once you've read all the facilities offered at this campsite, you'll be amazed to discover that there's a deluxe category to boot. So, if the pine forest, resort-style pool and private beach aren't enough, find your bliss in the higher-category cabins. Accommodating three to six, they come with satellite TV, air conditioning and two bathrooms.

🍴 Eating & Drinking

As is the case for hotels, Lignano has a plethora of restaurants and bars, in many cases combined. Head out of the centre for refined, top-level dining destinations, or stay in the centre for a festive, holiday vibe. To avoid long, hunger-inducing waits, remember to book ahead on weekends.

🍴 Sabbiadoro

Oasi del Pesce
STREET FOOD €

(☑ 342 189 49 80; www.oasidelpesce.it; Viale Europa 146; grilled fish from €5.90; ⊙ 11.30am-3.30pm & 5-10pm) With its long benches, convivial vibe and simple, cheap, authentic grub, this place feels like a village food fest. It's no coincidence: an initiative of the Trieste Fishermen's Cooperative, it proclaims itself a permanent 'Fish Festival'. Great for kids and those who love a crowd.

Sacheburache
OSTERIA €€

(☑ 0431 714 98; www.sacheburache.it; Via Genziana 2; meals €20-35; ⊙ 6-11pm Mon, 11am-2pm & 6-11pm Tue-Sun) It's hard to find an *osteria* as authentic as this one in Lignano. Head in for simple, top-quality specialities from the region (above all the wine and prosciutto), served by affable staff. You'll find it right under the former aqueduct.

Farmacia dei Sani
OSTERIA €€

(☑ 0431 700 00; Via Latisana 44; meals €25-35; ⊙ 10.30am-2.30pm & 5.30pm-midnight; 🤶) Although busiest at aperitivo hour, the curiously named 'Pharmacy of the Sane' is also open for lunch and dinner, when it serves a seafood-centric menu. Hung with reproduc-

tion Warhols and the work of other artists, its trump card is its young, lively atmosphere. (Don't miss a trip to the bathroom for an unexpected surprise.)

Marechiaro
RESTAURANT €€

(☑ 0431 716 73; www.ristorantemarechiaro.com; Viale Italia 72; meals €40; ⊙ noon-3pm and 6-11pm Mon & Wed-Sun) Marechiaro's seafood dishes steer on the side of tradition, with the odd detour into more adventurous territory; there's also pizza for those not keen on surf. The restaurant itself is named after the Neapolitan coastal village, and its large seafront terrace, attentive service and use of southern ingredients gives the place a decidedly Mediterranean vibe.

Da Miro
RESTAURANT €€

(☑ 0431 705 75; Via Lagunare 31; meals €35; ⊙ 11.30am-2.30pm & 6-10pm) This thatched restaurant recalls the old *casoni* (temporary fishermen's houses) that once peppered the coast.

It's an atmospheric spot (especially outside the high season), flanked by stored boats and Lignano's busy dock. Both the fried morsels and grilled fish are tasty. It's a good option if you're travelling with children, though service can be slow at times.

Bidin
WINE BAR €€

(☑ 0431 719 88; www.ristorantebidin.com; Viale Europa 1; meals €40; ⊙ 11am-2pm & 7-10pm Thu-Tue) Highly regarded by the locals, Bidin is a step above the general standard in this town. Feast on carefully prepared Friulian fare and seafood dishes that greatly respect the produce.

The setting is enchanting and the service meticulous.

Rosa
RESTAURANT €€/€€€

(☑ 0431 701 48; Via Latisana 156; meals €30-60; ⊙ noon-2.30pm & 7-10.30pm) That Rosa's prices are higher than the average is justified: when it comes to quality, the restaurant tops the list in Lignano. It's a homely place, with fresh seafood cooked traditionally or using worldly recipes.

⭐ Terrazza di Crema
BEACHCLUB, RESTAURANT €€/€€€

(☑ 0431 700 51; Via Carso 45; mains €13-22; ⊙ 9.30am-2pm & 6.30-11.30pm; 🤶) It's an appealing set-up: a series of personal 'pagodas' on a timber terrace overlooking the sea. Breeze on salty skin, feast on shellfish and toast with a *vino* (or perhaps a mojito). Are you in Lignano, Miami or Saint Tropez?

The venue is also a popualr *aperitivo* spot, when it moonlights as a waterfront cocktail bar.

Divino WINE BAR
(☏0431 706 10; Via Udine 72; ⊙10.30am-2pm & 5pm-2am, closed Thu in winter) Divino deserves a mention for (at least) two reasons. Firstly, it's one of the few places in Lignano that's low-key, tranquil, almost silent. Secondly, a browse of the wine list reveals a decent number of biodynamic drops. Prefer something else entirely? Cocktails and other libations are also available.

Pineta

La Buca dei Papi WINE BAR€€
(☏0431 42 22 79; Tana del Gambero 4; meals €35-45; ⊙7pm-2am) An historic restaurant in Pineta, as well as one of the best known in Lignano, La Buca dei Papi is especially popular with families. While the main drawcard is signora Lola's homemade pasta, Gianni's wine options are also worthy of a nod. Arguably a little expensive, but within reason.

Perbacco WINE BAR
(☏0431 42 21 13; Viale a Mare 17/25; ⊙11am-3am) Under the same management as Tenda, wine bar Perbacco is a big hit with younger locals. The fit-out is more Carnia than Lignano: think dark-timber furniture and a cosy vibe befitting of a mountain setting. Nevertheless it's perfect for an *aperitivo,* with top-notch *vino* from carefully chosen wineries.

La Pagoda BAR
(☏0431 42 27 38; Alberto Kechler promenade; ⊙8.30am-3am; 🛜) On Sabbiadoro's landmark Terrazza a Mare (accessed from the pier), this bar also sits in the middle of the sea. That said, this one is less chic. Always buzzing, it's especially busy around *aperitivo* time.

Riviera

Al Cason RESTAURANT, GELATERIA €€ /€€€
(☏0431 42 30 29; www.ristorantealcason.it; Course of the Continents 167; meals €35-60; ⊙11am-3pm and 6pm-midnight) Fabulously set on the Riviera marina, this restaurant offers fiery sunsets over the sea and evenings under the stars. Although in business since 1967, it's kept up with the times, both in look and culinary offerings. Staunch traditionalists needn't fret: you'll find old-school razor clams and scallops too (as long as you don't mind the price tag).

☆ Entertainment

Mister Charlie CLUB
(www.mrcharlie.net; Via Tagliamento 2, Lignano Pineta; ⊙11pm-4am Tue & Fri, 9pm-4am Sat) Nightclub may not be quite the right word to describe Mr Charlie, shaking Lignano's booty for over 40 years. The venue's different areas and music offerings make all generations feel at home. Get down to the latest summer anthems or get nostalgic with retro Italian classics.

★Tenda BAR
(☏0431 42 21 33; www.tendabar.it; Piazza Marcello D'Olivo 7, Lignano Pineta; ⊙8am-4am Mar-Sep) Apparently, if you haven't been to Tenda, you haven't really been to Lignano. And while personal tastes may vary, for many, having a drink at Tenda is a quintessential part of the Lignano experience. True to its name, the hotspot is located in a giant tent (*tenda* is Italian for tent) in the centre of Pineta, with a sea of alfresco tables, indoor and outdoor bars, DJs and a lively, exuberant atmosphere at any time of the day.

Club Italia CLUB
(☏0431 704 44; Via Udine 103, Lignano Sabbiadoro; ⊙evenings 11pm-5am) Closed on our last visit, this Sabbiadoro nightclub is usually a go-to for those wanting to dance until the wee hours.

Zoos, Parks & Theme Parks

It's easy to spend a fun day or more at one of Lignano's seven parks, which range from the zoological to the waterslide variety.

Parco Zoo Punta Verde ZOO
(☏0431 42 87 75; www.parcozoopuntaverde.it; Via G. Scerbanenco 19/1; adult/reduced €15/12, discount with FVG Card; ⊙9.30am-6pm May–mid-Jul & mid-Aug–mid-Sep, to 7pm mid-Jul–mid-Aug, to 5pm mid-late Sep, only Sat & Sun Oct & Nov) Opened in 1979, this progressive zoo focuses on animal conservation and includes a research centre aimed at raising awareness about sustainability and environmental protection. Part of its revenue goes towards conservation and development projects in the Americas, Asia and Africa. The exhibits themselves are informative and engaging for all ages.

One highlight is the chance to get up close and help feed the lemurs (€8; maximum eight people). To participate, you'll need to **book ahead** (call or email info@parcozoo puntaverde.it; ⊙ 10am & 11am Mon, Wed, Fri & Sun Jun-Sep).

Aquasplash   THEME PARK
(☑ 0431 42 88 26; www.aquasplash.it; Viale Europa, Lignano Sabbiadoro; adult/reduced per day €25/20, afternoon only €20/18, discount with FVG Card; ⊙ 10am-6pm Jun–mid-Sep) Italy's king of water parks. To reach its squeal-inducing medley of swimming pools, slides and climbing ropes, catch bus A2. Suitable for all ages, including little ones.

Parco Junior   AMUSEMENT PARK
(☑ 0431 72 13 70; www.parcojunior.it; Via Centrale 16/b, Lignano Sabbiadoro; admission free, coin-operated games from €2; ⊙ 2.30-8pm Mon-Sat & 10.30am-8pm Sun early-mid May & early-mid-Sep, 10.30am-10pm Jun & early-mid-Sep, 10.30am-mid-night Jul & Aug) In the centre of Lignano Sabbiadoro, Parco Junior is by far the best option in the area for younger kids. The amusement park includes the Junior Express train, much loved by little ones.

L.Hub Park   SPORTS PARK
(☑ 0431 40 90 40; Viale Europa 102; ⊙ 24hr) `FREE` Sports fields, running track, foosball and a half pipe.

Strabilia Lunapark   AMUSEMENT PARK
(www.lunaparkstrabilia.com; Viale Europa, Lignano Sabbiadoro; free admission, coin-operated games from €2; ⊙ 8pm-1am Jun-Sep) It might be the Ferris wheel, or perhaps it's the scent of cotton candy, but there's something utterly romantic about this Luna Park, which has delighted both adults and children for generations.

I Gommosi   THEME PARK
(Raggio delle Capelonghe, Lignano Pineta; adult/reduced €13/9; ⊙ cloudy 10am-11.30pm, sunny 5-11.30pm mid-May–mid Sep) At this family-run theme park, kids under 12 enjoy no time limits on any of the offerings, among them zorb balls and a swimming pool that is packed with toys.

Opening hours are weather dependent as the sun can overheat the rubber equipment.

🛍 Shopping

Thanks to 750 shops and extended summer trading hours, shopping seems to be the most popular pastime in Lignano after hitting the beach.

For a little retail therapy, stroll Sabbiadoro's pedestrianised **Viale Venezia**, **Via**

Tolmezzo and **Via Udine** or Pineta's Viale a Mare (nicknamed **il Treno**), home to everything from designer threads to the everyday essentials.

Island Surf   SURF & CO
(☑ 0431 42 22 48; www.islandsurf.it; Corso degli Alisei 52; ⊙ 9.30am-1pm & 5-11pm summer, 9.30am-1pm & 3.30-7.30pm rest of yr) The place for surfing gear, particularly Lignano's specialities: kitesurfing and windsurfing.

Libreria Pineta   BOOKS
(☑ 0431 42 28 02; Radius of the Ostro 42; ⊙ 9.30am-12.30pm & 4.30-7.30pm) If you've run out of reads for the beach, drop into this bookshop in Pineta.

❶ Information

INTERNET ACCESS
Free wi-fi is available at most cafes and bars, as well as at 24 of the 37 bathing establishments in Lignano.

MEDICAL SERVICES
Lignano Emergency Department (☑ 118; Via Tarvisio 5/b)

POST
Lignano Sabbiadoro post office (☑ 0431 40 93 11; Viale Gorizia 37/39; ⊙ 8.20am-7pm Mon-Fri, to 1.35pm Sat) In winter, only open in the morning.

Lignano Pineta post office (☑ 0431 42 73 36; Piazza Rosa dei Venti 24; ⊙ 8.20am-1.35pm Mon-Fri, to 12.35pm Sat)

TOURIST INFORMATION
Lignano Pineta Infopoint (☑ 0431 42 21 69; Via dei Pini 53; ⊙ 9am-12.30pm & 2.30-5.30pm Apr-Oct)

Lignano Sabbiadoro Infopoint (Map p116, E5; ☑ 0431 718 21; Via Latisana 42; ⊙ varies, on our last visit 9am-1pm & 4-8pm summer, 9am-1pm & 2-6pm Mon-Sat, 9am-1pm Sun winter) Sabbiadoro's well-stocked tourist office can help with every aspect of your trip. It also sells the FVG Card.

❶ Getting There & Away

BOAT
TPL FVG (☑ 800 05 20 40, mobile 040 971 23 43; https://tplfvg.it/it/il-viaggio/servizi-marittimi) sails between Lignano and Marano (€3.55, 40 minutes, departures from Lignano in Viale Italia 74 at 10am, noon, 5pm & 7pm year-round, also 11.15pm Jul & Aug; bike €0.90). Bicycles are permitted at the captain's discretion, and only from Monday to Friday (7pm service excluded). To reach the dock, take bus AS from the bus station and alight at Via Latisana 5.

Moorings

With some 5000 berths in eight docks, Lignano Sabbiadoro is one of the largest tourist ports in Europe, so finding a mooring shouldn't be too tricky.

Darsena Porto Vecchio (☑ 0431 72 31 83; www.lignanosabbiadoro.it/portovecchio/doveit.htm; Viale Italia 50, Lignano Sabbiadoro)

Marina Punta Faro (☑ 0431 703 15; Via Monte Ortigara 3; www.marinapuntafaro.it; Lignano Sabbiadoro)

Marina Uno (☑ 0431 42 86 77; www.marina-uno .com; Viale Adriatico 39, Lignano Riviera)

Marina Punta Verde (☑ 0431 42 71 31; www. marinapuntaverde.it; Via G. Scerbanenco 17/1, Lignano Riviera)

Aprilia Marittima (☑ 0431 531 23; Via del Coregolo 3; Aprilia Marittima)

BUS

TPL FVG (☑ 800 05 20 40, mobile 040 971 23 43; https://tplfvg.it) runs frequent buses from Lignano Sabbiadoro to nearby locations. Buses leave from the new **bus station** in Via Amaranto. Bus 500 and 515 connect with Udine (€7.15, 75 to 90 minutes, 12 daily), passing through Latisana from where you can take the train to Trieste. To reach Marano (€6.05; 80 minutes) you'll need to transfer in Latisana, San Giorgio di Nogaro or other locations. For timetables and all routes, see the website.

CAR & MOTORCYLE

From Trieste Take the A4 to Palmanova, continue towards Venice, exit at Latisana and follow the signs for Lignano; the entire trip takes around 80 minutes.

From Milan Take the A4 exit at Latisana and follow the signs to Lignano.

Parking

In the summer, parking in Lignano is not easy. Your best best is to find a spot on one of the streets parallel to the coast: the further from the water, the better your chances. Street parking is €0.90 per hour between 9am and 10pm. On the Lungomare Trieste there's a daily flat rate of €8. For those after a longer-term solution, there are monthly (€80) and seasonal (€155) passes.

The following are supervised car parks:

Parcheggio Venezia (☑ 0431 72 00 86; Via Treviso 21, Lignano Sabbiadoro; hourly/daily €1/10)

Luna Blu Parking (☑ 800 14 43 28; Via dello Stadio 2, Lignano Sabbiadoro; hourly/ daily €1/15)

TRAIN

Trains do not run to Lignano: if you are travelling by train, the most convenient station to go too is Latisana, from where ATVO buses reach Lignano (€4.50).

ⓘ Getting Around

Venice Marco Polo is the closest airport to Lignano. Dedicated Express shuttles run to/from Lignano in summer (⊙ 16 Jun-31 Aug). Alternatively, catch ATVO bus 8 to Latisana and switch to TPL FVG bus 455.

Trieste Ronchi dei Legionari airport If flying into Treviso, you'll need to reach Trieste and transfer to a Lignano-bound service there.

PUBLIC TRANSPORT

Bus

TPL FVG (☑ 800 05 20 40, mobile 040 971 23 43; https://tplfvg.it) See the website or download the TPL FVG app for routes and timetables.

The AS summer shuttle (navetta estiva) connects the new bus station (Via Amaranto) with Sabbiadoro in 12 minutes.

A single ticket costs €1.35 and is valid for 60 minutes (four hours on Sunday). A daily ticket costs €4.60.

Taxi

Summer Taxi (☑ 345 262 64 64; www.taxilignano.com)

Taxi Service Lignano (☑ 335 658 61 82; www. taxiservicelignano.it)

THE LAGUNA DI GRADO & MARANO LAGUNARE

The 9000 hectares of clayey soil and brackish water situated between the mouth of the Tagliamento and the Canale Anfora make up the Grado and Marano lagoon, a particularly well-preserved natural environment. Aside from the *briccole* (wooden navigation poles) that guide boats through the canals, there are few signs of human intervention here; those that do exist blend seamlessly into the landscape as a result of careful conservation efforts.

The area is well known for its birdwatching and wild horses, with some of the old *casoni* (temporary fishermen's homes made of cane and wood) now handy refuges for those fishing for the perfect wildlife photograph. For food lovers, the area is the place to hunt down Grado's famous *boreto alla graisana,* a fish stew made with the day's catch.

In this silent, timeless landscape, the rhythm of daily life has always been determined by the tides (right down to its modern fishing tourism) and exploring the area by boat is essential to understanding its history and amphibious culture.

From here, tours lead to millenary towers, Byzantine mosaics and churches that seem to magically float on water.

❶ Getting There & Away

BOAT

TPL FVG (☑ 800 05 20 40, mobile 040 971 23 43; https://tplfvg.it/it/il-viaggio/servizi-marittimi) sails between Grado and Trieste (single/return €10.20/15.30; ⊙ Tue-Sun, from Trieste 8am, 1pm & 6pm mid-Jun-early Sep, 8am & 5.30pm Sep-early Oct, from Grado 9.40am, 2.30pm & 7.30pm mid-Jun-early Sep, 10am & 7.30pm Sep-early Oct). A twice-daily service (Tue-Sun) sails between Grado and Lignano (⊙ varies seasonally, see website). From Lignano, you can reach Marano (€3.55, 40 minutess, ⊙ from Lignano Sabbiadoro 10am, noon, 5pm & 7pm Jun-Sep, also 11.15pm Jul & Aug; from Marano 9am, 11am, 2pm & 6pm Jun-Sep, also 10.30pm Jul & Aug; bike €0.90 at captain's discretion).

Foci dello Stella To explore the area by boat, you'll need to join a tour in Marano Lagunare or Lignano (for more information contact the Lignano Sabbiadoro tourist office, p122).

Grado Moorings

Lega Navale Italiana (☑ 0431 817 06; www.lnigrado.it; Mandracchio & ex Riva Brioni 10)

Darsena Navigare 2000 (☑ 0431 801 83; www.hotelsanremogrado.it; Isola della Schiusa, Riva Garibaldi)

Darsena San Marco (☑ 0431 815 48; www.darsenasanmarco.it; Località Testata Mosconi 1)

Porto San Vito (☑ 0431 835 00; www.portosanvito.it; Riva Giovanni da Verrazzano 1)

Marina Primero (☑ 0431 89 68 80; www.marinaprimero.com, Via Monfalcone 16)

BUS

TPL FVG (☑ 800 05 20 40, mobile 040 971 23 43; https://tplfvg.it) buses connect the **bus station** in Grado (Piazza Carpaccio, between Porto Mandracchio and Isola della Schiusa) with Udine (buses 400, 401 and 402; €5, 75 minutes, roughly every hour) via Aquileia (€2.25, 12 minutes) and Palmanova (€3.50, 45 minutes).

Buses 461, 462 and 465 offer six services between Udine and Marano Lagunare between 6.15am and 6.30pm (€5; 70 to 90 minutes).

There are several options from Marano to Lignano (€6.05; 80 minutes), requiring a change in Latisana, San Giorgio di Nogaro or another town.

CAR & MOTORCYCLE

From Trieste or Udine Take the A4 from Trieste or the A23 from Udine to Palmanova. You'll reach Grado after Cervignano. Continue on towards Venice and then exit at Porpetto for Marano Lagunare.

TRAIN

The two closest train stations to Grado are Cervignano–Aquileia–Grado and Monfalcone. From either you'll need to continue on a TPL FVG bus route.

The handiest stations for Marano Lagunare are Latisana or San Giorgio di Nogaro, from where you'll need to continue by bus.

Marano Lagunare

POP 1737 / ELEV 2M

Marano is one of the least spoilt and fascinating places in the area, a secluded, quiet oasis in sharp contrast to nearby Lignano and Grado and their tourist hordes. The village is located just east of the mouth of the Stella River, and while it flanks the lagoon it doesn't directly overlook it. Directly opposite Marano are the string of islands that guard the lagoon (nominally Isola Marinetta and Isola di Sant'Andrea), making the town the perfect launching pad for boat tours.

Built a bit like Venice, at the heart of a small archipelago, Marano has always distinguished itself as a fishing centre and a garrison, a function that, in around 1000 CE, it carried out under the control of Aquileia. From 1453 it was occupied, then purchased, by the Venetians, whose legacy remains especially visible today. In the town and on the surrounding islets, you can still see the *cippi di conterminazione*, Istrian stone pillars that marked the beginning of territories under La Serenissima's control. In the heart of town, **Piazza dei Provveditori** claims the **Loggia Maranese**, a portico where public meetings were once held, and the 32m-high **Torre Millenaria**, likely used as a watchtower since at least 1066. At the tower's base are the busts of the Venetian administrators who clinched control of the town. Opposite it stands **Palazzo dei Provveditori** (Palace of the Administrators).

Up until the 19th century, Marano was completely surrounded by walls, no doubt an impressive sight for those sailing in from the lagoon. Today, only the **Bastione di Sant'Antonio** remains, though its charm is slightly obscured by the historic Maruzzella canned-tuna factory.

Just like the waters that flow through the lagoon's contorted channels, life in Marano flows quietly. At times, it can seem absent altogether. But then the fiery setting sun sets the sea alight and life stirs once more. White wine is poured and raw clams and grilled eels are served.

☞ Tours

Boat & Bike Tours

The same tour companies that depart from Lignano organise boat tours and fishing trips out of Marano. **Battello Santa Maria** (☑339 633 02 88; www.battellosantamaria.it; boarding in Piazza Cristoforo Colombo; tours €25-70) runs half-day tours of the Stella River, Aquileia and Grado, with the added option of a dinner cruise. Keep an eye on the program: summer tours often feature a small live orchestra. The company also operates the **Battello Pinta**, which runs a boat & bike tour on Mondays and Fridays. This tour sails up the Stella River, passing the historic *casoni* (traditional fishermen's huts), to Titiano. From here, you can cycle back to Marano through the woods. A third boat, *Nina*, is used for sailing trips.

For other mini cruises, contact the long-established **Nuova Saturno** (☑0431 678 91, 335 536 86 85; www.saturnodageremia.it; boarding in Piazza Cristoforo Colombo), which operates highly popular tours of the Stella River, traditional *casoni* and Isola delle Conchiglie, with onboard lunches and tastings, as well as visits to hidden lagoon wineries. **LadyE** (☑338 203 71 60; Riviera boarding 24 May) offers similar routes but aboard a smaller boat. Don't forget your sunscreen.

★ Festivals & Events

Processione di San Vito   JUNE

On 15 June (or the following Sunday), a long procession of boats take to the lagoon to ward off dangers faced by fishermen and to commemorate those lost at sea; a ritual dating back to the 14th century.

🛏 Sleeping

Hotel Stella d'Oro   HOTEL €€

(☑0431 670 18; www.stelladoro.info; Piazza Vittorio Emanuele II 11; d from €70; ❄ 🛜) Ideal for those wanting to slumber in the historic centre, a stone's throw from a canal that leads into the lagoon. While the woody, retro rooms might clash a little with the building's modern look, the place is nonetheless a very comfortable place to stay. The hotel restaurant is renowned in town.

JO Hotel   HOTEL €€€

(☑0431 64 02 59; www.johotel.it; Via Udine 7/9; s €55-60, d €80-90; ❄ ❄ 🛜) A well-equipped, three-star hotel offering good wi-fi, minibar, secure parking and an internal garden. Staff are helpful and a good source of tourist information.

🍴 Eating

Alla Nave   OSTERIA €

(☑0431 64 00 86; Marii Square 5; meals €20; ⊙7am-midnight Thu-Mon, to 7.30pm Tue) This convenient old *osteria* offers unbeatable atmosphere and authenticity, right down to the *ciacola* (chitchat) of the old regulars drinking at the bar. Settle in on the flower-fringed terrace on the square or among the slot machines inside and tuck into fresh, simple seafood: raw, lightly seared with salicornia or faithfully prepared using old local recipes. Prices are reasonable and reservations always a good idea (booking is a must on weekends).

Al Molo   OSTERIA € /€€

(☑0431 64 02 39; Riviera 24 May 1; meals €20-25) What was once a fishmonger is now a seafood *osteria*, serving up fresh surf cooked simply and deliciously (the fried options are especially good). Expect a super-casual vibe.

Barcaneta   TRATTORIA €€

(☑0481 674 10; www.trattoriabarcaneta.com; Marii Square 7; meals €30-35; ⊙noon-2pm & 7-11pm Mon, Tue & Thu-Sun) As is often the case in seaside villages, the best options here are based on the day's catch (usually presented as the day's specials). Expect unique, creative dishes, with exceptional *antipasti* and a very long list of desserts.

SEA & LAGOON MARANO LAGUNARE

DON'T MISS

WILDLIFE

At the western edge of Marano lies the wonderful, 121-hectare **Riserva Naturale della Valle Canal Novo** (☑0431 675 51; www.parks.it/riserva.valle.canal.novo/index.php; Via delle Valli 2; adult/reduced €3.50/2.50; ⊙9am-5pm Tue-Sun Oct-May, to 6pm Jun-Sep). While not the only wetland in the area, it's one in which you can truly immerse yourself in nature and get up close to the wildlife; the reserve's old *casoni* (traditional fishermen's huts) are especially handy for birdwatching and photography. At the entrance, a traditional *casone* (farmhouse) has been converted into a visitor centre (packed with information) and *osteria* serving surf and turf dishes.

Porta del Mar
TRATTORIA **€€**

(☑0431 64 00 60; Via Porto del Friuli 2; meals €30-32; ☺9am-3pm & 5-11.45pm Mon, Tue & Thu-Sun) A more relaxed alternative to Barcaneta, Porta del Mar offers the same quality in a more casual format. The refreshed dining room offers glimpses of the town's old walls. You'll find it directly opposite the old fish market.

Alla Laguna
OSTERIA **€€** /**€€€**

(☑0431 670 19; www.vedovaraddi.it; Piazza Garibaldi 1; meals €35-45; ☺noon-3pm & 7-9.45pm Tue-Sun, closed 3 weeks in Nov & Sun in winter) The quintessential old-school *osteria* (albeit renovated) in which to feast on grilled eel and fish *antipasti*. While it's not the only place in Marano specialising in fresh fish (served impeccably may we add), it trumps the competition for history and location, not to mention its air conditioning and acceptance of all credit cards.

 Drinking & Nightlife

620 Passi
BEER

(☑333 729 24 30; Via Synod, 8; ☺5pm-1.30am Tue, 10am-2pm & 5pm-1.30am Wed-Sat, 10am-11pm Sun) For those who don't live on fish and white wine alone, there's this beer bar. Not only does it pour excellent brews, it serves canapés and Trieste-style cooked ham. It's also good for a cocktail.

Riserva Naturale delle Foci dello Stella

Of the deltas that form the frayed edge of the northern Adriatic, that belonging to the Stella River is perhaps the least known and one that begs for exploration. It's an **area** (☑0431 675 51; www.parks.it/riserva.foci.stella;

L'ISOLA DELLE CONCHIGLIE

The **Isola di Martignano** is known as a sinuous piece of paradise, famed for its flora, fauna and expanse of sea shells (hence its nickname 'Island of the Sea Shells'). The island is in fact a lido, separating the Adriatic Sea from the Marano lagoon. Its beaches are sandy and shallow for several metres, while the strong wind that blows in from the mainland makes it a popular destination for kite surfers.

☺24hr) rich in birdlife and soul-stirring views, a place where river sediment stretches out into the lagoon like a low promontory on which water and light interact to mesmerising effect. Given its beauty and natural abundance, it's not surprising that the area is a nature reserve; one only accessible by boat. Numerous cruises depart from Lignano, Grado and, above all, Marano, sailing to the delta and then up the Stella to the river hamlets of Precenicco and Palazzolo. From Precenicco itself, Houseboat (www.houseboat.it/info/precenicco-2) operates cruises down the river and into the lagoon.

Not only is the Riserva Naturale delle Foci dello Stella a fantastic **birdwatching** spot (species include marsh harriers, mute swans and herons), it's also worth exploring for its lush natural landscapes, villages of *casoni* (traditional fishermen's huts) that face east for shelter from the bora and tramontana winds, and chats with local fishers.

For a truly unique experience, visit the **Bilancia di Bepi** (☑340 363 67 33; Location Fraida, Palazzolo dello Stella; excursions €25-30, family €69). It's run by Daniele, a young Friulian who inherited a farmhouse on the Stella from his grandfather and decided to open it to visitors. The house is connected to a *trabucco* – known locally as a *bilancia* (weighing scale) – a huge, motor-powered fishing net that is lowered into the water to catch fish. You'll often see it in action and you're also welcome to enjoy the catch. Daniele also organises enjoyable cruises of the lagoon and Isola delle Conchiglie, and rents out kayaks too. In the farmhouse kitchen, note the autographed photograph of Ernest Hemingway; Daniele's grandfather was a friend of the famous wordsmith.

Grado

POP 7971 / ELEV 2M

Venice today seems an urban anomaly, an outlandish, one-off experiment. But there was a time when many settlements along the upper Adriatic followed a similar template. Grado is one example. Like Venice, the island was permanently settled by hinterland refugees pushed into the marshes by the barbarian invasions of the 5th and 6th centuries. And like La Serenissima, its brightly coloured abodes breathe life into a monochromatic lagoon landscape (especially in winter).

Nicknamed L'Isola del Sole (The Island of the Sun), Grado was a favourite destination of the Austrian bourgeoisie between the 19th and 20th centuries. At the time, the town was busy reinventing itself as the 'Portofino of the Upper Adriatic'. However, the history of this place goes much deeper. In 568, the patriarchal seat, previously in Aquileia, was moved right here. This was followed by the construction of the important basilicas of Sant'Eufemia and Santa Maria delle Grazie. When Aquileia regained its political and religious importance (as well as its patriarch), Grado tightened its relationship with Venice.

Alas, as Venice's own power and prestige grew, Grado's own splendour diminished, the city raided by the Franks, Saracens and the patriarchs of Aquileia. The patriarchs of Grado themselves were increasingly chosen from among Venetian patricians, until, in 1451, the patriarchate was moved to Venice altogether.

From that moment, the island returned to its humble fishing roots, fighting for its survival. After the Treaty of Campo Formio, Grado followed the fate of the rest of Friuli and in 1918, when it was united with Italy, it had already metamorphosed from a fishing village to a seaside resort.

In 1936, the island was connected to the mainland by a bridge, over which thousands of tourists head to savour Grado's timeless atmosphere, beautiful beaches, celebrated dishes and many outdoor activities.

◉ Sights

Basilica di Santa Eufemia   PLACE OF WORSHIP
(☑ 0431 801 46; Campo Patriarca Elia; ⊘ 8am-7pm)
Simply follow Grado's omnipresent bell tower to reach the brick-and-sandstone Basilica of Sant'Eufemia, built on the site of the 4th-century *basilichetta* (little basilica) of Petrus. The current church has a tripartite facade marked by two portals and three windows. Inside, three naves are supported by 10 columns on each side. The columns were upcycled from older buildings, evident in the mismatching capitals. Dating from the late 6th century, the spectacular **floor mosaic** will leave you speechless, especially if you haven't yet been to Aquileia (home to an even larger one, p132). This one covers an area of 700 sq m, its symphony of Latin text, biblical scenes, floral motifs and geometric patterns partly obscured by the church pews.

Other notable features include the hexagonal stone **ambo**, crafted in the 13th century and supported by six columns adorned with foliated capitals. Like the floor mosaic, the dome is also influenced by the Byzantine style. Reliefs, frescoes and sculptures are scattered through the interior, on the pillars of the pulpit, in the apse and in the left aisle, where you'll find the venerated Madonna degli Angeli (linked to Perdòn de Barbana, p130). In the right aisle is the **mausoleum**, which reveals traces of the earlier church. Here, look for the monogram of Elia (Helias Episcupvs), the patriarch who consecrated the church in 579. The door on the far right leads to the **Museo Lapidario**, which houses local artefacts from various eras.

To the left side of the basilica lies the octagonal **baptistery**. Dating from the 5th century, it's home to a marble baptismal font. The basilica's 42m-tall **bell tower** hails from the 15th century: the weathervane statue of St Michael crowning it is a symbol of the city.

Chiesa di Santa Maria delle Grazie   PLACE OF WORSHIP
(☑ 0431 801 46; Campo dei Patriarchi; ⊘ 8am-7pm)
The somewhat modest dimensions of this basilica belie its importance. Here since 401, it preserves precious mosaics: note the depiction of a fish, an ancient symbolic representation of Christ that is the only example of its kind in Grado.

Piazza Biagio Marin   PIAZZA
This piazza harbours the remains of a third basilica, the 4th-century **Basilica della Corte**. Purpose-built walkways traverse the ruins, which are evocatively lit up at night. The square once housed the Roman *castrum* (fort).

Lungomare Nazario Sauro   ESPLANADE
Grado's seaside promenade runs along a breakwater built by the Austrians in 1885 to protect against storm surges. Its relaxed atmosphere and panorama – especially beautiful on clear days – makes it a popular spot for a *passeggiata* (stroll).

Porto Mandracchio   PORT
Commissioned by the Austrians in the 19th century, the Mandracchio was subsequently transformed into a larger port in the shape of an inverted Y.

It's one of the most atmospheric corners of the city: in the morning, dozens of fishermen arrange their nets on its banks, seagulls chasing the fishing boats out and back into the harbour. Come afternoon, the same nets dry lazily in the sun.

Grado

0   1000 m
0   0.5 miles

N

Laguna di Grado

Mare Adriatico

SP19

Via Ascoli
Viale del Turismo
Via Italia
Viale Kennedy
Via del Sole
Via Vespucci
Viale dei Morieri
Riva Ugo Foscolo
Via G. Galilei

Riva Grandi Navigatori
Riva Garibaldi
Via Arte
Riva Sant'Andrea
Riva Slataper
Via Carducci
Via Alighieri
Viale Regina Elena

Riva Gregori
Via Grego
Via Roma

Viale Europa Unita

SR352

Via Trieste
Via Sant'Agata
Via Ariosto
Via Lugnan
Via Flume
Via Marchesini
Via Aquileia
Via Pola
Via Pisa
Via Milano

Grado

◉ Sights

1	Basilica di Santa Eufemia	C3
2	Chiesa di Santa Maria delle Grazie	C3
3	Lungomare Nazario Sauro	C4
	Parco delle Rose	(see 9)
4	Piazza Biagio Marin	C3
5	Porto Mandracchio	C3

🏖 Beaches

6	Lido di Fido	F3
7	Spiaggia Costa Azzurra	A2
8	Spiaggia Grado Pineta	off map G2
9	Spiaggia Principale GIT	D3
	Terme Marine & Parco Acquatico	(see 9)

☉ Activities, Courses & Tours

	ASD Fairplay	(see 7)
10	Mauro Bike	C3
11	Motoscafisti Gradesi	C3
12	Società Canottieri Ausonia	B2
13	TaxiBoat	C3

🛏 Sleeping

14	Grand Hotel Astoria	C3
15	Hotel alla Città di Trieste	C3
16	Hotel Hannover	C3
17	Isola del Paradiso	off map C1
18	Tenuta Primero	off map G2

✖ Eating

19	Ai Ciodi	off map A1
20	Al Canton de la Bira	B3
21	Al Pontil de' Tripoli	D2
22	All'Androna	C3
23	Da Ovidio	C3
24	Laura e Christian	C3
25	Mandracchio	B3
26	Ostaria De Mar	C3
27	Zero Miglia	C2

⊜ Shopping

28	L'Anzolo	C3
29	La Brocca Rotta	C3
30	Market	B3

SEA & LAGOON GRADO

Beaches

There are three beaches in Grado: (from west to east) Spiaggia Costa Azzurra, Spiaggia Principale GIT and Spiaggia di Grado Pineta. The latter is furthest from the town and frequented mainly by kite surfers.

The sweeping expanse of sand that makes up **Spiaggia Principale GIT** (Grado Impianti Turistici; ☑ 0431 89 91 11; www.gradeit.it; Viale Dante 72; admission €3, with sun lounge €6-9) enjoys direct sunlight all day. It also has a plethora of bathroom facilities. Heading east along here, you'll reach the string of facilities managed by Grado Impianti Turistici: treat yourself to a spa treatment in the hot sand therapy zone or, if you insist on a full tan, opt for the gender-segregated **Solarium** (☑ 0431 89 92 20; ☺ 9.30am-6pm May-Sep).

The **Terme Marine (Marine Baths)** (☑ reservations 0431 89 93 09; ☺ Apr-Nov, see www.gradeit.it for details) include an indoor hydrotherapy pool and the type of spa treatments that made Grado famous during Austrian rule.

Just beyond the thermal baths is the **Parco Acquatico** (☑ 0431 89 93 50; adult/child €15-19/10-12, afternoon €10-13/7-8; ☺ 10am-7pm), a water park with a curvaceous, 85m seawater pool equipped with spa jets, swim current facilities for those who like to swim against the tide, and waterslides and diving boards.

Beyond it lies **Lido di Fido** (☑ 0431 89 92 20; umbrella & beach equipment for 2 & dog bed from €25), a fully equipped beach for dogs and their human sun seekers.

Spiaggia Grado Pineta is Grado's eastern-most beach and one loved by kite surfers, who flock to Grado to ride their boards. The beach includes bathing establishments and a dog-friendly section aptly named **Spiaggia di Snoopy** (Snoopy Beach; www.spiaggiaairone.it).

The least developed and furthest beach from the centre is **Spiaggia Coasta Azzurra**, known locally as *spiaggia vecja*. It's largely a free beach, making it a very popular spot. The water is deeper and the beach includes a number of kiosks. **ASD Fairplay** (☑ 346 366 78 66; http://asdfairplay.it/it/grado.html, info@asd-fairplay.it) rents out canoes and SUP (stand-up paddle boards), has personal trainers, and runs beach soccer, tennis and volleyball tournaments.

🏃 Activities

Grado's many bike paths make it easy to pedal between beaches. **Mauro Bike** (☑ 324 600 92 63; www.maurobike.com; Riva Scaramuzza 8/a; ☺ 8am-12.30pm & 2.30-7pm Mon-Sat, 8am-12.30pm Sun) rents bicycles.

BIAGIO MARIN: THE POET OF GRADO

Grado's main piazza is dedicated to the town's lauded poet Biagio Marin (1891–1985), much loved throughout Friuli Venezia Giulia. The region's lagoon, light and seafaring ways echo in his highly vernacular compositions, written mainly in dialect. Among the few works written in Italian is *Acquamarina*, released in 1973. Marin spent time living in various countries, amassing a large volume of work and winning a number of important literary prizes, among them the Bagutta and the Viareggio. In 1981, Marin was nominated for the Nobel Prize in Literature. Despite his fame, he remained indelibly tied to his beloved Grado. In 1925, while director of the tourist office, he promoted the opening of the tranquil **Parco delle Rose** (Map p128), a 30-sq-metre park close to the beach.

🚣 Courses

Società Canottieri Ausonia   ROWING
(☑ 0431 803 05; Molo Torpediniere 4) Rowing courses and equipment rental.

👉 Tours

Motoscafisti Gradesi   ISOLA DI BARBANA
(☑ 0431 801 15; www.motoscafistigradesi.it; Riva Scaramuzza, Isola della Schiusa) With its fleet of four motorboats, Motoscafisti Gradesi can zip you across to the island of Barbana for a short 30-minute tour or to other lagoon destinations.

TaxiBoat   SURROUNDS
(☑ 334 727 52 54; www.taxiboat-grado.com; Riva San Vito; per person €10-20) Family-run business specialising in trips from Grado to the island of Barbana, to the islands occupied by the *albergo diffuso* Porto Buso, as well as to the hugely popular Isola di Anfora. Very convenient if you're staying near the Mandracchio.

⭐ Festivals & Events

Perdòn de Barbana   JULY
One of Grado's historical traditions, this long procession of boats sees a statue of the Madonna transported to the Isola di Barbana as a *grazie* for delivering the town from the plague in 1237. A spectacular, moving event.

🛌 Sleeping

★ Isola del Paradiso   CAMPING €
(☑ 0431 820 61; https://isoladelparadiso.com/it; Isola Volpera; basic/serviced pitch €4.50/15, bungalow €100; P ⊗ ⓡ ⓣ ⚡ 🎾) This campsite's strength is its extraordinary setting, on an island accessible by car, halfway between Grado and Aquileia, in the middle of the lagoon. The camping facilities are limited and the whole place is quite rudimentary, but you will find a beach and swimming pool.

★ Hotel Hannover   HOTEL €€
(☑ 0431 822 64; www.hotelhannover.com; Piazza 26 Maggio 10; d with breakfast from €90; P ⊛ ⓡ) An elegant hotel with a narrow facade that makes it look like it's stuck between buildings. In reality, the rooms are huge and bright, with windows that look out at the marina. There's also an onsite restaurant and sophisticated bar with a terrace overlooking the street.

Parking is available but must be booked in advance (€18 per day).

Hotel alla Città di Trieste   HOTEL €€
(☑ 0431 835 71; www.hotelcittaditrieste.it; Piazza 26 Maggio; s/d €80/110; P ⊛ ⓡ) Wake to the sight of fishing boats returning to harbour at this hotel, which overlooks the Mandracchio. Centrally located, its rooms offer restrained style and a standard befitting of its three-star category.

Ask the concierge for a list of restaurants that have deals for hotel guests.

Tenuta Primero   RESORT €€€
(☑ 0431 89 69 00; www.tenutaprimero.com; Via Monfalcone 14; bungalow €210; P ⚡ ⓡ 🎾 ⚡) Luxury within reach of nature: this resort has endless services and the price includes the use of the swimming pool and various sports fields, sun beds on the beach, yoga and pilates classes as well as bike rental. It is also connected to the Grado Golf Club.

★ Grand Hotel Astoria   HOTEL €€€
(☑ 0431 835 50; www.hotelastoria.it; Largo San Grisogono 3; d €169-240; P ⊛ ⓡ ⚡ 🎾) While Grado isn't short of large hotels, the wonderfully hospitable Astoria tops the list. The property includes 126 superb rooms, excellent facilities and secure parking. The proverbial cherry, however, is its top-floor poolside restaurant, the highest in Grado. Feast your eyes.

🍴 Eating & Drinking

While there's no shortage of local seafood specialities, classics like *boreto* (local fish stew) or *bisato in spéo* (roasted eel) have helped make Grado a standout culinary destination in the region. Reservations are essential in summer and on weekends.

Ostaria De Mar
WINE BAR €

(☎ 0431 856 10; Piazza XXVI Maggio 4; wines by the glass €3-6, fish sandwiches €10; ⏱ 8am-10pm Tue-Sun in winter, 8am-midnight daily in summer, closed 3 weeks Nov) With the chug of fishing boats in the background, Ostaria De Mar's outdoor tables are a fine spot to quaff a *vino* while nibbling on a fish sandwich or plate of anchovies, or to sip an aperitif while deciding on where to dine. Post-dinner, head back for a well-mixed cocktail.

Laura e Christian
PASTA € /€€

(☎ 0431 826 87; www.ristorantelauraechristian. it; Via Gradenigo 27; meals €20-25; ⏱ noon-10pm Mon & Wed-Sun; d/q €95/130; ❄ 🐕) You know the feeling: sun-kissed and salty skinned, you wrap up another long, 'exhausting' day at the beach and are suddenly overcome by an intense, primal craving for spaghetti with seafood. When it hits, satiate your craving here. There's a hotel onsite too; handy for any carb-induced coma.

Da Ovidio
RESTAURANT €€

(☎ 0431 804 40; www.ristorantedaovidio.com; Via Marina 36; meals €25-30; ⏱ noon-2pm & 6.30-10pm Mon & Wed-Sun, 6.30-10pm Tue) You'll find the greatest hits of Grado's seafood repertoire (and a few unexpected extras) here, prepared and served with attention to detail. The princely *antipasto misto* (mixed *antipasto*) is exceptional.

Al Pontil de' Tripoli
SEAFOOD €€

(☎ 0431 802 85; www.alpontildetripoli.it; Riva Garibaldi 17, Isola della Schiusa; meals €30; ⏱ 7-10pm Apr-Sep) Secluded from the clamour of the city centre and overlooking the lagoon and its poignant sunsets, this dinner-only restaurant could be the trump card on a romantic evening. Bond over silky *pesce crudo* (raw fish), conversation-friendly finger foods or perhaps a first-course eaten directly (and lustfully) from the pan.

⭐ Zero Miglia
SEAFOOD €€

(Fishermen's Cooperative; ☎ 0431 802 87; www.zero miglia.it; Riva Dandolo 22; meals €30-40; ⏱ noon-2pm & 6-9pm Mon & Wed-Sun) Zero Miglia is a simple, straightforward affair, run by the local Fishermen's Cooperative. Overlooking Grado's fishing fleet, it serves impossibly fresh seafood: try the *crudo* (raw fish) to quench any doubt.

The cuttlefish, mussels, sea bass, amberjack and mullet are equally impressive, cooked just the way any expert local *nonna* (grandmother) would.

⭐ Ai Ciodi
RESTAURANT €€

(☎ 335 752 22 09; www.portobusoaiciodi.it; Isola di Anfora; meals €30-40; ⏱ kitchen 11.30am-4pm) First thing to do is call ahead and book. Next, contact the TaxiBoat and set sail for the Isola di Anfora. Once there, soak up the timeless atmosphere of the lagoon, perched on a wooden bench, feasting on freshly fried seafood, grilled eel and crisp white wine.

Mandracchio
BISTRO €€

(☎ 333 117 65 21; Piazza Marinai d'Italia 10; meals €30-40; ⏱ 11am-2.30pm & 5.30-10.30pm Mon, Tue & Thu-Sun) Although a tad expensive, Mandracchio nails it on many fronts: spaciousness, friendly vibe and, most importantly, quality (which exceeds most expectations). And while facing stiff competition in this town, its *boreto* (local fish stew) is utterly delicious. The marina views are free.

All'Androna
TAVERN €€

(☎ 0431 809 50; www.androna.it; Calle Porta Piccola 4; meals €40; ⏱ 6-11pm Mon-Fri, noon-3pm & 6-11pm Sat & Sun) Although fans of authentic trattorias may turn up their noses at the polished mise-en-scène, it's worth giving All'Androna a chance. Firstly, there's the atmospheric location on a hidden street. Then there's the cooking: refined and creative, but never too detached from tradition. Bistro-only service at lunch.

Al Canton de la Bira
BEER

(☎ 335 815 55 55; Via Duca d'Aosta 1; ⏱ 10am-midnight Thu-Tue, also 5pm-midnight Wed Jun-Aug) Punters head here for the beers (which have their fair share of admirers).

But if you need to line your stomach, you'll also find tasty sandwiches and decent fried calamari.

🛍 Shopping

L'Anzolo
CRAFTS

(☎ 0431 87 62 21; Via Caprin 52; ⏱ 10am-7pm Mon-Fri) Handmade mosaics, ceramics, majolica, paintings and cups inspired by the colours and Zen-like tranquility of the landscape.

SEA & LAGOON GRADO

La Brocca Rotta
BRIC-A-BRAC

(☑389 182 24 07; Campo Porta Nuova 19; ⊙10am-1pm & 4-7pm Mon-Fri, 10am-midnight Sat & Sun in summer, 10am-6pm Sat & Sun in winter) A shop and cafe in one, where you can browse the shelves and trunks.

Market
GROCERIES

(Piazza Duca d'Aosta 30; ⊙7am-1pm & 4.30-8pm) Grado's 'Restaurant Row' also claims this well-stocked undercover market, ideal for both self-caters and those wanting to take home some local delicacies. Fill the larder with Friulian specialties, organic produce and local wines.

❶ Information

INTERNET ACCESS
Free wi-fi is readily available in Grado, especially on the beaches.

MEDICAL SERVICES
Ospedale S. Polo di Monfalcone (☑0481 48 71 11; Via Luigi Galvani 1, Monfalcone)
Tourist Medical Service (☑0431 87 81 54)

POST
Post Office (☑0431 89 65 11; Via Caprin 23; ⊙8.20am-1.35pm Mon-Fri, to 12.35pm Sat)

TOURIST INFORMATION
Grado Infopoint (Map p128, C3; ☑0431 87 71 11, 335 770 56 65; cnr Piazza XXVI Maggio & Campo Porta Nuova 26; ⊙varies seasonally) Sells the FVG Card. For current tourist office opening times call or email info.grado@promoturismo.fvg.it.

❶ Getting Around

TO/FROM THE AIRPORT
The closest airport to Grado is Ronchi dei Legionari (www.triesteairport.it).

CYCLING
Cycling paths abound in Grado, allowing you to explore the entire area around the city. Bikes are permitted on ferries; consider booking a boat-and-bike sightseeing tour (p125).

PUBLIC TRANSPORT
Bus
TPL FVG (☑800 05 20 40, mobile 040 971 23 43; https://tplfvg.it) Given Grado's compact size, chances are you won't be needing public transport. One exception is Grado Pineta, reachable on bus 37. A single ticket costs €1.35 and is valid for 60 minutes (four hours on Sundays). A day ticket is €4.60. Tickets are free for FVG Card holders. For routes and timetables, see the website or download the TPL FVG app.

Taxi
TaxiBoat (☑334 727 52 54, 339 532 90 64; www.taxiboat-grado.com; Riva San Vito 5)

AQUILEIA & SURROUNDS

You merely need to glance at a map to realise the flat, marshy land between the A4 motorway and the sea is where the Romans chose to found their colonies and cities. Note the straight road (ruler-straight between the coast and Cervignano del Friuli), an ancient route which runs from Grado and Udine to Aquileia, one of the most important cities of its time and one of Friuli Venezia Giulia's most important historic and artistic destinations.

❶ Getting There & Away

BUS
TPL FVG (☑800 05 20 40, mobile 040 971 23 43; https://tplfvg.it) Aquileia is located on the Udine–Grado route: catch bus 400, 401 or 402 (€5.05, 50 minutes from Udine; €2.25, 10 minutes from Grado). Buses pass through Palmanova and Strassoldo (€4.35, 50 minutes from Udine; €3.50, 10 minutes from Grado).

CAR & MOTORCYLE
Having your own vehicle is arguably the best way to move around this area. From the A23 (from Udine) or A4 (from Trieste), take the Palmanova exit and follow the signs for Aquileia. Torviscosa is located on the SS14 halfway between the regional border and Monfalcone. To reach the Riserva Naturale della Foce dell'Isonzo e Valle Cavanata, follow the signs for Redipuglia, then those for the *riserva* (very well signposted).

TRAIN
Trenitalia (www.trenitalia.com) services run frequently from Udine (30 minutes; €3.50) to Cervignano del Friuli (Cervignano-Aquileia-Grado station), from where a bus service runs to other towns.

Aquileia
POP 3199 / ELEV 49M

Aquileia may now be a modest town of 3000 or so, but a millennium ago, it enjoyed the status afforded to London and Paris today. Between late-antiquity and the early Middle Ages, Aquileia was one of the most important spiritual and political centres on the Italian peninsula, a fact echoed in its imposing Basilica di Santa Maria Assunta. While it may appear out-of-scale set against the modern town and plain, the basilica's grandeur was befitting of a centre of global renown. By the 6th century, a then 700-year-old Aquileia even rivalled Rome and Byzantium for religious importance.

You can explore beautiful 3D reconstructions of Roman Aquileia at www.fonda zioneaquileia.it, an excellent prelude to any real-life visit. Waiting for you on the ground is an expansive archaeological area that will lead you back to the days of the Roman Empire, the Sack of Aquileia, the invasion of the Lombards and the formative years of the Western Church. All of Aquileia's attractions can be visited with the FVG Card Aquileia, a combination ticket (€15) available for purchase at the Infopoint (p136).

History

The Roman colony of Aquileia was founded in 181 BCE to defend the border from the threat posed by the Barbarians to the east. From its inception, the city was the base for military campaigns against the Histri and Carni that inhabited the Friuli. It became a *municipium* after 89 BCE, which allowed its inhabitants to acquire Roman citizenship. Aquileia soon became an important administrative, political and commercial centre, as well as the capital of X Regio, the 10th region of Imperial Rome.

In the first centuries of the Common Era, the city was a strategic centre for the spread of Christianity in Italy's northeast. In 300 CE, during the rule of Maximian, it became one of the capitals of the Roman Empire, ushering in the construction of grand public and private buildings. During the 4th century, the diocese of Aquileia acquired ever greater importance in the Christian world, controlling a vast region that included suffragan dioceses (such as Iulium Carnicum, today's Zuglio) dependent on the archbishop and extending beyond Italy's modern borders.

Aquileia managed to fight off attacks by Alaric and the Visigoths in 401 and 408; it took Attila to give it the *coup de grâce,* on 18 July 452, or so the story goes. Subsequent archaeological discoveries, including recent ones, indicate that 5th-century Aquileia was anything but ransacked and defeated.

In the 6th century, after the Schism of the Three Chapters in which the archbishops of Milan and Aquileia broke away from the official lines dictated by the Roman Empire, the Church of Aquileia declared its autonomy from Rome and Byzantium and promoted itself to the status of patriarchate. However, in 606, the patriarchate split in two and a patriarch independent from that of Aquileia was installed in Grado. While the Aquileian patriarch now supported Rome, his Grado rival backed the tricapitoline theses. This ideological split corresponded to the political one: the area around Aquileia was under Lombard control while the one around Grado was under Byzantine control. In the 8th century, Cividale was chosen as the new strategic seat of the patriarchate before finally returning to Aquileia in the 11th century. This move was orchestrated by patriarch Poppo of Treffen, who helped revive the once powerful city. It was during this period that the Basilica of Santa Maria Assunta underwent a major renovation, which included construction of the bell tower.

The patriarchs' power came to an end in 1420 with the Venetian dominion of Friuli. From 1509, Aquileia became part of the Holy Roman Empire. After the Treaty of Campo Formio, it became part of the Habsburg coast. The town's Italian history begins only after WWI, when Aquileia was annexed to the Kingdom of Italy.

◉ Sights

★ Basilica di Santa Maria Assunta

PLACE OF WORSHIP

(☏ 0431 910 67; www.basilicadiaquileia.it; Piazza Capitolo 1; adult/reduced Basilica & Cripta degli Affreschi €3/2.50, with Cripta degli Affreschi & Cripta degli Scavi €5/4, all sites €10/7.50, free with FVG Card & FVG Card Aquileia; ⊙ 10am-6pm Mon-Sat, noon-6pm Sun Mar & Oct, 10am-7pm Mon-Fri, 10am-6pm Sat & noon-7pm Sun Apr-Sep, 10am-4pm Mon-Fri Nov-Feb) Founded during the time of the first edicts and councils, Aquileia's basilica is one of the most important churches of the medieval period. It was in 313, the year of the Edict of Milan, that Bishop Theodore of Aquileia decided to build a place for worship consisting of two halls (one of which stood on the site of the current basilica). Indeed, the basilica you see today is a fusion of centuries of nips, tucks and extensions, from the Romanesque to the Gothic to the Renaissance. In the 4th century, this corner of the city was a commercial district, with some of its warehouses incorporated into the original church. Centuries earlier, it was the site of a stately Augustan villa, whose mosaics are visible in the Cripta degli Scavi.

The current building is the result of major alterations and restoration commissioned by

SEA & LAGOON AQUILEIA

patriarch Poppo of Treffan in 1031, works that spanned many years and included construction of the 73m-tall bell tower, reconstruction of the capitals and the addition of the apse frescoes. In the nave, Romanesque arches were replaced with Gothic ones in the 14th century, while the Renaissance saw the addition of a main altar in the apse, marble panels in the Cripta degli Affreschi, and the stairs.

Dedicated to Our Lady of the Assumption and the saints Hermagoras and Fortunatos, the basilica is accessed from the entrance on its southern side. Step inside and (discreetly) gasp at the 4th-century floor mosaic, which, at 750 sq metres, is the largest and oldest in the Western world. Dating back to the original Theodorian basilica, the mosaic's panels represent various scenes. While the symbolism behind panels like the *Fight of the Rooster and the Turtle* is ambiguous, others are clearer, depicting wealthy Roman patrons and biblical scenes such as the *Stories of the Prophet Jonah*. At the end of the right aisle you can admire the frescoed chapels of St Ambrose and St Peter. Behind the altar, don't miss the 12th-century **Cripta degli Affreschi**, where frescoes depict the trials and tribulations of the saints Hermagoras and Fortunatos. The left transept houses sarcophagi, bas-reliefs and frescoes. Beyond the left nave, close to the basilica's entrance, the **Cripta degli Scavi** (adult/reduced €5/4 with Südhalle, Domus & Palazzo Episcopale) harbours the oldest and least decipherable of the mosaics. The fantastical animals and plants depicted in the northernmost section of the work are the least tied to traditional Christian iconography. Instead, they reveal the cultural ties the ancient city enjoyed with the East, in particular with Alexandria in Egypt. At the beginning of the left aisle you'll pass the 11th-century Holy Sepulchre, a replica of the original in Jerusalem.

The 11th-century **Chiesa dei Pagani** and 4th-century **baptistery** (adult/reduced €5/4 with Basilica and Südhalle, free with FVG Card & FVG Card Aquileia; ⊙ same as the basilica) are connected to the church via a portico. The octagonal baptistery is particularly interesting. From it, one had access to two rooms, one to the north and the other to the south. The latter, the Aula Cromaziana, is better known as **Südhalle** as it was discovered in 1893 by Austrian archaeologists. Both rooms were decorated with floor mosaics laid between the late 4th and early 5th centuries; a large section remains visible in the Südhalle. You'll find another mosaic inside the basilica's **campani-**

le (adult/reduced €2/1; ⊙ 10.30am-1.30pm & 2.30-6.30pm daily Apr-Sep, 10am-5pm Sat & Sun Oct), which offers a bird's-eye view of the basilica. (Note that the campanile was closed temporarily on our last visit.)

Domus & Palazzo Episcopale   RUINS
(Piazza Capitolo; www.fondazioneaquileia.it; adult/reduced €2/1, with Aula Cromaziana & Baptistery €5/4; ⊙ 10am-6pm Mon-Sat, from noon Sun Mar & Oct, 10am-7pm Mon-Sat, from noon Sun Apr-Sep, 10am-4pm Mon-Fri Nov-Feb) You can literally see the layers of history at this fascinating archaeological site, the most recent to open to the public. Overlapping floors reveal ruins from different eras, built one on top of the other over the centuries. Eye up the ruins of a 1st-century BCE city block (built outside the city walls), a dwelling from the 1st to 2nd century CE, a 4th-century apsidal hall, and extensive mosaics and walls belonging to the 5th-century bishop's palace.

Mercati Tardo Antichi   RUINS
(⎙ 0431 91 76 19; entrance from Via dei Patriarchi; ⊙ 9am-4pm Nov-Mar, to 6pm Apr & May, to 7pm Jun-Sep, 8.30am-6pm Oct) **FREE** To the south of the basilica lies a vast archaeological area. While not as striking as the others, it is of great historical importance and one that is still being excavated today. In 2020, a third square was unearthed on the site, testifying to the existence of a system of late-Roman squares (4th and 5th centuries) in the area now called Fondo Pasqualis. It's believed that there may be a fourth square yet to be unearthed. The entire district served as an interchange between the inland and coastal roads, evident in the circular embankments to the south that supported the defensive wall.

The three market squares have different configurations, suggesting that each specialised in a particular category of goods. Together, they constituted a sort of 'shopping centre' that was the soul of what appears to have been a flourishing, powerful city (a Byzantine gold coin unearthed here attests to this theory). It's an especially interesting proposition given that the era has traditionally been associated with serious decline.

★ Museo Archeologico Nazional   MUSEUM
(⎙ 0431 910 16, 0431 910 35; www.museoarcheologicoaquileia.beniculturali.it; Via Roma 1; adult/reduced €7/2, free with FVG Card & FVG Card Aquileia; ⊙ 10am-7pm Tue-Sun, last entry 6pm) Together with the basilica, this archaeological mu-

seum is an unmissable pitstop in Aquileia. Its collection consists solely of local archaeological finds, painting a vivid picture of the city's glorious past. The horde includes sculptures, coins, engraved gems, glass and amber objects. The courtyard houses the lapidary and its booty of epigraphs, stelae and mosaics (some truly impressive). The museum's nautical section houses the remains of a Roman boat found near Monfalcone.

Grande Mausoleo Candia   MAUSOLEUM

(Via Giulia Augusta) What you see today is a reconstruction from 1956. Nonetheless, this monumental tomb is an arresting sight. The urns were stored in the central block, upon which stands a columned shrine crowned with a conical roof and topped with a sculpted pine cone (a funerary symbol). Designed for an important magistrate of the Augustan age, the monument is guarded by two stone lions. A little further along Via Giulia Augusta lies a section of the Decumanus Major, the east–west road that sliced through the ancient city. The thoroughfare is dedicated to Aratria Gallia, an affluent Aquileian who financed its restoration in the 2nd century.

Forum & Roman Basilica   RUINS

(Via Giulia Augusta, intersection with Via Gemina) Although what remains of the Roman forum is hardly monumental, it makes for a satisfying sight. (This may, in part, be due to having already caught a glimpse while travelling along the state road.) The forum developed at the intersection of the *cardo* (Via Iulia Augusta) and *decumano*; reconstructed in 1939, the site include a series of columns that once supported the portico, relics of the beautiful flooring, and the remains of a Roman basilica.

Sepolcreto   RUINS

(☑0431 91 76 19; Via 24 Maggio; ☉9am-4pm Nov-Mar, to 6pm Apr & May, to 7pm Jun-Sep, 8.30am-6pm Oct) **FREE** In Roman times, Aquileia was a large city and its cemetery was decidedly larger than the portion you see today. Despite this, the five burial enclosures that flank what was once a secondary road leading out of the city are of great historical and artistic importance. The plots belonged to five wealthy Aquileian families: (in order) Stazia, an anonymous family, Giulia, Trebia and Cestia. Monuments and tombs adorn the plots, the earliest dating from the 1st century CE. The fourth plot was used until the 4th or 5th century, as indicated by the late-antiquity

style of its sarcophagi. Some of these are set on supports to show the elevation at which they were found.

Porto Fluviale Romano   RUINS

(Via Sacra) In Roman times, a mighty river crossed through the eastern part of Aquileia, where the city's *porto fluviale* (river port) pulsated with trade and travellers. Ruins of the ancient port – dating from the 2nd century BCE – survive, including the pier and quay where boats once moored. The river itself was diverted in the 4th century, with only a stream flowing through the area today. It makes for an intriguing sight, especially when considering the 50m-wide behemoth that flowed through here some 2000 years ago.

Domus di Tito Macro   RUINS

(☑0431 91 76 19; by prebooked guided tour only) **FREE** Set between two *decumani* (east–west Roman streets) south of the city and measuring 1700 sq metres, this is one of the largest Roman-era residences found in northern Italy. If you've already been to the Museo Archeologico Nazionale, you'll be interested to know that the famous mosaics depicting the Rape of Europa, vine branches tied with a bow and an 'unswept floor' hail from this very site. The villa was inhabited continuously from the 1st century BCE to the 6th century CE and its name refers to its wealthy Aquileian owner Tito Macro, whose initials (T. MACR) were found inscribed on an unearthed stone weight.

The first atrium-style Roman dwelling found in Aquileia, Domus di Tito Macro was an ambitious building. The modern roof and shutters that enclose the ruins today help to articulate both its vastness and the series of indoor and outdoor spaces that constituted its design. The site's strength are the floor mosaics, some featuring abstract patterns evoking Persian rugs, others depicting more figurative scenes. Beautiful mosaics grace the *tablinum* (the landlord's reception room), while the rear part of the house overlooked an alfresco courtyard.

Museo Paleocristiano   MUSEUM

(☑0431 910 35; Piazza Pirano 1; ☉8.30am-1.30pm Tue-Thu & Sat, 2.30-7.30pm Fri) **FREE** Until 1961 it was the late antique and early Christian section of the National Archaeological Museum, but now it is a museum in itself, very important for learning about the history and development of Christianity on this site. The exhibition consists mostly of early Christian mosaics and funerary inscriptions and is located inside a beautiful agricultural building built on the remains of a basilica from the first centuries of Christianity.

🛏 Sleeping & Eating

Camping Aquileia
CAMPING €

(☑ 328 331 00 65; www.campingaquileia.it; Via Gemina 10; adult/3-11yr €8.50/6, standard pitch €12, bungalows from €63; P 🛜 🖳 🕸) A friendly campsite with good facilities, including a swimming pool, restaurant and market. Look westward and you'll notice a row of cypress trees between which you'll catch a glimpse of the Roman-era river port.

Ostello Domus Augusta
HOSTEL €

(☑ 0431 910 24, reservations 331 104 13 17; www.ostelloaquileia.it; Via Roma 25; s/d/tr €28/46/64, rm with 4/5 beds €84/100, €20 surcharge for check-ins after 9pm; check-in ⊙ 5-9pm; P 🛜) A good option if you intend to stay in Aquileia for more than the standard half-a-day sojourn. It's a no-frills, 92-bed hostel, within walking distance of the archaeological ruins and city centre, and with helpful staff happy to offer tips on local sightseeing. If arriving outside of check-in hours, call the number posted on the door.

Casa Delneri
B&B €€

(☑ 0431 911 71; Via XXIV Maggio 18; d €110; P 🛜 🕸) An elegantly restored, modernised country house that welcomes guests with its lovely garden (complete with chaise longues). Rooms are bright, comfy and cosy: some are in the attic while others crank up the atmosphere with exposed beams and stonework. It's a special spot, with a refined tranquility that's much harder to find on the coast. It's also a stone's throw from the Sepolcreto.

Pasticceria Mosaico
CHOCOLATE €

(☑ 0431 91 95 92; www.pasticceriamosaico.com; Piazza Capitolo 17; ⊙ 9am-7pm Sep-Jun, 8am-8pm Jul & Aug) Coffee, pastries and, above all, exquisite chocolates in the shadow of the Basilica. The latter can also be sampled and bought from **Cocambo** (Viale Stazione 2/a). Among the offerings are a handful of gluten-free and vegan options.

Al Granaio
RESTAURANT €€

(☑ 339 725 88 94; Via Tiel 24; San Lorenzo di Fiumicello; meals €35; ⊙ noon-2.30pm & 6.30-10pm Tue-Sun) Tucked away in the flat countryside of lower Friuli, this old farmhouse is now a

culinary hotspot. Local wines and flawlessly cooked meats. Try the deer if it's on offer.

🛍 Shopping

Souvenir Shop
SOUVENIRS

(Basilica di Aquileia; ⊙ same as the basilica) Near the basilica, this prosaically named enterprise peddles numerous items, from books and devotional objects, to fabulous DIY mosaic kits inspired by those of Aquileia.

ℹ Information

Aquileia Infopoint (☑ 0431 91 94 91; Via Giulia Augusta 11; ⊙ 9am-1pm & 1.30-5.30pm Mon-Sat, 9am-1pm Sun Nov-Feb, 9am-1pm & 2-6pm Mar-Sep, 9am-1pm & 1.30-5.30pm Oct) Head here to buy the FVG Card, the FVG Card Aquileia or to join a guided tour. Note that opening times may vary seasonally.

Torviscosa
POP 2686 / ELEV 3M

If you find yourself travelling between Aquileia and Palmanova, stop in Torviscosa for a few hours.

Up until the early 20th century, this area was a malaria-riddled swampland. Ambitious public works beginning in the 1920s saw the area drained and reclaimed, leading to Torviscosa's inauguration in 1938. A curious, at times ghostly place, the town is a unique example of a planned Fascist settlement, built entirely using Fascist principles and design, right down to the street furniture. The town's kingpin, around which everything else was built, was the SNIA Viscosa plant, an enormous factory dominated by soaring, cylindrical towers. The original vision for Torviscosa was of a self-sufficient settlement manufacturing rayon (viscosa), using cellulose extracted from the *Arundo donax* (giant reed) prevalent in the area. Alas, the scheme soon bankrupted and the town's chemical plants now focus mainly on pharmaceuticals.

The promoter of this utopian dream was Franco Marinotti. A managing director of SNIA, he chose architect Giuseppe de Min to design the town. In 1940, Torviscosa separated from the municipality of San Giorgio di Nogaro, officially becoming autonomous and spreading westward.

Although designed to accommodate 20,000, the town's population never exceeded 4000. The *centro storico* (historic centre) is fascinating in an understated way, its streets home to well-preserved Fascist-era architecture. Wander the town and you'll stumble up-on council houses once inhabited by factory workers and managers, as well as theatres, churches and schools, the town hall, and a 47m-high observation tower built in 1962.

The **Centro Informazione Documentazione** (☑ 0431 92 79 29, 335 762 57 61; http://cid.comune.Torviscosa.ud.it; Piazzale Marinotti 1; ⊘ 3-7pm late Jul-early Nov) exhibits scale models of Torviscosa and Italy's SNIA Viscosa factories, posters from the 1920s and various artefacts that recount the history of the place.

✖ Eating

La Tavernetta TRATTORIA €€
(☑ 0431 920 39; www.tavernettamalisana.it; Piazza della Fontana 8, Malisana; meals €30; ⊘ 10am-10pm Mon, Tue & Thu-Sat, to 3pm Wed & Sun, closed Sun in Aug) Torviscosa is the place to sample so-called *cucina autarchica* (autarchic cuisine), which stems back to Fascist times. Try the *surrogati* (surrogates), homegrown alternatives to international edibles, in the town's restaurants. You'll need to book ahead to sample the self-sufficient menu, where recipes from the 1930s are recreated using strictly Italian ingredients.

Strassoldo

POP 707 / ELEV 2M

A village of Cervignano del Friuli, Strassoldo pops up like a desert oasis on the flat Friuli plain. It's an idyllic place, famously built around two castles – Castello di Sopra (Upper Castle) and Castello di Sotto (Lower Castle) – and, subsequently, between two churches, the 18th-century Chiesa di San Nicolò and the Chiesa di San Marco. The village itself is enchantingly entered through a whimsical looking, 17th-century portal, leading to the **Castello di Sotto**. Built in 1360, the hulking castle is surrounded by a park and canals in an area well known for its natural springs. A small bridge leads to the **Castello di Sopra**, which dates from 1322. Beside it lies the **Chiesa di Santa Maria in Vineis**, home to fascinating frescoes.

✖ Eating

Al Cavallino FRIULIAN €
(☑ 0431 93 94 13/333 649 10 22; www.fricheria alcavallino.com; Via Taglio 4; frico €7.60; ⊘ 11.30am-3pm & 5.30pm-2am Mon-Wed & Fri, 10am-2am Sat & Sun) *Frico* (a cheese and potato pancake) is to Friuli what pizza is to Campania. That said,

we're not sure how the staunchest traditionalists would feel about the dozens of versions offered by signor Renzo. Perhaps the disarming smile and passion conquer all.

Riserva Naturale della Foce dell'Isonzo & Valle Cavanata

Between Grado and Monfalcone lies the mouth of the Isonzo River, a protected area which includes the municipalities of Staranzano, San Canzian d'Isonzo, Grado and Fiumicello. After significant conservation work, the area now claims an excellent nature reserve, known for its unique horses and abundant birdlife (including numerous migratory species).

The **Isola della Cona** (Visitor Centre ☑ 333 405 68 00; www.riservafoceisonzo.it; adult/reduced €5/3.50; ⊘ 10am-4pm Mon-Wed & Fri-Sun), the reserve's main land mass, is famous throughout the region for its herds of rare-breed Camargue horses. That said, it is the area's birdlife that really stands out for twitchers across the country. The reserve is well equipped for birdwatching, with well-positioned observatories, some of which occupy old fishermen's huts. A loop trail reaches all of the lookouts (don't miss the Osservatorio Marinetta). Each offers a different perspective on the ponds, meadows and marshes, and all make for great vantage points if you're taking photographs.

The panoramic boardwalk views and the chorus of birdsong in the woods are enough reward for your journey. Inside the building, close to the visitor centre, **Bar al Pettirosso** is a little eatery serving tasty first courses as well as sandwiches. It shares the same opening hours as the reserve.

South of the mouth of the Isonzo, at the easternmost part of the Laguna di Grado, you can visit the 250-hectare **Riserva Naturale della Valle Cavanata** (☑ 340 400 57 52; www.vallecavanata.it; Via Grado 1; visitor center ⊘ 10am-5pm Mon-Wed & Fri-Sun Apr-Oct, 10.30am-3.30pm Sat-Mon Nov-Mar), a former fishing farm turned nature reserve. Here, the break between land and water is more definitive and less marshy than it is in Riserva Naturale della Foce dell'Isonzo, creating a different atmosphere. That said, twitchers (on foot or bicycle) can still spot a plethora of water birds here, along trails that lead between woodland and water.

The reserve also claims the Laboratorio Didattico di Casa Spina and various bird-watching lookouts (binoculars can be borrowed free of charge from the visitor centre). To reach Valle Cavanata, head out of Grado towards Monfalcone and follow the signs.

🛏 Sleeping & Eating

★**Caneo** HOTEL € /€€
(☑ 0431 88 44 26; www.caneo.it; Strada del Caneo 1, Punta Sdobba; d with breakfast €50-90, half-board €90-110; meals €25-35; ☺ restaurant 12.30-3pm & 7-10pm; ℗ ❋ ☎) Located at the beginning of Punta Sdobba, a low promontory on the southern bank of the Isonzo River, this hotel immerses guests in the sweeping, big-sky wetlands that define this corner of Italy. Rooms are refurbished, luminous and cater to those with limited mobility.

The restaurant serves excellent fish-of-the-day dishes, while a network of wooden walkways lead out into beautiful natural landscapes (with small pagodas perfect for reading a book). Staff are well-versed in things to do and see in the local area.

MONFALCONE

POP 28,339 / ELEV 7M

For those arriving from the Friulian coast (or from the Carso), Monfalcone marks a rather sudden change of scenery. Here, the landscape is dominated by industry: hydroelectric plants, warehouses, cotton mills.

While the city is not the region's pin-up, it is home to one of Italy's most important open-air museums, the **Parco Tematico della Grande Guerra** (☑ 0481 49 42 29; www.turismofvg.it/parco-tematico-della-grande-guerra-di-monfalcone; ☺ year-round) FREE. Dedicated to WWI, the museum is divided into three themed sections, with walking routes that lead through bunkers and trenches of various war fronts. Along the paths you'll see the Rocca di Monfalcone, a circular fortification with a central tower that dates from the 5th century; today it houses the **Museo della Rocca** (Via E. Valentinis 134; ☺ 9am-2pm Sun & holidays) FREE, a local speleology museum. In the mountains above Monfalcone, the Pro Lo-co Fogliano Redipuglia organises **Paths of Peace** (www.prolocofoglianoredipuglia.it/sentieri-di-pace), a series of half-day excursions focussed on various aspects of WWI and the Carso region.

The ground floor of the former workers' hotel in **Panzano**, a neighbourhood built in the 1920s to house shipyard employees, claims the **Museo della Cantieristica di Monfalcone — MuCa** (☑ 0481 49 43 75; www.mucamonfalcone.it; Via del Mercato 3, Località Panzano; adult/reduced €7/5, free with FVG Card; ☺ 10am-6pm Mon & Fri-Sun Oct-May, to 7pm Jun-Sep). Through engaging, modern displays, it tells the story of the Monfalcone and its shipyard, considered one of Italy's major industrial hubs. You'll need to book ahead to join the fascinating guided tour of the shipyard itself (see the museum website for times and to book).

The remainder of the building is occupied by the **Nuovo Albergo Operai** (☑ 388 404 14 66; www.nuovoalbergooperai.it; Via del Mercato 5; s/d €55-96/75-130; ℗ ❋ ☎), an interesting place to slumber considering its history.

ℹ Information

IAT (☑ 0481 28 23 52; www.visitmonfalcone.it; Via Sant'Ambrogio 21; ☺ varies, call ahead) provides information on the area's trails and themed itineraries.

ℹ Getting There & Away

BUS

TPL FVG (☑ 800 05 20 40, mobile 040 971 23 43; https://tplfvg.it) bus G51 runs between Monfalcone and Trieste (€3.50, 40 minutes, roughly every 30 minutes). Buses G1, G7 and G8 run between Monfalcone and Gorizia (€4.35, one hour, roughly every 30 minutes).

CAR & MOTORCYLE

From Trieste Drive along the *lungomare* (seafront) towards Duino and then take the SS14.

From Milan Take the Venezia-Trieste, exit at Palmanova and follow the signs.

TRAIN

Trenitalia (www.trenitalia.it) runs trains from Venice Mestre (from €10.75, 90 minutes) and from Trieste (from €3.50, frequent services, about 30 minutes).

Udine & Surrounds

Includes ➡

Udine 141
Palmanova 154
Clauiano 157
Codroipo 157
San Daniele del Friuli . . 159
Pinzano
al Tagliamento 164
Osoppo 164
Ragogna 165
Gemona del Friuli 166
Venzone 167
Tarcento 169
Artegna 170
Lusevera 171

Best Authentic Osterie

➡ Osteria Pieri Mortadele (p150)
➡ La Polse (p150)
➡ Osteria e Locanda al Cappello (p151)

Best Wine Bars

➡ Al Pignolo (p152)
➡ La Trappola (p162)

Why Go?

Behind the vestiges of a medieval past lies a gentle soul here. Discover it starting in Udine: the region's second largest city is the city of Tiepolo and arcaded *loggias,* wine bars and jazz clubs.

Leaving the towns behind, the countryside will dominate the view out your window, dotted with castles and 18th-century villas.

To the south, don't miss the starry city (Palmanova) and the city of sundials (Aiello), before a salute to Villa Manin, the residence of the last doge.

Then to the north, between San Daniele, Gemona and Venzone, you'll find excellent food – celebrated with festivals and tastings – and signs of a past worth delving into.

When to Go

Given Friuli's infamously fickle skies, no one season trumps another, with each offering a unique take on the city and its province. Spring and summer are hot, with verdant hills and cooling walks through the woods. Autumn explodes with colour and succulent produce, while winter lures with warming soups, village fairs, markets and the ice-covered Tagliamento.

Udine & Surrounds Highlights

1 Piazza della Libertà
(p141) Admire the Venetian touch of this square and its surroundings in Udine.

2 Gallerie del Tiepolo
(p145) This Udine gallery is a must.

3 Palmanova (p154) Not so much a city as an urban ideal.

4 Aiello del Friuli (p159) Learn how to tell the time in the land of sundials.

5 Villa Manin (p157) Home of the last doge of Venice.

6 San Daniele del Friuli (p159) There's good reason why its prosciutto is so, so famous.

7 Lago di Cornino (p164) Close encounters with emerald waters and griffon vultures.

8 Gemona del Friuli (p166) and **Venzone** (p167) Tales of the terrible earthquake of 1976.

9 Pinzano al Tagliamento (p164) Where the view from the bridge is spectacular.

UDINE

POP 99,402 / ELEV 113M

Udine's reputation as a dull, lacklustre destination died years ago. Today, the university town buzzes with pubs, *osterie,* restaurants, shopping, and hip bars and clubs.

And while it might be small and easily covered on foot, Udine's attitude is anything but provincial. Sophisticated and ambitious, it claims several Tiepolo frescoes and an internationally renowned museum of modern and contemporary art.

On the weekend, Piazza San Giacomo and surrounds heave as locals come out to play, hopping between taverns in search of the next *tajut* (glass of red wine) and lining their bellies with *mortadella,* prosciutto and cheese.

When the weather is warm, restaurants open their patios on the old irrigation canals. Indeed, as you wander around the historic centre, you'll often hear the gentle sound of flowing water. If the sound doesn't remind you of Venice, the city's architecture will, its squares and streets revealing traces of Udine's days under Venetian rule.

History

Although Udine is first mentioned in a document from 983 CE (when its castle was donated to the patriarch of Aquileia by Emperor Otto II), the area on which the city stands was inhabited as early as Roman and Lombard times. When the patriarchs moved the seat of the patriarchal palace from Cividale to Udine in the 13th century, the city grew in population and importance.

Conquered by Venice in 1420, it remained under La Serenissima's control for nearly 400 years. Indeed, Venice chose it as the seat of the Venetian lieutenancy in Friuli, and in a short time the city's appearance was transformed.

After the 1511 earthquake, which razed part of the historic centre to the ground, the area around the castle was expanded, followed by the city centre itself. With the signing of the Treaty of Campo Formio in 1797, Friuli fell to the French before passing to the Habsburgs.

In 1848, its inhabitants rose up against the Austrians in the First Italian War of Independence, but were defeated and their city severely bombarded. Austrian rule lasted until 1866, when Udine and part of Friuli were annexed to the Kingdom of Italy. During WWI, the city became an important logistics hub,

housing the Italian supreme command, military hospitals and an ammunition depot. As a result, it was nicknamed 'Capital of the Great War'. After the war, Udine became the capital of the Province of Friuli before suffering further damage during the Allied bombings of WWII.

Following the disastrous earthquake of 1976 (see p169), Udine's city council and residents played an active role in organising aid for the region's reconstruction.

⊙ Sights

★ Piazza della Libertà PIAZZA

(Map p144) Elegant and petite, some call Piazza della Libertà the most beautiful Venetian square on the mainland. Already a lively commercial hub in the Middle Ages, its large trade in wine saw it named 'Piazza del Vino'.

Yet, it's the Venetians who left the greatest legacy, expanding the square several times and adding numerous architectural beauties. Among these is the pink and white Palazzo Comunale (Town Hall). A commanding, Venetian-Gothic building, its famous portico (1457) is named **Loggia del Lionello** after the goldsmith who designed it.

Across the piazza, the 16th-century **Loggia di San Giovanni** was once connected to the castle. Home to a chapel dedicated to the fallen, the building's **clock tower** is modelled on the one in Venice's Piazza San Marco. Perched atop are two copper *mori* (Moors), dutifully striking the hours. The current timekeepers were added at the end of the 19th century to replace older wooden versions. In the past, the pair weren't call *mori,* but the Italian (left) and the German (right). This reflected two ways of telling the time: in the old Italian way of dividing the dial into 24 hours and starting from sunset, and in the German style of dividing the dial into 12 hours.

The Renaissance-era Carrara Fountain and a column-perched Lion of San Marco (1539) adorn the centre of the square, whose numerous statues also include the neoclassical Statue of Peace, donated by Franz Joseph I of Austria to commemorate the Treaty of Campo Formio. Beside it, the Statue of Justice gazes towards the Loggia del Lionello as if to warn the city councillors to govern righteously. The square also claims 17th-century depictions of Hercules and Cacus, better known in the city as Florean and Venturin.

UDINE & SURROUNDS UDINE

Udine

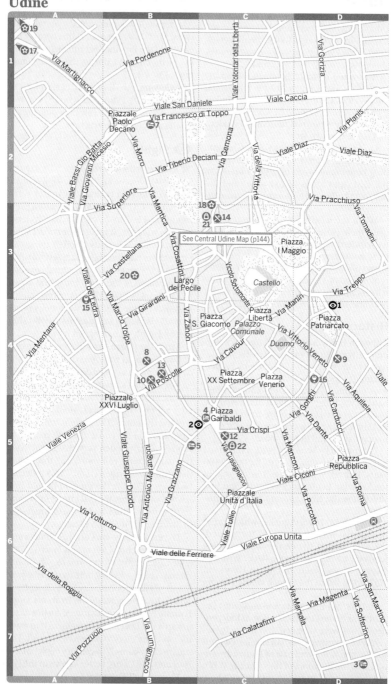

See Central Udine Map (p144)

Udine

⊙ Top Sights
1 Museo Diocesano &
   Gallerie del Tiepolo D4
2 Museo Etnografico del Friuli B5

⊟ Sleeping
3 Al Fari D7
4 Al Vecchio Tram C5
5 Hotel Allegria B5
6 Hotel Clocchiatti Next E2
7 Hotel Suite Inn B2

⊗ Eating
8 Al Vecchio Stallo B4
9 Aquila Nera D4
10 Biffi B4
11 Mamm E3
12 Osteria ai Barnabiti C5
13 Osteria Toscano B4
14 Trattoria ai Frati C3

⊙ Drinking & Nightlife
15 Liberty A4
16 The Black Stuff D4

✪ Entertainment
17 Arci Cas*Aupa .... off map A1
18 Caffè Caucigh C3
19 Stadio Friuli .... off map A1
20 Visionario B3

⊟ Shopping
21 C.L.U.F. C3
22 Wool Style C5

Porticato del Lippomano　HISTORIC BUILDING
(Map p144; Piazzale Patria del Friuli 2) From the Loggia di San Giovanni, past the Arco Bollani – designed by Palladio in 1556 and crowned by the Lion of San Marco – you enter this breathtaking portico. Leading up towards the Colle del Castello, it's one of Udine's architectural highlights, commissioned by Lieutenant Tommaso Lippomano in 1487 on a site once crossed by the city's 13th-century walls. The portico's columns and arches are highly atmospheric, especially when casting arabesque shadows. Tip: head up just in time for sunset.

Castello　CASTLE
(Map p144; Piazzale Patria del Friuli 1) It's hard to ignore Udine's hilltop castle, which, according to a document from 983 CE, occupies the site of an ancient *castrum* (Roman fort).

Central Udine

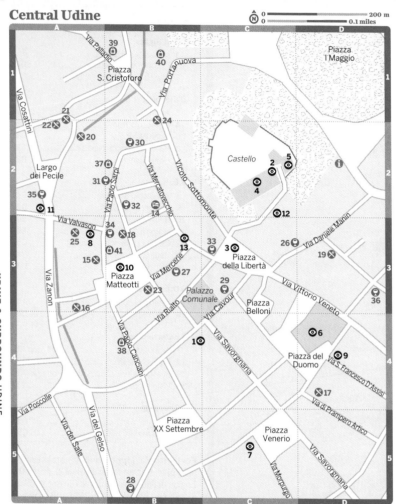

The patriarchs of Aquileia subsequently established their headquarters here, before the complex was destroyed in 1511 and replaced with the current castle, begun in 1517. Recently restored, its style is more noble residence than fortress, reflected in the sumptuousness of its frescoed Salone del Parlamento (Hall of the Parliament) and in the rooms that house the Civici Musei.

A venue for summertime concerts and events, the square in front of the palace is home to the **Casa della Contadinanza**. Here, representatives for the local peasantry gathered with the blessing of the Venetian Republic, which wanted to diminish the power of the pro-German nobility. Although the building dates from the 16th century, it was dismantled and rebuilt in its current location in 1931.

Today, it houses a **restaurant** (☎ 0432 50 96 96; Colle del Castello; meals €25; ☺ 9.30am-8.30pm Tue-Sun) with a beautiful view of the hill and mountains. On clear days, the peaks of the Julian and Carnic Alps rise above the Udine plain like giant dinosaur crests.

★ Civici Musei   MUSEUMS

(Map p144; ☎ 0432 127 25 91 switchboard & guided-tour bookings; www.civicimuseiudine.it; Colle del Castello 1; adult/reduced €8/4, with Casa Cavazzi-

Central Udine

◎ **Top Sights**

1 Casa Cavazzini – Museo d'Arte
   Moderna e Contemporanea............B4
2 Civici Musei...C2
3 Piazza della Libertà C3

◎ **Sights**

4 Castello C2
5 Chiesa di Santa Maria di Castello C2
6 Duomo D4
7 Ex Chiesa di San Francesco..................C5
8 Galleria Tina Modotti............................A3
9 Oratorio della Purità.............................D4
10 Piazza Matteotti/
    Piazza San Giacomo.......................B3
11 Porta Torriani A2
12 Porticato del Lippomano C2
13 Via Mercatovecchio...............................B3

◎ **Sleeping**

14 Mercatovecchio Luxury Suites.............B2

◎ **Eating**

15 Al Tagliato...A3
16 Alla Ghiacciaia A3
17 Alla Tavernetta.......................................D4
18 Antica Maddalena B3

19 Ex Provinciali...D3
20 Gabin A2
21 L'Alimentare A1
22 La Polse A2
23 Mezza Libbra B3
24 Osteria Pieri Mortadele.........................B1
25 Vitello d'Oro A3

◎ **Drinking & Nightlife**

26 Al Pignolo..C3
27 Alle Volte B3
28 Buca di Bacco...B5
29 Caffè Contarena C3
30 Da Michele B2
31 Da Teresina A2
32 Lume B2
33 Metropolis...C3
34 Osteria e Locanda al Cappello...............B3
35 Quinto Recinto A2
36 Taverna dell'Angelo D3

◎ **Shopping**

37 Cityalps B2
38 Galleria Bardelli B4
39 Kobo Shop B1
40 Libreria Editrice Odòs B1
41 SeR B3

ni & Museo Etnografico del Friuli €10, free with FVG Card; ⊙ 10am-6pm Tue-Sun, last admission 5.30pm) The castle houses five different collections, all interesting and covered by the one ticket.

The **Museo Archeologico** exhibits local and donated archaeological items, among them mosaics and urns. The sprawling **Galleria d'Arte Antica** has a reproduction of Caravaggio's St Francis, several stunning Tiepolos, as well as works by Giovanni da Udine and Giovanni Antonio de' Sacchis (also known as Pordenone).

Those interested in modern history will enjoy the **Museo Friulano della Fotografia** and its collection of Friulian images captured over the past two centuries. The **Museo del Risorgimento** traces the history of the region, from the fall of the Venetian Republic to Italy's unification, while the **Galleria dei Disegni e delle Stampe** is a must for lovers of old maps and prints.

Chiesa di Santa Maria di Castello
PLACE OF WORSHIP

(Map p144; ⊙ closed for restoration at time of research) One of Udine's oldest churches, the Chiesa di Santa Maria del Castello is of-

ten overlooked by those who head straight from Piazza Libertà to the castle museums. And yet, its bell tower (which, like the facade, was designed by Gaspare Negro in the 16th century) is crowned by one of the city's most famous (and visible) landmarks: the **Angelo del Castello (Angel of the Castle)**, a hollow bronze statue that rotates according to the wind.

The current church occupies the site of an earlier religious building said to have already existed in the 8th century. Inside is a series of Romanesque frescoes executed by Girolamo da Padova in the 14th century: seek out the *Deposizione della Croce (Deposition of the Cross)*, *Morte della Madonna (Death of the Madonna)* and *Battesimo di Cristo (Baptism of Christ)*.

★ Museo Diocesano & Gallerie del Tiepolo
MUSEUM

(Map p142; ☑ 0432 250 03; www.musdioc-tiepolo .it/ Piazza Patriarcato 1; adult/reduced €8/6, free with FVG Card; ⊙ 10am-1pm & 3-6pm Mon & Wed-Sun, last admission 30min before closing) Home to the patriarchs of Aquileia between the 17th and 18th centuries, Palazzo Patriarcale claims

THE TRUE MAGICIAN OF PAINTING

Counted among the greatest exponents of 18th-century Italian art and defined by his contemporaries as 'the true magician of painting', **Giambattista Tiepolo** (1697–1770) arrived in Udine in June 1726 to create the frescoes in the Duomo's Cappella del Santissimo Sacramento and remained in the city until 1740. During this period, he also painted the altarpiece of *patron saints Hermagoras and Fortunatus,* and a series of Roman history scenes now housed in the museums of St Petersburg, New York and Vienna. Tiepolo returned to Udine in 1759 upon the invitation of the new patriarch Daniele Dolfin. With his son Giandomenico (one of 10 children), he began work on the masterpieces in the Oratorio della Purità and also painted a beautiful altarpiece for the Chiesa di Santa Chiara delle Benedettine in Cividale, now kept in Dresden.

Tiepolo's works bewitch on many levels, from the perspective of the scenes and gaze of the subjects, to the tales his brushstrokes tell. It's easy to spend much of one's Udine sojourn seeking out the Venetian's masterpieces, which are scattered among several sites. Among them is the Museo di Arte Antica di Udine, the Musei Civici (Room X) and the Castello's beautiful Salone del Parlamento, whose southern wall features a monochrome fresco depicting the *Triumph of Christians over the Turks after the Battle of Lepanto*). Of course, don't forget the frescoes in the Oratorio delle Purità or, if you're heading to the coast, the 254 Tiepolo drawings in the collection of the Museo Sartorio (p63) in Trieste.

frescoes that helped launch Tiepolo into the artistic stratosphere. Above the Staircase of Honour is *Fall of the Rebel Angels,* the first work Tiepolo executed in the city. Other masterpieces by the Venetian heavyweight include his depiction of *Solomon's Judgment,* as well as famous scenes from Genesis.

On the first floor, don't miss the room of wooden carvings, which offers a taste of the carving the region (particularly Carnia) is famous for. On the second floor, seek out the library: dating from 1708, it holds more than 12,000 historic volumes.

Duomo
PLACE OF WORSHIP

(Map p144; ☑0432 50 53 02; www.cattedrale udine.it; Piazza del Duomo; ☉7am-noon & 4-6.45pm) Tweaked several times over the centuries, Udine's 13th-century cathedral is the city's largest place of worship. Before stepping inside, cast your eye over the facade, whose Gothic main entrance, the **Portal of Redemption,** features a lunette with 14th-century bas-reliefs. The canopy above the entrance is a 20th-century addition.

Around the corner to the left, at the base of the bell tower, is the **Portal of the Coronation.** Executed in the late 14th century, it's crowned by a group of sculpted saints, sadly ravaged by time and smog.

Inside the cathedral you'll find a suite of 18th-century side chapels that harbour precious altars, statues and paintings. Tiepolo fans will find his works in the Cappella del-

la Santissima Trinità, the Cappella dei Santi Ermacora e Fortunata, and the Cappella del Santissimo Sacramento. (In the right nave, don't miss the small but exquisite altarpiece depicting the *Resurrection,* also by Tiepolo.)

Dating from 1441, the octagonal bell tower was built on an earlier baptistery, hence its somewhat squat appearance. The baptistery and Cappella di San Nicolò currently house the **Museo del Duomo** (☑0432 50 68 30; Piazzetta Bertrando; donation welcome; ☉10am-noon & 4-6pm Mon & Wed-Sat, 4-6pm Sun), which exhibits works and objects related to the era of the patriarchs (in particular to the life of Bertrando) and frescoes by Vitale da Bologna. Among these objects is Betrando's show-stopping marble sarcophagus (1348). Supported by five chiselled saints, the work is considered a masterpiece of Gothic sculpture.

The two 14th-century statues adorning the rear exterior of the baptistery (visible from Via Vittorio Veneto) depict the Virgin Annunciate and the Archangel Gabriel.

Oratorio della Purità
PLACE OF WORSHIP

(Map p144; Piazza del Duomo; ☉10am-noon Mon, Wed, Thu & Fri or on request, contact the Museo del Duomo) Right beside the Duomo, this oratory was founded in 1760 on the site of an old theatre. Cardinal Daniele Dolfin commissioned both its construction and the lively, monochromatic frescoes by Giambattista Tiepolo and son Giandomenico inside. Giambattista also executed the ceiling fresco *Assunta*, considered a masterpiece of its kind.

⭐ Museo Etnografico del Friuli   MUSEUM

(Map p142; ☑ 0432 12 72 92, civic museums 0432 12 72 591; www.civicimuseiudine.it; Giacomelli Palace, Via Grazzano 1; adult/reduced €5/2.50, with castle & Casa Cavazzini €10, free with FVG Card; ☺ 10am-6pm Fri-Sun) Also known as the Nuovo Museo delle Arti e delle Tradizioni Popolari (New Museum of Popular Arts and Traditions), this place is a real gem. Not only is its setting, **Palazzo Giacomelli**, fabulous, the museum ditches fusty, dusty displays for engaging, contemporary exhibits that offer a glimpse into Friulian life.

The region's unique heritage and traditions are explored through numerous themes, including folk festivals, daily life, music, religion, games, *fogolâr* and costumes. A visit here will help make any trip through Friuli Venezia Giulia a richer, more meaningful experience.

Piazza Matteotti   PIAZZA

(Map p144) Known as Piazza delle Erbe (Square of the Herbs) to romantics and Piazza San Giacomo to its faithful, Piazza Matteotti was, until the 1980s, a rather infamous area. Today, it's Udine's buzzing, communal lounge room, its cafes and bars drawing everyone from spritz-sipping parents to young, after-dark party goers.

The square's centrepiece **fountain** dates from 1543, while the **column** topped with a statue of the Virgin hails from 1487. Noble, medieval buildings flank the piazza, some still adorned with decorative frescoes. At its western end is the **Chiesa of San Giacomo**, distinguished by the stone shells decorating its facade; a symbol of the saint, protector of pilgrims. The church was built at the behest of the Brotherhood of Furriers and dates back to 1398, though the facade was restored and the chapel added at a later date.

Via Mercatovecchio   STREET

(Map p144) Centuries ago, the defensive walls and moat that surrounded the Colle del Castello passed near Via Mercatovecchio, the first area to develop outside the castle walls. It was here that the market took place, hence its name: 'Old Market St'.

Although the stalls have given way to fashionable boutiques, the gently curving street retains its historic elegance, with some of its *palazzi* deserving more than a quick glance. Among these is 16th-century **Casa Sabbadini**, decorated with a fresco by Giovanni Battista Grassi dating from 1554; note the depiction of Jupiter in the centre. In the corner of the building, beside the fresco, you'll notice a small ring from which a flag once marked the finish line of the city's Palio.

A little further on is 17th-century **Palazzo del Monte di Pietà**; once home to around 30 artisan shops and warehouses, it's now home to Italian bank Cassa di Risparmio. Look up to appreciate its pair of elegant three-light windows, then step under its five-arched portico to enter the small **Cappella di Santa Maria del Monte di Pietà**: the chapel's late 17th-century frescoes are the work of Giulio Quaglio, while the altar is by Heinrich Meyring (Enrico Merengo).

⭐ Casa Cavazzini – Museo d'Arte Moderna e Contemporanea   MUSEUM

(Map p144; ☑ 0432 127 37 72; www.civicimusei udine.it; Via Cavour 14; adult/reduced €5/2.50, free with FVG Card; ☺ 10am-6pm Tue-Sun) Revamped by the Italian starchitect Gae Aulenti, 16th-century Casa Cavazzini houses Udine's Museum of Modern and Contemporary Art. Spread over three floors where old meets new, the collection showcases top-tier 20th-century artists such as Giorgio de Chirico, Giorgio Morandi and the Basaldella brothers. Many of the works were donated to the city by the artists themselves after the 1976 earthquake. Also noteworthy is the museum's FRIAM collection of American art from the 1960s and 1970s, also donated by the artists after the devastating quake.

Ex Chiesa di San Francesco   GALLERY

(Map p144; Largo Ospedale Vecchio) Altered several times between its construction in 1259 and the 18th century, it would take a comprehensive, postwar restoration to reveal many of this former church's early features. The rose window punctuating its gabled facade dates from 1435, while the simple, single nave interior now functions as a striking venue for temporary art and photography exhibitions (the deconsecrated church is one of Udine's Civic Museums). If the lighting isn't too dim, you might make out the 14th-century frescoes decorating the walls.

Galleria Tina Modotti   GALLERY

(Map p144; ☑ 0432 127 25 91 Civic Museums of Udine; Via Paolo Sarpi; ☺ open during exhibitions & events) One of the world's most famous photographers, Tina Modotti, was born in Via Pracchiuso, opposite Osteria e Locanda al

UDINE & SURROUNDS UDINE

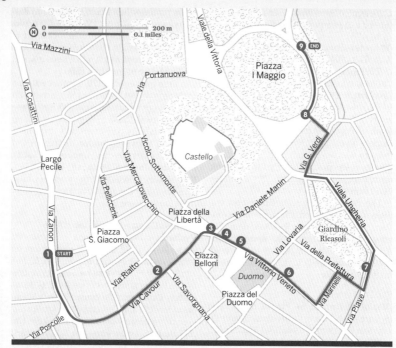

Walking Tour
Along the Medieval Canals

START VIA ZANON
END PIAZZA PRIMO MAGGIO
LENGTH 2KM; 1 HOUR

In the Middle Ages, Udine was crossed by six small, artificial canals that charged the city, powering local mills and factories. In addition to the Ledra River, two survive: the *roggia di Udine* (Udine canal) and the *roggia di Palma* (Palma canal). Their course is fragmented, occasionally disappearing under the streets and reappearing a few blocks later.

This walking tour explores both the lesser-known face of Udine and what remains of its 16th-century architecture.

Start from ① **Via Zanon**, along the Udine canal, overlooked by Osteria Alla Ghiacciaia (p150), and continue south. Turn left into Via Poscolle and continue along it to ② **Via Cavour**; note the dainty decorative elements on the building on the corner with Via Canciani.

Once in Piazza della Libertà, turn right into ③ **Via Vittorio Veneto** and continue. Near the Duomo, at number 18, you will see the ④ **Palazzo della Forza Concina**, with its neoclassical facade, and the 17th-century ⑤ **Palazzo Strassoldo** (number 20). At number 36, ⑥ **Palazzo Tinghi** preserves fragments of frescoes by Pordenone. At the intersection with Via Marinelli, turn left and then right into Via della Prefettura.

Walk along the canal on Via Piave and you'll enter ⑦ **Giardino Ricasoli**, a tranquil oasis adorned with exotic species, flower beds and graceful swans. In this area, the Palma canal is visible for a few hundred metres.

Crossing the entire park you will come out in front of the Palazzo Patriarcale: continue along Via Verdi up to ⑧ **Piazza Primo Maggio**, the largest open space in the city and the site for fairs and events throughout the year.

Finish your wander by taking a look at the ⑨ **Santuario della Beata Vergine delle Grazie**. Founded in the 15th century, the church now sports a neoclassical facade with Corinthian columns that blends well with its surrounds.

Cappello (p151). The city's Art-Nouveau former fish market is now a gallery named in her honour, with a diverse program of photography exhibitions. Like the ex Chiesa di San Francesco, the gallery is another of Udine's Civic Museums.

Porta Torriani
GATE

(Map p144; Via Torriani) Medieval Udine was protected by numerous defensive walls. At the end of the 15th century, there were five, expanding from the castle to the current ring road. The best surviving relic from this system is Porta Torriani (also known as Torre di Santa Maria, formerly known as Porta Nuova). Other medieval gates still visible in the city are **Porta Manin** (1273–99), **Porta Aquileia** (circa 1440) and **Porta Villalta** (1436).

Festivals & Events

Far East Film Festival
APRIL

(www.fareastfilm.com) A week-long celebration of East Asian cinema, both contemporary and classic. Expect screenings, talks, workshops and Asian bites too.

vicino/lontano
MAY

(www.vicinolontano.it) A five-day culture fest, with debates, art installations, photography exhibitions and the awarding of the international Premio Terzani, one of Italy's most prestigious literary prizes.

Udin&Jazz Winter
WINTER

(www.euritmica.it) Although the Udin&Jazz summer festival has moved to Grado, Udine hosts winter concerts in the warmth of its Teatro Comunale Palamostre. Expect high-profile international acts, as well as young Italian talent.

Sleeping

Al Fari
GUESTHOUSE €

(Map p142; ☑ 339 145 34 33; Via Melegnano 41; r from €50; P ✽ 🕿) A cosy little *pensione* (guesthouse) a stone's throw from the train station, with good quality rooms and compact apartments. There's a small, soothing garden and private parking.

Hotel Allegria
BOUTIQUE HOTEL €€

(Map p142; ☑ 0432 20 11 16; www.hotelallegria.it; Vicolo Chiuso 1; r from €69; P ✽ 🕿) It may occupy a 15th-century building in the centre of town, but this svelte hotel opts for minimalist, contemporary interiors. Its 21 rooms are spacious, well furnished and lined with beautiful parquet flooring. Rates include a generous breakfast buffet and the property also hosts an excellent **restaurant** (☑ 0432 255 08; Via Grazzano 18; meals €30; ⊘ 7-10pm Mon, noon-2pm & 7-10pm Tue-Sat, noon-2pm Sun) which reinterprets traditional Friulian dishes. Hotel parking is a pricey €11 per day.

★ Hotel Suite Inn
HOTEL €€

(Map p142; ☑ 0432 50 16 83; www.suiteinn.it; Via di Toppo 25; r from €85; P ✽ 🕿) A 15-minute walk from the Duomo and close to the motorway exit, this homely, warmly welcoming hotel offers consistently clean, tastefully decorated rooms. The icing on the cake is its generous, high-quality breakfast.

★ Mercatovecchio Luxury Suites
HOTEL €€

(Map p144; ☑ 0432 50 00 27; www.mercatovecchio.it; Via del Carbone 1; ste from €100; P ✽ 🕿) Not only is its location behind Via Mercatovecchio appealing, this wonderfully comfy hotel ups the ante with its super-friendly staff, chic vibe and six themed suites. The latter find their inspiration in various corners of the world, from Morocco to India to Russia.

Hotel Clocchiatti Next
HOTEL €€

(Map p142; ☑ 0432 50 50 47; www.hotelclocchiatti.it; Via Cividale 29; r from €85; P ✽ 🕿) It might sit just outside the historic centre, but once you've stretched out on its veranda, surrounded by cedars and bamboo, you won't mind the 10-minute walk into the city centre. Rooms are modern, spacious and tastefully furnished, and the staff take care of their guests like family.

Al Vecchio Tram
HOTEL €€

(Map p142; ☑ 0432 50 71 64; www.hotelvecchiotram.com; Via Brenari 28, cnr of Piazza Garibaldi; r from €99; ✽ 🕿) A small hotel with sharp, contemporary styling in the heart of the city. Rooms are minimalist and bright, and the attic suites particularly beautiful; check the hotel website for any good deals.

Eating

Rich in tradition, Udinese cuisine is hearty, with robust flavours and high-quality products. *Frico* dominates the scene (see p151) and is always paired with polenta and a *tajut*, the local term for a glass of wine (also known as *nero*). Local cuisine is served at the numerous *osterie* (taverns) in the historic centre, distinguished by their *fogolâr* (hearth), around which Friulian families once gathered for lunch and dinner. Although uncommon in private homes these days, many of the region's restaurants still feature them, even if only for decorative purposes.

Mamm
DELI €

(Map p142; ☎ 342 619 18 01; Largo del Teatro; focaccia from €2; ⏱ 11.30am-2.30pm Mon, 11.30am-2.30pm & 6.30-10pm Tue-Thu, to 10.30pm Fri & Sat) A hip, bike-themed joint peddling delicious, high-quality *panini* (sandwiches). The focaccias are utterly delicious and pimped with the region's top ingredients.

Opposite it lies **Mamm Pane** (⏱ 7.30am-2.30pm Mon-Sat), a spin-off bakery also serving breakfast.

★ La Polse
OSTERIA €

(Map p144; ☎ 0432 29 47 94; https://osteriala polse.business.site; Via Raimondo D'Aronco 23; bruschetta from €2.50; ⏱ 8.45am-midnight) That the first *bruschetta* is complimentary here not only speaks volumes about La Polse's easy vibe, but also about the actual addictiveness of the *bruschettas* themselves. Drool over the various options, scribbled down on a big blackboard.

★ Osteria Pieri Mortadele
OSTERIA €

(Map p144; ☎ 0432 50 92 34; www.pierimortadele .com; Via Bartolini 8; platter per 100g from €4; glasses €1-5; ⏱ 10am-10pm Mon-Sat) A must in Udine, this simple, authentic *osteria* features a large central table where it's easy to strike up a conversation. Wines range from house to non-house drops, while bites include cult-status *mortadella*. You'll usually find one weighing almost 300kg on the counter, eaten at the speed of light and served at all hours with a splash of salt and lemon.

There's a second branch at Piazzale Giobatta Cella 4.

Alla Ghiacciaia
OSTERIA €

(Map p144; ☎ 0432 50 24 71; Via Zanon 13; mains €5.50-12; ⏱ 11am-3pm & 6pm-midnight Mon-Fri, 10am-3pm & 6pm-midnight Sat & Sun) Sporting a fabulous terrace overlooking weeping willows and the canal on Via Zanon (see walking tour, p148), this charming tavern serves hearty Friulian grub, from *frico* and prosciutto San Daniele, to *cjarsons* (potato ravioli).

Mezza Libbra
BURGERS €

(Map p144; ☎ 0432 61 87 46; www.mezzalibbra .com; Piazza Matteotti 1; burgers €7-10; ⏱ 9.30am-midnight) When you just can't face another *frico*, Mezza Libbra comes to the rescue. Flanking Udine's showpiece piazza, it's a hit with young locals, who chomp on tasty burgers made with fresh, quality ingredients (including 100% Italian beef). It can get crowded on weekends, so book ahead.

Al Vecchio Stallo
FRIULIAN €

(Map p142; ☎ 0432 212 96; Via Viola 7; meals €20; ⏱ 11am-3pm & 7pm-midnight Mon, Tue & Thu-Sun) The classic Italian *osteria*, right down to the easy, no-frills vibe and checkered tablecloths. Those who love to learn the lowdown on their food will appreciate the cook, who (when in the mood) explains everything in detail. Top choices include the *musetto e brovada*, as well as the shank.

Gabin
PIZZA €/€€

(Map p144; ☎ 0432 29 43 02; Via dei Rizzani 19; pizzas €10-20; ⏱ noon-3pm & 6.30-11pm) Not your stock-standard pizzeria, Gabin is all about creative combinations and fastidiously selected locavore ingredients. Granted, prices exceed the average, but so does the quality and overall experience.

Osteria ai Barnabiti
FRIULIAN €/€€

(Map p142; ☎ 0432 251 50; www.enotecaosteria .it; Piazza Garibaldi 3/a; meals €20-30; ⏱ 10am-11.30pm Mon-Fri, 11am-2.30pm & 6-11.30pm Sat in winter, 10am-3pm Mon-Sat in summer) A woody, homely tavern serving excellent Friulian dishes and fine *vino*. One of the house specialties is *tazzelenghe*, a wine hailing from the Colli Orientali (ask the barkeep to explain the origin of the name).

While a tasting menu is offered in the evenings, those with less ravenous appetites can drop by for a spritz, cheeses and cold cuts.

Ex Provinciali
ITALIAN €/€€

(Map p144; ☎ 0432 51 20 73; www.exprovinciali. it; Via della Prefettura 3; meals €20-30; ⏱ 11am-1am Mon-Sat) Ex Provinciali's cook hails from Cremona, which translates into Friulian cooking with creative Lombard twists. House specialities include freshly made tagliatelle with orange and asparagus.

Biffi
PIZZA, FRIULIAN €€

(Map p142; ☎ 0432 29 71 86; Via Poscolle 59; meals from €20; ⏱ noon-3pm & 7pm-midnight Tue-Sun) A popular, cacophonous, spacious pizzeria whose offerings include a hyper local *frico* pizza. Pie aside, Biffi also plates up classic Friulian dishes, both turf and surf.

★ L'Alimentare
DELI €€

(Map p144; ☎ 0432 50 37 27; www.lalimentare. it; Via D'Aronco 39; meals from €25; ⏱ 10.30am-2.30pm Mon, 10.30am-2.30pm & 6-10pm Tue-Thu, to 10.30pm Fri & Sat) An Udine hotspot for years, this gourmet deli and eatery peddles delicious tartare, starters and tastings of local wines and craft beers in a tranquil, relaxed atmosphere. Its take-home Friulian products are reasonably priced.

Trattoria ai Frati
FRIULIAN €€

(Map p142; ☑0432 50 69 26; www.trattoriaaifrati.it; Piazzetta Antonini 5; meals €25; ⊗bar 8.30am-midnight Mon-Sat, restaurant noon-2.45pm & 7-10.30pm Mon-Sat) Leaving Udine without a meal at this historic trattoria would be a mistake. A traditional *fogolâr* welcomes diners, who tuck into house-made pasta and *frico* while card-playing, *tajut*-swilling veterans chatter and bellow in the background.

If you're keen on a view of the canal, head up to the fabulous first-floor terrace.

★ Antica Maddalena
FRIULIAN €€

(Map p144; ☑0432 50 05 44; www.anticamaddalena.it; Via Pellicerie 4; meals €30-35; ⊗6pm-midnight Mon, 11am-3pm & 6pm-midnight Tue-Sat) A small, family-run restaurant with a penchant for culinary brilliance.

Osteria Toscano
TUSCAN €€

(Map p142; ☑0432 50 53 36; Via Poscolle 49; meals € 30-35; ⊗12.30-2pm & 7.30-10pm Mon-Fri, 7.30-10pm Sat) True to its name, Osteria Toscano finds its inspiration in the simple, strong flavours of Tuscan cooking. The menu includes dishes like *pici cacio e pepe* and pappardelle with wild boar, with recipes handed down from mother to son.

The cellar has an exceptional inventory of wines, Friulian and otherwise, while the lovely courtyard is just the ticket for those wishing to dine al fresco.

Al Tagliato
ITALIAN €€€

(Map p144; ☑0432 174 38 87; www.altaglia.it; Via Paolo Sarpi 4/c; meals from €25; ⊗11.30am-10.30pm Tue-Sun) If you're not too fussed about being fussed over, opt for an outdoor table and enjoy a quick bite while watching the passing parade. Bites include excellent canapés, salads and Friulian 'tapas', with discounted Americano cocktails on Tuesdays.

Alla Tavernetta
FRIULIAN €€€

(Map p144; ☑0432 501 066; www.allatavernetta.com; Via Artico di Prampero 2; meals from €30; ⊗noon-3.30pm & 7pm-midnight Tue-Sat, also noon-6pm Sun in summer) In a tranquil location and with outdoor seating, Alla Tavernetta faithfully celebrates Friulian culinary traditions. Top-notch seafood dishes include excellent scallops, complimented by a carefully considered selection of regional wines.

F IS FOR FRICO

Your culinary memories of Friuli will most likely feature *frico*, one of the region's most iconic bites. Served hot and accompanied by baked polenta, it's made up of very simple ingredients: cheese (usually Montasio) and potatoes, pan cooked to an omelette-like consistency. Its many variations include the addition of onions or speck, with every corner of the region claiming its own traditional recipe. If you find yourself addicted and need a stash to take home, you'll find it in convenient vacuum packs at many local grocery stores.

Aquila Nera
FRIULIAN €€/€€€

(Map p142; ☑392 654 01 38; www.aquilanera.biz; Via Piave 2/a; meals €35-45; ⊗11am-3pm & 7-11.30pm Mon-Sat) If these walls could talk they'd tell the story of Italy; it's said that Aquila Nera was already in business in the days of revolutionary Giuseppe Mazzini and the Risorgimento.

Recently reopened, this historic tavern remains true to Friulian food and wine, with everything from the appetisers to the desserts utterly delicious.

Vitello d'Oro
FRIULIAN €€€

(Map p144; ☑0432 50 89 82; www.vitellodoro.com; Via Erasmo Valvason 4; meals €45-55; ⊗7-10.30pm Mon, noon-2.30pm & 7-10.30pm Tue & Thu-Sun, Tue-Sat in summer) Founded in 1849, this local veteran given traditional dishes modern tweaks.

Seafood is the house speciality, paired with produce from the Friulian countryside.

🍷 Drinking & Nightlife

★ Osteria e Locanda al Cappello
OSTERIA

(Map p144; ☑0432 29 93 27; www.osteriaalcappello.it; Via Paolo Sarpi 5; ⊗10.30am-3pm & 5.30-11pm Tue-Fri, 10am-3pm & 5.30pm-midnight Sat, 10am-3pm & 5.30-9pm Sun in winter) True to its name (*cappello* is Italian for 'hat'), this *osteria* is hung with hundreds of caps and hats under which jovial crowds guzzle prosecco and nosh on *crostini*. It's the kind of place you plan on having a quick drink and end up staying all night.

Indeed, the place even has six **rooms** (☑335 676 78 30; s/d with breakfast €75/120).

★**Al Pignolo** WINE BAR
(Map p144; ☑349 359 93 59; Via Manin 6; ⊙11am-midnight) Petite and refined, this wine bar takes its *vino* seriously: expect the barkeep to give you a detailed rundown of the wine you're drinking, from provenance and history to tasting notes.

Metropolis BISTRO
(Map p144; ☑0432 60 46 58; Via Mercatovecchio 1; ⊙11am-1am) A hip spot in an unbeatable location, Metropolis flanks Porticato del Lippomano, where you can sit down for a fabulous aperitif, surrounded by the city's nightlife. Booze-soaking small plates are on standby.

Lume PUB, RESTAURANT
(Map p144; ☑0432 172 10 10; Via Pellicceria 11/a; ⊙6pm-2am Tue-Sun) A pub with neighbouring restaurant, separated by an eyewear store. Ideal for a predinner tipple, it pulls cool types sauntering down Via Pellicceria.

Caffè Contarena CAFE
(Map p144; ☑0432 51 27 41; www.contarena.it; Via Cavour 1; ⊙8am-3.30pm Mon, 8am-late Tue-Sat, 8.30am-late Sun) Chic, magnificent Contarena is one of Udine's most famous cafes, a coffee-scented, Art-Nouveau veteran a stone's throw from Piazza della Libertà.

Da Michele OSTERIA €
(Map p144; ☑391 394 41 00; Via Paolo Sarpi 18/a; ⊙11am-midnight) The classic Friulian tavern, with terracotta barrel vaults, prosciutto hanging from the walls, and an unpretentious vibe. Low prices, loads of wines and tasty canapés making for one perfect *aperitivo*.

Alle Volte COCKTAIL BAR, OSTERIA
(Map p144; ☑0432 163 70 69; www.osteriallevolta.it; Via Mercatovecchio 4; cocktails €15-20; ⊙bar 9am-3pm & 6pm-late, restaurant noon-2.30pm & 7-11.30pm Mon-Sat) Easy to miss (the entrance is in an alley off Via Mercatovecchio), Alle Volte pours some of Udine's finest cocktails. Hidden at the back is an *osteria*, where you can lunch under an atmospheric brick-vaulted ceiling.

Quinto Recinto BAR, RESTAURANT
(Map p144; ☑327 287 74 12; Largo dei Pecile 3; cocktails €8, meals €10-20; ⊙7.30am-midnight Mon-Thu & Sun, until 1am Fri & Sat) Cyclist-friendly drinking holes with adjoining bike workshops are all the rage in Italy and this is Udine's offering. Sip *vino* or slurp an Italian craft brew while talking cadence, brakes

and grand tours. The in-house eatery is a very popular lunch spot.

Buca di Bacco WINE BAR
(Map p144; ☑348 902 53 32; Via Battisti 21; ⊙10am-3pm & 6-11pm Mon-Sat) Buca di Bacco is known for its *aperitivo*-hour *grissinone al prosciutto*, a huge, crispy breadstick wrapped in the region's famous ham. Wash it down with a well-chosen Friulian wine.

Taverna dell'Angelo PUB
(Map p144; ☑0432 50 77 52; Via Lovaria 3/d; ⊙7pm-2am Mon-Sat) It's wise to hit this pub on a full stomach given its impressive selection of Scottish whiskeys, cognacs and spirits may see you itching to sample several. Alternatively, line your belly with its delicious *panini* and appetisers. Those who simply must pair their tipple with a cigar can do so too, with a dedicated smoking room onsite.

The Black Stuff PUB
(Map p142; ☑0432 50 83 96; www.theblackstuff.it; Via Gorghi 3/a; ⊙6pm-2am) An easy-going Irish pub serving high-quality beer and regular live music; check the website for upcoming events.

Liberty COCKTAIL BAR
(Map p142; ☑333 160 21 31; www.facebook.com/libertyudine; Viale del Ledra 56; ⊙6pm-3am Mon-Sat) Picky cocktail drinkers adore Art Nouveau-inspired Liberty, whose dexterous barkeeps concoct impressive libations. Prices are higher than the norm, but so is the standard. Jazz fans take note: the venue hosts the occasional live gig.

Da Teresina OSTERIA
(Map p144; ☑348 928 08 06; Via Paolo Sarpi 10/a; ⊙5pm-midnight Mon-Thu, to 1am Fri, noon-2.30pm & 5pm-1am Sat, noon-2.30pm & 5-11pm Sun) Arguably the humblest, least pretentious of the options on Via Paolo Sarpi, this classic, well-lit tavern has a charming courtyard occasionally bustling with high-spirited, graduating students. Drinks include an interesting selection of local craft beers.

☆ Entertainment

Caffè Caucigh CAFE, PUB
(Map p142; ☑0432 50 27 19; caffecaucigh.wixsite.com/caucigh; Via Gemona 36; ⊙7am-11pm Tue-Fri, to midnight Sat, 8am-10pm Sun) The Friday jazz jams at Caucigh (Udine's oldest cafe) draws audiences from across the city. If

you're nearby and it's the right day, don't miss the experience.

Visionario
CINEMA

(Map p142; ☑0432 22 77 98; www.visionario.info; Via Asquini 33; ☺30min before the first screening) An interesting multiplex cinema screening a mix of new-release blockbusters and independent flicks, both new and classic. In the summer, exhibitions and special events are organised onsite too. If you're driving, free parking is available out the front.

★Arci Cas*Aupa
MUSIC

(Map p142; Via Val d'Aupa 2; www.casaupa.org; ☺varies; 🛜) Udine's only real concert hall hosts weekend DJ sets, live concerts and all kinds of activities. The venue is part of the ARCI cultural association, so you'll need a membership card to enter; these are readily available at the venue. To get here, take bus 2 from the train station.

Stadio Friuli
FOOTBALL

(Map p142; ☑0432 54 49 11; Piazzale Repubblica Argentina) Even if you're not a soccer fan, cheering on the city's beloved Udinese team with Friulian die-hards is solid good fun. The fastest way to score tickets is at tobacconists; don't forget your photo ID. To reach the stadium (known as Dacia Arena), catch bus 9 from the station.

🔒 Shopping

Galleria Bardelli
ARCADE

(Map p144; ☑0432 50 46 53; www.galleriabardelli .com; Via Canciani 15) Even if you're not seeking retail therapy, it's worth strolling through Galleria Bardelli to experience Udine's elegant side. Long the city's commercial hub, it's a pleasant and lively place lined with major international brands. The gallery itself is always open, unlike the shops inside.

Kobo Shop
MUSIC & BOOKS

(Map p144; ☑338 326 12 44; Via Palladio 7; ☺9.30am-1pm & 3.30-7.30pm Tue-Sat) Lovers of design, comics, music and counterculture should make a beeline for this shop as soon as they set foot in Udine. Stocked with hard-to-find items, it's the kind of place where you'll want to buy everything on display.

SeR
MILLINERY

(Map p144; ☑0432 29 99 45; serconcettiperuomo .it; Via Paolo Sarpi 3; ☺9.30am-12.30pm & 3.30-7.30pm Tue-Sat) Rubbing shoulders with Osteria e Locanda al Cappello, this shop sells all kinds of quality men's hats and accessories. Styles range from aristocratic to hipster.

Cityalps
OUTDOOR

(Map p144; ☑0432 148 22 50; www.cityalpstore.it; Piazza Guglielmo Marconi 5/a; ☺9.30am-12.30pm & 3.30-7.30pm Tue-Fri, 9.30am-7.30pm Sat) If you fancy hitting the Alps but have only packed a swimsuit, Cityalps has everything you need for a high-altitude adventure, from snug socks and running shoes, to waterproof jackets and headlamps.

Wool Style
FASHION & ACCESSORIES

(Map p142; ☑333 736 17 92; www.facebook. com/WoolStyle2018; Via Cussignacco 4/b; ☺9am-12.30pm Mon-Wed, 9am-12.30pm & 3.30-7pm Sat) When temperatures drop, this little store will keep you snug with its booty of bold, contemporary garments, handmade using high-quality wool. Pick up anything from jackets and sweaters to scarves.

★C.L.U.F.
BOOKS

(Map p142; ☑0432 29 54 47; Via Gemona 22; ☺9am-12.30pm & 3.30-7pm Mon-Sat) An erudite bookshop with a thoughtful selection of titles, some of which are hard to find elsewhere (especially its illustrated books). Friendly, helpful staff seal the deal.

Libreria Editrice Odòs
BOOKS & MAPS

(Map p144; ☑0432 20 43 07; www.odos.it; Vicolo della Banca 6; ☺9.30am-12.30pm & 4-8pm Tue-Sat) A bookshop specialising in travel, complete with an in-house travel publishing company focussed on the Balkans. Stock up on travel tomes and maps covering every corner of the globe, including cycling maps of Friuli Venezia Giulia.

ℹ Information

TOURIST INFORMATION

Udine Infopoint (Map p144, D2; ☑0432 29 59 72; www.turismofvg.it; Piazza 1° Maggio 7; ☺9am-1pm & 2-5.30pm Mon-Sat, 9am-1pm Sun) Udine's tourist office provides free maps and information on sights and activities in and around the city. It also stocks audio guides and the FVG Card (see p53). Opening times vary seasonally.

ℹ Getting There & Away

BUS

Udine's bus station (Map p142, E6; ☑0432 50 69 41; Viale Europa Unita 35/8) is located some 200m from the train station and connected to it by an underpass. Facilities include a left-luggage office.

TPL FVG (☑ 800 05 20 40, mobile 040 971 23 43; https://tplfvg.it) operates frequent buses from Udine to Trieste (€7.65, 2hr 10min), Gorizia (€5.70, 2hr 15min) and Pordenone (€7.65, 2hr). It also offers good connections to destinations within Udine province, including Palmanova (€3.85, 40min), Gemona del Friuli (€4.35, 1hr 6min), Venzone (€5.05, 1hr 38min) and San Daniele del Friuli (€4.35, 1hr). For all routes, timetables and fares, see www.mycicero.it/tplfvg-go.

CAR & MOTORCYLE
From Milan Take the A4 and exit at Palmanova, continuing towards Udine on the A23 Palmanova–Udine–Tarvisio.

TRAIN
From Stazione Centrale (Map p142, D6; Viale Europa Unita 90) Trains connects Udine with the whole region, including Trieste Airport. Frequent services to Milan run via Venezia Mestre (from €56.55, 5hr 6min).

🛈 Getting Around
BICYCLE
Some say that the best way to appreciate Udine is on a bicycle, and a number of hotels offer bike rental. Alternatively, you can use the city's bike-sharing service **UDINEbike**. For information on how to use it, see www.comune.udine.it/udinebike.

PUBLIC TRANSPORT
Bus
TPL FVG (☑ 800 05 20 40, mobile 040 971 23 43; https://tplfvg.it) manages Udine's public transport. Udine's compact city centre makes public transport unnecessary in most cases, though buses are useful for reaching neighbouring towns. Most routes run from around 6.10am to 11pm.

Taxi
Radiotaxi Udine (☑ 0432 50 58 58; www.taxiudine.it) Open 24 hours.

T-car (☑ 0432 449 66) Services Udine and its surrounds.

THE PLAIN SOUTH OF UDINE

As you leave Udine heading south, you'll have the chance to appreciate some of Friuli's Renaissance legacies, from the fortress city of Palmanova, to Villa Manin, last residence of the doge of Venice. In between is a tapestry of charming villages, steadfast medieval castles and old city walls and towers. While public transport reaches all the destinations mentioned following, interchanges and exhausting waits make driving your easiest option

for exploring the area. If you do opt for public transport, plan your trip carefully in advance.

🛈 Getting There & Away
BUS
TPL FVG (☑ 800 05 20 40, mobile 040 971 23 43; https://tplfvg.it) runs buses from Udine to Palmanova (€3.85, 50min) via Clauiano (€3.85, 40min). Between 6.55am and 7.40pm, buses run frequently between Udine and Codroipo (€4.35, 40min).

CAR & MOTORCYLE
Palmanova is very conveniently located at the intersection of the A4 (Venice–Trieste) and A23 (Udine–Tarvisio) motorways, with the city centre a few minutes' drive from the Palmanova exits. From Palmanova, the SP33 heads north to Clauiano, another of Italy's most beautiful villages. If heading to Codroipo from Milan, take the A4 towards Trieste and exit at Latisana.

TRAIN
Trenitalia (www.trenitalia.com) From Udine, trains reach Palmanova on the Udine–Cervignano line (€2.95, 12min, roughly hourly). Direct services also run between Udine and Codroipo on the Venice–Udine line (€3.50, 14min, roughly half-hourly). See the website for details.

Palmanova
POP 5312 / ELEV 27M

Palmanova is more than an historic, Unesco World Heritage–listed town. It's a life-size model of a Renaissance utopian city. While the best place to fully appreciate its shape – a nine-pointed star – is from the air (consider taking a hot-air balloon flight on Easter Monday, p156), a quick Google image search will reveal its extraordinary layout. That said, Palmanova leaves its mark at street level too: from its three city gates, each street leads straight to central Piazza Grande, closed to traffic and often bustling with local festivals and fairs. Best of all, even the most disorientated of visitors will find it difficult to get lost: after all, Palmanova is a mere 650 Venetian steps (circa 1.6km) wide.

⦿ Sights
★ Fortifications   DEFENSIVE WALLS
Construction on the fortress of Palmanova began in 1593 at the behest of Venice, which was concerned about Habsburg and Ottoman incursions. Its design adhered to the principles of Renaissance military architecture, which reflected advancements in ballis-

Palmanova

Palmanova

◎ Sights

1	Duomo	B2
2	Palazzo del Governatore delle Armi	C3
3	Palazzo del Monte di Pietà	C3
4	Palazzo del Provveditore Generale	B3
5	Piazza Grande	B3
6	Polveriera Napoleonica Garzoni	C2
7	Porta Aquileia	B4
8	Porta Cividale	C2
9	Porta Udine	B2

⊜ Sleeping

10	Zona 30	C2

⊗ Eating & Drinking

11	Caffetteria Torinese	B2
12	Il Melograno	C3
13	Osteria Campana d'Oro	B2
14	Terra Madre 1891	B3

🛍 Shopping

15	Palmanova Outlet Village	off map C4

tic techniques. The result is a striking, star-shaped fortification designed to withstand the trajectory of cannons. It's possible to walk or cycle along the entire ramparts, passing old moats, bulwarks and Napoleonic **powder kegs** like the Garzoni, open to the public during exhibitions. The ramparts form the innermost circle of walls and give access to the city through three gates: **Porta Aquileia, Porta Udine** and **Porta Cividale**. Head through them to see the old wheels once used for lifting the drawbridges, as well as the paths once roamed by soldiers on patrol. Just outside the ramparts are the **rivellini**, built by the Venetians in the 17th century to defend the city gates and the weaker flat sections of the first circle of walls. In 1806, Napoleon added an additional defensive element to prevent enemy fire from reaching the heart of the fortress and had the **lunettes** of the outer circle of walls built. Aligned to form a trio of nine-pointed stars, the three concentric walls are connected to each other by a series of tunnels, winding for hundreds of metres at a depth of 9m.

Restored by a group of speleologists, the passageways are accessible to the public; contact the tourist office to find out more information.

Piazza Grande   PIAZZA

Nowhere is a town square quite as central as it is in Palmanova. On a map, Piazza Grande (formerly Piazza delle Armi) is a veritable bullseye, from which city streets shoot out in every direction. The square's most important building is the **Duomo**, a gleaming baroque beauty dating from the 17th century. Other notable buildings flanking the hexagonal piazza include **Palazzo del Provveditore Generale** (1611), **Palazzo del Monte di Pietà** (1666) and **Palazzo del Governatore delle Armi** (1613).

🏃 Activities

Fvgnordicwalking   NORDIC WALKING

(www.facebook.com/fvgnordicwalking) A nice way to appreciate the zig-zag pattern of the Palmanova ramparts is to grab some poles and go Nordic walking along the entire route. Alternatively, rent a mountain bike and pedal between ravelins and lunettes; trail signs will guide you.

✨ Festivals & Events

Pasquetta sui Bastioni   MARCH/APRIL

Easter Monday is one of the best times to visit Palmanova, as the day is celebrated on the city's ramparts. Events include hot-air balloon rides, which offer an unforgettable view of the city's distinctive star shape. For little ones, there's carriage rides and kite-making workshops.

Palma alle Armi   SEPTEMBER

If you happen to be in Palmanova in September and spot knights charging the city walls on their steeds, shouting 'War!' and duelling, don't panic: it's merely a military re-enactment that takes the city back to 1615 for three atmospheric days.

🛏 Sleeping

★**Zona 30**   B&B €€

(☎ 328 008 10 78; www.zona30.eu; Via Pasqualigo 5; r from €78; P ❄ 🛜) A brand-new, bike-friendly B&B, with three smart, contemporary rooms and one enthusiastic team. If you're travelling by bike (worth considering given the area is especially suitable for riding), you'll appreciate the safe storage area, not to mention the bike workshop and e-bike charging station. Don't have a bike? No problem: they rent them.

🍴 Eating & Drinking

★**Caffetteria Torinese**   BAR €

(☎ 0432 92 07 32; www.caffetteriatorinese.com; Piazza Grande 9; mains €7-13; ⊙ 6.30am-midnight Mon, 7.30am-midnight Tue & Thu, 7.30am-1am Fri & Sat, 8am-11pm Sun; 🛜) Going strong since 1938, the Torinese was voted 'Best Bar in Italy' in 2014. Years later, it hasn't lost its lustre. Classic *caffè con brioche* (coffee with croissant) aside, the veteran serves up fantastic dishes prepared with seasonal ingredients. if it's October, feast on truffles (or the salted cod, oysters or snails).

Terra Madre 1891   ITALIAN €

(☎ 0432 93 25 03; Borgo Aquileia 1; meals from €20; ⊙ 7am-10pm) Entering Palmanova from Porta Aquileia you'll stumble upon this cheery place, where you can tuck into succulent prosciutto platters, wash down *aperitivo* bites

---

PEOPLE POWER & UNESCO

Just over a decade ago, Palmanova's mighty Renaissance walls were a sorry sight. Vegetation had literally swallowed the fortifications and park, and the place where many locals had spent the happiest moments of their childhood had almost disappeared under a blanket of brambles.

In 2011, the local administration launched a clever operation which saw over 3000 volunteers help clean them up, and within two short weeks, the walls had been returned to their former glory.

It was well worth the effort: in 2017, Palmanova was declared a Unesco World Heritage site (together with Bergamo, Peschiera del Garda, Zadar and Sibenik in Croatia and Cattaro in Montenegro) as an important Venetian work of defence between the 16th and 17th centuries.

> **ⓘ BICIBUS**
>
> Friuli Venezia Giulia has always been bike-friendly, with many kilometres of cycling trails spread across the region. Equipped with special bike wagons, **Bicibus** (📞 800 05 20 40; www.tplfvg.it; 🕒 toll-free number 6am-10pm) services allows cyclists to hop on and off buses along the Alpe Adria (p242) bike trail.
>
> Bicibus services run between Grado-Gorizia-Cormòns, Udine-Palmanova-Aquileia-Grado, Udine-Latisana-Ligna-no and Maniago-Gemona. For Bicibus guidelines and timetables, check the website.

with a Sauvignon, or swoon over the outstanding, homemade *tagliolini*.

Il Melograno   FRIULIAN €€
(📞 0432 92 02 71; www.ilmelograno.online; Contrada Villachiara 34; meals from €25; 🕒 noon-2.30pm & 6-11.30pm) A spacious, bright restaurant which is especially ideal for groups (even if it can get very crowded on weekends, especially outdoors).

In addition to local specialities, the place pours an interesting selection of craft beers. Gluten-free dishes available.

Osteria Campana d'Oro   FRIULIAN €€/€€€
(📞 0432 92 87 19; www.osteriacampanadoro.it; Borgo Udine 27; meat menu €25-35, seafood menu €35-45; lunch & dinner Wed-Sat, lunch only Mon & Sun) This is one of Palmanova's finest restaurants, with impeccable service that never feels stuffy and polished Friulian dishes made strictly with locally grown and seasonal ingredients.

If they're on the menu, try the Montasio flan and eggplant gnocchi.

🛍 Shopping

Palmanova Outlet Village   OUTLET MALLS
(📞 0432 83 78 10; www.palmanovavillage.it; SP125, Km 1.6, Joannis-Aiello del Friuli; 🕒 10am-8pm) A popular mall 5km southeast of central Palmanova, with over 90 outlets offering good discounts on Italian and international fashion, accessories, beauty and homewares.

ⓘ Information

Palmanova Infopoint (Map p155, B2; 📞 0432 92 48 15; Borgo Udine 4; 🕒 9am-1pm & 2-6pm summer, 9am-1pm & 1.30-5.30pm Mon-Sat, 9am-1pm

Sun winter) Visitor centre with audio guides and information on sights, activities and exhibitions in and around town. It also sells the FVG Card.

Clauiano

POP 457 / ELEV 36M

A hamlet located a few kilometres north of Palmanova, Clauiano is on the list of the most beautiful villages in Italy.

A perfectly intact medieval creature, it charms its visitors with its distinctive stone abodes, marked by magnificent courtyards and large doors with white-stone frames.

To savour the place, enjoy a lazy amble through its *centro storico* (historic centre): on weekend mornings, the stillness that cloaks its streets borders on eerie.

Clauiano was born from the merging of two villages that during the Middle Ages had developed around the Chiesa di San Giorgio and the Chiesa di San Martino.

The two churches were connected to each other by a road which would eventually become the state route leading from Palmanova to Trivignano.

The oldest part of the village, located around the Chiesa di San Giorgio, dates from the 15th century.

✪ Festivals & Events

Borgo in Fiore   APRIL
Blooming in early April, Clauiano's flower festival brings together local artisans and nurseries. Flowers and plants of all kinds enliven the village, as well as art exhibitions, stalls and floral-themed cultural events.

ⓘ Information

Infopoint (Via della Filanda 1, in the Spazio Espositivo courtyard; 🕒 8am-8pm) Provides useful information to cyclists travelling on the Alpe Adria trail.

Codroipo

POP 16,069 / ELEV 43M

Stupendous **Villa Manin** (📞 0432 82 12 11; www.villamanin-eventi.it; Piazza Manin 10) has no shortage of admirers. And, in fact, as you approach the complex you will grasp its charm and importance: the last doge of Venice in Friuli (Ludovico Manin) resided here.

This importance is also underlined by the splendid architecture: designed in the mid-17th century, the villa owes its present appearance to a restoration that took place in the 18th century, which has made it in effect a baroque masterpiece.

The 17-hectare park is full of fountains and statues that seem to be waiting for your photographs. The park hosts concerts and other events, especially in summer, and Villa Manin also hosts various art exhibitions.

In the vicinity of the villa, also in Codroipo, is the headquarters of the **National Aerobatic Team**. From March to September it is possible to attend training: see the PromoTurismo FVG website (www.turismofvg.it/live-freccia-tricolori).

Heading towards San Martino, a few kilometres south of the villa, the wonderfully nostalgic **Museo Civico delle Carrozze d'Epoca** (☑ 0432 91 24 93 Via San Pietro 6, Località San Martino; adult/reduced €3/2; ⊕9am-3pm Fri, 2-6pm Sun) showcases 44 carriages built between the 19th and 20th centuries in various parts of the world, as well as period toys in wood, tin, fabric and porcelain.

If you plan on visiting the museum, also stop in at trattoria **Da Vanda** (☑ 0432 90 00 29; Via Erminia 9, Località San Martino; meals €20-30; ⊕11.30am-2pm Mon & Tue, 11.30am-2pm & 7-9pm Thu- Sun), popular with locals and serving standout *frico* and *salame all'aceto* (salami with vinegar).

ⓘ Information

IAT (☑ 0432 82 12 57; Passariano hamlet, Piazzale Manin 10, Barchessa di Levante; ⊕10am-7pm Tue-Sun) Tourist office at Villa Manin, with information on Codroipo, its surrounds, and the rest of Friuli Venezia Giulia.

A SKYSCRAPING CAMPANILE

Traveling along the road that connects Palmanova to Codroipo, you'll notice a bell tower standing out on the horizon. It belongs to the **Duomo di Mortegliano** (☑ 0432 76 00 50; Piazza San Paolo 2), a beautiful neo-Gothic church from 1890 that claims one of the region's most precious wooden altars.

Yet, what makes this church truly unique is its octagonal, brick-and-concrete bell tower: at 113.2m, it's the highest in Italy.

Its construction began in 1958 following the demolition of the previous tower, damaged after WWI.

THE HILLS NORTH OF UDINE

The hills immediately north of Udine harbour some of the Friuli's most picture-perfect villages, and each has its drawcard: birds, butterflies, secret rooms, even mummies. Mixed in among them is a healthy dose of castles and villas. This area was one of the worst affected by the 1976 earthquake (see p169), with beautiful Gemona and Venzone still bearing signs from the deadly event. South of these villages, palates and minds are stimulated in the prosciutto factories and bookstores of San Daniele. If you have your own wheels, cruise aimlessly through the hills, following your instincts or the Tagliamento River. Wherever you land, Friulian history and culinary traditions await, at evocative ruins, ramshackle farmhouses and, last but never least, the local *osteria*.

ⓘ Getting There & Away

BUS

TPL FVG (☑ 800 05 20 40, mobile 040 971 23 43; https://tplfvg.it) runs buses to every municipality in Udine province. Frequent services run from Udine to San Daniele (€1.65, 32min), which continue through to Fagagna (€2.75, 35min) and Montegnacco (€4.35, 1hr). Also from Udine, buses reach Gemona (€3.50, 39min), Venzone (€5.05, 49min), Pinzano al Tagliamento (€4.25, 50min), Forgaria nel Friuli (€5, 56min), Ragogna (€4.25, 46min via San Daniele) and Osoppo (€5.05, 1hr 34min via Majano or Gemona). For Lago di Cavazzo, bus 170 from Udine to Tolmezzo (€6.65, 1hr 12min) also passes through Cavazzo Carnico (€6.65, 49min).

CAR & MOTORCYLE

From Udine, simply exit north on the A23 and follow the signs. The road is particularly beautiful towards Gemona and Venzone, often skirting or crossing the Tagliamento River.

TRAIN

Trenitalia (www.trenitalia.com) trains on the Udine–Tarvisio line stop at Gemona (€3.25, 1hr, half-hourly) and Venzone (€4, 1hr). Neither San Daniele or Osoppo is serviced by passenger trains; the most convenient station is Udine, from where you can continue by bus.

Fagagna

POP 6068 / ELEV 177M

It's not so much the road signs as the gob-smacking number of white storks and ibises in the sky that confirm you've arrived

AURELIO IN THE TOWN OF SUNDIALS

It all started about 20 years ago, when **Aiello del Friuli** resident Aurelio Pantanali decided to 'fill in' an asymmetrical void in the facade of his building by drawing a sundial. Not only did his research into gnomons, shadow lengths and hour-lines turn into a personal passion, it sparked a town-wide craze, with everywhere from churches and schools to private homes getting in on the act with their own personalised timepieces.

Today, this modest settlement of 2200 inhabitants has broken records by claiming over 100 sundials, earning it the moniker **'Town of Sundials'**. Aiello even hosts an annual sundial competition, in which four new sundials are subject to a popular vote.

If possible, join a **guided tour** (Circolo Culturale Navarca; ☑0431 99 87 70, 324 777 65 84; www.ilsoleeiltempo.it; Via Marconi; €80), which lasts around two hours and is more fascinating than you may think. Clued up on the technical specifics of these ancient solar clocks, you'll never look at a shadow in quite the same way. If you're not driving, public transport connects the town to Udine, Grado and Gorizia.

in Fagagna. (If you've brought your binoculars, now would be a very good time to make use of them.)

Birdlife centre **Oasi dei Quadris** (☑331 978 85 74; www.oasideiquadris.it; Via Caporiacco; adult/reduced €4/3; ⊙varies, closed Sep–mid-Mar) extends some 100 hectares around the village. Created to safeguard local flora and fauna, it's a good spot for **birdwatching** and nature walks.

Fagnana is another of Italy's most beautiful villages, and at the top of the hill, you can visit what remains of the **castle**. Little is known of its history; it's believed to date back to at least the 10th century, but only a few ruins remain, including the crenellated, fairytale tower.

The hill itself offers a commanding view of the plain around Udine.

Next to the castle you will find the **Chiesa di San Michele in Castello**, built sometime before the 13th century and renovated in the 16th century.

Fagagna also claims **Cjase Cocèl** (☑0432 80 18 87; www.museocjasecocel.it; Via Lisignana 40; adult/reduced €3/2.50; ⊙varies, generally 9.30am-12.30pm Mon-Fri, Sat & Sun by appointment), which sheds light on local peasant life and toil between the 19th and 20th centuries. Set up in an old rural house, the child-friendly museum includes a dairy where cheese is still produced today.

⭐ Festivals & Events

Corse dai Mus   SEPTEMBER
A historic donkey race held in Fagagna on the first Sunday in September since 1861.

✗ Eating

★San Michele   RESTAURANT €€
(☑0432 81 04 66; www.sanmicheleristorante.com; Via Castello di Fagagna 33; meals from €35; ⊙10.30am-3pm & 5.30pm-midnight Wed-Sun) If it's sunny, grab a seat in the garden; in case it gets cold there's the warmth of the *fogolâr* inside.

Occupying a 13th-century building at the foot of the castle, San Michele plates up ambitious traditional dishes, from saffron risotto with shellfish to duck breast casserole.

Al Bàcar   FRIULIAN €€€
(☑0432 81 10 36; www.al-bacar.ory.it; Via Umberto I 29; meals from €35; ⊙7.30am-10.30pm Mon-Sat) Once an *osteria,* Al Bàcar has evolved into a sophisticated restaurant serving refined, beautifully presented dishes flaunting high-quality, seasonal ingredients.

San Daniele del Friuli

POP 7989 / ELEV 252M
Thanks to its world-famous prosciutto, San Daniele del Friuli is a holy grail for food lovers. Yet ham is only one of the town's specialities. The other is trout, which is bred in the Tagliamento River and meticulously smoked at less than 30°C.

Moreover, San Daniele is more than its celebrated edibles and salt-of-the-earth appearance. Dig deeper and you'll discover a surprisingly cultured place of libraries, precious manuscripts and unexpected artistic treasures. So, before succumbing to its sweet, nutty, smoky flavours, feed mind and spirit with a wander through its streets, churches and historic *palazzi*.

San Daniele del Friuli

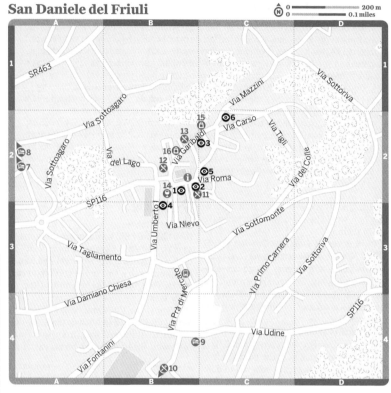

San Daniele del Friuli

⦿ Sights

1	Biblioteca Guarneriana	B2
2	Casa del Trecento	B2
3	Chiesa di Sant'Antonio Abate	C2
4	Consorzio del Prosciutto di San Daniele	B3
5	Duomo	C2
6	Porta Gemona (Portonat)	C2

🛏 Sleeping

7	Casa Rossa Ai Colli	off map A2
8	Cascina Pittiani del Lago	off map A2
9	Mezza Mela	B4

✴ Eating

10	Ai Bintars	off map B4
11	Al Bersagliere	B2
12	Meister	B2
13	Osteria di Tancredi	B2

🍷 Drinking & Nightlife

14	La Trappola	B2

🛍 Shopping

15	Adelia	C2
16	Squisito	B2

⦿ Sights

Biblioteca Guarneriana　　　LIBRARY
(📞 0432 94 65 60; www.guarneriana.it; Via Roma 1, guided tours for groups by reservation; ⊙ Old Section 9am-noon & 3-6pm Wed, 3-6pm Sat, or on request, closed Aug, Modern Section 9am-noon & 2.30-

6.15pm Tue-Fri, 9am-noon Sat) Beside the Duomo, Palazzo Comunale houses one of Italy's first public libraries. Its namesake is humanist Guarnerio d'Artegna, who donated his personal treasures to the village in 1466, among them illuminated manuscripts, bibles, maps and more. Today the library is divided into two areas, *antica* (historic) and *moderna* (modern), both awash with priceless treasures. Among these are two editions of Dante's *Divine Comedy*: one an illuminated, late 14th-century manuscript, the other a single sheet of microscopic calligraphy.

PromoTurismo FVG organises guided tours of the library (free for FVG Card holders).

Duomo   PLACE OF WORSHIP
(Piazza del Duomo; ⊘7am-6.30pm) The grand staircase and portal statues set a majestic tone at the Duomo di San Michele Arcangelo. A gleaming, baroque beauty, the cathedral owes its current look to the early 18th-century renovation of a pre-existing church. Slip inside to admire its biblically themed, 16th-century frescoes. The bell tower to the right also hails from the 16th century: begun in 1531, it was never completed.

Chiesa di Sant'Antonio Abate   PLACE OF WORSHIP
(Via Garibaldi; ⊘8am-6.30pm) Consecrated in 1308, this now deconsecrated Romanesque church houses one of the finest fresco cycles in Friuli Venezia Giulia (proudly referred to as 'Our Sistine Chapel' by locals).

It's an extraordinary union of storytelling, colour and movement, both mesmerising and luminous. The frescoes were painted by Martino da Udine (known as Pellegrino da San Daniele) in around 1500.

Casa del Trecento   HISTORIC BUILDING
(Via Roma 18) This building is either very robust or very lucky: not only has it withstood seven centuries of wars and invasions, it also dodged the bombs that decimated much of San Daniele between 1944 and 1945. Indeed, not even the quake of 1976 could bring it to its knees. Consequently, it's now the oldest building in town. Once occupied by a pawnshop, it currently houses the Associazione Nazionale Alpini (National Alpine Association). If the office is open, feel free to have a snoop inside.

Porta Gemona (Portonat)   GATE
(Via Mazzini) That Porta Gemona (Portonat to the locals) recalls Udine's Arco Bollani is no coincidence: both were designed by Renaissance starchitect Andrea Palladio. This is the only old city gate still intact. Inserted into a tower that was part of the medieval castle, it connects Via Mazzini and Via Andreuzzi.

★★ Festivals & Events

Aria di Festa   JUNE
(www.ariadifesta.it) In late June, San Daniele becomes the epicentre of a four-day festival of banquets, demonstrations and parties. Concerts are held throughout the town, food producers open their doors to the public, and revellers tuck into copious amounts of prosciutto.

🛏 Sleeping

Mezza Mela   B&B €
(www.mezzamela.eu; Via Udine 20; 1/2/3 guests with breakfast per person €32/30/28; ℗❋🤶) If you fancy snoozing in the historic centre, keep in mind this very simple but clean, bright, good-value B&B. The three bedrooms come with private bathroom, independent entrance and a pleasant terrace.

LAND OF HAM

The origins of the **Consorzio del Prosciutto di San Daniele** (Prosciutto San Daniele Consortium; ☑ 0432 95 75 15; https://prosciuttosandaniele.it; Via Ippolito Nievo 19) lie in 1961, when local citizens and producers united to protect the name and quality of their ham. Regulations for each stage of the production process were imposed to ensure a consistently high standard, ultimately leading to Prosciutto San Daniele's DOP appellation in 1996.

To this day, the town's prosciutto is produced using traditional methods: only the hind legs of Italian-reared pigs are used, seasoned preservative-free up to the thirteenth month from the beginning of the process.

The consortium unites some 20 local producers (both large and family-run), with a strict border marking the DOP area. Nine of these producers offer factory tours (highly recommended), while all have retail outlets. Quality is consistent across the board and a complete list of producers (with contacts for booking guided tours) is available on the consortium's website.

The property was temporarily closed while researching, so call first.

Casa Rossa Ai Colli
AGRITURISMO €€

(☎ 0432 03 01 15; www.casarossaaicolli.it; Via Ai Colli 2, Ragogna; s/d with breakfast from €55/80; P 🛜) Picture a restored farmhouse from 1906, an enchanting garden, wooded hills and distant mountains and you have this wonderful *agriturismo*. Rooms are well appointed and San Daniele a few minutes' drive away.

Cascina Pittiani del Lago
AGRITURISMO €€

(☎ 348 883 07 73; Via Ragogna 80; s/d with breakfast from €45/90; P ❄ 🛜 ☀) Another bucolic beauty not far from the centre, this well-equipped farmhouse comes with a swimming pool. Shrouded in silence, it's an ideal place to unplug, decompress, enjoy hearty breakfasts and gaze out over the hills. Furthermore, it's a stone's throw from Lago di Ragogna.

🍴 Eating

Chances are you're in town for its eponymous prosciutto, which you can sample at the town's prosciutto factories or at its dining tables. Just don't forget to sample the town's other cult-status bite: smoked trout.

Meister
CAFE €

(☎ 333 313 14 31; www.meistercafe.it; Piazza Vittorio Emanuele II 2; meals €15-20; ⊗ 8am-6pm Tue-Sun) Meister wears many hats: cafe, bistro, bar and bookshop. It's a fetching place, especially if you score a seat on the terrace overlooking the square.

It's also a passionate *locavore,* with everything from the asparagus and Montasio, to the craft beers and Collio wines, hailing from the area.

Al Bersagliere
FRIULIAN €/€€

(☎ 0432 95 71 42; www.albersagliere.it; Via Roma 16; meals €20-30; ⊗ 10am-10pm Wed-Mon) Entering Al Bersagliere, the scent of hand-cut *prosciutto crudo* sets mouths watering. Wipe away the drool and scan the menu, which offers all kinds of local specialities, a ton of sausages, and all at reasonable prices.

★ Ai Bintars
FRIULIAN €/€€

(☎ 0432 95 73 22; www.aibintars.com; Via Trento & Trieste 67; meals €20-30; ⊗ 12.30-2.30pm & 7.30-9.30pm Mon, Tue & Thu-Sun, 12.30-2.30pm Wed) A historic *osteria* with checkered tablecloths, wooden chairs and a splendid Berkel slicer carving through 1500 hams a year. Indeed, the focus here is on San Daniele's famous prosciutto, with a supporting cast of cheeses and

morsels sott'olio (in olive oil). Pair with a good Friulian wine and toast to simple pleasures.

Osteria di Tancredi
FRIULIAN €€

(☎ 0432 94 15 94; www.osteriaditancredi.it; Via Monte Sabotino 10; meals €25-30; ⊗ noon-2.15pm & 7-10pm Mon, Tue & Thu-Sun) Whet the appetite with *prosciutto crudo* or house salami and speck, before moving onto Friulian classics like *frico*, rabbit with herbs, delicious apple gnocchi and *cjarsons*.

There's a focus on seasonality and the recipes of the Val Pontaiba, and if you're keen on trying the so-called 'queen of San Daniele', this is the right place: the trout is always Tagliamento fresh.

🍷 Drinking & Nightlife

★ La Trappola
WINE BAR

(☎ 0432 94 20 90; www.enotecalatrappola.it; Via Cairoli 2; ⊗ 10am-10.30pm Tue-Sun) There's something magical about quaffing Friulian *vino* in a cosy, vaulted space dating from the 1300s (or in a snug, equally historic alley) and that is precisely what you'll be doing at this atmospheric *enoteca*. Swill from an impressive list of local, regional and international wines (or slurp a craft beer) while imagining the 700 years of tales these walls could tell.

🛍 Shopping

Squisito
FOOD & DRINK

(☎ 0432 94 31 13; www.squisitosandaniele.it; Via Garibaldi 1; ⊗ 9.30am-7.30pm Tue-Sat) A charming providore where you can buy prosciutto, tea, coffee and chocolate (after having rigorously sampled them, naturally). You'll also find a good selection of spices, jams and honey, with all products hailing from local farms. If you find yourself peckish, sit at a table and grab a bite.

★ Adelia
FOOD & DRINK

(☎ 0432 94 04 56; www.adeliadifant.com; Via Garibaldi 27; ⊗ 10am-1pm & 4-7pm Tue-Sat, 10.30am-1pm & 2.30-6pm Sun) If you love chocolate, this artisan chocolatier will leave you gaga. Stock up on superlative chocolate blocks, bars and pralines, made onsite using local ingredients (the liquorice-infused chocolate is phenomenal) or a cheeky drop of grappa. The shop also stocks its own line of liqueurs.

ℹ Information

Ufficio Turistico Pro San Daniele (Map p160, B2; ☎ 0432 94 07 65; www.infosandaniele.com; Via Roma 3; ⊗ 9.30am-12.30pm & 3-6pm Mon-Fri,

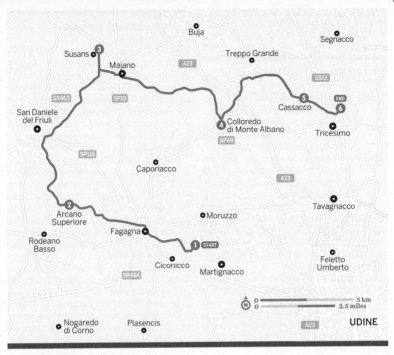

Cycling Tour
Roaming Castles

START FAGAGNA
END TRICESIMO
LENGTH 40KM; 4HR

Start in Fagagna's surrounds, at the **1 Castello di Villalta** (☎ 0432 80 01 71; www.castello divillalta.it; Via Castello 27, Villalta di Fagagna), one of the region's most beautiful castles. Destroyed, rebuilt and extended several times over the centuries, its origins lie in the 12th century; note the Ghibelline merlons crowning its stoic walls.

Continuing towards **2 Rive d'Arcano** (Località Arcano Superiore 11/c), a couple of kilometres to the east, another castle emerges, its double walls topped with Guelph merlons. Although the Castello di Arcano is a private residence, it's clearly visible from the vicinity and surrounding vineyards. Just before the castle is **Arcania winery** (☎ 0432 80 95 00; www. castellodiarcano.it), which produces and sells various types of organic wine at competitive prices.

Continuing towards Colloredo, turning at Majano, you'll arrive at **3 Castello di Susans** (☎ 0432 94 80 90; www.castellodisusans.com; Via Castello, Susans di Majano), a Medici residence from 1636 with four large towers.

Further towards **4 Colloredo di Monte Albano**, in a setting of moraine hills and gravel-rich meadows, you'll spot an imposing 14th-century fort in which 19th-century Italian writer and patriot Ippolito Nievo lived and wrote his classic novel *Confessions of an Italian*. Damaged several times over the centuries, the fort received its final blow from the earthquake of 1976. Now under reconstruction, the village that flanks it remains an atmospheric place.

From Colloredo you'll reach **5 Castello di Cassacco** (www.consorzio castelli.it; Via Cassimberg 10). Perched on the edge of a hill, it dates from 1200, with two large, well-preserved towers and a walled enclosure.

Close by, immersed in a small wood, is 17th-century **6 Castello Tricesimo** (Via del Castello 28; Località Fraelacco), home to a sanctuary run by Franciscan nuns.

10am-12.30pm & 3.30-6pm Sat & Sun) Tourist office with information on sights, exhibitions and activities in and around the town.

Pinzano al Tagliamento

POP 1497 / ELEV 206M

True to its name, the village of Pinzano enjoys an idyllic position by the region's longest river, the Tagliamento. To fully appreciate this setting, stop at the clearing before the **Ponte di Pinzano (Pinzano Bridge)**, which connects the town to San Pietro di Ragogna.

It's believed that the two banks were connected for centuries by numerous means, from wooden bridges to boats. It was only in the early 20th century that a permanent crossing was built, though its strategic location proved somewhat problematic: in November 1917, after the Battle of Caporetto, the bridge was partly destroyed by retreating Italian troops.

Provisionally restored in the 1920s, the current cantilevered structure dates from a 1970s restoration. Today it's one of the most popular places from which to admire the Tagliamento, especially for motorcyclists here to experience San Pietro di Ragogna's exhilarating hairpin turns.

If you have time up your sleeve, stop in petite Pinzano to view the Pordenone frescoes inside **Chiesa di San Martino**.

Art lovers looking for a true treasure, however, shouldn't miss the hamlet of Valeriano, a few kilometres further south.

Here you'll find the **Chiesa di Santa Maria dei Battuti**, whose gracefully simple facade is adorned with monochromatic frescoes. To the right of the entrance is a depiction of *St Christopher* by Marco Tiussi (1532); the trio to the left are saints Valerian, John the Baptist and Stephen, executed by Pordenone along with the *Magi* above them.

Directly above the entrance is the *enthroned Madonna,* depicted with the coat of arms of the noble Savorgnan family. The portal itself dates from 1499 and is the work of Giovanni Antonio Pilacorte. The original paintings are kept inside the church, built at the behest of the Battuti Christian confraternity.

Other treasures inside the building include a wonderful *Nativity scene* by Pordenone and a marble altar. The latter is a copy of an even more precious wooden altar moved to Palazzo Ricchieri in Pordenone.

Forgaria nel Friuli

POP 1722 / ELEV 270M

West of the Tagliamento and close to the Prealpi Carniche (Carnic Prealps), the nondescript village of Forgaria is known for the unforgettable **Riserva Naturale Regionale del Lago di Cornino** (☑ 0427 80 85 26; www.riservacornino.it; Via Sancornino 81; by donation; ☉ varies seasonally), a nature reserve sprawling more than 500 hectares around a pristine lake with dazzling emerald waters.

Here, an international project to protect the griffon vulture has been underway for more than 20 years, so look up to spot dozens of them hurtling through the sky. From the visitor centre, follow the trail past the large aviaries where tawny owls, griffon vultures and a handsome eagle-owl are kept, until you reach a viewing terrace overlooking the vulture rookery.

From the village, a series of simple, well-marked hiking trails lead around the lake and up **Monte Prat** (841 m), which offers an impressive view of the Tagliamento River.

One of these trails, the **sentiero Sompcornino-Ledrania-Peonis** is a bit more demanding: around 5km long and with an elevation gain of 450m, it will take about 2.5 hours to complete.

Keep an eye out for vipers, but don't forget to look up to catch impressive griffin vultures, as well as buzzards, kites and peregrine falcons.

ⓘ Information

Centro Visite della Riserva Naturale Regionale del Lago di Cornino (☑ 0427 80 85 26; www.res ervacornino.it; Via Sompcornino 81) can give you the lowdown on Grifone Project and also manages the guided tours in the reserve. Check the website for opening times as they vary seasonally.

Osoppo

POP 2829 / ELEV 184M

Osoppo was once famous for hosting Rototom Sunsplash, one of the most important reggae festivals in Europe and an event which brought 200,000 people to the area annually. The event moved to Benicàssim, Spain, in 2010. Yet, dreadlocks and congo drums aren't the only memories here.

The town stands at the foot of a historic hill, whose memory is full of episodes of resistance (against the Austrians in the Risorgimento and against the Nazi-Fascists when the Osoppo Brigade was established).

The entire urban layout of the city is designed for military purposes; in particular, if you are traveling by car you will sometimes notice, on the side of the road, parts of the ancient fortifications now in ruins.

Today Osoppo is mainly known for its fortress, which has been declared a National Monument.

★**Fortezza di Osoppo**　　　FORTRESS
(Via Olivi 5) Part of the Upper Tagliamento-Fella barrage, the Osoppo Fortress is an example of buildings erected from the Middle Ages to the 19th century adapted for defensive purposes, in this case the First War of Independence (1848).

The hill itself has occupied a strategic position since Roman times: the salt route and roads connecting Aquileia to northern Europe passed through here.

Designed to defend the eastern border of the Austro-Hungarian Empire, the fortress became useless after Italy entered the war in 1915, as the Italian army had advanced past the old border. As a result, it was disarmed and used as a warehouse before becoming a residence.

Restored after the earthquake of 1976, it's now an architectural Matryoshka doll of buildings and eras. The labyrinthine complex spans a very large area so give yourself time to explore its trenches, tunnels and defensive walls, not to mention the magnificent views of both the Tagliamento River and Friulian hills.

The hilltop fortress is accessible by car. After parking near the bar, you'll stumble upon the curious **Chiesa di San Pietro**. Note the Corinthian half-columns and neoclassical portal, which date from the 17th century. The building occupies the site of a 13th-century church, whose apse and raised presbytery survive.

The building was renovated in the Middle Ages and then demolished. Towards the end of the 18th century, it was transformed into a warehouse before being used for military purposes during the Risorgimento. What you see today is the result of the restoration that followed the 1976 earthquake.

Continuing around the hill, you'll notice the scattered remains of Roman and medieval settlements: flooring in *cocciopesto* style, the foundation of buildings, sepulchres and tombs.

ℹ Information

IAT Osoppo (☑ 0432 89 93 50, 345 314 67 97; Piazza Napoleone 5)

Ragogna

POP 2819 / ELEV 235M

Located near San Daniele, Ragogna offers what are arguably the best views of the Tagliamento River.

Start with the ones enjoyed from **Castello di San Pietro di Ragogna** (☑ 340 841 54 10; www.volontariatorar.it/il-castello-di-san-pietro-di-ragogna; Frazione San Pietro; ⊙ 2.30-6.30pm Sat & Sun Apr-Oct), a 6th-century castle overlooking the river bed.

Medievalists and book lovers take note: the castle houses the Scuola Italiana Amanuensi e l'Opificium Librorum (open by appointment), a sort of living museum that recreates a fully functioning medieval scriptorium.

Next to the castle is the **Chiesa di San Pietro di Ragogna**, whose roots lie in the 8th century. The village also claims one of the few 'official' beaches on the Tagliamento, complete with restaurant, kiosk and summertime concerts.

Numerous trails belonging to the Routes of the Great War start from here. Following the signs for **Monte di Ragogna** (512m), you'll arrive at a clearing at the top of Monte Muris: emerging out of nowhere is the **Chiesa di San Giovanni in Monte**, a beautiful stone church dating from the 13th century.

Destroyed and rebuilt several times, especially between 1915 and 1918, it was dedicated to the Alpine troops of Friuli in 1947.

The marked trails on the mountain lead to various vantage points from where the view of the river is breathtaking.

And if the trenches and tunnels you stumble upon intrigue you, the village itself houses the **Museo della Grande Guerra di Ragogna** (☑ 0432 95 40 78; www.grandeguerra-ragogna.it; Via Roma 23, San Giacomo di Ragogna; ⊙ 3.30-6pm Tue, Thu, Sat & Sun) FREE.

The museum focuses on the events of WWI that took place between Ragogna, San Daniele and Forgaria nel Friuli; note the meticulously detailed model, a valuable resource for understanding the lay of this land in wartime.

ℹ Information

Pro Loco di Ragogna (☑ 328 266 06 25; www.prolocoragogna.it; Via XXV Aprile 2/a) Offers valuable tourist information; handy for planning local trips in the area.

Lago di Cavazzo

ELEV 195M

Another surprise awaits on the left side of the Tagliamento River between Gemona and Venzone: Lago Cavazzo. Also known as Lago dei Tre Comuni (Lake of the Three Municipalities), this is the largest natural lake in Friuli Venezia Giulia thanks to the abundance of subterranean springs, common throughout the Prealpi Carsiche (Carso Prealps). The lake extends for more than 6km and you can walk or cycle along its perimeter, enjoying commanding views of Monte Festa and Monte San Simeone.

On weekends, the lakeside park is swarmed by locals, who head here for picnics and boat trips. Watersport enthusiasts can canoe, windsurf and sail, while those after something more low key can settle for a quiet ride on a pedal boat.

Campers will appreciate the lakeside campground.

🏃 Activities

Nautilago　　　　　　　　WATER SPORTS
(📞 0432 97 92 88; www.nautilago.com; Via Tolmezzo 58, Trasaghis Frazione Alesso) If you're interested in sailing or kayaking, contact this association (you may need to provide medical documentation confirming good health so ask in advance). Various regattas are organised throughout the year.

🛏 Sleeping

Camping Lago 3 Comuni　　　　CAMPING €
(📞 0432 97 94 64; www.lago3comuni.com; Via Tolmezzo 52, Trasaghis Frazione Alesso; adult/reduced from €5.50/4, small pitch €7-11, large pitch €17-19; ⊗ 8am-11pm Apr-Sep; 🅿) A well-organised, well-equipped campsite by the lake. Free power and hot showers.

Gemona del Friuli

POP 10,734 / ELEV 272M

Gemona, like nearby Venzone, was one of the villages most affected by the 1976 earthquake (see p169). While life has long since returned to normal, with most of its buildings and monuments rebuilt, the tragedy lives on in the photographic displays that pop up in the narrow streets that cross the *centro storico* (historic centre).

Enter it through Porta Udine, the only one of Gemona's seven medieval gates still standing. Give yourself about an hour to explore the village, whose most important landmark is the Romanesque-Gothic **Duomo di Santa Maria Assunta**. Gothic architecture, which spread through Europe between the 12th and 14th centuries, had less of a revolutionary impact in Italy than it did in other parts of Europe. Instead, selective Gothic elements, such as rose windows, were often introduced to Romanesque buildings. Gemona's Duomo is a fine example of this phenomenon.

In addition to the three rose windows, the cathedral's facade features a 7m-high statue of St Christopher (patron saint of pilgrims and travellers), sculpted around 1332. Above the entrance, nine sculptures depict scenes of the Epiphany; note the three slumbering *magi* on the right.

While the earthquake spared the facade, it destroyed the Duomo's bell tower and one of the side naves, since rebuilt.

Flanking the cathedral is **Via Bini**, dotted with porticoed, 16th-century *palazzi,* some of which retain fragments of 13th-century frescoes.

Palazzo Gurisatti houses the **Cineteca del Friuli** (📞 0432 98 04 58; www.cinetecadelfriuli.org; Via Bini 50; ⊗ 9.30am-1.30pm & 2-5.30pm Mon-Thu by appointment), a *cinemateque* which, alongside Cinemazero di Pordenone, organises silent-film festival Le Giornate del Cinema Muto.

ECOMUSEO DELLE ACQUE DEL GEMONESE

The open-air, multisite **Ecomuseo delle Acque del Gemonese** (📞 338 718 72 27, www.ecomuseodelleacque.it; Largo Beorcje 12, Gemona) explores local history and culture by researching the waterways of the Gemona area, an alluvial plain near the Tagliamento River, formed by the retreat of a glacier 10,000 years ago. Five nearby municipalities have joined the project: Artegna, Buja, Majano, Montenars and Osoppo. The museum's headquarters are in Ospedaletto di Gemona, where you'll also find a milling museum and education lab.

Fans of 15th- and 16th-century art will appreciate **Museo Civico Palazzo Elti** (☑ 0432 97 13 99; Via Bini 9; ☺ same as the IAT tourist office) **FREE**, which showcases artists from the Veneto and Friuli regions, including Pellegrino da San Daniele and Pomponio Amalteo. The museum sits inside the beautiful, 14th-century Palazzo Elti, also destroyed in 1976 and subsequently rebuilt.

Climb the Salita dei Longobardi, a stairway that leads to the top of the Colle del Castello, for the best view over the village. The castle itself is only partially accessible due to ongoing renovation work following the 1976 earthquake. Along the way, historic photographs show the village before and after that fateful year.

Not far from the Duomo, you can also quickly visit the **former Chiesa di San Michele** (☑ 0432 97 13 99; Largo Porta Udine; ☺ on request), built inside the city walls in 1447 and rebuilt outside them at the end of the 19th century, next to Porta Udine. Destroyed by the earthquake and rebuilt once more, it now houses a series of small frescoes from nearby churches.

Wandering down from Via Bini towards Via Caneva you'll pass **Chiesa della Beata Vergine delle Grazie**, whose portal and staircase were the only original 16th-century elements to survive the earthquake.

Finally, the **Museo della Pieve e Tesoro del Duomo** (☑ 0432 98 06 08; Via Bini 50; ☺ 10.30am-12.30pm & 3-7pm Sun & holidays) houses a collection of religious artworks, including paintings, sculptures and furnishings by local artists from the 13th and 14th centuries.

The examples of illuminated manuscripts from the 12th to 14th centuries are beautiful, as is the cathedral's treasury, whose pieces include precious Friulian goldsmithing from the 15th century.

🏃 Activities

Thanks to its natural assets, the area around Gemona draws active types practising a wide range of sports. You'll find a range of adrenaline-pumping options, from hiking and cycling, to rock climbing and paragliding, on the **Sportland** (www.sportland.fvg.it) website, an initiative aimed at promoting the area and its plethora of activities.

Soaring behind the Duomo is Monte Glemina, whose south-facing wall is ideal for climbing.

Volo Libero Friuli   GLIDING
(www.vololiberofriuli.it; Via Pralungo 9/2) This outfit runs paragliding and hang-gliding flights from Monte Cuarnan (Gemona) and Monte San Simeone (Bordano). See the website for information.

🍴 Eating & Drinking

Osteria Rive Grande   ITALIAN €€
(☑ 0432 97 28 51; Via Liruti 10; meals from €20-25; ☺ 11.30am-2.30pm & 6-9.30pm Tue-Sun) A lovely little restaurant peddling local cuisine and more, including a delicious carbonara famous throughout the village and decent risottos.

For the purists, local grub includes *frico*.

Pan & Salam   WINE BAR
(☑ 346 289 22 49; Via Bini 2; platters €8, glass of wine €1.30-5; ☺ 10am-10pm Tue-Sun; 🛜) Youthful, relaxed and armed with an excellent playlist, this *enoteca* pours a wide choice of local and nonlocal wines, as well as serving hot or cold dishes, from cheese and charcuterie platters to gnocchi with sausage and radicchio.

Weekend *aperitivo* sessions often feature live music.

ℹ️ Information

IAT Office - Infopoint Gemona Turismo (☑ 0432 98 14 41; www.gemonaturismo.com; Via Bini 9; ☺ 10am-12.30pm & 2.30-6pm Tue-Sun Nov-Mar, daily Apr & May, 9.30am-1pm & 3-7pm daily Jun-Oct) Provides information on sights, activities and exhibitions in Gemona, as well as maps.

Venzone

POP 1941 / ELEV 230M

Strolling its snug, storybook streets, it's hard to believe that Venzone was reduced to rubble in the earthquake of 1976. Faithfully rebuilt, it was named 'Borgo dei Borghi' (Village of Villages) in 2017.

While some argue that Venzone 2.0 is a little too perfect, there's no denying the charm of the place. Surrounded by medieval walls, it stands at the foot of the mountains, just south of where the Tagliamento and Fella rivers meet.

Leave your car in one of the free car parks outside the walls and slip into its lavender-scented streets.

The heart of the medieval village, founded around 1000 CE, is **Piazza del Municipio**. The square claims **Palazzo Comunale**, built between 1490 and 1510 in Venetian

THE BUTTERFLIES OF BORDANO

Especially popular with children, the **Casa delle Farfalle** (House of the Butterflies; ✆0432 163 61 75; www.bordano farfalle.it; Via Canada 5, Bordano; adult/reduced €5/4, €8/6 including greenhouses, under 3yr free; ⏰10am-6pm year-round, greenhouses late Mar-late Sep) is the main attraction in **Bordano**, a village on the left bank of the Tagliamento between Gemona and Venzone. Recreating habitats from various parts of the world, its three large greenhouses are aflutter with thousands of butterflies and various invertebrates. To fully enjoy their colours, visit in the morning when the sun is high in the sky.

The site includes the recently inaugurated **MUFFFA**, a museum with an interesting collection of moths.

style and home to a small photographic exhibition dedicated to the village and the 1976 earthquake.

Nearby, Palazzo Orgnani Martina houses **Tiere Motus: Storia di un terremoto e della sua gente (Tiere Motus: History of an Earthquake & its People;** ✆ 328 593 05 17; Via Mistruzzi 4/9; adult/reduced €5/4; ⏰ 3-7pm Fri, 9am-1pm & 3-7pm Sat & Sun)), a poignant exhibition recounting the tragedy and subsequent reconstruction of Friuli's affected areas.

In the same building you'll find the arguably less-gripping **Foreste, uomo, economia nel Friuli Venezia Giulia** (Forests, Humankind, Economy in Friuli Venezia Giulia; ✆ 0432 98 52 66; ⏰ 2-6pm Sat, also Sun May-Oct) **FREE**, which traces the biodiversity of the region with information about local flora and fauna.

Less central but easily reached is the **Duomo di Sant'Andrea** (⏰9am-5pm winter, to 7pm summer). Built of local white stone around the 14th century, the cathedral is Venzone's most important building, with a Romanesque style, Latin cross plan and 14th-century frescoes.

Severely damaged in the earthquake, it was rebuilt by anastylosis, a technique in which a building is recomposed using as many of the original pieces as possible.

Thankfully, Venzone's status as a national monument meant that restorers had a wealth of archived photographs to work with. Be-

side the cathedral, the **Cappella Cimiteriale di San Michele** (€1.50; same hours as the Duomo) houses five of the circa 15 mummies salvaged from the cathedral's ruins.

Curiously, the mummification process happens naturally here, caused by a fungus that dehydrates corpses in the tombs.

🏃 Activities

Hiking

From Venzone, various trails lead into the Parco Naturale Regionale delle Prealpi Giulie (p238). Others cross the Tagliamento River valley.

Giro delle Malghe　　　PANORAMIC TRAIL
(CAI trail 705; from Borgo Pragiel to the Ungarina alpine hut; elevation gain 1060m, 8km, 5hr) A beautiful walk that winds along the southern slope of Monte Plauris passing various *malghe* (alpine huts). Depending on the time of year, you might stumble upon the transhumance of local cattle.

Mountain Biking

The Anello della Venzonassa (Venzonassa Ring) is a 40km circuit from Venzone. Follow the road to the village of Sottomonte north of the town. For information, see www.pedalegemonese.it (in Italian).

🍴 Eating

Alla Vecchia Concordia　　　CAFE €
(✆ 0432 98 51 51; Piazza Municipio 6; ⏰ 7am-11pm Mon-Wed & Fri-Sun) Simple pleasures are this cafe's forte, where even the humblest toasted sandwich, chocolate or glass of *vino* lift the mood.

If it's summer, kick back at a table on Venzone's main square. If not, take refuge in the elegant dining room.

Locanda al Municipio　　　FRIULIAN €€
(✆ 0432 98 58 01; Via Glizoio di Mels 4; meals €23-28; ⏰ 8.30am-11pm Tue-Sun) A solid restaurant right next to the town hall loggia. Friulian flavours dominate, from excellent game to seafood dishes. If you fancy staying overnight, the property also offers five **rooms** (s/d with breakfast €37/65).

ℹ️ Information

Pro Loco Pro Venzone (✆ 0432 98 50 34; www.venzoneturismo.it; Via Glizoio di Mels 5/4; ⏰10am-1pm & 3-6pm Tue-Sun) Tourist office near Palazzo Comunale.

COLLI ORIENTALI

Scattered with vineyards, *agriturismi,* abandoned fortresses and silk-spinning mills, the gently rolling hills nestled between the Chiampon, Stella and Bernadia mountains are a veritable compendium of Friulian history and traditions.

Known as the Colli Orientali (Eastern Hills), they make for an easy day trip, hunting castles (both robust and ruined), soaking up soft, verdant landscapes, and quaffing the fruits of the area's mild climate and ancient, lauded viticulture.

ℹ Getting There & Away

BUS

From Udine, **TPL FVG** (☑ 800 05 20 40, mobile 040 971 23 43; https://tplfvg.it) buses reach all the towns mentioned in this section. Very frequent services run to Tarcento (€4.35, 42min), Artegna (€4.35, 55min), Faedis (€3.85, 30min), Nimis (€4.35, 30min), Attimis (€4.35, 35min), Manzano (€4.35, 49min), Lusevera (€5.05, 64min) and Buttrio (€3.25, 43min).

CAR & MOTORCYCLE

Having your own vehicle allows you to reach all the main destinations of the Colli Orientali quickly. if you're heading in from Udine, take the A23 (Palmanova–Tarvisio) and exit at Udine Nord. From there, follow the signs for Tavagnacco and Tricesimo, then continue on the SS13.

Once in Tarcento, follow the signs for the towns listed in this section.

TRAIN

Tarcento (Via della Ferrovia) is the only train station in the Colli Orientali di Tarcento. It's located on the Pontebbana line (Udine–Tarvisio), with frequent services to Udine (€3.25, 30min).

Tarcento

POP 8877 / ELEV 230M

Wedged between the Julian Prealps, the Tagliamento River and the Valle del Torre, Tarcento is considered the capital of the Colli Orientali. In the centre of town you'll find the 15th-century **Duomo**, as well as 17th-century residence **Palazzo Frangipane**.

A little more than a century ago the town was a popular holiday resort, a golden era echoed in **Villa Moretti**, a white Art-Nouveau show-off with four reddish towers in the nearby hamlet of **Coia**.

Climbing to the top of the hill you'll see what remains of the hamlet's 12th-century **Castellaccio di Coia** (Cjscjelat). Eight-hundred metres up **Monte Bernadia**, on the other hand, you'll find a **blockhouse** built in WWI.

🏃 Activities

In Tarcento we recommend the **sentiero Tai roncs dal sorêli**, a beautiful walking trail that skirts the main attractions of the town. If you like waterfalls, hit the **sentiero di Crosis (Crosis Trail)**.

THE TRAGEDY OF 1976

On 6 May 1976, news bulletins reported a powerful earthquake '120km from Venice'. For Italy, it felt like the sudden discovery of Friuli Venezia Giulia. Isolated for years, the region was suddenly an international headline.

Striking halfway between Artegna and Osoppo, the 6.4 temblor was felt as far away as Rome, Germany, Belgium and Czechoslovakia. Many towns near the epicentre were destroyed, including Gemona del Friuli, Osoppo and Venzone. Further destruction came in the form of two strong aftershocks on September 11 and 15. Almost 1000 people lost their lives in the tragedy, with some 100,000 people displaced, 18,000 homes destroyed and another 75,000 damaged. Entire villages were evacuated, with families temporarily moved to hotels or the homes of relatives and friends in safer locations.

The earthquake sparked a sense of solidarity never before seen in Italy. Friulians who had emigrated abroad sent aid and the country proved strong, united and determined to rebuild: as the local priests and bishops shouted to politicians, 'First the houses, then the churches'. Venzone received special attention. Architecture faculties at universities across Europe introduced a 'Restoration of Venzone' course, aimed at bringing new ideas and approaches to rebuilding the medieval town.

Almost half a century later, the wounds of 1976 are still felt, in the exhibitions of various local museums and in the heartfelt stories of the people you will meet.

🛏 Sleeping

Lì dai Tôs   B&B €

(☑ 0432 78 35 35; www.lidaitos.it; Via Natisone 3, Tarcento Frazione Loneriacco; d €50-60; 🛜) An excellent option if you fancy lingering in the Colli Orientali, this welcoming B&B is clean, luminous and complete with terrace and garden. Its trio of double rooms can be transformed into triples and quadruples if required.

ℹ Information

Associazione Pro Tarcento - IAT office (☑ 0432 78 06 74, 377 167 88 41; www.protarcentoud.com; Palazzo Frangipane, Piazza Roma; ⊙ 3-6pm Fri, 10am-1pm & 3-6pm Sat & Sun Apr-Oct & 8 Dec-6 Jan). On our last visit, the tourist office had been temporarily moved to the Biblioteca Civica Pierluigi Cappello (Pierluigi Cappello Public Library), at Via Divisione Julia 13 due to renovations.

Artegna

POP 2805 / ELEV 210M

A quick detour northwest of Tarcento, Artegna should not be missed. The town sits close to a hill once home to an ancient Roman settlement and still graced by 13th-century **Castello Savorgnan** (☑ 328 302 06 82; www.castello diartegna.it; by donation; ⊙ 10am-12.30pm & 3.30-7pm Sat & Sun). Returned to its former glory after a post-quake restoration, the castle is small but majestic. Beside it is the **Chiesa di San Martino**, a building from 1205 with a very troubled history. Like the castle, the church was the target of hostilities from its Gemonese neighbours, who besieged and destroyed it in 1299. Resurrected, the church was subsequently damaged by earthquakes and wars; what you see today is the fruit of a 16th-century restoration. The church's 14th-century bell tower is capped by a statue of an angel (similar to that of Udine's Chiesa di Santa Maria di Castello) and was once connected to a long-gone fortification. Waiting inside the church are 16th-century frescoes by Giampaolo Thanner.

ℹ Information

Associazione Pro Artegna (☑ 351 820 77 75; www.proartegna.com; Centro Polifunzionale, Via Vicenza; ⊙ 8am-10am Sat or by appt)

Magnano in Riviera

POP 2307 / ELEV 201M

Magnano is another town where a pleasant stop can take up an afternoon. Severely damaged by the 1976 earthquake, its main attraction is its storybook **Castello di Prampero**, perched on the hill to the west of town. In 1227, the castle passed hands from the lords of Pramperg to the nobility of Gemona. The complex was almost destroyed by a popular revolt, fire and earthquake in the 16th century, before being repeatedly renovated between the 16th and 17th centuries. While the

---

TASTING ACADEMY & DOC DEGUSTATIONS

The wine-making heart of the Colli Orientali is **Corno di Rosazzo**, whose 18th-century Villa Nachini Cabassi houses the Consorzio Colli Orientali del Friuli Venezia Giulia and the recently inaugurated **Tasting Academy** (www.colliorientali.com/tasting-academy), the place to taste wines from the local area. If you're driving between Buttrio and Manzano, however, organise a tasting at one of the wineries in the DOC Friuli Colli Orientali area. Among these, we recommend:

Marina Danieli (☑ 0432 67 32 83; https://marinadanieli.estate; Via Beltrame 77, Buttrio; ⊙ 9am-6pm Mon-Fri, Sat & Sun by appt)

Count D'Attimis-Maniago (☑ 0432 67 20 27; www.contedattimismaniago.it; Via Sottomonte 21, Buttrio; ⊙ 8.30am-noon & 1.30-5.30pm Mon-Fri, 8.30am-12.30pm Sat)

Petrucco (☑ 0432 67 43 87; https://vinipetrucco.it/it; Via Morpurgo 12, Buttrio; ⊙ 8am-6pm Mon-Fri, to 1pm Sat)

Tami (☑ 347 753 18 95; www.vinitami.com; Via Roma 50, Buttrio; ⊙ 5.30-8pm Tue-Fri, 10.30am-1pm & 5.30-8pm Sat, 10.30am-1pm Sun)

Buiatti (☑ 0432 67 43 17; www.buiattivini.it; Via Lippe 25, Buttrio; ⊙ 8am-8pm)

Colutta (☑ 0432 74 03 15; www.colutta.it; Via Orsaria 32, Manzano; ⊙ 8am-5pm Mon-Fri, to noon Sat, Sun by appt)

castle is private property (and partially under restoration), walking around the medieval behemoth is a joy in itself.

 Information

Pro Loco Magnano in Riviera (☑ 0432 78 34 25, 347 898 05 59; Via Prampero 3)

Nimis

POP 2596 / ELEV 207M

Famous above all for its wines, the town of Nimis is speckled with the remains of medieval buildings, though little of that past remains. You're better off heading to the nearby hamlet of **Ramandolo** to savour its famous eponymous wine, the first to receive DOCG status in Friuli.

From Nimis, the hamlet can also be reached via the **passeggiata del Ramandolo (Ramandolo promenade)**, a beautiful walking trail surrounded by vineyards.

 Eating

Osteria di Ramandolo   FRIULIAN/WINE BAR €€ (☑ 0432 79 00 09; www.osteriadiramandolo.it; Via Ramandolo 22, Nimis; meals €30-35; ⊙10.30am-3pm & 5-11pm Tue-Fri, 10.30am-11pm Sat & Sun) Yes, the view over hills and vineyards from the terrace is mesmerising, but the local dishes at this *osteria* are equally deserving: try the free-range guinea fowl. The owners even make their own Ramandolo.

Attimis

POP 1704 / ELEV 195M

Attimis' **Museo Archeologico Medievale** (☑ 329 899 36 16; Via Principale 99; adult/reduced €3/2; ⊙10am-7pm Sun), also known as the Museo della Terra dei Nove Castelli (Museum of the Land of the Nine Castles; contact the Pro Loco tourist office for information) exhibits relics from the feudal era. If this fails to rouse your interest, the town is also a launching pad for numerous short walks through the woods. Follow the signposts and you'll pass the vestiges of crumbled manors and castles, as well as survivors like the 11th-century **Castello di Partistagno**, composed of a beautiful tower house.

 Activities

Plant lovers will appreciate the whimsically named **Sentiero dei Folletti (Trail of the Sprites)**, lined with medicinal plants, and the **Sentiero delle Streghe (Trail of the Witches)**, suitably laced with toxic species.

ℹ **Information**

Pro Loco Attimis (www.prolocoattimis.it; Via Adelaide Ristori 14)

Faedis

POP 2823 / ELEV 176M

Enveloped in the lush greenery of the Julian Prealps, the village of Faedis is dotted with medieval castles and fortifications, among them the 12th-century **Castello di Zucco** and the **Castello di Cucagna**. If you're suffering fort fatigue, visit the **Chiesa della Madonna in Castello**, whose fragments of frescoes date from medieval times. Alternatively, forget churches and forts altogether and simply luxuriate in nature or good wine: the Refosco here is superb.

ℹ **Information**

Pro Loco Faedis (www.prolocofaedis.it; Via Monsignor Pelizzo 11)

Lusevera

POP 601 / ELEV 504M

Legend has it that Lusevera's name originates from the Latin *'lux vera'*, which is what Julius Cesar reputedly called the place upon seeing it kissed by the sun. Ironically, the town is well known for the anything-but-luminous **Grotta Nuova di Villanova** (☑ 320 455 45 97; www.grottedivillanova.it; Villanova delle Grotte 3; adult/reduced €9/7, free with FVG Card; ⊙varies seasonally), a grotto whose 8km of tunnels can be partially explored on a guided tour. Times vary seasonally so consult the website, call ahead or email reservations@grottediv illanova.it. From Lusevera, as well as from Venzone, you can also access the Parco Naturale Regionale delle Prealpi Giulie (p238).

🏃 **Activities**

Climbing

Not far from the Parco Naturale Regionale delle Prealpi Giulie visitor centre (p238) is the fantastic Ai Ciclamini climbing wall, which offers varying degrees of difficulty.

Hiking

Each of the towns of the Colli Orientali offer different trails through woods and hills: there are many and all are well signposted. In Lusevera, in the middle of the Julian Prealps, the wheelchair-accessible **sentiero dei Ciclami (Trail of the Cyclamen)** is a worthy option. At the Piana dei Ciclamini you can opt for the **sentiero natura Valle Musi (Valle Musi Nature Trail)**. Traversing the slopes of the Musi chain, the beautiful path can be completed in a couple of hours. The elevation gain is a slight 200m, making for an effortless hike through woods and pastures to the headwaters of the Torre River.

Cross-country skiing

Cross-country ski enthusiasts can enjoy the **Passo Tanamea**, a 5km trail loop that winds its way through the woods.

❶ Information

Centro Visite del Parco Naturale delle Prealpi Giulie (☑0433 53 53 4; www.parcoprealpi giulie.it; Piazza del Tiglio 3, Prato Resia; ☉office 9am-1pm & 2-5pm Mon-Thu, 9am-1pm Fri) Lusevera belongs to the area of the Julian Prealps Park. At the foot of the Monti Musi chain, in the Alta Val Torre, this visitor centre includes a photo exhibition on the valley. The centre also has a guesthouse: if you're interested in staying overnight, contact the centre in advance.

Buttrio

POP 3890 / ELEV 79M

Buttrio's history takes one back many centuries, with both the Lombards and Charlemagne passing through here. The village was once ruled by counts and lords, whose grand residences stud the surrounding hills. Aside from its wineries (see p170), the only reason to head here is **Castello di Buttrio**(☑0432 67 30 40; www.castellodibuttrio.it; Via Morpurgo 9; s/d from €150/170; ❏❅☎), a historic property turned luxury wine resort surrounded by renowned vineyards. Even if you don't stay overnight, it's worth visiting the villa-castle (perhaps with the excuse of buying a couple of excellent bottles). Hardcore wine connoisseurs might also consider visiting the **Museo della Civiltà del Vino** (Via Morpurgo 8; ☉by appointment) **FREE**. Housed inside Villa di Toppo Florio, its collection of tools and machinery tell the story of the winemaking process, from harvest to storage.

❶ Information

Pro Loco Buri (☑0432 67 35 11; www.buri.it; Via Elio Morpurgo 8; ☉9.30am-12.30pm Tue-Sat, also 3-6pm Thu & Fri) This tourist office is proactive about promoting the area and often organises food and wine events.

Manzano

POP 6199 / ELEV 71M

About 15km from Buttrio, Manzano claims the atmospheric **Abbazia di Rosazzo** (☑0432 75 90 91; www.abbaziadirosazzo.it; Piazza Abbazia 5; ☉9am-12.30pm & 2.30-6pm summer, closes 30min earlier rest of yr except Sun). While its origins aren't clear, the site already housed a church and monastery dedicated to St Peter in around 1000 CE, later renovated. The abbey occupies a strategic position and was transformed into a defensive fortress around the 15th century. In times of peace it served as the summer residence of the bishops of Udine. Inside, you'll glimpse fragments of 16th-century frescoes, while moving towards the cloister and garden, beyond the splendid Sentiero delle Rose (Path of the Roses), you'll reach the real highlight here: a heavenly view of the Collio.

Cividale del Friuli & the Valli del Natisone

Includes ➜

Cividale del Friuli 175

Valli del Natisone 181

San Pietro al
Natisone 182

Prepotto............ 182

San Leonardo 183

Stregna 183

Grimacco........... 184

Drenchia 184

Savogna............ 184

Pulfero 185

Best Ancient Treasures

➜ Museo Cristiano & Tesoro del Duomo (p175)

➜ Tempietto Longobardo & Monastero di Santa Maria in Valle (p176)

➜ Santuario della Beata Vergine di Castelmonte (p182)

Best Restaurants

➜ Al Campanile (p179)

➜ Al Monastero (p179)

➜ Alla Frasca (p180)

Why Go?

Heading west from Udine, the area between Cividale and Slovenia shifts between plains and mountains. The Natisone and its tributaries have shaped magnificent valleys, as lively in summer as they are desolate in winter. This is a land of Romans and Lombards, of folklore and well-worn traditions. In these valleys, talk is of wild herbs, war and witches. It is also home to some rather unique sweets.

Home to Unesco World Heritage sites of exceptional beauty, the town of Cividale del Friuli makes history and archaeology buffs swoon. It's an enchanting place, evocatively set up by its storybook entrance, the Ponte del Diavolo (Devil's Bridge).

When to Go

The Valli del Natisone are consummate chameleons. In wild winter weather or midweek in low season, they can feel almost ghostly – a sweep of semideserted villages and abandoned railways, mountain-clutching hermitages and wilderness. Come summer or the holidays, the villages are abuzz with life, bonhomie, local festivals and hikers.

Cividale del Friuli & the Valli del Natisone Highlights

1 Ponte del Diavolo (p175) An unexpected glimpse of the Natisone.

2 Museo Cristiano & Tesoro del Duomo (p175) An extraordinary collection merging history and new technology.

3 Tempietto Longobardo & Monastero di Santa Maria in Valle (p176) A unique relic of a civilisation with few remaining traces.

4 San Pietro al Natisone (p182) Gateway to the Valli del Natisone.

5 Santuario della Beata Vergine di Castelmonte (p182) Climb the steps and enjoy the view.

6 Cisgne (p183) The ghostly lure of an abandoned village.

7 Stregna (p183) A village of traditional stone abodes with balconies.

8 Grotta di San Giovanni d'Antro (p185) Harbouring a beautiful subterranean church.

CIVIDALE DEL FRIULI

POP 10,991 / ELEV 135M

That Cividale is one of the region's greatest enigmas makes perfect sense: after all, most of the town's assets lie hidden away. You'll need to dig deep, at times even head underground, to find them.

Start by crossing the Ponte del Diavolo (Devil's Bridge) on the Natisone River to reach the old city, where history has left various traces of centuries past, from the Tempietto Longobardo, Ratchis Altar and Callisto baptismal font, to other small, scattered treasures that together have earned the town's historic centre Unesco World Heritage status.

Don't be shy: peek into backstreets, courtyards and churches and Cividale's many secrets will unfurl.

Interestingly, the town also hosts Mittelfest, a festival of Central European theatre that attracts thousands each year.

History

Founded in the mid-2nd century BCE as a *castrum* (Roman fort), Cividale was elevated to the rank of forum (trade centre) by Julius Caesar himself. The forum's name, Iulii, would later shape that of the entire region: Friuli. Roman relics are scattered throughout the town, among them a *domus* (private house) in the courtyard of the town hall, various mosaics, and the ruins of ancient spas and necropolises.

Strategically positioned, Cividale became the Lombard capital in 568 with the name of Civitas Fori Iulii. Burnt down by the Avars in 737, it rose again as the seat of the Patriarchate of Aquileia, chosen by Callisto to defend against barbarian incursions from the east.

A few years later, the Carolingians took control of the Duchy of Friuli, thus ending the era of the Lombards and turning the town over to the Holy Roman Empire. The baptismal font in the Museo Cristiano dates back to this period.

Up until the 13th century, Cividale was one of the most important economic centres of Friuli, challenging Udine's commercial dominance of the area. Falling to Venice in the early 15th century, the town was subsequently passed to Austria with the Treaty of Campo Formio in 1797.

Only after the third war of independence, in 1866, was it annexed to the Kingdom of Italy together with the rest of Friuli.

Despite suffering extensive damage in both World Wars and the 1976 earthquake,

ⓘ MUSEUM DISCOUNTS

If you plan on visiting more than one museum in Cividale, you can save a few euros by purchasing a **multi-attraction ticket** (three museums €9), available from any of the participating sights (Museo Archeologico, Museo Cristiano and Tempietto Longobardo).

If you're feeling charitable, you can also buy a *biglietto sospeso* (literally, 'suspended ticket'), set aside for someone unable to pay the admission.

For further information, call the **ticket office** (☏ 0432 70 08 67).

If your trip includes other cities (and museums) in the region, opt for the FVG Card (see p53) instead.

Cividale has since been restored to its former splendour.

◉ Sights

Ponte del Diavolo   BRIDGE

(Corso Paolino d'Aquileia 19 A dizzying gateway to the old city, the soaring 'Devil's Bridge' offers a magnificent view of the Natisone River. Built in 1442 to replace an older wooden crossing, the bridge was rebuilt post-WWI after retreating Italian troops blew it up. The double-arched behemoth is a commanding sight, 48m long and 22m high.

Legend has it that the locals asked the devil himself to help construct it. He agreed but it was on the condition that he could take the soul of the first creature to cross it. Cunningly, the locals sent an animal across first, saving one of their own from eternal damnation.

★ **Museo Cristiano & Tesoro del Duomo**   MUSEUM

(☏ 0432 73 04 03; Via GB Candotti 1; adult/reduced/8-18yr €4/3/2, with Tempietto Longobardo & Museo Archeologico Nazionale €9/6/3, with FVG Card & under 8yr free; ☺ 10am-1pm & 3-5pm Wed-Sun Oct-Mar, to 6pm Apr-Sep) If the idea of a museum dedicated to religious art elicits a yawn, this museum will come as a pleasant surprise. In fact, some pieces in the Lombard and Treasury collections will leave you gobsmacked.

Seek out the **Ratchis Altar**, take a seat and enjoy the show: as the lights dim, LED lights begin to colour in the altar's bas-reliefs like a high-tech colouring book, returning the

Cividale del Friuli

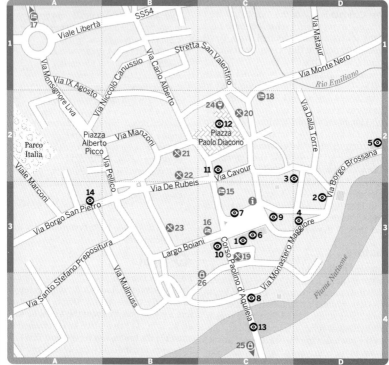

8th-century marvel to its original, Technicolor glory. It is hands down one of the most effective uses of multimedia technology in any museum in Italy.

Behind the altar (commissioned by Duke Ratchis, king of the Lombards, in honour of his father), lies the **baptismal font of Callisto**. Dating from 730, the octagonal piece features Corinthian columns connected by arches decorated with geometric and symbolic motifs.

★**Tempietto Longobardo & Monastero di Santa Maria in Valle** CHAPEL
(☑0432 70 08 67; www.tempiettolongobardo.it; Via Monastero Maggiore 34; adult/reduced/8-18yr €4/3/1.50, with Museo Cristiano, Tesoro del Duomo & Museo Archeologico Nazionale €9/6/3, with FVG Card & under 8yr free; ☺10am-1pm & 2-5pm Mon-Fri, 10am-5pm Sat & Sun Oct-March, 10am-1pm & 3-6pm Mon-Fri, 10am-6pm Sat & Sun Apr-Sep) Beyond the cloister of the riverside Monastero di Santa Maria in Valle, lies this small, early-medieval building, one of few surviv-

ing examples of Lombard architecture in Italy. Not much is known about its origins: it was apparently built in the 8th century as a chapel of the adjacent monastery.

Awaiting behind its barrel-vaulted apse is a series of magical Byzantine frescoes and stuccoes: the six female figures depicted above the lunette are very rare and exquisite examples of Lombard art in Italy.

From the church, cross the footbridge over the Natisone for a great photo vantage point.

Museo Archeologico Nazionale MUSEUM
(☑0432 70 07 00; www.museoarcheologicocividale.beniculturali.it; Piazza Duomo 13; adult/reduced €4/2, with Museo Cristiano & Tempietto Longobardo €9/6, with FVG Card & under 8yr free; ☺9am-2pm Mon, 8.30am-7.30pm Tue-Sun) Designed by Renaissance starchitect Andrea Palladio, the Palazzo dei Provveditori Veneti makes a suitably handsome setting for Cividale's archaeological museum.

Cividale del Friuli

◉ Top Sights
1 Museo Cristiano & Tesoro
     del Duomo C3
2 Tempietto Longobardo & Monastero
     di Santa Maria in Valle D3

◎ Sights
3 Casa Medievale D2
4 Centro Internazionale
     Vittorio Podrecca D3
5 Chiesa dei Santi Pietro
     e Biagio D2
6 Duomo C3
7 Galleria De Martiis C3
8 Ipogeo Celtico C4
9 Museo Archeologico
     Nazionale C3
10 Palazzo Comunale C3
11 Palazzo Levrini-Stringher C2
12 Piazza Paolo Diacono C2
13 Ponte del Diavolo C4
14 Porta di San Pietro A3

⊜ Sleeping
15 Dai Toscans C3
16 Domus Iulii C3
17 Locanda al Castello .... off map A1
18 Locanda al Pomo D'Oro C2

⊗ Eating
19 Al Campanile C3
20 Al Duca C2
21 Al Monastero B2
22 Alla Frasca.. B2
23 Alla Speranza.. B3

◎ Drinking & Nightlife
24 Enoteca L'Elefante................................. C2

⊙ Shopping
25 Al Ponte .... off map C4
26 MADA C4

Spanning two floors, the collection includes priceless Roman, early Christian and medieval treasures. On the ground floor, it's the mosaics that stand out, sourced from Roman houses discovered in the town. Upstairs, a cache of local Lombard-era items includes sculptures, decorative objects, jewellery and coins found in the necropolises.

The museum also includes a small Jewish lapidary, while under the portico at the entrance is a slot with an inscription that says 'Contro Ministri dei Direttori di Mani Morte' (Against Ministers of the Directors of Mani Morte).

Apparently, citizens were permitted to post anonymous accusations of misconduct against the ministers in charge of the Church's real estate. These assets were part of the so-called ecclesiastical mortuary, which – due to the argument that church assets could not be handed down – rendered them exempt from state inheritance taxes.

Galleria de Martiis
MUSEUM

(Palazzo de Nordis; ☑ 0432 71 04 60; www.palazzo denordis.it; Piazza Duomo 5; adult/reduced €8/5, with FVG Card free; ☉ 10am-1pm & 2-5pm Mon-Fri, 10am-5pm Sat & Sun Oct-Mar, 10am-1pm & 3-6pm Mon-Fri, 10am-6pm Sat & Sun Apr-Sep) The namesake of this gallery of modern and contemporary art is Friulian entrepreneur Giancarlo De Martiis, who generously donated his private collection to the town.

While highlights include works by Henri de Toulouse-Lautrec, Karel Appel and Afro Basaldella, there's also an interesting collection of pieces by avant-garde Eastern European artists.

Duomo
PLACE OF WORSHIP

(☑ 0432 73 04 03; Piazza Duomo; ☉ 7am-7pm) Dedicated to Our Lady of the Assumption, Cividale's cathedral was built in 1457, on the site of an 8th-century church commissioned by patriarch Callisto. Completion took many years, reflected in the building's Venetian-Gothic and Renaissance elements.

Three portals decorated the simple facade, behind which lies a triple-nave interior. On the main altar is a medieval altarpiece, made of 123 silver plates and depicting patriarch Pellegrino II.

The left nave harbours a 13th-century wooden crucifix.

Palazzo Comunale
HISTORIC BUILDING

(Corso Paolino d'Aquileia) Directly opposite the Duomo lies Cividale's town hall. Sporting a beautiful arcade of pointed arches, the brick *palazzo* was erected in 1588 on the site of a 13th-century building. The remains of a Roman-era *domus* were discovered in the town hall's inner courtyard.

ANOTHER DIG, ANOTHER LOMBARD

As is often the case in Italy, construction sites in Cividale commonly unearth ancient objects and structures, keeping archaeologists on their toes. Found beneath gardens, parks and basements, many date from the town's Roman and Lombard periods, testaments to the layers of history lurking beneath. Unearthed right below the Museo Archeologico Nazionale, for example, were the ruins of late Roman dwellings (a conveniently located find indeed).

One of the latest discoveries took place in Grupignano, not far from the Lombard necropolis 'Gallo'. Here, another burial ground has emerged, consisting of 17 burials plots (10 intact) dating back to between the 2nd and 6th centuries CE.

Archaeologists aren't the only ones who bring to light traces of Cividale's past. The earthquake of 1976 may have caused damage and loss of life, but it inadvertently revealed beautiful frescoes hidden behind stucco for centuries.

A case in point is **Palazzo Levrini-Stringher** (Corso Mazzini 16), built in the early 16th century and remodelled two centuries later. Shaking from the quake caused the modern plaster to collapse in places, uncovering 16th-century frescoes now widely visible (between Via Cavour and Via Carlo Alberto).

In front of the building is a commanding bronze statue of Julius Caesar. The work is a 1935 copy of the Roman marble sculpture gracing the council chamber of the Campidoglio in Rome.

Centro Internazionale Vittorio Podrecca
MUSEUM

(☑ 0432 70 08 67; www.centropodreccasignorelli.it; Via Monastero Maggiore 38; adult/reduced €3/2, 8-18yr €1, FVG Card & under 8yr free; ⊙ 10am-1pm & 3-6pm Mon-Fri, 10am-6pm Sat & Sun Apr-Sep, 10am-1pm & 2-5pm Mon-Fri, 10am-5pm Sat & Sun Oct-Mar) Cividale is the birthplace of Vittorio Podrecca (1883–1959), one of Italy's most famous puppeteers, and this museum houses a rich and colourful collection of puppets belonging to the master (alongside the prized possessions of noted collector Maria Signorelli).

If you're travelling with children, don't miss it. Buy tickets at the Tempietto Longobardo.

Ipogeo Celtico
HYPOGEUM

(☑ 0432 71 04 60; Via Monastero Maggiore 4; ⊙ 10am-noon & 2.30-4.30pm; hours may vary, contact InformaCittà) **FREE** Unless you're claustrophobic, there's a certain thrill in descending deep into the bowels of Cividale.

Lurking below is this hypogeum, created from a series of natural cavities near the Natisone's embankments. Riddled with mysterious niches and eerie stone masks, it's not clear whether it was an ancient prison or a cemetery.

To access the site, ask for the keys at InformaCittà (p180) or at the Tempietto Longobardo (p176).

Piazza Paolo Diacono
PIAZZA

(Piazza Paolo Diacono) Cividale's fountain-graced, cafe-speckled main square once hosted the town's vegetable market. These days, it's where the locals mingle every afternoon and evening. The charming, gelato-hued buildings that flank it were built between the 12th and 18th centuries; partially frescoed number 29 hails from the 1300s.

The piazza is also home to Monte di Pietà, a charitable pawnbroker established in 1700 to counter the power of Cividale's money lenders.

Casa Medievale
HISTORIC BUILDING

(☑ 0432 71 04 60; Stretta T Cerchiari 2; ⊙ 10.30am-12.30pm & 3-7pm Sat & Sun) Cividale's oldest surviving abode is also known as the 'Goldsmith's House' and in the second half of the 14th century gold was indeed worked inside.

The building is the original one, right down to the small window on the first floor; the other doors and windows here were later additions.

Porta di San Pietro
LANDMARK

(btwn Viale Guglielmo Marconi & Via Borgo San Pietro) Porta di San Pietro takes its name from a nearby church. In the 16th century, under Venetian rule, it became the town armoury, leading to the moniker 'Arsenale Veneto'. Prior to this, the town's armaments were stored in the Palazzo Comunale.

Chiesa dei Santi Pietro e Biagio
PLACE OF WORSHIP

(Via Borgo Bossana; ☺on request) It's worth passing by this church dedicated to St Peter and St Blaise, if only to admire its magnificently frescoed facade, executed by an unknown artist in 1508. Despite having faded, the works retain a lively quality. Lurking inside are even older frescoes from the 14th century.

✦✦ Festivals & Events

Messa dello Spadone
JANUARY 6

Another of Friuli's historical re-enactments, this tradition dates back to 1366. At a mass given in Latin, the priest thrusts a vibrating, 15th-century sword to symbolise the Church's power and to recall patriarch Marquardo von Randeck's entry into Cividale. The service is followed by a historical procession in period costume.

Mittelfest
JULY

(www.mittelfest.com) Cividale's best-known festival celebrates Central European culture. Concerts, readings, theatre, dance and puppet shows are held across the town.

★ Palio di San Donato
LATE AUGUST

Friuli Venezia Giulia has no shortage of historical re-enactments and this is one of the oldest and most atmospheric. Held since 1548, it sees the entire town in medieval costumes, with different neighbourhoods competing in running and archery tournaments, and festive streets abuzz with jugglers, fire eaters and artisan shops.

Running over three days, it's unmissable if you're in the area.

🛏 Sleeping

Domus Iulii
B&B €/€€

(☎333 673 70 42; www.domusiulii.it; Largo Beata Bonaventura Boiani 8; r from €55; 🛜) A small, family-run B&B located in an old building in the centre. While the four rooms on offer here are not huge, they're welcoming and well furnished.

Breakfast follows the Friulian standard: healthy and generous.

Dai Toscans
B&B €€

(☎349 076 52 88, 349 324 89 97; www.daitoscans.it; Corso Mazzini 15/1; s/d/tr €60/80/110; 🛜) In a building that for centuries housed a noble family of Tuscan origins, this refined B&B has five rooms (including two triples) furnished in a vaguely 19th-century style, with wooden furniture, coats of arms and drapes.

It's centrally located on pedestrianised Corso Mazzini (something to keep in mind if arriving by car).

Locanda al Pomo D'Oro
INN €€

(☎0432 73 14 89; www.alpomodoro.it; Piazza San Giovanni 20; s/d/tr €60/90/110; 🛜) Its location in a more isolated corner of the historic centre only accentuates the tranquility at this beautiful inn, converted from an old *xenodochio,* a hostel for travellers in times gone by. Today's guests have much more modern digs at their disposal, with clean, bright rooms and a panoramic terrace (perfect for an *aperitivo*).

The inn has an annex in Stretta San Valentino 14, 150m from the main building.

Locanda al Castello
HOTEL €€

(☎0432 733 242; www.alcastello.net; Via del Castello 12; r from €99; 🛜 ♿) If you feel the sudden urge to say 'I love you', the terrace at this romantic 19th-century castle is the place to do it.

Converted into a hotel, the property includes an excellent restaurant and wellness centre complete with swimming pool. All 27 rooms are rather sumptuous, with classic furnishings.

🍴 Eating & Drinking

★ Al Campanile
BAR, TRATTORIA €/€€

(☎0432 73 24 67; www.alcampanile.com; Via GB Candotti 4; meals €15-25; ☺10am-3pm & 6-11pm Tue-Sun) Here's an *osteria* that gets straight to the point: good food, few frills and, above all, bargain prices. The interior doesn't stand out for its bold design, but you're here for the unfailing quality and friendliness. The *frico* is so good that you may just fall in love with the chefs.

★ Al Monastero
OSTERIA €/€€

(☎0432 70 08 08; www.almonastero.com; Via Ristori 9; meals €20-30; ☺noon-2.30pm & 7-10pm Tue-Sat, noon-2.30pm Sun) As soon as you enter this *osteria* you'll find yourself clutching a glass of red wine, produced at the family wineries.

Sit yourself in front of the fireplace, in a room furnished in rustic Friulian style, and tuck into local specialities, in particular the *cjarsons,* potato-dough ravioli typical of Carnia.

FROM CIVIDALE TO NEW YORK CITY

Well before their success in TV and the restaurant business, the Bastianich family had decided that the area around Buttrio was the ideal place to grow grapes: today, their vineyards occupy almost 32 hectares, producing 270,000 bottles of wine annually. Eighty percent of these are white, among them Friulano, Sauvignon and more complex wines like Vespa Bianco and Bastianich's cult-status Plus.

By booking in advance you can visit the **Bastianich winery** (☑0432 70 09 43; www.bastianich.com; Via Darnazzacco 44/2, Gagliano, Cividale del Friuli; tastings 4/6 glasses €15/22; ☉cellar door & tastings 9.30am-noon & 2-5pm Mon-Fri, 11am-5pm Sat & Sun) and taste them with sommelier and manager Wayne, an affable character with a contagious passion for *vino*.

The Bastianichs – Italians who migrated to the USA, then Americans who returned to Italy – have always had a soft spot for Friuli, considering its climate and soil excellent for winemaking.

Needless to say, their own efforts to produce and promote their wine have played no small role in the renaissance of Friulian wines worldwide.

Al Duca
HAMBURGERS, PIZZA €€

(☑0432 171 15 31; Piazza Paolo Diacono 8; meals from €20-30; ☉noon-3pm & 6-11pm) Here the pizza is high-crusted and the burgers are gourmet and the piazza-side terrace the perfect place to eat them (perhaps with a craft beer in hand).

First and second courses are also offered, including a luscious carbonara.

Alla Speranza
OSTERIA €€

(☑0432 73 11 31; Piazza Foro Giulio Cesare 16; meals €30-35; ☉10.30am-2.30pm & 6-10pm Wed-Sun, 10.30am-2.30pm Mon) If you're craving seafood, this historic tavern is the right place for it, with a generous selection that includes grilled sea bass, sea bream fillet and seafood linguine.

If you're particularly famished and fancy a classic, the *gran fritto di pesce* (mixed platter of fried seafood) is both generous and delicious.

Finish it all off with a glass of *mandarinetto*, a mandarin-based liqueur.

★Alla Frasca
MUSHROOMS €€

(☑0432 73 12 70; www.allafrasca.it; Stretta Bernardino De Rubeis 10A; meals €35-40; ☉11am-2pm & 7-10.30pm Tue-Sun) The menu at Alla Frasca ranges from snails *bourguignonne* to oven-cooked lamb chops with vegetables and mashed potato.

The speciality here though is porcini mushrooms, paired with house or other wines of your choosing.

The atmosphere is super traditional and there is a nice garden where you can eat in summer.

Enoteca L'Elefante
WINE BAR

(☑333 830 87 00; Piazza Paolo Diacono 19; ☉10am-2.30pm & 5-10pm Mon-Fri, 10am-10pm Sat & Sun) A very popular wine bar and bottle shop, which offers a wide selection of Friulian drops. Food options range from bite-sized, *vino*-friendly snacks to more substantial options.

🛍 Shopping

Al Ponte
LOCAL SPECIALITIES

(☑338 167 54 74; Corso Paolino d'Aquileia 14; ☉9am-7pm) This family-run 'little shop of flavours' stocks a wide range of regional delicacies at competitive prices.

If you're in the market for a culinary memento of the area, focus on *gubana* or *strucchi* (see p183), which are produced by in-house pastry chefs.

★MADA
CLOTHING

(☑347 173 33 42; www.facebook.com/MADAtemporarylab; Largo Bojani 27; ☉10am-12.30pm & 3-7pm Mon-Sat) In Italian, the shop's name is an acronym for Hands, Art, Woman, Craftsmanship, four words that encapsulate the philosophy, passion and creativity encapsulated in the creations of MADA's female founders. High-quality, sustainable clothing, accessories and gifts.

ℹ Information

TOURIST INFORMATION

InformaCittà (Map p176, C3; ☑0432 71 04 60; www.cividale.net; informacitta@cividale.net; Piazza Duomo 5; ☉10am-1pm & 2-5pm Mon-Fri, 10am-5pm Sat & Sun Oct-Mar, 10am-1pm &

3-6pm Mon-Fri, 10am-6pm Sat & Sun Apr-Sep) All the local tourist information you need, plus the keys to the Ipogeo Celtico (Hypogeum).

ⓘ Getting There & Away

BUS

Centro Intermodale di Cividale (☑ 0432 73 37 16 ticket office, 0432 58 18 44 general information) Cividale's main bus station, located near the new railway station. Bus frequency varies seasonally.

TPL FVG (☑ 800 05 20 40, mobile 040 971 23 43; https://tplfvg.it) operates buses to Udine (€2.95, 19 minutes, frequent departures) and to other major regional destinations, including San Giovanni al Natisone (€2.95, 43 minutes) and the Tarcento area (€3.50, 40 minutes), passing through Nimis (€3.50, 25 minutes) and Faedis (€2.25, 14 minutes).

It also runs buses to Gorizia (€4.25, 78 minutes) via Cormòns (€2.95, 35 minutes).

CAR & MOTORCYLE

Cividale is located 16km from Udine, 34km from Gorizia and 68km from Trieste.

From Udine, follow the SS54 (Cividale is after Remanzacco).

From Trieste, follow the signs for Sgonico, then at the Udine–Venezia junction continue on the E70 towards Gorizia, switching to the SR356 for Cividale.

Just before the Devil's Bridge, Piazza della Resistenza is a good option for parking. Note that some areas of the *centro storico* (historic centre) are ZTL zones, with limited access.

TRAIN

From Cividale del Friuli station (located at the Centro Intermodale di Cividale), trains run to Trieste (€12.20, 2 hours), Gorizia (€7.20, 75 minutes) and Pordenone (€7.95, 66 minutes).

Ferrovia Udine–Cividale (☑ 0432 73 10 32, www.ferrovieudinecividale.it) is a regional line connecting the two cities (€2.55/2.95, with FVG Card free, 20 minutes, hourly from 7am-11pm Sun & holidays, hourly from 6am-10pm Mon-Sat); one bike permitted per carriage (up to five per train).

ⓘ Getting Around

TO/FROM THE AIRPORT & TRAIN STATION

To reach Ronchi dei Legionari airport, you'll need to transfer to the E51 line in Udine, operated by **TPL FVG** (☑ 800 05 20 40, mobile 040 971 23 43; https://tplfvg.it; €5, 1 hour, roughly hourly from 5pm to 10pm).

TAXI

Autonoleggio De Michieli (☑ 339 659 10 14) Car rental.

VALLI DEL NATISONE

Northeast of Cividale, between the Natisone, Alberone, Cosizza and Erbezzo Rivers, sprawl the Valli del Natisone ('Sclavanìe' in the Friulian language), connecting Cividale with the Valle dell'Isonzo and forming part of the so-called Slavia Friulana.

The Valli del Natisone are a peculiar place, laced with abandoned railways, war trenches and legends of witches with backward feet (see p185); indeed, you'll even find a Buddhist retreat. The influence of neighbouring Slovenia is palpable in everything from the cooking to the language (Proto-Slavic is spoken in some towns).

While **Monte Matajur** (1641m) dominates the valleys, travelling through here delivers ever-changing panoramas, alternating between expanses of pink crocuses cut by streams of blue and green, grottoes, vineyards and churches set in rock.

Winter isn't the ideal time to visit, with dangerous hairpin bends, snow-blocked roads and semideserted villages.

Between April and September, however, the Valli del Natisone offer the best of summer. Suddenly, the slope-clutching villages stir from their slumber and lush, fragrant landscapes awash with wildflowers, chestnuts, ashes and limes beckon hikers and mountain bikers.

🏃 Activities

Wherever you stop in the valleys, you'll have miles of trails to hike, whether for a few hours or a full day. Details on many of the trails can be found at www.caicividale.it and www.lintver.it.

The Alpe Adria Trail also passes through the Valli del Natisone.

ⓘ Information

Pro Loco Nediške Doline/Valli del Natisone Valleys (☑ 339 840 31 96, 0432 727 490; www.nedi skedoline.it; Via Alpe Adria 13/01; ⊙ 10am-1pm & 2.30-5.30pm) In addition to providing you with all kinds of information on the valleys, this tourist office organises interesting literary itineraries in the footsteps of Carlo Emilio Gadda as part of the broader Great War itineraries.

ⓘ Getting There & Away

BUS

From Cividale del Friuli, **TPL FVG** (☑ 800 05 20 40, mobile 040 971 23 43; https://tplfvg.it) buses will reach all of the destinations found in this chapter, including San Pietro al Natisone (€1.65, 10 minutes),

Prepotto (€2.25, 15 minutes), San Leonardo (€1.65, 20 minutes), Stregna (€2.95, 30 minutes), Drenchia (€3.30, 30 minutes), Savogna (€2.25, 18 minutes), Puilfero (€2.25, 14 minutes) and Udine (€4.35, 57 minutes). The ride from San Pietro al Natisone to Prepotto costs €2.95 (30 minutes). At the time of our research there were no direct buses to Grimacco, much less to Topolò.

If you don't have a car you'll need to get from Cividale to Clodig (€2.95, 29 minutes) and from there continue on foot for a couple of kilometres.

CAR & MOTORCYLE

Weather and road conditions permitting, driving is the most convenient way to enjoy the entire Valli del Natisone area, cutting out the waiting time for public transport.

Hairpin bends are common here, so drive carefully, especially on your way back from the local taverns (random breath tests are carried out frequently by police). If you plan on enjoying one of the local festivals, work out your designated driver in advance or stay overnight.

To reach the valleys from Cividale, follow the signs for San Pietro al Natisone. From there, all the roads leading to the various villages branch off.

For San Giovanni d'Antro, Pulfero and Stupizza follow the SS54; for Savogna take the SP11, while for Grimacco take the SP45 (which leads to the main sites of the Great War of the Valli del Natisone). The SP47 leads instead to Stregna and San Leonardo.

For Castelmonte, follow the SP19, then turn at the crossroads with the SP31. All the villages are well signposted.

San Pietro al Natisone

POP 2106 / ELEV 175M

Any jaunt in the Valli del Natisone will commence from this little hillside village, from where various trails reach the surrounding mountains (Matajur, San Giorgio and San Bartolomeo).

Slovenian is spoken fluently by a large part of the population, and the town harbours top-notch gelaterie and pastry shops where you can sample authentic *gubana* and other sweets from the valleys. The small, 13th-century **Chiesa di San Quirino** is also worth a visit, reputedly built on the site of a temple of Diana.

🏃 Activities

San Pietro al Natisone is the starting point of the 14km **Monte Roba hiking trail**, which spans elevations of 174m to 1641m and leads to the top of Matajur in half a day.

Between Montemaggiore and Prepotto you'll find the **Italia trail**, which rejoins that of Monte Roba.

🍴 Eating & Shopping

Dorbolò SWEETS

(☑ 0432 72 70 52; www.gubanedorbolo.com; Via Alpe Adria 81; ⊙ 7.30am-7pm Mon & Wed-Sun) Sweet tooths from across the region travel to San Pietro for Dorbolò's *gubana*.

That said, the focaccias on offer here are pretty good too, as are the edibles that use local valley chestnuts. The onsite bar has outdoor seating, handy for an *aperitivo* at any time.

ℹ️ Information

IAT Valli del Natisone (☑ 349 324 11 68, 339 840 31 96; www.nediskedoline.it; Via Alpe Adria 13/01, San Pietro al Natisone; ⊙ 10am-1pm & 2.30-5.30pm)

Prepotto

POP 733 / ELEV 105M

As you head towards Prepotto you'll begin to get an idea of the rural architecture of the area.

From the town itself, signs lead to the **Santuario della Beata Vergine di Castelmonte** (☑ 0432 73 10 94; www.santuariocastelmonte.it; ⊙ 7.30am-7pm summer, to 6pm winter). It's believed that a Christian place of worship already existed here around the 5th to 7th century, even if one of the first documents to mention the sanctuary 'only' dates from 1200.

It appears that the complex was already an important religious centre by then and a fortified village was built around it in the mid-13th century.

To reach the complex, you'll need to climb 118 steps (or take the lift), an effort compensated by magnificent views of Monte Nero, Cima Fredda, and the Natisone and Judrio Rivers. Inside the sanctuary, highlights include a Black Madonna with Child dating from 1479.

Beneath the church, in the crypt, is a room laden with curious votives donated by the faithful over the years.

Perched on a hillside, the medieval village of **Castelmonte** is a striking sight. You will get a good view of it from the panoramic road that leads there, as well as from the Grotta

GUBANA & OTHER VALLEY SPECIALITIES

Although found across the region (and especially in Cividale), *gubana* is a typical sweet of the Valli del Natisone. The snail-shaped cake is made of baked sweet pastry, filled with a rich combination of walnuts, raisins, pine nuts, sugar, lemon peel and a splash of liqueur. Although usually eaten at Christmas and Easter, it's available year round.

According to tradition, *gubana* is an edible wish for luck and prosperity: indeed, in the *Gubane* dialect it means just that. The term itself reputedly hails from a Slovenian word for 'curl', which echoes the shape of the cake. The filling used for *gubana* is also used in *strucchi* (or *strucoli,* or *strucoleti*), little bundles of shortcrust pastry.

Slovenia's culinary influence in the Valli del Natisone goes beyond sweet treats. Local menus will often feature *štakanije* (mashed potatoes with courgettes, usually served in summer), *šličnjaki* (wheat-flour dumplings) and various soups, including corn, pumpkin and chestnut soups (especially popular in Stregna). Many recipes are rich in herbs, and dishes abound with trout and malga goat's milk cheeses served with conserves. Mouth watering? Head to Dorbolò in San Pietro al Natisone.

di San Giovanni d'Antro (p185), with eyes facing to the right.

❶ Information

Pro Loco Prepotto (☑ 331 112 24 35; Via XXIV Maggio 17; ⊘ varies) Check its Facebook page (www.facebook.com/prolocoprepotto) for information on events.

San Leonardo

POP 1050 / ELEV 168M

San Leonardo is a small town in the Valli del Natisone, made up of hamlets scattered along the Cosizza and Erbezzo streams. The surrounding mountains are riddled with caves, the most famous of which is the 700m-deep **Grotta Star Čedad**, located near the Kot waterfalls. Unfortunately, accessing the cave is a complicated affair, requiring climbing equipment and mountaineering skills.

Much easier to reach is the village of **Cisgne**. The village had slowly begun to depopulate in the 1950s, until it was completely abandoned in 1976.

Despite not having suffered significant damage in the 1976 earthquake, its last remaining inhabitants were forced to move down to the valley floor.

Today, the abandoned village – where leafy branches grow out of windows – is a strange and poignant sight.

Many visitors reach Cisgne by bike or on foot, travelling along a dirt road that starts from the church of Cravero, a hamlet a few kilometres to the north.

Stregna

POP 316 / ELEV 404M

Continuing from San Pietro along the SP47 you enter the heart of Friuli's Slavia area, with its traditional, balcony-adorned stone houses, stables, barns and kilns. These are especially prevalent in Tribil, the loftiest village.

Tranquility is an art form in Stregna, where you'll spot villagers young and old sunbathing, strolling along the mule tracks of **Monte Cum** (917m) or chatting by the Judrio stream.

If it's open, pop inside the 15th-century **Chiesa di San Pietro Apostolo**.

Throughout the area – whose 21 hamlets claim a total headcount of 400 – you'll notice wayside shrines peppering the landscape.

Arriving in Stregna by car is a highlight in itself, with views that alternate between streams, storybook bridges and dizzying cliffs.

✺ Festivals & Events

Burnjak OCTOBER
(Tribil Superiore) The third Sunday in October is dedicated to chestnuts, with concerts, markets, exhibitions and walks in the valleys that involve the whole village (which does not equate to a massive crowd).

❶ Information

Pro Loco Stregna (☑ 339 360 78 62; www.prolocostregna.altervista.org; Frazione Tribil Superiore 50)

Grimacco

POP 307 / ELEV 248M

From Stregna, a further 20 minutes on the SP45 will lead you to Grimacco.

The town is mainly known for one of its hamlets, Topolò, an enchanting village (population 30) that tumbles down the hillside between Monte Colovrat and Monte San Martino.

Every summer, the village revives the Valli del Natisone with its Stazione di Topolò, a highly atmospheric festival of music, art, theatre and juggling.

Several hiking trails also start from Topolò: follow the red and white signs scattered along the way.

✦ Festivals & Events

★ Stazione di Topolò   JULY

(Postaja Topolove; www.stazioneditopolo.it) If you're around in July, try not to miss this charming, three-week festival. It draws artists, musicians, jugglers and hippies from all over northern Italy for a colourful, spirited shindig.

⌑ Sleeping

Albergo Diffuso Valli del Natisone   ALBERGO DIFFUSO €/€€

(☑338 202 59 05; www.slow-valley.com; houses per person €23-35, hostel from €22/33; ⓟ) In Grimacco and Stregna, an eclectic medley of abodes (including 18th-century farmhouses), make up this *albergo diffuso*; ask if the especially picturesque Casa Krajnova is available.

Each abode has its own unique character and all are located in postcard-pretty locations.

Drenchia

POP 100 / ELEV 663M

Drenchia, north-east of Topolò, is home to the Museo all'Aperto del Kolovrat (Kolovrat Open Air Museum). Occupying the 'third Italian defensive line', the museum route is a fascinating one, extending along the Kolovrat plateau bordering Slovenia and retracing some of the most strategic areas of WWI.

Italian soldiers were stationed here for entire winters to control the enemy and, in 1917, suffered an attack by the troops of notorious German captain Erwin Rommel.

If you're interested in the itinerary (which can be completed in a couple of hours), continue from Drenchia towards Slovenia and stop before the former national mountain pass (on the Passo Solarie). You'll find a car park near the monument dedicated to Riccardo di Giusto, the first Italian soldier to fall in WWI. A little further on, the sealed CAI 746 hiking trail begins and you'll recognise the open-air museum's information panels. Continue along the route to the Zagradan Pass (1042m), then to Monte Piatto, where you'll see the remains of machine-gun pits and barracks. Turning at the last fork on the left will lead you back to the car park.

✕ Eating

Al Colovrat   OSTERIA €€

(☑0432 721 104; Località Clabuzzaro; meals from €20-30; ☉lunch & dinner Fri-Mon) On weekends you risk not scoring a table without a reservation: the quality of food at this *osteria* attracts food lovers from all over the area.

❶ Information

Pro Loco Matajur (prolocomatajur@gmail.com; Montemaggiore 44)

Savogna

POP 351 / ELEV 235M

Savogna stretches out between the Valle dell'Alberone and the slopes of Matajur (1641m), on whose summit the Slovenian border runs.

From Savogna, a 20-minute drive towards Slovenia on Via Blasin (prepare for hairpin turns) leads to Polava, where Buddhist centre Cian Ciub Ciö Ling (www.cianciubcioling.com) seemingly appears out of nowhere; you'll recognise it by the Tibetan prayer flags waving from the pagoda.

Even if Buddhism doesn't rock your boat, the centre is so unexpected that it deserves a snoop. Among other things, it organises seminars and meditation courses, and once received a visit from the Dalai Lama. There's no onsite parking, so leave your car on the right side of the road.

⚡ Activities

From Savogna you can reach the Rifugio Pelizzo (Pelizzo Refuge; 1325m), from where it's another 45-minute hike up to the summit of Mount Matajur. Your reward is an unforgettable view of the Julian Alps. Dominating the mountain summit is the Chiesa del Cristo Redentore.

Eating

Péstrofa AGRITURISMO €€
(☑ 0432 71 41 72; https://friuli.vimado.it; SP11 Cedron; meals from €20-30; ⊘ 11am-11pm Fri-Sun)
If you travel to the area on the weekend, this farmhouse will be your *caravanserai,* a place to recharge your batteries. The house speciality is trout, farmed in a small lake in front of the building.

ⓘ Information

Pro Loco Matajur (prolocomatajur@gmail.com; Location Montemaggiore 44)

Pulfero

POP 849 / ELEV 184M

Pulfero is one of the towns of the Valli del Natisone with the most notable history. The road that crosses the village was an important junction towards Tarvisio and Carinthia. It was already in use during the time

of the Romans, who fortified the area to defend it from invasions. In the Lombard period, Pulfero belonged to the Gastaldia of Antro, an administrative region which later belonged to the Patriarchate of Aquileia and to Venice.

Coming from San Pietro al Natisone, travelling along the right bank of the river, you'll pass through Biacis, where you can visit the **Chiesa di San Giacomo**, a delightful church dating back to the period of the patriarchs. Destroyed by an earthquake in 1511, it has been rebuilt and restored several times since.

Next to it lie the remains of a tower and parts of a defensive system, both of which belonged to the Lombard-era **Castello di Ahrensperg**.

Following the signs for Antro, you will reach the **Grotto di San Giovanni d'Antro** (☑ 339 777 93 67; www.grottadantro.it; Località Antro Pulfero; adult/reduced €7/5; ⊘ by reservation only; see website), with its **subterranean church** (€5 for church admission up to the display cases, without access to the tourist nature trail).

The complex is built around a natural cavity, used for both religious and defensive purposes over the centuries. It once included the Castello di San Giovanni, of which little remains now.

Beyond the staircase that ascends the rocky cliff face of Monte Mladesena (459m) lies the chapel, home to a beautiful, 18th-century wooden altar, tombstones and fragments of medieval frescoes.

Although the cave extends for more than 4km, only a few hundred metres are accessible to the public. It was here that the fossilised remains of *Ursus Spelaeus,* the cave bear, were found.

🏃 Activities

From **Centro visite Villaggio degli Orsi di Stupizza** (☑ 333 924 68 02; Località Stupizza Pulfero) a series of hiking routes start in Pulfero.

The most beautiful of these is the 7km-long Stupizza–Pradolino trail, which leads between Monte Mia (1237m) and Lubia (1052m) and along the ruins of Predrobac, a rural village dating from the early 20th century.

Intrepid hikers can detour towards the *malga* (alpine hut) of **Monte Mia**, though this means a steep journey of almost 15km: think carefully before committing.

DO YOU BELIEVE IN THE KRIVAPETE?

If you happen to chat with a local of the Valli del Natisone, ask them to tell you a story about the Krivapete: chances are they'll remember a tale or two from childhood.

Part of local folklore, the Krivapete are similar to witches, with green hair and backward feet (their name derives from the Slovenian *kriv,* twisted, and *peta,* heel). Defiant and mysterious, they enjoy living isolated lives out in nature. Alas, they're also partial to kidnapping and eating children.

The Krivapete inhabit the darkest and most remote corners of the Valli, such as caves and precipices. Conveniently, the fear of encountering these creatures has kept generations of children away from the most dangerous parts of the valleys.

And while no one has ever met one, who's to say what lurks in the wilder corners of this strange and brooding land?

🛏 Sleeping & Eating

Alla Trota
HOTEL, TRATTORIA €

(☎0432 72 60 06; www.allatrota.com; Via Specognis 9, Pulfero; s/d €38/60, half board/full board €40/50, breakfast €4, meals €15-25; ⊙Tue-Sun; Ⓟ) Have you ever tasted trout with polenta? At this historic family-run trattoria, they fish it straight out of the Natisone and cook it in the oven or with white wine. If you don't like fish, go for game or seasonal mushrooms.

The property enjoys an enchanting location on the river, with some rooms serving up panoramic valley views.

Gastaldia D'Antro
HOTEL, TRATTORIA €€

(☎0432 70 92 47; www.gastaldiadantro.it; Via Antro 179, Pulfero; r with breakfast per person €35; ⊙restaurant Wed-Sun; Ⓟ) In a renovated medieval building, this hotel offers five very simple rooms, all with private bathroom and outdoor garden.

The location is enchanting, overlooking the entire valley.

The popular onsite restaurant cooks up Friulian dishes. In season, try the pumpkin curry. On any day, don't miss the *antipasti*.

Pordenone, the Magredi & the Valli Pordenonesi

Includes ➜

Pordenone..........189
Sacile..............195
Caneva.............197
San Vito
al Tagliamento......198
Valvasone..........199
Spilimbergo.........200
The Magredi........201
Vivaro.............202
The Valli
Pordenonesi........203
Polcenigo..........204
Maniago............205
Travesio............206
Clauzetto..........208

Why Go?

Friuli Venezia Giulia is a land of rivers, lakes and lagoons, its aqueous nature giving light and liveliness to landscapes and towns. The province of Pordenone, awash with mountain torrents and unexpected springs, is living proof.

In the Magredi, a rocky steppe unique in Italy, the Meduna and Cellina Rivers sink underground before resurfacing as a tangle of renamed waterways crossing valleys and plains to the sea. These navigable canals made the fortune of these places, connecting towns and locals to the power and grandeur of Venice. Today, La Serenissima's legacy lives on in many forms, among them in Pordenone's colourful facades, the warehouse buildings that grace Sacile's Piazza del Popolo, and the glittering mosaics of Spilimbergo.

Beyond these big hitters of Friuli's southwest are its lesser-known wonders, from solitary castles to Benedictine abbeys. Not surprisingly, water also powers two of the area's most famous crafts, blacksmithing and bladesmithing, traditions alive and well in Maniago and on alpine slopes.

Best Osterie

➡ Al Marescial (p207)
➡ Lataria dei Magredi (p203)
➡ Vecia Osteria del Moro (p194)

Best Local Experiences

➡ Exploring the Magredi on foot (p201)
➡ Taking part in a mosaic course in Spilimbergo (p200)
➡ Buying knives in Maniago (p205)

When to Go

Home to beautiful, easily traversed plains, welcoming cities and weather that's rarely inhospitable, this is a destination for all seasons. Spring and summer undoubtedly stand out with their bumper offering of music events, not to mention their optimal conditions for many activities, from pulse-racing canyoning and gliding, to more meditative options such as horseback riding in the Magredi.

Pordenone, the Magredi & the Valli Pordenonesi Highlights

1 Pordenone (p189) An open-air art gallery.

2 Sacile (p195) On the placid Livenza, once a strategic link between the town and Venice.

3 San Vito al Tagliamento (p198) Hidden views and a sweeping square awash with light.

4 Valvasone (p199) Castle still intact, its historic quarter will catapult you back to medieval times.

5 Abbazia di Santa Maria in Silvis (p199) A Benedictine archetype in Sesto al Reghena.

6 Spilimbergo (p200) More frescoed buildings, plus mosaics and summertime tunes in the squares and streets.

7 The Magredi (p201) A universe to explore and above all understand.

8 Grotte Verdi di Pradis (p208) The ideal setting for canyoning.

PORDENONE & THE PLAIN

Pordenone

POP 51,568 / ELEV 24M

Since Roman times, Pordenone's importance was tied to its strategic access to both the Livenza and Meduna Rivers, trade superhighways connecting the Adriatic Sea to Europe's north.

Under the dominion of the Habsburgs and the patriarchs of Aquileia, river trade flourished as Pordenone exploited its location between Trieste and Venice. Commercial success led to substantial growth and Pordenone was declared a city in 1314. Falling to Venice in 1508, a new port was built in the city in 1537.

After the collapse of the Venetian Republic and a period of Napoleonic rule, Pordenone returned to the Habsburgs. Construction of the Pontebbana road and the railway (1855) saw local manufacturing flourish in the 19th century, while 1866 saw the city annexed to the Kingdom of Italy.

Although WWI and the crisis of 1929 inflicted a severe blow to the city's profitable cotton-processing industry, it found new vigour after WWII with Zanussi, a family-owned business which became an important European manufacturer of household appliances. The company was acquired by Sweden's Electrolux in 1984.

◉ Sights

Duomo PLACE OF WORSHIP
(Piazza San Marco) Pordenone's late-Gothic cathedral was built between the 14th and 15th centuries to replace its 13th-century, Romanesque predecessor. The unfinished facade includes a sculpted portal by Giovanni Antonio Pilacorte, crafted in 1511. Awaiting inside are frescoes, paintings, religious artefacts and the **Altarpiece of San Marco**. Built between 1219 and 1417, the Duomo's soaring bell tower (79m) is crowned by an octagonal spire dating from 1616–21.

The single-nave **interior** harbours some important artworks by the city's Renaissance master Pordenone (see p193). Among these is a stunning altarpiece depicting the *Madonna della Misericordia* (1515), located in the first side chapel to the right. Also on the right is an octagonal pillar decorated with frescoes of *Sant'Erasmo* (1524) and *San Rocco* (1523);

the latter, a self-portrait by Pordenone, exemplifies his great expressive ability. On the same pillar, the *Madonna col Bambino* is also attributed to the artist.

Palazzo Comunale HISTORIC BUILDING
The most iconic of Pordenone's civic buildings is also its town hall, built in the Gothic style between 1291 and 1365 as the seat of the city council. A bookend to Corso Vittorio Emanuele II, the building is both fascinating and indecipherable with its jumble of styles and elements. Among these is a large loggia, Gothic windows, a balcony and a centrepiece clock. The latter, added in 1452, vaguely recalls the famous timepiece in Venice's Piazza San Marco.

Galleria d'Arte Harry Bertoia ART GALLERY
(☏0434 39 29 35; www.comune.pordenone.it/galleriabertoia; Corso Vittorio Emanuele II 60; opening hours & admission vary) While the exhibitions here vary constantly (see the website), what never changes is the beauty of Palazzo Spelladi, whose origins lie in the 14th century. The gallery's namesake is Harrfy Bertoia (1915–78), an important figure of 20th-century design and creator of the Diamond chair (1952), described as a 'sculpture of steel and air'.

Museo Civico d'Arte ART MUSEUM
(☏0434 39 29 35; www.comune.pordenone.it/it/comune/il-comune/struttori/museoarte; Palazzo Ricchieri, Corso Vittorio Emanuele II 51; adult/reduced €3/1, free with FVG Card; ⊙3-7pm Thu-Sun) Close to Palazzo Comunale lies Palazzo Ricchieri, a typical Venetian-style residence now home to a museum known for its well-curated and engaging exhibitions. The collection itself includes Friulian and Veneto artworks from the Middle Ages onwards, including canvases, drawings, frescoes, wooden sculptures, furniture, jewellery and ceramics.

The **picture gallery** claims paintings by Pordenone and Michelangelo Grigoletti. Check the website for what's on.

Pordenone

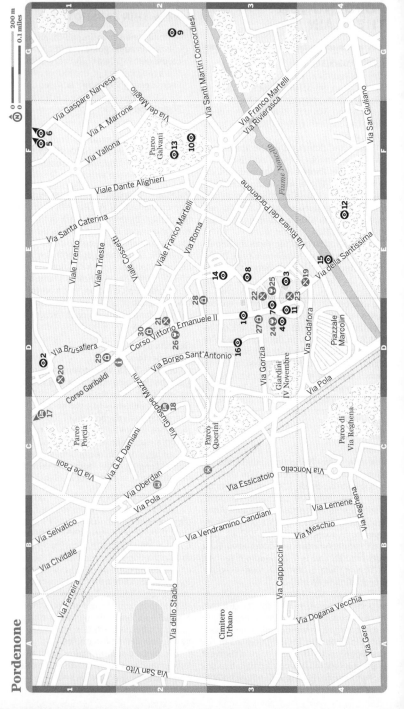

Pordenone

⊙ Top Sights

1 Corso Vittorio Emanuele II......................D3

◉ Sights

2 Chiesa di San Giorgio Martire..............D1
3 Duomo...E3
4 Galleria d'Arte Harry Bertoia.................D3
5 Immaginario Scientifico............off map F1
6 Museo Archeologico
del Friuli Occidentale ....off map F1
7 Museo Civico d'Arte...............................D3
8 Museo Civico di Storia Naturale.............E3
9 Museo Diocesano di Arte Sacra............G2
10 PAFF! Palazzo Arti Fumetto Friuli..........F2
11 Palazzo Comunale..................................D3
12 Parco Fluviale del Noncello...................E4
13 Parco Galvani...F2
14 Piazza della Motta..................................E3
15 Ponte di Adamo ed Eva..........................E4
16 Vicolo delle Mura...................................D3

⊜ Sleeping

17 Giardino in Città......................off map C1
18 Park Hotel Pordenone...........................C2

⊗ Eating

19 Al Gallo..E4
20 Da Cico...D1
21 Ovest..D2
22 Vecia Osteria del Moro..........................E3
23 Zampolli..E3

⊙ Drinking & Nightlife

24 Caffè Municipio......................................D3
25 Enoteca al Campanile.............................E3
26 Peratoner...D2

⊙ Shopping

27 Dimore...D3
28 Libreria al Segno....................................D2
29 Libreria Quo Vadis.................................D1
30 Nanà...D2

★ **Corso Vittorio Emanuele II**   STREET

Expect to stroll this pedestrian thoroughfare often during your Pordenone sojourn. Running between Piazza Cavour and the Noncello River, its appeal is three-fold. Firstly, there's the local atmosphere, which you can soak up on a walk, bike ride or sipping a spritz. Secondly, there are its historic porticoes, the second longest in Italy (after Bologna) and lined with a plethora of shops and historic cafes. Thirdly, you have its famous, frescoed facades, which make the Corso a veritable open-air art gallery, over 600m long.

Among the more restrained of the Corso's frescoed buildings, Casa Scaramuzza (no 49, overlooking Palazzo Comunale) is a highlight. Heading up the street, Palazzetto Cattaneo (no 54) reveals fragments of 16th-century frescoes, while opposite, Casa Vianello (no 45) sports magnificent 14th-century decorations.

The frescoes adorning Palazzo Mantica (no 52) – depicting mythological figures Milo of Crotone and Marcus Curtius – are attributed to Pordenone. Frescoed facades aside, some of the Corso's buildings harbour fascinating relics from the city's past. The courtyard of Palazzo Policreti (no 16), for instance, reveals the only remaining stretch of Pordenone's ancient city walls.

When you reach Casa Pittini (no 21), turn into Via del Cristo, which you'll recognise by the beautiful shrine to the Madonna. The shrine belonged to the Confraternita dei Bat-

tuti, a confraternity once based nearby. At the end of the street is the Chiesa di Santa Maria degli Angeli (or del Cristo), built in 1309. Note its elegantly sculpted portals, dating from 1510 and attributed to Pilacorte.

Continuing north, past Piazza Cavour, take pedestrianised **Corso Garibaldi**, which, despite its lack of porticoes, is an equally pleasant strip to wander. The street formed the axis for Pordenone's expansion after the 17th century and harbours some interesting works of architecture.

Among these are Palazzo Pera and Palazzo Sbrojavacca, which together house the seat of the Province of Pordenone.

Piazza della Motta   PIAZZA

This has been Pordenone's market square since the Middle Ages and its cheery, boisterous, well-stocked market runs every Wednesday and Saturday morning. On market days, you'll hardly notice the buildings surrounding the 15th-century piazza, among them the former Biblioteca Civica (Public Library), the Palazzo del Monte dei Pegni (dating from 1768) and the 15th-century Chiesa di San Francesco. The church cloister is often open for cultural events.

**Chiesa di San
Giorgio Martire**   PLACE OF WORSHIP

(☑ 0434 266 81; www.parrocchiasangiorgiopn.it; Largo San Giorgio 8/a) Originally built in 1588, this church underwent several nips and tucks

THE LONG LOST WALLS

Walking up Corso Vittorio Emanuele II from Palazzo Comunale, the first alleyway to your left is known locally as **Vicolo delle Mura**.

It leads beneath Palazzo Gregoris to Via Gorizia, where the city gate Porta dei Cappuccini once stood. In fact, a good section of Via Gorizia flanks what little remains of Pordenone's old city walls. For centuries, this once high and sturdy barrier helped defend the city from uninvited guests, among them the Turks in 1499. By the time Napoleon's army set about dismantling the walls in 1796–7, they surrounded the entire Contrada Maggiore, with two main towers (Trevisana and Furlana) and 16 supporting ones.

With its flower-graced balconies and tranquil gardens, Vicolo delle Mura hardly paints a warlike picture today. Yet, this very street once bustled with heavily armed soldiers. Indeed, it was once called *degli Andadori* (of those who go), a nod to the soldiers who roamed the walls.

until its consecration in 1873. Its most prominent (and peculiar) feature is the bell tower. Designed by Giovanni Battista Bassi and built in 1852, it could be described as colossal classical column crossed with a lighthouse. Inside the church, highlights include the two stoups and paintings by Gaspare Narvesa and Michelangelo Grigoletti.

Museo Civico di Storia Naturale   MUSEUM
(☑0434 39 29 50; www.comune.pordenone.it/it/comune/il-comune/strutture/museostorianaturale; Via della Motta 16; adult/reduced €3/1, free with FVG Card; ⊙3-7pm Thu-Sun) This museum is a useful stop on any trip to the Dolomites, with geological exhibits, over 10,000 minerals, display cases teeming with insects and birds, and an impressive cast of taxidermic animals. There's even a Wunderkammer laden with a thousand oddities, including three-legged chickens, two-headed calves and a unicorn's horn.

Parco Galvani   PARK
(Via Vallona 55; ⊙6.30am-9.30pm Mar-Oct, 7am-8.30pm Nov-Feb) FREE This park was once the garden of a villa belonging to the noble Galvani family, who lived here in the 18th century. The grounds are expansive, making them

an ideal place to explore on bike. At the entrance is **MIRA**, a lakeside trail leading past a wide variety of roses. The park is also home to **PAFF! Palazzo Arti Fumetto Friuli** (☑0434 39 29 41; https://paff.it; ⊙3-8pm Tue-Fri, 10.30am-1pm & 3-8pm Sat & Sun), a unique museum dedicated to the art of comic books and illustrations, with exhibitions, workshops and various special events.

Museo Diocesano di Arte Sacra   MUSEUM
(☑0434 52 43 40; www.diocesi.concordia-pordenone.it; Via Revedole 1; ⊙9am-1pm Tue-Thu & Sat, 4-6.30pm Fri) FREE Pordenone's museum of sacred art claims a formidable cache of religious treasures – paintings, sculpture, vestments, reliquaries – spanning the 7th to the 20th centuries.

Parco Fluviale del Noncello   PARK
(Via della Santissima) This swathe of green extends beyond the **Ponte di Adamo ed Eva (Bridge of Adam & Eve)**, so called for the two statues that guard it. In truth, the figures depict Jupiter and Juno. The current bridge was completed in 1925 to replace an earlier, 18th-century crossing. Note the moveable central timber section, designed for the passage of boats to a river port that was never completed. Interestingly, the two walkways at the base of the bridge served as crossings for the animals used to tow the vessels. One of the two walkways remains accessible on foot.

The park itself is a wonderful spot in the warmer months, especially for a bike ride.

The small church at its centre is the **Chiesa della Santissima Trinità**, erected in 1550 and featuring an octagonal bell tower. Today, it's a shrine to the fallen of WWI and WWII, as well as a place of worship for the Orthodox community.

Museo Archeologico del Friuli Occidentale   MUSEUM
(☑0434 54 14 12; www.comune.pordenone.it/it/comune/il-comune/struttori/museoarcheologico; Via Vittorio Veneto 19-21; adult/reduced €3/1, free with FVG Card; ⊙3-7pm Sat & Sun by reservation only) Back in Pordenone's Roman days, a vast burial ground extended from the current Via Veneto to the walls of medieval **Castello dei Conti di Ragogna**. These days, the castle's frescoed interior houses Pordenone's archaeological museum.

Focussing on western Friuli, its booty includes prehistoric items from Piancavallo and Iron-Age relics from Gradisca. There are numerous Roman finds, especially from local necropolises, as well as an interesting section illustrating the castle's own stages of construction.

Immaginario Scientifico INTERACTIVE MUSEUM

(✔0434 54 24 55; www.immaginarioscientifico.it/sedi/pordenone; Via Vittorio Veneto 31, Località Torre di Pordenone; adult/reduced €6/4, free under 6yr & with FVG Card; ⊙10am-6pm Sun, planetarium hourly from 3pm) Like the one in Trieste, this science centre serves up fun science experiments to enjoy with your little Einsteins.

⭐ Festivals & Events

Pordenonelegge SEPTEMBER

(www.pordenonelegge.it) Top choice for bookworms, this literature festival is held in mid-September. A program of author talks, panel discussions and readings dish up all the latest on the Italian literary scene.

🛏 Sleeping

Giardino in Città B&B €

(✔0434 36 62 88; www.giardinoincitta.it; Via Montereale 45; s/d €45/70; P 🅿 ✳ 🛜) A 10-minute walk from the centre, this excellent B&B has three large rooms with private bathroom, as well as numerous common areas that include a kitchen, TV room and lovely garden. No pets allowed.

Park Hotel Pordenone HOTEL €€

(✔0434 279 01; www.parkhotelpordenone.it; Via Mazzini 43; s/d €88/105; P ✳ 🛜) All the usual perks of the Best Western chain: modern, well-equipped rooms, a good bar, excellent breakfast and a handy location halfway between the centre and the train station. Rooms are small but comfortable, and the free bike rental is an added sweetener. Secure, private parking (€9 per night) is available 150m from the hotel.

🍴 Eating

Zampolli SWEETS €

(✔0434 52 08 74; Piazza San Marco 10; ⊙8am-1pm & 3-11pm Tue-Sat, to 8pm Sun) In the shadow of the Duomo, this calorific veteran exudes old-world charm. The artisanal pastries are tempting, and best washed down with coffee, tea or glass of prosecco while admiring the simple, elegant lines of the cathedral bell tower.

Ovest BISTRO €€

(✔0434 203 37; Via Cesare Battisti 2; meals €25-30; ⊙noon-2.30pm & 7-10pm Mon-Thu, to 10.30pm Fri & Sat; 📶) A popular lunch spot for local office workers and executives, but equally fine for a post-sightseeing *aperitivo* or dinner. Working from a small, open kitchen, young, creative chefs concoct high-quality, modern dishes, from reimagined pasta classics to vegetarian bites.

As good for a light meal as it is for a three-course feast.

Da Cico RESTAURANT, PIZZERIA €€

(✔0434 273 12; https://dacico.it; Largo San Giorgio 4; meals €20-30; ⊙11am-3pm & 6pm-midnight Mon-Sat, to 11pm Sun; 📶) Family-friendly Da Cico serves tasty meat, fish and vegetarian-friendly dishes, as well as decent pizzas. You can choose between classic pizzas or *spianate,* large, thin-crust pies you can top with your own choice of fresh, quality ingredients. The small outdoor tables offer a unique view of the city.

PORDENONE OF PORDENONE

Whether you're in Pordenone, another corner of Friuli Venezia Giulia, or another Italian city altogether, chances are you'll come across one of Italy's lesser-known 16th-century masters: Giovanni Antonio de 'Sacchis (1483–1539). Born in Pordenone and therefore nicknamed 'Il Pordenone', the Renaissance great had a knack for balancing grandiose classical narratives with a popular sensibility, wisely tweaking the proportions of each according to the commission's provenance, urban or rural. A pupil of Giorgione, Pordenone achieved great success, becoming a serious rival to Titian. The Friulian painter became the subject of a *damnatio memoriae* of sorts, his legacy undermined by a number of Venetian art critics whose loyalties were with Titian. Indeed, questions surround Pordenone's sudden death, which took place while delivering tapestry designs to Ercole II d'Este in Ferrara. According to the art-world rumour mill, Pordenone was poisoned on the orders of Titian himself.

★ Vecia Osteria del Moro
OSTERIA €€

(📞 0434 286 58; www.laveciaosteriadelmoro.it; Via Castello 2; meals €30; ⊙ noon-2.30pm & 7.15-10.30pm Mon-Sat) Relaxed but somewhat more refined than the standard tavern, Vecia Osteria del Moro sets an atmospheric scene with its original 19th-century prints. The menu includes all the local Pordenone specialities; during Lent, don't miss the *renga* (herring), a fusion of Venetian and Friulian cuisines. There's a good choice of wines, with the option to open a bottle and only be charged for the amount consumed.

Al Gallo
SEAFOOD €€€

(📞 0434 52 16 10; www.ristorantealgallo.com; Via San Marco 10; meals €50-60; ⊙ noon-2.30pm & 7-10.30pm Tue-Sat, noon-2.30pm Sun) Heading down from Piazza San Marco towards the Noncello River, you'll pass this elegant, historic restaurant to your left, atmospherically set beneath the porticoes. From the *antipasti,* to the *primi* and *secondi,* the star ingredient here is seafood.

🍷 Drinking & Nightlife

★ Caffè Municipio
HISTORIC CAFE

(📞 0434 52 27 86; www.caffemunicipiopn.it; Corso Vittorio Emanuele II 58; ⊙ 7am-1am) Overlooking Pordenone's historic town hall, Caffè Municipio is a local institution. It's also the place to try Pordenone's famous *centino*.

The local aperitif was originally called the *Trentino* as it cost 30 *lire* (*trenta* is Italian for '30'), becoming the centino when its price hit 100 *lire* (*cento* means '100'). Despite further inflation, the name has stuck. The drink it-

---

DON'T MISS

THE PATENTED BISCOTTO

Pordenone's signature sweet is the **Biscotto Pordenone**. Just ask the Chamber of Commerce, which registered the trademark and attributed the original to **Gelateria Pasticceria Montereale** (📞 0434 36 51 07; www.biscottopordenone.it; Via Montereale 23; ⊙ 7.30am-8pm Mon, to 9pm Wed-Fri, 7.30am-1pm & 3.30-9pm Sat & Sun), where it's still made to a 1940s recipe. In 2004, the Ministry of Agriculture got in on the act, declaring the biscuit a typical product of Friuli. The cult-status bite is made using local wheat and corn flour, raw almonds (grown locally since Roman times) and grappa.

---

self is a riff on the Americano, served in the vintage glass and perched on a rather unique coaster. *Cin cin!*

★ Peratoner
CHOCOLATE

(📞 0434 52 00 14; Corso Vittorio Emanuele II 22/b; ⊙ 8am-9pm Tue-Sun) The undisputed go-to for hot chocolate, time-warped Peratoner is also a fine place to start the day. Choose from a bounty of luscious pastries, brioche and *cornetti,* whose variety of fillings include chocolate (naturally).

Enoteca al Campanile
WINE BAR

(📞 0434 52 06 28; Via del Campanile 1; ⊙ 6pm-midnight Tue-Thu, 11am-2.30pm & 6pm-midnight Fri-Sun) You'll find wines from all over Italy at this tiny, soulful wine shop, set at the foot of a bell tower in a medieval corner of the city. The handful of outdoor tables are highly coveted in the summer, where peckish punters quaff and nibble on *vino*-friendly charcuterie and small plates.

🛍 Shopping

Mercatino dell'Antiquariato
ANTIQUES

(Corso Vittorio Emanuele II) Pordenone's antiques fair is held on the last Sunday of the month from September to June. Scour the stalls for vintage treasures or simply take in the Corso at its most colourful.

Libreria Quo Vadis
TRAVEL BOOKS

(📞 0434 24 75 60; www.quovadislibris.com; Corso Garibaldi 4/c; ⊙ 9am-noon & 3.30-7pm Tue-Sat) Expect to get seriously itchy feet at this bookshop, which specialises in travel guides, travel narratives and maps. There's a particular focus on Friulian, Balkan and Eastern European themes and subjects.

Libreria al Segno
BOOKS

(📞 0434 52 05 06; www.libreriaalsegno.com; Vicolo del Forno 2; ⊙ 9am-12.30pm & 3.30-7.30pm Tue-Sun) A huge bookshop near Corso Vittorio Emanuele II, not far from the Chiesa di Santa Maria degli Angeli. Despite its size, the sole focus here is books, so don't expect the gadgets and stationery found at other big bookshops. It's also a publishing house, with a large catalogue covering both local and wider-ranging themes.

Nanà
CLOTHING

(📞 0434 24 71 19; Corso Vittorio Emanuele II 9/a; ⊙ 9am-12.30pm & 3.30-7.30pm Tue-Sat) From bohemian prints to Scottish patterns, inspiration comes from far and wide at this eclectic, affordable fashion boutique, with various branches across Italy's northeast.

Dimore
(☑ 0434 212 65; www.dimore-concept.com; Corso Vittorio Emanuele II 56/c; ⊙ 10am-12.30pm & 3.30-7pm Tue-Sun) Drop in for homewares and furnishings, personal accessories and various brilliant concepts that might include designer pots that germinate plants directly from the seed. You'll find it under the porticoes near Caffè Municipio.

ℹ Information

EMERGENCY
Fire Brigade (☑ 0434 39 11 11; Via Internal 14)
Police (☑ 0434 23 81 11; Piazzale Palatucci 1)

MEDICAL SERVICES
Ospedale Santa Maria degli Angeli (☑ 0434 39 91 11; www.aopn.sanita.fvg.it; Via Montereale 24)

TOURIST INFORMATION
Pordenone Infopoint (map p190, D2; ☑ 0434 52 03 81; www.turismofvg.it; Palazzo Badini, cnr Via Mazzini & Piazzetta Cavour; ⊙ 9am-1pm & 1.30-6pm) Well-stocked and very central. Also rents out city audio guides (see p189).

ℹ Getting There & Away

AIR
The closest airport is **Treviso Antonio Canova Airport** (TSF; SR515, ☑ 0422 31 51 11; www.trevisoairport.it; Via Noalese 63E), accessible from Pordenone via the A28 (68km) or by train (80 minutes). Alternatively, **Venice Marco Polo Airport** (VCE; ☑ 041 260 61 11; www.veniceairport.it; Viale Galileo Galilei 30/1, Tessera) is connected to Pordenone by **ATVO** bus 68 (one-way/return €13.50/21.70).

BUS
Flixbus (☑ 02 947 59 208; www.flixbus.it) and **Buscenter** (☑ 06 164 160; www.buscenter.it) connect Venice to Pordenone with two early-morning services (€13, 75 minutes).

TPL FVG (☑ 800 05 20 40, mobile 040 971 23 43; https://tplfvg.it) buses connect Pordenone to other towns on the plain. Bus P33 reaches Sacile (from €2.25, 30 to 50 minutes) and Caneva (€2.95, 35 minutes, 13 daily between 7am and 7pm). Bus P22 (30 minutes via Zoppola) and bus P55 (40 minutes via Fiume Veneto) serve San Vito al Tagliamento (€3.50). Bus P18 line reaches Valvasone (€3.50, 35 minutes, 8 daily) and Spilimbergo (€4.25, 50 minutes, 25 daily between 6am and 10.30pm), while bus P19 connects Spilimbergo with Casarsa della Delizia and San Vito al Tagliamento (€3.50, 35 minutes, roughly hourly). To reach Casarsa della Delizia (the nearest train station), take bus P19.

CAR & MOTORCYLE
From the A4 (Turin–Trieste) motorway, switch to the A28 (Portogruaro–Conegliano), which reaches Pordenone and the Friulian Dolomites.

Sacile lies 13km from Pordenone along the SS13. From Sacile, the SP12 leads to Caneva. To reach the archaeological site, head out of Caneva to Sarone and then follow the signs on the foothill road.

To reach Valvasone, exit the A4 at Portogruaro, switch to the SS13 up to Casarsa della Delizia, then follow the signs.

Spilimbergo lies 33km from Pordenone. To reach it, take the Cimpello–Sequals motorway link, exit at Tauriano and follow the signs for Spilimbergo. If you're traveling on the A4, exit at Portogruaro (if you're eastbound) or Palmanova (westbound), follow the signs to Pordenone, then those for Spilimbergo.

Parking
GSM Pordenone (☑ 0434 20 90 98; www.gsmpn.it; Via Colonna 2) manages parking in the city. Hourly rates range from €0.40 to €1.40 depending on the area (⊙ 8am-7pm Mon-Fri, 8am-6pm Sat).

Parcheggio Candiani (☑ 0434 52 01 47; Via Candiani 26; €0.40 per hr, free for the first hr; ⊙ 24hr) Ideally located beside the train and bus station (map p190, C2), a short walk from the centre.

TRAIN
Trains runs frequently between Pordenone and Venice, from where connecting services reach Milan and Rome. Services run from 5am to 11pm, with one-way tickets starting from €8. The travel time between Venice and Pordenone is around 75 minutes.

ℹ Getting Around

TPL FVG (☑ 800 05 20 40, mobile 040 971 23 43; https://tplfvg.it; Piazzale Caduti di Nassiriya e di tutte le Missioni di Pace 1, c/o Stazione Ferroviaria di Pordenone; ☑ 0434 22 44 44 ticket office ⊙ 6.45am-7.15pm Mon-Sat) Manages public transport in Pordenone and its province. A single ticket in the city is €1.35 (valid 60 minutes) or €1.65 (valid 75 minutes).

Sacile
POP 19,842 / ELEV 25M

Sacile's history is indelibly tied to the Livenza River. Falling under Venetian control in 1420, the town enjoyed three bustling, prosperous centuries due to its river trade. Timber for Venice's gondolas was shipped from here, as were goods destined for northern Europe.

Even today, the Venetian influence lingers, in Sacile's canals and bridges, historic warehouses and double entrances (from the street and from the river). Wandering around, you'll soon understand why the town was once known as 'The Garden of La Serenissima'.

◉ Sights

Although it straddles two river islands and their surrounds, Sacile's historic centre is easy to navigate on foot. Its main landmark is the **Duomo** (Piazza Duomo 4; ⊙ 9am-noon & 3-7pm), dedicated to San Nicolò (patron saint of sailors and merchants) and idyllically set by the riverfront.

Sporting a Renaissance facade, the cathedral harbours colourful 15th- and 16th-century frescoes and a plaque commemorating the 1454 burial of David, son of Ottoman sultan Murad II. As the fortifications of Torrione di San Rocco and Foro Boario testify, 15th-century Sacile occupied a strategic position for the Venetians, who were no strangers to Ottoman incursions.

Your explorations will probably start in **Piazza del Popolo**, which still retains the look of an old dock. Indeed, this was the arrival point of boatmen sailing along the Livenza and was therefore considered the city gate. Now home to bars and restaurants, it's a good spot to soak up Sacile's sleepy atmosphere.

Flanking the square is **Palazzo del Comune**, built in 1483, as well as a number of 16th-century buildings. Among these is Palazzo Fabio-De Zanchis (no 18), decorated with the traces of mythologically themed frescoes.

Heading northeast on Viale Zancanaro you'll cross a bridge. Note the building to your right, which is marked with bullet holes. These were fired by soldiers returning from Caporetto.

The building itself is **Palazzo Ragazzoni** (☑ 0434 78 71 37; Viale Zancanaro 2; ⊙ by request), which, in the 16th century, belonged to Giacomo Ragazzoni, a famous and wealthy Venetian merchant.

Inside is a series of exceptional 16th-century frescoes by Francesco Montemezzano, a pupil of Veronese (don't miss those in the Salone degli Imperatori).

From Piazza del Popolo, Via del Popolo heads south to the 17th-century Ponte della Pietà, which crosses the slower branch of the Livenza.

Waiting across the water is the jewel-box Chiesa di Santa Maria della Pietà, an oratory sporting a charming loggia. Take a moment here to watch the river flow tranquilly below.

★☆ Festivals & Events

Sagra dei Osei   SEPTEMBER
(www.prosacile.com) Held on the first Sunday of September, Sacile's Bird Festival is a must if you're in the area.

With origins in the town's medieval bird market, the event includes avian displays and a bird-singing competition.

🛏 Sleeping & Eating

Hotel Due Leoni   HOTEL €€/€€€
(☑ 0434 78 81 11; www.hoteldueleoni.com; Piazza del Popolo 24; s/d/jnr ste with breakfast & undercover parking €86/120/150; 🛜❄) This is the yellow building on the main square of Sacile, decorated with the traditional flags and two very Venetian stone lions. The comfortable front rooms overlook the bright and bustling square. Onsite perks include a spa and excellent breakfast.

Cellini   RESTAURANT, PIZZERIA €
(☑ 0434 728 68; cellinisacile.weebly.com; Via Pietà 20; meals €30; pizzas €7-15; ⊙ noon-3pm & 6-11pm Tue-Sun) The pizza here is quite popular and the rest of the surf-based menu caters for most tastes.

Yet what makes this place really special is its setting, with some tables on a terrace jutting out into the river and others on Piazzetta Antonio Pasqual, right beside the Duomo and its bell tower.

La Piola   PORK RIBS €
(☑ 0434 78 18 93; www.lapiolasacile.it; Piazza del Popolo 9/d; pork ribs €12; ⊙ noon-2.30pm & 7-10.30pm Tue-Sun) This restaurant specialises in *puntine* (pork ribs), cooked on the grill over a wood fire and served with potatoes and a simple pinch of salt. For those not keen on too much meat, the *antipasti* and dishes of the day come to the rescue.

The onsite wine bar offers 400 different drops.

Trattoria Cavour   RESTAURANT €€
(☑ 0434 714 89; www.trattoriacavour.com; Via Cavour 31; meals €30; ⊙ noon-2pm & 7pm-1am Mon-Fri, 7-9pm Sat) Sporting a stylish, contemporary fit-out and riverside garden terrace, locals have been flocking to Cavour for a quick coffee, business lunch or dinner (family or romantic) for almost 60 years. While the menu nods to Sacile's river location, it also draws on the sea, hinterland fruit and vegetables, and regional meats.

🍷 Drinking & Nightlife

Caffè Commercio
CAFE

(☑ 0434 73 51 83; Piazza del Popolo 11; ⊘ 7am-midnight) This historic cafe peddles excellent desserts that could easily stand in for a proper meal. (We won't tell your doctor, scout's honour.)

Antica Sacile
WINE BAR

(☑ 340 835 33 24; Piazza del Popolo; ⊘ 7.30am-1am Mon & Wed-Sun, from 2.30pm Tue) In the heart of town, this is the main go-to for coffee, *aperitivo* or a nightcap. Sacile's Venetian influence is clear in the usually generous selection of *cicheti* (Venetian tapas). If the weather's not too hot or cold, kick back at an outdoor table and take in the piazza action.

La Bottega di Bacco
WINE BAR

(☑ 0434 721 70; Viale Zancanaro 19; ⊘ 9.30am-1pm & 3.30-7.30pm Mon-Sat) A traditional, intimate wine bar serving *ombre* (the Venetian term for glasses of wine) and snacks. Perfect if you're in the mood to strike up a conversation (or simply eavesdrop).

🛍 Shopping

Grosmi
COFFEE

(☑ 0434 715 97; Via Garibaldi 6; ⊘ 8.30am-12.30pm & 2.30-7.30pm Mon-Sat) Passion and competence drive this gorgeous little shop, peddling quality coffee beans and blends from all over the world.

ℹ Information

IAT di Sacile (☑ 0434 73 72 92; www.visitsacile. it; Via Mazzini 11; ⊘ 9am-noon & 2-6pm Mon-Fri in winter; 3-6pm Mon, 9am-12.30pm & 3-6pm Tue, Thu & Fri, 9am-12.30pm Wed, 9am-1pm Sat & Sun in summer) Tourist office, a few steps from Piazza del Popolo.

Caneva

POP 6330 / ELEV 57M

Located 6km northwest of Sacile, between hills and the Cansiglio plateau, this little village stands out for its **Castello di Caneva** (☑ 0434 795 10; ⊘ outside always open, inside by prior booking). The castle dates from at least 1034, the year in which, according to documents, Emperor Conrad II offered the manor to Popone, Patriarch of Aquileia. For all we know, it may have already existed. Its strategic position becomes clear as you head up to the castle, from where the surrounding territory unfurls like a map. You'll need to book ahead to visit the castle interior, though the storybook exterior and breathtaking views are reward enough.

Within the perimeter of the ruined castle walls is the 11th-century **Chiesa di Santa Lucia**, home to Renaissance frescoes. On the climb up to the castle, you'll pass the Chiesa di San Tommaso: the lower part, from the base to the entablature, comes from a demolished 16th-century theatre, while the upper part dates from the postwar period. Waiting inside are beautiful frescoes by Giovanni di Min (a follower of Canova), including *The Fall of the Rebel Angels*.

Be careful not to confuse the bell tower of the church with the castle; the latter is another couple of kilometres further up the hill. Mercifully, it's possible to cover most of the route by car, with only the last few metres requiring foot work.

Caneva, however, is more than its castle. Italy's passion for cycling is celebrated at its curious **Museo di Ciclismo Toni Pessot** (☑ 0434 79 74 60; Via Trieste 51; ⊘ on request) ‎🆓FREE, which showcases various items belonging to cycling champions and, incongruously, the boxing gloves of local World Heavyweight Champion Primo Carnera.

Northeast of the town, on the banks of the Livenza, lies the archaeological site of **Palù di Livenza** (http://palu.incaneva.it). In the upper Paleolithic, the area was home to a large and important pile-dwelling settlement, carbon dated to between 4500 and 3800 BCE. The many artefacts found here – among them flake tools, fragments of oars and axes, and the wooden remains of huts – are now on display at the Museo Archeologico del Friuli Occidentale in Pordenone (p192).

While there are no actual ruins to see, the site's location on the Livenza River makes it a beautiful spot. In 2011, it became a Unesco World Heritage Site as part of a series of prehistoric pile-dwelling sites around the Alps. Nineteen of these lie in Italy.

Even older are the flint instruments discovered near Bus de la Lum north of Caneva, believed to belong to hunters camping around the Foresta del Cansiglio in 11,000 BCE.

ℹ Information

Associazione Pro Castello Caneva (procastello .incaneva.it)

Sovrintendenza per i Beni storici per il Friuli Venezia Giulia (☑ 040 452 75 11; www.sabap. fvg.beniculturali.it) For information on the Palù di Livenza archaeological site.

Comune di Caneva (☑ 0434 79 74 11; Piazza Martiri Garibaldini 8) Also useful for information on Palù di Livenza.

San Vito al Tagliamento

POP 15,157 / ELEV 30M

Located west of the river, San Vito al Tagliamento is one of the prettiest towns in Friuli Venezia Giulia. Predominantly medieval in style, it was a stronghold of the patriarchs of Aquileia, who controlled it until the mid-18th century. Looking more like a noble residence than a fortification these days, the castle (home of the patriarchs) survives, as do parts of its bailey and the moat.

Piazza del Popolo is the heart of the town and most of the main sights are located on (or just off) it. Top billing goes to the **Duomo** (Chiesa dei Santi Vito, Modesto e Crescenzia), built between the 15th and 17th centuries and flanked by a sinuous, 73m-high bell tower. Behind it lies the **Chiesa di Santa Maria dei Battuti** (Via Bellunello 18; ⊘ 9am-7pm), built in 1360 and featuring a Renaissance facade and beautiful apse decorated in the 16th century. Further along Via Bellunello stands the 12th-century **Torre of San Nicolò**. Known as Scaramuccia, this was San Vito's eastern city gate, where sections of the old city walls remain visible today.

Other beautiful buildings on Piazza del Popolo itself include the 17th-century **Palazzo Altan Rosa**, which incorporates Torre Grimana and a neoclassical oratory. The complex harbours beautiful frescoed ceilings and the **Museo della Vita Contadina Diogene Penzi** (☑ 0434 83 32 75; ⊘ 9am-12.30pm Mon-Fri, reservations recommended) FREE.

The building with the frescoed facade is **Palazzo Fancello**, directly opposite which stands Palazzo Comunale.

The latter claims a beautiful loggia and the jewel-box **Teatro Giangiacomo Arrigoni** (☑ 0434 802 51; Piazza del Popolo 38; same times as the IAT tourist office) FREE.

Yet, it's the square's crenellated Torre Raimonda that attracts the most attention from visitors. Another of San Vito's medieval gates, it's especially photogenic at sunset.

Fans of prehistoric art (or Roman coins) can visit the **Museo Civico Federico De Rocco** (☑ 0434 804 05, reservations 0434 83 32 95; Via Amalteo 1; ⊘ first Sun of the month or by reservation), located inside the tower. The collection showcases local archaeological finds, including protohistoric artefacts from the necropolis of San Valentino and other objects dating from the late 1st century BCE to the 4th century CE.

On the opposite side of Piazza del Popolo is Via Bellunello, which runs along the south side of the Duomo.

🛏 Sleeping & Eating

Patriarca HOTEL, RESTAURANT €€
(☑ 0434 87 55 55; www.hotelpatriarca.it; Via Pascatti 6; s/d from €55/75; P ❄ 🤶) If San Vito's charm has won you over and you want to stay, this hotel – a stone's throw from the Torre Raimonda – will have you slumbering in the heart of the historic centre. Of its 28 rooms, 11 come with spa bath.

La Corte di Rosa B&B €€
(☑ 327 300 44 73; www.lacortedirosa.com; Via Madonna di Rosa 35; s/d €60/80; ⊘ reception 8.30-10am & 5-7pm; P ❄ 🤶 🐾) A little out of the way, this B&B is located near the Santuario della Madonna di Rosa, where a miraculous apparition of the Virgin took place in 1655. The B&B itself occupies a 19th-century building, with clean, bright rooms and comfy furnishings.

Al Colombo TRATTORIA €
(☑ 0434 801 76; Via Roma 4; meals €20; ⊘ noon-2pm & 7.15-9pm Tue-Sat, noon-2pm Sun) Just beyond Torre San Nicolò is this authentic, old-fashioned trattoria, animated with friendly chatter. Tuck into simple, homestyle cooking that marry local tradition with the kitchen's own culinary flair.

Trattoria al Vecchio Castello OSTERIA €€
(☑ 0434 83 32 71; Via Marconi 14; meals €25-30; ⊘ noon-2pm & 7.15-9pm Tue-Sat, noon-2pm Sun) Located between Piazza del Popolo and Piazzetta Pescheria, this tavern serves Pordonone specialities in a suitably traditional space, complete with Venetian-style terrazzo flooring and a period counter. In summer, tables are available in the small garden. Consider booking ahead.

Osteria Al Rustico TRATTORIA €€
(☑ 0434 83 42 09; www.osteriaalrustico.com; Piazza Centrale 4, Località Prodolone; meals €25; ⊘ 9.30am-2pm & 5.30-11pm Tue-Sat, 9.30am-3pm Sun) Prodolone is a beautiful rural village about 1km northwest of San Vito, complete with old water mill, churches and a frozen-in-time atmosphere.

If you're peckish, choose this rustic trattoria, serving meat dishes (including game) at reasonable prices.

THE FRIULIAN MIDDLE AGES

From San Vito al Tagliamento, it's worth heading south as far as the Veneto border to visit two very special medieval treasures. The first is the town of **Cordovado**, considered one of Italy's most beautiful villages and encircled by near-perfectly preserved medieval walls. The village itself is a jumble of buildings dating from the 13th to 16th centuries. Among these is Palazzo Piccolomini-Freschi, surrounded by a splendid 19th-century garden, and Palazzo Agricola, whose small medieval church preserves a fresco attributed to the school of Giotto. The **Castello di Cordovado** (☑ 338 444 37 27; www.castellodicordovado.com; Via Castello 3; garden & village €10, garden only €8, under 12yr free; ☺ 10am-6pm Sat & Sun on request) was built on the site of a Roman *castrum* (fort) that stood guard over a ford of Via Augusta, located on a now dried-up branch of the Tagliamento River. The site was the border of the Patriarchate of Concordia Sagittaria, of which it was a fiefdom.

A little further west of Cordovado, **Sesto al Reghena** is home to the Romanesque **Abbazia di Santa Maria in Silvis** (☑ 0434 69 90 14; www.abbaziasestoalreghena.it; Piazza Castello; ☺ 9.30-11.30am & 3.30-5.30pm Mon-Sat, 3.30-5.30pm Sun) FREE, a large Benedictine abbey whose roots lie in the 8th century. Inside is a cycle of frescoes from the Giotto and Rimini schools, whose various depictions include tales relating to St Benedict, St Peter and the Virgin. Seek out the *Lignum vitae*, which portrays the meeting of the living and the dead. The crypt harbours a wonderful early-medieval relief as well as a Venetian-Byzantium depiction of the *Annunciation* from the 13th century.

ℹ Information

IAT di San Vito al Tagliamento (☑ 0434 84 30 30; www.comune.san-vito-al-tagliamento.pn.it or www.facebook.com/IAT-San-Vito-1040761281 85029; Piazza del Popolo 13; ☺ 9.30am-12.30pm & 3-6pm Mon-Fri, 10am-12.30pm & 3-6pm Sat & Sun)

Valvasone

VALVASONE ARZENE: POP 3904 / ELEV 59M

The village of Valvasone lies on the west bank of the Tagliamento, where, in the Middle Ages, a ford allowed the safe passage of travellers and pilgrims. The name of the town derives from Wolfe Höfe ('farm of the wolf'), most likely a reference to the coat of arms of the noble Valvasone family, depicting a black wolf on a white background. Given its storybook medieval appearance, it's not surprising that Valvasone is considered one of the country's most beautiful villages. It's also a popular spot for weddings, lending it the nickname 'Village of Brides'.

Piazza Castello is home to Valvasone's **castle** (☑ 0434 89 88 98; admission per person €4; ☺ booking required at least 10 days in advance for groups of at least 10 people), which on first impression looks more like a cluster of village buildings. The complex, which follows the circular form of an earlier watchtower, was expanded several times until the 19th century. The site itself has been continuously inhabited since the late Roman period. A gate replaced the ancient drawbridge which crossed the now-dry moat. Inside, the castle's numerous riches include allegorical frescoes, a private chapel and what claims to be Italy's smallest theatre. Now a national monument, the castle's guests have included Napoleon.

The well-preserved village is a pleasure to wander. Piazza Castello, anchored by a 14th-century well, is surrounded by medieval abodes adorned with Venetian-style porticoes and windows, as well as a 15th-century water mill. **Piazza Libertà** claims 18th-century Palazzo Comunale, still occupied by the local council.

If you drop by the **Duomo** (preferably in the morning or early afternoon as the parish priest keeps the lights off), you can admire the oldest organ in Europe. Dating from 1532, it's still in working order; during mass, its sound fills the square. Not far from here is the **Chiesa dei Santi Pietro e Paolo** (☺ 9am-6pm), also home to 16th-century frescoes.

Just outside Valvasone's defensive walls is the former Convento dei Serviti, built in the 17th century, partly demolished in the 19th century and recently restored.

⚜ Festivals & Events

Medioevo a Valvasone   SEPTEMBER
(www.medioevoavalvasone.it) On the first weekend in September, locals party like its 1399 by dressing up as knights, damsels and players and celebrating in the village's highly atmospheric, torch-lit streets.

ℹ SELF-GUIDED TOWN TOUR

The Valvasone tourist office rents out audio guides which offer commentary on 11 sights around the village. The self-guided tour takes about an hour.

🛏 Sleeping

Giardino in Corte   B&B €€
(☑ 338 589 94 20; www.bbgiardinoincorte.com; Via Bando 2; s €40-45, d €70-80; 🕿) Occupying a late 17th-century residence, this B&B sets a nostalgic scene with its period furniture and original furnishings. Green thumbs will appreciate the fabulous garden.

Casa Menini   B&B €€
(☑ 340 599 31 36/0434 890 21; www.casamenini.it; Via Cesare Battisti; s €40-50, d €75-85; 🕿) If you need a break from all the medieval bingeing, reconnect with the modern world at this B&B, located in a recent build. Its three rooms feature muted palates and contemporary furnishings, while the communal areas are so wonderfully hushed you'll forget you're in the heart of the village.

🍴 Eating & Drinking

Trattoria La Torre   TRATTORIA €
(Piazza Castello 11; meals €20; 🕑 noon-2pm & 7-10pm Tue-Sat, noon-2pm Sun) It's located near one of the entrances to Piazza Castello and has an adjoining winery where, if you're not in the mood for regional grub, you can stop for a simple glass of *vino* in a medieval setting.

Osteria Pozzodipinto   RESTAURANT €€
(☑ 0434 89 89 63; www.osteriapozzodipinto.it; Via Pozzodipinto 44; meals €30; 🕑 11am-3pm & 6pm-midnight Mon, Thu & Fri, 11am-3pm Tue, 10am-3pm & 6pm-midnight Sat & Sun) Contemporary, forward-thinking, yet respectfully in sync with the area's traditions, Osteria Pozzodipinto celebrates seasonality and quality wines. Its wintertime *cena degli ossi* (dinner of the bones), for example, celebrates an old local tradition in which the meat on the bone of pigs slaughtered to make salami is slowly boiled and shared among friends.

Wolf   WINE BAR
(☑ 0434 89 90 82; Largo Isonzo 1; 🕑 9am-1am Mon, Tue & Thu-Sat, 10am-1am Sun, 9am-3pm Wed) Right behind the Duomo, new-school Wolf is a great spot for a drink (or bite) in a relaxed, upbeat atmosphere.

ℹ Information

IAT Valvasone (☑ 0434 89 88 98, 375 632 63 97; info.valvasone@gmail.com; Piazza Castello 14; 🕑 10am-noon & 3-5pm Mon & Wed-Sun) Tourist office.

Spilimbergo

POP 11,961 / ELEV 132M

Infectiously cheerful Spilimbergo was a county seat in the Middle Ages, making it a fairly important place at the time. Its name derives from the noble Spengemberg family, who were counts here between the 11th and 12th centuries. Many of Spilimbergo's medieval buildings survive today.

The town's main square is Piazza Garibaldi, skirted by its main thoroughfare Corso Roma. Lined with bars, restaurants and shops, the street cuts through the historic centre and leads towards the **Duomo** (🕑 8.30am-6.30pm). Completed in 1359 and consecrated in 1453, the Duomo contains a frescoed apse and 16th-century organ. Beyond Piazza del Duomo, which takes on a quiet, surreal atmosphere at night, is Spilimbergo's privately owned **castle** (not open to the public). Built around a riverbed of the Tagliamento, it's one of the most spectacular examples of an aristocratic residence in Friuli Venezia Giulia. With a known history dating back to the early 11th century, the castle has been enlarged several times over the centuries. The result is a series of stylistically diverse buildings arranged in a semi-circle. In the south wing is the magnificent, 15th-century Palazzo Dipinto, whose facade frescoes are attributed to Andrea Bellunello.

Like many other places in this area, Spilimbergo has its own nickname: 'City of the Mosaic'. The modern mosaic technique, known as the 'indirect' technique and developed by Sequals-born Gian Domenico Facchina (see p206) was born here and is taught at the town's **mosaic school** (☑ 0427 20 77; https://scuolamosaicistifriuli.it; Via Corridoni 6; 🕑 office 8am-noon & 1-4pm Mon-Fri, visits 10am-12.30pm & 4.30-8pm Jul & Aug, varies rest of yr) , established in 1922.

🎉 Festivals & Events

Folkest   JULY
(www.folkest.com) In July, Spilimbergo's squares and bars host a program of folk music in all its forms, performed by ensembles and orchestras from across the globe.

🛏 Sleeping

Relais la Torre
HOTEL €€

(📞 339 269 77 17; www.relaislatorre.com; Corso Roma 28; s with breakfast €60, d with breakfast €75-80; 🅿 ❄ 🛜) This meticulously kept B&B occupies a large, light-filled medieval attic.

Its double suites are bright and elegant, decorated with period or contemporary furniture and each with a private living room. Free undercover parking is located 200m from the property.

La Macia House
B&B €€

(📞 338 762 58 68; www.lamaciahouse.it; Corso Roma 84; s/d €55/80; 🅿 ❄ 🛜) Three rooms and a mini-apartment in a thoughtfully restored building in the town centre. The furniture is new but classic in style, and the small bar and warmth of the heritage building make this hotel an intimate, welcoming place to slumber. Parking is free and the place very good value for money.

🍴 Eating & Drinking

Osteria Al Bachero
OSTERIA €

(📞 0427 23 17; www.osteriabachero.com; Via Pilacorte 5; meals €20; ⊙ 9.30am-2pm Mon, 9.30am-2pm & 6-10pm Tue-Sat) Take a Puglian sailor, drop him in Friuli, and Osteria Al Bachero is what you get. While a traditional *fogolâr furlàn* burns lazily in the middle of the dining room, punters tuck into cod, tripe and other authentic Friulian classics, cooked using local produce.

Al Buso
OSTERIA €

(📞 0427 20 14; Via Simoni 8; platters from €4.50, first courses €5-6; ⊙ 9.30am-2pm & 4.30-10.30pm Mon-Thu, to midnight Fri, 8am-midnight Sat) An authentic, historic tavern. Step inside for the conviviality, *musetto* (a type of *cotechino*), platters of delicious cured meats and glass or two of *vino*. You might even catch some live music (not uncommon in Spilimbergo).

Trattoria Tre Corone
TRATTORIA €€

(📞 0427 504 38; Via Volpe Marco 11; meals €25; ⊙ 11am-3pm & 6-11.30pm Mon-Thu, to 1am Fri, 10.30am-1am Sat & Sun) A side street off Corso Roma leads to this trattoria, tucked under the porticoes and complete with crackling wintertime fireplace.

Service is warm and familial, perfectly complimenting a repertoire of comforting surf and turf dishes. The *baccalà* (salted cod) and meat dishes are very popular.

La Torre
RESTAURANT €€/€€€

(📞 0427 50 55 55; www.ristorantelatorre.net; Piazza Castello 8; meals €30-60; ⊙ noon-2pm & 7-10pm Tue-Sat, noon-2pm Sun) Just getting here after dark – which involves crossing evocative Piazza Castello – is memorable. So too is the restaurant's actual location, inside Spilimbergo castle's frescoed Palazzo Dipinto.

The focus here is on regional cooking, spanning land and sea, and cooked to exceptionally high standards. Indeed, no restaurant quite captures Spilimbergo's essence like this one.

Enoteca La Torre
WINE BAR

(📞 0427 29 98; Via di Mezzo 2; ⊙ 11am-2.30pm & 6-11pm Mon-Thu, to midnight Fri-Sun) Set at the foot of a medieval tower, this *enoteca* lures with its soft lighting and solid timber tables. At the counter, wines and grappas are poured for Spilimbergo's night owls.

There's often someone tickling the ivories and, during Folkest, the wine bar hosts jazz concerts.

Food is available for the peckish.

ℹ Information

IAT Spilimbergo (📞 0427 22 74; Piazza Duomo 1; iat@comune.spilimbergo.pn.it) Tourist information, with a focus on the mosaic school.

THE MAGREDI

Of all of Friuli Venezia Giulia's unique and idiosyncratic offerings, the Magredi is one of the most surprising.

Roughly translating as 'Lean Land', the name refers to the desolate, flat grasslands between the **Cellina** and **Meduna** riverbeds on the slopes of the Friulian Dolomites. On a map, the rivers form a distinct 'V' shape. Within it, the Magredi steppe sprawls out towards a seemingly infinite horizon.

Wildflowers splash colour across a landscape alive with rare and precious birds, among them the striking Eurasian stone-curlew.

Until recently, the area was an immense training ground for armoured vehicles from the nearby Aviano military base.

Today, the Magredi is a protected nature reserve and a symbol of Slow Travel, whose big skies and vastness have a way of sparking wanderlust.

The Magredi

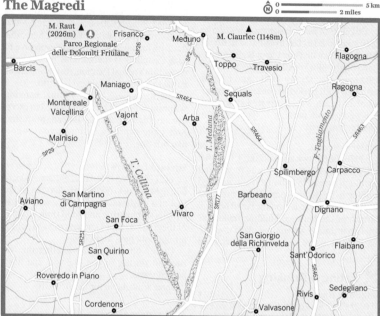

N ☉ 0 — 5 km
0 — 2 miles

Vivaro

POP 1287 / ELEV 138M

The little town of Vivano sits at the southern end of the steppe, close to the confluence of the Cellina and Meduna rivers. Its compact *centro storico* (historic centre) claims a 14th-century mill and a number of old dairies, some of which have been converted into museums or public spaces.

The town is an excellent base for those wishing to explore the area; the one and only *agriturismo* here has no shortage of beds. Staying overnight will give you the opportunity to join a bike or horseback tour of the Magredi.

If you'd rather explore the area independently, simply head out of town in any direction and within a few short kilometres, the Magredi's distinct, desert-like landscape will emerge.

🏃 Activities

Driving is the best way to fully enjoy the Magredi. Once you're near the steppe, you can leave your car at the edge of the ford and continue on foot, following the stones.

If you have an off-road vehicle or dirt bike, avoid the temptation to put the pedal to the metal: this is strictly forbidden in some parts.

In addition to organising excursions in the area, Gelindo dei Magredi can offer advice on how to get around.

🎊 Festivals & Events

Magraid   JUNE
(Triathlon Team; ☎ 0434 54 18 44; www.magraid. it; Viale della Libertà 75, Pordenone) This is a three-day, 100km running race through the Magredi.

The race is divided into three stages (25km, 55km and 20km), with less gruelling options including Nordic walking and simple 6km and 12km walks between the Cellina and Meduna Rivers.

🛏 Sleeping & Eating

Gelindo dei Magredi   AGRITURISMO €€
(☎ 0427 970 37; www.gelindo.it; Via Roma 14; s/d €70/95, meals €20-30; ☺ noon-3pm & 7-11pm Tue-Sun; ☀ P ☀ ☏) A portion of the Magredi is occupied by a large estate belonging to Piero, a passionate entrepreneur whose *agriturismo* takes his father's name.

Pretty much the only accommodation that is available in the area, the family-friendly property offers a range of different rooms (housed in numerous rustic buildings) and a campsite.

There's also a riding club, both indoor and outdoor riding stables, a swimming pool and restaurant, all set on a working property whose range of products include wine, vegetables, meats, cheeses, jams, juices and condiments.

The welcome is warm and the suite of experiences offered include wine and cheese tastings, hikes and horseback excursions.

Lataria dei Magredi RESTAURANT €€
(☑0427 970 99, 335 717 08 08; Vicolo Centrino 12; meals €20-30; ☺7-11pm Sat, noon-3pm Sun) Run by Gelindo dei Magredi, this welcoming restaurant occupies a carefully restored building that once housed the historic Vivaro Social Dairy.

The menu on offer here is a virtual love letter to the region and its culinary traditions; the fried bites are exceptionally light and best washed down with one of the estate's own wines.

ⓘ Information

Consorzio Pro Loco Dolomiti Friulane e Magredi (☑0427 76 44 38; www.prolocodolomitifriulanemagredi.it) has a tourist office in Vivaro (☑0434 970 15, Vicolo Centrico 14) with information on local nature trails, tours and farm gates. Call ahead as the office is staffed by volunteers and not always open.

ⓘ Getting There & Away

BUS
TPL FVG (☑800 05 20 40, mobile 040 971 23 43; https://tplfvg.it) Bus P24 runs between Pordenone and Vivaro (€4.25, about 35 minutes, six daily).

Bus 16 runs between Maniago and Vivaro (€2.95, 30 minutes, three daily).

CAR & MOTORCYLE
From Pordenone, take the SS13 to Roveredo in Piano, then follow the signs for the SP53. Cross the ford on the Cellina River and follow the signs for Vivaro.

From Spilimbergo, you will need to head towards the SP53 and cross the ford on the Meduna River; continue through to Basaldella, after which lies Vivaro.

TRAIN
Maniago is the most convenient train station. Trains runs to Pordenone via Sacile (€4.75, 1 hour 40 minutes, four daily).

THE VALLI PORDENONESI

Bordered by the Livenza and Tagliamento Rivers and the mountains to the north, the province of Pordenone is a soft, genteel land, with six streams shaping a suite of small valleys. Crossing them all is the Strada Pedemontana Provinciale (Pedemontana Provinciale Road). Between Polcenigo and Tramonti, the road crosses a pocket of the region in which you'll find a curious hybrid Friulian-American culture, shaped by the local Aviano military base and the thousands of US soldiers it attracts.

Sleepy and rural, the Valli Pordenonesi (Pordenone Valleys) offer a string of outdoor activities, from canyoning and paragliding, to mountain biking through the woods. Those wanting to slow the pace can retreat to a designer treehouse, amble along gurgling streams or seek out the traces of wolves and bears.

Come summer, cool down in the crystal-clear waters of Cerdevol Curnila while gazing out at the Dolomites.

La Luna Turismo Essenziale (☑347 520 64 31; laluna@turismoessenziale.it) is a handy resource for those wanting to explore the less-trodden corners of the region, offering tailored tours, activities and experiences across the province.

ⓘ Getting There & Away

BUS
TPL FVG (☑800 05 20 40, mobile 040 971 23 43; https://tplfvg.it) From Pordenone, buses P13 and P14 reach Maniago (from €3.50, 55 minutes), while buses P12 and P33 reach Polcenigo (€2.95, 40 to 55 minutes, 15 daily between 10am and 12.30pm); other routes require a transfer in Aviano.

Bus P28 runs one daily direct service from Pordenone to Meduno (€4.25, one hour); all other P28 services require a change in Maniago (€2.25, 15 minutes, 17 daily between 6.30am and 7pm). From Maniago, bus P51 is the most convenient for reaching Sequals (€2.95, 15 minutes, seven daily).

From Spilimbergo, buses P26 and P27 reach Travesio (€2.50, 15 to 25 minutes, eight daily between 6am and 5pm), while bus P25 reaches Clauzetto (€3.50, 45 minutes, 10 daily).

CAR & MOTORCYLE
Maniago is the most important road junction for this area. To reach it from Pordenone, take the

SR251. From here, take the SR464 for Sequals and Spillimbergo.

From Sequals, the SR552 leads to Meduno while the SP33 reaches Travesio.

From Travesio, the SP22 continues to Clauzetto.

TRAIN

From Sacile, trains reach Maniago (€2.10, 34-39 minutes, seven daily) and Budoia-Polcenigo station (€1.35, 13 minutes, seven daily).

For all the other destinations in this section, the reference station is Pordenone.

Polcenigo

POP 3099 / ELEV 42M

It takes a simple wander around Polcenigo to understand why it's on Italy's 'Most Beautiful Villages' list. Known as the *scrigno verde* (verdant treasure chest) and within striking distance of the Riserva Naturale delle Prealpi Carniche, it's a lush, watery, luxuriously leafy place. From its historic centre, walking trails lead to natural springs and, further along, to mountains, sinkholes and alpine pastures.

From Polcenigo you can walk to the hamlet of Gorgazzo, to see the **Buco del Gorgazzo**, an underwater cave which is the source of the Gorgazzo stream. As inviting as its dazzling emerald waters look, swimming in this natural pool is dangerous and prohibited. Not far from here are the **headwaters of the Livenza**, as well as the 16th-century **Chiesa della Santissima Trinità**, home to interesting frescoes, sculptures and a beautiful 17th-century wooden altar.

Looking up, you'll spot the **Castello di Polcenigo**. An 18th-century villa, it's built on the remains of a medieval fortification, itself perched on remains dating from late antiquity. Due to its strategic position, Polcenigo was subject to raids. It was also on the Via Ungaresca, which in the early Middle Ages was the main artery connecting the March of Treviso (a medieval territory in modern-day Veneto) to Friuli.

Polcenigo houses the quirky **Museo dell'Arte Cucinaria dell'Alto Livenza** (☑ 0434 740 16; www.ecomuseolisaganis.it; Piazza del Plebiscito 1; ⊙ on request) FREE, which you might consider for a quick visit. During the 20th century, the Upper Livenza area witnessed a relatively large emigration of cooks who, most notably after WWII, took their culinary skills to all corners of the country.

🎊 Festivals & Events

Sagra dei Sest   SEPTEMBER

This basket fair has been celebrated for almost 350 years. Although the craft's impor-

---

LIS AGANIS: FROM MYTH TO MUSEUM

In the complex system of Friulian myths and ancestral beliefs, *Lis Aganis* are fairies who also take the form of animals who live around waterways or in caves, two defining aspects of the region's landscape. Similar creatures are found in various countries that straddle the Alps, albeit with different names and characteristics.

One very old tale in the Val Colvera recounts the story of a woman with many children to raise. One day she meets a salamander on the banks of a stream and helps it to give birth. As a sign of gratitude, the salamander (who is actually an Agana) gives her a ball of wool whose thread never runs out. With it, the woman makes sweaters and socks for her children as well as those of other mothers. It's said that the magical ball of yarn is still passed on, hand to hand. The story is a beautiful metaphor for a tradition that hails from nature and which is shared by, and provides for, many. It also symbolises the thread of memories and knowledge rooted to the earth.

As the bearers of these balls of wisdom, *Lis Aganis* are perfect namesakes for the **Ecomuseum Lis Aganis** (☑ 0427 76 44 25; Via Maestri del Lavoro, 1, Maniago), a network of 29 sites (known as 'cells') dedicated to showcasing and preserving the region's age-old traditions. Scattered throughout western Friuli, between Caneva, Maniago, the Valli Pordenonesi and the Dolomites, the sites are categorised by theme (water, stones or crafts) and include everything from local ethnographic museums and cultural associations to villas and walking trails. Together, they offer opportunities to partake in workshops, acquire knowledge and directly experience local heritage. On your travels, information panels pointing out the sites and their stories appear unexpectedly, a bit like ethereal *Lis Aganis*.

tance has faded over the years, the event serves up an authentic slice of village culture and atmosphere with its convivial, communal tables, regional dishes, and craft demonstrations.

Eating

Apicoltura il Gorgazzo KIOSK €
(☑ 344 270 47 96; www.apicolturagorgazzo.it; Via Giuliana 10; ⊘ 9.30am-7.30pm) For a natural, alternative snack, this apiary kiosk, located near the beautiful Gorgazzo, peddles waffles with fruit from local producers, ice cream with honey and toasted peanuts, even honey beer. All its products (including honey, *naturalmente*) can also be purchased at **Spaccio del Miele** (⊘ 9.30am-7.30pm).

🛍 Shopping

Re Caprone FARM GATE
(☑ 348 120 74 88; Località Dietro Piante 14; ⊘ 5-7pm Mon-Fri & Sun, 10am-noon & 4.30-7pm Sat) Sarah took over the reins of this goat farm and small artisan dairy in 2016. She produces and sells aged cheese, *caciotta* (including spiced varieties), ricotta, even goat's milk–based desserts, all utterly delicious. She also stocks prosecco, refosco, pinot grigio and ribolla, also made here too. An *agriturismo* and educational farm are also in the pipeline.

❶ Information

Pro Loco Polcenigo (☑ 328 756 04 65; www.pro locopolcenigo.com; Piazza Plebiscito 3)

Maniago

POP 11,586 / ELEV 286M

Maniago marks the transition zone between the Magredi and the mountains, and a good place to appreciate its setting is from the panoramic lookout of the **Castello di Maniago**. You can reach the castle on foot by taking Via Castello from beautiful **Piazza Italia** in the town centre. Maniago is also known as 'the city of knives', a reference to its very long tradition of bladesmithing. The craft itself is indelibly tied to the town's geography, with mountain waters flowing into local rivers and canals to power the mills that in turn powered the tools used by the blacksmiths and bladesmiths. Originally, local artisans focussed on making agricultural tools such as scythes and hatchets, and to this day, the *britola* pruning knife (widespread throughout Italy's northeast) remains Maniago's most famous souvenir.

Knives aside, the town's modern industry produces a variety of metal items; chances are you've used a bottle opener made right here. Its very first knife factory is now the **Museo dell'Arte Fabbrile e delle Coltellerie** (☑ 0427 70 90 63; Via Maestri del Lavoro 1; adult/reduced €4/2, free with FVG Card; ⊘ 10am-1pm & 2.30-5.30pm Mon & Thu-Sun, 10am-1pm Tue & Wed), which offers a sharp rundown on the history of blades and pocket knives, including the demand for Maniago-made weapons on Hollywood film sets.

🛏 Sleeping & Eating

Albergo Leon d'Oro HOTEL €€
(☑ 0427 711 18; www.facebook.com/leondoroma niago; Piazza Italia 1; s/d €40/75; 🅿 🛜) Reinvigorated after a significant restoration, Hotel Leon d'Oro is the most classic spot in town, with breakfast served in a room overlooking the square. Management changed hands in June 2021; check the hotel's Facebook page for updates.

Trattoria Casasola RESTAURANT €€
(☑ 0427 54 02 28; Via Piave 57; meals €30-35; ⊘ noon-2.30pm & 6.30-10pm Mon & Thu-Sun) This historic tavern dates from 1910. Today, it's a cosy restaurant run by Florina and Marian, who serve Pordenone specialities – most notably the Peta di Noè Antonini and Asìno cheese – as well as tweaked classics like *mesta*, a dish of polenta and milk from Carnia.

🛍 Shopping

L'Arte del Coltello CRAFTS
(☑ 0427 70 93 13; www.maserin.com; Piazza Italia 46; ⊘ 9am-12.30pm & 3.30-7.30pm Mon, Tue & Thu-Sat) Switchblade, dagger, cooking, table, creative or traditional: whatever type of

high-quality, locally made knife you're looking for, you'll find it here.

Consorzio Coltellinai Maniago
CRAFTS

(📞 0427 717 44; www.consorziocoltellinai.it; Piazza Italia 11; ⏰ 8.30am-12.30pm & 3-7pm Mon, Tue & Thu-Sat) This consortium of 46 small, local cutlery and tool makers sells everything from hunting and kitchen knives, to gardening hand tools, corkscrews and potato peelers. All the best local products under the one roof.

Antonini Noè
BUTCHER

(📞 0427 710 32; www.noeantonini.it; Via Piave 86; ⏰ 9am-1pm Mon-Wed, 9am-1pm & 4-9pm Thu-Sat) Together with the butcher Bier (p208), this is the only *pitina* producer that follows the very strict regulations set out by the Slow Food organisation. Needless to say, *pitina* maker Noè is passionate about his work, having even uncovered historic recipes from the family archives. Among these are secret formulas for making *salame di Barba Nane,* a cured meat dating from Friuli's Austro-Hungarian days. Other delicacies are also available and can be enjoyed onsite.

ℹ️ Information

IAT di Maniago (turismo.maniago.it) Located at the Museo dell'Arte Fabbrile e delle Coltellerie ticket office.

Sequals

POP 2187 / ELEV 270M

Slumbering between the Meduna and Cosa streams, and bordering the hills that morph into the Carnic Prealps and the Dolomites, Sequals' name is tied to professional boxer Primo Carnera and to Gian Domenico Facchina, inventor of the 'indirect' mosaic technique. Facchina's legacy lives on in the mosaics peppered across the town, especially near the artist's former abode.

Close to it (and well signposted) lies Art-Nouveau **Villa Carnera** (📞 0427 78 91 11; http://villacarnera.com; Via Roma 12; ⏰ by reservation May-Oct) FREE, the former home of the town's (literally) gigantic boxing champion. Today, it's a house-museum documenting Primo Carnera's life and career.

🛏️ Sleeping & Eating

Sasso d'Oro
AGRITURISMO €€

(📞 0427 935 87; www.sassodoro.pn.it; Frazione Solimbergo, Via del Capitel 4; s/d/tr with breakfast €45/65/80; full pitch/under 6yr €10/free, breakfast €6; 🅿️ ❄️ 🛜 ♿) Surrounded by greenery, Sasso d'Oro is located in the rural centre of Solimbergo, a hamlet of Sequals.

Crisp, clean and welcoming, the farmhouse includes a camping area, especially suitable for campervans and caravans. Simple rooms, natural surrounds and a swimming pool make this a great place to recharge your batteries. Ecofriendly credentials include solar-heated water and jams and preserves made using fruit from the organic farm (the breakfast is delicious).

The farm cultivates truffles and, to top it off, has an airfield and hangar for microlights: the team will gladly help organise a tandem flight above Sequals. Free bicycles are also available.

Al Fogolar da Mander
TRATTORIA €€

(📞 0427 930 71; Via Garibaldi 5, Località Solimbergo; meals €20-25; ⏰ 11am-2pm Mon, 11am-11pm Wed-Fri & Sun, 6.30-11pm Sat) Overlooking Solimbergo's low-key square, this authentic, country trattoria has been in business for 130 years.

Complete with fireplace, exposed timber beams and hanging copper pots, it draws workers at lunch in the week and local revellers in the evening, here for the grilled meats (mixed grill €12 to €20) and friendly vibe.

ℹ️ Information

Pro Loco Sequals (📞 347 285 59 90; www.prolocosequals.it; Via Roma 10/2)

Travesio

POP 1789 / ELEV 226M

On first impressions, Travesio looks like an uninspiring ghost town, caught between the Meduna and Tagliamento Rivers. Don't be fooled. Its 12th-century **Chiesa di San Pietro** (📞 0427 900 72; Via Riosecco 54) claims many of the Pordenone artworks found in the region. The church's frescoes, executed by the Friulian master between 1516 and 1526, represent stories from the life of St Peter and other biblical scenes. The altarpiece, on the other hand, was painted by Pomponio Amalteo in 1537.

For food lovers, there's Al Marescial, a fabulously authentic Friulian trattoria with a renowned selection of local cheeses.

A little further west towards Meduno, the tiny Travesio hamlet of **Toppo** is another local village to make it onto the list of Italy's most beautiful villages. On the hill, you'll notice the evocative, crenellated **ruins of Toppo's castle**.

Tackle the climb to the ruins (free to visit) and your reward is a spectacular view that takes in the Meduna and Cosa valleys, as well as the Tagliamento River.

To reach the castle from the town square, take Via Verdi to the stream, then continue on foot for 1km along the paved road (closed to traffic).

✵ Festivals & Events

Marcia e Sagra delle Rane   APRIL
On the first two weekends in April, Usago – a southern hamlet of Travesio – comes alive for its frog festival. Expect food and wine stands, live music and plenty of other entertainment. On the last Sunday, the festival wraps up with a noncompetitive march along various routes.

⌂ Sleeping & Eating

Alle Genziane   AGRITURISMO €
(☑ 0427 900 13; www.allegenziane.it; Location Praforte 30; s/d incl breakfast €40/70, discounts for multiday stays; ℙ) The simple, clean rooms at this *agriturismo* open onto a first-floor veranda perfect for relaxing, reading or planning day trips.

The downstairs restaurant serves honest, authentic grub, with many ingredients coming straight from the farm.

The estate enjoys the cooling effect of its location at the foot of the Prealps, which is also a handy midway point for exploring both the mountains and the valleys. The owners have even opened a shop selling house-made delicacies and other quality gourmet products; it's located in a former dairy in Travesio's town square.

★ Al Marescial   TRATTORIA €
(☑ 0427 900 12; www.marescial.it; Via Villa 105; meals €15-20; ⊙ 9am-3pm & 6-10pm Tue-Sun, closed a few weeks in Oct) What's not to love about this place? Not only is the setting utterly authentic (think *fogolâr*, summer patio and homespun Friulian hospitality), the short list of *piatti del giorno* (daily specials) is top notch. Signora Rina makes almost everything from scratch, bar the selection of local valley cheeses (for which the trattoria is also renowned). If you're after a quick nibble, the latter can be enjoyed at the counter.

ⓘ Information

Pro Loco Travesio (☑ 339 211 00 55; www.face book.com/proloco.travesio)

CULINARY HIGHLIGHTS IN THE HILLS

Many of Friuli Venezia Giulia's gastronomic traditions converge in these misty hills, and scattered through them are some exemplary restaurants and *osterie*.

In Meduno, both locals and far-travelling gastronomes raise their forks at **La Stella** (☑ 0427 861 24; Via Principale 38, Meduno; meals €50; ⊙ Sat & Sun, call ahead). One of the region's top culinary destinations, it's a homely trattoria, with strictly local dishes and wines, and no written menu.

Famous for its red onion, Cavasso Nuovo is home to another foodie favourite, **Ai Cacciatori** (☑ 0427 77 78 00; Via Diaz 4, Cavasso Nuovo; meals €30; ⊙ 12.30-3pm Thu & Sun, 12.30-3pm & 6-10.30pm Fri & Sat), which, despite its modern takes on local traditions, hasn't lost its traditional trattoria soul. If it's on offer, try the *cestino di frico con gnocchi passati al Montasio, cipolla di Cavasso e pitina croccante* (Montasio cheese, Cavasso onion and crispy *pitina* gnocchi served on *frico*).

Meduno

POP 1534 / ELEV 313M

A small town lost in the hills, Meduno began life in the 11th century. For centuries a strategically important gateway to the Val Tramontina, it remains the entry point into the valley, itself shaped by the Meduna stream. The setting is beautiful and lends itself to an array of thrilling outdoor activities.

🏃 Activities

Hiking

From Meduno you can hit numerous walking routes in the valley. Following the trails to Val Colvera, you'll cross the Valle del Muiè and Malga Valinis, reaching the summit of **Monte Valinis** (1102m). The trail is quite easy; needless to say, the view from the finish line will repay any effort.

Paragliding

The plain below the ruins of the Castello di Toppo (between Meduno and Travesio) and the slopes of Monte Valinis are popular paragliding spots, with fantastic views. There are several options: click onto **www.parapen diobiposto.it** for a directory of instructors operating in Meduno or contact **Marco Zon-ca** (marco-zonca.blogspot.it).

🛏 Sleeping & Eating

Al Castello GUESTHOUSE €
(📞 347 454 48 10 Nicola, 347 260 00 84 Cristina; alcastello.weebly.com; Via Castello 9, Località Top-po; s/d from €30/40, min stay 2 nights, breakfast €5; P ✳ 🛜) Located in a little piece of para-dise, near the ruins of the medieval fortifica-tion of Toppo (p206), halfway between Me-duno and Travesio.

The rooms are simple, modern and very spacious. Right by the foothills.

Vanin Sentiero Valinis PUB, GELATERIA
(📞 0427 861 16; Piazza Miani 1; ⊘ 4.45pm-1am Tue-Sun) You'll feel like you're hanging out at a friend's house at this village pub, especially on Thursdays, when culinary-themed eve-nings are held in the garden. It's a hit with locals of all ages, who head in for *vino*-fuelled catch-ups.

Bier BUTCHER
(📞 0427 861 89; www.macbier.it; Via Roma 1; ⊘ 8am-12.30pm Tue-Sat, 4-7pm Thu-Sat, 8.30am-12.30pm Sun) When it comes to *pitina* (cured 'meat-ball' salami), farm-to-table Bier knows its stuff. Operating in the square since 1875 and run passionately by Antonella and Filippo, it produces three types of the local special-ity using its own meat: the Val Tramontina (Slow Food presidium) variety, the so-called 'historical' version, and the traditional one.

ℹ Information

Pro Meduno (www.facebook.com/ProMeduno; Via del Municipio 15)

Clauzetto

POP 389 / ELEV 558M
The best way to reach Clauzetto and the Grotte Verdi di Pradis area is on the SP22, weaving your way between the cooling banks of the Molino, in an ever-increasingly ver-dant landscape dotted with peculiar-looking roofs and bell towers. The highest of the lot rises over Clauzetto, itself dubbed the 'Bal-cony over Friuli'. On clear days, you can see the Adriatic Sea from the village. At night, the sky is awash with stars.

THE BALOTE

Balote (*balotes* in the plural) is a typical dish of the Val Cosa, most particularly of Clauzetto. A vegetarian 'meatball' of sorts, it's made with polenta and Mon-tasio cheese and baked *au gratin* until the cubes of Asìno cheese in the centre melt to perfection.

Each year, Clauzetto celebrates the dish with its own festival, the **Fieste da la Balote**(www.turismofvg.it/eventi/la -fieste-da-la-balote).

It's said that, once upon a time, pro-spective grooms would offer *balotes* to the family of their future bride. If the family placed them on the hearth, it symbolised their approval.

The mountains behind Clauzetto – **Mon-te Pala** (1231m), **Monte Taiet** (1369m) and **Monte Ciaurlec** (1148m) – form the Valle di Pradis, an area with one of the highest con-centrations of caves and gorges in Europe.

The hamlet of **Pradis di Sotto** is home to the **Grotte Verdi** (📞 0427 803 23; www.grottedi pradis.it; combined ticket with the Museo della Grot-ta adult/reduced €5/3; ⊘ varies, check website), a huge, partially accessible grotto that har-bours a sanctuary dedicated to the Virgin.

The site also claims the **Museo della Grot-ta Cave** (www.grottedipradis.it; combined tick-et with Grotte Verdi adult/reduced €5/3; ⊘ varies) and its collection of local paleontology and archaeology. From the grotto, it's a 207-step walk down into the gorge of the Cosa stream, passing waterfalls and the odd rainbow.

🏃 Activities

4Lander House Food Sport Relax CANYONING
(📞 333 507 98 98; www.4lander.it/it/canyoning; Via Pradis di Sotto 101) This co-op organises can-yoning adventures along the stream that me-anders into the Pradis caves, complete with professional guide and equipment.

Expect to rock climb, hike and even swim. The outfit also operates a free-spirited restau-rant and bar.

Hiking Monte Taiet HIKING
On the road from Clauzetto to Pradis di Sotto, in front of the quarry on the right (Via delle Cave), is a sign that marks the start of CAI walking trail no 820. Easy parking is avail-

able 100m further on, on the left, from where the trail to Ciaurlec begins.

Following the signs, take the track that exits the village just after the chapel dedicated to San Francesco and that skirts the dry riverbed bed up to a fountain with trail markers.

The well-marked trail winds through a thicket of beech, hazel, juniper and lodgepole pine. Exiting it, the view opens up, offering a glimpse of Monte Pala and the scree at the base of Monte Dagn. A little further on is a view of the plain, the Tagliamento River and, above it, the Taieit ridge. Once you hit an altitude of 1309m, the most interesting part of the hike begins.

🛏 Sleeping & Eating

Balcone sul Friuli   ALBERGO DIFFUSO €€
(📞331 248 32 97; www.balconesulfriuli.it; Via Fabricio 17; r from €55; 🅿❊🛜) True to the philosophy of the *albergo diffuso,* Balcone sul Friuli has breathed new life into unused old buildings. The hotel reception is in Clauzetto, with the actual abodes scattered in the val-

leys (though all within a few minutes by car). All you have to do is choose from which one you'd like to soak up the lofty views.

Albergo Corona 2.0   HOTEL, RESTAURANT €€
(📞0427 805 20; Via Fabricio 14; meals €35; ☺8am-11pm Mon-Sat, to 9pm Sun) Both the restaurant terrace and hotel rooms offer exceptional views of the plain. The former is the place to try Clauzetto's famous *balote* (cheese-filled polenta balls). The deliciousness of the food here makes up for the patchy service and higher prices.

Ai Mulinars   TRATTORIA €€
(📞0427 806 84; www.ristoranteaimulinars.it; Via della Val Cosa 83; meals €20-25; ☺12.30-2pm & 7.30-10pm Tue-Sun) Another traditional Friulian trattoria serving good food and heartfelt hospitality. Expect time-worn regional recipes and a few revamped classics, devoured in an isolated, thoughtfully renovated farmhouse (along the SP22 that leads from Travesio to Clauzetto) near Lake Tui.

The Mountains

Includes ➡

Piancavallo 211
Friulian Dolomites . . . 214
Erto & Casso 216
Cimolais. 219
Barcis. 221
Forni di Sopra &
Forni di Sotto 224
Carnic Alps 226
Tolmezzo 227
Ampezzo 229
Sauris. 230
Prato Carnico 232
Sappada. 234
Zuglio 235
Julian Prealps 238
Julian Alps 240
Tarvisio. 242

Best Activities

➡ Skiing and hiking in Tarvisio (p242) and Sella Nevea
(p245)

➡ Trekking in the Friulian
Dolomites (p225)

Why Go?

Colossal peaks, remote, one-of-a-kind villages, fertile valleys, snow-covered sanctuaries, ravines carved by emerald
streams, immense fir forests, caves, even Roman ruins: all
this awaits in the Friulian mountains, which stretch from
Carnia in the west to the Julian Alps in the east.

A historical region with a palpable identity, Carnia includes part of the Friulian Dolomites and the mountains that
flank them to the north and east. With the upper course of
the Tagliamento as its backbone and Tolmezzo as its capital,
the area's heritage is made up in equal measure of natural
alpine beauty and idiosyncratic villages. Each of these has
its own claim to fame, whether it be clocks, *salumi* (cured
meats) or its very buildings. Further east, the area of the Julian Alps is famous for its remote valleys, places where centuries of isolation manifest themselves in autonomous cultures and languages with long, deep connections to their
counterparts in Austria and Slovenia.

While both the Romans and Venetians saw these mountains as a border zone, for the Friulians, they had always
been the heart of a larger Alpine–Adriatic area which finds
its natural capital in the resort town of Tarvisio.

When to Go

Carnia is best experienced in summer, when you can enjoy
breathtaking hikes in the Friulian Dolomites and take refreshing dips. The Julian Alps, however, are at their peak
in winter, when ski facilities are in full swing and abundant snowfalls blanket Tarvisio and Sella Nevea. Seasonality is less of a factor in Piancavallo or Sappada, where you
can enjoy both summer hikes and winter skiing, with stunning views year round.

PIANCAVALLO

POP 95 / ELEV 1280M

Piancavallo sits on a plateau north of Pordenone, between **Monte Cavallo** (2251m), the Friulian Dolomites and the last offshoots of the Cansiglio Forest. The first place in Italy to guarantee snow using snow machines, the village is primarily a tourist spot, with hotels and a ski centre built in the 1960s. Indeed, Piancavallo has acquired a certain fame thanks to the prestigious competitions it has hosted, including the FIS Alpine Ski World Cup and the Ski Mountaineering World Cup.

While Piancavallo attracts active types with its countless, family-friendly activities, it also offers more relaxing pursuits, not to mention stunning natural beauty.

The top of Monte Cavallo is so close you'll feel that you can almost touch it with your fingertip, while the road leading down the mountain's southeastern flank serves up a gobsmacking panorama. On clear days, it's a view that takes in the plain's rivers, Aviano military base and Magredi, all the way south to the glistening lagoons and Adriatic Sea.

 Activities

SUMMER ACTIVITIES

Tobogganing

PromoTurismo FVG　　　　TOBOGGANING

(☑0434 65 52 58; www.turismofvg.it; Piazzale Tremol) Comfortable **two-seater mountain-coaster sleds** (adult/group €5/3.50; ☉1.30-4pm Sat & Sun winter & Christmas period, 9.30am-5pm Sat & Sun summer, daily mid-Jul–Aug) that zip between meadows and woods on a 1km route suitable for all ages; children under 10 years of age ride free. The starting point is located between Palaghiaccio and the base of the Tremol 1 chairlift.

Hiking

Tabacco (www.tabaccoeditrice.it) topographical hiking map in hand, hit the trails around the **Sauc** mountains (1646m), **Cornier** (1767m) and **Tremol** (2000m); trails cover all bases, from short to longer, relatively easy to challenging.

One easy trail from the centre of Piancavallo is the **Passeggiata delle Malghe**, which leads past beech woods, sinkholes and grassy valleys, with sweeping views of both the Dolomites and the plain (on clear days you can spot Trieste and Venice). From the roundabout in Piancavallo, head up Via Collalto, pass the sign for the Chiesetta degli alpini and, on your left, take the path marked 'Passeggiata delle Malghe'.

Paragliding

Gliders shouldn't overlook Piancavallo, which hosts international competitions attracting some of Europe's top talent. During these events, onlookers are often treated to unscheduled spectacles as professionals take to the skies.

Centro Friulano Parapendio　TANDEM FLIGHTS

(☑347 442 13 20; www.centrofriulanoparapendio. it) Offers tandem flights above Aviano and Piancavallo. On clear days, the views are utterly breathtaking.

Adventure Parks

Rampypark　　　　　　　　ZIPLINING

(☑345 015 54 36; www.rampypark.it; Via Monte Cavallo; adult/reduced/infant €23/14-20/4; ☉10am-4.30pm daily Jul & Aug, 1-4.30pm Fri & Sun Jun, 10am-4.30pm Sat & Sun Sep) Young and old can indulge their inner Tarzan or Bear Grylls at this ziplining adventure park, whose treetop routes range from breezy to challenging.

WINTER ACTIVITIES

Skiing & Snowboarding

With 51 hectares of downhill **ski slopes** and 30km of cross-country trails, Piancavallo holds its own as a ski resort. Snowboarders can get their kicks at the Snowboard Funk Park, assuming you don't mind music blaring loudly.

Skiers will find two refreshment points at high altitude: **rifugio Baita Arneri** (uphill from the first section of the chairlift, 1640m) and **Val dei Sass** (at the chairlift stop, 1850m), where, however, it is not possible to stay overnight.

PIA.NO.　　　　　　　　　SKI RENTAL

(Piancavallo Noleggi; ☑0434 65 50 24; www.pianca vallonoleggi.it) Rents out skis, snowboards, helmets and other equipment. Outlets include **Noleggio Roncjade** (☑0434 65 53 53; Via Sandro Pertini 4) and **Noleggio Palantina** (☑0434 65 50 24; Piazzale della Puppa 1).

YEAR ROUND

Palasport Piancavallo　　　SPORTS CENTRE

(☑0434 65 55 79; piancavallo1265.com; Via Barcis 5) A sports centre with basketball and volleyball courts, five-a-side football fields and trampoline for acrobatic thrills. Those seeking calmer pleasures can hit the Palapredieri ice rink.

The Mountains Highlights

1 Parco Naturale delle Dolomiti Friulane
(p215) Explore the pristine Friulian Dolomites in this 37,000-hectare park.

2 Sappada (p234)
Germanic conversations and the headwaters of the Piave.

3 Campanile di Val Montanaia (p219) A trek with spirit-lifting views.

4 Malga Priu (p242)
Slumber up a tree inside a high-tech 'pine cone'.

5 Monte Zoncolan (p236)
Heaven or hell for cyclists and motorists.

6 Sauris di Sopra & di Sotto (p230) Two villages suspended in time.

7 Pesariis (p233) This 'city of clocks' is not the only reason to visit Val Pesarina.

8 Santuario del Monte Lussari (p243) In a fairytale landscape, the Marian sanctuary is bewitching in every season.

9 Forra del Cellina (p221) An old state road leads to a jaw-dropping canyon.

Courses

Piancavallo's safe, tranquil environment makes it an ideal location for teaching little ones to ski. It's just as suitable for adult snow bunnies wanting to improve their downhill or cross-country skills, or perhaps learn how to snowboard.

The following ski schools can help with all of the above.

Scuola Italiana Sci Aviano Piancavallo
(✓ 0434 65 50 79; www.scuolasciavianopianca vallo.it; individual lessons per hr €36-39)

Scuola Italiana Sci Piancavallo (✓ 0434 65 52 16; www.scuolasciavianopiancavallo.it; individual lessons per hr €36-39)

Sleeping & Eating

Campeggio Luna CAMPGROUND €
(✓ 393 640 48 02; www.campeggioluna.it; Piazzale Martiri della Libertà, 1; pitches €18-21; ⊗ Dec-Apr & mid-Jun–mid Sep) Marcello and his family have dedicated themselves to this campsite since 2015, constantly adding new features, from a playground to a BBQ area. The lunar-like setting is unbeatable.

1301 Inn HOTEL €€
(✓ 0434 65 55 79; www.1301inn.it; Via Barcis 15; s/d with breakfast €60/110; P ⊛) It's hard to miss this mammoth hotel. Comprising of 37 rooms, it includes a bar, buffet restaurant, brand-new wellness area and, appropriately, a ski room.

Genzianella OSTERIA €€
(✓ 339 694 42 31; www.lagenzianella.eu; Piazzale della Puppa; meals €25; ⊗ 12.15pm & 7-10pm Dec-Mar & Jun-Sep) At the base of the Casere chairlift and accessible on foot or skis, this welcoming, comfy hangout is just the antidote to chilly temperatures and post-ski fatigue. Re-energise with generous portions of local alpine grub.

Taverna all'Urogallo TRATTORIA €€
(✓ 0434 65 54 00; Piazzale della Puppa 1; meals €25; ⊗ noon-2.30pm & 7-9.30pm Thu-Tue) A traditional trattoria in Piancavallo serving excellent, season-based mountain cooking. Specialities include an onion-free *frico* and *urobistecca* (an epic Angus steak), kept fine company by goulash, pork ribs, trout cooked three ways, and in the autumn, an abundance of mushrooms and herbs.

The place is renowned for its wines and schnapps, so raise your glass.

Festivals & Events

Rally Piancavallo SPRING
(www.rallypiancavallo.com) A classic car rally attracting participants and spectators from everywhere, with a vintage car parade to boot.

ℹ Information

Infopoint PromoTurismo FVG Piancavallo
(✓ 0434 65 51 91; Via Collalto 1; ⊗ 9am-1pm & 2-6pm Dec-Mar & Jun-Sep)

Informazioni Impianti PromoTurismo FVG
(✓ 0434 65 52 58; Piazzale Tremol)

ℹ Getting There & Away

BUS

TPL FVG (✓ 800 05 20 40, mobile 040 971 23 43; https://tplfvg.it) During the tourist season, bus P20 connects Piancavallo to Pordenone via Aviano.

CAR & MOTORCYLE

Coming from Trieste/Udine on the A4, take the Portogruaro exit and continue on the A28 towards Pordenone until you see the signs for Piancavallo.

FRIULIAN DOLOMITES

The Friulian Dolomites (Dolomiti Friulane) are bordered to the north, west and east respectively by the **Tagliamento**, **Piave** and **Meduna** Rivers. Like a colander, the southern side is an escape route for many other rivers flowing towards the plain. Water defines this stretch of the mountains, its wealth of creeks, brooks, canals, artificial lakes and waterfalls coloured apple green to dazzling aquamarine.

It's a wild place of impenetrable woods, ravine-carving torrents and rocky peaks that pierce clouds and scrape the sky. At the base of the range, villages appear out of nowhere, keeping a watchful eye at the entrance to the valleys.

The Dolomites are part of the **Parco Naturale delle Dolomiti Friulane**, which spans almost 37,000 hectares and is visited by 400,000 people annually.

The park is a pristine wilderness, free of villages and bitumen (bar the road that leads to the Rifugio Pordenone). Don't expect to find bins either, so make sure you're able to take your litter away with you.

The area includes over 230km of marked hiking trails, with an additional 130km of secondary routes. Tackle them on foot or on a mountain bike. Alternatively, combine a hike with rock climbing (alone or accompanied by a mountain guide).

However you visit the park, be open to a rugged, active, hands-on experience. Your reward: unforgettably epic, ever-changing landscapes, from the cathedral-like peaks of the Monfalconi to the huge stone spire of the Campanile di Val Montanaia.

Ski resort Forni di Sopra aside, the Friulian Dolomites have few facilities for visitors in winter. This lack of development is a plus for some, who head here to snowshoe and ice climb. Road accessibility during this period is highly dependent on weather conditions: some roads remain closed between November and April, among them the Passo del Rest (Rest Pass) between Andreis and Valcellina.

If you are planning a winter trip, head here during Carnivale, when festivals and folk traditions are celebrated in the villages.

This said, spring, summer, and to a lesser extent autumn, are the ideal seasons to access the area's magnificent peaks, alpine refuges and forest-hidden caves, not to mention make the most of its rivers and lakes with invigorating swims.

Park Access

The Parco Naturale delle Dolomiti Friulane is accessible from the villages that surround it. In each you'll find a visitor centre (listed in this chapter), where you can access information and maps, as well as visit an exhibition on local history or geography. Opening hours at the centres vary considerably so always check before heading in. For more information, see www.parcodolomitifriulane.it.

ℹ️ Information

Ente Parco Naturale Dolomiti Friulane (☑ 0427 873 33; Via Roma 4, Cimolais) Manages the park and its visitor centres.

Guide Alpine FVG (☑ 0433 26 60; www.guide alpinefvg.it; Via Matteotti 16, Tolmezzo) A group of mountaineering professionals organising climbing, hiking and trekking adventures throughout the region.

ℹ️ Getting There & Away

BUS

TPL FVG (☑ 800 05 20 40, mobile 040 971 23 43; https://tplfvg.it) Bus P32 runs from Pordenone, Maniago and Montereale Valcellina to Barcis (€5, 50 minutes), Claut (€7.15, 75 minutes), Cimolais (€7.15, 90 minutes), Erto and Casso. Another useful line, from Claut, is the P69. Bus P28 runs one daily direct service between Pordenone and the towns of the Val Tramontina.

Other routes reach the valley in about two hours, with a change required in Maniago (bus P14 and then bus P28). Other options include further changes; see the TPL FVG website. For the Valle del Tagliamento (Tagliamento Valley), right up to Forni di Sopra (€10.40, two hour 20 minutes), take bus 100 from Udine to Tolmezzo and then bus 110 from Tolmezzo to the Passo della Mauria (Mauria Pass).

CAR & MOTORCYLE

The SR251 is the panoramic road that connects Montereale Valcellina to Barcis and continues to Cimolais, Erto and Casso along the entire

---

PARCO NATURALE DELLE DOLOMITI FRIULANE

Established in 1996 and accessible by hiking trails only, the **Parco Naturale delle Dolomiti Friulane** (☑ 0427 873 33; www.parcodolomitifriulane.it) protects a huge expanse of wilderness in western Friuli.

As it wasn't completely covered by ice during the Ice Ages, the area is particularly rich in flora and fauna. Species found here include the largest orchid in the Alps, the splendid Lady's Slipper *(Cypripedium calceolus)* and the Froelich's Gentian, endemic to the alpine pastures of the Eastern Alps. Commonly found critters include golden eagles, chamois, ibex and marmots.

The park includes nine visitor centres, listed on its website and located in the main valleys and at major points of interest. It also manages an information centre at the Diga del Vajont, p217). Open during the main tourist periods, the centres provide updated information on nature trails, activities, accessibility and other aspects of the park.

The centres also host exhibitions and offer guided hikes.

Its main branch is the **Cimolais Visitor Center** (☑ 0427 873 33; www.parcodolomiti friulane.it; Via Roma 6; ⊙ 10am-noon & 2-5pm Sat & Sun Oct-May, 10am-noon & 2-6.30pm Sat & Sun Jun, Jul & Sep, 10am-noon & 2-6.30pm daily Aug), home to the park's administrative headquarters.

Friulian Dolomites

0 — 5 km
0 — 2 miles

Lorenzago di Cadore
SS51
Pieve di Cadore
Lago di Pieve di Cadore
M. Tiarfin (2417m)
Sauris di Sotto
Lago di Sauris
Forni di Sopra
Ampezzo
Veneto
Cima Cadin (2385m)
SS52
Forni di Sotto
Mediis
Campanile di Val Montanaia (2173m)
M. Pramaggiore (2479m)
F. Piave
M. Duranno (2652m)
Cima Postegae (2347m)
M. Chiarescons (2168m)
M. Citta (2191m)
Parco Naturale Regionale Dolomiti Friulane
Val Vaiont
Cimolais
M. Caserine (2309m)
Tramonti di Sopra
Val Settimana
Casso
Erto
M. Dosaip (2062m)
Tramonti di Sotto
Longarone
Claut
Lago di Cà Selva
Lago di Tramonti
Val Tramontina
F. Piave
M. Toc (1921m)
M. Raut (2026m)
Poffabro
Meduno
Col Nudo (2472m)
Barcis
Andreis
Frisanco
Travesio
Ponte nelle Alpi
Crep Nudo (2207m)
Lago di Barcis
Maniago
Val Colvera
SR464
A27

Valcellina. At the confluence of the Cellina and Settimana streams, in the area known as the Pinedo, the SP5 shoots northeast towards Claut and Lesis.

The Val Tramontina is crossed by the SR552, which starts near Ampezzo (p229) in the north and ends in Meduno in the south. From here it connects easily with the rest of the region's road network.

From the A23 (Udine–Tarvisio), exit at Carnia-Tolmezzo, then follow the SS52 and the signs for Forni. From the A27 (Venezia–Belluno), exit at Cadore-Dolomiti, take the SS51 for Cortina, then the SS52 for Passo della Mauria; at that point you'll be in the Valle del Tagliamento, where the two towns are located.

The secret Val Colvera is not especially accessible. From Valcellina (SR251), you can it reached by car via the SP63; from the plain (Maniago and Pordenone) take the SP26.

TRAIN

The most convenient stations for reaching the Friulian Dolomites are in Veneto: Longarone for the Val Cimoliana and Calalzo di Cadore for the Val del Tagliamento. On the Friulian side, the most practical station is Maniago, useful for reaching the Cellina and Colvera Valleys.

Erto & Casso

POP 370 / ELEV 775M

Erto and Casso sit on opposite slopes of **Monte Toc** (1921m). Although the hamlets are located in the same valley, each has its own dialect; while Erto's is a mix of Ladin and Friulian, Casso's has Venetian influences. On top of this, each has its own distinct architecture. Both are beautiful and worth a visit.

The only aspect that truly unites the two villages is the exodus of many of its inhabitants, a result of both the Vajont disaster and the general challenges of living in such a remote corner of the region.

◉ Sights & Activities

Coming from the Passo Sant'Osvaldo (Sant'Osvaldo Pass), along the state road, one inevitably notices a change in the overall landscape. While the mountains remain, the valley disappears.

For 50 years, the latter has been blanketed by **the Monte Toc** landslide, which still makes its presence felt when the odd boulder tumbles down into the silence.

Looking up at the southern slope, you'll notice the bare face of the mountain. It was from here that an immense mass of rock broke away, causing one of Europe's biggest catastrophes.

A little further on, on the northern side of the road, Erto Nuova is an unfortunate example of a 'new town', built to house those who returned a decade after the landslide. It's home to a handful of guesthouses, a hotel, eateries, a bank and pharmacy.

On the other side of the highway is the old town, **Erto Vecchia**, made up entirely of traditional stone buildings. Wandering its handful of streets, the sense of abandonment is palpable. Graffiti riddles some of the buildings: while some of it condemns those responsible for the Vajont disaster, other messages are eerily hopeful, as if written by ghosts. A well-signposted interchange leads to **Casso**, high up on the northern side of the valley.

Due to its position, the town was less severely affected by the landslide and is therefore better preserved. Its spectacular stone tower-houses, declared a national monument in 1976, are worth a look. Walking uphill from the village, paths lead to panoramic ledges which offer a good overview of the landslide. Gazing out, consider the mega tsunami caused when the mountainside smashed into the Vajont dam. Consider also the boulders that reached the former elementary school.

The latter site is now home to the Nuovo Spazio di Casso, an experimental centre for contemporary alpine art and culture.

Don't leave town without visiting the **Diga del Vajont**. The guided tour leads along the walkway crowning what was, until recently, the tallest dam in the world. While looking out at what remains of the valley, the guides give a gripping, detailed account of the 1963 tragedy, as well as pointing out some other points of interest. Among these is the road that the German general Erwin Rommel had opened here in WWI.

Between the junction for Casso and the junction for Erto is the **Falesia di Erto (Erto Cliff)**, a well-known and freely accessible **crag**.

Divided into two sectors (one for beginners and one for more experienced climbers), it's considered a mecca for climbers, with around 120 possible routes.

It's especially unique for its overhang, which shelters ascending climbers on those pesky rainy days.

THE VAJONT DAM & THE TRAGEDY OF 1963

Crossing this part of the Dolomites, it's worth stopping at the former **Diga del Vajont** (☑ 0427 873 33; www.parcodolomitifriulane.it; 3hr tour adult/reduced €10/5, 40min dam walkway visit €5; ☺ varies, see website or call). A masterpiece of 20th-century hydraulic engineering, the dam was the tallest in the world when completed in 1960 (it's now the fifth tallest).

The dizzying structure was built to turn the Valle del Vajont into an artificial basin, although concerns about possible landslides and subsidence involving the surrounding mountains had been raised from its conception. After all, neighbouring **Monte Toc** (1921m) owes its name to the Friulian word for 'failure', precisely because of its tendency to shatter.

On the evening of 9 October 1963, with the reservoir completely full, 300 million cubic metres of Monte Toc's slope collapsed. In just 40 seconds, 48 million cubic meters of water were lifted, creating an 80m wave that crashed into the villages on the banks. Another 170m wave plunged into the Piave Valley from a height of 400m, razing entire towns and communities, including Longarone. While the dam itself remained largely intact, almost 2000 lives were lost.

The tragedy extended far beyond that fateful autumn night, with the evacuation of the valley's inhabitants, especially those of Erto, the substantial 'militarisation' of the area, and a long, taxing investigation into the catastrophe. Sadly, the Vajont catastrophe was not a simple case of bad luck: too many technical considerations and concerns were overlooked or omitted.

Today, tour guides at the dam site offer comprehensive, factual insight into the events that led up to the disaster, allowing visitors to form their own opinion on one of modern Europe's most devastating chapters.

THE NEVER-ENDING LANDSLIDE

The 1963 Vajont dam tragedy (p217) was a largely human-made 'calamity'. Monte Toc was well known for shedding chunks of itself and the unnerving sound of crashing boulders, especially at night, remains the mountain's warning to ambitious engineers and architects to leave it alone. Six decades on, the fateful landslide of 9 October 1963 remains active, forever shifting.

Driving along the picturesque road that towers above it, the scale of the landslide becomes apparent. Take a good look at the trunks of the trees. Those that are straight signify trees that have shot up after the landslide. Those with a conspicuous curve at the base of their trunk denotes trees caught in the landslide, which have managed to survive by growing crooked out of the debris over time.

From the Diga del Vajont, drive eastward along the SR251 for less than a kilometre. After passing the car park and, after it, the bus parking area, take the small road on your right (which may be in poor condition in winter), and drive over the landslide, until you rejoin the main road some 6km later. Down below, the Vajont stream still flows between the boulders.

🛏 Sleeping & Eating

Located at the entrance to Erto Nuovo, **Trattoria Julia** (🗹 0427 87 90 80; Via IX October 32; meals €20; ⊙ 7.30am-3pm Mon, Tue & Thu, to 10pm Fri & Sun, to 9pm Sat) serves simple, hearty mountain dishes that will set you up for a deep, sound sleep. You can indulge in the latter at **La Voce del Tempo** (🗹 042 766 04 36; www.bblavocedeltempo.com; Via Roma 135; s/d €60/100; 🛜 🐾), a new, well-kept B&B in Erto's strangely enchanting old town.

ℹ Information

Erto & Casso Visitor Centre (🗹 0427 873 33; Return Square 3; ⊙ 10am-noon & 2-6pm Jun-Aug, Jan & Feb, Sat & Sun only rest of yr) Located in Erto, this is one of the most important and comprehensive interpretive centres for both the Vajont disaster and the area's history and traditions. Further information can be found at the Diga del Vajont(p217) information centre.

Val Zemola

Detaching itself from the Valle del Vajont (where Erto and Casso are located), Val Zemola is a 5km-long valley stretching north–south in the Duranno-Preti group of the Friulian Dolomites. Although small, the valley is wild, secluded and crossed by Zemola stream. While there are no towns located here, you will find numerous mountain huts which welcome hikers, climbers and locals from neighbouring valleys who come here for some quiet time with 'their' mountains.

🏃 Activities

You can enter Val Zemola by using the sealed road (follow the signs for Val Zemola) leading north from Erto Nuovo to **Casera Mela** (🗹 333 785 79 08; www.caseramela.it; Val Zemola, Erto & Casso; overnight stay €23; ⊙ Jun-Sep, weekend only or by reservation Apr, May, Oct & Nov), where it's possible to park. A beautifully positioned mountain hut, La Casera is as handy for a snack as it is for an overnight stay.

SUMMER ACTIVITIES

Canyoning

The southern part of Val Zemola has fixed anchors suitable for canyoning. The number of equipped abseils is 12, the highest of which measures 20m. During the descent you pass through particularly beautiful and characteristic environments, the most famous of these is the rotating pool, in which the water rotates counterclockwise and allows canyoners a fun digression on the subject.

Hiking

In Val Zemola it is possible to enjoy some wonderful excursions. The **Path no 374** (difference in altitude 1100m, 6hr 30min) is part of **the Val Zemola ring** and, through larch and mountain pine woods, reaches the plateau of the **Maniago Refuge** (🗹 0427 87 91 44 , 338 169 74 79, 338 533 74 60; Val Zemola, Erto & Casso; overnight stay/half board €20/50; meals €20-25; ⊙ every day 20 Jun-20 Sep, Sat & Sun rest of the year depending on weather conditions) in about an hour and 30 minutes; at 1730m, it's a privileged point to admire the valley.

The path continues among the pines, then on a grassy ridge, until it reaches the bare rock. You then reach the Forcella del Duranno at 2217m (one hour 30 minutes from the refuge). Along the same path you return to the Maniago Refuge and continue to the junction with **Path no 381** (difference in altitude 1100m, 5hr) which leads to Casera Bedin, which is located on a panoramic hill at an altitude of 1711m.

Cimolais

POP 350 / ELEV 652M

The mountains are at their most rugged and strikingly beautiful in Cimolais, home to the headquarters of the Parco Naturale delle Dolomiti Friulane. From the village, hikers set off for the Campanile di Val Montanaia, a towering rock formation soaring some 300m into the sky. First successfully scaled in 1902, the geological giant is the stuff (professional) climbing dreams are made of.

Handy village facilities include an ATM and a petrol station; consider that the next petrol station heading west is in Erto, after the Sant'Osvaldo Pass.

🏃 Activities

SUMMER ACTIVITIES

Campanile di Val Montanaia   HIKING

While every Dolomite group has its iconic peak, the undisputed star of the Friulian Dolomites is an imposing rock pinnacle. With its summit sitting 2173m above sea level, the tower's base is reached along a challenging trail of scree and a steep, rocky stream bed.

The starting point for the hike to the Campanile di Val Montanaia is the **Rifugio Pordenone** (☑ 0427 873 00/335 522 49 61; www.rifugio pordenone.it; Val Cimoliana; meals €20-25.50; overnight stay/half-board €22/53; ⊗ mid-May–Sep), accessible from Cimolais in about three hours on foot or 30 minutes by car.

From here, you'll need to follow a section (elevation gain 900m, 2hr 30min) of the longer **trail 353** (elevation gain 1100m, 3hr 45min), which leads through the Forcella Montanaia to the Rifugio Padova (p225). The trail is difficult to decipher; follow the *omini di pietra* (men of stone), stone piles left by previous hikers. Beyond another leg-breaking stretch of scree lies the base of the monumental *campanile*.

While its sky-scraping presence is nothing short of spectacular, so too is the view over the valley. Muscles weary, enjoy a well-earned rest at the little Bivacco Perugini (Perugini mountain hut).

If you don't feel like climbing to the base of the Campanile di Val Montanaia, two lookouts (a five-minute walk from each other) offer views of the tower.

To reach them from the Pordenone Refuge, take **trail 352** (elevation gain 330m, 1hr). While not very demanding, the trail is very popular in the middle of the day.

Pianpinedo   WILDLIFE PARK

(☑ 0427 873 33; www.parcodolomitifriulane.it; Via Vittorio Emanuele II; adult/reduced €3/2; ⊗ 9am-6pm Sun Jun-late Jul & Sep–mid-Oct, daily late Jul-Aug) On the road between Claut and Cimolais, Pianpinedo is an ideal pitstop if you have kids in tow. Three trails lead through the park, offering close encounters with deer (including roes), ibex and chamois. Information panels shed light on the area's various botanical species.

Little ones might also enjoy the small sensory trail at the visitor centre, which explores the forest and creatures living within it. Entry to the park is directly opposite the Dolomia bottling plant.

🛏 Sleeping & Eating

⭐ **Bresin**   CAMPGROUND €

(☑ 335 526 97 62; 850m beyond the end of Via XIX Ottobre; adult/reduced €6/4; site €8 plus €2 for electricity; ⊗ mid-Jun–mid-Sep) This basic campground has two sections: one with driveways for permanent campers and a meadow for those passing through (or for those who simply prefer grass).

The setting is breathtaking and the campground an ideal base camp if you're planning a hike up to the Campanile di Val Montanaia. You'll find it along the road leading to the Rifugio Pordenone (p225).

Margherita   HOTEL/RESTAURANT €€

(☑ 0427 870 60, 335 702 43 23; Via Roma, 7; s/d €55/80; meals €30-35; ⊗ noon-2.30pm & 7-9pm Tue-Sun; 🅿) In 2019 what was once called Locanda Margherita celebrated 50 years of activity. It is nice to stop here in one of the simple rooms of the hotel or chat with the managers and other guests about the best routes to take in the wild Dolomites, in front of a good *frico,* a homemade lasagna and excellent house wine.

ℹ Information

Ente Parco Naturale Dolomiti Friulane (☑ 0427 873 33; Via Roma 4, Cimolais)

Claut

POP 883 / ELEV 613M

Claut's main claim to fame is **dinosaur footprints**, imprinted in a boulder near Val di Giere. To see them, follow the road from Claut to Lesis. Passing the latter, continue through the valley until you reach the car park for **Casera Casavento** (☑ 348 492 09 26; Valcellina, Lesis; meals €25), set in a pasture encircled by majestic peaks.

From here, it's a short hike to the Triassic theropod's footprints, found by chance by students on a field trip in 1994.

The largest village in the Valcellina, Claut also attracts walkers, cyclists and whitewater rafters, not to mention families seeking a getaway in lush, tranquil surrounds.

If you're intrigued by its traditional stone houses, pay a visit to the **Museo della Casa Clautana** (☑ 0427 87 80 78; www.parcodolomitifriulane.it; Piazza San Giorgio 4; ⊙ 3.30-6.30pm Sat & Sun Jun-late Jul, daily late Jul-Aug, Sun early–mid-Sep, by appt other periods) `FREE` to explore their interiors and learn about the customs and traditions of the area's peasant past.

🏃 Activities

SUMMER ACTIVITIES

⭐ **Landre Scur** CAVE
(Trail 962, Casera Casavento–Landre Scur, elevation gain 380m, 2.3km, 1hr 30min) From the Casera Casavento car park, a relatively easy forest trail with only one steep, short uphill stretch reaches Landre Scur ('Dark Cave'). Hidden in the woods and only recently discovered, the cave has a wide, almost perfectly square opening.

Inside the natural 'hall', a second, 2m-wide portal leads to 4.5 kilometres of tunnels, suitable for experienced cavers only.

YEAR ROUND

Tree Village THEME PARK
(☑ 333 386 63 63; www.montagna.es/tree-village; Via Val Settimana; P) The first of its kind in Italy, this village of wooden treehouses includes an organic garden, hiking trails and cables that allow guests to 'fly' between the treetops. A dream for kids.

🍴 Eating

Corona OSTERIA €€
(☑ 0427 87 81 77; Via Pinedo, 30; meals €25; ⊙ bar 7am-8pm, restaurant noon-2pm & 7-9pm Tue-Sun) Located at the intersection between the SR251 and the SP5 for Claut, this handy tavern pulls everyone from forest rangers and mountain guides, to hikers and holiday makers. Together, they tuck into simple, hearty first and second courses based on game, mushrooms and cheese.

Val Settimana

From the Valcellina, several side valleys wind their way northwards, long, wide and enclosed at their upper ends. The Val Settimana is a typical example, running roughly north–south from Claut, near which the Settimana stream flows into the Cellina River.

The valley is crossed by a partly sealed, partly unsealed road (not always crossable) which fords numerous times over the torrent and reaches the **Rifugio Pussa** (Whatsapp ☑ 349 620 05 18; www.rifugiopussa.com; overnight stay/half-board €20/40; ⊙ Jun-Sep; P).

The mountain hut is located in a dense forest of fir and beech, and offers the usual mountain-hut facilities. The hut's name translates to 'stink', a nod to the nearby sulphur spring.

While the valley doesn't have a significant elevation gain, it is quite long (14km), making it ideal for **mountain biking** (about 1hr 30min). Immediately after the bridge that crosses the Settimana stream towards Claut, the slow but steady climb begins. Surrounded by boulders, woods and mountains that become pointier and more rugged along the way, the road leads to the Rifugio Pussa, sitting some 940m above sea level. Pay attention to the fords and drains that cross the road as they're quite slippery.

🏃 Activities

SUMMER ACTIVITIES

Hiking

From the Rifugio Pussa it's possible to hit some fascinating high-altitude routes and enter the wild heart of the Friulian Dolomites. **Trails 366A** (elevation gain 180m, 70min), **366** (elevation gain 1388m, 5hr) and **370** (elevation gain 1536m, 6hr) lead to the Rifugio Pordenone; two of these (366A and 366) also reach the Rifugio Flaiban Pacherini (p225).

Trail **364** (elevation gain 1050m, 5hr 30min leads to Forni di Sotto, while **trail 376** (elevation gain 990m, 6hr) leads to Lesis, from where you can reach the dinosaur footprints, and to Claut.

WINTER ACTIVITIES
Ski Mountaineering & Snowshoeing

Using snowshoes or climbing skins, it's possible to climb up to **Casera Pradut** (☎ 345 828 93 07; Claut; overnight stay/half-board €25/45) in winter, reached through dense coniferous woods. Despite the low altitude, abundant rainfall means that the area is often well-covered with snow.

From Casera Pradut, **trail 961** (www.cai-fvg.it) leads to the Baldàs pass (1749m), below the summit of Monte Resettum. The beautiful descent on skis leads through a tract of forest that's not too dense.

To reach Lesis from Claut, you'll need to drive. Leave your car at the car park (the road beyond it isn't maintained so it may be heavily snow-covered) and take the signposted trail to the right among the trees until you reach the Casera Pradut clearing.

Barcis

POP 237 / ELEV 409M

Barcis is a small village reflected in the waters of **Lago di Barcis**, a strikingly beautiful reservoir which takes on an incredible aniseed-emerald hue in the summer. Fringed by woods and a crown of mountains, the artificial lake is often frozen in the winter.

◎ Sights & Activities

Palazzo Mocenigo-Centi   HISTORIC BUILDING

Historically and architecturally, Palazzo Mocenigo-Centi is the most valuable building in the entire valley, combining elements of Valcellina's rustic style with those of Venetian architecture. In the 17th century, it was home to the noble Venetian Mocenigo family, lords of Valcellina.

Last century, it was inhabited by the Centi family, who also ran it as an inn. Set on fire by the Nazis in 1944 as a revenge act against the partisans, the restored stone beauty now houses the reception of the Albergo Diffuso di Barcis.

★ Forra del Cellina   CANYON

(Visitor Centre ☎ 0427 873 33; Località Ponte Antoi; ☺ 2-5pm Sun) There are many canyons, gorges and ravines in the Dolomites, but the Forra del Cellina is especially fascinating.

The largest canyon in Friuli Venezia Giulia, it's easily accessible thanks to the old **ANAS state road** (adult/reduced €3/2; ☺ 10am-6pm; compulsory helmet provided at entrance), now accessible on foot or by hopping aboard the comfortable **Valcellina tourist train** (☎ 0427 503 16; www.friulviaggi.it; 8 trips daily, €4-7; Apr-Oct; ☺ Antoi bridge ticket office 10am-12.15pm; Barcis-Souvenir Boz ticket office 2.30-3.30pm & 4.30-5.30pm).

Sentiero del Dint   HIKING

(Trail 997, elevation gain 120m, 2hr) An easy, 4km walk with excellent lookouts over the Cellina gorge, accessible year round.

Sightings of eagles are common as Andreis is home to a rehabilitation centre for injured birds of prey.

⌂ Sleeping & Eating

Camping San Francesco   CAMPGROUND €

(☎ 0427 763 66/331 945 09 10; www.campingbarcis.it; Località Ribe; site/adult/child €10/8/4) The ideal base camp for walks and treks in the Valcellina, and equally suited to those wanting to simply enjoy the intense blue of Lago di Barcis.

The town centre, Cellina Gorge, lakeside promenade and other local attractions are within walking distance, and there's a lakeside parking zone for camper vans located nearby.

★ Albergo Diffuso   APARTMENTS €/€€

(☎ 333 163 13 33; www.albergodiffusobarcis.it; Via Garibaldi 13; apt €70-157; P ☎) Choose from 23 holiday apartments, located in traditional, restored buildings around Barcis.

The reception building is located in Palazzo Mocenigo-Centi.

Aquila Nera   WINE BAR/RESTAURANT €€

(☎ 0427 763 90; Via Roma 18; meals €25; ☺ 10am-11pm; kitchen 12.30-2.30pm Tue-Sun; also 8-9.30pm Sat) Armed with a long wine list, small verandah and welcoming, atmospheric fit-out, this small *enoteca* offers a few daily food specials, as well as cured meats and freshly made *frico*.

Dolce e Salato   DELI

(☎ 346 120 94 91; Piazza Vittorio Emanuele II; ☺ 7.15am-8.30pm summer, reduced hrs winter) If you're in a hurry or simply don't feel like a sit-down meal, hit this place for picnic provisions or a made-to-order sandwich from the deli.

ⓘ Information

Pro Barcis - IAT di Barcis (☎ 0427 76 300; www.barcis.fvg.it; Piazza Vittorio Emanuele II 5; 10.30am-12.30pm & 3-6pm daily mid-Jun–mid-Sep, Sun only rest of yr)

Andreis

Not far from Barcis is historic Andreis. Known for its distinct **abodes**, adorned with wooden balconies and external stairs, this is a village of farmhands and artisans. It once produced bone and ox-horn combs and snuffboxes, sold across the valleys and around the world.

While its **Museo Etnografico dell'Arte e della Civiltà Contadina** (0427 760 07; Piazza Centrale; ⊙ on request) displays a collection of objects, work tools, clothes and handicrafts from a now waning agricultural civilisation, the entire village is an open-air museum of sorts, its timeless streets scattered with information panels recounting its history.

Andreis lies 6km east of the Riserva della Forra del Cellina.

🏃 Activities

SUMMER ACTIVITIES

Nordic Life Park HIKING

(Giovanni Bertagno 📞 335 526 97 62; Franco Polo 📞 334 814 95 98) Andreis' network of eight walking trails span different lengths and levels of difficulty: choose one that's right for you and follow the corresponding colour.

Frisanco & Val Colvera

POP 568 / ELEV 550M

One of the Dolomites' wildest valleys, Val Colvera is encircled by steep slopes reflected in its lakes and basins, and while it might be small, its configuration allows for many hours of exploration.

The valley links Val Cimoliana to the south and Val Tramontina to the east, and the best place to eye up its traditional architecture – made of raw-cut sandstone or limestone and decorated with wonderful timber balconies similar to those in Andreis – is in the medieval village of Frisanco.

Temporary exhibitions are held in the former town hall, **Palazzo Pognici** (Via Valdestali 1), allowing visitors to snoop around its interior.

From here, a two-minute walk west leads to the **Chiesa di Sante Fosca e Maura** (0427 780 14; Via Canonica). Originally from the 15th century, the church was remodelled five centuries later, with interior decorations dating from 1939 and post-Friuli earthquake.

In the immediate vicinity of the village lies the Foresta di Frisanco, a lush, leafy forest where you can enjoy easy walks and reach the **Chiesa della Madonna della Stangada**, located some 2km from the free car park (Parcheggio Comunale Gratuito) in the centre of town.

🏃 Activities

SUMMER ACTIVITIES

Hiking & Mountain Biking

Val Colvera promises memorable hiking and cycling romps, with trail information available at the Poffabro visitor centre and other information centres throughout the Parco Naturale delle Dolomiti Friulane.

Especially beautiful trails here include one along the **torrente Colvera (Colvera stream)**, which runs parallel to the SP26 and leads through gorges, and the long **Sentiero Beato Pier Giorgio Frassati** (trail 899, elevation gain 1100m, 5hr 30min) that loops between Frisanco, Poffabro, Andreis, Fanna and Maniago, passing numerous well-preserved places of worship en route.

Poffabro

A hamlet of Frisanco, Poffabro is an architectural jewel, its old stone houses cascading down the mountainside like a landslide. Included on the list of Italy's Most Beautiful Villages, the place is especially photogenic in the spring, with Monte Raut soaring in the background and village flower boxes bursting with colour.

Come Christmas, dozens of *presepi* (nativity cribs) decorate its balconies. The visitor centre occupies the former dairy, with a ground-floor exhibition exploring the history of Friulian dairies, including the *latteria di Friscano* (Friscano Dairy).

Upstairs, nature exhibitions focus on the Parco Naturale delle Dolomiti Friulane and Val Colvera.

🛏 Sleeping & Eating

Agna Lussieta GUESTHOUSE €

(📞 333 899 45 84, 338 459 51 16; Via Zorza; per person €30) Located in the heart of historic Poffabro, accessible only on foot, two stone houses host the trio of double rooms that make up this simple, tranquil, family-run guesthouse.

La Pignata TRATTORIA €€

(📞 340 611 26 53; Via Colussi 8; meals €25; ⊙ 11am-2.30pm & 6-9.30pm Mon & Wed-Sun) Thankfully, the food at this simple trattoria equals the charm of its commanding terrace, looking

PITINA, PETUCCIA & PETA

While they might sound like a Friulian nursery rhyme, *pitina, petuccia* and *peta* are in fact three signature edibles of the Valcellina and Val Tramontina.

The best known of the three is *pitina,* a cured 'meatball' originally hailing from Tramonti, today a Slow Food presidium. Local butchers peddle different versions of the speciality, born of the need to preserve hunted game through the year.

Chamois and roe deer were once the main ingredients, salted and seasoned using various herbs (including wild rosemary), then rolled in corn flour and smoked on the *fogher* (traditional Friulian hearth). After a period of maturation, the *pitinas* were sliced like a salami and eaten raw.

The same method was used on a goat or sheep that had been injured or that had died, given that this was more convenient than slaughtering the beast.

Today, the mutton variety is more frequently served in restaurants and sold in shops, although the venison version has not completely disappeared. Either way, today's *pitina* has been refined for modern palates, with a little pork or lard added to the mix.

Valcellina, on the other hand, is known for its *petuccia.* Although substantially the same thing, wild fennel and juniper berries are added to the mix of salt, black pepper and garlic, producing aromas reminiscent of those encountered on alpine hikes. A magnum version of *petuccia* is produced in the Valcellina village of Andreis. Known as *peta,* it's round, flat and can weigh up to a kilogram.

out over green hills and Poffabro's charming stone abodes.

Standout dishes include *frico* and homemade tagliatelle with mushrooms.

ℹ️ Information

Poffabro Visitor Center (📞 0427 873 33; Piazza XX Settembre 1; ⊙ 3.30-6.30pm Aug; for other periods see website)

Val Tramontina

TRAMONTI DI SOPRA: POP 284 / ELEV 420M
TRAMONTI DI SOTTO: POP 343 / ELEV 366M

Despite its wild first impression, Val Tramontina reveals a softer, gentler side of the Dolomites. Marking the eastern border of the group, the valley coaxes visitors with magnificent walks, refreshing summertime river swims, and some of Friuli's finest, most intriguing gastronomic specialities.

All three of the valley's hamlets are called Tramonti: di Sopra, di Mezzo and di Sotto. It's an apt name (*Tra-i-monti* means 'between the mountains') given that the valley is enclosed by a dense ring of wild, wooded peaks.

Tramonti is the home of *pitina,* a cured 'meatball' made of game or mutton, and the valley's inhabitants were once known for their crafts, particularly basketmaking, stonemasonry and, above all, tinsmithing.

From Tramonti, numerous easy hikes lead along the Meduna and the other local streams, including Rio dei Gamberi, Torrente Viellia and Torrente Silisia. Hike towards the trails that lead to **Monte Rest** (1782m) and your reward is an unforgettable panorama.

The Grotte Verdi di Pradis are also easily accessible from here: about 4km south of Tramonti di Sotto, along the SR552, take the deviation for the SP57, from where the caves are a further 12km.

👁️ Sights & Activities

Lago di Tramonti　　　　　　　　　LAKE
(SR552) Lago di Tramonti is the largest and most picturesque of all the area's lakes. In dry periods, you'll be able to spot the remains of an old village, now submerged. The lake is a popular fishing spot, and also a lovely spot for a lakeside walk or canoeing session.

Pozze Smeraldine &
Lago del Ciul　　　　　　　　　　LAKES
As the name suggests, the waters of the little-known 'Emerald Pools' are an inviting, jewel-like green well worth a trip.

Leave your car at the dedicated car park and continue on foot, keeping an eye on the signs.

You'll spot the natural pools beyond the Sgurlina spring: to reach them, follow the stream bed to the left.

Continuing uphill along **trail 386**, you'll pass the abandoned village of Frassaneit, once populated by woodcutters. Some 2.5 hours from the start of the trail you'll reach dam-enclosed Lago del Ciul.

Walking a further 20 minutes, at the other end of the lake, you can cross the Selis suspension bridge.

🛏 Sleeping & Eating

Da Febo HOTEL/RESTAURANT €
(☑392 843 90 66; Pecol 1/a; s/d €30/55; meals €25; ◔noon-10pm) Occupying an enviable position on Lago di Tramonti, Febo offers travellers very simple yet creatively furnished rooms.

The same can be said of its restaurant dishes, which gives classic, homestyle recipes imaginative touches.

Borgo Titol AGRITURISMO €
(☑345 244 95 41; www.borgotitol.com; Località Titol 1; d €65) Standing out against the mountains on the road to the Pozze Smeraldine (p223), this stone abode keeps things homely with its wooden interiors and simple, traditionally furnished rooms.

Expect peace, tranquility and the option of a meal made using local ingredients, from cured meats to cheeses.

★ Antica Corte OSTERIA, HOTEL €€
(☑331 790 03 33, 346 810 20 90; Piazza Santa Croce 5, Tramonti di Sotto; s/d €40/75 May-Sep only, meals €25-30; ◔noon-2pm & 6-9pm Wed-Sun) Its bar never short of boisterous, *vino*-guzzling locals, this wine shop and eatery flanks a small piazza in the centre of Tramonti di Sotto.

Food options marry tradition, creativity and sophistication, whether it be cured game (the local speciality) or a dish of gnocchi with snail *ragù*. Reservations are recommended on weekdays.

🛍 Shopping

La Tana delle Pitine FOOD & DRINK
(☑393 147 77 33; Via Sisto 1, Tramonti di Sopra; ◔8am-noon & 3-7pm Mon-Sat) *Pitina* (a cured, smoked 'meatball' made using a mix of game and beef) hails from here and this place produces one of the best.

WORTH A TRIP

MOUNTAIN SAFARI

The SR552 of the Passo Rest, which connects Tramonti di Sopra and di Sotto with Ampezzo (p229), leads through some of the region's wildest landscapes.

ℹ Information

Tramonti di Sopra Visitor Centre (☑0427 873 33; Via Villaggio 6 Maggio 3; ◔variable hrs, daily Aug). See website for updated opening times.

Forni di Sopra & Forni di Sotto

FORNI DI SOPRA: POP 908 / ELEV 907M
FORNI DI SOTTO: POP 551 / ELEV 777M

Now separate municipalities, Forni di Sopra and Forni di Sotto were once united in an autonomous territory under Venetian control. The latter is the 'youngest' of the two, rebuilt from scratch after the Nazis burnt it down in WWII. Forni di Sopra escaped the bombings and, as a result, is much more atmospheric, its traditional stone abodes flanked by pretty churches and encircled by majestic peaks. Wooden sculptures decorate the streets, testament to the area's long wood-carving tradition.

Forni di Sopra is the only ski resort in the Friulian Dolomites, with ski lifts on Monte Varmost and runs that are well-trodden hiking trails in the summer. In season, rhododendrons, buttercups, lilies and orchids carpet the valleys. If you're lucky, you might even spot a primula auricola, a springtime flower that sprouts from the crevices.

◉ Sights

Museo Rurale Fornese MUSEUM
(☑0433 88 67 67; Via Madonna della Salute 3; Frazione Vico; ◔contact tourist office) FREE The strongpoint of this ethnographic museum is its location: the historic Casina da Vic dairy.

It's an evocative place to explore the area's dairy traditions, with a collection that includes large boilers and other vintage machinery used for making milk and cheeses.

Museo 'Il Filo dei Ricordi' MUSEUM
(☑0433 88 67 67; Ciasa dai Fornès, Frazione Cella; ◔contact tourist office) FREE Carnia is traditionally renowned for its weavers, so much so that the 'Cràmars' (hailing from the Gorto and San Pietro Valleys) and the 'Tesseri' or 'Tisidous' (from the Socchieve and Tagliamento Valleys) would spend the winters in Venice and Habsburg Austria, where their skills were in great demand.

The craft is explored at this 17th-century rural abode, which includes a section dedicated to *scarpéts*, exclusive velvet shoes typical of the Carnia region.

🏃 Activities

SUMMER ACTIVITIES

Canyoning

Scuola di Alpinismo del FVG   CANYONING
(www.fornidolomiti.it) If you're keen on canyoning along the Tolina and Rassie rapids, this outfit has a host of alpine guides at the ready.

Trekking

⭐ **Anello delle
Dolomiti Friulane**   TREKKING
(https://tabaccomapp-community.it/it/percorso/17880-ring-of-the-dolomites-friulane) This five-day hiking adventure takes you into the wild heart of these mountains.

Tobacco's 02 topographic map will guide you from Rifugio Giaf to enchanting **Truoi dai Sclops** (CAI trails 361, 369, 362, elevation gain 1000m, 6hr) and Forcella Urtisiel in a series of unforgettable vistas. You can start the hike from any of the *rifugi* (mountain refuges or huts) on the circuit, which are all accessible from the valley.

For instance, you could start from Rifugio Flaiban-Pacherini, head up to Passo di Suola, cross Forcella Rua Alta and Forcella Pramaggiore – Pramaggiore's summit is the highest (2478m) and most panoramic – and descend through the Val dell'Inferno and **Val Postegae** (CAI trails 363, 366, 362, elevation gain 800m, 5-6hr).

From **Rifugio Pordenone** (p219) set out to tackle the magnificent Val Montanaia. Beyond the Campanile di Val Montanaia (p219), Forcella Montanaia (CAI trail 353) leads to Val d'Arade and, at the end of it, the vast meadow which claims Rifugio Padova, also accessible from Veneto.

Forcella Montôf   HIKING
(Trails 215 & 214, elevation gain 1060m, 6hr) A nature trail leading through woods and clearings up to the crags of the Brutto Passo and Passo dello Zauf (2013m).

Anello di Bianchi   HIKING
(Trails 346, 340, 354, 342, from Forni di Sopra, elevation gain 300m, 3hr 30min) Panoramic trail in the heart of the Parco delle Dolomiti.

Alle Malghe Tartoi e Tragonia   HIKING
(Trails 208 & 211, elevation gain 700m, 5hr) A trail traversing woods towards the *malghe* (alpine huts) of Forni di Sopra, all of which are connected. Along trail 211, the **Malga Varmost** (☑349 452 16 94; Varmost chairlifts, Forni di Sopra) is a good place to stock up on dairy products.

Rifugio Flaiban-Pacherini (☑0433 885 55; Forni di Sopra)

Rifugio Giaf (☑338 785 63 38; www.rifugiogiaf.it; Località Coston di Giaf, Forni di Sopra)

Rifugio Som Picol (Varmost chairlifts, Forni di Sopra)

Adventure Parks

Dolomiti Adventure Park   ADVENTURE PARK
(☑328 184 19 88; www.fornidolomiti.it; Località Santaviela; adult €15, child €5-10; ⊙10am-7pm Sat & Sun Jun & Sep, 10am-7pm daily Jul & Aug) On the banks of the Tagliamento River, this all-ages adventure park gets the adrenalin pumping with seven trails equipped with aerial walkways, tightropes, nets and a recently added Powerfan that will have you 'bungee jumping' 15m from a tree. Geronimoooo!

Via Ferrata

Adventure Climb Varmost   CLIMBING
(www.for-adventure.it) Tackle gorges, sheer walls, suspension bridges and ascents on this climbing route to the summit of Varmost; *via ferrata* climbing kits can be rented at the Dolomiti Adventure Park.

If you're not feeling especially adventurous, opt for the undemanding walking trail to the summit instead.

WINTER ACTIVITIES

Skiing & Ice Skating

Located on the slopes of the Davost and Varmost mountains, Forni di Sopra's handful of ski runs deliver extraordinary scenery without the crowds and high prices of other Dolomite resorts.

Aside from its 15km of downhill runs, the resort claims an important cross-country skiing centre, with a large 13km ring. Two kilometres of the circuit, the *pista* **Tagliamento** (⊙6-8pm Mon & Wed), is floodlit, allowing for an evening ski. There's also an outdoor ice rink and, for young snow bunnies, **Fantasy Snow Park** (☑328 184 19 88; www.fornidolomiti.it), complete with tunnels, rafts and trampolines.

For ski-equipment rental, contact **Dolomiti ski-bar** (www.dolomitiskibar.it; Via Nazionale 8, Forni di Sopra), which will put you in touch with signor **Roberto** (☑380 329 33 99), also the right person to ask about ski lessons at the **'3s' ski school** (Via Tagliamento 22, Forni di Sopra).

Equipment rental is also available from **Sherpa** (☑0433 88 67 35; Via Nazionale 168, Forni di Sopra). For lessons, you can also check out the **Scuola Italiana Sci Forni di Sopra** (☑ 0433 882 46; www.scuolascifornidisopra.it).

YEAR ROUND

Indoor Climbing & Swimming

Centro Sportivo Polifunzionale SPORTS CENTRE
(☑ 0433 880 56, 335 48 49 96; ☺ 8am-1pm; Località Davost, Forni di Sopra; ☺ 4-7.30pm mid-Jun–Sep & winter) Sports centre with indoor pool, gym, wellness centre and indoor rock climbing.

🛏 Sleeping & Eating

Camping Tornerai CAMPGROUND €
(☑ 0433 880 35; www.campingtornerai.it; Location Stinsans 11; adult €5.60, child €3.60-4.60, site €8-11) A beautiful campground, encircled by the mighty Dolomites and graced with a sweeping field, majestic old trees and a storybook reception building.

Birrificio Foglie d'Erba BEER, PIZZA €
(shop ☑ 347 355 51 97; www.birrificiofogliederba.it; Via Nazionale 14; ☺ 3.30-6.30pm Tue-Sun; pizzeria ☑ 329 464 26 30; Via Nazionale 85-87; meals €15; ☺ 6.30pm-midnight Wed-Sun Oct–mid-Jun, extended hours summer) While the pizzas here hit the spot, the real drawcard at this much-loved microbrewery is its range of aromatic craft beers. The brewery has a second point of sale at the bottom of the ski lifts.

Antica Osteria la Speranza FRIULIAN €€
(☑ 345 979 70 59; Via degli Orti 1; meals €25; ☺ 10am-10pm Mon & Wed-Sun) Setting a cosy scene with its *fogolàr* and patio, this intimate *osteria* nourishes diners with hearty, Friulian mountain grub; just the ticket after a day on the slopes or hiking trails. Note the 'Negozio alla Speranza' above the entrance, here since 1875.

ℹ Information

Parco Dolomiti Friulane Visitor Centre (☑ 0427 873 33; Via Vittorio Veneto 1; ☺ 10am-noon & 3.30-6.30pm daily Aug, Fri-Sun rest of year) The best of the valley's visitor centres, with generous information on outdoor activities and the area.

CARNIC ALPS

The western part of the Friulian Alps is located in Carnia, the historical region which also includes part of the Dolomites, but extends mainly to the north and east of the Dolomite group.

In Carnia, nature and the built environment form a pleasing balancing act. The glorious mountains that frame the valleys are softened by centuries of human intervention, visible in passionately tended pas-

Carnic Alps

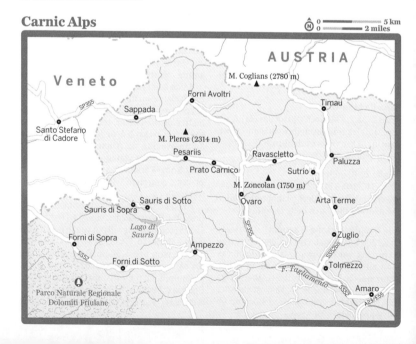

tures and woods, and charming mountain huts and bivouacs.

The region has always been crossed by *cramârs*, street vendors who sold spices and fabrics across the Alps in winter, and by the *portatrici carniche,* Carnic women of steel who carried food and ammunition to soldiers in WWI in wicker panniers.

Here, villages are built with the stones that tumble from the peaks and shaped over time by wind and other elements. While some of these villages are distinguished by their unique architecture, such as the *stavoli* (local barns), others, like clockmaking Pesariis, are famed for their traditions.

Some towns recall events that underline the gritty combativeness of the area's inhabitants; the first Partisan Republic was established in Ampezzo in 1944.

Inside dark, guarded alpine cellars, cured meats and cheeses ripen, forming an important part of the region's gastronomic heritage. In these parts, wild herbs are king and used in a variety of local dishes, including *cjarsons*, Carnia's exquisite stuffed ravioli.

History

The Carnians settled in the area in the 5th century BCE and, according to the ancient Greek historian Polybius, were 'proud and warlike'. In the Middle Ages, Carnia became a flourishing centre of trade, prompting the patriarchs of Aquileia to fortify its capital, Tolmezzo, with 18 watchtowers. Ruled by Venice for several centuries, the area (along with the other former Venetian territories) fell under Austrian control before being passed to Italy in 1866.

The area's greatest entrepreneur was Jacopo Linussio, whose 18th-century textile factory played a pivotal role in the birth of blue jeans. During WWI, Carnia was the battleground between Italy and the Austro-Hungarian empire, a bloody chapter remembered in the trenches and bomb craters that litter the Carnic landscape.

🛈 Getting There & Away

BUS

Tolmezzo is the area's main transport hub.

TPL FVG (☑ 800 05 20 40, mobile 040 971 23 43; https://tplfvg.it) buses 100, 150 and 440 run between Udine and Tolmezzo (€6.05-6.65, 45-75min, numerous trips between 6.20am & 8.15pm). Bus 440 connects Trieste to Tolmezzo (€14.55; 2hr 15min, one daily). Alternatively, catch bus G51 to Udine and continue to Tolmezzo on bus

TAGLIAMENTO

Carnia is not all Dolomite peaks. There is, for example, the Valle del Tagliamento, through which the region's longest and most important river flows. Stretching 170km, the Tagliamento and its tangled channels are responsible for a complex river ecosystem. The section of the waterway closest to the Dolomites is considered 'young', its very source not far from the Mauria Pass, right by the border of Friuli Venezia Giulia and Veneto. From there it begins its journey though a lush, high-altitude landscape of woods and heavy winter snows, skirting the border with Carnia to the north.

100. From Tolmezzo, bus 110 reaches Ampezzo (€3.50) – connected by bus 112 to Sauris –, Socchieve (€2.95) and Forni di Sopra (€5); bus 130 reaches Sutrio (€2.95) and Terme di Arta (€2.25); buses 140 and 145 reach Zuglio (€1.65, 10-30min, frequent); bus 120 reaches Comeglians (30min), from where bus 124 continues to Prato Carnico and Pesariis (10min; €3.50). Bus 125 runs between Comeglians and Ravascletto.

CAR & MOTORCYLE

From Udine, follow the signs for Gemona on the E55, then continue on the SR512. At the junction for Amaro, head towards Tolmezzo. Ampezzo is located in the Valle del Tagliamento, about 20km from Tolmezzo along the SS52. Prato Carnico is 25km from Tolmezzo. From the SS52, take the SR355 to Comeglians, then follow the signs for Prato Carnico. Beyond it is Osais, followed by Pesariis.

TRAIN

Udine is the most convenient station, from where buses depart frequently to Tolmezzo. Carnia station is another option, although connecting bus services are much less frequent. For times, see www.trenitalia.com.

Tolmezzo

POP 10,051 / ELEV 323M

In name and in fact, Tolmezzo is 'in the middle' of Carnia and is historically its capital. The town has found itself on the routes from the plains to Austria for centuries, and it remains a key junction in the area's road system. Tolmezzo is also a handy base for exploring the four corners of Carnia.

Small but lively, it's a pleasant place to spend the night between hikes, skis, climbs and other adventures in the mountains. The town itself has its drawcards, from its traditional architecture to the postcard-pretty neighbourhood of Borgàt.

◉ Sights

A visit to Tolmezzo will start from **Borgàt**. The town's historic centre, it's structured around two parallel streets: Via Roma and Via Cavour (which becomes Via Renato del Din, then Via Linussio, heading south).

Both thoroughfares skirt Piazza XX Settembre, where you can admire the 18th-century Duomo di San Martino, designed by Domenico Schiavi. The porticoed streets leading off the square are flanked by numerous noble buildings, including Palazzo Garzolini and Palazzo Frisacco, built between the 18th and 20th centuries, and 17th-century Palazzo Campeis. The latter houses the **Museo delle Arti Popolari Luigi e Michele Gortani** (☑0433 432 33; www.carniamusei.org; Via della Vittoria 2; adult/reduced €6/4, free with FVG Card; ⊙9am-1pm & 3-6pm Tue-Fri, from 10am Sat & Sun May-Sep, 9am-1pm & 3-5pm Tue-Fri, from 10am Sat & Sun Oct-Apr), an ethnographic museum whose cache includes Carnic craftwork and everyday objects from the 14th to 19th centuries. Highlights include exquisite fabrics, wooden credenzas, masks and musical instruments.

Heading north of Borgàt on the trail that leads up the hill overlooking the town, you'll notice **Torre Picotta**. The watchtower looked out over Tolmezzo from the 15th century until WWII, when it was destroyed

by the Germans. Today, it's the only vestige of the town's medieval fortification, together with the **Porta di Sotto**, an old city gate in the historic centre.

Prà Castello claims the ruins of **Castello di Tolmezzo**. Built during the final years of Aquileian rule in Carnia, a period which lasted from 1077 to 1420, the castle immediately became the area's most important as the seat of the steward of Carnia. As the Aquileian patriarch's representative, the steward was tasked with looking after temporal interests, protecting citizens, making the streets safe and judging 'civil and criminal' matters.

⌷ Sleeping & Eating

Albergo Diffuso
Tolmezzo   ALBERGO DIFFUSO €€
(☑0433 416 13, 331 802 83 83; www.albergodiffuso tolmezzo.it; rates vary; P) This 'widespread hotel' comprises 14 properties (some beautiful, others more ordinary), located in central Tolmezzo and the surrounding hamlets. Its reception is located in the underpass connecting Piazza XX Settembre to Piazza Centa; contact the office or check the website for rates and facilities, which vary between the properties.

Albergo Roma   HOTEL €€
(☑0433 46 80 31; www.albergoromatolmezzo.it; Piazza XX Settembre 14; s/d from €50/90; P 🛈) Accommodating visitors since 1889, the centrally located Albergo Roma was once Tolmezzo's most prestigious hotel. While it's since lost some of its sheen – the rooms and service could aim a little higher – it remains one of Carnia's most prolific hotels.

Handy facilities include undercover parking and a bar with a traditional *fogolàr*. The latter attracts no shortage of patrons, both hotel guests and passersby.

Al Borgat   OSTERIA € / €€
(☑0433 94 96 57; Piazza Mazzini 7/b; meals €20-25; ⊙10am-2pm and 5-9pm Mon-Sat; ☑) Filled to the brim with bottles, this warm, historic tavern captures the spirit of its namesake neighbourhood. Regulars congregate at the vast counter in the front room, while those after a calmer, more intimate vibe bunker down at tables in the second room.

The kitchen takes its *frico* very seriously, offered alongside other delectable local dishes; for a taste of the mountains, order the *crespelle alle erbe* (pancakes with herbs).

DON'T MISS

PIETRA VIVENTE

From the centre of Tolmezzo, Via Illegio leads to **Illegio**. Mentioned by 8th-century historian Paolo Diacono (Paul the Deacon), the jewel-box mountain village has its roots in the 4th century. Ambling its cosy, time-warped streets you'll stumble upon the **Mulin dal Flec**, a 16th-century mill still in operation today. Meanwhile, a trail from the village leads to the lofty church of **Pieve di San Floriano**, built between the 9th and 10th centuries. To get here from Tolmezzo, catch bus 104 (€1.35, 15min, 10 daily).

Drinking & Nightlife

Caffetteria Manzoni   CAFE
(☑ 0433 89 03 55; Piazza XX Settembre 10; ☺ 7am-
9pm Mon & Wed-Sun, extended hours summer; 🛜)
Situated slap-bang on the main square, Manzoni is Tolmezzo's landmark cafe, a spacious,
relaxed affair with a good selection of wines
and DJ sets on Saturday evenings. If you're
a sweet tooth, find your bliss in the strudel
or *frittelle*.

Shopping

Manin   PASTRY SHOP
(☑ 0433 405 73; www.facebook.com/pasticceria
manin; Piazza Garibaldi 14; ☺ 6.30am-1pm & 3-7pm
Mon-Sat, 8am-12.30pm Sun) Taste Carnia's sweet
side at Manin, which peddles delectable
cakes, pastries, chocolates and more.

ℹ Information

Tolmezzo Infopoint (☑ 0433 448 98; www.turis
mofvg.it; Via della Vittoria 4; ☺ 9am-1pm & 2-6pm
Mon-Sat winter, 9am-1pm & 2.30-6.30pm Mon-
Sat summer) Provides information on Carnia and
Tolmezzo, including skiing and accommodation.

Ampezzo

POP 942 / ELEV 560M

Ampezzo sits peacefully in the Alta Val Tagliamento (Upper Tagliamento Valley). During
the Resistance, this territory was controlled
by anti-fascist partisans and in the months
of September and October 1944, Ampezzo
was the capital of the 'Free Republic of Carnia', a fact proudly declared at the entrance
to the town.

It's a pleasant place, graced with traditional Carnic houses and home to the modern **Museo Geologico della Carnia** (☑ 0433
48 77 79, 335 769 78 38; www.carniamusei.org; Piazza Zona Libera 1944; ☺ 9.30am-12.30pm & 3-6pm
Tue-Sun Jun-Sep, Oct-22 Dec on request, 3-6pm daily except Dec 23-Jan 6, 3-6pm Sat & Sun Feb-May)
FREE, which delves deep into the area's geology and environment. Its other drawcard
is the **Foresta di Ampezzo**, a soothing forest of beech, fir and larch sprawling to the
southern shores of Lago di Sauris.

Following the signs pointing the way from
the Museo Geologico della Carnia, you'll hit
the **Plan dai Cjavai** nature trail. Sealed at the
beginning, the easy route leads into the forest to Pocion, a clearing adjacent to the choke
of the Teria stream. Bring a picnic and, if the
weather is warm, your swimsuit.

THE CHURCH & THE OSTERIA

Located near Socchieve, a few kilometres
from Ampezzo, **Nonta** is easy to miss
(look closely to find the sign along the
SS52). While it might be tiny – think four
houses, one charming church and an inn
that has always been run by the same
family – the village encapsulates the very
essence of Carnia, from its breathtaking
vistas to its atmosphere and flavours.

Take a seat at **Osteria di Nonta**
(☑ 0433 805 96; Via San Maurizio 1; meals
€30; ☺ reservations only) and comfort-
ed by the *fogolàr*, enjoy Elvira's authentic Carnic dishes. There is no menu; simply trust the cook. Belly full, contemplate
the beauty of tradition while your coffee brews in the moka pot. You may never want to leave.

Not far from Ampezzo lies the **Biotopo di
Sella di Cima Corso**. An ecological term, *biotopo* (biotope) refers to a small area that dif-
fers from its surrounding environment due
to its flora or fauna.

In Cima Corso, this point of difference is a
peat bog. Glacial in origin, it harbours a rich
collection of extremely rare botanical species (both at a regional and national level).
A number of signposted, ecofriendly routes
allow you to visit the zone, which lies southwest of Ampezzo.

To reach it from the village, head west on
the SS52 and pull into the car park adjoining Osteria Monte Jof. From here, follow the
stretch of road to the dirt track that leads to
the biotope.

🛏 Sleeping & Eating

Primavera   AGRITURISMO €
(☑ 0433 804 52; www.agriturismoprimavera.it; Località Gof 1; s/d €45/70; 🅿) ⌀ Situated at the
edge of the village, about 450m beyond the
Museo Geologico della Carnia, is this welcoming, sustainably minded farmhouse.
Savour the farm's homegrown products by
the *fogolàr* in the dining room and slumber
peacefully in the handful of simple rooms
upstairs.

From the property, numerous undemanding walks lead through the surrounding
area, among them the Plan dai Cjavai nature trail.

🔒 Shopping

Carniagricola FOOD & DRINK
(✆ 0433 807 05; www.carniagricola.it; Via Nazionale 106; ⊘ 8am-12.30pm Mon-Sat, also 4-7pm Fri & Sat)
Do not underestimate this shop, indicated only by the word 'butcher', with the windows on Via Nazionale, the main street of Ampezzo. You can buy quality meats, cheeses and cured meats here (try a fresh salami).

ⓘ Information

Ampezzo Carnico Tourist Office (✆ 0433 807 58; www.ampezzocarnico.it; Via Nazionale 80; ⊘ varies) For current opening times, see www.facebook.com/ufficioturisticoampezzo.

Sauris

POP 394 / ELEV 1212M

The winding, 15km road from Ampezzo to Sauris leads past *malghe* (alpine huts), pastures and dazzling lakes, into rocky tunnels, and through fairytale forests seemingly made for elves and goblins.

About halfway along the route is **Lago di Sauris**, whose impossibly turquoise waters draw canoeists and fisherfolk alike. At the end of your journey, Sauris appears like a happy oasis hidden in the mountains.

To the locals, Sauris is Zahre, and their unique dialect is closer to Austrian German than Italian. The municipality is made up of four hamlets: Sauris di Sopra (Upper Sauris), Sauris di Sotto (Lower Sauris), Lateis and La Maina. Sauris di Sotto is nestled in a large clearing, while Sauris di Sopra guards the road that leads to the Sella di Razzo pass (1760m) in Veneto.

⊙ Sights

Sauris di Sotto and di Sopra can be visited quickly and offer magnificent views of the surrounding mountains, especially during summer (in winter, check the weather before proceeding and remember the obligatory snow tyres or chains on board).

Sauris di Sotto is the larger of the two hamlets, home to a ski slope, ski lift and the **Santuario di Sant'Osvaldo**. The latter, a pilgrimage site, reputedly houses the thumb of the patron saint of Venetian goldsmiths. The hamlet also claims **Prosciuttificio Wolf Sauris** (✆ 0433 860 54; www.wolfsauris.it; Sauris di Sotto 88; ⊘ shop 8.30am-12.30pm & 3-7pm Mon-Sat, 9am-7pm Sun in summer, 9am-7pm daily Aug, factory by appointment), a family business that has been producing IGP-appellation prosciutto for 150 years.

Climbing up to the centre of Sauris di Sopra, you'll notice the **Chiesa di San Lorenzo**. Austrian-Gothic in appearance, the church was built between the 15th and 16th centuries. The village itself is even tinier and more secluded than Sauris di Sotto, its photogenic cluster of stone and wooden abodes occupied by the *albergo diffuso*.

For a crash course in local traditions, drop by the small **Centro Etnografico Haus van der Zahre** (✆ 0433 862 62; www.sauris.org/musei/centro-etnografico-haus-van-der-zahre; Località Sau-

---

COSSACKS IN CARNIA

Their name rooted in the Turkish word *qazaq* ('free man'), the Cossacks began life as a group of soldiers escaping Tsarist power in the 15th century. Becoming part of an autonomous community of mercenaries and soldiers, they eventually formed an outpost of the Russian Empire, becoming part of the army. When the Nazis invaded the Soviet Union in 1943, the Cossacks enlisted with the Germans, who in return promised them autonomy and a return to their own land. In the meantime, however, they were moved to other parts of Europe to free their soldiers from territorial control duties.

So it was that in July 1944, some 22,000 Cossacks and their families settled in Carnia, promised to them as Kosakenland in Nord Italien. To the Carnians, however, their arrival was nothing short of an occupation. Many locals were displaced, while others were forced to live among people whose traditions and customs were incompatible with their own. With the advance of the Allies in 1945, the Cossacks' hope of gaining Carnia fell apart and the occupiers fled en masse to Austria, where they surrendered to the British. Little did they know, however, that the Yalta Agreements stipulated that all Soviet prisoners were to be sent back to the USSR. Officers were to be shot and their families deported to Siberia. Upon hearing this news, many Cossacks preferred death to the gulags, committing mass suicide by throwing themselves into the Drava River.

ris di Sopra 3/a ; ⊙ 10am-noon & 3-6pm Mon & Thu-Sun) **FREE**. Set up in a 19th-century barn, the museum offers an interesting collection of historical local work tools, objects and artefacts, as well as informative, temporary exhibitions exploring a culture that stretches back to the 13th century. (It's always a good idea to contact the museum or village tourist office before visiting as opening times are subject to change.)

Sauris di Sopra also claims its own acclaimed craft beer **Zahre** (brewery ☑ 0433 86 14; www.zahrebeer.com; Sauris di Sopra 50; ⊙ 9am-5pm Mon-Fri), while its intimate main piazza is the starting point for the 'rite' of the Carnevale di Saurano (p232).

Separated by 3km of winding road, both hamlets are scattered with fantastical statues and wooden carvings, revealing the fine line between the real and the fantastical in this remote, magical corner of the region.

 Activities

SUMMER ACTIVITIES
Hiking & Cycling
The dense network of trails that were traditionally used by Saurian farmers and forest workers doubles as spectacular hiking and cycling trails.

The Sauris tourist office (p232) offers a 'Camminare per scoprire Sauris' (Walking to Discover Sauris) brochure marking four trails. Trail 2 revolves around the area's unique *stavoli*, traditional buildings used to store hay.

Standout CAI trails include the **Sentiero delle Malghe** (CAI trail 204-206-218; elevation gain 700m, 5hr), which runs from Sauris di Sopra towards the Sella di Festons (1860m), skirting the side of Mount Pieltinis and its pastures before descending along Mount Rinder Park.

The superb route connecting **Sauris to Forni di Sopra** (CAI trail 209; elevation gain 1300m, 6hr), considered the 'Two Pearls of the Alps', leads through a bucolic landscape of streams, mountain huts and meadows.

WINTER ACTIVITIES
Snowshoeing & Snowmobiles
The area has interesting routes for snowshoers: Sauris di Sopra–Ruke-Sauris di Sopra (7km); Sauris di Sopra–Hinter Eike–Sauris di Sotto (7km); Sauris di Sotto–Eimblat de Ribm–Lateis (7km).

Too tiring? **Contact Sauris Motoslitte Tour** (☑ 335 703 48 10; www.saurismotoslittetour. it) to book a snowmobile excursion.

MUSEUMS OF CARNIA

The **CarniaMusei** (www.carniamusei. org) museum network is a cross-border initiative with Austria, launched in 1998 to better promote Carnia's unique cultural heritage.

Originally, the network consisted of five museums: **Museo delle Arti Popolari** (p228) in Tolmezzo, **Museo Archeologico** (p236) in Zuglio; **Museo Geologico della Carnia** (p229) in Ampezzo, **Galleria di Arte Moderna Enrico De Cilla** (☑ 0433 77 70 23; Palazzo della Biblioteca; adult/reduced €2.60/1.60; ⊙ 4-6pm Sat, 3-6pm Sun May-Sep, closed Oct, Nov & Feb-Apr) in Treppo Carnico, and **Museo Storico della Grande Guerra** (☑ 0433 77 91 68; ex Scuola Materna; adult/reduced €3/free; ⊙ 9am-noon & 2-6pm Sat & Sun Oct & Jun, 2.30-6.30pm Tue-Fri, 9am- noon & 2.30-6.30pm Sat & Sun Jul & Sep, 9am-noon & 3-7pm Tue-Sun Aug) in Timau.

The network has since expanded, including a number of other small museums and private collections. For information on the latter, contact the **CarniaMusei office** (☑ 0433 48 77 79).

Skiing & Ski Mountaineering
Inexperienced skiers and those more interested in appreciating the landscape than breaking records aren't overlooked in Sauris. Downhill runs include both an easy and intermediate option, equipped with artificial snow and night-time lighting. Given the limited choice, a half-day ski pass should suffice.

Conversely, there's also no shortage of options available for ski mountaineers, with several panoramic routes on Monte Bivera (2474m) and Monte Rucke, running for several kilometres.

There are also two cross-country circuits: a medium-level loop called Untervelt (7.5km) and an easy loop called Plotze (1.5km).

⭐ Festivals & Events

Sauris has a rich heritage of traditions, culture, architecture and gastronomy, and the best time to experience it all is at Carnivale, one of the oldest and most enchanting in Italy.

Carnevale Saurano
FEBRUARY

The Carnival of Sauris is held on the Saturday before Ash Wednesday, with floats, traditional costumes, wooden masks, and an atmospheric, lantern-lit walk through the forest at night. Led by mythical creatures Rölar and the Kheia, festivities include music, dancing, bonfires and mulled wine. Truly magical.

Festa del Prosciutto
JULY

Prosciutto, raw, sweet or smoked, is the star at this food festival, complete with tasting stalls, market, live music and performances.

🛏 Sleeping & Eating

Sauris is famous for its prosciutto and speck, with cured meats a staple at local bars and cafes. Furthermore, many local *salumifici* (cured-meat producers) have designated tasting areas for visitors.

★ Albergo Diffuso
ALBERGO DIFFUSO €€

(☑ 0433 862 21; www.albergodiffusosauris.com; Via Sauris di Sopra 7/g; rates vary; 🔊) A veritable mini district, this 'widespread hotel' occupies a number of lovingly restored timber stables in Sauris. Guests have access to a sauna and wellness centre, not to mention the blissful silence that cloaks the area at night. An ideal place to recharge.

Alla Pace
RESTAURANT, HOTEL €€

(☑ 0433 860 10; www.ristoranteallapace.it; Frazione Sauris di Sotto 92; meals €30; ⊙ noon-2pm & 7.30-9pm, closed Tue & Wed out of season) The Schneider family runs this historic inn from 1804, dishing out local specialities (try the excellent *tris di primi alle erbe*) and mouthwatering desserts. Upstairs, Meublé Schneider offers seven **rooms** (s/d €50/90) furnished in rustic alpine style, as well as a generous breakfast buffet.

🛍 Shopping

Zahre
FOOD & DRINK

(☑ 327 831 45 35; www.zahre.it; ⊙ 10.30am-4.30pm) While Wolf's fame is well deserved (see p230), it's not the only producer of cured meats in the area. At this magnificent store, Zahre (whose own factory is in nearby Ampezzo) peddles a drool-inducing number of local and regional cured meats and cheeses, which gluttons are free to sample.

Tessitura di Sauris
WORKSHOP

(☑ 0433 862 08; www.tessiturasauris.com; Sauris di Sotto; ⊙ 10am-noon & 2-6pm Mon-Fri, 10.30am-noon & 3-5.30pm Sat & Sun in winter, 9am-noon &

DON'T MISS

ORIAS STAVOLI

Carnia and Canal del Ferro are speckled with curious stone buildings called *stavoli*. While you may think they're mountain huts, they're actually traditional animal shelters; the word *stavoli* hails from the Latin *stabulum* (stable). You'll find many scattered throughout the Friulian Alps and Stavoli is also the name of a village near Moggio Udinese, only accessible on foot. The picturesque Val Pesarina claims one of the most photogenic *stavoli* settlements, **Orias**, whose 12 well-preserved stone charmers look straight out of a fairytale. To get here by car, follow the signs from Prato Carnico. Alternatively, tie your shoelaces and hike here from Osais or Pieria.

2-6pm Mon-Fri in summer) Sauris' weaving heritage lives on at this traditional workshop. Wonderfully atmospheric, it's a good place to learn about the craft, which once saw women cultivating the crops and men operating the loom.

ⓘ Information

IAT di Sauris (☑ 0433 860 76; www.sauris.org; Sauris di Sotto 91/a; ⊙ 9am-1pm Mon, 9am-1pm & 2-6pm Thu-Sun year round, also 11am-7pm Wed in high season) Not far from the base of the ski lift, this tourist office is well stocked with information on Sauris, Carnia and surrounds.

Prato Carnico

POP 874 / ELEV 686M

Prato Carnico is one of the main municipalities of the magnificent **Val Pesarina**, a narrow, east–west valley flanked to the north by bare, rugged peaks and to the south by verdant pastures, woods and softer, rounder summits.

The valley's tallest peak is **Monte Clap Grande** (2487m). The municipality itself is made up of 10 tiny hamlets, all built beside the Pesarina stream. The area was once the land of anarchists, who gravitated around the Casa del Popolo. While little remains of that period, the mountain hamlets are nonetheless fascinating.

The main village houses the 19th-century **parish church**, whose treasures include two locally carved altars from the 16th and 18th centuries. The latter features paintings illustrating the *Passion of Christ*.

Heading from Tolmezzo towards Pesariis, you'll pass through **Osais**. Made up of a dozen stone houses, its frescoed **Chiesa di San Leonardo** (☺ on request) stands out for its Austrian-style bell tower.

🛏 Sleeping

Zoncolan   ALBERGO DIFFUSO €€

(☎ 0433 67 80 28; www.albergodiffusozoncolan.it; reception in Via Caduti 2 Maggio, Ovaro; accommodation €60-70, min 3-night stay) With its reception in Ovara, this 'widespread hotel' offers accommodation in beautifully renovated houses in Ovaro and Raveo, many with garden and games for kids. The hotel itself is named after Monte Zoncolan, which casts its shadow over the area.

ℹ Information

Pro Loco Valpesarina (☎ 0433 694 20; www.prolocovalpesarina.it; Frazione Pesariis, Prato Carnico) Tourist office offering detailed information on Prato Carnico and Pesariis. Local information is also available at the Museo dell'Orologeria Pesarina ticket counter.

Pesariis

POP 178 / ELEV 750M

Of the many picturesque villages dotting Carnia, Pesariis vies for the title of most charming. Its unique stone buildings, crowned with steeply pitched, shingled roofs, were meticulously rebuilt after the 1976 earthquake, resulting in a particularly pretty village.

A hamlet of Prato Carnico, Pesariis gets its name from the customs weighbridge once used for the transit of goods between Carnia and Comelico (*pesare* means 'weigh' in Italian). The village's 19th-century church houses an 18th-century marble altar.

◉ Sights

Museo dell'Orologeria Pesarina   MUSEUM

(☎ 0433 690 34; www.carniamusei.org; adult/reduced €3/1.50, adult/reduced guided tour €4/2, free with FVG Card; ☺ 10am-1pm & 2-6pm Sat & Sun May-Jul, Sep & Oct, 10am-1pm & 2-6pm Sun Mar & Apr, 10am-1pm & 2-6pm daily Aug–mid-Sep, 10am-4pm 8, 9, 16 Dec & 22 Dec-6 Jan) Clocks have been made in Pesariis for 400 years, and the Solari factory has been making them for three solid centuries. The famous flip clock was invented here and the factory's timepieces can be found everywhere from train stations to airports.

This museum explores the evolution of timekeeping and clockmaking, from the artisanal to the industrial and highly technological. The venue also forms part of the **Percorso dell'Orologeria Monumentale**, a self-guided walking tour exploring Pesariis' eclectic cache of timepieces.

Casa Bruseschi   MUSEUM

(☎ 338 346 05 95; www.facebook.com/museobruseschi; Frazione Pesariis 37; minimum donation €1; ☺ Sat & Sun Jul, daily Aug & 26 Dec-6 Jan, by appointment) In 1963, Dorina Bruseschi, the last member of one of the most important families in the village, bequeathed her home (next to the church) to the parish, which turned it

---

OFF THE BEATEN TRACK

VAL DEGANO

Home to the region's highest peak (**Mount Croglians**, 2780m), a visit to Val Degano feels a bit like rummaging through Friuli's proverbial attic. Start in **Comeglians** and head to lively **Rigolato** and its pretty timber houses. Further along, a stone's throw from the Austrian border, **Forni Avoltri** is known for its biathlon (ask the guesthouse at the base camp for information).

It's not its only draw, however, with beautiful hiking trails, a 4km cross-country skiing loop (which becomes a roller-skiing track in summer) and a shooting range for .22 air rifles. It also claims the **Museo Etnografico Cemout chi erin** (☎ 0433 722 02; Corso Italia 3; ☺ 5-6.30pm & 8.30-10pm Tue-Sat, 10am-noon & 4-6.30pm Sun Jul–mid-Sep, by appointment rest of year) **FREE**, which shares its address with a war museum.

From Forni Avoltri, the climb to Friuli's rooftop leads to **Collina**, a village surrounded by alpine wilderness. You have two options here: slumber in the village, at a hotel such as **Cogliand** (☎ 0433 720 06; s/d €30/52) or **Volaia** (☎ 0433 720 13; s/d €35/62), or leave the car behind and hike up to a high-altitude *rifugio* (mountain hut) such as **Rifugio Marinelli** (☎ 0433 77 91 77; www.rifugiomarinelli.com; overnight stay/half-board €22/55).

CAMMINO DELLE PIEVI

Somewhere between a pilgrimage and a long hike or pedal, the **Cammino delle Pievi** (☑ 345 913 06 72; www.camminodellepievi.it) is a fantastic way to explore Carnia on foot or by bike. The trail, divided into 20 stages, leads past 10 local churches from Tolmezzo to Zuglio. It's not especially demanding and can be tackled whole or in part. For maps and other information, see the trail website.

into the Museum of the Carnic House. The house is highly regarded for both its architectural and ethnographic value.

 Activities

Cascata di Fuas   HIKING

This easy, 20-minute trail starts east of the village centre and leads to the Cascata di Fuas (Faus Waterfall), hidden away in the forest. It's signposted, but those wanting further information will find it at the Museo dell'Orologeria Pesarina ticket counter. (Don't forget to wear suitable footwear.)

Pesariis to Osais   HIKING

If you're after a pleasant amble, consider visiting the valley's two most atmospheric villages on foot. Just south of Pesariis and Osais, 1.5 km of dirt road connects the centres without too much difficulty.

🛏 Sleeping & Eating

There are four restaurants in Pesariis and all of them are decent. While this guidebook reviews two which offer accommodation, it's also worth mentioning **Ristorante da Sardo** (☑ 0433 690 58; Pesariis 123; meals €20; ☺ 8am-8pm Tue-Sun), a foodie favourite since the 1950s, and **Osteria Ri-Creativa** (☑ 366 128 86 35; Pesariis 124; meals €20; ☺ 10am-2pm & 5-9pm Mon, Thu & Fri, 10am-11pm Sat & Sun), which serves a mix of regional classics, pizzas and specials that might include paella.

★ Inn Pik   INN €€

(☑ 0433 09 67 47; www.osteriainnpik.com; Pesariis 70; apt from €90; ☺ tavern 5-11pm Fri, from 9am Sat & Sun) Cosy, vaulted Inn Pik peddles traditional dishes (meals €25) in a labyrinthine 17th-century abode. Grazers can enjoy tastings in the rustic larder, hung with salami.

Sot la Napa   AGRITURISMO €€

(☑ 0433 69 51 03, 0433 693 79; www.sotlanapa.it; Pesariis 61; s/d €46/70, meals €25; ☺ kitchen noon-2.30pm & 7-10pm daily mid-July–mid-Sep & Christmas holidays, same hours Fri dinner-Mon lunch rest of the year; ☺) This thoughtfully restored 17th-century farmhouse comes with 10 comfy rooms, a farm gate, and a restaurant with a soothing *fogolàr* and strictly seasonal dishes. It's the kind of place you could easily wile away a few days, eating well and snoozing soundly *sot la napa* (under the chimney cap).

Sappada
POP 1317 / ELEV 1250 M

Included among the Borghi Più Belli d'Italia (Italy's Most Beautiful Villages), Sappada stretches out beneath a crown of mountains in charming fashion. Valhalla for snow lovers, it can just as easily be appreciated for its picturesque summertime hikes.

The village's German pedigree is evident in both its dialect and its architecture, from its signature Blockbau houses (composed of interlocking timber beams) to its pair of Nordic-style churches.

Sappada's origins lie in the early Middle Ages: wanting to populate the area, the Patriarch of Aquileia summoned a group of families from Bavaria to settle in the area.

In September 2017, Sappada hit the headlines after the Italian Senate approved the municipality's 2008 request to leave the province of Belluno for that of Udine, therefore leaving Veneto and joining Friuli Venezia Giulia.

A referendum held in 1852 had produced the opposite result, with 100% of local voters (consisting only of the heads of families) choosing to pass from the Austrian-ruled province of Udine to that of Austrian-ruled Belluno. In short, in these parts, borders are a somewhat mercurial concept.

◉ Sights & Activities

A simple stroll through Sappada will lead you to all its points of interest. Start in the district of **Mühlbach**, or Rio dei Molini, whose cascades form the Rio Mühlbach.

Continue to the district of **Cretta** to admire **casa s'Paurn** (no 17), dating from the first half of the 18th century, and **casa Milpar's'Ènders** (no 28). Cascatelle houses the **Piccolo Museo della Grande Guerra** (☑ 0435 46 91 31; ☺ 10am-noon & 4-7pm Tue-Fri Jun-Sep).

The districts of **Cottern** and **Hoffe** are the most interesting part of town, while the names of the subsequent districts – Fontana, Krattern, Soravia – move seamlessly between German and the Venetian and Friulian dialects. Here, **Casa-Museo della Civiltà Contadina** (☑ 0435 46 91 31; www.carniamusei.org; adult/under 14yr €1.50/free; ☺ 5-7pm Mon, Wed & Fri Jun, Jul & Sep, daily Aug) is located in the masterfully restored **Puicher s'Kottlars Haus/Schtol**.

At the eastern end of the village, **Cima Sappada** harbours **Žepòdarkirche**, an 18th-century church dedicated to St Osvaldo, as well as the **Museo Etnografico Maestro Giuseppe Fontana** (☑ 0435 46 91 31; www.carniamusei.org; adult/under 14yr €1.50/free; ☺ 5-7pm Tue, Thu & Sat Jun, Jul & Sep, daily Aug).

From Cima Sappada, a long walking trail leads through an idyllic landscape to the headwaters of the Piave, one of Italy's most important and symbolic rivers. (If you're feeling lazy, you can drive the 7.5km route.)

Once you've ticked off the sights, you can devote yourself to local activities. Winter offers 15km of slopes for **Nordic skiing** and 20km for **alpine skiing**. Kids can get their kicks at **Nevelandia** (www.nevelandia.it; Borgata Bach 92; see website for times and fees or contact the tourist infopoint ☑ 0435 46 91 31), while both young and old can learn to ski at the **Scuola sci Sappada Ski** (www.scuolascisappada.com).

Winter options also include climbing frozen waterfalls, snowshoeing and snow mountaineering. Come summer, hikes, *via ferratas* and less taxing e-bikes await. For more information, see www.sappadadolomiti.com.

🛏 Sleeping & Eating

Hotel Haus Michaela   HOTEL **€€**
(☑ 0435 46 93 77; www.hotelmichaela.com; Borgata Fontana 40; d from €110; 🅿 🛜 ❄ 🛗) This fetching, spacious property features timber-clad rooms with breathtaking views and beautifully detailed bathrooms, not to mention a large outdoor swimming pool, sauna and Jacuzzis (one of which sits by large windows offering an alpine backdrop).

Le Coccole   B&B **€€€**
(☑ 0435 46 99 26; www.bblecoccole.it; Borgata Lerpa 88; d €180; 🅿 🛜 🛗) The name of this B&B roughly translates to 'The Pampering', which might allude to the soothing beauty of the mountains, the pristine white of the snow or the gurgling streams. Then again, it could just as easily refer to the private Jacuzzi, soft sheets and warm sensation of timber beneath your feet. Rooms are contemporary, minimalist yet wonderfully cosy.

Rifugio Sorgenti del Piave   FRIULIAN **€**
(☑ 0435 46 92 60/334 779 91 75; Località Val Sesis; meals €15-20; ☺ 7am-9.30pm; 🍽) You're practically in Austria on the slopes of Monte Peralba, where this mountain-hut restaurant serves generous portions of local, seasonal nosh (head in for dinner if possible). The property also offers 20 beds, making it a convenient base for hiking the area's many trails.

★**Ristorante Mondschein**   FRIULIAN **€€**
(☑ 0435 46 95 85; www.ristorantemondschein.it; Via Bach 96; meals €35-40; ☺ 9am-11pm Wed-Mon) Hospitable, family-run Mondschein serves world-class dishes that fuse alpine produce, local traditions and contemporary finesse. The end result are creations like thyme and porcini risotto with blueberry cream or mountain-pine gnocchi. In winter, crank up the thrill factor by heading in on a snowmobile.

ℹ Information

Sappada Infopoint (☑ 0435 46 91 31, 335 108 59 32; Borgata Bach 9)

Zuglio

POP 561 / ELEV 429M

Located on the right bank of the Bût stream, Zuglio lies on a historically important route linking Italy and Austria. Although lacking blockbuster sights, the **Valle del Bût** has its fair share of local historical attractions, making it worth a quick visit. Known as Iulium

---

TERME DI ARTA

To soothe weary muscles, follow the signs between Zuglio and Sutrio for **Arta Terme** (☑ 0433 92 93 20; www.termediarta.it; Via Nazionale 1; swimming pool adult/child €11/8 Mon-Fri, €13/8 Sat & Sun, treatment prices vary; ☺ see website), a historic thermal spa making good use of the Pudia spring.

Located in the beautiful Palazzo delle Acque, the venue includes a thermal pool and a long list of treatments and services, from facials, massages and mud baths, to manicures, pedicures and hair cuts.

Carnicum in Roman times, the town was also once an episcopal seat ruled by Aquileia. Today, it's the largest archaeological area in Carnia.

History

Around 50 BCE, present-day Zuglio was inhabited by Carnian Gauls. With the arrival of the Romans, who founded a fortified outpost, then a *municipium* and finally a colony, Forum Iulium Carnicum became a city of great strategic importance.

The northernmost colony in Italy, it was a decisive garrison along the Via Iulia Augusta, the road that connected Aquileia to Aguntum in Noricum (located in present-day central Austria).

The colony fulfilled its military function for many centuries; not only was it part of the defence system of the eastern Alpine arc of the Praetura Italiae et Alpium (a territory garrisoned by forts and troops), but during the age of Constantine it was also incorporated into the long-gone Claustra Alpium Iuliarum, imposing defence walls that stretched from Rijeka to Carinthia.

Invasions by the Visigoths in 401, the Huns in 452 and the Lombards in 568, marked the end of Zuglio's Roman era.

The town experienced a rebirth under Aquileian rule, playing the role of episcopal see between the 4th and 8th centuries.

⊙ Sights

The village's very modest Roman relics (which include a mosaic floor) belonged to an ancient basilica, temple and forum. The latter was framed by limestone porticoes, of which only the column bases remain.

Many of the artefacts unearthed, among them amphorae, jugs, epigraphs and statues, are on display at the **Museo Archeologico Iulium Carnicum** (☑ 0433 925 62; www.carnia-musei.org; Via Giulio Cesare 19; adult/reduced €3/2, free with FVG Card; ⊙ 9am-noon Fri, 9am-noon & 3-6pm Sun Oct-Feb, 9am-noon & 3-6pm Fri & Sat Mar-May, 9am-noon Thu & Fri, 9am-1pm & 3-6pm Sat & Sun Jun-Sep), housed inside Palazzo Tommasi Leschiutta.

Also worth a visit is the lofty church of **Pieve di San Pietro in Carnia**, located 4km from the centre of town. Built in 1312 on the site of an older building, it's among the oldest churches in Friuli, with an asymmetrical appearance resulting from numerous nips and tucks.

THE FEARSOME KAISER

'Kaiser' is the nickname given to **Monte Zoncolan** (1750m), a hulking giant rising between Comeglians and Sutrio. The mountain forms part of Italy's world-famous cycling race, the Giro d'Italia, and heading here, one cannot fail to notice the myriad of enthusiasts trying their hand (and glutes) at what is a beast for *grimpeurs* of all abilities.

The mountain is so steep and leg-breaking that cyclists didn't have the proper gears to face it until 1997. Indeed, cycling champion Gilberto Simoni once said that the easiest section of the Zoncolan equals the more challenging sections of the entire Tour de France.

Of course, you can always drive up, from where the views are nothing short of gobsmacking.

While its stone bell tower is crowned by an onion-shaped dome, its interior harbours 18th-century paintings, a Baroque organ and a beautiful Gothic polyptych carved, painted and gilded by Domenico da Tolmezzo.

⭐ Festivals & Events

Bacio delle Croci   MAY
On Ascension Sunday, each of the churches in the valley carries its own cross, adorned with fluttering multicoloured ribbons, to the mother church of Pieve di San Pietro, to re-enact the symbolic 'kissing of the crosses'.

Sutrio

POP 1240 / ELEV 570M

Also nestled in the Valle del Bût, Sutrio casts an enchanting spell with its traditional stone abodes, lovingly rebuilt after the 1976 earthquake.

The village is especially magical at Christmas, when magnificent nativity cribs (including life-sized models) decorate its every corner.

The most famous of these is the **Presepe di Teno** (☑ 0433 77 89 21; Via Roma 60; ⊙ 10am-noon & 4-7pm Jun-Sep & Christmas period, by appointment rest of the year) **FREE**, lovingly created and embellished over 30 years by artisan Gaudenzio Straulino (Teno).

Carnia's proud tradition of woodcarving manifests itself in the wooden statues that adorn Sutrio's Yuletide cribs.

✪ Festivals & Events

Fasin la Mede
JULY

On the last Sunday in July, Monte Zoncolan erupts in a celebration of peasant rituals, from haymaking and dancing in the meadows, to hearty feasting.

Fums Profums Salums
NOVEMBER

While everyone agrees that Carnia produces excellent cured meats, there's less consensus on the best ways to make it. On the third Sunday of November, local families present their own versions and recipes, hoping to impress the judges.

Get busy: you have an entire village to sample!

🛏 Sleeping & Eating

Borgo Soandri
ALBERGO DIFFUSO €

(📞 0433 77 89 21; www.albergodiffuso.org; Via Linussio 1; accommodation €22-31.50; ⊘ reception 9am-noon & 2-6pm Mon-Sat; P 🛜) It's a good idea to book ahead at this *albergo diffuso*, whose collection of holiday apartments are scattered across Sutrio.

The reception is in the heart of the village and its friendly staff are happy to share information on things to do and see in the area. If there's no-one manning reception, ask at Osteria da Alvise.

Osteria da Alvise
FRIULIAN €€

(📞 0433 77 86 92; www.osteriadaalvise.it; Via I Maggio, 5; meals €25-30; ⊘ noon-2.30pm & 7.30-9.30pm Thu-Tue) Upbeat and relaxed, da Alvise serves excellent grub. If you love your game, ask whether the venison stew is cooking.

The *osteria* also has five **rooms** (€30-40 per person including breakfast; ❄ 🛜) if you fancy snoozing overnight.

Alle Trote
FISH €€

(📞 0433 77 83 29; Località Peschiera; meals €30; ⊘ 10am-11pm Wed-Mon) Punters don't come here for the designer fit-out or fancy plating: they come here for the fresh, delicate trout, raised and fished a few steps away. Fried, grilled, or served *involtini* style (rolled up with seasonal vegetables), it makes for a welcome break from *frico* and prosciutto.

The property also includes a **guest house** (d €75; P 🛜).

La Colonie
FRIULIAN €€

(📞 348 441 82 89; Via Enzo Moro; meals €25; ⊘ 11am-11pm Fri-Sun) Above the town, at the beginning of the road leading up Monte Zoncolan, this *osteria* marries Friulian culinary traditions and a minimalist, contemporary sensibility. Side perks include a stunning view and live music.

ℹ Information

PromoTurismo FVG Arta Terme (📞 0433 92 92 90; Via Nazionale 1; ⊘ 8.30am-12.30pm Tue, 8.30am-12.30pm & 2-6pm Wed-Sat, 10am-2pm Sun) and **Pro Loco Sutrio** (📞 0433 77 89 21; www.prolocosutrio.it; Via Linussio 1; ⊘ 9am-noon & 2-6pm Mon-Sat, to 19 Aug & in winter) Both tourist offices offer information on the valley villages and Terme di Arta.

Ravascletto

POP 497 / ELEV 952M

While a mention of this town and the Valcaldain which it lies might leave you indifferent, the peaks and ski runs of nearby Monte Zoncolan (1750m) are likely to grab your attention a little quicker. The infamous 'Kaiser' stage of the Giro d'Italia passes near Ravascletto on the climb up to Ovaro and the village is a popular tourist destination year-round, with winter snow sports and summer hiking and cycling. The best time to visit, however, is in the quieter periods of autumn and spring, when you can better appreciate its natural beauty and the slow pace of mountain life.

🏃 Activities

SUMMER ACTIVITIES

Hiking & Cycling

From Ravascletto and throughout the Valcalda you can hit dozens of hiking trails, mainly to the *malghe* (alpine shepherd's huts). Cyclists are equally spoilt for choice, with several well-signposted trails of varying difficulty scattered throughout the Zoncolan area. The tourist office has detailed maps of all the official routes for both standard and mountain bikes.

Malghe dello Zoncolan
HIKING

(CAI trail 170, from the Ravascletto cable car, elevation gain 1000m, 3hr) In search of the perfect view over the valleys, passing Malga Marmoreana and the Sella to the top of Monte Zoncolan, home to several *rifugi* (mountain huts).

Rifugio Tamai (☑ 371 109 87 78; https://rifugio tamai.it; Monte Zoncolan)

Baita Goles (☑ 346 403 34 00; www.baitagoles. it; Monte Zoncolan)

Rifugio Cocul (☑ 0433 77 52 33; www.cocul.it; Monte Zoncolan)

Baita da Rico (☑ 331 689 23 83; www.baitada rico.it; Località Ciarcenal, Monte Zoncolan)

WINTER ACTIVITIES

Skiing, Snowboarding & Snowshoeing
Most of Monte Zoncolan's slopes face east, which means you'll always ski with the sun in your favour. The cable car reaches 1730m, with huts and refreshments available at high altitude. The mountain's 24 pistes cover all levels; pros will enjoy breathtaking views on the two black runs. Those wanting to practise their jumps can do so at the **Freestyle Snow Park Arena**, while options also include snowshoeing and after-dark snowcat tours. For equipment rental try **Noleggio Sci Morassi** (☑ 0433 662 33, info@morassi sport.it; www.morassisport.it; Via L. De Infanti 5/a; ⊙ 8am-7pm).

🐾 Courses

Scuola Italiana Sci Carnia (☑ 0433 660 43; www.scuolascicarniazoncolan.it; individual lessons €40-43 per hr) Ski school.

Ski Academy Zoncolan (☑ 366 100 55 26; www.skiacademyzoncolan.it; Via Roma, 9, Sutrio) Individual & group lesson packages available, see website.

🛏 Sleeping & Eating

Albergo Pace Alpina   HOTEL & CAMPING €/€€
(☑ 0433 660 18; www.pacealpina.it; Via Valcada 13; r with breakfast per person €37, site €9, adult/reduced €7/5.50, meals €24; ⊙ noon-3pm & 7-9.30pm; 🅿 🛜) 🍴 Depending on the season, the Alpine-style, timber rooms at this hotel, steps away from the ski lifts, overlook ski slopes or grassy meadows.

Adorned with copper pots and a summertime verandah, the welcoming restaurant is a fine spot to tuck into *cjarsons*, goulash and *frico*, or pizza.

Located behind the building, the tranquil **Zoncolan campground** is clean and orderly and suitable for camper vans (which will require a minimum two-night stay). On-site facilities here include a bike workshop, and the entire complex uses renewable energy sources.

❶ Information

Infopoint Zoncolan–Ravascletto (☑ 0433 660 33; www.turismofvg.it; Via Monte Zoncolan 84) Offers information on all the area's tourist facilities.

JULIAN PREALPS

A prelude to the higher peaks of the Julian Alps, the Julian Prealps rise between the Tagliamento and Isonzo Rivers. Bookended by Carnia to the west and Gorizia Collio to the east, the area is as unique for its culture as it is for its fauna and flora. Closed, remote valleys have shaped one-of-a-kind customs, crafts and traditions, while the area's geological history has left its own idiosyncratic legacies, visible along the Via degli Antichi Ghiacciai.

In order to protect its rich heritage and natural beauty, the **Parco Naturale Regionale delle Prealpi Giulie** (☑ 0433 535 34; www. parcoprealpi giulie.it; Prato di Resia) was established in 1996. The park is crossed by dozens of well-maintained, user-friendly trails, safely leading to the most secluded and spectacular corners of the Julian Prealps. You'll even find a trail called 'Per Tutti' (For All), suitable for both children and elderly explorers.

❶ Information

Parco Naturale Regionale delle Prealpi Giulie Visitor Centre (☑ 0433 535 34; www.parcopreal pigiulie.it; Piazza Tiglio 3, Prato di Resia; ⊙ 9am-1pm & 2-5pm Mon-Fri, daily in summer) The centre includes an **exhibition** (adult/reduced €2/1) highlighting the park's trails, whose themes range from geology to biodiversity and sustainability.

❶ Getting There & Away

BUS
TPL FVG (☑ 800 05 20 40, mobile 040 971 23 43; https://tplfvg.it) Bus 193, which from Tolmezzo (€4.25) passes through Resiutta (€1.75) and Prato di Resia (€1.55), terminates in Stolvizza (20min, four daily).

CAR & MOTORCYLE
To reach Resia and Resiutta from the A23, exit at Gemona or Carnia and continue on the SS13.

Val Resia

RESIA: POP 936 / ELEV 492M
In this part of Europe, it's hard to find a place that feels more remote than the Val Resia. Wild, secluded and home to unique flora and fauna, the valley is traversed by

the Resia stream, which descends from the **Monte Canin** (2587m) on its journey towards the Fella.

The area is famous for its eponymous sweet garlic, which you can buy from Slow Food producers (www.slowfood.it) or taste at **Bar All'Arrivo** (☑339 225 74 03; Via Udine 31, Località Stolvizza; ⊙8am-midnight Fri-Wed in summer, closed lunch in winter).

Practically closed off from the rest of the region, the valley has developed its own traditions, music and dances, as well as a semi-itinerant lifestyle. Indeed, the valley is home to a community with Slavic roots, whose dialect, Resian, is related to Slovene. (Not that you'd call it a dialect in these parts; linguistic identity is felt strongly among the locals, who consider Resian a proper language.)

Its origins are said to lie in the 7th century, when Slavic tribes settled in the area. Over time, the valley's isolation created a linguistic enclave, allowing Resian to develop independently. Today, the valley's bilingual signs are in Italian and Resian, a constant reminder of Val Resia's wonderful peculiarity.

Resia is fiercely parochial in both its costumes and customs, with each of its six hamlets speaking a different shade of Resian.

Two hamlets that particularly stand out are Prato di Resia, home to the **Parco Naturale Regionale delle Prealpi Giulie visitor centre** (⊙9am-1pm & 2-5pm Mon-Fri, daily in summer) and Coritis, the starting point for many hiking trails.

Among Val Resia's unique traditions is the *arrontino,* a roaming artisan grinder (usually a traveller or emigrant) who sharpened blades at home in the valley and further way in Austria, Hungary and beyond.

In Stolvizza, the **Museo dell'Arrotino** (☑0433 535 54, 333 125 32 99; www.arrotinivalresia.it, for reservations info@arrotinivalresia.it; Località Stolvizza, Via Monte Sart 12/a; admission €2.50; ⊙10am-1pm & 2-4pm Wed-Sun) explores the itinerant aspect of the trade, including the clever use of bicycles to power the grinder. Once handed down from father to son, the ancient craft continues today, with about 20 *arrontini* active in the valley.

🏃 Activities

You haven't truly seen the Val Resia without a hike. Big on wow factor, trails include less arduous options for those who prefer leisure over endurance.

Via degli Antichi Ghiacciai HIKING
(elevation gain 650m, 5hr 30min) Suitable for most fitness levels, this trail follows quiet, sealed roads to natural wonders that speak of the area's geological history.

Monte Guarda TREKKING
(CAI trail 741, elevation gain 1289m, 8hr) A challenging, undulating route stretching almost 16km. The trail starts from the Sella Carnizza pass (1086m), passing Malga Nischie and Malga Coot before reaching the summit of Monte Guarda (1720m).

Fontanone Barman HIKING
(CAI trail 703, elevation gain 850m, 3hr) Beyond the town of Lischiazze, on your left, is a large car park. From it, a trail leads up the valley of the Rio Nero. Once you enter the beech grove, leave the path and follow the sound of water to a 70m-high waterfall, whose crystalline waters form an enchanting emerald lake.

🎭 Festivals & Events

Carnevale Resiano FEBRUARY
(Püst; www.resianet.org/site) Held in the hamlet of San Giorgio/Bila from Fat Thursday (the Thursday before Lent) to Ash Wednesday, this is a highlight of the Resian calendar, with five days of fun and folklore that includes the traditional *resiana* dance and typical musical instruments like the *cïtira* and *bünkula.*

Expect to see hundreds of locals here donning hats, curious-looking local masks and white costumes adorned with colourful ribbons.

ℹ️ Information

Pro Loco Val Resia (☑0433 533 53; www.resianet.org; Via Prato 7/a, San Giorgio di Resia) Tourist office.

Resiutta

POP 275 / ELEV 316M

Resiutta sits in the valley of the **Canal del Ferro**, right at the entrance to the Val Resia. Here, the northern slopes of **Monte Plauris** (1958m) have been mined intensely since the end of the 19th century.

At the **Mostra della Miniera del Resartico** (☑0433 55 02 41; www.parcoprealpigiulie.it; Via Roma 32; ⊙9am-1pm & 2-5pm Sat & Sun Jun, Jul & Sep, 9am-1pm & 2-5pm Tue-Sun Aug) **FREE**, you can learn about the less-than-ideal life of miners of the past and step inside a reconstructed mining tunnel.

Not far from the mine is the **Galleria Ghiacciaia di Resiutta** (📞 0433 55 02 41; Via Udine; admission €1; same hrs as Mostra della Miniera del Resartico), excavated in 1844 to store ice used to refrigerate beer. Behind the project was a group of Carinthian entrepreneurs, who decided to utilise the waters of the Resia to produce low fermentation beer (hence the need for ice).

At the brewery itself, also located in Resiutta, the famous Dormisch beer was born in 1881.

Ten years later, with the creation of the Ledra canal in Udine, production was moved to the city and, in the 1950s, taken over by Peroni. The cavernous icebox and Resiutta factory, abandoned at the end of the 19th century, are all that remain of Dormisch's glorious past.

Not that beer lovers need to fret: since 2001, the village has been producing Birra di Resiutta, a craft brew you can savour at **Al Buon Arrivo** (📞 0433 512 07; Viale Udine 25; half a chicken with potatoes €8.30; ⊙ 11am-11.15pm Tue-Sun, daily Jul & Aug).

The brewery-pub is also known for its rotisserie chicken, which feeds famished motorists, truckers and the throng of cyclists on the Alpe Adria cycling route.

JULIAN ALPS

The Julian Alps constitute Italy's most easterly mountain range, though much of it is actually located in neighbouring Slovenia.

The chain includes the massifs of Monte Santo di Lussari, Mangart, **Jôf di Montasio** (2755m, the tallest peak on the Italian side and the second tallest overall), Jôf Fuart and Monte Canin.

After the Passo del Predil, the Alps enter Slovenian territory where the highest peak, **Triglav**, soars 2864m above sea level.

Compared to the nearby Carnic Alps, the Julian Alps are rockier and more rugged, with four small glaciers to boot: one on Triglav, two on Jôf di Montasio and one on Monte Canin.

The Italian section of the chain is roughly divided in two by the majestic **Valcanale**, a valley of villages and dense forests (p241) that starts in Pontebba and continues through to Malborghetto Valbruna and Camporosso in Valcanale. Here, the Hotel Spartiacque marks the watershed separating the catchment areas of the Danube and Po rivers.

Further east, towards Slovenia, lies Tarvisio, the largest tourist hub in the area.

Julian Alps

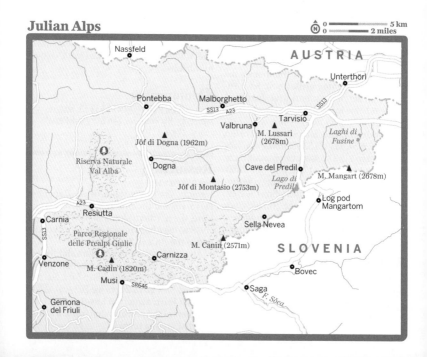

Beyond it, the Valcanale crosses the Valle di Rio del Lago before finally reaching Fusine Valromana and its lakes (p244).

The Valle di Rio del Lago leads south to Sella Nevea, where the Val Raccolana begins and rejoins the Prealps.

That the Julian Alps recall the name of one of ancient Rome's oldest patrician clans, the *gens* Julia, is no coincidence. Between 18 and 12 BCE, the area fell under Roman administration, and during the following two centuries, the influence of these Romanised mountains reached the city of Emona (modern day Ljubljana).

When the Roman Empire fell, so too did the region's political unity. Consequently, the region became a political border zone, first between the Habsburg and Venetian dominions and later between Europe's western and eastern blocs.

Culturally, the Julian Alps marked the confluence of the Latin, Germanic and Southern Slavic worlds, and to this day, the area remains an important area of exchange between central Europe, the Mediterranean and the Balkans.

ℹ️ Getting There & Away

BUS

TPL FVG (☑ 800 05 20 40, mobile 040 971 23 43; https://tplfvg.it) manages bus services from Udine to Tarvisio via Malborghetto Valbruna (bus 200, €10.20; 90min to 2hr, 8 trips between 7am & 8pm) and Chiusaforte, from where you can reach Sella Nevea (bus 191, €2.25).

CAR & MOTORCYLE

Reaching Tarvisio is a cinch: the town is connected to Udine by the A23, which runs through the entire Valcanale, and is a 15-minute drive from the motorway exit.

Sella Nevea and Fusina Valromana are located along the panoramic SS54.

Malborghetto Valbruna

This village was known as Bonborghetto (Good Hamlet) before Habsburg conflicts, a period of economic and social crisis, and repeated Venetian raids led to a name tweak (Malborghetto means 'Bad Hamlet'). That said, it's not certain whether its original medieval name reflected favourable conditions. It may in fact hail from Bamberghetto, a nod to the bishops of Bamberg who ruled the entire Valcanale.

The village is a good base for summer and winter activities, though its strongpoint is the 16th-century **Palazzo Veneziano**, home to the **Museo Etnografico** (☑ 0428 649 70; Via Bamberga 52; www.canaldelferro-valcanale.uti fvg.it; adult/reduced €3/1.50; ⊙ 10.30am-12.30pm & 3-6pm Tue-Sun). The museum includes an interesting section on the Foresta di Tarvisio; don't miss the 400-year-old **lime tree** in the courtyard.

Directly opposite the *palazzo* is the **parish church**. Established in the 15th century and rebuilt in the early 19th century, it's dedicated to the Visitation of the Virgin Mary and to St Anthony.

Note the lunette above the side portal, decorated with a 15th-century fresco of the Nursing Madonna surrounded by fluttering angels.

The client who commissioned the work makes a cameo in the bottom left corner.

You won't have trouble finding directions for **Animalborghetto**, an easy trail that winds its way through the village and its surrounds. The trail introduces children to the world of the forest and its creatures.

Malborghetto Valbruna's westernmost hamlet is Bagni di Lusnizza, famous for the sulphurous waters of the Rio Zolfo.

A PRECIOUS POCKET OF GREEN

A living, breathing organism lies at the gates of Tarvisio. Ancient and enormous, the **Foresta di Tarvisio** is a 24,000-hectare wood that constitutes the largest state-owned forest in Italy outside a designated nature park. It's also one of the country's most precious natural areas, with one of the most complete fauna systems in the Alps.

The forest supplies 15,000 cubic metres of timber annually to the valley's inhabitants, who are entitled to it according to mountain customs. Its high-quality spruce is particularly valuable and used to make musical instruments, hence its name, *abete di risonanza* (resonance fir).

🛏 Sleeping & Eating

★ Malga Priu
TREEHOUSES €€€

(☑ 331 102 59 89; Località Ugovizza; overnight stay, dinner & breakfast €260; ☺ Fri-Sun May, Jun & Sep, daily Jul & Aug) Picture two little abodes shaped like pine cones and nestled in the canopy of a tree.

Then imagine each with mod cons and located on the edge of the forest, steps away from a *malga* (mountain hut), in one of the region's most beautiful settings. This is exactly what awaits at Malga Priu.

To reach it, follow Via Uque from Ugovizza and leave your car at car park no 2. From here, the property is a 1.5km walk. If it's raining or you're having trouble, the managers can pick you up by car.

Tarvisio

POP 4113 / ELEV 732M

Besides being the most important mountain resort in Friuli Venezia Giulia, Tarvisio is also the closest Italian town to Austria (not to mention a stone's throw from Slovenia). Given this, it's not surprising that the town serves up a (somewhat stereotyped) concentration of Italy, from *limoncello*-packed shop windows to big bowls of *impepate di cozze* (peppered mussels).

Nonetheless, a Habsburg air lingers in this long, sinuous town, whose restaurants, shops and large hotels are mainly concentrated on its two main streets: Via Roma and Via Vittorio Veneto. And while it may be popular year round for its beautiful surroundings, the town centre itself is also worth a visit.

Tarvisio's most popular and worthy attraction is the **Chiesa Fortificata di San Pietro e Paolo** (☑ 0428 23 95; ☺ sunrise-sunset), built in 1445 and located in the centre of town.

Surrounded by defensive walls, it incorporates two medieval towers, one hexagonal and one circular, believed to date from the 12th century. The fortified complex served as a shelter for locals during the highly destructive Ottoman raids of 1478 to 1492. Inside the church you'll find 16th-century frescoes along the aisles and in the apse.

Walk or cycle up to the top of Boscoverde to ponder the Austrian victory that drove out the French army in 1809. Crowning the low hill is an imposing monument honouring the Austrian rifleman of the Napoleonic wars. Not far from here, a path leads to the paradisal **Orrido dello Slizza**, a lush, verdant canyon formed by the emerald waters of the Slizza stream.

At a certain point along the canyon's route you'll stumble upon the iron bridge of the old Tarvisio–Ljubljana railway line, abandoned many years ago. Built in around 1870 and considered a masterpiece of engineering, the bridge soars 63m above the water and can be crossed on foot.

🏃 Activities

SUMMER ACTIVITIES

The Tarvisian summer is packed with events and activities. Contact any of the **TurismoFVG tourist offices** (www.turismofvg.it) for information on tandem paragliding and hang-gliding flights from Monte Lussari.

Hiking

Walk to Monte Borgo
HIKING

A two-hour, muscle-warming walk around Tarvisio, from Via delle Pinete to the slopes of Monte Borgo.

Somdogna
HIKING

(CAI trail 611, from Malga Saisera to Sella Somdogna, 2hr) Leading to the Rifugio Grego (1389m), this nature trail passes glacial lakes, woods and sites associated with WWI.

Tarvisio-Rifugio Zacchi
ALPE ADRIA TRAIL

(AAT Trail T5, 18.8km, 6hr) Part of the Alpe Adria Trail, this route winds from Tarvisio to the

---

DON'T MISS

FROM THE ALPS TO THE ADRIATIC

Spanning three countries, 43 stages and 750km, the **Alpe Adria Trail** (http://alpe-adria -trail.com) starts in Carinthia, Austria, crosses the Hohe Tauern National Park and descends through Slovenia to the Italian coastal town of Muggia, crossing the Julian Alps, Valli del Natisone and Carso en route. The entire trail is well managed and marked, and you can tackle its entire length or any number of its 20km-long stages; stage T4 passes through Tarvisio. The two-wheeler version of the Alpe Adria Trail is the **Ciclovia Alpe Adria** (www. alpe-adria-radweg.com). Running from Grado to Salzburg, Austria, the partly sealed cycling trail also passes through the Tarvisio area.

PILGRIMAGE TO THE MOUNTAIN

One of Tarvisio's main attractions, **Monte Lussari** (1789m) is accessible via **gondola lift** (☑ 0428 65 39 15; round trip adult/reduced €14/11.50, free with FVG Card; ☺ 9am-4pm Dec-Easter Mon, 9am-5.30pm Mon-Sat, 8.30am-6.15pm Sun Jun-Sep, to 11pm Aug) or, in summer, by hiking through the forest on the Sentiero del Pellegrino. On the summit, the starting point for fantastic hikes and dizzying ski runs, you can visit the **santuario mariano** (Marian sanctuary; ☑ 0428 630 57; www.lussari.eu; ☺ same times as cable car), around which the village has developed. Especially beautiful in the snow, the sanctuary's origins lie in the 14th century. Destroyed several times by war and inclement weather, the current structure was built in the early 20th century and restored in 2000. As a pilgrimage site for believers from three nations (Italy, Austria and Slovenia), the church has become a symbol of fellowship, with highly evocative masses celebrated in German, Slovenian and Italian. The village itself, a storybook tableau of alpine abodes and deep-green firs, has places to eat and sleep (p244) if you fancy lingering on the mountaintop.

Rifugio Zacchi (Zacchi Refuge), passing through the Laghi di Fusine (Fusine Lakes).

Saisera Wild Track   HIKING
Fifteen kilometres of undemanding trails that cross woods and pockets of pristine nature to the foot of Jôf di Montasio.

Rifugi (Mountain Huts)
Locanda al Convento (☑ 338 178 11 33; www.refugealconvento.it; Località Monte Lussari 184; half-board adult/teen/child €85/59.50/42.50) More hotel than stock-standard mountain hut.

Mount Lussari (☑ 0428 632 42; www.rifugioalpinomontelussari.it; Località Monte Lussari 17; B&B/half-board per person €40/50; ☺ late Nov-Easter Mon & late May-early Oct)

Rifugio Zacchi (☑ 0428 78 60 64; www.rifugiozacchi.it; Località Conca delle Panze; r €24, breakfast €8, half-board per person €35-50, full-board per person €45-60; ☺ by reservation on weekends)

Rifugio Pellarini (☑ 349 280 92 82; www.facebook.com/RifugioPellariniTarvisio; Località Carnizza di Camporosso; B&B/half-board per person €26/39)

WINTER ACTIVITIES
Skiing, Ski Mountaineering & Snowshoeing
When the Tarvisio ski slopes open annually, professional mountain guides offer a string of activities to choose from. In addition to **downhill skiing** (daily ski pass adult/senior/child €35/31/26), **cross-country skiing** and **ski mountaineering** (particularly popular in Tarvisio), you can snowshoe day or night (especially beautiful at midnight) or take a horse-drawn sleigh ride.

For details, contact the Tarvisio Infopoint (p245) as soon as you arrive in town. For equipment rental, contact:

Baldan Sport (☑ 0428 22 39; www.baldansport.com; Via Roma 59; ☺ 9.30am-1pm & 3-7pm Tue-Sat, 10.30am-1pm & 3.30-7pm Sun)

Lussari Sport (☑ 0428 630 34; www.lussari.com; Via Alpi Giulie 44; ☺ 9.30am-1pm & 3.30-7.30pm Mon-Sat, 10am-1pm & 4-7pm Sun)

Snow Parks
Gold Snow Park   SNOW PARK
(☑ 0428 65 39 15; www.turismofvg.it; Via Priesnig 34) Snowboarders, take note: you'll find three different rails, six boxes and five kickers of different sizes at this snow park.

If you're scratching your head, don't fret: snowboarding rookies are welcome here too.

Area Snow & Fun   SNOW PARK
(Piana dell'Angelo; admission €5; ☺ 10am-4pm Tue-Sun) A 30,000-square-metre adventure snow park for little ones in Piana dell'Angelo, halfway between Tarvisio and Camporosso.

YEAR ROUND
Palaghiaccio Pontebba   ICE SKATING
(☑ 0428 905 26; www.ghiacciopontebba.it; Via Mazzini, Pontebba; adult/reduced €7/6, with skate rental adult/reduced €11/9, free with FVG Card; ☺ varies) Modern, multipurpose skating and ice-hockey rink.

↻ Courses
Ski Schools
Scuola Italiana Sci Evolution 3 Lands (☑ 0428 64 41 91, 366 520 99 07; www.e3l.ski; Piazzale Nuova Priesnig; individual lessons per hr from €35)

Scuola Sci di fondo Camporosso (☎ 0428 404 74; www.lussari.com; Via Alpi Giulie; contact school for rates)

Scuola Sci di fondo Valcanale (☎ 0428 631 43; Via Saisera, Valbruna; lessons weekdays/weekends €35/40, €10 for each additional person)

✦ Festivals & Events

No Borders Music Festival   JULY-AUGUST (www.nobordersmusicfestival.com) Music as a cultural expression capable of breaking down linguistic, ethnic and political borders is at the heart of this summer festival, which aptly crosses numerous musical genres, from rock to classical.

Krampus   DECEMBER
On 5 December, Tarvisio's procession for St Nicholas is enlivened by the *krampus,* half-human, half-goat creatures who stalk through the crowd looking for naughty children. Tempering their raids is St Nicholas,

who distributes sweets to good children and coal to the brats.

🛏 Sleeping & Eating

There is no shortage of accommodation in Tarvisio, which is just as well given the high number of visitors, especially in winter. Options range from self-contained apartments and guesthouses (ideal for longer stays), to B&Bs and all manner of hotels, some of which have highly regarded restaurants. Note that many of the larger hotels require a minimum stay of three or seven nights.

Those after solitude are better off choosing a room or apartment in one of the cottages or mountain chalets on the edge of town (or just outside it).

Alternatively, if you fancy slumbering at high altitude, consider crashing at one of the *rifugi* (mountain huts) in Sella Nevea. For accommodation rates, availability and bookings, drop by the tourist office.

OFF THE BEATEN TRACK

LAKES, MINES, BORDERS

Heading north towards the Austrian border, the SS54 unloads its final curiosities. Among these is the **Miniera di Raibl – Cave del Predil** (Parco Internazionale Geominerario del Raibl; ☎ 0428 87 65 36; www.museitarvisio.it; Via Miniere, ticket office in Largo Mazzini 7, Cave del Predil; adult/reduced €8/6, free under 6yr & with FVG Card; ⊙ 10am-1pm & 3-6pm May-Sep, 10.30am-12.30pm & 2.30-5.30pm Sat & Sun Oct-Apr), once an important lead and zinc mine established under Austro-Hungarian rule. Management of the mine became tricky when the Habsburg dominions were carved up between Italy, Austria and Yugoslavia: suddenly the 120km of tunnels, arranged over 19 levels, found themselves astride the border. The mine and miners continued to belong to the three nations, with a Guardia di Finanza (Financial Police) post deep underground to control unauthorised attempts by Yugoslavian workers to flee. In 1990, the old mine became the Raibl International Geomining Park, which can be partially explored on foot and miniature railway. Don't forget to bring a warm jacket; it's bone-chillingly cold in the mine.

Further north on the SS54 are the glacial **Laghi di Fusine (Fusine Lakes)**. Consisting of a Lago Superiore (Upper Lake), Lago Inferiore (Lower Lake) and Laghi Piccoli (Small Lakes), the lakes occupy a basin in the Valcanale on the slopes of **Mangart** (2677m). This is one of the coldest areas of Italy and in winter the lakes freeze and are covered in snow. In summer, snow melted, the waters are dazzlingly crystalline. You can explore the lakes on the **Giro dei due Laghi**, a trail that connects the bodies of water and leads to the Rifugio Zacchi (p242; follow the signs).

The area is also famous for its **Scuola Internazionale di Mushing** (☎ 348 268 58 67, 348 374 51 19, 0428 65 13 31; www.ararad.net; Via Verdi 21, Fusine in Valromana). The first mushing school to open in Italy, it offers mere mortals the exhilarating thrill of steering a dog sled; the experience begins with a short technical introduction and within an hour you'll find yourself tightening the reins and tearing between the mountains.

Day wrapped up, recharge at **Edelweiss** (☎ 0428 610 50; www.albergo-edelweiss.com; Via dei Laghi 8; d €90, half-board/full-board per person €60/70; P 🛜), whose rooms overlook emerald waters. If you can't stay overnight or don't have time for lunch, at least consider a drink on the lakeside terrace.

★ **Valle Verde** HOTEL, RESTAURANT €€
(📞0428 23 42; www.hotelvalleverde.com; Via Priesnig 48; s from €50, d €120; 🅿✳🛜🏊) Gianni de Cilla is the soul of this place, overseeing everything from the bike hire to the fit-out of the spacious, comfy rooms. The real apple of his eye, however, is the hotel restaurant, considered one of the village's top dining spots for both its revamped local classics and impressive wine list (passionately compiled by Gianni himself).

Foresta di Tarvisio ALBERGO DIFFUSO €€
(📞0428 30 03; www.leresidenzedirutte.it; Località Rutte Piccolo 8; rates vary; ⏱reception 9.30am-12.30pm) A 'widespread hotel' with 39 rooms and 81 beds dispersed across the town. Reception is located at the address listed above.

Hotel Edelhof HOTEL, RESTAURANT €€
(📞0428 400 81; www.hoteledelhof.it; Via Armando Diaz 13; s €75-92, d per person €52-72, half-board €69-89; 🅿🛜) Set in a traditional alpine building on the edge of the forest, the Edelhof has many rooms; warm, welcoming interiors; and a beautiful spa. The highly regarded inhouse **restaurant** (meals €25-35) specialises in game.

Hotel Trieste HOTEL, RESTAURANT €€
(📞0428 22 14; www.ristorantetrieste.it; Via Dante 44; s/d/t/q € 55/80/100/120; 🅿🛜) A clean, restrained hotel at the eastern entrance to the town. Its 25 simple rooms (two of which cater for guests with limited mobility) feature immaculately clean linen, while hotel facilities include a small but pleasant spa and a free shuttle to the station and ski lifts.

The **restaurant** (meals €25; ⏱noon-9.30pm) serves local cuisine, but by virtue of the owners' origins also offers delicious pizzas and seafood dishes. Sauté of mussels with mountain vista, anyone?

Rosengarten B&B €€
(📞0428 66 88 32; www.rosengartentarvisio.com; Via Bamberg 3; d/q € 120/200; 🅿✳🛜🏊) Of the many B&Bs along the route to the Laghi di Fusine, this is one of the newest. Pamper yourself in the spa, kick back on a deckchair in the garden, and start the following day right with the appetising breakfast. Room types vary, with some rather spacious options.

Miramonti FRIULIAN €€
(📞0428 20 50/347 543 03 40; Via Dante 73; meals €60, tasting menu €25-55; ⏱7am-11pm Mon-Sat) What was (and in part still is) the old village bar has evolved into a Tarvisian fine-dining hotspot. Savour next-level alpine dishes made with local produce, from wild herbs and mushrooms, to lichen.

Hladik FRIULIAN €€
(📞0428 66 83 43; Via Romana 33; meals €25-30; ⏱11am-2pm & 5.30-9pm Wed-Sat) A small restaurant with only 25 covers, Hladik serves handsomely presented Friulian cuisine in a homely, vaulted space filled with locals (a rarity in Tarvisio). The soups, prepared by the owner's wife, are excellent, and the wine list is long. Don't miss it.

🛍 Shopping

Dawit FOOD, CRAFTS
(📞0428 630 12; www.dawit.it; Via Alpi Giulie 30; ⏱6am-8pm Mon-Sat, to 6pm Sun; closed Mon afternoon in low season) What started out as a bar in the 1950s is now this engaging shop, peddling locally made edibles as well as more-or-less authentic handicrafts. True to its origins, it still serves *vino,* cheese and other grazing options to enjoy onsite.

ℹ Information

MEDICAL SERVICES

Tarvisio Outpatient Clinic (📞0428 29 31; Via Vittorio Veneto 74)

PHARMACIES

Spaliviero (📞0428 20 46; Via Roma 18, Tarvisio; ⏱9am-12.30pm & 3-7pm Mon-Sat)

TOURIST INFORMATION

Tarvisio Infopoint (📞0428 21 35; www.turismofvg.it; Via Roma 14; ⏱9am-1pm & 3-7pm daily winter & summer, 8.30am-12.30pm & 2-6pm Mon-Sat, 8.30am-12.30pm Sun spring & autumn) Tarvisio's tourist office peddles information about the town, Valcanale and surrounds, as well as road conditions.

Sella Nevea

ELEV 1190M

Despite its relatively low elevation, the hamlet of Sella Nevea isn't short of winter snow. This is due to its location in a basin between Monte Canin (2587m) and the Jôf di Montasio, which is exposed to the cold winds from Eastern Europe. The hamlet is reached from Piazzale Slovenia, from where ski lifts reach the slopes and *rifugi* (mountain huts).

In the winter, Sella Nevea sits in the heart of the downhill ski runs, which beckon alpine skiers and snowboarders.

Cross-country skiers, on the other hand, hit the area's Pista del Camet.

In summer, the hamlet is the starting point for hikes into lush, flower-strewn valleys. A few kilometres from Sella Nevea, a trail leads around beautiful **Lago del Predil**, surrounded by woods and small sand-and-pebble inlets. Frozen in winter, the lake draws canoers and windsurfers in the summer.

Botany fans shouldn't miss the **Sentiero Botanico del Bila Peč** (1600m, elevation gain 150m, 1hr); starting from the Rifugio Gilberti, the trail leads towards Monte Canin, home to many endemic plant species. Heavy snowfall combined with the valley's strong solar radiation has created a very unique natural habitat combining cliffs, scree, grasslands, moors and valleys.

The trail itself is divided into 21 flora stops, four panoramic stops and five habitat areas, with information panels along the way.

If you're lucky you might spot the famous alpine poppy, Traunfellner's buttercup, alpine flax or yellow bonarota.

For a trail brochure with detailed map, stop by the visitor centre.

🛏 Sleeping

There's no better way to enjoy Sella Nevea's wild beauty than by sleeping in a *rifugio* (mountain hut). While blankets are provided, guests are obliged to bring a sleeping bag to slumber in.

Celso Gilberti   MOUNTAIN HUT €

(☑0433 540 15; www.facebook.com/irenepittino; Via Friuli 1, Località Conca Prevala; bed from €40; ⊘mid-Dec–Apr & mid-Jun–Sep) A super-cosy mountain hut in the Monte Canin group, located a stone's throw from the ski fields and lifts. There are six double rooms and a large 10-person room, and the hut serves excellent local dishes and desserts. It also often hosts tastings of Friulian cured meats and wines, as well as themed parties that attract punters from across the valley.

Giacomo di Brazza   MOUNTAIN HUT €

(☑340 630 50 34, 346 228 00 72; www.facebook.com/rifugiodibrazza; Montasio plateau; beds starting from €10-45; ⊘ Jun-Oct) A 30-minute walk from the Altopiano del Montasio car park, this hilltop hut offers a splendid view from its terrace.

Understand Friuli Venezia Giulia

HISTORY 248

At the crossroads of two regions, this borderland has long been a cultural melting pot, witnessing centuries of war, heroic deeds, fraternity and division.

ARTS & LITERATURE.........................261

Friuli Venezia Giulia has drawn lifeblood from its rich cultural tapestry to produce a surprising and varied artistic heritage in every sphere, from music and literature to architecture.

FOOD & WINE 274

In the seemingly endless repertoire of regional food and wine specialities, one thing remains constant: excellence.

ENVIRONMENT.............................283

Friuli Venezia Giulia's rich biodiversity manifests itself in a variety of landscapes, harbouring a wealth of indigenous flora and fauna.

History

The history of Friuli and the history of Venezia Giulia run almost parallel, finally meeting up in recent times. From Trieste to the Carnic Alps, from Aquileia to Cividale, the region's backstory is that of a borderland that has witnessed the rise and fall of empires, the redrawing of borders, opposing blocs, lacerating tensions and sensational recoveries. Friuli echoes Venetian elegance, Venezia Giulia the memory of the Habsburgs and the Belle Époque. Together, their inhabitants reflect the meeting of people from the Balkans, Central Europe and the sea.

Prehistoric Traces

In prehistoric times, the land now known as Friuli Venezia Giulia was traversed by nomadic hunter-gatherers. Few traces of this period remain. North of Trieste, in Visogliano, unearthed human bones and tools have been dated back to the Lower Palaeolithic period, some 400,000 years ago.

In 1994, a school group on a field trip to Casera Casavento in the Parco delle Dolomiti Friulane accidentally discovered the footprints of a theropod, a dinosaur that roamed the region more than 200 million years ago.

Cave settlements appeared on the Karst plateau around 7000 years ago, while from 5000 BCE, in the Neolithic age, farming villages began springing up. Archaeological finds also attest to intensive trade with the Po Valley and the eastern shore of the Adriatic. These groups built complex pile-dwelling settlements, such as that of Palù sul Livenza.

Starting from the Middle Bronze Age (around 1500 BCE), fortified villages known as *castellieri* were established in the region, particularly in Istria. Often built on higher ground, rendering them more easily defensible, these *castellieri* consisted of one or more concentric defensive walls harbouring small settlements. Over the centuries, many *castellieri* were converted into Roman settlements.

The Celts & the Romans

The first Celtic tribes, arriving from Asia, settled in the Danube region in the second millennium BCE before expanding into France, the Iberian Peninsula and the British Isles from the 8th century CE. While the Celts were a collection of peoples with the same linguistic and cultural heritage, they lacked political unity. Nevertheless, they were able to

TIMELINE	5000 BCE	1500–1000 BCE
	The first organised groups of people practising agriculture emerge.	The territory of present-day Friuli is populated by Paleovenetian and Illyrian tribes. *Castellieri* begin to dot the land.

unite against common enemies, as the Gauls did against Julius Caesar, albeit with little luck.

The Celtic Carni crossed the Alps in the 4th century BCE and settled in present-day Friuli, where they came into contact with the Venetians who were already living there. The Celtic influence lives on in some of the region's river names and customs, such as the lighting of winter-solstice bonfires at higher altitudes *(pignarûl)* and the launching of flaming fir wheels from the mountains of Carnia *(cidulas)*.

Buoyed by their victory over the Carthaginians and intent on securing the territories of northern Italy, the Romans entered the region a little over a century later. According to Roman historian Livy, the colony of Aquileia was founded in 181 BCE, destined to become a Roman stronghold along what was already a very fragile border. Aquileia and the surrounding area quickly gained importance as a trading hub, bolstered by the Romans' impressive road network: the Via Flavia connected Trieste, Pola and Fiume, the Via Annia ran between Adria, Padua and Mestre, while the Via Postumia crossed northern Italy from Aquileia to Genoa.

Although the Carni initially resisted the Roman advance, they gave in to Consul Marcus Aemilius Scaurus in 115 BCE. In return, they obtained the territory between the Livenza River and the Julian Alps, though they were progressively absorbed into Latin culture over the centuries.

Other Roman towns developed in the first century BCE. Among these were *Forum Iulii* (Cividale del Friuli), built on settlements dating back to the Palaeolithic period, and *Iulium Carnicum* (Zuglio), located on the road that crossed the Alps and reached Norico, a region that included part of present-day Austria, Bavaria and Slovenia.

Augustus' territorial reorganisation of Italy included Friuli in the X Regio, called *Venetia et Histria,* with Aquileia as its capital.

The city became extraordinarily rich and lively, a hub of trade and ideas. After the Edict of Milan (313 CE) it was appointed bishopric and began enjoying the ecclesiastical and political prestige that would culminate in the Patriarchate.

The Barbarians & the End of the Empire

While Aquileia itself prospered, the Western Roman Empire – established after emperor Diocletian split the Empire in two in 286 CE – was in the grip of a spiralling crisis. The collapse of its internal structures was compounded by the growing pressure of barbarian incursions. The roads built by the Romans would now lead Alaric and his Visigoths to Rome, which they sacked in 410. And while Aquileia had managed to fend off Alaric, it fell to Attila's Huns, who razed it to the ground in 452.

In 476, the Germanic general Odoacer deposed the last Roman emperor, 14-year-old Romulus Augustulus. The year commonly marks the end

---

In his book *I senzastoria. Il Friuli dalle origini a noi* (1977), Tito Magnacco offers an expansive exploration of the region's history from a unique perspective; that of the peasants, labourers and 'little people' usually overlooked in history's grand narratives.

HISTORY THE BARBARIANS & THE END OF THE EMPIRE

Becoming a forum by decree of Julius Caesar, Cividale was one of northeastern Italy's most important centres in late antiquity. The contraction of its Latin name, *Fr Iulii*, would give rise to the region's own name, Friuli.

---

181 BCE	238 CE	381
The Romans establish Aquileia to protect the regions of northern Italy from Celtic tribes on the northern borders.	Emperor Maximinus Thrax and his son are murdered at the gates of Aquileia after his army loses confidence in him.	The Council of Aquileia, promoted by Saint Ambrose and presided over by the city's bishop, Valerian, condemns the Arian doctrine.

of antiquity and the beginning of the Middle Ages. These two eras were linked by the Romano-Barbaric kingdoms, political entities that arose as the Western Empire weakened and formed the basis for a developing European civilisation.

Odoacer saw himself as the representative of the Eastern Emperor Zeno in Italy, whose support he needed to consolidate his position on the peninsula. Not trusting Odoacer's expansionist ambitions, Zeno, in 488, urged Theodoric the Great, King of the Ostrogoths (long since federated with Byzantium) to invade Italy and take possession of it.

Yet, not even Theodoric managed to enthuse Zeno, who counted on the war to weaken both his contenders. Odoacer was defeated and killed in 493, a year that marked the beginning of Italy's Ostrogothic rule.

It was a prosperous period for Friuli, thanks to Theodoric's policy of continuity with Roman traditions, agreement with the other Romano-Barbaric kingdoms and good relations with the local population.

> Legend has it that when Aquileia was conquered by Attila, its inhabitants hid their most precious possessions in a pit that has never been found.

The Lombards & the Duchy of Friuli

When Theodoric died in 526, his reign was already starting to show signs of weakening. The following year, the young Justinian I took the Byzantine throne, remaining in office for almost 40 years and leaving a deep mark on Europe.

Justinian I managed to regain provinces in Africa and the larger Mediterranean islands before taking on the Ostrogothic Kingdom in Italy in the Gothic War.

Worn down by the fighting, Italy's northern regions offered little resistance to the invading Lombards, who left Pannonia in 569 under the leadership of King Alboin.

The first years of Lombard rule in Italy were uncertain and marked by conflicts between the monarchy, established in the capital Pavia, and the warrior leaders who had led the military operations. The latter, called *duces*, or duchi (dukes), took control of small-to-medium territories, known as *ducati* (duchies).

The first to be established was the Duchy of Friuli. With Cividale as its capital, it was governed by Gisulf I, nephew of Alboin. The king considered Friuli the bridgehead for any incursion into Italy, therefore installing numerous garrisons and armed strongholds.

One of the most influential duchies of the Lombard kingdom, the territory faced difficult moments in the 7th and 8th centuries due to palace conspiracies and attacks by the Avars and Slavs. Among its succession of dukes was Pemmo (Pemmone), whose long dispute with the patriarch of Aquileia saw him deposed by King Liutprand and replaced by Pemmo's son, Ratchis. The latter became king of the Lombards in 744.

> We owe the *Historia Langobardorum*, one of the most important and comprehensive historical sources of the time, to 8th-century Cividale native Paul the Deacon.

539	590	774
The Goths attack Trieste and free it from Byzantine control. The city then passes to the Lombards in 590.	The first duke of Friuli, Gisulf I, dies fighting the Avars.	Charlemagne conquers Italian territory and proclaims himself king of the Franks and Lombards. The Carolingian reign begins.

Five years later, Ratchis' brother Aistulf, also a Duke of Friuli, assumed the throne in Pavia.

Rise & Fall of the Carolingians

Alarmed by Aistulf's ambitions, Pope Stephen II called the Franks to Italy, who dissolved the Lombard state in less than 20 years. Conquering Pavia in 774, Charlemagne proclaimed himself king of the Franks and Lombards and reorganised the kingdom on the Frankish model. The last known Lombard duke of Friuli was Hrodgaud (Rodgand), who resisted the Franks until his death in 776. In 781 Friuli became part of the *Regnum Italiae*.

Under the Carolingians, the Duchy of Friuli was converted into a *march* in 846, overseen by duke-turned-marquis Eberhard of Friuli. *March* was the name given to the empire's frontier territories, considered challenging to govern and requiring a particularly heavy military presence.

Despite this, the Carolingian empire had already started crumbling after the death of Charlemagne, and the struggle for control of Italy also involved Friuli. Marquis Berengar was crowned king of Italy in 888 and again in 898, before becoming emperor of the Holy Roman Empire in 915.

This, however, did not bring good fortune to Friuli. At the beginning of the 10th century, the region suffered a series of terrible Hungarian raids known as the *Vastata Hungarorum*. Devastated, the Friulian countryside remained severely depopulated for years.

The March of Friuli was united with that of Verona and, when the Ottonian dynasty imposed its hegemony on Italy, fell under Carinthian control. During what was a politically challenging period, the region began defining and refining its own language, which gradually detached itself from its Latin, Celtic and Lombard foundations to become the language of the locals.

In the course of the 10th century, a large number of castles were built in Friuli. Unlike the walled villages common throughout much of Italy, these Friulian castles were proper strongholds inhabited by the area's feudal lord. These *castellans* had relatively limited powers over their possessions: political authority was exercised by the Patriarchate of Aquileia, which played a major role in Friuli's reconstruction at the turn of the year 1000.

The Days of His Grace (1960), a historical novel by Nobel Prize–winning writer Eyvind Johnson, is set around Cividale at the time of the transfer of power between the Lombards and Charlemagne's Franks.

The Patriarchate of Aquileia

The Patriarchate of Aquileia became both an anchor and a beacon of hope for a region attempting to recover from the Hungarian raids. This function had already been carried out after the fall of the Western Empire, when the diocese of Aquileia had carried out a systematic program of evangelisation, constructing churches across the Friulian territory.

781	888	1077
The Duchy of Friuli is incorporated by the *Regnum Italiae* and entrusted to the son of Charlemagne, Carloman (Pepin of Italy), who is a child at the time.	Berengar, Marquis of Friuli and grandson of Louis the Pious, becomes king of Italy. He is crowned emperor in 915.	The Patriarch of Aquileia obtains feudal investiture. From this date until 1420 the patriarchs are also princes of the empire and dukes of Friuli.

As a border region, Friuli was no stranger to instability, and for its frightened, disorientated inhabitants, the authorities were a familiar rock in a sea of general anarchy.

Christendom itself was facing division and doctrinal disputes, particularly on the question of the nature of Christ. This had culminated in the Schism of the Three Chapters in 554. Disagreeing with the official line dictated by Emperor Justinian and ratified, with some hesitation, by Pope Vigilius, the bishopric of Aquileia broke its communion with Rome and the Church of the Empire.

Further religious and political division was just around the corner. When the Lombards invaded northern Italy in 568, Paulinus I, bishop of Aquileia, took refuge in Grado, which remained under Byzantine control.

In 607, Bishop Candidianus, loyal to Rome, took office in Grado, while the schismatic John I was appointed in Lombard-ruled Aquileia.

Although Aquileia was reconciled with the pope in around 700, the rivalry between the two cities would continue for over four centuries. Often, it was the the emperors who settled their disputes.

As a reward for his loyalty to Henry IV, Holy Roman Emperor, the Patriarch of Aquileia was granted the feudal investiture of Duke of Friuli and the title of prince in 1077.

The Friulian territory thus came out of the sphere of influence of its more powerful neighbours and regained an autonomous political identity under the authority of the patriarch.

Among those who held this office were Wolfger von Erla (1204–18), a shrewd diplomat who relaunched Aquileia's trade, his successor Berthold (1218–51), who fought against Ezzelino da Romano and brought the Patriarchate to its maximum territorial expansion, and Raimondo Della Torre (1273–99), who courageously defended Aquileia from Venice.

During the 14th century, Cividale and Udine competed for the role of main city of the Patriarchate. Towards the end of the century, a real war of succession ensued, involving Hungary, which sided with Cividale, and Venice, allied with Udine. Cividale prevailed, but its adversaries refused to recognise the victory. In 1382, meanwhile, Trieste had become part of the Habsburg dominions.

The fate of the Patriarchate was, however, sealed. Caught in the conflict between the Empire and Venetian Republic, Patriarch Louis of Teck chose the imperial faction. Accordingly, Venice declared war, invading Friuli and inflicting significant devastation.

In 1419 the Venetians took Cividale, with Udine capitulating the following year. And so, the Patriarchate finally came to an end, reduced to the sole lordship of Aquileia in all its decadence.

A curious tradition traces the custom of 'April Fools' Day' back to a miracle that took place in Aquileia in the 14th century: the pope, invited to lunch by the patriarch Bertrand, is said to have gotten a fishbone stuck in his throat. Having fallen asleep without being able to extract it, he found it prodigiously placed on a tray the next morning, hence the traditional ban on eating fish on 1 April and the association between this date, fish and unbelievable events.

1318	1508	1514
A fierce fire tears through Pordenone, destroying most of the old town's wooden houses.	The War of the League of Cambrai breaks out: a coalition of European states attempt to counter the expansion of the Venetian Republic. Two factions emerge in Friuli, one desiring a return to Venetian rule, the other loyal to the Habsburgs.	The war ends: Venice retains the Friulian territories while Gradisca d'Isonzo and Gorizia pass to Austria.

THE OTTOMAN RAIDS OF THE 15TH CENTURY

For Europe, the powerful Ottoman Empire remained a threat for centuries and the regions that most often bore the brunt of its force were the Republic of Venice and the Habsburg Empire. Towards the end of the 16th century, Friuli suffered numerous raids that often took the local garrisons by surprise, causing serious devastation and loss of life.

In 1477, the pasha of Bosnia, İskender Mihaloğlu, led some 10,000 men across the Isonzo River and unleashed them in the Friulian countryside after having ambushed the garrison of Gradisca. In October 1499, an even larger Ottoman force pounced on the region of Pordenone, raiding, fighting and looting as far as the vicinity of Conegliano in present-day Veneto. Once again, the Venetians' response was inadequate: the Ottoman brigades, fast and difficult to locate, held La Serenissima's soldiers in check for weeks. Wanting to give Friuli's defenders a safe and solid base, the Venetian Republic commissioned the fortress of Palmanova a century later.

The Venetian Age

With Venice's victory, Friuli became part of the Domini di Terraferma (Mainland Dominions), which together with the Dogado and the Stato da Màr formed the three divisions of the powerful Venetian Republic.

Little changed in the social order: feudal relations were maintained and local customs and traditions were generally respected. For the Venetians, the territory was considered a buffer state against possible threats from the North and East.

The 15th century was defined by Ottoman incursions. Crossing the Balkans, and clashing with Albanians, Serbs and Hungarians en route, they invaded Friuli, hungry for loot.

In 1508, the War of the League of Cambrai broke out, ignited by a coalition of European states determined to curb the Venetian Republic's expansion. The conflict brought years of poverty to Friuli and rekindled historic tensions between feudal lords, the bourgeoisie and the peasantry.

Two factions were created: one united the newly established nobility, rural communities and others sympathetic to the Venetian Republic, while the other was formed by old aristocratic families interested in the privileges that annexation to the Habsburg Empire would bring.

For Friuli, 1511 was a particularly challenging year. Not only did a peasant revolt see castles and estates systematically torched, the region was struck by a devastating earthquake and plague. The war itself finally came to an end in 1514: Venice essentially regained the territories

1593	1615–17	1751
Work begins on the fortress city of Palmanova, designed by engineers Marcantonio Martinengo and Giulio Savorgnan in the shape of a nine-pointed star.	Venetians and Habsburgs clash over the fortress of Gradisca. Venice's position in the Adriatic is strengthened by the end of the hostilities.	Pope Benedict XIV suppresses the Patriarchate of Aquileia and establishes the archdioceses of Udine and Gorizia.

that were under its rule at the outbreak of the conflict, while the county of Gradisca d'Isonzo and Gorizia passed to Austria.

To stem the danger of popular uprisings, the Venetians established the Contadinanza in 1533. Innovative for Europe, the representative body was elected by the peasants to defend their own interests, with the right to both propose and veto laws in Parliament.

The introduction of corn and potatoes in the 16th century mitigated the effects of famines and epidemics, just as the cultivation of rice and its integration into the local diet helped tackle pellagra (a deficiency disease) and improve the living conditions of farmers.

The first stages of industrialisation in the region unfurled in the mid-18th century. While these were often hindered by the Venetian authorities, bound to old patterns and threatened by change, they were embraced with more enthusiasm in Gorizia, where the Austrians gave ample freedom to the first entrepreneurs.

Napoleon implemented various political and civil reforms: the elimination of feudalism and privileges, the introduction of the decimal metric system, the establishment of the land and building *cadastre* and the application of civil law. Less favourable aspects of Napoleonic rule, however, included the systematic pillage of artworks kept in Friuli.

The French & the Austrians

With the Treaty of Campo Formio (1797), signed at the end of the Italian Campaign, Napoleon wrapped up over a millennium of Venetian Republic rule. Present-day Friuli was divided into departments: Tagliamento (including Treviso), Adriatico (including Venice) and Illirico (Trieste, Gorizia, Dalmatia, Istria and Croatian Littoral).

The new ideas and principles that inspired the French conquest were highly favoured by younger locals, many of whom were inspired enough to enrol as volunteers in Napoleon's army.

With the Restoration of 1814, Friuli was restructured, joining the newly constituted, Austrian-controlled Kingdom of Lombardy-Venetia. During this phase, Trieste, which the Austrians had declared a free port in 1719, began its ascent to the rank of Central European metropolis, with a booming population and a cultural scene that blossomed up until the 20th century.

On the economic front, the manufacturing of silk and metals reached peak prosperity between the 17th and 19th centuries. Yet, while the number of workshops and spinning mills increasing exponentially during this period, working conditions were terrible. Spinning mills continued to operate using manual labour and wages were barely enough to feed the workers.

The situation was complicated by the crisis in the agricultural sector, competition from Chinese silk and a string of endemic crop diseases, from the downy mildew that affected potatoes to the phylloxera that decimated vineyards.

1719	1762	1797
Trieste is proclaimed a free port, facilitating trade between the Adriatic and the Danube hinterland and prospering as a result.	Udine's Società di Agricoltura Pratica is founded, the second of its kind in Italy after Florence's Accademia dei Georgofili, and the first to establish prizes for solving agronomic problems.	With the Treaty of Campo Formio, signed at the end of the Italian Campaign, Napoleon imposes French rule on Friuli and Veneto.

WAR ON THE ISONZO

The Isonzo River is remembered for the 12 battles in which Italian and Austro-Hungarian troops contested Friuli during WWI. The first four battles were fought in 1915 and led to paltry territorial and strategic gains given the efforts and losses on both sides. Marshalled by Italian general Luigi Cadorna, an offensive in August 1916 captured Gorizia, though it failed to penetrate the Austrian front. The following year's initiatives, aimed at Trieste, had the same outcome.

The Italians suffered terribly in the last battle of the Isonzo. Known as the Battle of Caporetto, it began on 24 October 1917 and led to the collapse of the Italian front. Startled by the deep penetration of an Austro-German contingent led by a young Erwin Rommel, the Italians retreated hastily. Accompanied by tens of thousands of terrified Friulian civilians, they made it to the Piave River, where the last line of defence had been established to prevent the enemy from entering the Po Valley.

More than 600,000 Italian soldiers deserted or surrendered during the battle, with Austria gaining control of Friuli entirely and holding onto power until the final Italian victory in November 1918.

Irredentism & WWI

With the Third Italian War of Independence (1866), fought as a secondary front in the Austro-Prussian conflict, the Italians gained control of Veneto and Friuli, excluding the provinces of Gorizia and Trieste, which remained with Austria. Meanwhile, in Trieste in 1863, Gorizian linguist Graziadio Isaia Ascoli proposed the name *Venezia Giulia* to replace *Litorale* (Küstenland), used by the Austrians to indicate the empire's coastal region.

Together with Trentino and Alto Adige, Venezia Giulia remained an Italian-inhabited area controlled by Austria after the process of Italian unification (1860–70). Consequently, a movement known as Irredentism was formed after 1870, determined to free Italian territories from foreign rule. Trieste was an important hub for Irredentists, who operated more or less as secret associations disseminating patriotic propaganda.

Known as the Great War, WWI hit Friuli and the Isonzo Karst particularly hard. Its victims were not only the fighters, of whom an appalling number lost their lives, but also the civilian population, whose houses, roads, infrastructure and crops were destroyed.

Friuli and Venezia Giulia were the scene of numerous bloody battles. After two years of substantial equilibrium, maintained at the cost of immense sacrifices and tens of thousands of war dead, the Austrians broke through the Italian front at Caporetto (25 October 1917) and swept into Friuli.

The fall of the Venetian Republic is described in Ippolito Nievo's novel *Confessions of an Italian* (1867). Set between the end of the Venetian Republic and 1848, it recounts a period of political and social unrest, patriotism and transition.

1815	1864	1866
After the fall of Napoleon, Friuli becomes part of the Kingdom of Lombardy-Venetia, controlled by Austria.	Maximilian I sets sail from Trieste to Mexico. His reign will end three years later, when he is tragically shot.	After the Third Italian War of Independence, the Italians gain control of Friuli, excluding Gorizia and Trieste. The province of Udine is the largest in Italy.

Not wanting to leave anything to the enemy, the retreating Italians destroyed almost everything in their path, from bridges and factories to houses. As a result, the prized Pezzata Rossa cattle breed was almost wiped out, together with an incalculable number of other grazing and working animals.

With the help of the Allied powers, however, Italy managed to turn the tide of the conflict: on 3 November 1918, the Italian cavalry entered Udine and on the same day a division of *bersaglieri* (Italian troops) landed in Trieste. In the course of the war more than 20,000 Friulians had died or suffered serious injuries.

Fascism & WWII

The victory brought Italy some territorial expansions, even if not all requests were accepted at the peace table. Following the acquisition of Gorizia and Trieste, around 400,000 Croats and Slovenes, former subjects of the defeated Austro-Hungarian empire, were incorporated into the new borders of the kingdom, towards which integration policies were practically nil.

In Friuli, as in the rest of the country, postwar tensions proved a fertile ground for the rise of fascism. The problems were many: frustrations with a victory that had not kept all its promises, heated social and class conflicts, the difficult reintegration of veterans into civilian life, the stunted recovery of the impoverished countryside and the fear of Communism, not to mention the ineffectiveness of weak and irresolute governments.

Driven by the middle classes and the agrarian bourgeoisie, fascism infiltrated the country and its institutions with intimidation and squad violence against opponents. In this climate, Narodni Dom, a cultural hub for Trieste's Slovenian minority, was set alight on 13 July 1920.

The Fascist regime made unscrupulous use of the Friulian community to rouse anti-Slavic sentiment, fuelling a nationalism that Italy's victory had not abated. The authorities chose a markedly repressive approach towards Friuli Venezia Giulia's ethnic minorities.

The Slavic and German communities were penalised robustly: languages other than Italian were restricted or forbidden (including, to a lesser extent, Friulian) and both surnames and town names were Italianised. The emigration of farmers to the colonies of Cyrenaica and, later, Ethiopia was encouraged; many Friulians were also involved in the reclamation of the Agro Pontino (Pontine Marshes).

The early stages of WWII seemed favourable to the Italians, at least on the eastern front. Italy participated in the partition of Yugoslavia, swiftly brought to its knees by the German army, and obtained the Slovenian province of Ljubljana and part of Dalmatia (including most of the is-

In April 1944, the Nazis carried out two vengeful massacres in Trieste. On 3 April, 71 people were slaughtered in Poligono di Opicina; on 23 April, 51 hostages were hanged along the steps of Palazzo Rittmeyer.

1882	1915	1917
Guglielmo Oberdan, an irredentist from Trieste, is hanged by the Austrian authorities in the courtyard of Trieste's Caserma Grande.	The supreme command of the Italian armed forces is established in Udine, the Italian city closest to the Isonzo Front.	The collapse of the Italian front after the Battle of Caporetto brings Austro-Hungarian troops back to Friuli.

lands). It also indirectly assumed control of Croatia. Declared an independent state, it was entrusted to Prince Aimone, Duke of Aosta, who never actually performed any effective functions.

Within a few months, however, the Italian war machine began to break down and the first forms of armed resistance to the regime were reported, though these were dismissed as a simple police problem by the authorities.

After the armistice of 8 September 1943, Friuli, like the rest of central and northern Italy, was occupied by the Germans. The provinces of Udine, Trieste, Gorizia, Pola and Fiume, under the name Adriatisches Küstenland, Litorale Adriatico, came under the direct administration of the Reich, represented by the Gauleiter of Carinthia, Friedrich Rainer, a fervent Nazi who harboured particular anti-Italian sentiments.

During the Italian Social Republic, two partisan units emerged: the communist-inspired Brigate Garibaldi (Garibaldi Brigades) and the Brigate Osoppo-Friuli (Ossopo-Friuli Brigades), made up of liberals, socialists and Catholics. On 7 February 1945, 17 partisans of the latter unit were killed by communist patriots in the so-called Porzûs massacre.

The partisan struggle was especially fierce in Friuli. Liberated territories remodelled themselves as autonomous, self-governing entities, such as the Partisan Republic of Carnia. Bloody battles and German reprisals were common. Numerous villages in Carnia and the Udine area, including Nimis, Attimis and Faedis, were set on fire.

Summary executions and deportations were also frequent. Trieste's Risiera di San Sabba became a detention and sorting centre, witnessing the slaughter of war hostages, partisans, political prisoners and Jews. Of the 5000 Jews that were resident in Trieste before the war, more than 700 were deported to concentration camps, with only some 20 later returning.

The End of the War & the Trieste Question

In April 1945, the war in Italy came to an end, with Udine liberated on 1 May 1945. The Yugoslav Fourth Army and the British Eighth Army (commanded by General Bernard Freyberg) converged on Trieste. On 1 May, the Yugoslavs arrived on the outskirts of the city and engaged the German contingents that still held out.

The next day, in an atmosphere of great tension, Freyberg's New Zealanders arrived in the city and received the Germans' surrender. Thus a stalemate loomed: with overlapping occupation zones, diplomats set to work to avert a potentially devastating crisis between the victorious powers.

On 9 June, the Anglo-Americans decreed the passage of Trieste and Gorizia under their control, to which Marshal Tito agreed. The final

The trial of two men responsible for crimes and atrocities at the Risiera di San Sabba took place in 1976. While one of the two defendants had since died, the other, Joseph Oberhauser, was sentenced to life in prison in absentia. Germany refused to extradite him to Italy as extradition agreements between the two countries only covered crimes committed after 1948. Nonetheless, the trial was historically significant for breaking the silence on the San Sabba tragedy.

HISTORY THE END OF THE WAR & THE TRIESTE QUESTION

1919	1920	1922
The Treaty of Saint-Germain-en-Laye assigned eastern Friuli to the Kingdom of Italy. In September, Gabriele D'Annunzio's legionaries depart Ronchi to occupy Fiume.	With the Treaty of Rapallo, Italy maps out its border with the Kingdom of Serbs, Croats and Slovenes (Yugoslavia) and acquires Gorizia and Trieste.	In the days following the March on Rome, fascist squads sweep across the region.

peace treaty, signed two years later, assigned a large part of Venezia Giulia to Yugoslavia.

A new political entity, known as the Free Territory of Trieste, was created as its capital. The territory was divided into two parts: Zone A, from Duino to Muggia, administered by the Anglo-Americans, and Zone B, from Koper to Novigrad, given to the Yugoslavs.

Fear of persecution and revenge led thousands of Italians to leave Istria as exiles. Their concerns were justified: during and after the war, a large number of Italians in Yugoslav-controlled areas were thrown (alive or murdered) into the *foibe* (deep sink holes) that litter the Karst in what is known as the Foibe massacres.

The process that would bring Trieste back under Italian control began in 1953 and faced strong Yugoslav opposition. The situation was indeed a delicate one.

Not only was the city an important pawn on the international chessboard, the climate in the city itself was volatile, with no shortage of pro-Italian demonstrations and street protests (one of which had cost the lives of six demonstrators).

After about a year of negotiations, the parties finally reached an understanding. On 5 October 1954, the London Memorandum was ratified, assigning, with minor adjustments, Zone A to Italy and Zone B to Yugoslavia.

On 26 October the *bersaglieri* entered Trieste to a rousing welcome and the Anglo-American administration handed the reins to the Italians. The London Memorandum was officially provisional in nature and spoke of administration, not sovereignty. The latter was sealed with the Treaty of Osimo, signed on 10 November 1975.

Reconstructing a New Region

The 1947 Constitution merged Friuli and Venezia Giulia into a single region. In the 1948 elections, the first in the newly formed Italian Republic, the Democrazia Cristiana (DC; Christian Democracy) party asserted itself decisively in the country and in Friuli, albeit with some differences between provinces.

In Udine the DC obtained almost three times as many votes as the left-wing Fronte Democratico Popolare (Popular Democratic Front), while in Gorizia, mainly due to the votes of the Monfalcone shipyard workers, the extent of the victory was more modest.

In 1962, in view of the region's special geopolitical position, Friuli Venezia Giulia was granted the special status provided for in the Constitution. Six year later, in 1968, the region's provinces of Trieste, Gorizia and Udine were joined by Pordenone.

The University of Udine is the only one in Italy established through a citizens' initiative bill. In 1976, after the earthquake, local institutions set about collecting the required 50,000 signatures for the petition. More than 125,000 people signed, many of them living in the tent cities set up in response to the quake. The university was founded in 1978.

1944	1947	1954
The Partisan Republic of Carnia is founded. Inhabited by about 90,000 people spread over 38 municipalities, it's an important bastion of freedom and civic engagement.	In the new formed republican Italy, Friuli and Venezia Giulia are merged into a single region.	With the London Memorandum, Trieste returns under Italian administration. Italy and the US agree to establish a NATO base at Aviano airport.

Postwar reconstruction was slow and arduous. Although the retreating Germans had spared several industrial sites, a shortage of raw materials hindered recovery. Unemployment and lack of opportunities revived emigration, further fuelled by an agricultural crisis. As the years went by, the situation improved markedly on the wave of Italy's economic boom. While Allied bombings in WWII had destroyed much of Trieste's industry (including its shipyards), these losses were partially compensated by the city's new function as Friuli Venezia Giulia's capital city, which created new jobs in sectors like public administration.

Two disasters struck Friuli in the 1960s and 1970s. On 9 October 1963, a massive landslide on Monte Toc crashed into the Vajont Dam reservoir, creating a mega tsunami that wiped out the town of Longarone and several other municipalities in the area.

More than 1900 people are believed to have perished in the tragedy, which resulted from incompetence, an underestimation of geological risks and the guilty silence of various insiders.

The event made a deep impression on Italians, who were equally indignant at the lenient sentences handed down to those in charge of the public and private companies involved in the dam's construction.

Thirteen years later, on 6 May 1976, a devastating 6.4-magnitude earthquake struck near the town of Gemona, followed by a further two strong quakes in September.

Almost 1000 lives were lost and dozens of villages destroyed. On both occasions, the people of Friuli picked themselves up and promptly set about rebuilding their devastated homeland.

Beyond the Iron Curtain

Although Winston Churchill didn't coin the term 'Iron Curtain', he made it famous, citing Trieste as its southern end. Gorizia too was at the border of Europe's Eastern and Western blocs, the city split in two by a fence running straight through Piazza della Transalpina.

While 83% of the province was ceded to Yugoslavia, most of Gorizia city remained with Italy. In 1947, city districts outside the Italian zone were reorganised into the municipality of Nova Gorica, which became the capital of the Isonzo area assigned to Yugoslavia.

The dissolution of the blocs and of Yugoslavia, coupled with Slovenia's entry into the European Union (2004) and its signing of the Schengen Agreement (2007), resulted in the dismantling of the region's borders: physical, ideological and, albeit with more difficulty, cultural. The taxing bureaucratic procedures that had hindered freedom of movement between Italy and its neighbour suddenly vanished.

Although now two different cities in two different countries, Gorizia and Nova Gorica were once again united.

A referendum to establish the province of Alto Friuli (Upper Friuli) took place on 21 March 2004: 54% of the nearly 40,000 voters voted no.

1964	1984	1999
The first regional elections are held in Friuli Venezia Giulia: the Christian Democrats win over 43% of the vote. The region's first president is Alfredo Berzanti.	The Swedish Electrolux Group acquires Zanussi, a historic Pordenone-based manufacturer of household appliances.	Parliament passes a law that officially recognises the existence of a Friulian-speaking linguistic minority.

A Quality Life

In *Sole 24 Ore's* 2021 report on Italy's most liveable towns and cities, three centres in Friuli Venezia Giulia made the top 10, with Udine in ninth place, Pordenone in seventh and Trieste topping the list altogether. Bragging rights aside, the results revealed a sustained, upward trend in the region's quality of life.

Friuli Venezia Giulia's efforts to better valorise its traditions, enhance its environmental credentials and improve sustainability are paying dividends, including in its tourism sector. After the Valsugana in Trentino, the Tarvisio area was the second eco-sustainable destination in Italy recognised by the Global Sustainable Tourism Council (GSTC), an independent, nongovernmental organisation managing global standards for sustainable travel and tourism.

Despite the challenges of the COVID-19 pandemic, the region is also the only one in Italy to have recorded employment growth (albeit minimal), even in 2020. This resilience is due in part to Friuli Venezia Giulia's favourable geopolitical position: being at the crossroads of important trade routes, it has been able to rely on exports as a driving force of a robust economy.

2007	2016	2018
Slovenia becomes a full member of the Schengen area, resulting in the permanent removal of the border dividing Gorizia and Nova Gorica.	A constitutional law amends the statute of Friuli Venezia Giulia and deletes its four provinces. The region is reorganised into UTI (Intermunicipal Territorial Unions).	The 29 April regional elections see a victory for the center-right coalition: Massimiliano Fedriga, a member of the Lega Nord, becomes the president of Friuli Venezia Giulia.

Arts & Literature

For centuries, the multiculturalism that underpins Friulian and Julian culture has expressed itself in its brushstrokes and buildings, literature and crafts. From the mosaicists of Aquileia to those of Spilimbergo, from Tiepolo to Pordenone, from Biagio Marin and Italo Svevo, to Umberto Saba, James Joyce and Claudio Magris, from medieval organs to the pop-rock of Elisa, Friuli Venezia Giulia's artistic legacy is nothing short of extraordinary.

Architecture

Many of Friuli Venezia Giulia's cities and towns are veritable museums, recounting centuries of gripping history through the complex layering of palaces, castles and humbler abodes.

The region's architectural highlights include a small but significant cachet of Roman ruins, magnificent Byzantine basilicas, castles, and stately Venetian, Habsburg and Art-Nouveau palaces.

An awareness of architecture's various styles helps to better understand a city's past (and through it its present). This is especially true in Friuli Venezia Giulia, whose historical twists and turns are reflected in the forms and nuances of its buildings.

Indeed, in few regions is the very image of a city so clearly linked to specific historical and cultural developments. Here, architecture clearly tells the region's story, so look up and look down, and let its stones, bricks and mortar fill you in on Friuli Venezia Giulia's rollercoaster ride through time.

The Roman Empire

When it comes to the region's Roman past, everything revolves around Aquileia. Founded in 181 BCE, its strategic proximity to both the sea and central Europe quickly made it one of the Empire's main centres. Originally a military camp, Aquileia was upgraded to *municipium* in 89 BCE before becoming the capital of the X Regio in Augustan times. Little of the ancient city's flourishing theatres, spas, forums and markets remain, due in part to Attila's destructive tour of 452 CE. Much of what does remain flanks Via Giulia Augusta, including part of the colonnade that graced the 2nd-century forum.

Basilica of Aquileia: The Guide Book to the Reading of the Mosaics (Gaspari, 2011), by Renato Iacumin, is a valuable compendium for visiting Aquileia.

In Trieste, the relics of ancient Tergeste, a Roman colony from the middle of the 1st century BCE, are scattered everywhere. Colle di San Giusto was the city centre, from where Tergeste's long-gone city walls descended to the sea.

Visible at the top of the *colle* (hill) are the remains of the forum (a large paved area and traces of the basilica) and a colonnaded street. At the foot of the hill, not far from Piazza Unità d'Italia, lies the well-preserved Roman theatre, believed to date from the early 1st century CE.

Byzantines & Lombards

With the fall of the Western Roman Empire, the Byzantine era began. Freedom of worship had spawned ever-growing Christian communities, resulting in the construction of many basilicas across the region. The

In 2020, Trieste launched *Un mare di archeologia* (A Sea of Archaeology), an annual festival engaging young people with its rich archaeological heritage through technology and fun.

first of these were built by the Romans, who found their inspiration in the regal palace halls of the eastern Mediterranean. To illuminate their interiors, the nave was built higher than the side aisles, allowing the upper section of the walls (the clerestory) to be lined with windows.

As Christianity spread, so too did the need for larger places of worship. Consequently, the Roman-style basilica, which had been a symbol of Roman civic life, was adapted. While little of its structural form changed, its use did.

While Roman basilicas had been busy, chaotic places where daily activities took place along the aisles, the revised Christian version saw the buildings divided into two rigidly defined zones: one reserved for the officiating clergy (the presbytery, which adjoined the apse), the other for the faithful masses.

Among the most important places of worship of the period are the 11th-century Basilica of Santa Maria Assunta in Aquileia (based on an earlier 4th-century basilica), the 6th-century basilicas of Santa Eufemia and Santa Maria delle Grazie in Grado, and the 14th-century Cattedrale di San Giusto in Trieste, also built on the remains of an earlier early-Christian basilica (part of whose original floor survives).

If Lombard architecture intrigues you, Cividale should be the first town on your hit list. Starting life as a *castrum* (Roman fort), it was elevated to the rank of forum by Julius Caesar before eventually becoming a *municipium*. In 569 the Lombards elected it the seat of the duchy and embellished it with fine works of art that survive to this day.

Today Cividale is one of the seven Italian places that together form Unesco's 'Lombards in Italy: Places of Power (568–774)' World Heritage site, rendered significant due to its preserved Lombard art. In the Gastaldaga – the palace of the *gastaldo,* lord of the city – you can visit the Tempietto Longobardo, a breathtaking masterpiece of architecture, mosaics, frescoes and decorative stucco.

Romanesque & Gothic

The region's undisputed Romanesque-era jewel is Sesto al Reghena's Abbazia Benedettina di Santa Maria in Silvis, built in the 8th century and later fortified. Muggia, on the other hand, claims the Basilica di Santa Maria Assunta.

The prodigious statue of St Christopher gracing the facade of the Duomo di Gemona dates from 1332. Sculpted by Griglio da Gemona and made by joining six blocks of stone, the 7m-tall figure is one of the most impressive statues of the Friulian Gothic period. Miraculously, both the statue and the Duomo's facade withstood Friuli's violent 1976 earthquake.

In the mid-12th century, a bold French innovation emerged that turned ecclesiastical architecture on its head. Known as Gothic architecture, it offered a new way of unloading weight.

While Romanesque churches were entirely supported by their walls, resulting in bulky buildings with no large windows, Gothic churches allowed the weight to be discharged onto pillars, assisted by rampant arches and buttresses.

As a result, church walls slimmed down, rose higher and accommodated generously proportioned windows that flooded the interiors with light.

Yet, despite its popularity across Europe, the new French style roused less interest in Italy (at least initially). South of the Alps, hulking Romanesque churches dabbled lightly with the style, whether through the addition of ribbed vaults, a spire or a rose window.

Significant examples of this 'Italian Gothic' style include Gemona's 14th-century Duomo di Sant'Andrea and Venzone's Duomo di Santa Maria Assunta, both partially damaged by the 1976 earthquake and rebuilt.

Built between 1291 and 1395, Pordenone's Palazzo del Comune is also representative of the Friulian Gothic style, as is the picturesque Duomo di Muggia with its strikingly curvaceous facade.

UNESCO WORLD HERITAGE SITES IN FRIULI VENEZIA GIULIA

➡ Aquileia and the Basilica di Aquileia: since 1998 (p132)

➡ Dolomites (Provinces of Udine and Pordenone): since 2009 (p214)

➡ Tempietto Longobardo and the Monastero di Santa Maria in Valle (Cividale del Friuli): since 2011 (p176)

➡ Prehistoric pile dwellings around the Alps at Palù di Livenza - Santissima di Livenza (Polcenigo): since 2011 (p197)

➡ The Venetian works of defence at Palmanova: since 2017 (p154)

Venetian Rule

Friuli's Venetian history began in 1420, the year in which the region's cities began a profound urban transformation. Seigniorial palaces, monuments and seats of power arose, with many of the finest examples found in Udine. Among these is Niccolò Lionello's Loggia del Lionello and Tommaso Lippomano's Loggia del Lippomano.

Private palaces enriched the entire Friulian plain, many of which can still be admired today in the area's many villages. The most beautiful and richly frescoed *palazzi* can be found along Pordenone's *corsi* (boulevards), around Udine's Piazza San Giacomo, or in Spilimbergo, between the castle and the old town.

Working between Udine and Pordenone in the second half of the 16th century, celebrated Renaissance architect Andrea Palladio brought a wave of classicism to the architecture of the time: you will find works by the Veneto-born master in Udine (Arco Bollani) and in San Daniele (Porta Gemona, adapted from the design for Arco Bollani).

The 17th century also lavished Friuli Venezia Giulia with grand architectural statements. In addition to a string of religious and political buildings, fountains, monuments and, in some cases, entire cities made their debut.

Palmanova was one of the century's most ambitious architectural feats: a star-shaped fortress town built according to the principles of a Renaissance utopian city.

The 17th century also delivered some magnificent Baroque assets, among them Villa Manin in Codroipo, residence of the last doge, and the Duomo di San Daniele, revamped by Domenico Rossi in the latter part of the 1600s.

> Udine's current Loggia del Lionello is not the 15th-century original. The building was rebuilt after the devastating fire of 1876, faithfully reproducing Niccolò Lionello's design.

The Habsburgs & the Rebirth of Trieste

Between the 17th and 18th centuries, the Gorizia area ushered in a wave of new buildings sporting decorative elements inspired by Central Europe's Baroque style. One example is Gorizia's Chiesa di Sant'Ignazio. Begun in 1654 and completed in the 1700s, its bell towers are crowned by distinct, onion-shaped domes.

Indeed, many churches and chapels were built in this period, commissioned by the various religious orders.

In Trieste, though, the 17th century left no architectural works of particular note: the only significant Baroque building in the city is the Chiesa di Santa Maria Maggiore, erected at the behest of the Jesuits.

Trieste, however, underwent much more significant transformations starting from 1719, when it was declared a free port by Austria. Particularly loved by Maria Theresa of Austria, the city was endowed with a new district, the Borgo Nuovo or Teresiano, requested by the empress.

> Maria Theresa of Austria (1717–80) devoted herself so passionately to the rebirth of Trieste that she completely reshaped its urban structure. The Borgo Teresiano is named in her honour.

When Napoleon ceded Friuli to the Habsburg Empire in 1797, the port of Trieste entered a new golden age, becoming one of Europe's great cosmopolitan cities. Its booming population included a new bourgeoisie with an appetite for luxury and the money to obtain it.

In the following years, the city gave birth to numerous prolific shipping and insurance companies, specifically Lloyd Triestino, Assicurazioni Generali and Riunione Adriatica di Sicurtà.

Piazza Unità d'Italia was given its present form and the buildings that still surround it sprang up. Among these is Palazzo del Municipio (1875), built in the 19th-century eclectic style, and the neoclassical headquarters of Assicurazioni Generali (1884). The latter is crowned by a fascinating frieze depicting an anthropomorphised Trieste.

To its right is the past, represented by painting, sculpture, architecture, Roman antiquity and wisdom (depicted as the Owl of Athena). To its left is the future, portrayed by a traveller's suitcase, a locomotive, pincers and gears symbolising technology.

The 18th century also saw the creation of the city's Borgo Giuseppino (between Via Diaz, Via Cadorna and Via del Lazzaretto Vecchio) and Borgo Franceschino (around Viale XX Settembre).

The region's 19th-century architecture took on the late Baroque and neoclassical tones in vogue throughout Europe. In Trieste, this classical revival inspired a string of magnificent buildings, among them Palazzo della Borsa Vecchia, Teatro Nuovo, Casa Steiner and Palazzo del Tergesteo. Meanwhile, the eclectic style also popular in the 1800s would shape the city's seafront Castello di Miramare, canal-side Palazzo Gopcevich and Teatro Rossetti.

Written by Leone Veronese and Armando Halupca, the Italian-language *Trieste nascosta* (2005) is packed with interesting information about the city's art and architecture, with a focus on historic buildings and traces of the past.

From Art Nouveau to Reconstruction

As the 20th century dawned, Art Nouveau (known as 'Liberty' or *floreale* in Italy) spread across the region. The style challenged the architectural sobriety that had come before it, resulting in buildings like Trieste's Casa Bartoli, Casa Polacco, Cinema Eden and Pescheria Centrale.

SEEKING PORDENONE

Pordenone's frescoes are scattered throughout Friuli (particularly between Pinzano al Tagliamento and Travesio), and art lovers who take the time to seek them out will discover an extraordinary artist. The following are some of his finest works:

➡ *Santi Rocco ed Erasmo (Saints Roch and Erasmus*, 1506, fresco on a pillar, and *Madonna della Misericordia col Bambino (Virgin of Mercy with Child)*, 1515, altarpiece; in the Duomo di Pordenone (p189)

➡ *Trinità (Trinity)*, c 1530–35, in the Duomo di San Daniele del Friuli (p161)

➡ *Assunzione della Vergine (Assumption of the Virgin)*, *Caduta di Simon Mago*, *Conversione di San Paolo (Conversion of St Paul)*, 1524, organ doors, and *Scene della vita della Vergine (Scenes from the Life of the Virgin)*, 1524; in the Duomo di Spilimbergo (p200)

➡ *Noli me tangere*, 1535, oil on canvas, in the museum of the Duomo di Cividale del Friuli (p177)

➡ *Gigantomachia (Gigantomachy)*, 1535, frescoes, Udine, Palazzo Tinghi (p148)

➡ *Natività (Nativity)*, 1527, in the Chiesa di Santa Maria dei Battuti in Valeriano (p164), and *Madonna col Bambino (Madonna and Child)*, 1525, in the Chiesa di San Martino in Pinzano (p164)

➡ *Cristo (Christ)*, 1516, *Pietà*, 1526, *Adorazione dei Magi (Adoration of the Magi)*, 1526, *Decollazione di San Paolo (Beheading of St Paul)*, 1526, and *Conversione di Saul (Conversion of Saul)*, 1526; in the Chiesa di San Pietro in Travesio (p206)

Beyond the capital, fine examples of the style include Villa Moretti in Coia, near Tarcento, and Casa Micoli in Udine.

The 20-year Fascist period saw the construction of vast mansions and the founding of Torviscosa. Rationalist in design, the town was envisioned as a self-sufficient entity, encompassing industry, agriculture and residential areas.

The postwar period was defined by major reconstruction throughout Friuli Venezia Giulia, with notable architects of the period including Marcello d'Olivo. In 1952, he designed the masterplan for Lignano Pineta, a coastal town whose spiral-shaped streets found their muse in the garden-city of the Renaissance.

Another 20th-century architect who left his mark on the region is Gino Valle, whose creations include thermal baths in Arta Terme, the Zanussi offices in Porcia, and the tomb of film director Pier Paolo Pasolini in Casarsa della Delizia.

Painting

Some of Friuli Venezia Giulia's oldest brushstrokes date from the Romanesque period, and, once more, the heart of the scene is Aquileia. The basilica's apse harbours a series of frescoes dating from Patriarch Poppone's reign, as well as an umissable depiction of *The Deposition* in the crypt.

Romanesque frescoes also adorn the Basilica of Santa Maria Assunta in Muggia Vecchia, while Trieste's Cattedrale di San Giusto claims Romanesque mosaics. Also valuable are the miniatures of the Byzantine Bible, preserved in San Daniele's Biblioteca Guarneriana.

Of the few Gothic works to survive in Friuli Venezia Giulia, the frescoes inside Sesto al Reghena's 14th-century Abbazia Santa Maria in Silvis, executed by painters of the Giotto school, are a highlight.

To the northeast, Vitale da Bologna worked in Udine from the second half of the 14th century. Together with his collaborators, the Bologna-born painter executed numerous frescoes in the city's churches. Among these are scenes from the Old and New Testaments inside the Duomo.

The region's first painters of national significance came to prominence in the Renaissance. Eminent among them was Bellunello (Andrea di Borlotto, 1430–94), whose works include *Crocifissione e santi* in the Civici Musei di Udine and a triptych inside the Chiesa di San Floriano in Forni di Sopra. Equally regarded is Pellegrino da San Daniele (Martino da Udine, 1467–1537), responsible for the frescoes inside San Daniele's Chiesa di Sant'Antonio Abate.

The region's undisputed Renaissance superstar, however, is Pordenone (Giovanni Antonio de' Sacchis, 1484–1539). Among his many masterpieces is *La Madonna della Misericordia* (1515) in the Duomo di Pordenone and *Noli me tangere* (1535) in the Duomo di Cividale. Pomponio Amalteo, Pordenone's son-in-law, was another great figure of 16th-century Friulian art, creating scenes from the life of the Virgin and the childhood of Christ (1545) in the Chiesa dei Battuti in San Vito al Tagliamento.

Between the 17th and 18th centuries, painting in the region was affected by geopolitics. While areas in the east were essentially inspired by the Baroque of central Europe, those under Venetian influence, including Udine, courted artists of the caliber of Tiepolo.

Indeed, the Venetian master's arrival in Udine in 1726 heralded a golden age for painting in Friuli.

Tiepolo stayed in the city long enough to leave immense masterpieces in Palazzo Patriarcale, Duomo and nearby Oratorio della Purità. His brushstrokes would also grace many of Udine's noble abodes: *La caduta degli angeli ribelli* (*The Fall of the Rebel Angels*, 1726), *Il Giudizio di*

If you fancy learning more about Giambattista Tiepolo and his son Giandomenico, writer Alvise Zorzi's Italian-language *L'Olimpo sul soffitto: I due Tiepolo tra Venezia e l'Europa* (2006) offers an engaging account of the great artists' lives.

Salomone (*The Judgement of Solomon,* 1726–29) and *L'Assunta* (*The Assumption,* 1759) are just some of his works one can admire in the city. Other prolific artists active in the region during this period were Antonio Carneo (1637–92) and Sebastiano Bombelli (1635–1719): many of their creations are now housed in the Civici Musei di Udine.

Much like the architecture of the time, 19th-century painting was inspired by classicism. While ancient mythology was a common theme, so too were local landscapes and portraits of the bourgeoisie: some of these works now hang in the civic museums of Trieste and Udine.

The region's most successful 19th-century artists were Palmanova-born Bernardino Bison and his Triestine pupil Giuseppe Gatteri, Gorizia's Francesco Caucig and Giuseppe Tominz, Udine's Odorico Politi, and Pordenone's Michelangelo Grigoletti. Talented female painters also distinguished themselves in 19th-century Friuli Venezia Giulia: among them Marianna Pascoli Angeli (1790–1846), a portrait painter from Monfalcone taught by Antonio Canova.

Friuli Venezia Giulia's 20th-century art was influenced by the avant-garde movements that shaped the century, and many local artists of the period emerged from Friuli's Second Biennial (1928). Avant-garde painter Fred Pittino produced frescoes for Udine's Duomo and was also one of the directors of the Spilimbergo Mosaic School.

The works of fellow avant-gardists Alessandro Filipponi and Anton Zoran Mušič can be found in Udine and Gorizia, while those of the lauded Basaldella brothers (sculptors Dino and Mirko, and painter Afro) are scattered across various modern art collections.

Another of the region's modern greats is Luigi Spazzapan, whose hometown of Gradisca d'Isonzo houses a museum dedicated to the celebrated painter.

Born an Austro-Hungarian citizen in Habsburg-era Trieste, Gillo Dorfles (1910–2018) was an artist, art critic and professor of aesthetics. Befriending writer Italo Svevo in his youth and buying books from Umberto Saba, the formidable intellectual spent his long life witnessing the evolution of 20th-century art. Dorfles celebrated his 106th birthday by presenting his latest book, *Gli artisti che ho incontrato (The Artists I Have Met)* at the Auditorium del Museo Revoltella in Trieste.

Contemporary Art

Although Friuli Venezia Giulia isn't especially known for its contemporary art scene, its handful of dedicated museums and galleries don't disappoint. Fans should head to Udine, whose Casa Cavazzini – Museo di Arte Contemporanea is the region's most important contemporary art museum.

Pordenone's Parco Galvani is home to Pordenone Arte Contemporanea (PArCO), while Monfalcone's Galleria Comunale di Arte Contemporanea houses a collection dedicated to Tranquillo Marangoni, one of the area's most important printmakers.

In Codroipo, Villa Manin regularly hosts modern art exhibitions, while the cross-border CarniaMusei project includes Art Park in Verzegnis, where contemporary artists create outdoor sculptures and installations that fit harmoniously into the natural landscape.

Mosaics

Friulian mosaics can be divided into two categories: ancient mosaics of the Aquileian school and modern mosaics developed by Giandomenico Facchina and belonging to the Spilimbergo school.

The former represents the classical tradition, which reached its apex with the colourful mosaics of Rome and Byzantine. In Friuli Venezia Giulia, the genre shines in the floor mosaic in the Basilica di Aquileia. Commissioned by Bishop Theodore in the early 4th century and originally covering an area of 1500 square metres, it's the largest floor mosaic in Europe, adorned with human figures, animals and biblical scenes.

Other fine examples of the genre await in Grado's Basilica di Santa Maria delle Grazie and Basilica di Santa Eufemia, where the focus is geometric.

The modern mosaic style originated in Friuli itself in the early 20th century. Its inventor was Giandomenico Facchina, whose so-called 're-verse' technique revolutionised mosaic production and design global-ly. Together, Spilimbergo and Sequals are the heartland of this tech-nique and their streets, monuments and churches adorned with doz-ens of examples.

Sculpture & Decorative Arts

The Lombards left precious examples of goldsmithing and stucco work: you'll find superb examples of gold jewellery, fibulae and crosses from the 6th to 8th centuries at the Museo Archeologico di Cividale.

The region's most important sculptural piece is the Lombard-era Altar of Ratchis, housed in Cividale's Museo Cristiano. Commissioned by Patriarch Callisto and crafted between 737 and 744, the karst-stone altar is adorned with bas-reliefs which, thanks to modern technolo-gy, can now be viewed in their original, Technicolor splendour. The town also claims the Battistero di Callisto Baptistery (737), an octago-nal baptismal font which contributed to Cividale's accession to Unes-co's World Heritage list.

The Romanesque period also produced valuable sculptures and bas-reliefs: Grado's Basilica di Santa Eufemia claims a whimsical, 13th-century *ambo* (pulpit) that recalls the turret of a Persian palace. Meanwhile, superb 14th-century altarpieces are scattered across the region. Among them is the 123-plate, silver altarpiece of Patriarch Pel-legrino II in Cividale's Duomo. Also notable is the altarpiece inside Gra-do's Basilica di Santa Eufemia, created in 1372.

Influenced by the Lombard-Venetian tradition, Friuli Venezia Giulia develop its own sculptural style in the Gothic period. Examples can be found in the Duomo di Gemona and that of Venzone, whose bas-reliefs and sculptures date from between the 13th and 14th centuries. Many of the marble urns and sarcophagi present in the region's churches, such as the 14th-century Arca del Beato in Udine's Duomo, also date from the Gothic era.

It was, however, working with wood that Friulian sculptors real-ly distinguished themselves artistically. In the heavily wooded moun-tain areas, a fine tradition of woodcarving developed between the 15th and 16th centuries, prevailing over stone carving due to its lower cost.

Some of the greatest woodcarvers belonged to the Scuola Sanvitese (Sanvitese School), founded by Bartolomeo da San Vito. In Carnia, Do-menico da Tolmezzo established the equally distinguished Scuola Tol-mezzina, whose legacy continues today. The region's most prized wood-carving is a Statue of St Euphemia, housed in Udine's Museo Diocesa-no di Arte Sacra.

Between the 18th and 20th centuries, the region produced a signifi-cant number of neoclassical altars, fountains and funerary monuments. Many were crafted in Trieste.

Music & Theatre

Friuli Venezia Giulia's traditional music developed in conjunction with the spread of Christianity, making sacred music one of its oldest surviv-ing forms of musical expression. During this time, the first local choirs were formed and the first liturgical dramas sung.

The region's organs are a testimony to this period, some of which are many centuries old and still functioning. Among these are the organs inside the Duomo di Spilimbergo and Duomo di Valvasone. The latter organ, dating from 1532, is the oldest in Europe.

The region's secular music took off from the 1500s, finding an almost spontaneous form of expression in dancing. In 16th-century Udine,

Sutrio is the epicentre of Friuli's woodcarving tradition. Although its most important sculptures are fea-tured in its Yuletide *presepi* (nativity cribs), works by Carnic woodcarvers grace the village year round. Each September, local and international artisans are show-cased at Sutrio's Magia del Legno (Magic of Wood) festival.

ARTS & LITERATURE SCULPTURE & DECORATIVE ARTS

dancing was permitted anywhere and at any hour, with the city council even employing a dedicated orchestra of woodwind and string players. Eventually, municipalities across the region organised plays and comedies featuring private musicians.

One notable Friulian musical tradition is the *villotta*, a polyphonic composition for three or four voices. In it, a soloist is accompanied by a choir, the latter chanting original nursery rhymes while a group of people dance around a couple (usually lovers). While its origins stem back as early as the 15th century, the Carnic tradition spread like wildfire from the 19th century onward.

With the rising popularity of theatre from the 17th-century onward, Friuli's musical tradition found a new bedfellow. In 19th-century Trieste, in particular, a plethora of theatres drew large crowds with their operas and operettas.

The town of San Vito al Tagliamento claims one of the smallest theatres in Italy, tucked away inside Palazzo Comunale.

Concerts and performances were organised everywhere and the city, revelling in its Belle Époque, was also busy producing symphonies. Interestingly, attending the opera became a custom not only for the region's bourgeoisie, but also for its working class.

Among the region's most important theatres are the Politeama Rossetti in Trieste, Teatro Verdi in Gorizia and its namesake in Pordenone. While sharing the same name, the two theatres are very different in appearance: while Gorizia's version occupies a 19th-century building, Pordenone's occupies one of Friuli Venezia Giulia's most interesting contemporary buildings.

Seventies counterculture and Pordenone's Great Complotto punk scene of the 1980s are distinctive, defining moments in the region's modern music scene.

The rise of punk in the Pordenone plain turned the province into one of Italy's punk-music hubs (alongside Bologna and Florence), with dozens of punk-rock and new-wave bands emerging in the area.

In 2009, singer-songwriter Luigi Maieron set to music an early one-act play by Pier Paolo Pasolini, *I turcs tal Friûl* (1944), which compares the 1499 Turkish invasion of Friuli to the passage of Allied bombers in WWII. Also an author, Maieron's novel *Te lo giuro sul cielo* (2018) is a tribute to Carnia.

That both Tre Allegri Ragazzi Morti, an indie-rock band formed in 1994, and Prozac+, a pop-punk group founded in 1995, hail from Pordenone is no coincidence.

The leads in both bands, Davide Toffolo and Gianmaria Accusani, played together in Futuritmi, an outfit that emerged from the Great Complotto. These days, Accusani plays in Sick Tamburo, a highly regarded band from Pordenone.

Udine, on the other hand, is a jazz town: you can catch live jam sessions at many venues (among them Liberty and, on Friday nights, Caffè Caucigh. Each June, the city hosts Udine Jazz, one of Italy's most important jazz festivals.

Well-known names associated with *la canzone friulana* (popular Friulian songs) include Beppino Lodolo, Luigi Maieron and Lino Straulino, whose music is found in many of Friuli Venezia Giulia's record stores.

Interestingly, the region's retro and folk tunes have inspired some unlikely contemporary musicians, who adapt and rework the music into new forms. Among them are Arbe Garbe, FLK and DLH Posse, who mash-up Friuli's old-school tunes and language with punk, rock or hip hop.

In Friuli Venezia Giulia today, music and film are channels of cultural exchange between Italy, Austria and Slovenia, a fact reflected in the many multicultural festivals that fill the region's summers. Among them is Trieste's biannual Guča sul Carso, a music festival whose Balkan air is reminiscent of Serbia's Guča Trumpet Festival.

The artist who unites music and cinema at the highest level is electronic music composer Teho Teardo. The Pordenone native has written soundtracks for prolific Italian film directors Gabriele Salvatores, Paolo Sorrentino (above all for his film *Il Divo*) and Guido Chiesa.

On the mainstream music front, Friuli Venezia Giulia is also the birthplace of Elisa Toffoli (aka Elisa). Originally from Monfalcone, the singer-songwriter found fame in 2001 thanks to a song that evocatively describes the almost psychogeographical nature of 'Tramonti a Nord-Est' (Sunsets in the Northeast), something you're bound to experience on your travels in the region.

Film

Friuli Venezia Giulia's plethora of cinemas are a testament to the Friulians love of the movies. Trieste's own film industry experienced a boom in the 1960s, so much so that plans were made for the city to become the 'Hollywood of the Adriatic', with the Montebello studio as its nexus. The city's trump card was its proximity to a variety of landscapes, from the Trieste coast and Carso, to Friuli's plains and mountains. For film directors, this equated to cheaper set design and post-production costs.

Pordenone has also played a role in the region's cinematic history. In 1978, the city launched Cinemazero, a cultural association and film centre which continues to celebrate, analyse and preserve screen culture, both local and international.

Location scouts were quick to realise the visual potential of Friuli Venezia Giulia and the region appears in many films, among them some true masterpieces. Francis Ford Coppola shot several scenes of *The Godfather* (1974) in Trieste, while Charles Vidor aimed his camera at Venzone in *Farewell to Arms* (1957). Venzone was also a shooting location in Pasquale Festa Campanile's *The Girl and the General* (1967), starring Virna Lisi, while Udine is a backdrop in Mario Monicelli's classic *The Great War* (1959).

Notable films which focus on Friuli Venezia Giulia's own history and culture include Oreste Biancoli's *Black Feathers* (1952). Starring Marcello Mastroianni and Marina Vlady, the classic film sheds light on several events during WWII, particularly those involving Carnia and the Cossacks.

Matteo Oleotto's *Passeranno anche stanotte* (2002) is an interesting co-production between Italy and Slovenia: shot in four days, it recounts the tale of an immigrant's border crossing during the Cold War.

Oleotto is also behind the David di Donatello–nominated, cross-border comedy *Zoran, My Nephew the Idiot* (2013), which stars Giuseppe Battiston, one of Friuli's most prolific actors.

The idyllic Laghi di Fusine show their dark side in Andrea Molaioli's successful debut feature *The Girl by the Lake* (2007), which, thanks in part to Toni Servillo's performance as Commissario Sanzio, has received numerous awards.

Meanwhile, Trieste appears in several recent films, including Gabriele Salvatores' *The Invisible Boy* (2014) and its 2018 sequel. Trieste-based director Katja Colja chose the Barcola waterfront to represent the protagonists' connection to the sea in *Rosa* (2019), while Mauro Mancini shot some scenes for *Thou Shalt Not Hate* (2020) inside Trieste's synagogue.

Literature
Friulian-Language Literature
The earliest-known poems written in the Friulian language date from the 14th century. Courtly in nature, they were produced by notaries: an important *Schola notariorum* was active in Cividale in the 14th century.

Cinephiles will find their Valhalla at Gemona's Cineteca del Friuli. Home to thousands of meticulously archived films, the cinémathèque's highly regarded collection includes over 1000 silent films, cartoons and a variety of documentaries, particularly on WWI.

Travelling cinephiles keen on visiting film locations in Friuli Venezia Giulia should check out www.cineturismo fvg.com, which offers themed itineraries and a round-up of all the films and TV shows shot in the region, either by genre or by location.

The notary Antonio Porenzoni, for example, wrote his amorous ballad *Piruç myo doç inculurit* on the blank page of one of his deeds.

The Venetian hegemony of the 15th century saw Friulian literature become more 'mainstream'. Consequently, the region's native language was temporarily relegated to more administrative duties, such as humanist Pietro Capretto's *Constitutioni della Patria del Friouli (Constitutions of the Friulan Motherland)*. In its preface, the author declares that he chose the Friulian language because the Tuscan dialect (on which standard Italian is now based) was 'too obscure to the Friulian people'.

Pordenone-born Guarnerio d'Artegna played a crucial role in enriching the region's print landscape. The humanist and passionate bibliophile donated his collection of 173 literary manuscripts to the church of San Daniele on the condition that a library would be established and made accessible to all who wished to consult it. Consequently, the Biblioteca Guarneriana was founded on 8 October 1466, becoming one of Italy's first public libraries.

The re-emergence of Friulian in mid-16th century poetry was a rebellious act, used in deliberate opposition to the more courtly Tuscan dialect.

The 17th century delivered a trio of Friulian literary greats: Eusebio Stella, known for his licentious poems, Ciro di Pers, and, chiefly, Ermes di Colloredo. Considered the father of Friulian literature, di Colloredo ditched the broader Italian style to produce literary works that were proudly, distinctly regional, and a language that would become the basis for contemporary Friulian.

While Friuli Venezia Giulia produced little literature of great significance in the 18th and early 19th centuries, the mid-19th century saw the emergence of one of its most important literary figures: Pietro Zorutti. Between 1821 and 1867 the poet published his popular 'Strolic', an annual almanac of poetry written in the Friulian language.

> Linguistics lovers familiar with (or curious about) Friulian will appreciate Carla Marcato's language guide *Il lessico friulano* (2014).

FRIULIAN

A romance language belonging to the Rhaeto-Romanic language group (don't call it a dialect!), Friulian has been officially recognised as a historic minority language since 1999. The language is protected, hence the region's bilingual signs. Like all languages, it has dozens of variations and nuances, undetectable to the untrained ear but crystal clear to the Friulians. While some say that 'proper' Friulian is the version spoken in Udine (Central Friulian), it's not uncommon to hear other areas claiming the title, from Gorizia to Pordenone.

The following is a list of basic terms in Friulian:

Greetings & Basic Conversation

Hello.	*Bundì, buinesere*
Goodbye.	*Mandi.*
Excuse me.	*Che mi scusi.*
I'm sorry.	*Mi displâs.*
Please.	*Par plasê.*
Thank you.	*Gracîs.*
You're welcome.	*Di ce?*
Yes.	*Sì.*
No.	*No.*

Signs

Open	*Viârt*
Closed	*Siarât*
Entrance	*Jentrade*
Information	*Informasions*
Toilet/Restroom	*Le tualet*
Ladies	*Feminis*
Gents	*Omps*
Exit	*Jesude*
Prohibited	*Proibît*

In the 20th century, Friulian stepped out of the regional wings and onto the national stage thanks to Pier Paolo Pasolini. During his sojourn in Friuli in the 1940s, the renowned writer and film director promoted Friulian-language literature, publishing his own collection of Friulian poetry, *Poesie a Casarsa*, in 1942. Interestingly, the last book published by the writer was also a collection of poems in Friulian, *La nuova gioventù* (1974).

In addition to penning award-winning novels in Italian, Carlo Sgorlon also published three in Friulian: *Prime di sere* (2005), *Il Dolfin* (1993) and *Ombris tal infinît* (2010) .

Between the 19th & 20th Centuries

Between the 19th and 20th centuries, Trieste and Venezia Giulia provided a fertile ground for writers, who found inspiration in the area's cosmopolitanism, borderland position and search for a defined cultural identity, not to mention the strong sense among Trieste's intellectuals of being called to a kind of mission.

The greatest and most prolific writers of this period are Italo Svevo and Umberto Saba. Svevo (the pseudonym of Ettore Schmitz, 1861–1928) straddled two worlds: that of business from which he hailed (his father was a Jewish-German merchant) and the world of literature, with which he had a conflicting relationship.

Hostile to ideological positions and alignments, and a friend of James Joyce, another great writer who spent many years living in Trieste, Svevo wrote three great novels, *Una vita* (1892), *Senilità* (1898) and *La coscienza di Zeno* (1923).

Umberto Saba (1883–1957), from a Jewish family on his mother's side, steered clear of the main literary currents of his time. Very attached to the city of Trieste, in which he ran a bookstore for years, the writer made everyday life the main subject of his intimate, confessional poems, which often conformed to 19th-century poetic metre. Originally published in 1921, Saba's vast collection of poems, *Il Canzoniere*, was supplemented in 1947 and finally revised and further supplemented posthumously in 1961.

Alongside Svevo and Saba, the literary landscape of the period included other important writers and poets, many of whom were intense, tormented figures. Despite ending his life at a very young age, Gorizia's Carlo Michaelstaedter (1887–1910) produced a large volume of work, examining in his short stories, essays and poems the relationship between the individual, life and death.

The intellectual Scipio Slataper (1888–1915), who perhaps best embodied the very essence of being Triestine, began his career by contributing to Giuseppe Prezzolini's *La Voce*. His works, which include diaries and epistolaries, are marked by strong moral tensions, a poetically tragic sense of life, and the lure of the wilderness. Slataper, whose only novel is *Il mio Carso* (1912), was killed in battle on Monte Podgora.

Carlo Stuparich (1894–1916) left only one work, a collection of poems and letters called *Cose ed ombre di uno*, published posthumously in 2006. Like Slataper, he too fell in WWI: killed on Monte Cengio at the age of 21, he was awarded the gold medal for military valour in memoriam.

Stuparich's brother Giani (1891–1961) oversaw the publication of his late sibling's work, as well as that of Stuparich. Also a writer who had fought on the Italian front, Giani Stuparich himself produced various short stories and essays, as well as the memoir *Trieste nei miei ricordi* (1948).

ARTS & LITERATURE LITERATURE

Corinna Opara's guidebook *Three Days in Trieste: Five Itineraries In and Around Town* (Beit, 2013) offers five routes for exploring the city. It also contains a reprint of an 1858 guidebook: it's up to you to find out what has changed since then.

The Biblioteca Guarneriana in San Daniele claims two especially curious items: the world's smallest book and a micrographic edition of Dante's *Divine Comedy*. Consisting of tiny characters indecipherable to the naked eye, miniature texts were highly fashionable among 19th-century bibliophiles.

Contemporary Writers

In his *Istrian Trilogy*, consisting of the novels *Materada* (1960), *La ragazza di Petrovia* (1963) and *Il bosco di acacie* (1966), Istrian writer Fulvio Tomizza (1935–99) recounts the dramatic tale of those forced to leave their Istrian homeland and expresses nostalgia for his native land, passed to Yugoslavia in 1954. The vicissitudes of 20th-century Istria are also the focus of his novel *La miglior vita*, recipient of the prestigious Strega Prize in 1977.

Enzo Bettiza (1927–2017), world-renowned journalist, essayist and novelist, published numerous books over more than 60 years. Among them are *Il fantasma di Trieste* (1958), *I fantasmi di Mosca* (1993) and *Esilio* (1996).

The great essayist Claudio Magris (1939–) is one of Friuli Venezia Giulia's most influential figures. His most famous works include *Danubio* (1986), *Trieste: Un'identità di frontiera* (2015) and *Microcosmi* (1997), for which he won the Premio Strega in 1997. The internationally acclaimed writer and academic immerses readers in the intellectual world of 20th-century Trieste in *Ti devo tanto di ciò che sono* (2014), which reveals the correspondence between Magris and his teacher Biagio Marin, an intellectual and poet from Grado.

Nominated for the Nobel Prize in Literature several times, Slovenian-speaking Triestine writer Boris Pahor (1913–2022) traces key episodes of the Italian and Slovenian 20th century from first-hand experience. His novel *V labirintu* (Dentro il labirinto, 1984) transports readers to 1940s Trieste, weaving individual stories into the broader narrative of world conflicts and the contrasts between Italians and Slovenes.

His most famous book, *Nekropola* (Necropoli, 1967), focuses on the history of a concentration camp, offering a different view of political deportation from Italy and the persecution of the Slavs.

For a somewhat unconventional read about Pahor's life and thoughts, *Quello che ho da dirvi – dialogo tra generazioni lontane un secolo* (2015) documents the dialogue between a centenarian Pahor and six Gen-Z 18 year olds.

Journalist Paolo Rumiz (1947–) has long chronicled Trieste, Istria and the Balkans: his book *È oriente* (2005) includes a piece entitled *Il frico e la jota*. Along with Rumiz, Italy's most successful Friulian writers are Mauro Covacich (1965–), a journalist and writer of travel stories, and Mauro Corona, whose novel *La voce degli uomini freddi* (2013) placed him among the five finalists for the 2014 Campiello Prize.

Another writer worth mentioning is Gian Mario Villalta (1959–). Poet, playwright, novelist and artistic director of the Pordenonelegge festival, his *L'apprendista* (2020), nominated for the Strega Prize, delves deep into the heart of Friulian village life.

Several books by Milanese-born, Carnia-based writer and publisher Paolo Morganti are set in 16th-century Friuli. His latest novel, *Fantasmi in viaggio* (2021), however, is a wonderfully surreal declaration of love for the Northeast; a supernatural road trip in which a bus full of luminary literary ghosts head to a conference in Gorizia.

Fans of detective fiction can immerse themselves in the icy wilderness of Friuli's mountains as Commissioner Teresa Battaglia solves crimes in Ilaria Tuti's (1976–) series of best-selling novels, among them *Fiori sopra l'inferno* (2018), *Ninfa dormiente* (2019) and *Figlia della cenere* (2021).

Another outstanding younger writer is Pordenone-born Enrico Galiano (1977–), whose debut novel *Eppure cadiamo felici* garnered significant attention upon its release in 2017.

Inaugurated in 1994, the 'Latisana per il Nord-est' International Literary Prize is reserved for writers born or resident in the area between Friuli Venezia Giulia, Trentino-Alto Adige, Veneto, Slovenia, Austria and Croatia, and whose works are set in these territories.

Trieste in Five Books

La città celeste, by Diego Marani (2021)

Trieste di carta. Guida letteraria della città Paper Trieste, by Gianni Cimador (2020)

Trieste. Un'identità di frontiera, by Angelo Ara and Claudio Magris (2015)

Trieste sottosopra: quindici passeggiate nella città del vento, by Mauro Covacich (2006)

Trieste and the Meaning of Nowhere, by Jan Morris (2001)

The work's focus is adolescence, a subject Galiano knows well given his experience as a teacher. The writer is also behind 'Cose da prof,' a web series viewed more than 20 million times.

Germany, too, has brought Trieste and its surrounds back into the spotlight, with Trieste-based German writer Veit Heinichen showcasing the city in works like *Triest: Stadt der Winde* (Trieste: La città dei venti, 2005).

In his more recent novel *Die Zeitungsfrau* (La giornalaia, 2016), Heinichen combines detective fiction with forays into the history of art and Trieste itself.

Food & Wine

The cuisine of Friuli Venezia Giulia is the lovechild of Venetian, Slavic and Central European flavours, and its culinary traditions are fiercely protected and flaunted. From the mountain specialities of Carnia to the lagoon specialities of the Adriatic, each corner of the region offers its own distinct culinary experiences. Many recipes have humble origins, created in times when necessity demanded the use of leftovers and the storage of food for the winter. The result is simple but friendly. Of course, there's nothing meagre about the region's wines. Here, 20,000 hectares of vines claim no less than 10 DOC and four DOCG areas. From the vino and salumi (cured meats), to the cheeses and the honey, the common factor in Friuli is excellence.

Bread, Polenta & Sweets

Friuli Venezia Giulia's bread-making tradition is associated with the *pancogole,* women bakers who roamed the streets of Trieste, bread basket balanced on their heads. Their fame as bakers (and possibly as equilibrists) reached the Hapsburg courts in the 18th century.

One fruit of this tradition is the *biga servolana,* a type of bread that takes its name from Trieste's Servola district and is made by combining two loaves in a single piece. You'll find it baking in every oven in Venezia Giulia.

Another favourite in Trieste is the *cornetto istriano,* a croissant-shaped pastry introduced by immigrant Istrian bakers.

Typical of the province of Udine is the *grispolenta,* a large breadstick made of corn and wheat flour, oil and lard.

The *rosetta* has Austro-Hungarian roots (it was once known as kaiser bread), its five-petalled, flower-shaped bun often garnished with sesame and poppy seeds.

Produced by the Regional Agency for Rural Development (ERSA), the beautifully illustrated *Cibario del Friuli Venezia Giulia, Atlante dei Prodotti della Tradizione* (Ersa, 2015) offers a wealth of information on the region's culinary specialities.

Richer and more elaborate are the *pan de frizze* – made with wheat and rye flour, lard, pork crackling *(frizze)* and eggs – and the *pan di sorc,* a round loaf with a dark crust, yellow crumb and polenta-like aroma. The yellow hue comes from the corn flour, which is blended with rye and wheat flour, dried figs, wild fennel and raisins. Originating in the Gemona area and traditionally consumed at Christmas, it's one of the region's Slow Food darlings.

The peasant dish par excellence, polenta is a staple across the region. Usually yellow, it tends to get whiter (and, in home kitchens, have a runnier consistency) the closer you are to the coast. Introduced to Europe by explorers returning from the 'New World', polenta soon spread to the Friuli plain: in Udine, corn was sold in the markets as early as the second half of the 16th century. Corn flour is available in many varieties in the region: corn from Carnia is excellent, while the area around Tarvisio cultivates *resia corn,* whose distinctive grain fades from yellow to red. Mortegliano, on the other hand, is known for its premium-quality *Blave di Mortean.*

Flour is also a staple in most of Friuli Venezia Giulia's sweets. The region, despite its impoverished past, has a repertoire of festive treats. Carnia is famous for its *biscotti esse* (S-shaped biscuits), made using flour,

TYPICAL DISHES

Mouth watering at the thought of sampling Friuli Venezia Giulia's flavours? Look out for the following classics on the region's menus:

➡ Trieste: *jota* (soup with beans, potatoes and cabbage, sauerkraut and, occasionally, sausage or *cotechino*), goulash, *struccolo de pomi* (apple strudel), *presnitz* or *cuguluf* (or Kugelhupf, a sort of *panettone* with Viennese roots), *sardoni fritti e impanati* (fried crumbed sardines), *ribaltavapori* (smelt), *baccalà alla triestina* (Trieste-style stockfish), *brodetto di pesce* (fish stew), *scampi alla busara* (scampi in a rich tomato sauce), *mussoli* and *dondoli* (types of molluscs), *sarde in savôr* (sweet-and-sour sardines), *prosciutto cotto di Trieste* (Trieste cooked ham), *gnochi de susini* (gnocchi with plums) and *lepre alla boema* (sweet-and-sour hare sauce with polenta).

➡ Gorizia: potato gnocchi with plums (topped with melted butter, cinnamon and sugar), *patate in tecia* (pan-fried potatoes), *kaiserfleisch* (smoked pork loin sprinkled with freshly grated horseradish and served with sauerkraut), *ljubljanska* (schnitzel stuffed with ham and cheese), *rosa di Gorizia* (a rose-shaped radicchio) and Cormòns prosciutto.

➡ Udine: *frico* (potato, onion and Montasio cheese pancake), *musèt e la brovada* (local sausage with fermented turnip), *gubana* (snail-shaped cake stuffed with walnuts, pine nuts, vanilla, lemon peel, sugar and grappa), white asparagus from Tavagnacco, white truffle from Muzzana del Turgnano, prosciutto from Sauris, borlotti beans and pork shank from Carnia, *cjalzons* (ravioli stuffed with ricotta and herbs, seasoned with melted butter, smoked ricotta and cinnamon) and *malga* (mountain cheese).

➡ Pordenone: *pitina* (cured and smoked meatball), Asìno cheese, *formai del cit* (a spreadable cow-milk cheese), *figo moro di Caneva* (Caneva fig), Ovoledo potatoes, Cavasso red onion and *biscotto Pordenone*.

butter, sugar and vanilla, and flavoured in different ways depending on the area (most often with lemon or Marsala). Flour, sugar, almonds, eggs, coarse salt, aromatics and a dash of alcohol underscore sweet-and-salty *biscotti Pordenone,* which enjoy their own registered trademark. Almonds decorate spicy *biscotti pevarins,* while blanched almonds conspire with flour, sugar, eggs and honey in the occasionally pink-hued *favette treistine,* another Habsburg heirloom.

Made in Resia, in the Tarvisio area of Friuli Venezia Giulia, oven-baked *buiadnik* is a festive dessert consisting of dried and fresh fruit, corn flour and wheat. *Colaz,* a ring-shaped cake made of wheat flour, butter, sugar and spices, is eaten in the area between Udine and Pordenone. Traditionally, it was offered to children on their confirmation day by their godparents.

It's impossible to write about Friulian sweets without mentioning *gubana* and *strucchi,* both typical of the Valli del Natisone.

Gubana is a snail-shaped cake made of stuffed leavened dough and baked in the oven.

Strucchi contain the same filling (walnuts, pine nuts, vanilla, lemon peel, sugar and grappa) but are shaped like small rectangles and fried.

Easter staples include the *pinza triestina,* a leavened cake prepared in Venezia Giulia, and the *presnitz,* which has Central European origins. The latter, produced between Trieste and Gorizia, consists of puff pastry and a spiral-shaped filling made from dried fruit. Similar, though more moist and fluffier, is *putizza,* made with leavened dough and decadently filled with dried fruit, apricot jam, cocoa and rum.

In 2017, after a long dispute with Veneto, the region won the right to claim *tiramisu* as its own, with the coffee-soaked dessert added to its list of traditional regional dishes.

Alberto Tonizzo's *La cucina friulana dalle risorgive al mare* (De Bastiani, 2009) features recipes from the lower Friuli area and coast. For fans of Pordenone cuisine, there's Adriano Del Fabro's *Cucina friulana. Ricette tradizionali della provincia di Pordenone* (Terra Ferma Edizioni, 2009).

FOOD & WINE BREAD, POLENTA & SWEETS

Cheese

Friuli Venezia Giulia has a strong and ancient tradition of cheesemaking. Most of the region's cheeses hail from the mountainous Carnia area, whose *malghe* (alpine shepherd huts) have most prominently shaped the styles and characteristics of the region's offerings. *Malga* cheese can be sampled throughout the Alps, in particular in the area between Pordenone and Carnia. It's made by mixing raw cow's milk collected in the morning with semi-skimmed milk collected the previous evening. In some cases, goat's milk is used. The resulting curd is cooked, then brined before the wheels of cheese are ripened in the *malghe.* The ripening process is completed in a storeroom down in the valley.

Also worth a mention are Carnia's smoked goat and cow ricotta – processed in the *malghe* to help preserve the ricotta – and *ont,* a type of local ghee.

Over time, the farmers situated in the valleys have established dairy co-operatives equipped with better cheesemaking techniques, technology and work processes for the production of what are ever more sophisticated cheeses. Among these is *Latteria,* produced throughout the region (hence the usual inclusion of the place of origin in its name) using heat-treated milk and selected enzymes.

Across in the Carso, *Tabor* is produced in a similar manner using the milk of fodder-fed cows. Before maturing for at least a month, *Tabor* is immersed in brine for 24 hours.

Montasio is one of the most famous and iconic cheeses of Friuli Venezia Giulia, with its own DOP appellation to prove it. It has been produced on the Montasio plateau for almost a millennium, from where it has spread throughout the region over the years. The cheese is made using cow's milk aged from 30 days to three years, a factor which determines the cheese's flavour profile. Montasio is also the main ingredient of *frico,* one Friuli's most famous dishes.

Asìno is another of the region's signature cheeses. Available in two types (classic and soft), it's a salty, cow's milk cheese matured in special brines and produced between Clauzetto and Spilimbergo. Although its name means 'donkey' in Italian, it actually takes its name from Monte d'Asio. *Monte Re* cheese, on the other hand, is produced in a single dairy in Monrupino, on the border between Slovenia and the Trieste Carso. At one time it was made with a combination of goat, sheep and cow's milk; these days the latter is mainly used.

Originally from Carnia, *Formadi Frant* is made by mixing cheeses of different origin and maturity, adding salt, pepper, milk and cream, and storing the end product for 40 days. Originally conceived as a way of conserving perishable cheeses, its flavour is equally sweet and spicy. *Formai del Cìt* is a variant of *Formadi Frant* produced in Val Tramontina. It's aged for 10 days and stored in a stone vase called a *cit.*

Sot la Trape is made by soaking *caciotte* in pomace for several days before letting it age. The cheese is delicate and a little spicy, with a purplish or yellow rind (depending on whether it has been dipped in white or red grape must). While very common in Carnia, you'll also find it in Val Canale, where you can also taste the rare *Cuincîr,* a cream made

In the summer months, it's possible to stay overnight in one of the region's many *malghe* (alpine huts). Visit at the right time and you'll be able to help herd the cattle up towards the mountains or even partake in a little cheesemaking.

from fresh ricotta mixed with salt, pepper and wild fennel seeds, and aged for almost two months. Carnia, Val Canale and the whole area of the Friulian Dolomites are also known for *çuç di Mont*. Made with the milk of cows that graze in the *malghe* in summer, the cheese is aged for at least 45 days.

Pork

No ingredient quite defines the traditional cuisine of Friuli Venezia Giulia like pork, and the region's hams and sausages are renowned around the world. The proud tradition of curing and smoking meat has ancient Roman or Celtic origins, and every stage of the process is meticulously controlled to guarantee its famous quality.

The towns of San Daniele, Cormòns and Sauris constitute Friuli's *triangolo d'oro* (golden triangle) of prosciutto production, and each town's version has its own distinct characteristics. *Prosciutto San Daniele,* one of Friuli Venezia Giulia's best-known DOP products, is aged for at least 12 months. Cut into thin slices, this *prosciutto crudo* (raw ham) has a distinctly sweet, delicate flavour and is often served with figs or melon. *Prosciutto di Cormòns* is lightly smoked using cherry wood, bay leaf, herbs and other spices, while *prosciutto di Sauris* is smoked using beech wood.

Another smoked Friulian classic is speck, produced in Carnia and made from the upper, fatty part of the thigh. The area around Pordenone is known for *filon,* also lightly smoked but obtained from the lean, boneless loin.

Prosciutto crudo (cured ham) itself has absorbed influences from Central European. Throughout the region, but especially in Trieste and the Carso, the ham is usually baked in the oven for four hours in a leavened black bread dough, which is later removed. It's then served with mustard and *kren* (a horseradish-based sauce) and makes for a delicious *rebechin* (p76).

Sausages worth trying include Friulian salami, lightly spiced, with or without garlic. The humble origins of Friulian cuisine are reflected in the region's sausage making, which often uses the fattiest, cheapest cuts of pork. The results are excellent, if occasionally challenging for more delicate stomachs. Among these more robust classics is *coppa di testa*, whose name ('cup of head') alludes to its contents. *Linguâl* is made from pig's tongue, which is sometimes cut into pieces and mixed with other meats. Fatty meats and herbs conspire in *lujànie,* which is served cooked. *Muset* is one of the best-known Friulian sausages, made of lean pork, muscle, snout and lard; like *cotechino,* it's traditionally served with *brovada* (fermented turnips).

For intrepid food lovers there's *polmonarie*: traditionally made using the lungs, heart, kidneys and lard of the pig, it's smoked and matured for two weeks. Another hardcore sausage is the *sanganel,* which sees boiled pig's blood combined with fresh meat and lard. Typical of the area between Artegna and Buia, *crafût* is a crumbed liver meatball made using breadcrumbs, grapes, citrus peel, apples and spices, then squeezed into sausage casing. Also worth a mention is *marcundela,* a mix of liver, spleen, kidneys, lungs, belly fat and bloody meats wrapped in pork omentum and cooked in red wine (it can also be fried).

Lard is chopped, spiced and smoked for two months to make *argjel,* a spread that is typical of the Canal del Ferro and Val Canale areas. Although unappetising to look at, it's delicious spread on bread. Then there's *pestât*. Produced throughout Friuli by grinding fresh lard together with whatever vegetables one has at home, it's used to flavour a number of dishes.

In San Daniele alone, more than two million hams are produced annually, each one rigorously inspected by hand to guarantee its quality.

The word 'prosciutto' comes from the Latin *prae exuctus*, which means 'very dry'.

Sheep, Cattle & Game

Pork is not the only meat you'll encounter on your Friulian culinary adventures. After all, this region 'at the crossroads' has for centuries nourished locals, travellers and traders for whom pork is forbidden. Already in the 16th century, dozens of pork-free recipes had made their way here from Venice's Jewish Ghetto. One traditional meat that some may find surprising is goose, whose use is not limited to *foie gras*. Geese have long been reared in the area between Morsano al Tagliamento, Palmanova and Aiello del Friuli, and it's here that you can sample authentic goose salami, *prosciuttino, cotto d'oca* (stuffed, smoked goose) and *porcaloca,* similar to *cotto d'oca* but stuffed with pork. Just leave room for local goose breast and speck, the latter seasoned and smoked in a similar fashion to the pork version.

Cattle and sheep farms are widespread throughout Friuli Venezia Giulia. The region even claims its own breed of cow, the Pezzatta Rossa. Not only does it provide high-quality meat, but also prized milk used to make outstanding dairy products.

Brusaula, typical of Pordenone, is made using dried chamois meat (also beef or pork these days) preserved for many months. On the other hand, the Val Tramontina's *pitina* is a salami-type 'meatball' made from venison, goat or mutton.

Prized *cappone friulano* (Friulian capon) is also excellent. A young, neutered rooster fed on a diet of cereal and milk, it was once given as a gift by breeders to the landowners.

The Pezzata Rossa Italiana cow originated in Friuli at the end of the 19th century by crossing the Friulana and Simmenthal breeds. Once called the Pezzata Rossa Friulana, it spread from Italy's northeast to the rest of the country. It's not an especially common animal, with a population of around 400,000 in Italy today.

Fish

Given the dominance of rivers, lagoons and the sea in Friuli Venezia Giulia, it's not surprising that fish plays an essential part in local cooking. Top billing goes to trout, with the region accounting for 40% of national production. Curiously, while San Daniele is internationally renowned for its eponymous prosciutto, locals also celebrate the town for its smoked trout. Indeed, one of the two variants on the market is called *regina di San Daniele* (Queen of San Daniele). As is the case for meat and cheese, trout was originally smoked to preserve it over long periods of time.

Fish farms are common in the lagoon area between Grado and Marano, and many breed eels using historic methods. *Bisato in speo* is a simple dish of grilled eel, cooked with rock salt and bay leaves according to a traditional recipe of Laguna di Marano. In the area surrounding Grado, you can sample *matàn,* a delicacy in which eagle ray is sliced, hung and left to dry in the sun in the area's old *casoni* (fishermen's huts). Other Grado specialities include *sepe sofegae,* a type of stewed cuttlefish, and *boreto alla graisana,* a fish stew seasoned with garlic, vinegar and black pepper, and served with polenta.

Also worth tasting is the *mormora di Miramare,* a wild fish found on the sandy seabed between Barcola and Sistiana, and the classic *sardoni in savor* (fried sardines marinated in onion and vinegar the day before serving) or *soto sal* (sardines preserved in salt).

The Trieste coastline is known for its mussel farming. Called *pedocio de Trieste* by the locals, the mussels are selected on the basis of size and sold live, following a tradition that dates back to the 18th century. The Saccaleva squid is fished in the Gulf of Trieste (beams of light installed on the boats lure the critters to the nets) and served wonderfully fresh. Other molluscs found on the region's menus include *mussolo de scoio* collected from the rockier sections of the seabed, *dondolo,* or *tartufo di mare* (sea truffle) and *canocia de nassa* (mantis shrimp). The latter, also known as *cannocchia di nassa,* is caught using *nasse* (basket traps) and also sold live.

SMALL PRODUCERS WORTH SAFEGUARDING

Several traditional Friulian products claim the Slow Food Presidium brand (garlic from Resia, the onion from Cavasso and Val Cosa, *Formadi Frant*, *Formaggio dei Latteria Turnaria* (Latteria Turnaria Cheese), *çuç di Mont*, *pan di sorc*, *pestât di Fagagna*, *pitina*, *radic di mont* and *rosa di Gorizia*) and the attention of the Ark of Taste, created by Slow Food foundation to protect heritage foods endangered by large-scale industrial agriculture and environmental degradation. Regional edibles at risk of extinction include *Varhackara*, a pesto made with white lard, speck, smoked bacon and aromatic herbs. It's a typical product of Timau, a hamlet in the municipality of Paluzza (Udine province).

Fruit & Vegetables

Friuli Venezia Giulia's vegetable plots produce some unique varieties which have helped shape the region's culinary habits and identity. Among them is *aglio di Resia* (Resia garlic), known for its small, reddish bulb and rather strong flavour. The white asparagus grown in the provinces of Udine, Pordenone and Gorizia is fleshy, bitter-sweet and devoid of the stringiness of its better-known green relative. Some varieties of beans are also at risk of extinction, such as *cesarins,* which grows in Val Pesarina and resembles a pea (*cesarons* in Friulian), and *fasûi borlots* (borlotti beans), still shelled by hand and stored in jute bags. Different types of radicchio include the greenish, bitter-tasting *lidrìc cul poc,* found throughout the Friuli plain; the yellow-and-red hued *radicchio canarino*; and the *rosa di Gorizia,* which actually resembles a rose. A highly prized variety due to its labour-intensive cultivation, you'll find it in the Isonzo area, served raw and seasoned with oil and vinegar or in the form of a spread.

Fruit growing also has very ancient origins in these parts. You'll notice a profusion of jams and syrups, especially in the region's hilly and mountainous areas, where isolation from the cities made it necessary to preserve fruit. These areas are well known for *olivello spinoso* (seabuckthorn), a hardy shrub producing tart berries used to make syrups and jams (especially in Carnia). Other tasty syrups include one made by grinding raspberries, blueberries, black and red currants together, as well as syrups made with dandelion and elderberry. Originally created as thirst quenchers (to dilute in water) or cough remedies, these syrups have become a part of the region's culinary heritage.

Apples are used to produce tasty apple juice requiring no added sugar. Meanwhile, the region's most common native apple variety, *Zeuka,* is used to make a curious side dish that accompanies roasted meat. *Most,* on the other hand, is a cider produced from pears. The fruit is also used to create a fragrant spirit widespread in the Arta Terme area.

The region's *ciliegie* (cherries) are also prized. Don't miss the *duracina* cherry from Tarcento. Cultivated in the Udine area for more than a century, its plants grow free or in pots, and without the use of pesticides. Between May and June, cherries abound between Udine and the Collio, but also in the Carso: your nose will pick up the scent on the hillside trails.

Cultivated in the provinces of Udine and Gorizia, the *pesca insontina* (Isonzo peach) has a firm, yellow flesh. The white flesh of the *pesca triestina* (Trieste peach) becomes red closer to the pit, while the *pesca iris rosso* (red iris peach) features a firm, white flesh.

Harvested between July and August, the *figo moro* is a fig with a more elongated shape than the common variety. Its flavour is sweeter too.

Autumn brings an abundance of *castagne* (chestnuts) throughout the region: expect to forage or taste your fair share in the Alpine foothills.

Friuli Venezia Giulia's climate and soil have always favoured the cultivation of apples: the fruit was already a hit in Roman times, when locally grown *mazia* apples were sold across the empire.

In the Pordenone area, the *marrone di Vito d'Asio* (Vito d'Asio marron chestnut) is larger in size and used in exclusive food products.

Oil & Vinegar

Although butter shapes many of Friuli Venezia Giulia's traditional dishes, the region's soil, climate and *cultivars* (plant varieties cultivated through selective breeding) conspire to produce high-quality extra virgin olive oil. Generally, the local oil is known for its mild spice: those from the Trieste area tend to be more bitter, while those from hilly areas are sweeter. Outstanding options include Tergeste DOP oil (produced with olives from the Trieste area), oil from the Carso area, and that from the Colli Orientali del Friuli. The cultivation of olive trees was abruptly halted in the area between Udine and Gorizia after a severe frost in the winter of 1929. Thankfully, the groves are back, gracing the hills between Cormòns and Cividale.

The tradition of olive-oil production stands side by side with that of vinegar, whose Friulian roots date back to the time of the Romans and the Patriarchate of Aquileia. *Aceto di mela* (apple vinegar), commonly found in Carnia, and *salsa balsamica* (balsamic sauce), made from cooked must aged in wooden barrels, are particularly popular. Vinegar aficionados will appreciate the Subida di Josko Sirck, a beautiful vinegar factory in Cormòns.

Friuli Venezia Giulia's extra virgin olive oil is unique sensorially (the oil produced around Trieste is distinctly bitter) and nutritionally; it's packed with vitamins and antioxidants, and especially suitable for children and the elderly.

Honey

Until sugar made its grand debut in Europe, honey was the sweetener par excellence for centuries. Its production in Friuli Venezia Giulia is linked to a long tradition of beekeeping. In the Carso, look for *miele di acacia* (a very sweet, runny, straw-yellow honey) and *miele di marasca* (amber in colour and more bitter). The Valli del Natisone is known for *miele di castagno,* an amber-hued honey with a fairly strong bitter taste with hints of mint. Dandelion is used to create *miele di tarassaco,* a yellowish, creamy honey.

Wine

Wine-growing runs through Friuli Venezia Giulia's veins, and while the region's production represents only a small percentage of Italy's overall output, it compensates by crafting some of the country's most outstanding drops. Around 70% of Friuli Venezia Giulia's wines are (internationally acclaimed) whites, though its highly idiosyncratic reds are also often praised by discerning palates. The most evocative spot to savour these drops is at the wineries themselves, scattered throughout the region.

Friuli Venezia Giulia & Its Producers

Friuli Venezia Giulia grows an encyclopaedic number of grape varieties. Eighty percent of Italy's vine cuttings are grown here, not to mention 30% of those of the EU and 25% of those in the entire world. Winemaking is concentrated in the plains surrounding Pordenone and the hills flanking the Slovenian border, stretching along the Carso and down to the coast. The region's diversity of soils and microclimates are reflected in the diversity of its wines.

White Wines from Indigenous Vines

Friulano is one of the region's signature white wines. It was known as Tocai friulano until Hungarian winemakers won the legal battle to restrict the name Tokay to wines produced in Hungary's Tokay region. In truth, both are very different creatures: Hungary's Tokay is a dessert wine made from Furmint and Hárslevelü grapes, while Italy's dry, delicate Friulano is made with a grape related to Sauvignon Blanc. With or without the

WINE FESTIVALS

Festa del Vino di Bertiolo, Udine Second and third week of March.

Festa del Vino di Brugnera, Pordenone First 15 days of April.

Alla Corte del Refosco di Faedis, Udine Third weekend of April.

Sagra del Vino, Casarsa della Delizia, Pordenone Late April to early May.

Fiera dei Vini di Corno di Rosazzo, Udine Second weekend of May.

Mostra dei Vini di Sgonico, Trieste First weekend of June.

Fiera Regionale dei Vini di Buttrio, Udine Second weekend of June.

Ein Prosit, Malborghetto, Udine Third weekend of October.

addition of 'Tocai' to its name, Friulano remains one of the most popular wines in the region, a versatile *vino* that's a popular *aperitivo* drop at wine bars. The region's flagship white, however, is Picolit, which can be traced back to the 17th century. It's an especially rare, low-yielding variety, harvested late in the season and left to dry to increase its sugar concentration. The result is a sweet and fruity wine which pairs beautifully with intensely flavoured cheeses or regional desserts. If you like sweet wines, head to the Colli Orientali to savour Ramandolo DOCG. Made using Verduzzo Friulano, it's known for its honey notes and sweet (though not cloyingly so) flavour. The same variety is used in a diverse range of still and sparkling drops, from dry whites well suited to a plate of figs and *prosciutto di San Daniele,* to the fruitiest, most fragrant sweet wines.

Delicate, dry and fragrant, Ribolla gialla is mainly produced in the Collio. In the Carso, savour dry, fresh Vitovska, a variety which, like Ribolla, is also grown in nearby Slovenia. The Carso is also the place to try the excellent Malvasia istriana: elegant and aromatic, with notes of peach and apricot, it pairs perfectly with fish.

Orange (or skin-contact) wines are white wines vinified with the same technique used to produce reds. The end result is an orange-tinged wine with richer aromas and higher tannins. Friuli is the heart of Italy's expanding orange-wine industry, with some winemakers producing skin-contact drops according to all-natural and ancient techniques. These include ageing the wine in amphorae.

> About 80 million bottles of vino are produced annually in Friuli Venezia Giulia. Of these, more than 50 million are white wine.

Red Wines from Native Vines

When it comes to the region's repertoire of reds, Refosco dal peduncolo rosso stands out. Robust, full-bodied and intensely coloured, it pairs wonderfully with fatty meats. Also worth a mention is Schioppettino. It's said that the wine got its name from when bottle fermentation would cause the cork to explode (*scoppiare* means 'burst'). Low in alcohol, it's a fresh and fruity *vino* well suited to cured meats, first courses and cheese tastings. Tazzelenghe, on the other hand, is super intense, with an acidic, astringent taste (hence the name, which means 'tongue cutter'). The Carso produces timeless, ruby-red Terrano. Also called Sangue del Carso (Blood of the Carso), it's a robust, highly tannic drop perfect with braised meats and Trieste's famous *jota* (bean and sauerkraut stew). Another native red is Pignolo: fruity, slightly tannic and with notes of wild berries, it pairs well with beef or pork.

Beer

While Friuli Venezia Giulia is renowned for its wines, the breadth and quality of its beers are testament to a flair with hops. Craft breweries both big and small dot the region, generally producing unfiltered, unpasteurised and preservative-free brews. Bire, Italy's largest craft brewery, produces six types of beer in Udine and Trieste: pilsner, red ale, black, wheat, radler and ginger ale. Just north of Trieste, the hamlet of Sgonico claims Cittavecchia and Tazebao, while Sauris is home to Zahre Beer. In Cividale, you'll find Birra Gjulia, which has recently launched Koilìa, a gluten-free brew. San Giovanni al Natisone is home to Mastro Birraio, one of the oldest breweries operating in the region. Friuli Venezia Giulia's commercial breweries include historic Birra Moretti, established in 1859 in Udine. The city would subsequently welcome another commercial player: Birra Castello.

Coffee & Grappa

The people of Trieste are the largest consumers of coffee in Italy, guzzling up to twice the national per-capita average of 5kg. In this town, coffee is culture and its history is indelibly tied to its timeless cafes, customary meeting places for literary conversations. How you choose to sip your *caffè* will depend on a number of (at times highly idiosyncratic) factors: serving size, roast, brewing technique, whether you want your brew 'corrected' (a splash of grappa, perhaps?), right down to the shape and material of the cup. Since the 19th century, coffee has arrived here in the form of raw beans, then roasted at the plethora of *torrefazioni* (coffee roasters) scattered across the region.

It's believed that grappa was first produced in the Friulian town of Cividale, in the 6th century CE.

In Friuli, grappa is called *sgnape* and its tradition runs parallel to that of wine. Pomace brandy was already being distilled at the time of the barbarian invasions, the practice possibly introduced by the Burgundians. Nonino is one of the most famous and historic distilleries in the region (and in Italy), founded in 1897 and still in operation. It was the first company to market grappa in eye-catching bottles, leading to its widespread popularity. Today, numerous Friulian distilleries produce excellent grappas using the pomace of indigenous and non-indigenous grapes.

Environment

Friuli Venezia Giulia is one of Europe's most biodiverse regions. Despite occupying only three percent of Italy's landmass, it's home to one-third of the fauna found in the country. Furthermore, the region claims about one-tenth of Italy's endemic species, spread between its snow-capped mountains, lagoons, rivers, lakes and plateaus. Indeed, due to its geographic position, the region has an extraordinary diversity of natural environments located within short distances of each other. Add to this the unique takes each season brings and you have a region where no two trips will ever be the same.

Friuli Venezia Giulia can be divided into four broad geographic areas: the mountains of the north, the hills and plains of the centre, the sea and lagoons of the south, and the Carso (Karst) plateau of the southeast. On top of this is a local division determined by the Tagliamento River, one which gave birth to the colloquial expressions *di là da l'aghe* (beyond the waters) and *di ca da l'aghe* (on this side of the waters). *Di ca* refers to the Tagliamento's 'Left Bank' and *di la* to its right.

Mountains

The easternmost section of the Alps straddles the north of Friuli Venezia Giulia, ending with the softer forms of the Julian Alps. While this section of the Alps is somewhat lower in height – the region's highest mountain, Monte Coglians, is a relatively modest 2780m – its well suited to all matter of alpine sports. Indeed, the area of Sella Nevea, near Tarvisio, is one of the snowiest in Europe, with snow depths of up to 7m.

Starting from the northwest, on the border with Veneto, the region's Alps begin with the Dolomites, which belongs to the Carnic Prealps. To the east are the Carnic Alps, followed by the Julian Alps.

The Friulian section of the Dolomites is larger, wilder and less populated than the Trentino section (a plus for many hikers and campers). It's home to the Parco Naturale delle Dolomiti Friulane, a national park with visitor centres in each of its gateway towns, from Erto and Casso to Forni di Sotto (reached via Barcis and Maniago). All park access points lead to excellent treks and wildlife spotting, the latter a major drawcard to the region's mountains. While the golden eagle, marmot and Eurasian capercaillie (symbol of the national park) are the most famous residents, the area harbours many other species of diurnal and nocturnal birds of prey, as well as skunks, golden jackals and salamanders. If you're especially lucky, you may even spot one of the estimated 10 bears that roam the region. Two very elusive local predators whose numbers are on the rise are the lynx and the wolf: while spotting one remains extremely difficult, their presence has been increasingly detected across Friuli's alpine landscape.

Rising between the Dolomites and the Julian Alps, the Carnic Alps are characterised by pastures and alpine meadows, pine forests, mountain lakes and several unspoiled valleys. The headwaters of the Tagliamento River are found between Carnia and Belluno, on the Friulian side of the Mauria Pass, 1195m above sea level.

Friuli Venezia Giulia is home to 3094 species of flora, equating to just under half the number counted in the entire country. Of these, 28 are endemic to the region.

The Julian Alps, on the other hand, soar along the easternmost part of Friuli Venezia Giulia, towards the border with Slovenia. The main chain of the Julian Alps is the Jôf Fuârt-Montasio. A massif located to the northeast, its name derives from its two most important mountains, Jôf Fuârt (2666m) and Jôf di Montasio (2754m). An important 14th-century sanctuary sits on Monte Santo di Lussari, cloaked in snow in the winter and surrounded by lush alpine greenery in summer.

If heading to the Julian Alps from Udine, you can also visit the Julian Prealps, between Lusevera, Resia and Venzone. Stretching east to west, they're home to a beautiful regional park, as well as many trails leading through alpine meadows and the forests of beech and pine that surround Monte Plauris (1958m) and Monte Canin (2587m). Nearby is Val Resia, a tiny valley that has developed its own linguistic and cultural traditions.

In the winter of 2009, 645cm of snow fell in the Tarvisio area, smashing a 50-year record. This new record lasted five short years, with 670cm falling on Monte Canin in 2014.

Plains & Hills

The Friulian and Julian hills extend south of the mountain ranges, as well as close to the Slovenian border in an area known as Slava Friulana. Along the Tagliamento basin, as well as in some other corners of the region, the hills and their microclimate have made Friuli Venezia Giulia a world-famous wine-growing region, with nine DOC areas scattered throughout its four provinces. Two of the most formidable wine-producing areas are the Collio Gorizano (Gorizian Collio) and, north of Udine, the Colline Moreniche (Moreniche Hills).

Magredi & Springs

Extending in the northern part of the Friulian plain, the Magredi (literally 'lean lands') are an arid steppe grasslands, similar to those found in Central Asia and Eastern Europe. The aridity of the Magredi isn't climate driven (Friuli Venezia Giulia is one of Italy's rainiest regions), but caused by the permeable alluvial deposits of the Cellina and Meduna Rivers, which make the Magredi especially arid and barren in summer. The waterways themselves disappear underground, resurfacing further downstream as springs. Exploring the Magredi riverbed, you'll spot mosses, lichens, and fauna that includes the Eurasian stone-curlew, a ground-nesting bird that has adapted well to this environment.

While roe deer are a common sight, other typical species are easier to hear than see, among them the grey partridge and Eurasian skylark. Like other areas of Friuli Venezia Giulia, the Magredi are an important stop for many migratory birds, including cranes, storks and cuckoos. Further south, the Friulian plain becomes much wetter. Here, springs emerge and water abounds, shaping both the landscape and the lives of those who inhabit it. Between Polcenigo and Monfalcone, groundwater rises to the surface, generating numerous canals and wetland-like peat bogs, visible throughout the Pordenone area, right down to the coastal towns of Lignano and Grado.

On a satellite map, the Magredi area appears as an immense, white 'V'.

Sea & Lagoon

Sea

Variation also underscores Friuli Venezia Giulia's coastline, which stretches from Lignano to Muggia. To the west are the brackish waters of the Laguna di Grado e Marano, where three of the region's major rivers – the Tagliamento, Isonzo and Stella – reach the sea in a series of striking landscapes. The coast itself is sandier west of the Timavo River, with especially shallow waters between Lignano and Grado. Further east, the Costiera Triestina (Trieste coast) between Duino, Sistiana and Muggia is deeper and rockier, with pebble and gravel beaches.

NATIONAL PARKS, RESERVES & PROTECTED AREAS

Parco Naturale delle Dolomiti Friulane (p215) The Tagliamento and Piave rivers bookend a vast patch of land bursting with trails and activities.

Parco Naturale Regionale delle Prealpi Giulie (p238) A long, narrow national park packed with trails and places with strong gastronomic and cultural traditions.

Riserva Naturale delle Falesie di Duino (p86) Rising dramatically out of the Adriatic blue, Duino's precipitous cliffs are a photographer's dream.

Riserva Naturale della Foce dell'Isonzo & della Valle Cavanata (p137) Amble along the marshes, spotting thousands of migratory birds and rare Camargue horses.

Forra del Cellina (p221) Dizzying cliffs plunge into turquoise Cellina waters at this spectacular gorge between Barcis, Andreis and Montereale.

Riserva Naturale Regionale del Lago di Cornino (p164) As you stroll around this crystal-clear lake, don't forget to look up: there are griffon vultures in the sky.

Riserva Naturale Val Alba An alpine park in the Maggio Udinese area, crossed by the Rio Alba and Rio Simon, and peppered with rocky ridges, dense woods, streams and waterfalls.

Riserva Naturale della Val Rosandra (p90) Spectacular views of cliffs and overhangs, plus caves, historic mills and railroads, all a stone's throw from Trieste.

Riserve Naturali della Valle Canal Novo & delle Foci dello Stella (p125 and p126) Sail between fishing huts and reeds, where the views recall Southeast Asia.

Riserva Naturale Marina di Miramare (p85) Carso views and a WWF-managed pocket of ocean teeming with marine life.

Riserva Naturale Laghi di Doberdò e Pietrarossa Two karst depressions filled with lakes.

Riserve Naturali dei Monti Lanaro e Orsario Rolling hills and elevations.

Riserve Naturali del Rio Bianco e di Cucco Pine and larch forests among rugged cliffs.

The region's marine life is incredibly rich, with both Mediterranean and colder-water Atlantic species found in the Gulf of Trieste. Numerous species use the Upper Adriatic as a breeding ground, including blue sharks, spiny dogfish, smalltooth sand tigers and sea turtles. Flora and fauna are also abundant in the area adjacent to the Area Marina Protetta di Miramare (Miramare Protected Marine Area), whose most significant species is the *Fucus virsoides*. An endemic alga of the Upper Adriatic, it belongs to the family of brown algae, usually found in much cooler waters, including the polar regions. The reserve is rich in mussels, sea urchins, limpets and thoracica, and teems with sea bass, sea bream and mullet. In winter, numerous water birds descend on the Gulf of Trieste, among them goosanders, great grebes and cormorants. With a little luck, you might spot a bottlenose dolphin. For diving aficionados there's the Riserva di Miramare, home to sea anemones, Mediterranean fanworms, octopuses and spider crabs.

Lagoon

The coastal region that extends between the mouths of the Tagliamento and the Isonzo is the northernmost lagoon in the Mediterranean. It was formed in the last millennia, due to the rising sea water level.

In the Laguna di Grado e Marano, land, river and sea conspire to create unique habitats and rare, fragile ecosystems. The lagoon's mercurial landscape is composed of islets, salt marshes (expanses of clay that protrude a few centimetres above the water level) and sandbanks that appear and disappear at the whim of the winds, tides and currents. The lagoon covers an area of 16,000 hectares, its brackish waters a mix of fresh water from the Stella, Cormor and Aussa-Corno rivers and salt water from the Adriatic, the latter flowing in from Porto Lignano and Porto Andrea and Porto Buso.

Navigating the lagoon along its channels is a unique experience, not only for the atmosphere and views, but also for the fauna and vegetation, which changes according to the salinity level of the water. The area teems with waterfowl, whose species change with the season. Nesting season brings hawks, reddish egrets, and numerous reed-bed birds, including sedge warblers and Eurasian reed warblers, similar in appearance but very different in song. Come winter, the lagoon heaves with large flocks of migratory birds, among them dunlins, curlews and numerous species of ducks, such as the Eurasian teal, gadwall and garganey.

The Carso (Karst) Plateau

Cave cravers will find some magnificent examples in Friuli Venezia Giulia: Grotta Gigante in the Carso, Grotta di San Giovanni d'Antro in the Valli del Natisone, and the 7km-long Grotta Nuova di Villanova, among the largest in Europe.

Wedged between the Julian Alps and the Adriatic Sea, stretching south towards Slovenia and Croatia, the Carso (Karst) is an arid plateau of woods, meadows and large limestone formations. The latter, millennia in the making, have been shaped by the acidity in rain, which erodes the rock in a phenomenon known as karstification. Riddled with caves, cliffs and sinkholes, the plateau is much loved by speleologists. Among the most impressive formations is the Grotta Gigante, alongside the Postojna and Skocjan caves on the plateau's Slovenian side.

Carso plant species include the European smoke tree *(Cotinus coggygria),* whose vivid autumn foliage creates the so-called 'fire of the Karst'. Come March, it's the Mediterranean spurge *(Euphorbia wulfenii)* along Trieste's rocky coast that catches the eye with its dense clusters of greenish-yellow flowers. Among the Carso's fauna are the Etruscan shrew (the smallest mammal in the world), European cat snake, peregrine falcon and blue rock thrush.

Survival Guide

DIRECTORY A–Z 288

Accessible Travel 288
Accommodation. 288
Climate. 288
Discount Cards. 289
Eating. 289
Emergencies 289
LGBTIQ + Travellers 289
Local Media. 290
Medical Assistance 290
Money 290
Tourist Information 290

TRANSPORT 291

GETTING THERE &
AWAY 291
Air 291
Land 291
Sea .292
GETTING AROUND 292
Air .292
Bicycle 292
Boat 293
Bus .293
Car & Motorcyle 293
Train 294
LOCAL TRANSPORT. 294

Directory A–Z

Accessible Travel

Italy is not an easy country for travellers with disabilities. Cobblestone streets and pavements blocked by parked cars and scooters make getting around difficult for wheelchair users. And while many buildings have lifts, they are not always wide enough for wheelchairs. Not a lot has been done to make life easier for hearing- or vision-impaired travellers either. However, awareness of accessibility issues and a culture of inclusion are steadily growing.

If travelling by train, you can arrange assistance through SalaBlu online (https://salabluonline.rfi.it) or by calling 800 90 60 60 (from a landline) or 02 32 32 32 (from a landline or mobile).

Visit the information page of Rete Ferroviaria Italiana (www.rfi.it/rfi-en/for-per sons-with-disability) for full details of services offered and barrier-free stations. If travelling on Italo services, see the website (www.italo treno.it) for more information.

Online Resources

Accessible Europe (www.accessibleurope.com)

Disabili.com (www.disabili.com)

Lonely Planet (https://shop.lonelyplanet.com/categories/ accessible-travel.com) Download Lonely Planet's free Accessible Travel guide.

Luoghi della Cultura For information: www.accessibilitamusei.beniculturali.it/ luoghi-cultura/index?catego riald=&denominazione=

Parking For information: www.aci.it/i-servizi/ per-la-mobilita/aci-per-il -sociale/contrassegno -disabili.html

Accommodation

The main cities and most popular coastal destinations offer a plethora of accommodation options. In the countryside, *agriturismi* (farm stays) abound and these often occupy historic buildings and country houses converted into comfortable, affordable, modern digs. Another slumber option gaining popularity is the *albergo diffuso,* a concept in which self-contained (self-catering) apartments in neighbouring houses in a village are rented to guests through a centralised hotel-style reception. In some cases, apartments and hotels are aimed at a specific market, for instance Lignano's 'no kids' hotel (p119). In the hinterland and mountains, idiosyncratic accomodation spans classic *agritursimi* to whimsical tree houses.

Climate

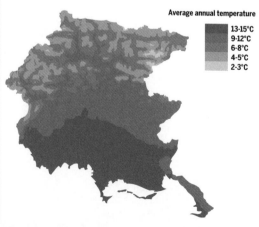

Average annual temperature

13-15°C
9-12°C
6-8°C
4-5°C
2-3°C

DISCOUNT CARDS

CARD	CONTACT	RATES
Camping Card International	☎ 055 88 23 91; www. campingcardinternational.com	€43/45, annual membership; one card per household only.
Hostelling International	www.hihostels.com	€20, annual individual membership valid in Italy and abroad
International Student Identity Card	www.isic.it	€13, valid until 31 December on the year of issue
Carta IoStudio – La Carta dello Studente	http://iostudio.pubblica. istruzione.it	distributed free to Italian high school students and valid until the completion of the school process

In this guidebook, accommodation is listed from cheapest to most expensive.

Online Resources

Agriturismi & B&Bs: www. turismofvg.it/agriturismo; www.agriturismo.it or www. agriturismo.net; www.bed -and-breakfast.it

Alberghi Diffusi: www. alberghidiffusi.it

Camping: www.camping.it; www.touringclub.it

Hostels: www.hihostels. com/it

Mountain Huts (Rifugi): www.cai-fvg.it; www.turis mofvg.it/montagna365/ rifugi

Discount Cards

FVG Card (www.turismofvg.it/ fvg-card), valid for 48 hours (adult/reduced €25/20) or seven days (€39/34), provides free admission to many sights as well as special deals and discounts. Local versions are also available: **FVG Card Aquileia** (www.turismofvg. it/fvgcard-aquileia; 24hr card 1 adult & 1 child under 12yr/12-18yr €15/7) and **FVG Card Tarvisiano FCC** (www.turismofvg.it/forest -camp-card), valid for 72 hours (adult/reduced €35/30) or seven days (€50/45).

Eating

Restaurants and other eateries reviewed in this guidebook are listed from cheapest to most expensive and, within each price category, by author preference.

Online Resources

Associazione Italiana Celiachia (Italian Celiac Association; www.celiachia.it)

Restaurants for Celiacs (www.ristorantiperceliaci.net)

Vegetarian & Vegan Restaurants (www.iomangio veg.it; www.ristorantiveg.com; www.veganhome.it)

Strada del Vino e dei Sapori (www.turismofvg.it/ strada-del-vino-e-dei-sapori)

Emergencies

All emergencies (police, ambulance, fire) ☎ 112
Coast Guard ☎ 1530

LGBTIQ+ Travellers

Online Resources

Arcigay - Arcobaleno Trieste Gorizia (www.arcigay trieste.it) organises various meet-ups for the LGBTIQ+ community, including Aperitivaqueer (on Thursdays), trips out of town and cultural events that keep queer life in Trieste vibrant.

Gayly Planet (www.weare gaylyplanet.com) is packed with up-to-date information on LGBTIQ+ friendly options for travellers, including beaches, bars, clubs, events and associations, in Italy and around the world.

Other general sites include the following: **ArciLesbica** (www.arcilesbica.it), **Gay.it** (www.gay.it) and **Quiiky** (www. quiiky.com).

PRICE GUIDE

Sleeping

Accommodation listings in this guidebook are categorised under the following price ranges:

€ Budget €70 or less

€€ Midrange €71-160

€€€ High more than €160

Eating

The following price categories refer to the cost of a three-course meal (excluding drinks):

€ Budget €20 or less

€€ Midrange €21-40

€€€ High more than €40

TRAVEL BOOKSHOPS

A good map of the region is a very useful tool while on the road. Also, consider that travel books can help you better understand the places you intend to visit. The following Italian bookshops specialise in travel:

CLUF (☑0432 295 447; www.facebook.com/libreria.cluf/; Udine)

Diari di Bordo (☑349 782 41 61; https://diaridibordo. jimdofree.com; Parma)

Geocart (☑011 749 33 69; www.geocart-torino.com; Turin)

Gulliver (☑045 800 72 34; www.gullivertravelbooks.it; Verona)

The globetrotter (☑011 473 28 15; www.ilgiramondo.it; Turin)

L'angolo dell'avventura (☑06 572 89 275; www.libreriaangoloavventurenelmondo.it; Rome)

LEG - Libreria Editrice Goriziana (☑0481 337 76; www.leg.it; Gorizia)

Libreria Accursio (☑051 22 09 83; Bologna)

Libreria Editrice Odòs (☑0432 20 43 07; www.odos.it; Udine)

Libreria On the Road (☑055 47 14 61; www.ontheroadlibreria.it; Florence)

Libreria Stella Alpina (☑055 41 16 88; www.stella-alpina. com; online bookshop based in Florence)

Libreria Viaggeria (☑0461 23 33 37; www.libreriaviaggeria. it; Trento)

Pangea (☑0498 76 40 22; www.libreriapangea.com; Padua)

Priamar Travel (☑019 82 09 01; www.priamarviaggi.com; Savona)

Transalpina - I (☑331 235 54 64; www.latransalpina.it; online bookshop)

Travel Bookshop (☑338 452 68 96; Monza)

VEL - La Libreria del Viaggiatore (☑0342 21 89 52; www. vel.it; Sondrio)

Gay-Friendly Beaches

Costa dei Barbari Located in Sistiana Mare; arrive by car, park near Maxi's restaurant and continue on foot. It is a naturist area in summer, frequented mainly by gay guys.

Liburnia Aurisina Gay beach near Trieste. Reach it via the Discesa Auguste Piccard.

Spiaggia naturista di Codroipo Large, tranquil, gay-friendly naturist beach on the Tagliamento River. Drive through Codroipo and turn right before the bridge (if coming from Udine).

Local Media

Trieste's main daily newspaper is *Il Piccolo*, with local, national and international news, including on the nearby Balkans. Outside Trieste, the most popular newspaper in the region is the *Messaggero Veneto*.

Medical Assistance

For a list of pharmacies in any municipality, see www. farmaciediturno.org.

Money

Italy's currency is the euro. Major credit cards such as Visa, MasterCard, Eurocard, Cirrus and Eurocheques are widely accepted. Amex is also recognised, although it's less common. ATMs (known as *bancomat*) are widely available.

Tourist Information

The official Friuli Venezia Giulia Tourist Board website (www.turismofvg.it) includes general information on sights and accommodation, and lists all of its tourist offices (Infopoints) across the region.

Trieste Infopoint (Map p58, B3; ☑040 347 83 12; www. turismofvg.it; Piazza Unità d'Italia 4/b; ⊗9am-6pm Mon-Sat, 9am-1pm Sun in winter, 9am-7pm daily in summer) has seasonal dates that can vary year to year.

The website www.discover-trieste.it offers valuable information on the region's capital, while www.pordenonewithlove.it is very useful if visiting Pordenone and surrounds. Another great online resource is www.parcodolomitifriulane.it.

In Udine, the **Info point** (Map p144, D2; ☑0432 29 59 72; www.turismofvg.it; Piazza 1° Maggio 7; ⊗9am-1pm & 2-5.30pm Mon-Sat, 9am-1pm Sun; times vary seasonally) is an excellent source of local travel info. For information on the Collio, contact the Cormòns **Infopoint** (Map p104, D2; ☑0481 38 62 24; www.turismofvg.it; Piazza XXIV Maggio 15; ⊗9am-1pm & 2-6pm)

In Cividale **InformaCittà** (Map p186, C3; ☑0432 71 04 60; www.cividale.net; informacitta@cividale.net; Piazza Duomo 5; ⊗10am-1pm & 2-5pm Mon-Fri, 10am-5pm Sat & Sun Oct-March, 10am-1pm & 3-6pm Mon-Fri, 10am-6pm Sat & Sun Apr-Sep) will help you access the Ipogeo Celtico.

Transport

GETTING THERE & AWAY

Air

Friuli Venezia Giulia Airport (☎0481 77 32 24; www.triesteairport.it; Via Aquileia 46, Ronchi dei Legionari) Located 33km from Trieste, 40km from Udine, 20km from Gorizia and 80km from Pordenone, with daily connections to major Italian airports and direct flights to London, Munich, Paris and Valencia.

The airport includes a tourist **Infopoint** (☎0481 47 60 79; www.turismofvg.it ⊘daily, hours vary).

For connections to the city centre, see p83.

Land

Bus

From **Trieste bus station** (☎040 203 40 17; www.autostazionetrieste.it; Piazza della Libertà 9; ⊘ticket office 6.30am-6.50pm Mon-Fri, to 2.10pm Sat & Sun), services run to Venice, Milan, Rome, Bologna and many other Italian cities. International destinations include Austria (Graz, Vienna), Romania and Bulgaria, as well as the main cities of Slovenia, Croatia and Serbia.

Long-distance bus companies serving Trieste include **FlixBus Italia** (☎02 94 75 92 08; www.flixbus.it) and **Floren-**tia Bus (☎055 96 70 24; www.florentiabus.it).

From **Udine bus station** (☎0432 50 69 41; www.autostazionediudine.it; Viale Europa Unita 35/8; ⊘ticket office 6am-7.50pm Mon-Sat, 7.20am-7.35pm Sun), companies including **Marino** (☎080 311 23 35; www.marinobus.it) and FlixBus run to numerous destinations.

Car & Motorcyle

Some useful websites for planning a road trip include the following:

ACI - Automobile Club d'Italia (☎06 499 81, roadside assistance ☎803 116; www.aci.it).

Autostrade per l'Italia (www.autostrade.it) Real-time traffic and toll calculation.

Google Maps (maps.google.it) **& ViaMichelin** (www.viamichelin.it/web/Itinerari) Both useful for plotting your route.

CCISS Viaggiare Informati (toll free ☎1518; 24hr; www.cciss.it) Realtime traffic updates.

Rai Isoradio (FM 103.3; www.raiplayradio.it/isoradio) Public service channel dedicated to mobility information.

Cycling

Cycling is the best way to get around towns where traffic can be a problem. If you're passionate about cycling and plan to pedal around the region, you'll find useful planning advice at **Federazione Italiana Amici della Bicicletta** (www.fiab-onlus.it, www.bicitalia.org).

If you plan on travelling by bike and train, consult **Trenitalia** (www.trenitalia.com/en/services/travelling_with_your_bike.html). If travelling on Italo services, see www.italotreno.it.

Train

Although Trieste Centrale is not a major Italian rail hub, services departing from the station do connect to the country's major high-speed rail network.

Among these is a direct service to Venice, from where high-speed trains travel across Italy. Udine is the

---

THINGS CHANGE

Fares, timetables and special offers can change frequently; the information provided in this chapter should therefore be taken as a general indicator. For up-to-the-minute details, check the company websites or consult a trusted travel agency.

terminus of four national lines that lead to Trieste, Tarvisio, Cervignano and Venice. From Udine, direct services also reach Vienna.

For routes, timetables and tickets, contact **Trenitalia** (24h ☑89 20 21 for bookings and CartaFRECCIA enquiries, 06 3000 for booking changes; www.trenitalia.com).

For real-time information on journey status, disruptions, cancellations and replacement services, see **Viaggiatreno Trenitalia** (www.viaggiatreno.it).

TRAIN STATIONS

Train stations are generally located close to the *centro storico* (historic centre) in Trieste, Udine and Pordenone. In smaller towns, they're generally located further out of the centre as they often serve more than one population centre.

Sea

The ports of Trieste and Monfalcone, located within close proximity of each other, host all passenger and freight services to and from the region.

From the Port of Trieste, ferries reach numerous destinations. A growing number of cruise ships also dock at the port.

The port sports a modern **passenger terminal** (www.triestoterminal.it).

An effort to reduce the number of cruise ships sailing into Venice has seen Trieste become an alternative

gateway to the region, with onward land and sea connections to Venice.

Cruise ship companies **MSC** (www.msccrociere.it) and **Costa Cruises** (www.costacrociere.it) anchor in Trieste.

Both offer reserved parking at the port, which also functions as a city car park (Parking Office ☑040 673 25 50).

The port's passenger terminal also caters to super yachts.

GETTING AROUND

Air

The Polo Intermodale is an elevated walkway connecting the airport terminal to the airport car parks, bus terminal and train station. The latter is on the Trieste–Venice and Trieste–Udine lines. For more detailed information, see www.triesteairport.it/it/airport/polo-intermodale.

TPL FVG (☑800 05 20 40 toll-free from landlines, 040 971 23 43 from mobiles; ☺6am-10pm; https://tplfvg.it) Bus G51 runs between the airport and Trieste half-hourly.

Radio Taxi Trieste (☑040 30 77 30; ☺24h; www.radiotaxitrieste.it) A ride from central Trieste to the airport costs €58 (fixed fare).

Radio Taxi Udine (☑0432 50 58 58; ☺24h; www.taxiudine.it) Minimum fare is around

€6.50. A ride to Trieste airport is €75 (fixed fare). From Udine, a trip to Venice airport costs €200 (fixed fare).

Many hotels offer shuttle services to/from the airport for guests.

Bicycle

Friuli Venezia Giulia is wonderfully suited to cycling trips, with a wide variety of landscapes catering to all levels and any number of interests.

While bike paths are not widespread in the cities, bicycles are a very common sight in the *centri storici* (historic centres) of places like Pordenone and Spilimbergo.

Inland, the king of cycling routes is the **Ciclovia Alpe Adria** (www.alpe-adria-radweg.com), which covers the 415km between Salzburg in Austria and Grado on the coast. The route spans the entire eastern part of Friuli from north to south, crossing all of the region's various landscapes and cultures.

Another interesting cycling route is the **Adriabike**. One section leads from Kranjska Gora in Slovenia to Trieste, while another runs from the Istrian port of Koper in Slovenia to Venice. For detailed route information, see www.turismofvg.it/it/86139/adriabike-itinera rio-complete.

An impressive number of cycling routes across the re-

TRAIN CARDS

Trenitalia (www.trenitalia.com) offers numerous discounts, promotions and special offers to customers. To make the most of these, it may be worth obtaining one of its various passenger cards.

Among these are the **Carta Verde** (for passengers aged 12 to 26) and the **Carta Argento** (for those over 60), both of which provide discounts on national and international tickets. Trenitalia's **CartaFRECCIA** allows you to accumulate points and take advantage of services and discounts throughout the country.

For more detail on Trenitalia's cards and offers, head to www.trenitalia.com and click on 'Offers'.

gion can be found at www.turismofvg.it.

Throughout the region, but especially between the coast and the Collio, you can take advantage of **Amare in Bici** (www.amareinbici.it), a network of cycling trails that connect the coast to villages and towns in the hinterland. Those cruising on e-bikes can easily recharge along the way (look out for the yellow totems).

Although not compulsory, wear a helmet, use bike lights and avoid busy roads.

You can carry a bike on all regional trains marked with the appropriate icon on the timetable, though you will need to pay a supplement (€3.50), valid for 24 hours.

Alternatively, you can buy a second-class ticket valid for the same route: validate the ticket before boarding the train.

Folding bikes and bikes that can be disassembled and placed in a bike-carrier bag can be carried free of charge (one bicycle per person; dimensions not exceeding 80x120x45cm).

Bicibus (https://tplfvg.it) is a service provided by TPL FVG that allows cyclists to travel around the region on buses equipped with special bike-carrying trailers, as well as on boat services connecting the major beach towns in summer. For more information (in Italian), head to the website, click on 'Il Viaggio', then 'Bicibus'.

Bicycles can be carried on local public transport and ferries. Conditions of carriage can vary between companies, so check their respective websites beforehand.

For more information on planning a bike tour in the region, contact the **Federazione Italiana Amici della Bicicletta** (http://fiab-onlus.it/bici/) and hit **Albergabici** (www.albergabici.it), an accommodation search engine which allows you to filter results based on accommodation type, services offered

and cyclist type (tourist, active, mountain biker).

Boat

Local boat services are managed by **TPL FVG** (☏800 052040 toll-free from landlines, 040 971 23 43 from mobiles, ⊙6am-10pm; https://tplfvg.it) and connect the coastal towns of Bibione, Lignano, Marano, Grado, Sistiana, Grignano, Barcola, Trieste and Muggia.

Other private companies operate different routes or offer similar services, usually at an agreed price.

Specific information is provided under the appropriate destinations throughout this guidebook.

Bus

The Friuli Venezia Giulia area is well served by Trasporto Pubblico Locale del Friuli Venezia Giulia **TPL FVG** (☏800 05 20 40 toll-free from landlines, 040 971 23 43 from mobiles; ⊙6am-10pm; https://tplfvg.it).

You may also find the following local websites useful:

➡ ATAP - Pordenone (www.atap.pn.it)

➡ Arriva Udine – Udine (www.arrivaudine.it)

➡ Azienda Provinciale Trasporti – Gorizia (www.apt gorizia.it)

➡ Trieste Trasporti – Trieste (www.triestetrasporti.it)

The user-friendly TPL FVG website allows you to consult timetables, plan your trip and buy tickets. Alternatively, download the very handy TPL FVG smartphone app.

The frequency of bus services varies with the seasons, especially on routes servicing alpine and coastal destinations. On Sundays, public holidays and in school-holiday periods, some services may run infrequently or not at all.

In larger cities, the bus station is often next to, or in the immediate vicinity of, the train station.

Tickets are usually purchased before travel, at the bus-station ticket offices (where timetables are also displayed) or from selected tobacconists. Tickets purchased on board are usually more expensive.

Car & Motorcycle

The whole region is traversed by superb, often breathtaking alpine roads bound to thrill motorcyclists: many ride to the Pinzano al Tagliamento area to enjoy hairpin bends and ascents.

The same can be said for the coastal road that leads to Trieste, and for those that lead along the gentle slopes of the Collio or the harsher ones of the Carso. Indeed, even the plains, especially the Magredi, are pleasant crossed on wheels.

Rental

When renting a vehicle, it's wise to choose comprehensive insurance that will cover you for any damage other than theft.

Younger drivers should enquire about any rental requirements (minimum age and licence) in advance.

All the major car rental agencies have pick-up locations at the airports, in each province's capital city and in the main tourist destinations that are covered in this guidebook:

Avis (☏06 452 108 391; www.avisautonoleggio.it)

Budget (☏199 30 73 73; www.budgetautonoleggio.it)

Europcar (☏199 30 70 30; www.europcar.it)

Hertz (☏02 696 82 445; www.hertz.it)

Maggiore (☏199 15 11 20; www.maggiore.it)

Train

Friuli Venezia Giulia's train network, which offers good connections to/from its main cities, is predominantly managed by **Trenitalia** (www.trenitalia.com).

FUC - Udine Cividale Railway (☑0432 58 18 44; www.ferrovieudinecividale.it) manages the regionally-owned section of the rail network connecting Udine to Cividale del Friuli. It's also a partner in MI.CO.TRA, a project aimed at improving cross-border public transport services. Trains between Udine and Villach (Austria) run four times daily, with weekend and holiday services continuing through to Trieste.

If you're relying on trains to get around, basing yourself in a city and exploring the surrounds by bus is your best bet in some areas. That said, having your own wheels will give you the most freedom and save you time waiting for connections.

LOCAL TRANSPORT

For information on local transport, consult the Getting There & Away section at the end of each individual destination.

Behind the Scenes

SEND US YOUR FEEDBACK

We love to hear from travellers – your comments keep us on our toes and help make our books better. Our well-travelled team reads every word on what you loved or loathed about this book. Although we cannot reply individually to your submissions, we always guarantee that your feedback goes straight to the appropriate authors, in time for the next edition. Each person who sends us information is thanked in the next edition.

Visit **lonelyplanet.com/contact** to submit your updates and suggestions or to ask for help. Our award-winning website also features inspirational travel stories and news.

Note: We may edit, reproduce and incorporate your comments in Lonely Planet products such as guidebooks, websites and digital products, so let us know if you are happy to have your name acknowledged. For a copy of our privacy policy visit **lonelyplanet.com/legal**.

WRITER THANKS

Luigi Farrauto

Thanks to Piero Pasini and Annalisa Bruni (*lǎoshī!*) for the coordination and lots of travel chit-chat. Thanks also to Silvia Castelli and the entire editorial team, who've been my second family for almost a decade.

Many years later, it's fair to say that you've become dear friends beyond the realm of work: Linda Marcuzzi, Giulia Cantone, Fabrice Gallina, Cristina Menis, Tatjana Familio and Diana Candusso. Some have had children, some have married, others have changed job, got a dog or left entirely. I left, but hope to return soon (perhaps without the need to take notes). Thanks also to the people who always welcomed me with equal affection, from the Colli Orientali to the *malghe*, from the Carso to the Natisone. And thank you to the Tagliamento River, which knows how to mesmerise me every time.

Many thanks also to Luigi and Daniele from www.wearegaylyplanet.com for your suggestions.

Also, an unreserved thank you to Arianna. I dedicate this guide to Fraintesa.

Piero Pasini

Friuli Venezia Giulia is not only a land that I love, but also a place where I have made many dear friends. I thank them for sharing their region and for helping me grasp aspects of it that I may have otherwise been unable to explore. Thanks also to the tourism board, tourist office staff and everyone else who gave up their time to assist me.

Special thanks to Michele Lestani, Roberto Scarpin and their merry troop of friends from Romans d'Isonzo, to Gianni De Cilla, Emanuele Zorino, Paola Musolino, Elisa Sabot, Sandro Lovato, Tiziana Zamai, Linda Marcuzzi, Tatjana Familio and for a reason I can't remember right now (though clearly worthy) my friend Federico 'Felix' Fedele... (Just kidding, he knows the reason... I think.)

Once again, a hug to my colleague Luigi Farrauto and a 'heart-eyes emoji' to Annalisa Bruni.

Thanks to Silvia Castelli, Angelo Pittro and Claudia Peruccio for trusting me once more. Dora and Elio, it's all for you. Chiara, it's all because of you.

ACKNOWLEDGEMENTS

Thanks to Giulia Cantone and Tatjana Familio of the PromoTurismoFVG press office for their advice.

Cover photograph: Palazzo Communale, Pordenone, Denis Vostrikov / Shutterstock ©.

CONTRIBUTING WRITERS

Cristian Bonetto translated this guidebook from Italian into English. He has written and researched dozens of Lonely Planet guides, and his musings on travel, food, culture and design appear in numerous publications around the world.

Luca Borghesio is a biologist researching environmental conservation for private companies and NGOs in Europe and East Africa, Luca wrote the Environment chapter.

Stefano Cena works as an editor at Italian publishing house EDT. He has written and edited history content in many Lonely Planet guides to Italy, including the History chapter in this guidebook.

Anita Franzon is a sommelier and contributes to several food and wine blogs. She wrote the Food & Wine chapter.

Jacopo Tomatis is a journalist, musicologist and, since 2008, the editor of *Il Giornale della Musica*. He wrote the music section in the Arts & Literature chapter.

THIS BOOK

This 1st edition of *Friuli Venezia Giulia* was translated into English by Cristian Bonetto. It was originally researched and written in Italian by Luigi Farrauto and Piero Pasini, and produced by EDT.

Product Editor Sasha Drew

Book Designer Ania Bartoszek

Thanks to Jim Brody, Melanie Dankel, Emily Huff, Rachel Imeson, Darren O'Connell, Angela Tinson

EDT Managing Editor Silvia Castelli

EDT Coordinator Annalisa Bruni

EDT Updates & Adaptations Paola Masi (coordination Luciana Defedele)

EDT Editors Annalisa Bruni, Angelica Taglia

EDT Layout Claudia Mastrogiacomo, Tiziana Vigna

EDT Cover & Colour Alessandro Pedarra (supervision Sara Viola Cabras)

EDT Cartographer Ivo Villa

EDT Production Alberto Capano

Index

A

abbeys, monasteries &
sanctuaries
Abbazia di Rosazzo 172
Abbazia di Santa Maria in
Silvis 199
Monastero di Santa Maria in
Valle 176
Santuario della Beata
Vergine 89
Santuario della Beata
Vergine di Castelmonte
182
Santuario della Madonna del
Lussari 243
Santuario di Sant'Osvaldo
230
accessible travel 288
accommodation 288-9, see
also individual locations
activities 42-5, see also
individual activities
Adriatic Sea 40-1
adventure parks, see theme &
adventure parks
Aiello del Friuli 159
air travel 291, 292
alps, see mountains
Ampezzo 229-30
Andreis 222
animals 283, 284-5, 286
aquariums 65
Aquileia 15, 16, 132-6, 261, **15**
archaeological sites 34-5
Arco di Riccardo 59, 60
Cividale del Friuli 178
Colle di San Giusto 57-8
Domus & Palazzo
Episcopale 134
Domus di Tito Macro 135
Fortezza di Osoppo 165
Forum & Roman Basilica 135
Mercati Tardo Antichi 134
Muggia Vecchia 91
Palmanova 154-6
Palù di Livenza 197

Porto Fluviale Romano 135
Sepolcreto 135
Teatro Romano 62
Trieste 60
architecture 261-5
art 265-7
art galleries, see museums
Art Nouveau 264-5
Arta Terme 235
Artegna 170
ATMs 290
Attimis 171

B

balotes 208
Barcis 221-2
Barcola 84-5
Barcolana 36, 72-3, **37**
Basovizza 87
beaches 17
Grado 129
Lignano Sabbiadoro 114-15
Marina di Aurisina 87
Sistiana 87
Trieste 71
beer 240, 281-2
bicycle travel, see cycling &
mountain biking
birdwatching 43, 284, 286, **42**
Fagagna 159
Forgaria nel Friuli 164
Isola della Cona 137, **40-1**
Lignano Sabbiadoro 118
Riserva Naturale della Valle
Canal Novo 125
Riserva Naturale delle Foci
dello Stella 126
biscotti 194, 274-5
boat tours 40-1, see also
canoeing
Grado 130
Lago di Cavazzo 166
Lignano Sabbiadoro 118
Marano Lagunare 125
boat travel 292, 293
books 269-73
bookshops 290
bora 36, 66
Bordano 168

bridges
Ponte del Diavolo 175
Ponte di Pinzano 164
budget 289
buffets 76-7
bus travel 291, 292
butterflies 168
Buttrio 172
Byzantine architecture 261-2

C

Campanile di Val Montanaia
219, **12**, **29**
Caneva 197-8
canoeing 45
Grado 129
Lago del Predil 246
Lago di Cavazzo 166
Lago di Tramonti 223
canyons & canyoning
Clauzetto 208
Forra del Cellina 221
Forni di Sopra 225
Orrido dello Slizza 242
Val Zemola 218
Capriva del Friuli 106
car & motorcycle travel 291,
293-4
Cormòns 103
Magredi, the 202
Passo Rest 224
Carnic Alps 226-38, **226**
Carso, the 12, 50-1, 88-90,
286, **51**, **12**
Carso Isontino 109
Casso 216-18
Castelmonte 182
castles 13
Castello dei Conti di
Ragogna 192
Castello di Arcano 163
Castello di Buttrio 172
Castello di Caneva 197
Castello di Cassacco 163
Castello di Colloredo di
Monte Albano 163
Castello di Cordovado 199
Castello di Duino 86, **41**
Castello di Gorizia 95-6

Castello di Miramare 85
Castello di Muggia 91
Castello di Polcenigo 204
Castello di Prampero 170
Castello di San Giusto 60,
62, **10**, **35**
Castello di San Pietro di
Ragogna 165
Castello di Spessa 106
Castello di Spilimbergo 200
Castello di Susans 163
Castello di Tolmezzo 228
Castello di Tricesimo 163
Castello di Udine 143-4
Castello di Valvasone 199
Castello di Villalta 163
Castello Savorgnan 170, **13**
cathedrals, see churches &
cathedrals
Cavasso Nuovo 207
caves 48
Buco del Gorgazzo 204
Grotta del Mitreo 86
Grotta di San Giovanni
d'Antro 185
Grotta Gigante 89
Grotta Nuova di Villanova 171
Grotta Star Čedad 183
Grotte Verdi 208
Landre Scur 220
cheese 276-7
chemists 290
children, travel with 46-8
churches & cathedrals
Basilica di Aquileia 133
Basilica di San Silvestro 58
Basilica di Santa
Eufemia 127
Basilica di Santa Maria
Assunta 133-4
Cattedrale di San Giusto
Martire 59-60
Chiesa dei Santi Pietro e
Biagio 179
Chiesa di San Giorgio
Martire 191-2
Chiesa di San Nicolò dei
Greci 66
Chiesa di Santa Maria delle
Grazie 127

Map Pages **000**
Photo Pages **000**

churches & cathedrals
continued
Chiesa di Santa Maria di Castello 145
Chiesa di Santa Maria Maggiore 59
Chiesa di Sant'Antonio Abate 161, **13**
Chiesa di Sant'Antonio Taumaturgo 67
Chiesa di Sant'Ignazio 97
Chiesa Serbo-Ortodossa di San Spiridione 67
Chiesa Votiva di Santa Maria del Mare 114
Duomo di Cividale del Friuli 177
Duomo di Gemona 262
Duomo di Gorizia 97
Duomo di Mortegliano 158
Duomo di Palmanova 156
Duomo di Pordenone 189
Duomo di San Daniele del Friuli 161
Duomo di Sant'Adalberto 102
Duomo di Udine 146
Oratorio della Purità 146-7
Pieve di San Pietro in Carnia 236
Santuario della Beata Vergine delle Grazie 148
Cimolais 219
cinema 269
Cisgne 183
Cividale del Friuli 14, 173-81, **174, 176**
accommodation 179
drinking 179-80
festivals & events 179
food 179-80
highlights 174
history 175
shopping 180
sights 175-9
tourist offices 180-1
travel to/from 181
travel within 181
Clauiano 157
Claut 220
Clauzetto 208
climate 288, see also individual regions
climbing 43
Erto & Casso 217
Forni di Sopra 226
Lusevera 171
Opicina 88
Parco Naturale delle Dolomiti Friulane 215

Map Pages **000**
Photo Pages **000**

Riserva Naturale della Val Rosandra 90
Sappada 235
Codroipo 157-8
coffee 78, 282
Colle di Santa Barbara 91
Colli Orientali 169-72
Collina 233
Collio, the 11, 93-4, 102-9, **94, 104, 11, 33**
Colloredo di Monte Albano 163
Comeglians 233
Cordovado 199
Cormòns 102-6, **104**
Corno di Rosazzo 170
Corso Garibaldi 191
Corso Italia 66
Corso Vittorio Emanuele II 191
Cossacks 230
Costiera Triestina 83-8
costs 289
courses
boating 118, 130
diving 117
rowing 118
sailing 117
skiing 214, 238, 243-4
windsurfing 117
cruise ships 292
currency 290
cycling & mountain biking 18-19, 43, 45, 291, 292-3
Ciclovia Alpe Adria 242
Collio, the 108, **108**
Cormòns 102-3
Grado 129
Lago di Cavazzo 166
Lignano Sabbiadoro 117, 118
Marano Lagunare 125
Opicina 88
Parco Naturale delle Dolomiti Friulane 214
Ravascletto 237, 238
Riserva Naturale della Val Rosandra 90
Sauris 231
Sentiero delle Vigne Alte 103
Trieste 71, **45**
Udine area 163, **163**
Val Colvera 222
Val Settimana 220
Venzone 168

D
Diga del Vajont 217, 218, 259
dinosaurs 47, 248
disabilities, travellers with 288
discount cards 52, 289

diving & snorkelling 44
Lignano Sabbiadoro 117
Riserva Naturale Marina di Miramare 85
Trieste 71
Dolegna del Collio 109
Dolomites, see Friulian Dolomites
Dorfles, Gillo 266
Drenchia 184
drinks 32-3, see also beer, coffee, grappa, wine & wineries
driving, see car & motorcycle travel
Duino-Aurisina 86-8

E
earthquake of 1976 169, 259
emergencies 289
environment 283-6
Erto 216-18
events, see festivals & events

F
Faedis 171
Fagagna 158-9
family travel 46-8
festivals & events 26-8, see also individual locations
Aria di Festa 161
Bacio delle Croci 236
Barbacan Produce 73
Barcolana 36, 72-3, **37**
Bioest 72
Borgo in Fiore 157
Burnjak 183
Carnevale di Muggia 91
Carnevale Resiano 239
Carnevale Saurano 232
Corse dai Mus 159
èStoria 98
Far East Film Festival 149
Fasin la Mede 237
Festa del Prosciutto 232
Fieste da la Balote 208
Fieste da Viarte 103
Folkest 200
Fums Profums Salums 237
Gusti di Frontiera 98
Horti Tergestini 72
Incendio del Mare 119
Krampus 244
Magraid 202
Marcia e Sagra delle Rane 207
Medioevo a Valvasone 199
Messa dello Spadone 179
Mittelfest 179
No Borders Music Festival 244
Nozze Carsiche 89

Olimpiade dele Clanfe 72
Palio di San Donato 179
Palma alle Armi 156
Pasquetta sui Bastioni 156
Perdòn di Barbana 130
Pic&Taste 16
Pordenonelegge 193, **28**
Premio Hemingway 118
Processione di San Vito 125
Rally Piancavallo 214
Sagra dei Osei 196
Sagra dei Sest 204-5
Stazione di Topolò 184
Sun & Run 119
SUP Race 119
Trieste Film Festival 72
Udin&Jazz Winter 149
vicino/lontano 149
wine festivals 281
film 269
fish 278
fishing 45
Lago di Tramonti 223
Lignano Sabbiadoro 118
Marano Lagunare 125
Fogliano Redipuglia 110
foibe 87
food 30-1, 274-80, 289, see also individual locations
balotes 208
biscotti 194, 274-5
buffets 76-7
cheese 276-7
costs 289
fish 278
frico 151, **31**
fruit 279
garlic 279
gubana 183
honey 280
olive oil 280
osmize 32, 86, **33**
peta 223
petuccia 223
pitina 223
polenta 274
pork 277
prosciutto 161, 232, 277, **30-1**
rebechin 76
Slow Food 279
vegetables 279-80
Foresta di Tarvisio 241
Forgaria nel Friuli 164
Forni Avoltri 233
Forni di Sopra 224-6
Forni di Sotto 224-6
Frana del Monte Toc 216, 218
frescoes 264, 265
frico 151, **31**
Frisanco 222-3

Friulian coast 112-38, **113**
Friulian Dolomites 12, 214-26, 283, **216**, **12**
Friulian language 270, 269-71
fruit 279
FVG Card 53, 289

G

gardens, *see* parks & gardens
garlic 279
gay travellers 289-90
Gemona del Friuli 166-7
golf 44, **44**
Gorizia 10, 16, 93-102, **96**, **10**
 accommodation 98-9
 drinking & nightlife 100-1
 entertainment 101
 festivals & events 98
 food 99-100
 highlights 94
 history 95
 shopping 101
 tourist offices 101
 travel to/from 101
 travel within 102
Gothic architecture 262
Gradisca d'Isonzo 109-10
Grado 126-32, **128**, **22-3**
grappa 32, 282
Grignano 85-6
Grimacco 184
gubana 183

H

Habsburgs 263-4
hang gliding 43, 45, 242
Hemingway, Ernest 115, 117, 118
hiking 18, 44, 45
 Alpe Adria 242
 Ampezzo 229
 Attimis 171
 Barcis 221
 Carnia 234
 Cimolais 219
 Claut 220
 Clauzetto 208-9
 Cormòns 103
 Forgaria nel Friuli 164
 Forni Avoltri 233
 Forni di Sopra 225
 Lago di Cavazzo 166
 Lignano Sabbiadoro 117
 Luserva 171-2
 Magredi, the 202
 Meduno 207
 Monte Guarda 239
 Opicina 88
 Parco Naturale delle Dolomiti Friulane 214
Pesariis 234

Piancavallo 211
Pulfero 185
Ravascletto 237
Riserva Naturale della Val Rosandra 90
San Michele del Carso 111
San Pietro al Natisone 182
Sappada 235
Sauris 231
Savogna 184-5
Sella Nevea 246
Tarcento 169
Tarvisio 242-3
Val Colvera 222
Val Resia 239
Val Settimana 220
Val Tramontina 223
Val Zemola 218-19
Valli del Natisone 181
Venzone 168
Vivaro 202
historic buildings & palaces
 Biblioteca Guarneriana 160
 Casa Bartoli 64
 Casa del Trecento 161
 Casa Medievale 178
 Casa Terni 64
 Casa Valdoni 64
 Domus & Palazzo Episcopale 134
 Hotel Balkan 64
 Palazzo Comunale (Cividale del Friuli) 177-8
 Palazzo Comunale (Pordenone) 189
 Palazzo Coronini Cronberg 98
 Palazzo del Governatore delle Armi 156
 Palazzo del Monte di Pietà 156
 Palazzo del Provveditore Generale 156
 Palazzo della Forza Concina 148
 Palazzo Lantieri 97
 Palazzo Levrini-Stringher 178
 Palazzo Mocenigo-Centi 221
 Palazzo Strassoldo 148
 Palazzo Tinghi 148
 Palazzo Vivanti-Ghiberti 64
 Palazzo Werdenberg 98
 Porticato del Lippomano 143
 Salone degli Incanti 64
 Sinagoga 98
 Stazione Campo Marzio 64
 Tempietto Longobardo 176, **14**
 Terrazza a Mare 114
 Villa Gattolini 114
 Villa Manin 157

history 18, 34-5, 248-60, *see also* WWI sites
 Carolingians 251
 Celtic period 248-9
 Duchy of Friuli 250-1
 fascism 256-7
 Habsburgs 263-4
 Iron Curtain 99, 259
 Irredentism 255
 Jewish history 69
 Lombards 250-1
 Ottoman Empire 253
 Patriarchate of Aquileia 251-2
 post-WWII period 258-9
 prehistoric period 248
 present-day period 260
 Restoration 254
 Roman period 248-50
 Venetian Age 253-4
 WWII 256-8
honey 280
horse-riding
 Lignano Sabbiadoro 117
 Sentiero delle Vigne Alte 103
horses 137, **11**
hypogea 178, 185

I

ice skating
 Forni di Sopra 225
 Tarvisio 243
Illegio 228
Isola della Cona 137, **40-1**
Isola di Anfora 130
Isola di Barbana 130
Isola di Martignano 126
Isonzo, the 93-4, 109-11
Isonzo River 109, 137, 238, **94**
Istria 90-2
itineraries 20-5, **20**, **22**, **25**

J

Jewish history 69
Julian Alps 240-6, **240**
Julian Prealps 238-40

K

kayaking 45
 Lago di Cavazzo 166
 Lignano Sabbiadoro 118
 Riserva Naturale delle Foci dello Stella 126
 Sistiana 87
kitesurfing 44
 Grado 129
 Isola di Martignano 126
knives 205
Krivapete 185

L

Laguna di Grado 123-32
lakes
 Laghi di Fusine 244, **19**
 Lago del Ciul 223
 Lago del Predil 246
 Lago di Barcis 221
 Lago di Cavazzo 166
 Lago di Cornino 164
 Lago di Ragogna 162
 Lago di Sauris 230
 Lago di Tramonti 223
language 269-71
LGBTQI+ travellers 289-90
libraries 160-1
Lignano Sabbiadoro 114-23, **116-17**
 accommodation 119-20
 activities 115, 117
 beaches 114-15
 courses 117-18
 drinking 120-1
 entertainment 121-2
 festivals & events 118-19
 food 120-1
 shopping 122
 tourist offices 122
 tours 118
 travel to/from 122-3
 travel within 123
Lis Aganis 204
literature 269-73
Lungomare Nazario Sauro 127
Lusevera 171-2

M

Magnano in Riviera 170-1
Magredi, the 187-8, 201-3, 284, **188**, **202**
Malborghetto Valbruna 241-2
Malga Priu 16, 242
Maniago 205-6
Manzano 172
Marano Lagunare 124-6
Marin, Biagio 130
Marina di Aurisina 87
markets
 Mercato Coperto di Corso Verdi 101
 Pordenone 193
 Trieste 72
Meduno 207-8
Miniera di Raibl – Cave del Predil 244
monasteries, *see* abbeys, monasteries & sanctuaries
money 289, 290
Monfalcone 138
Monrupino 89

monuments
  Faro della Vittoria 84
  Grande Mausoleo
    Candia 135
  Monumento Nazionale
    Foiba di Basovizza 87
  Ossario di Oslavia 101
  Risiera di San Sabba 48,
    70-1, 257
  Sacrario Militare 110
  Sacrario Oberdan 68
mosaics 266-7, **23**, **35**
motorcycle travel, *see* car &
  motorcycle travel
mountain biking, *see* cycling
  & mountain biking
mountains 17-18, 210-46,
  283-4, **212-13**
  Campanile di Val
    Montanaia 219, **12**, **29**
  Carnic Alps 226-38, **226**
  Colli Orientali 169-72
  Friulian Dolomites 12, 214-
    26, 283, **216**, **12**
  Jôf di Montasio 240
  Julian Alps 240-6, **240**
  Julian Prealps 238-40
  Monte Bernadia 169
  Monte Brestovec 111
  Monte Canin 239, 245
  Monte Cavallo 211
  Monte Ciaurlec 208
  Monte Clap
    Grande 232
  Monte Coglians 233
  Monte Cornier 211
  Monte Cum 183
  Monte di
    Ragogna 165
  Monte Glemina 167
  Monte Guarda 239
  Monte Lussari 243
  Monte Mangart 244
  Monte Matajur 181, 184
  Monte Pala 208
  Monte Plauris 239
  Monte Prat 164
  Monte Quarin 102
  Monte San
    Michele 111
  Monte Sauc 211
  Monte Sei Busi 110
  Monte Taiet 208
  Monte Toc 216, 217
  Monte Tremol 211
  Monte Tricorno 240
  Monte Valinis 207
  Monte Zoncolan 236, **24**
Muggia 90-2, **21**

museums 18
  Basovizza documentation
    center 87
  Casa Bruseschi 233-4
  Casa Cavazzini – Museo
    d'Arte Moderna e
    Contemporanea 147
  Centro Internazionale
    Vittorio Podrecca 178
  Civici Musei 144-5
  Civico Museo d'Antichità
    J.J. Winckelmann 62
  Civico Museo del Mare 65
  Civico Museo della Civiltà
    Istriana, Fiumana e
    Dalmata 63
  Civico Museo della Guerra
    per la Pace 'Diego de
    Henriquez' 69
  Civico Museo di Arte
    Orientale 62
  Civico Museo di Storia
    Naturale 69
  Civico Museo
    Sartorio 63-4
  Collezione Abarth
    Dorigo 205
  Ecomuseo delle Acque del
    Gemonese 166
  Ecomuseo Lis Aganis 204
  Ex Chiesa di San
    Francesco 147
  Galleria d'Arte Harry
    Bertoia 189
  Galleria de Martiis 16, 177
  Galleria di Arte Moderna
    Enrico De Cilla 231
  Galleria Tina Modotti
    147, 149
  Immaginario Scientifico
    85, 193
  Magazzino dei Venti 66
  Musei Provinciali, Borgo
    Castello 96
  Musei Provinciali, Palazzo
    Attems Petzenstein 98
  Musei Svevo e Joyce 57
  Museo Archeologico del
    Friuli Occidentale 192-3
  Museo Archeologico Iulium
    Carnicum 236
  Museo Archeologico
    Nazionale (Aquileia)
    134-5
  Museo Archeologico
    Nazionale (Cividale del
    Friuli) 176-7
  Museo Civico d'Arte 189
  Museo Civico di Storia
    Naturale 192
  Museo Cristiano & Tesoro
    del Duomo 175-6
  Museo d'Arte Moderna Ugo
    Carà 91
  Museo del
    Contrabbando 99
  Museo del Risorgimento 68

  Museo della Cantieristica di
    Monfalcone – MuCa 138
  Museo della Casa
    Carsica 89
  Museo della Comunità
    Ebraica di Trieste 'Carlo e
    Vera Wagner' 66
  Museo dell'Arrotino 239
  Museo dell'Arte Fabbrile e
    delle Coltellerie 205
  Museo dell'Orologeria
    Pesarina 233
  Museo Diocesano & Gallerie
    del Tiepolo 145-6
  Museo Diocesano di Arte
    Sacra 192
  Museo Etnografico del
    Friuli 147
  Museo Goriški 99
  Museo 'Il Filo dei Ricordi'
    224
  Museo Nazionale
    dell'Antartide 'Felice
    Ippolito' 70
  Museo Paleocristiano
    135-6
  Museo Revoltella 63
  Museo Storico della Grande
    Guerra 231
  Palazzo Coronini
    Cronberg 98
  Parco Tematico della
    Grande Guerra 138
  Villa Carnera 206
mushing 244
music 267-9

N
Napoleonica 88, **45**
national parks &
  reserves 285
  Oasi dei Quadris 159
  Parco Naturale delle
    Dolomiti Friulane 214,
    215-16, 283, **216**
  Parco Naturale Regionale
    delle Prealpi Giulie 238
  Riserva Naturale del Lago
    di Cornino 164
  Riserva Naturale della Foce
    dell'Isonzo 137-8
  Riserva Naturale della Val
    Rosandra 90
  Riserva Naturale della Valle
    Canal Novo 125
  Riserva Naturale della Valle
    Cavanata 137-8
  Riserva Naturale delle
    Falesie di Duino 86
  Riserva Naturale delle Foci
    dello Stella 126
  Riserva Naturale Marina di
    Miramare 85
newspapers 290
Nimis 171
Nonta 229

nordic walking
  Andreis 222
  Lignano Sabbiadoro 117
  Palmanova 156
  Vivaro 202
Nova Gorica 99

O
olive oil 280
Opicina 82, 88-9
Orias 232
Osais 233
Oslavia 101
osmize 32, 86, **33**
Osoppo 164-5

P
painting 265-6
palaces, *see* historic
  buildings & palaces
Palmanova 154-7, **155**
Panzano 138
paragliding & parasailing
  43, 45
  Gemona del Friuli 167
  Lignano Sabbiadoro 115
  Meduno 207-8
  Piancavallo 211
  Tarvisio 242
parks & gardens
  Giardino Pubblico 68
  Giardino Ricasoli 148
  Giardino Viatori 98
  Orto Botanico 70
  Parco della Rimembranza
    62
  Parco delle Rose 130
  Parco di San Giovanni 69-70
  Parco Fluviale del Noncello
    192
  Parco Galvani 192
  Parco Letterario
    Ungaretti 110
Pesariis 233-4, **19**
peta 223
petuccia 223
Pezzata Rossa Italiana
  cows 278
pharmacies 290
Piancavallo 14, 211, 214, **14**
piazzas
  Piazza Biagio Marin 127
  Piazza della Borsa 65-6
  Piazza della Libertà 141
  Piazza della Motta 191
  Piazza della Transalpina
    98, 99
  Piazza della Vittoria 97
  Piazza di Cavana 62-3
  Piazza Grande 156
  Piazza Marconi 90-1
  Piazza Matteotti 147

Piazza Oberdan 68
Piazza Paolo Diacono 178
Piazza Primo Maggio 148
Piazza San Giovanni 67
Piazza Unità d'Italia 53, 56-7
Piazza Verdi 65-6
Piazza Vittorio Veneto 68
Pinzano al Tagliamento 164
pitina 223
planning 16-48
budget 289
calendar of events 26-8
discount cards 53, 289
family travel 46-8
itineraries 20-5, **20**, **22**, **25**
repeat travellers 16
Poffabro 222-3
Polcenigo 204-5
polenta 274
Ponte del Diavolo 175
Ponte di Pinzano 164
Pordenone 15, 187-95, **188**, **190**, **15**
accommodation 193
drinking & nightlife 194
festivals & events 193
food 193-4
highlights 188
shopping 194-5
tourist offices 195
travel to/from 195
travel within 195
Pordenone, Il 193, 264, 265
pork 277
ports
Canal Grande 66-7
Le Rive 65
Mandracchio 91
Porta Gemona 161
Porta Leopoldina 95
Porto Mandracchio 127
Porto Vecchio 16, 70
Prato Carnico 232-4
Prepotto 182-3
prosciutto 161, 232, 277, **30-1**
Pulfero 185-6

R

Ragogna 165-6
Ravascletto 237-8
rebechin 76
reserves, see national parks & reserves
Resiutta 239-40
Rigolato 233
Rione San Giacomo 72
Risiera di San Sabba 48, 70-1, 257
Rive d'Arcano 163
Roman architecture 261, 262
rowing 118

S

Saba, Umberto 80, 271
Sacile 195-7
sailing 36-7, 44
Lago di Cavazzo 166
Lignano Sabbiadoro 117
Marano Lagunare 125
Muggia 91
San Daniele del Friuli 13, 159-64, **160**
San Dorligo della Valle 90
San Floriano del Collio 106-9
San Leonardo 183
San Martino del Carso 110
San Michele del Carso 111
San Pietro al Natisone 182
San Vito al Tagliamento 198-9, 268
sanctuaries, see abbeys, monasteries & sanctuaries
Sappada 16, 234-5, **24-5**
Sauris 230-2
Savogna 184-5
sculpture 267
Sella Nevea 245-6
Sequals 206
Sesto al Reghena 199
Sgonico 89-90
Sistiana 87-8
skiing 45
Forni Avoltri 233
Forni di Sopra 225-6
Lusevera 172
Nevelandia 235, **46**
Piancavallo 211, 214
Ravascletto 238
Sappada 235
Sauris 231
Tarvisio 243-4
Val Settimana 221
Slovenia 99
Slow Food 279
snorkelling, see diving & snorkelling
snow sports, see ice skating, nordic walking, skiing, snowboarding, snowshoeing, tobogganing
snowboarding 45
Piancavallo 211
Ravascletto 238
Tarvisio 243
snowshoeing
Parco Naturale delle Dolomiti Friulane 215
Ravascletto 238
Sappada 235
Sauris 231
Tarvisio 243
Val Settimana 221

spas
Arta Terme 235
Terme Marine 129
Spilimbergo 200-1, **22-3**
stand-up paddle boarding 45
Grado 129
Lignano Sabbiadoro 117
stavoli 232
Strassoldo 137
Stregna 183
sundials 159
Sutrio 236-7, 267
Svevo, Italo 57, 271
swimming, see also beaches
Forni di Sopra 226
Grado 129
Lignano Sabbiadoro 122
Trieste 71
synagogues 68, 98

T

Tagliamento River 13, 38-9, 227, **13**, **38-9**
Tarcento 169-70
Tarvisio 241, 242-5, **17**
theatre 267-9
Politeama Rossetti 80
Teatro Verdi 80, 101
theme & adventure parks 47
Adventure Park 87
Dolomiti Adventure Park 225
Parco Acquatico 129
Rampypark 211
Tree Village 220
Tiepolo, Giambattista 145-6, 265
tobogganing 211
Tolmezzo 227-9
Topolò 184
Torviscosa 136-7
tourist information 290
tours, see also boat tours, walking tours
Aiello del Fiuli 159
Grado 130
Lignano Sabbiadoro 118
Marano Lagunare 125
Trieste 71-2, 73
towers
Porta Torriani 149
Tor Cucherna 61
train travel 291-2, 294
trams 82
travel to/from Friuli Venezia Giulia 291-2
travel within Friuli Venezia Giulia 292-4
Travesio 206-7
trekking, see hiking

Trieste 9, 50-83, **54-5**, **58**, **5**, **8-9**
accommodation 73-4
activities 71
beaches 71
drinking & nightlife 77-9
entertainment 79-80
festivals & events 72-3
food 74-7
highlights 51
history 52-3, 263-4
shopping 80-1
sights 53-71
tourist offices 81-2
tours 71-2, 73
travel to/from 82-3
travel within 83
walking tours 60-1, 64, **61**, **64**

U

Udine 9, 139-54, **142-3**, **144**, **9**
accommodation 149
drinking & nightlife 151-2
entertainment 152-3
festivals & events 149
food 149-51
history 141, 263
shopping 153
tourist offices 153
travel to/from 153-4
travel within 154
walking tours 148, **148**
Unesco sites 263
Ungaretti, Giuseppe 110
University of Udine 258

V

Vajont dam tragedy 217, 218, 259
valleys
Canal del Ferro 239
Val Colvera 222-3
Val Degano 233
Val Pesarina 232
Val Resia 238-9
Val Settimana 220-1
Val Tramontina 223-4
Val Zemola 218-19
Valcalda 237
Valcanale 240
Valle Cavanata 137-8
Valle del Bût 235
Valle del Tagliamento 227
Valle del Vajont 217
Valle dello Judrio 109
Valli del Natisone 14, 173-4, 181-6, **174**
Valli Pordenonesi 16, 187-8, 203-9, **188**

Valvasone 199-200
vegetables 279-80
Venetian architecture 263
Venzone 38, 167-8, **39**
Via Cavour 148
Via Dante Alighieri 67-8
Via Mercatovecchio 147
Via Vittorio Veneto 148
Via Zanon 148
Viale XX Settembre 68
Vicolo delle Mura 192
vie ferrate
   Forni di Sopra 225
   Sappada 235
villages 18
Villaggio del Pescatore 88
Vivaro 202-3

W
wakeboarding 115, 117
walking tours
   Trieste 60-1, 64, **61**, **64**
   Udine 148, **148**
walks, *see* hiking
water sports 44-5, *see also*
   canoeing, diving &
   snorkelling, kayaking,
   sailing, swimming, wakeboarding, water-skiing,
   windsurfing
waterfalls
   Cascata di Fuas 234
   Fontanone Barman 239
   Val Rosandra 90
water-skiing 115
weather 288

wildlife parks & zoos
   Casa delle Farfalle 168
   Parco Zoo Punta Verde
      121-2
   Pianpinedo 219
windsurfing 44
   Lago del Predil 246
   Lago di Cavazzo 166
   Lignano Sabbiadoro 117
   Sistiana 87
wine & wineries 32, 107, 170,
   180, 280-1, **33**
woodcarving 267
WWI sites 18, 111, 255-6
   Barcola 84
   Carnia 231
   Carso Isontino 95, 109
   Drenchia 184

Faro della Vittoria 84
Fogliano Redipuglia 110
Gorizia 96
Monfalcone 138
Oslavia 101
Pinzano al Tagliamento 164
Ragogna 165
San Martino del Carso 110
San Michele del Carso 111
Sappada 234
Tarcento 169
Tarvisio 242

Z
zoos, *see* wildlife parks
   & zoos
Zuglio 235-6

Map Legend

Sights

- Beach
- Bird Sanctuary
- Buddhist
- Castle/Palace
- Christian
- Confucian
- Hindu
- Islamic
- Jain
- Jewish
- Monument
- Museum/Gallery/Historic Building
- Ruin
- Shinto
- Sikh
- Taoist
- Winery/Vineyard
- Zoo/Wildlife Sanctuary
- Other Sight

Activities, Courses & Tours

- Bodysurfing
- Diving
- Canoeing/Kayaking
- Course/Tour
- Sento Hot Baths/Onsen
- Skiing
- Snorkelling
- Surfing
- Swimming/Pool
- Walking
- Windsurfing
- Other Activity

Sleeping

- Sleeping
- Camping
- Hut/Shelter

Eating

- Eating

Drinking & Nightlife

- Drinking & Nightlife
- Cafe

Entertainment

- Entertainment

Shopping

- Shopping

Information

- Bank
- Embassy/Consulate
- Hospital/Medical
- Internet
- Police
- Post Office
- Telephone
- Toilet
- Tourist Information
- Other Information

Geographic

- Beach
- Gate
- Hut/Shelter
- Lighthouse
- Lookout
- Mountain/Volcano
- Oasis
- Park
- Pass
- Picnic Area
- Waterfall

Population

- Capital (National)
- Capital (State/Province)
- City/Large Town
- Town/Village

Transport

- Airport
- Border crossing
- Bus
- Cable car/Funicular
- Cycling
- Ferry
- Metro station
- Monorail
- Parking
- Petrol station
- S-Bahn/Subway station
- Taxi
- T-bane/Tunnelbana station
- Train station/Railway
- Tram
- U-Bahn/Underground station
- Other Transport

Routes

- Tollway
- Freeway
- Primary
- Secondary
- Tertiary
- Lane
- Unsealed road
- Road under construction
- Plaza/Mall
- Steps
- Tunnel
- Pedestrian overpass
- Walking Tour
- Walking Tour detour
- Path/Walking Trail

Boundaries

- International
- State/Province
- Disputed
- Regional/Suburb
- Marine Park
- Cliff
- Wall

Hydrography

- River, Creek
- Intermittent River
- Canal
- Water
- Dry/Salt/Intermittent Lake
- Reef

Areas

- Airport/Runway
- Beach/Desert
- Cemetery (Christian)
- Cemetery (Other)
- Glacier
- Mudflat
- Park/Forest
- Sight (Building)
- Sportsground
- Swamp/Mangrove

Note: Not all symbols displayed above appear on the maps in this book

OUR STORY

A beat-up old car, a few dollars in the pocket and a sense of adventure. In 1972 that's all Tony and Maureen Wheeler needed for the trip of a lifetime – across Europe and Asia overland to Australia. It took several months, and at the end – broke but inspired – they sat at their kitchen table writing and stapling together their first travel guide, *Across Asia on the Cheap*. Within a week they'd sold 1500 copies. Lonely Planet was born.

Today, Lonely Planet has offices in the US, Ireland and China, with a network of over 2000 contributors in every corner of the globe. We share Tony's belief that 'a great guidebook should do three things: inform, educate and amuse'.

OUR WRITERS

Luigi Farrauto

Gorizia, the Collio & the Isonzo; Udine & Surrounds; Cividale del Friuli & the Valli del Natisone Despite having a PhD in Design, Luigi's poor sense of direction led him to drawing maps. Formerly based in Porto, Amsterdam and Doha, he has been a visiting researcher at MIT Boston and an adjunct lecturer at various Italian universities. Today he lives in Milan, where, together with Andrea Novali, he opened 100km Studio, specialising in cartography and wayfinding. Passionate about ancient cartography and the Middle East, Luigi spends his spare time studying Arabic and Chinese.

Piero Pasini

Trieste & the Carso; Sea & Lagoon; Pordenone, the Magredi & the Valli Pordenonesi; The Mountains Born in 1980, Piero has a press pass in his pocket and a doctorate in Social History hanging on his wall. He has published several essays and collaborated with a number of Italian universities. Now roaming and writing for magazines and tour operators, Piero has also contributed to several Lonely Planet guidebooks covering Italy and the Balkans.

Published by Lonely Planet Global Limited
CRN 554153
1st edition – Mar 2023
ISBN 978 1 83869 618 4
© Lonely Planet 2023   Photographs © as indicated 2023
10 9 8 7 6 5 4 3 2
Printed in Singapore